Fodor's
World Weather Guide

Fodor's
World Weather Guide

E.A. Pearce and C.G. Smith

Random House
New York

Contents

Acknowledgements

In addition to the sources listed in the bibliography, the climatic data in the vast majority of the tables in this book has been adapted and, where necessary, converted to both Centigrade and Fahrenheit scales or inches and millimetre scales from the following publications of the British Meteorological Office. The data is reproduced in this form by permission of the Controller of Her Majesty's Stationery Office:

Tables of temperature, relative humidity, precipitation, and sunshine for the world.
Part I. North America and Greenland. Met. 0. 856a. HMSO, 1981.
Part III. Europe and the Azores. Met. 0. 856c. Met. 0 3, 1983.

Part IV. Africa, the Atlantic Ocean south of 35° N and Indian Ocean. Met. 0. 856d. HMSO, 1983.

Tables of temperature, relative humidity, and precipitation for the world.
Part II. Central and South America, West Indies and Bermuda. Met. 0. 617b: HMSO, 1959 (repr. 1984).
Part V. Asia. Met. 0. 617e. HMSO, 2nd edition 1966 (repr. 1979).

The British Meteorological Office has kindly made available further figures on hours of sunshine for the Fourth Edition of this book.

Bibliography

Additional data and valuable descriptions and explanations of the weather and climate of most countries and all regions of the world can be found in the following books. Climatic data is not always given in the standard form used in this book (as described on p. 25) and care is therefore needed in its interpretation.

These books are written for the specialist and are expensive. They will not be found in many public libraries but may usually be obtained on interlibrary loan through national central lending libraries.

W G Kendrew, *The Climates of the Continents*, Oxford University Press, London, 5th edition, 1961 (out of print).

H E Landsberg (ed.), *World Survey of Climatology*, Elsevier North Holland, New York, 15 volumes, 1969–84 (volumes 5 to 15 are concerned with regional climatology).

Willy Rudloff, *World-Climates, with tables of climatic data and practical suggestions*, Wissenschaftliche Verlagsgesellschaft, Stuttgart, 1981.

Glenn T Trewartha, *The Earth's Problem Climates*, University of Wisconsin Press, Madison, Wisconsin, 1981.

Memoranda with tables giving climatic data for numerous places are published by the national weather services of most countries. Such publications are often in a form not readily accessible or even comprehensible to the non-specialist.

However, such publications are usually available to the general public on application to the library or archive section of their national meteorological organization, which will often be willing to provide both information and advice for which a charge may be made.

How to use this book

This book provides both general explanations of weather and climate and details of the weather at specific places on the globe.

If you are in a hurry to find out about conditions in a particular part of the world, then turn to **Country by country weather**, starting on page 25. The short notes on page 25 will tell you how to use the information in the entries that follow – arranged in alphabetical order from Afghanistan to Zimbabwe. Or, use the **Index** at the back of the book to pinpoint quickly a specific place.

To find your bearings, it may also be useful to refer to the **Weather station maps** on pages 13–24. These show the locations of weather stations that recorded the information. You can infer that weather nearby will be very similar, but it is important to take into account the limits and extents of the weather regions laid out in the country by country descriptions.

If you have time, you may find that you get more out of information about particular places by first reading the general articles on weather at the beginning of the book.

The **Introduction** on pages 1–9 explains how personal comfort, and even personal well-being, can be affected by the unexpected combined effects of high heat and high humidity, or by the contrasting effects of combined low temperature and high wind. The introduction outlines the precautions that can be taken against every weather hazard from heatstroke to frostbite and offers advice on first-aid for those who fall victim. It also addresses the question whether the world's climate is changing.

On pages 10–11, you will find a classification of **The world's climate regions**.

On pages 431–3, there is a **Glossary** of technical and foreign terms used in the book.

Project management Stuart McCready, Denise Dresner

Editors Jane Anson, Clive Barratt, Ruth Barratt

Cartography Olive Pearson

Researcher William Blackwell

Production Tony Ballsdon

Typesetting, design, and page make-up Stuart McCready

Art editor Terence Caven

Introduction

It is never enough to know simply what temperatures you are likely to meet when you get there. Comfort – even our personal well-being – can vary enormously between places with much the same temperatures. How hot or cold we feel depends upon a precise combination of temperature, humidity, and wind.

Most of us know what temperature suits us best and when we feel most comfortable. We become accustomed to the range of temperatures of the country where we live. For most people temperatures below 18° C/64° F are too cool for sitting around. Temperatures above 30° C/86° F are too hot, particularly for strenuous exercise. Of course, these figures are only a general guide.

All temperatures in this book are shade temperatures. In the sun temperatures may be as much as 10–15° C/18–27° F higher in calm weather but much less in windy conditions. The same temperatures will not necessarily produce the same feeling of heat or cold indoors as distinct from outdoors, where wind and sun also play a part. This is where two other important factors come in: *humidity* and *wind*.

ITS NOT THE HEAT; IT'S THE HUMIDITY

How true this is! We can stand dry heat much better than damp heat which makes us feel listless and takes away energy. Humidity is the amount of moisture in the air. It can be measured in various ways, but the most usual is to described it as 'relative humidity'. Relative humidity is used throughout this book. It is expressed as a percentage.

A relative humidity of 100 percent means the moisture content of the air is the maximum possible at any particular temperature. The hotter the air the more moisture it can hold. So, at 26° C/79° F the air holds more moisture at 100 percent relative humidity than it does at 10° C/50° F at the same 100 percent relative humidity. When relative humidity is low, evaporation is rapid. Soil dries out, wet clothes dry quickly and perspiration evaporates from the skin. When relative humidity is high, clothes dry slowly and body sweat cannot evaporate easily.

In high temperatures with high relative humidity we feel sticky and hot; the higher the temperature the more we perspire and, as this perspiration cannot evaporate quickly, the more uncomfortable we feel. This is why in the tropics it feels very uncomfortable for part of, or even the whole of, the year, while

in hot and dry countries we can enjoy high temperatures as body sweat evaporates quickly.

Here are some examples. At a temperature of 21° C/70° F and a relative humidity of 100 percent some people will feel slightly uncomfortable in still air. Much the same effect is felt at around 27° C/81° F with a relative humidity of only 20 percent. If the humidity rises to 60 percent we feel very much hotter although the temperature is the same.

In a breeze the discomfort associated with humidity is greatly lessened. Even a temperature of 35° C/95° F and a relative humidity of 20 percent may not feel very uncomfortable in a strong breeze. In still air the same temperature and the same relative humidity would feel very hot indeed.

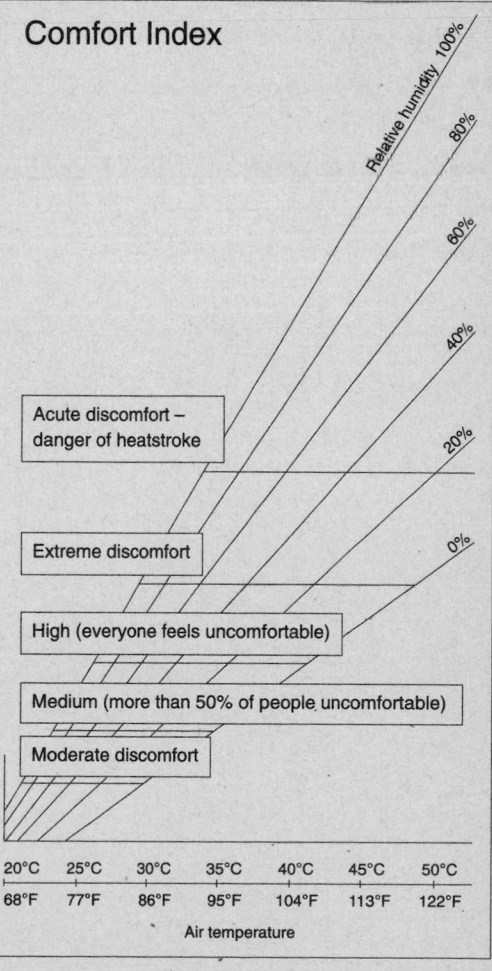

Comfort Index

Relative humidity 100% / 80% / 60% / 40% / 20% / 0%

Acute discomfort – danger of heatstroke

Extreme discomfort

High (everyone feels uncomfortable)

Medium (more than 50% of people uncomfortable)

Moderate discomfort

20°C	25°C	30°C	35°C	40°C	45°C	50°C
68°F	77°F	86°F	95°F	104°F	113°F	122°F

Air temperature

At temperatures below freezing point humidity makes almost no difference to how we feel because at such low temperatures the air can hold very little moisture. The popular belief that damp cold (raw cold) is more unpleasant than dry cold has some truth in it, but this expectation is likely to be realized mainly at temperatures above freezing point up to about 15° C/59° F. At low temperatures wind becomes much more important than humidity in determining how we feel.

USING THE COMFORT INDEX

The Comfort Index on page 1 shows how much discomfort you can expect as the weather gets hotter and stickier.

1. Temperatures are shown along the base line.
2. Relative humidity is shown by the diagonal lines.
3. The bands across the index describe how most people will feel in any combination of temperature and humidity 'in still air'.
4. To discover temperature/relative humidity conditions look up the average daily temperatures and relative humidity figures. Remember to match *maximum* temperatures with *afternoon* relative humidity figures.
5. Read off temperature from the base line and humidity from the diagonal lines. The band in which humidity and temperature intersect indicates the approximate discomfort you can anticipate.

Remember: *this index shows the conditions in still air.* Wind will reduce the effect of high humidity.

If you know the figures for temperature and relative humidity for the place you intend to visit, you can work out how you will feel on the Comfort Index. The example (right) for Singapore in January shows how to do it. Read off the average daily maximum temperature for January. It is 30° C/86° F. From the same graph you will see that the relative humidity in January is 78 percent (afternoon). The dotted line at 30° C/86° F intersects with 78 percent humidity in the band 'Everyone feels discomfort'. You will feel hot and sticky in Singapore in January.

BLOW, BLOW, THOU WINTER WIND …

How hot or cold we feel also depends on the strength of the wind. In hot climates and on hot days a brisk wind helps to keep us cool. In cold climates, and on days with very low temperatures, a strong wind makes us feel even colder.

This is because air moving rapidly past our body causes it to lose heat quickly. At high temperatures the evaporation of perspiration is one of the principal methods by which body temperature is regulated. When air temperature exceeds the normal skin temperature (about 34° C/93° F), as may happen in very hot, dry climates, the cooling power of the wind becomes critical.

In places such as Canada, the northern USA, and Russia, where very low temperatures and strong winds are normal in the winter, this cooling power is assessed by the Wind Chill Index (opposite). This indicates how any combination of wind speed and temperature can be read off as a particular degree of wind chill. It also shows why a temperature of 0° C/32° F and a wind speed of 50 kph/30 mph feels colder than a much lower temperature of -20° C/-4° F in completely calm conditions. This could be the difference between being exposed to the wind or being inside a tent.

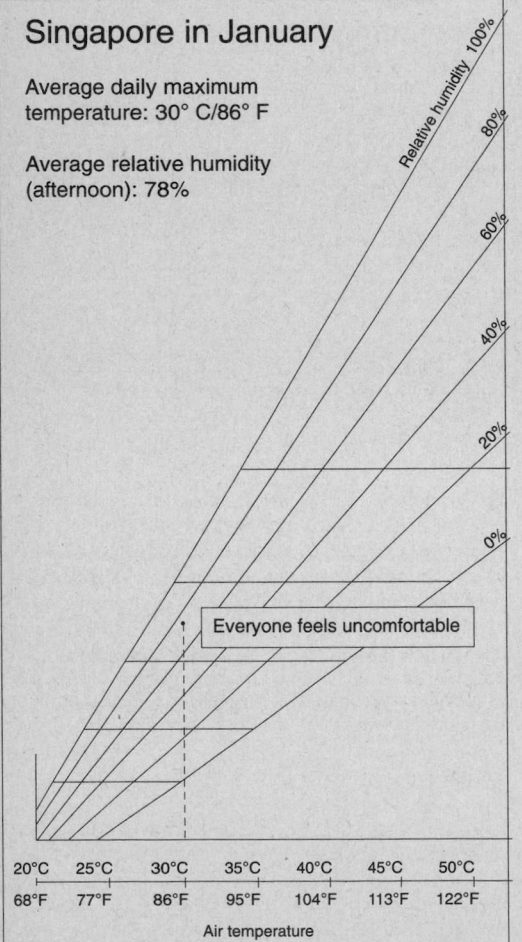

Singapore in January

Average daily maximum temperature: 30° C/86° F

Average relative humidity (afternoon): 78%

Relative humidity 100%

80%

60%

40%

20%

0%

Everyone feels uncomfortable

20°C	25°C	30°C	35°C	40°C	45°C	50°C
68°F	77°F	86°F	95°F	104°F	113°F	122°F

Air temperature

Because wind speed varies from place to place and even from hour to hour, it is not easy to provide meaningful wind statistics. Averages are of little value if gales occur on a few days and most days have light winds. As a general rule wind usually drops at night and increases by day, particularly on the coast.

We find that wind almost always increases as we climb hills and mountains – something amateur mountaineers should remember. Where strong winds are an important aspect of a country's weather they are described in the entry for that country.

In some countries, the USA for example, forecasts of wind speeds are given on television and radio. Newspapers also carry weather forecasts in which estimated wind speed may be given. If you know what the forecast wind speed is, then reference to the Wind Chill Index will give you a good idea of how you are going to feel. It works in much the same way as the Comfort Index.

Local winds are so important to the feel of the country that in some places they are given special names. Such winds may occur regularly at certain times of the day or at certain seasons of the year. A glossary of these major winds throughout the world is given on pp. 431–3.

In most parts of the world during warm, settled weather the daily onshore sea breeze is a regular feature of coasts and beaches. This usually begins about midday and can be useful in having a noticeable cooling effect. In some tropical and subtropical climates the onshore wind occurs at almost the same time each day.

When this breeze drops in the late evening the temperature can feel quite oppressive. In the early hours of the morning there may be a return land breeze blowing offshore, but this is usually less strong than the daytime sea breeze.

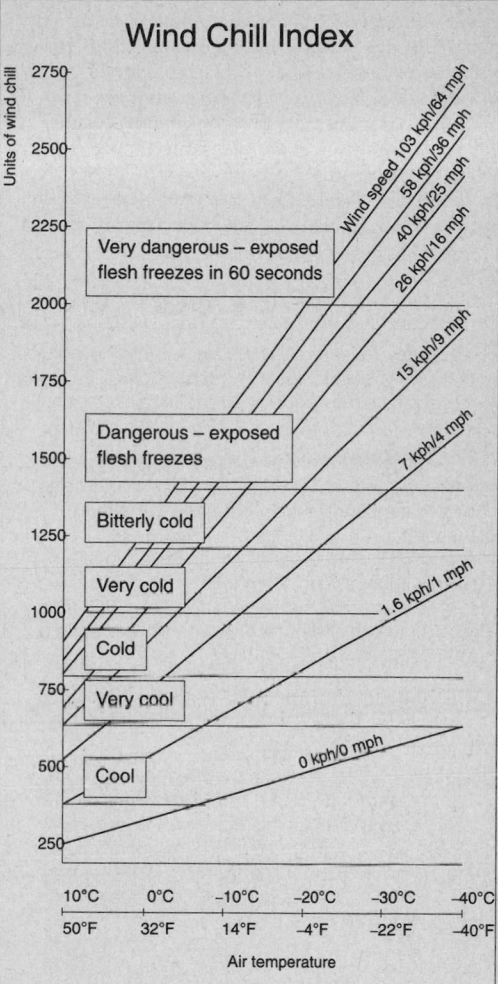

Wind Chill Index

HOW TO USE THE WIND CHILL INDEX

1. Temperatures are shown along the base line.
2. Wind speeds are shown by the diagonal lines.
3. The bands running across the index show how a suitably clothed person would feel.
4. Where a known temperature intersects with a forecast wind speed, conditions out of doors are shown.

Thus at a temperature of -5° C/23° F there is a danger of frostbite in a wind of 65 kph/40 mph. A sunny day will, of course, produce extra warmth the body can feel. This would not make much difference in extreme conditions of wind and cold, but it would appreciably affect comfort in calm conditions in temperatures down to -15° C/5° F. The Wind Chill Index was first developed, from experiments in the Antarctic, as an indication of safe conditions outside shelter. The units of wind chill on the left of the diagram show the rate of loss of heat from the body in kilogramme calories per square metre of body surface per hour.

HOT DAYS – COLD NIGHTS

In some countries there is a much greater difference between daytime and night-time temperatures than in other countries. The tables in this book give the average daily *maximum* and *minimum* temperatures for each month at a number of representative places in each country. The maximum temperature usually occurs just after midday and the minimum temperature just before dawn. The difference between these two is the *daily range of temperature* and is an important feature of the climate. It can also considerably affect our comfort.

On cloudy, rainy days the range of temperature may be quite small. In climates which are very sunny and dry, such as desert areas (for example, North Africa and Arizona, USA), there may be a very large daily range with surprisingly cold nights.

Be prepared for very chilly nights in desert and mountain areas where daytime temperatures may be either very hot or quite comfortable. As a general rule the range is greatest inland and least on the coast. For example, the average daily range of

Centigrade (Celsius) and Fahrenheit

The *Fahrenheit* temperature scale was introduced by the German scientist Gabriel Fahrenheit in 1714, and was the scale most widely used by English-speaking countries.

0° F was chosen as the temperature of a mixture of water, ice, and sal-ammoniac (the lowest artificially created temperature possible before the days of refrigeration), and 32° F as the freezing point of water. 96° F was chosen as the temperature of a healthy human being. From these fixed points the scale was extended below zero and above 96°. Thus the boiling point of water on the Fahrenheit scale is 212° F.

The *Centigrade* scale is the most widely used throughout the world and is recommended by the World Meteorological Organization.

First proposed by the Swedish astronomer Anders Celsius in 1742, it is based on two fixed points – the freezing and boiling points of water. The interval between is divided into 100°. Freezing point is 0° C and boiling point in 100° C. Minus temperatures on the Centigrade scale always indicate temperatures below freezing.

A quick way of converting Centigrade to Fahrenheit
For temperatures above 0° C double the Centigrade figure and add 30.

$$10° C \times 2 = 20 + 30 = 50° F$$

To convert Centigrade to Fahrenheit the reverse applies. Deduct 30 and halve the result.

$$70° F - 30 = 40 \div 2 = 20° C$$

The higher the temperature the more inaccurate this easy method becomes. Remember the method does not work below freezing point.

A more accurate method of conversion
This method is more accurate and, if you can memorize the following temperatures at 5° C and 9° F intervals, conversion is easy.

Freezing point is 32° on the Fahrenheit scale and 0° on the Centigrade scale. 1° C equals 1.8 ° F. Therefore 5° C equals 9° F, thus:

$$5° C \times 1.8 = 9° + 32° = 41° F$$

$$5° C = 41° F$$
$$10° C = 50° F$$
$$15° C = 59° F$$
$$20° C = 68° F$$
$$25° C = 77° F$$
$$30° C = 86° F$$
$$35° C = 95° F$$
$$40° C = 104° F$$

For temperatures below freezing:

$$-5° C = 23° F$$
$$-10° C = 14° F$$
$$-15° C = 5° F$$
$$-20° C = -4° F$$
$$-25° C = -13° F$$
$$-30° C = -22° F$$
$$-35° C = -31° F$$
$$-40° C = -40° F$$

If you use 2 as a multiplier instead of 1.8, the result is accurate enough for most purposes.

Temperature conversion table

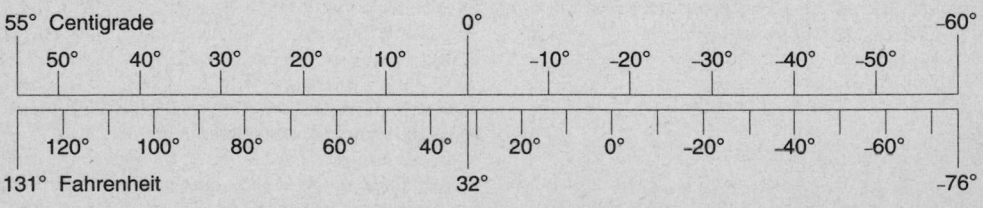

temperature at New Delhi (India) in May is 15° C/ 27° F. In August it is only 8° C/14° F. At Bombay the equivalent figures are 6° C/11° F and 5° C/9° F. At both places May is in the dry season and August in the wet season, but Bombay is on the coast whereas New Delhi is in the middle of India. By working out the range of temperature you will have a good idea of the clothes you need to take with you.

RAIN AND SNOW

As well as temperature, humidity, and wind, which together determine how hot or cold we feel, we are likely to be interested in rain and snow. We may wish to know not only the amount that falls but the probability of wet days. In this book the normal meteorological term 'precipitation' is used. This term includes all moisture falling on the ground whether it be rain, snow, sleet, hail, dew, or fog drip.

In most climates precipitation generally falls as rain. On high mountains, or in places with very cold winters such as Canada, Russia, parts of the USA, China, and Scandinavia, much of the precipitation may fall as snow. Snow, sleet, and hail are measured as the melted equivalent of rain. (30 cm/1 ft of snow is roughly equivalent to 2.5 cm/1 in of rain.)

As a general rule, at temperatures around 2° C/36° F, snow or sleet are as likely as rain. With temperatures at or below freezing point, precipitation is most likely to be snow. Freezing rain (rain falling when the temperature is below freezing point) is a rare occurrence but is a very serious danger on the roads, not least for those on foot.

In this book the average monthly precipitation is given. The average number of days with measurable precipitation is also given for each month. This may be a better guide to the raininess of a place, as some places have a relatively large monthly rainfall which falls for a few hours on one or two days. The two columns should be used in conjunction.

HOW WEATHER CAN VARY

It is impossible, without giving more figures than there is room for, to take account of the fact that, in many parts of the world, the weather is highly variable for at least part of the year. A month may include hot, sunny spells and wet, cloudy spells. In one July the weather may be more disturbed than in another. Similarly, one January may have much more snow than another.

Some indication of variability is given by the columns giving the highest and lowest temperatures recorded in each month. These figures indicate what the temperature *can* be. It is, of course, very unlikely that these extremes will be reached while you are visiting, even for a long stay, but the possibility exists! A month with an average daily minimum temperature below −2° C/28° F is likely to have frequent snow and, if the average daily maximum is 0° C/32° F or below, then snow may lie on the ground for long periods.

HOW HIGH WILL YOU BE?

The higher we go above sea level the colder it gets. As a general rule this fall in temperature is at the rate of 0.6° C/1° F for every 100 m/330 ft. This may not apply locally during the day, particularly if the sun is shining; but you will very soon be aware of it if the sky clouds over or you are in cloud.

Height above sea level can mean a wide range of day- and night-time temperatures. Nairobi (Kenya), at

Rainfall conversion table

inches/millimetres		millimetres/inches	
0.1	3	1	0.04
0.2	5	2	0.1
		3	0.1
0.3	8	4	0.2
0.4	10	5	0.2
0.5	13	6	0.2
0.6	15	7	0.3
0.7	18	8	0.3
		9	0.3
0.8	20		
0.9	23	10	0.4
		20	0.8
		30	1.2
1	25	40	1.6
2	51	50	2.0
3	76	60	2.4
4	102	70	2.8
		80	3.1
5	127	90	3.5
6	152	100	3.9
7	178		
8	203	200	7.9
		300	11.8
9	229	400	15.7
10	254	500	19.7
		600	23.6
		700	27.6
20	508	800	31.5
30	762	900	35.4
40	1016	1000	39.4

Hours of daylight by latitude

This table shows the varying length of day with latitude. Day length is here understood to be the period between the rising and setting of the sun. It does not include the period of twilight before and after sunrise and sunset. The length of the period of twilight increases from the equator to about 65° N and S where, on the longest day of the year, it lasts all night. On the equator twilight lasts about twenty minutes. At 30° N and S twilight lasts about thirty minutes before and after sunrise and sunset. At 50° N and S this period increases to about forty minutes. The term twilight here refers to 'civil twilight', which is the period during which the sun is not more than 6° below the horizon. Under clear skies and with good atmospheric conditions normal outdoor activities should be possible during the period of civil twilight. If the length of twilight is doubled and added to figures for day length given in the table below, it will give a good idea of the length of adequate daylight for each latitude.

Read the months on the left of the table for the northern hemisphere and the months on the right of the table for the southern hemisphere.

Length of day at selected latitudes

in hours and minutes on the 15th of each month

Month	Equator	10°	20°	30°	40°	50°	60°	70°	80°	Poles	Month
J	12:07	11:35	11:02	10:24	9:37	8:30	6:38	0:00	0:00	0:00	J
F	12:07	11:49	11:21	11:10	10:42	10:07	9:11	7:20	0:00	0:00	A
M	12:07	12:04	12:00	11:57	11:53	11:48	11:41	11:28	10:52	0:00	S
A	12:07	12:21	12:36	12:53	13:14	13:44	14:31	16:06	24:00	24:00	O
M	12:07	12:34	13:04	13:38	14:22	15:22	17:04	22:13	24:00	24:00	N
J	12:07	12:42	13:20	14:04	15:00	16:21	18:49	24:00	24:00	24:00	D
J	12:07	12:40	13:16	13:56	14:49	15:38	17:31	24:00	24:00	24:00	J
A	12:07	12:28	12:50	13:16	13:48	14:33	15:46	18:26	24:00	24:00	F
S	12:07	12:12	12:17	12:23	12:31	12:42	13:00	13:34	15:16	24:00	M
O	12:07	11:55	11:42	11:28	11:10	10:47	10:11	9:03	5:10	0:00	A
N	12:07	11:40	11:12	10:40	10:01	9:06	7:37	3:06	0:00	0:00	M
D	12:07	11:32	10:56	10:14	9:20	8:05	5:54	0:00	0:00	0:00	J

in September. The average daytime temperature is 24° C/75° F while the night-time temperature is 11° C/52° F. Mexico City, at over 2,300 m/7,500 ft, has almost identical figures for September. The nights in both places can be distinctly cool. Altitude figures are given for every place in this book so you can see how high you are going to be.

Remember also that the atmosphere becomes thinner at altitudes over 1,800 m/6,000 ft. The sun's rays (especially the ultraviolet light) are more powerful and you will tan – or burn – more quickly. Above these heights breathing and exertion become progressively more difficult. The body of a healthy person adapts to these conditions, but it may take you longer to climb or walk than you think. So do not forget that on mountains the temperature drops with height, especially in cloud, even more with wind, and much more at night. Always take warm clothing when walking or climbing.

COMPARE WHAT YOU KNOW WITH WHERE YOU ARE GOING

You may find it useful to compare the figures for your home area, where you know wheat the weather is like the whole year round, with the figures given for your destination. Work out:

Will it be hotter or colder by day and by night?

Is there a wide range of temperature between day and night?

Will humidity make it feel hotter than the temperatures suggest? Refer to the Comfort Index on p. 1.

Is it very wet and how many rainy days are there likely to be?

How much colder is it likely to be if you visit a place 1,000 m/3,000 ft higher than the nearest place for which figures are given? (Use the approximate rule given above.)

WHEN WEATHER CAN BE DANGEROUS

Most of us are unlikely to run into conditions of extreme heat or extreme cold, both of which in their different ways can be dangerous. But this can happen through accident, carelessness, or misadventure, so here is a brief description of the ways in which weather can be dangerous.

Too hot In high temperatures the body keeps cool by the evaporation of sweat from the skin. In low humidity evaporation occurs quickly and air, moved by wind or a fan, also increases evaporation. But there is an upper limit to the air temperature we can endure with comfort, even in low humidity. This is because in very high temperatures we may not be able to sweat fast enough to match the rate of evaporation. Also, the body can gain heat from very hot air. Increased wind speed will be even more dangerous because evaporation will be even faster.

Heat exhaustion When the body cannot lose heat fast enough there is a possibility of heat exhaustion. There is a feeling of lassitude, loss of appetite, and general discomfort. Visual hallucinations are possible and also vomiting. The sufferer should be moved to a cool place and drink salt and water to replace the sweat and salts lost through perspiration.

Heatstroke Heatstroke is a much more dangerous condition and, although rare, is more likely to follow from the less obvious condition of heat exhaustion. It can be fatal. Heatstroke is the result of the body's normal cooling mechanism ceasing to function. The skin becomes dry and body temperature starts to rise. The symptoms are burning sensations, dry skin, followed by feverish feelings. These symptoms can develop into restlessness, headache, and confusion. Unless treated at once body temperature will rise until the victim becomes unconscious, and death may follow.

For a person suffering from heatstroke, medical attention is necessary. The patient much be put in the coolest possible place and cooled as fast as possible. He or she should be splashed with cold water, or better still, iced water. Wrapping him or her in a wet sheet with a fan directed on the body will help to reduce body temperature quickly. Vigorous massage can also help.

Precautions There are, of course, precautions that can be taken against both heat exhaustion and heatstroke. When arriving in a very hot country do not overexert the body until you are acclimatized – about a week. Air travel is so fast that, unlike slow sea journeys, the body has no time gradually to acclimatize itself to high temperatures. Also, air conditioning in hotels, offices, etc., delays the process of acclimatization. Drink plenty of liquid, but not too much alcohol. Take more salt with food, or even salt tablets. Wear comfortable, light clothing and certainly avoid sunburn. The Comfort Index shows when a danger of heatstroke can arise, and the descriptions of the climate of hot countries indicate at what time of year the danger exists.

It is always sensible to adopt local customs in hot countries. The inhabitants *know* what it's like.

Too cold In very cold climates we put on more clothes – special clothing in polar regions – and we can keep relatively warm by generating body heat by walking or other activities. But if we stop moving, become tired, and remain in a strong wind below freezing, we can very soon become extremely cold. The main dangers of very cold climates and high mountains are hypothermia and frostbite.

Hypothermia Hypothermia, which is often called 'exposure', is the failure to maintain body heat. The possibility of hypothermia is greatly increased if clothes become wet; evaporation from wet clothes causes the body to lose heat even more rapidly. Rain and snow with a strong wind increase the danger.

Most cases of hypothermia out of doors occur through lack of proper clothing in mountains or at sea. Climbers and walkers who get lost and are forced to spend all night on a mountainside are risking hypothermia – especially if they are wearing light clothing. Even in a hut where they are out of the wind, hypothermia can occur if there are no blankets. Old people are particularly susceptible. At a very low body temperature (around 25–28° C/77–82° F) the condition becomes critical.

To counteract hypothermia, the body should be warmed by any means available. Rapid rewarming in a water bath of 40–45° C/104°–113° F is very important. If breathing has stopped, then artificial respiration and cardiac massage are required immediately.

Frostbite Frostbite is the extreme condition when the flesh freezes. It is most likely to affect the face, hands, and feet, and a bad case may mean the loss of limbs or other permanent injury. The affected parts should be rewarmed as soon as possible. If possible, rewarming in water no hotter than 40–44° C/104–

111° F will help a great deal. Water hotter than this increases pain and swelling. There should be no massage, no rubbing, and no exercise, and the affected part should not be bandaged.

The Wind Chill Index shows the temperatures and wind speeds at which danger of frostbite exists. Most people will never experience these conditions, but hypothermia can occur at low temperatures long before conditions approach the hazard of frostbite.

Is the climate changing?

The climate of the Earth has changed or fluctuated many times in the last 4,000 million years. The evidence for this can be found in rocks, fossils, and old landforms, such as glaciated mountains, fossil sand dunes, and coal deposits which are the relics of ancient tropical forests.

Until very recently it was the opinion of most scientists that major climatic changes, such as the retreat of the ice at the end of the last ice age some 10,000– 20,000 years ago, were slow and gradual. It was also thought that, while the climate might fluctuate over short periods of 30–100 years, this was around an average or norm not very different to that of the last 4,000 years. Recently, however, doubt has been cast on these assumptions and the subject of climatic change has become a matter of great concern. There are two reasons for this:

a Humans may now be responsible for causing significant changes of climate with harmful consequences.

b It is now known that some past changes of climate, such as the onset of ice ages, occurred more rapidly than had at one time been thought; namely, over less than a century rather than over several hundred years.

HOW HUMANS MAY BE BRINGING ABOUT CHANGES

The carbon dioxide problem The carbon dioxide (CO_2) content of the atmosphere has been increasing from an average value of 290 parts per million in the late 19th century to some 350 parts per million in 1990.

This is almost certainly a result of the great increase in the use of fossil fuels such as coal, oil, and natural gas which, when burned, release CO_2 into the atmosphere at a rate faster than it can be absorbed

by vegetation or the oceans. The destruction of forests, particularly in the tropics, adds to this effect.

Some estimates suggest that by the year 2050 the CO_2 content of the atmosphere may be double its present level.

CO_2 is called a *greenhouse gas* because in the atmosphere it acts, together with cloud and water vapour, to trap outgoing longwave radiation just as the glass in a greenhouse does. Thus an increase in this *greenhouse effect* would raise the Earth's surface temperature. The precise magnitude of this effect is uncertain; estimates range from 1–5° C/2–9° F. The effect would probably be greatest in high latitudes and least in the tropics.

The present pattern of climatic types could be drastically changed: some areas would benefit from the greater warmth but other areas could experience reduced rainfall, seasonal drought, or more frequent, severe storms. In the longer term the polar icecaps would melt and sea levels rise. At present evidence for the beginning of such changes is by no means clear, but a slight increase in surface temperatures in the sea may be the first sign of this effect.

A hole in the ozone layer Ozone is a gas that exists in very small amounts in the atmosphere but is particularly concentrated at high levels, about 30 km/100,000 ft up in the stratosphere. This layer protects the Earth from some of the harmful effects of solar radiation in the ultraviolet wavelengths. During the 1980s measurements of the ozone concentration in the stratosphere over the Antarctic showed a rapid decrease in the winter months – the 'ozone hole'.

The cause of this decrease is thought to be the release into the atmosphere of chlorofluorocarbons (CFCs). CFC gases are used in the manufacture of some types of plastic foam and are used in refrigerators and as propellants for aerosols.

A reduction or thinning of this high-level ozone layer would increase the risk of skin cancers in humans and have harmful effects on some crops, animals, and zooplankton. Chemical changes in the upper atmosphere as a result of the loss of ozone would also reinforce the greenhouse effect.

Acid rain and pollution from smoke and sulphur dioxide Since the Industrial Revolution and the great increase in the use of fossil fuels, industrial areas and great cities have experienced pollution in the form of smoke and sulphur dioxide in the atmosphere. This visible air pollution has been much reduced in the second half of the 20th century with the growing use of electrical energy. In large British towns, such as London, Birmingham, and Manchester, despite the increase of pollution from vehicle exhausts, the air is now much cleaner and fogs less dense and frequent than was the case in the early decades of the century.

However, when electricity is produced in large thermal power stations burning oil or coal, the gases released from the high chimneys are carried downwind for long distances. It is thought that this is one of the main causes of the acid rain which in quite remote rural areas has been blamed for leaf loss or the death of trees and the destruction of fish in freshwater lakes where this acid rainwater accumulates. Areas particularly affected are parts of Scandinavia, central Europe, and eastern Canada, and this is blamed on industrial emissions from factories and power stations in Britain, central and eastern Europe, and the United States.

ARE THE CHANGES SERIOUS?

There is no reason to believe that, over the next ten to twenty years, the climate in particular parts of the world will be very different from the descriptions and figures in this book. Occasional extreme events or spells of weather, such as occur at present, may well mask any longer-term change and make human influence on the weather difficult to detect for some time to come. One extreme winter or summer does not necessarily make for a change of climate.

Yet such changes are thought to be occurring and will be increasingly evident in the next fifty years. Even if drastic, immediate action is taken by the countries of the world to mitigate the effects of harmful pollutants such as CO_2 and CFCs, the consequences of the present levels of damage may be apparent for the next hundred years.

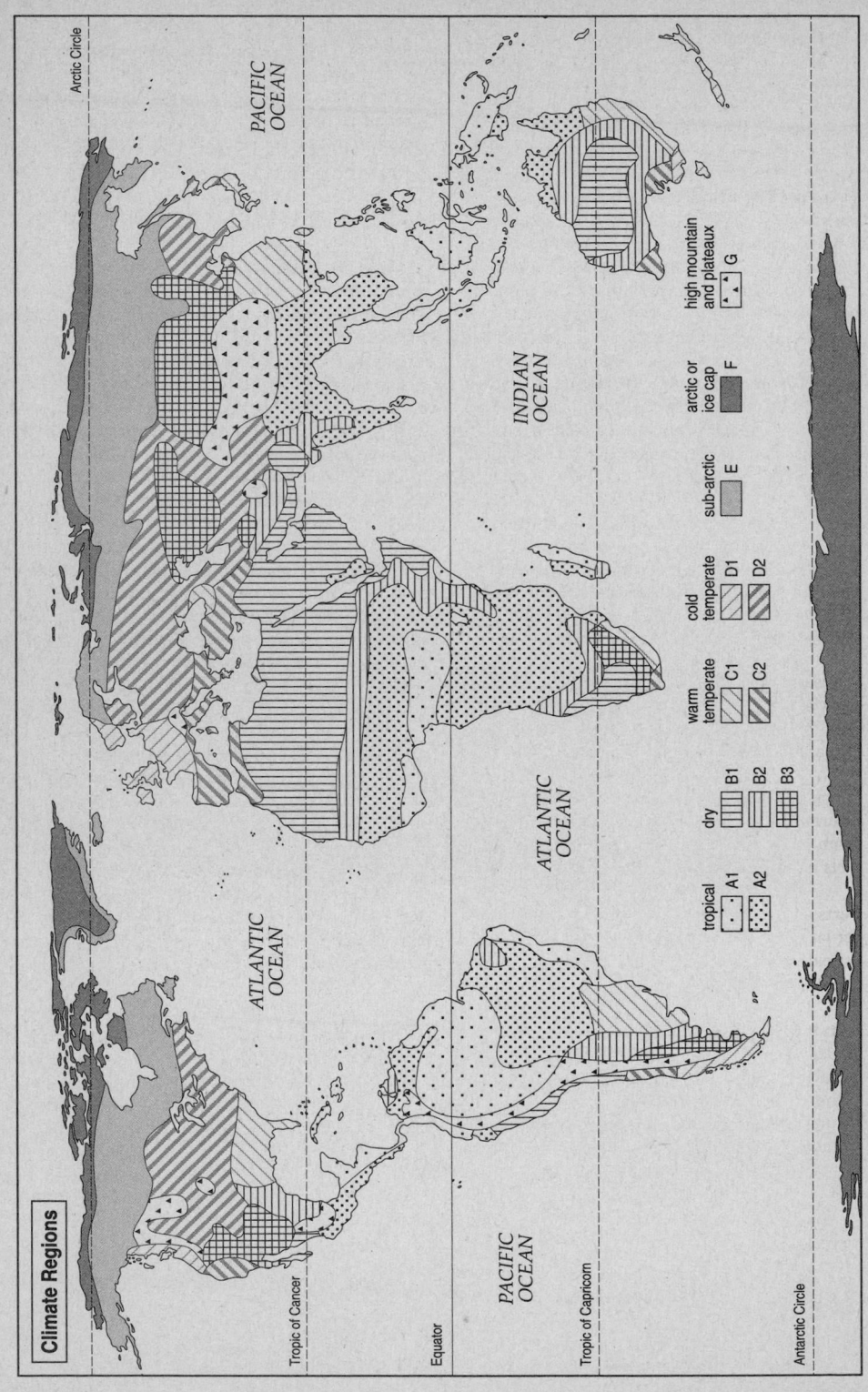

Climate Regions

tropical
A1
A2

dry
B1
B2
B3

warm temperate
C1
C2

cold temperate
D1
D2

sub-arctic
E

arctic or ice cap
F

high mountain and plateaux
G

The world's climate regions

Despite the complexity of climatic patterns produced by altitude, aspect in relation to prevailing winds, and proximity to the oceans, the general pattern of world climates has a certain logical simplicity. Broadly similar climates are found in different parts of the world in the same latitude and in similar positions on each continent. This is illustrated by the map of the Earth's climatic types on the facing page.

Here is a brief description of these climatic types:

A Tropical

A1 Often called *equatorial climates*. Here the weather is hot and wet around the year. These climates are found within about 5° of latitude north and south of the equator.

A2 Hot tropical climates with a distinct wet and dry season. They occur between roughly 5° and 15° north and south of the equator. In parts of south and southeast Asia the division between the wet and dry seasons is so clear that they are called *tropical monsoon climates*.

B Dry

B1 Hot deserts with little rain at any season and no real cold weather although temperature drops sharply at night. The Sahara desert and much of the Arabian peninsula are the best examples of this type.

B2 Tropical steppe or semi-desert with a short rainy season during which the rains are unreliable and vary much from place to place. Examples are found in the drier parts of India and the Sahel region of Africa.

B3 Deserts with a distinctly cold season. These occur in higher latitudes in the interior of large continents. The best examples are parts of central Asia and western China.

C Warm temperate

C1 Rain occurs at all seasons but summer is the wettest time of the year and temperatures then are warm to hot. Winters are mild with occasional cold spells. Much of eastern China and the southeastern states of the USA are in this category.

C2 Winters are generally mild and wet. Summers are warm or hot with little or no rain. This type of climate is often called *Mediterranean* because of its wide extent around that sea. It occurs in smaller areas elsewhere, such as central Chile, California, and Western Australia.

D Cold temperate

D1 The cool temperate oceanic type of climate. Rain occurs in all months and there are rarely great extremes of heat or cold. This climate is found in much of northwest Europe, New Zealand, and coastal British Columbia.

D2 Cold continental climates with a warm summer and a cold winter. Much of eastern and central Europe and central and eastern Canada and the USA have this type of climate.

E Sub-Arctic or tundra

The winters are long and very cold. Summers are short but during the long days temperatures sometimes rise surprisingly high. This type of climate occurs in central and northern Canada and much of northern and central Siberia.

F Arctic or icecap

In all months temperatures are near or below freezing point. Greenland and the Antarctic continent are the best examples of this type but it also occurs on some islands within the Arctic and Antarctic circles, such as South Georgia and Spitsbergen.

G High mountains and plateaux

Where land rises above or near the permanent snow line in any latitude the climate resembles that of types E and F. The largest extent of such climate is found in Tibet and the great mountain ranges of the Himalayas.

In Africa only the isolated peaks of Mount Kenya and Kilimanjaro and the Ruwenzori range are high enough to carry permanent snow. Similar mountain climates are more extensive in both North and South America.

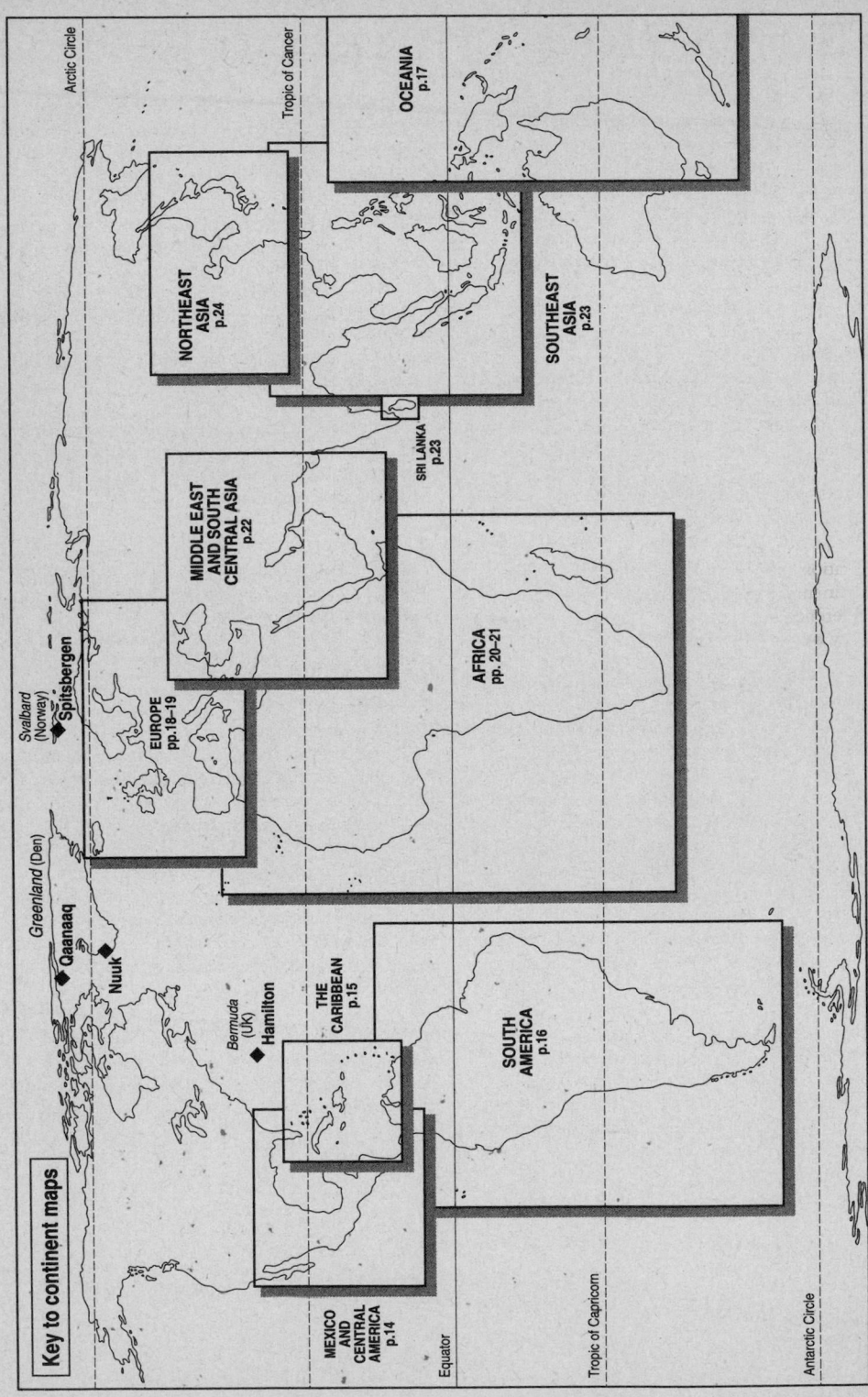

Key to continent maps

MEXICO AND CENTRAL AMERICA p.14

THE CARIBBEAN p.15

SOUTH AMERICA p.16

Bermuda (UK) ◆ Hamilton

Greenland (Den) ◆ Qaanaaq ◆ Nuuk

Svalbard (Norway) ◆ Spitsbergen

EUROPE pp.18-19

MIDDLE EAST AND SOUTH CENTRAL ASIA p.22

AFRICA pp. 20-21

NORTHEAST ASIA p.24

SRI LANKA p.23

SOUTHEAST ASIA p.23

OCEANIA p.17

Arctic Circle

Tropic of Cancer

Equator

Tropic of Capricorn

Antarctic Circle

Weather station maps

The tables of weather information in this book are based on readings from almost 500 weather stations around the world. The name of the town or city where the weather station is located appears in capital letters at the top left of each table. To help you see better what geographical area each table sheds light on, the locations of the weather stations are shown on the maps in this section and on individual country maps.

To find a weather station on the map, start with the world key map opposite. If the weather station you are looking for does not appear there, then turn to the page indicated for the appropriate continental or regional map. Towns and cities with weather stations that recorded the information used in the tables for this book are located by solid diamonds. Other towns and cities included to help you orient yourself are located by dots.

If the station you are looking for does not appear on the continental or regional map, you will find there a page reference for an individual country map in the **Country by country** guide – for example, Algeria

on p. 30. Individual country maps have been provided for selected entries. Most show, in addition to weather station locations and other towns and cities, the country's weather regions.

The division of countries into weather regions is necessarily approximate and it is important not to be misled by the clear boundary lines between regions on the maps that show them. The boundaries between weather regions can in reality be fairly broad zones where aspects of the physical geography make the usual gradual transition from one weather type to another sharper. The transition remains, all the same, a matter of degree. Where a country (for example, the United Kingdom or Ireland) has no sharp transitions from one weather type to another, the country map does not show weather regions.

Key
♦ Town or city with a weather station that recorded the information shown in one of the tables in the **Country by country weather** guide on pp. 25–429
• Other town or city
Δ Other frequently visited place

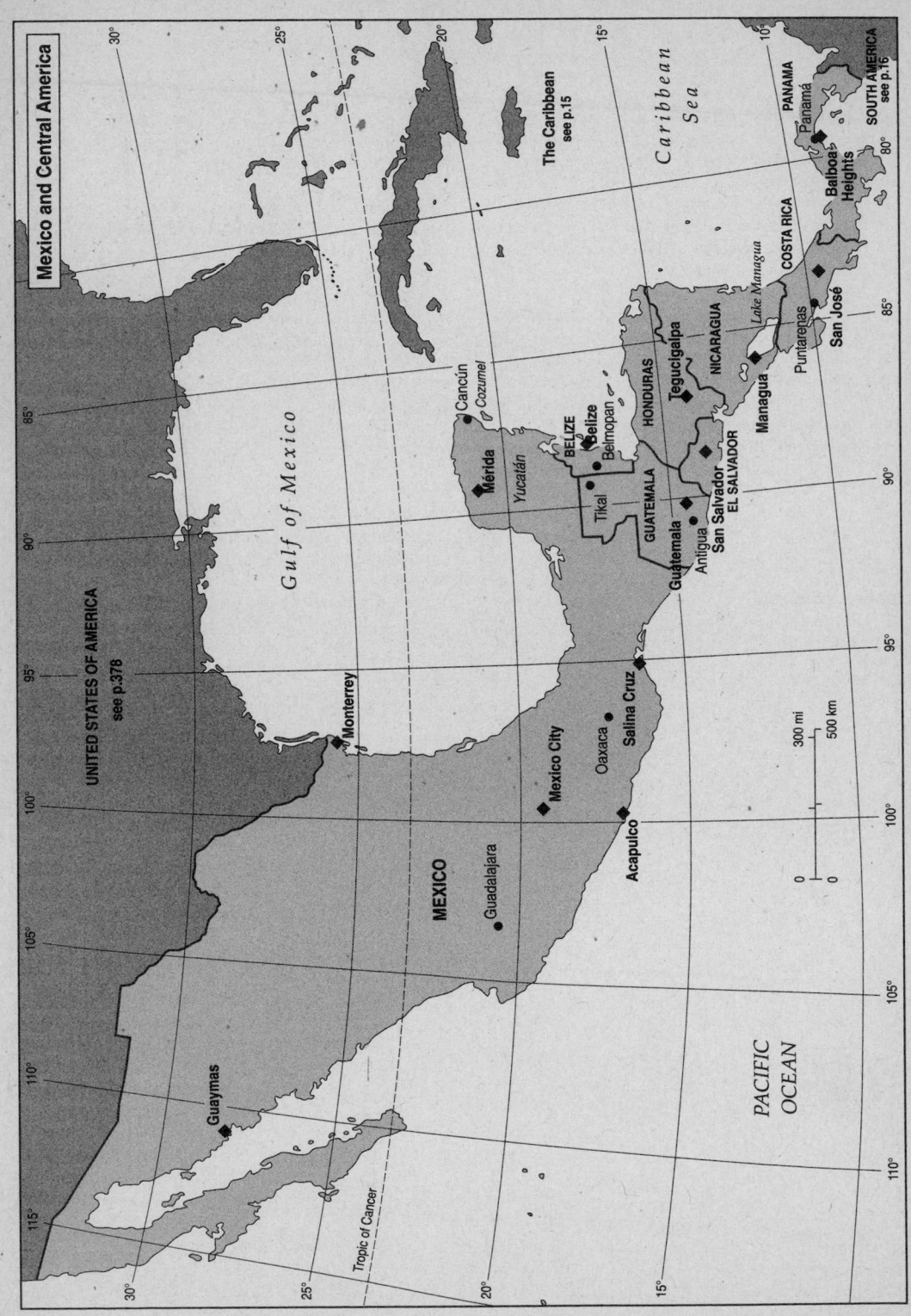

Mexico and Central America

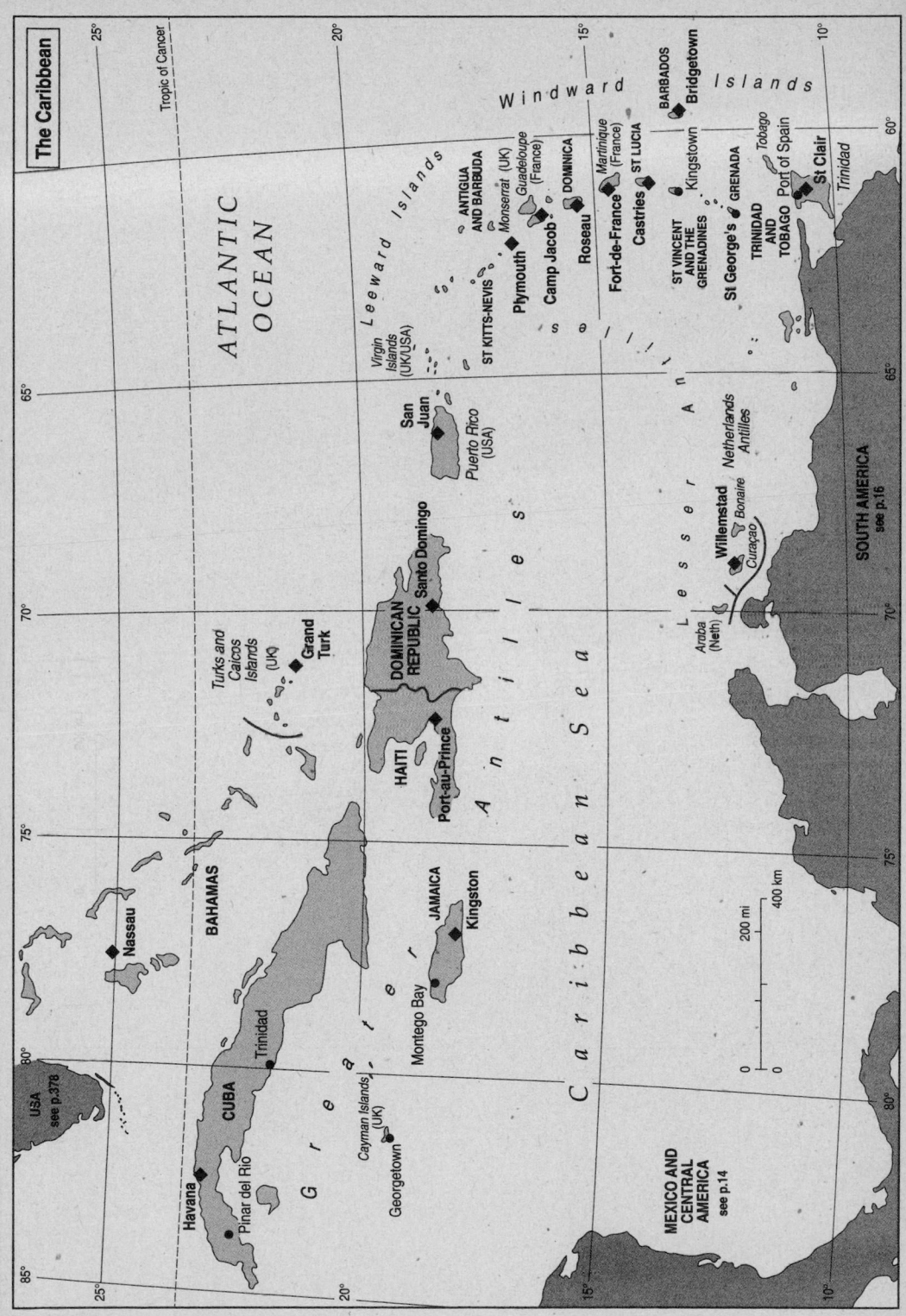

The Caribbean

Tropic of Cancer

ATLANTIC OCEAN

25° 20° 15° 10°

Windward Islands

BARBADOS Bridgetown

Leeward Islands

ANTIGUA AND BARBUDA
Monserrat (UK)
Guadeloupe (France)
Plymouth
Camp Jacob
DOMINICA
Roseau
Martinique (France)
Fort-de-France
ST LUCIA
Castries
Kingstown
ST VINCENT AND THE GRENADINES
GRENADA
St George's
TRINIDAD AND TOBAGO
Tobago
Port of Spain
St Clair
Trinidad

ST KITTS-NEVIS

Virgin Islands (UK/USA)

Lesser Antilles

San Juan
Puerto Rico (USA)

Netherlands Antilles
Willemstad
Bonaire
Curaçao

Aruba (Neth)

SOUTH AMERICA
see p.16

65° 70°

Turks and Caicos Islands (UK)

Grand Turk

DOMINICAN REPUBLIC
Santo Domingo

HAITI
Port-au-Prince

Antilles

Greater

75°

BAHAMAS
Nassau

JAMAICA
Kingston
Montego Bay

Caribbean Sea

80° 85°

USA
see p.378

CUBA
Trinidad
Havana
Pinar del Río

Cayman Islands (UK)
Georgetown

MEXICO AND CENTRAL AMERICA
see p.14

0   200 mi
0   400 km

25° 20° 15° 10°

MEXICO AND
CENTRAL AMERICA
see p.14

South America

90°   80°   70°   60°   50°

Maracaibo

Caracas

10°   10°

VENEZUELA   Georgetown
COLOMBIA   Santa Elena   Paramaribo
Bogotá   SURINAM   Cayenne
Andagoya   GUYANA   FRENCH
GUIANA

*Galápagos Islands
(Ecuador)*   Quito   Equator
0°   0°
ECUADOR   Riobamba
Seymour   Guayaquil   Iquitos
Island   Cuenca

Cajamarca   BRAZIL
PERU   see p.68

Machu
Picchu
10°   Lima   10°
Ica   Cuzco   *Lake
Titicaca*   Concepción
Arequipa   La Paz
BOLIVIA

PARAGUAY
20°   20°
Tropic of Capricorn
Asunción

CHILE
see p.99

30°   30°
ARGENTINA   URUGUAY
*PACIFIC   see p.37   Montevideo
OCEAN*

40°   40°

0   600 mi
*ATLANTIC
0   1200 km   OCEAN*
*Falkland
Islands
(UK)*
50°   Stanley   50°

90°   80°   70°   60°   50°   40°   30°

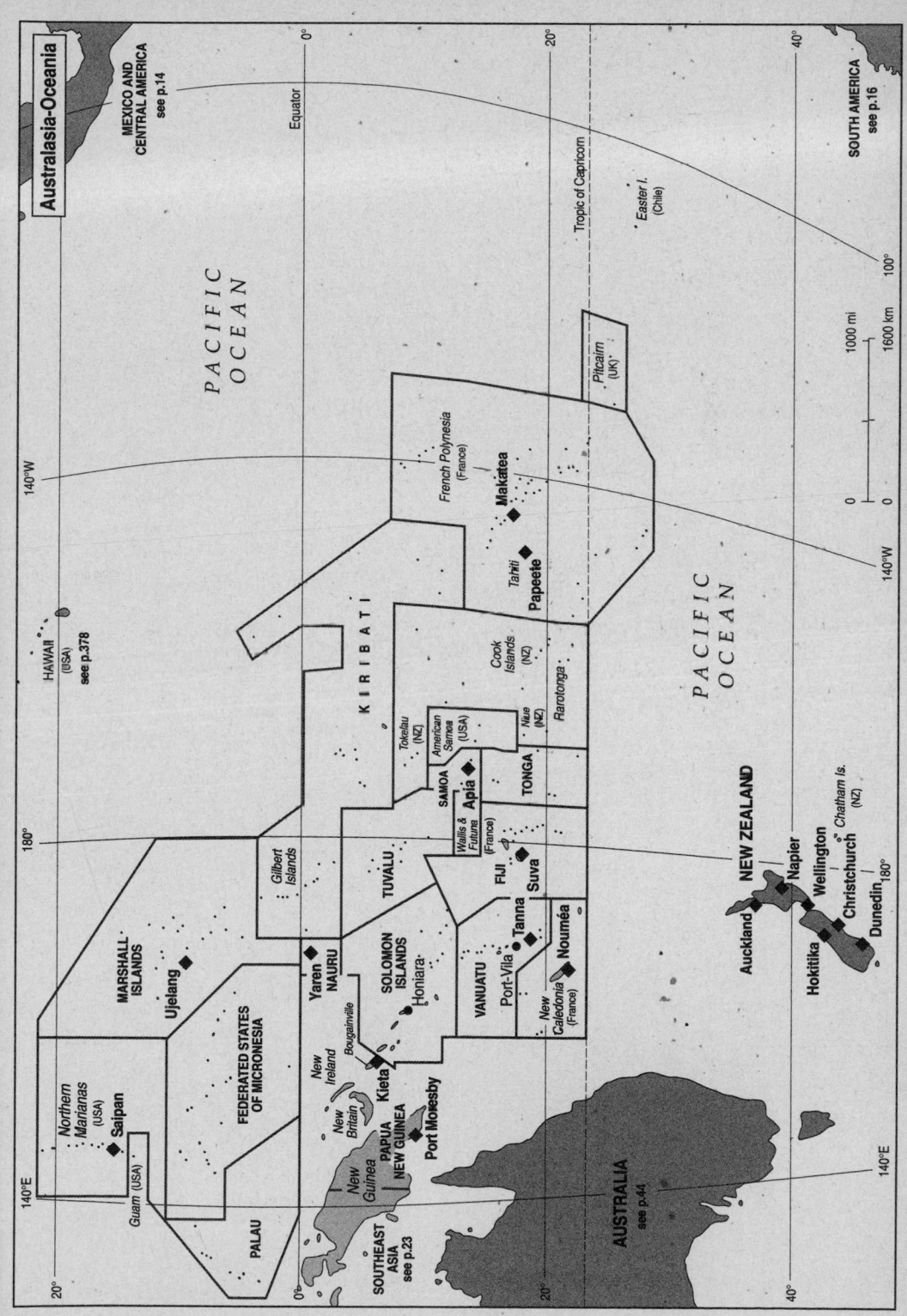

Australasia-Oceania

MEXICO AND CENTRAL AMERICA see p.14

SOUTH AMERICA see p.16

Equator

Tropic of Capricorn

Easter I. (Chile)

PACIFIC OCEAN

Pitcairn (UK)

1000 mi
1600 km

French Polynesia (France)

Makatea

Tahiti
Papeete

Cook Islands (NZ)

Rarotonga

PACIFIC OCEAN

HAWAII (USA) see p.378

KIRIBATI

Tokelau (NZ)

American Samoa (USA)

Niue (NZ)

SAMOA
Apia

Wallis & Futuna (France)

TONGA

Gilbert Islands

TUVALU

FIJI
Suva

NEW ZEALAND

Napier
Wellington
Christchurch
Chatham Is. (NZ)
Dunedin

Auckland

Hokitika

MARSHALL ISLANDS
Ujelang

Yaren
NAURU

SOLOMON ISLANDS
Honiara

Tanna

VANUATU
Port-Vila

Nouméa
New Caledonia (France)

FEDERATED STATES OF MICRONESIA

New Ireland

Bougainville

Kieta

New Britain

PAPUA NEW GUINEA
Port Moresby

New Guinea

Northern Marianas (USA)
Saipan

Guam (USA)

PALAU

SOUTHEAST ASIA see p.23

AUSTRALIA see p.44

PACIFIC OCEAN

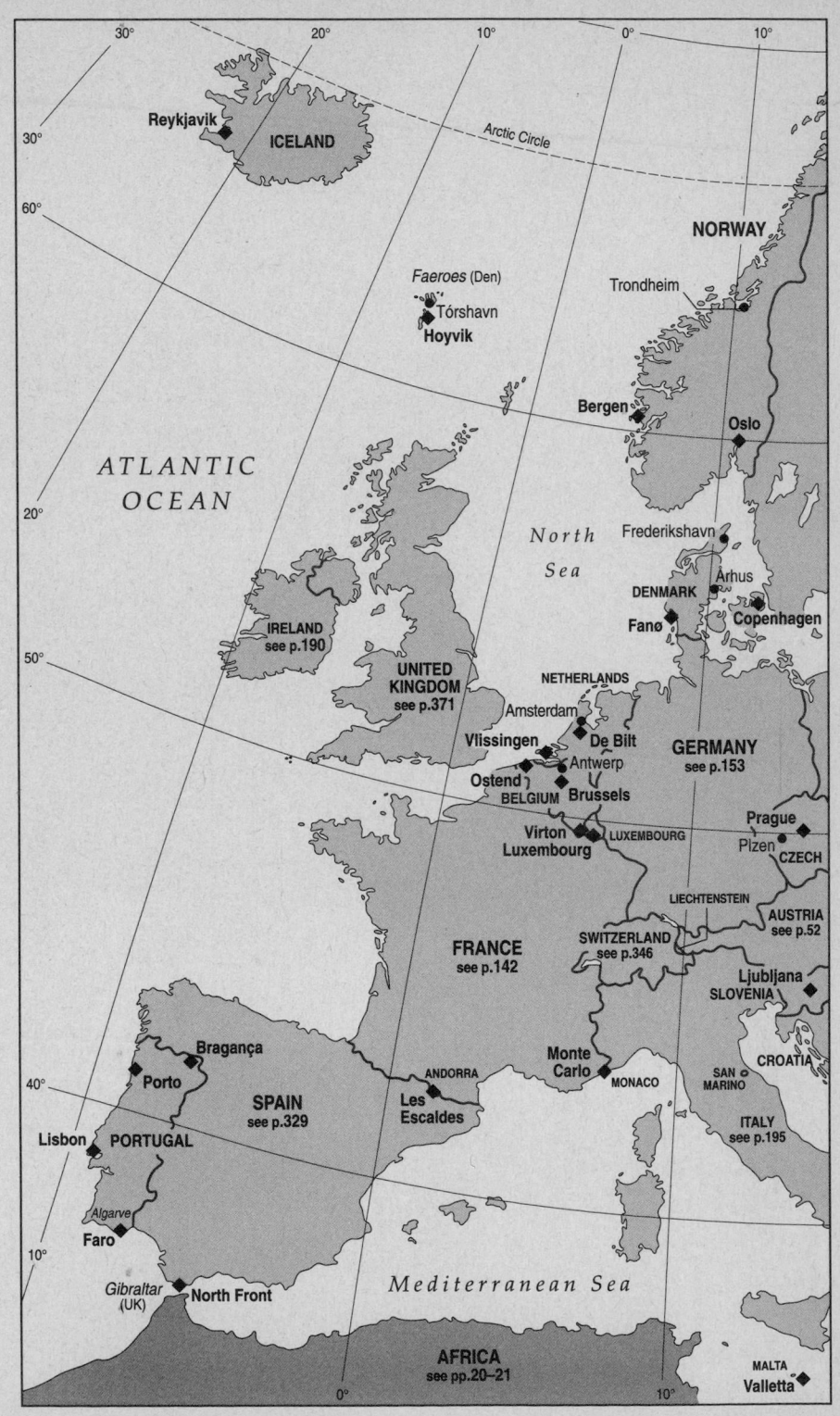

30°   20°   10°   0°   10°

Reykjavik ◆
ICELAND

Arctic Circle

30°

60°

NORWAY

Faeroes (Den)
Trondheim
◆ **Tórshavn**
Hoyvik

Bergen ◆

Oslo ◆

A T L A N T I C
O C E A N

20°

N o r t h
S e a

Frederikshavn

Århus

DENMARK

Copenhagen
Fanø ◆

IRELAND
see p.190

50°

UNITED
KINGDOM
see p.371

NETHERLANDS
Amsterdam
Vlissingen ◆ **De Bilt**
Antwerp
Ostend ◆ **GERMANY**
BELGIUM **Brussels** see p.153

Prague ◆
Plzeň ◆
CZECH

Virton ◆ LUXEMBOURG
Luxembourg

LIECHTENSTEIN

AUSTRIA
see p.52

FRANCE
see p.142

SWITZERLAND
see p.346

Ljubljana ◆
SLOVENIA

Bragança
◆ **Porto**

SPAIN
see p.329

Monte
Carlo ◆
MONACO

CROATIA

SAN
MARINO

40°

ANDORRA
Les
Escaldes ◆

ITALY
see p.195

Lisbon ◆ **PORTUGAL**

Algarve
Faro ◆

Gibraltar
(UK)   ◆ **North Front**

M e d i t e r r a n e a n   S e a

10°

AFRICA
see pp.20–21

0°   10°

MALTA
Valletta ◆

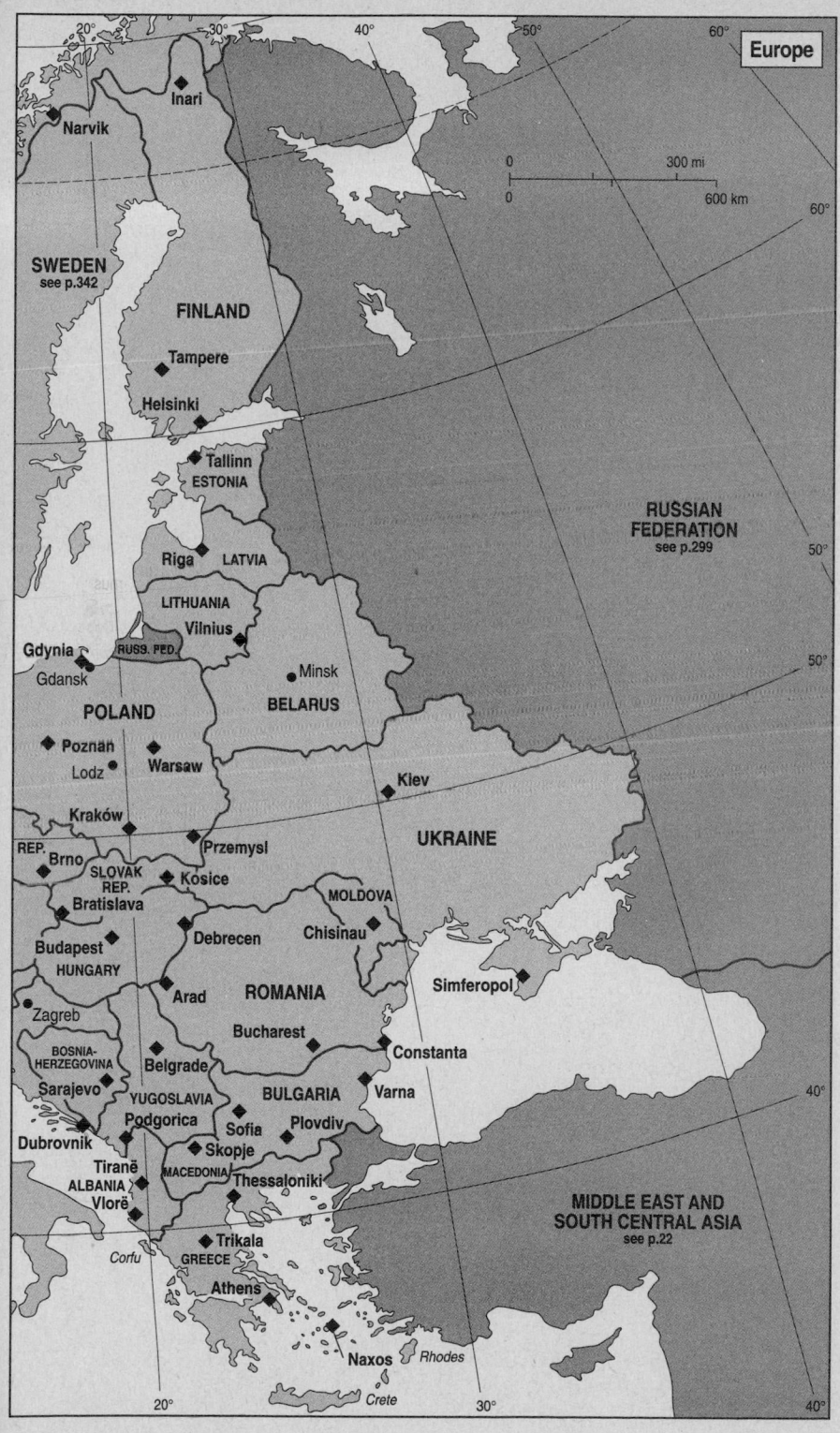

Europe

0   300 mi
0   600 km

SWEDEN
see p.342

FINLAND

Inari

Narvik

Tampere

Helsinki

Tallinn
ESTONIA

**RUSSIAN
FEDERATION**
see p.299

Riga   **LATVIA**

LITHUANIA
Vilnius

Gdynia   RUSS. FED.
Gdansk

Minsk

POLAND   **BELARUS**

Poznan
Lodz   Warsaw

Kraków

Kiev

REP.
Brno   Przemysl

**SLOVAK
REP.**
Bratislava   Kosice

UKRAINE

MOLDOVA

Budapest   Debrecen   Chisinau

HUNGARY

Zagreb   Arad   **ROMANIA**

Simferopol

**BOSNIA-
HERZEGOVINA**   Bucharest

Sarajevo   Belgrade

Constanta

Dubrovnik   **YUGOSLAVIA**   **BULGARIA**   Varna

Podgorica   Sofia   Plovdiv

Tiranë   Skopje
ALBANIA   **MACEDONIA**   Thessaloniki
Vlorë

**MIDDLE EAST AND
SOUTH CENTRAL ASIA**
see p.22

Trikala
Corfu   **GREECE**

Athens

Naxos   *Rhodes*

Crete

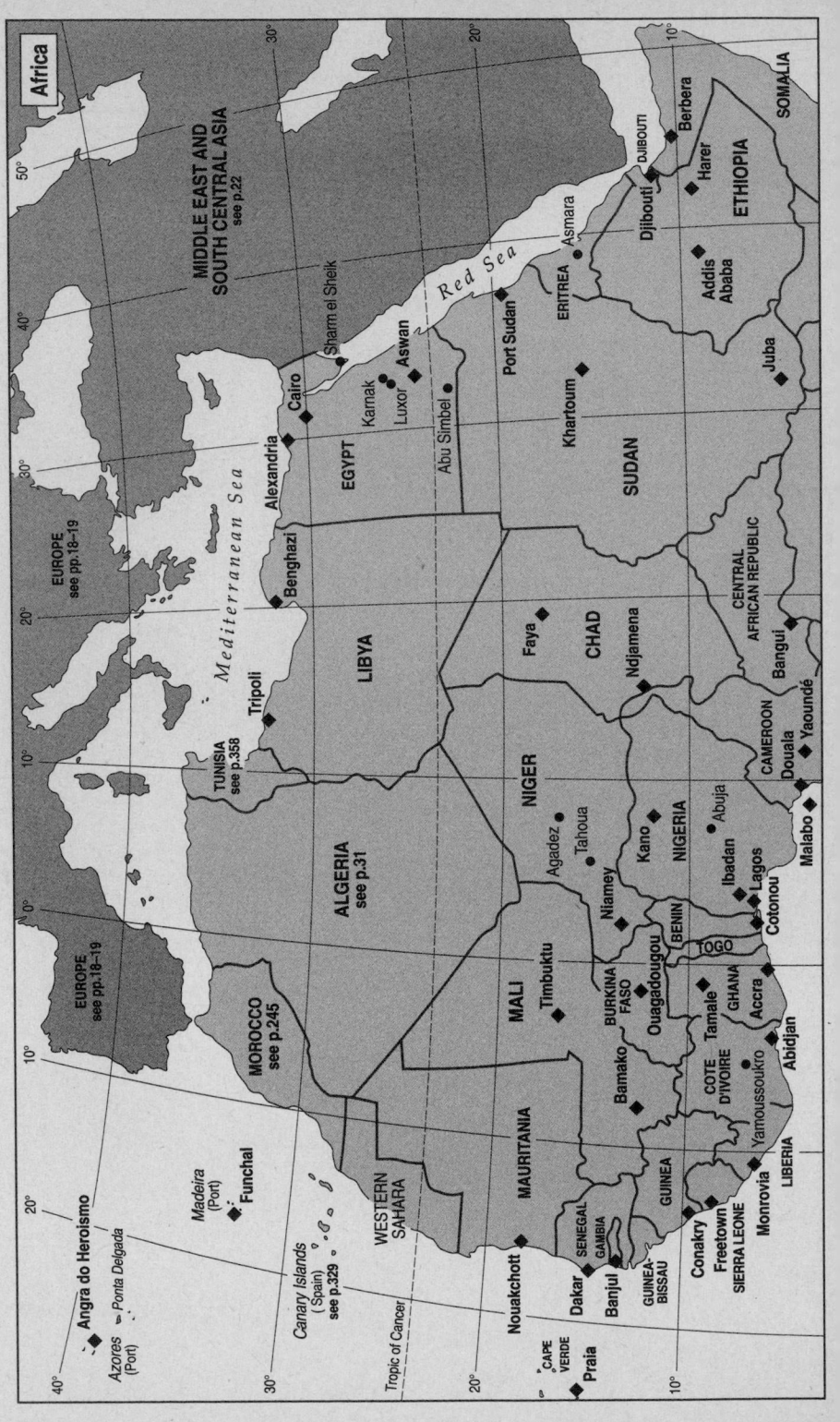

Africa

MIDDLE EAST AND
SOUTH CENTRAL ASIA
see p.22

EUROPE
see pp.18-19

Mediterranean Sea

Red Sea

Sharm el Sheik

Cairo

Alexandria

Benghazi

Tripoli

TUNISIA
see p.358

LIBYA

EGYPT

Karnak
Luxor
Abu Simbel

Aswan

Port Sudan

Asmara
ERITREA

DJIBOUTI
Djibouti
Berbera

Harer

Addis
Ababa

ETHIOPIA

SOMALIA

Khartoum

SUDAN

Juba

Faya

CHAD

Ndjamena

CENTRAL
AFRICAN REPUBLIC

Bangui

CAMEROON
Douala
Yaoundé
Malabo

NIGER

Agadez
Tahoua

Niamey
Kano

Abuja

NIGERIA

Ibadan
Lagos
Cotonou

BENIN

TOGO

GHANA
Accra

Abidjan

COTE
D'IVOIRE

Yamoussoukro

LIBERIA

Monrovia

SIERRA LEONE
Freetown

Conakry

GUINEA

Tamale

BURKINA
FASO

Ouagadougou

Bamako

MALI

Timbuktu

ALGERIA
see p.31

MOROCCO
see p.245

WESTERN
SAHARA

MAURITANIA

Nouakchott

SENEGAL
Dakar
GAMBIA
Banjul
GUINEA-
BISSAU

CAPE
VERDE
Praia

Canary Islands
(Spain)
see p.329

Madeira
(Port)
Funchal

EUROPE
see pp.18-19

Angra do Heroismo

Azores
(Port)
Ponta Delgada

Tropic of Cancer

50°
40°
30°
20°
10°
0°
10°
20°
30°
20°
10°
0°
10°
20°
30°
40°

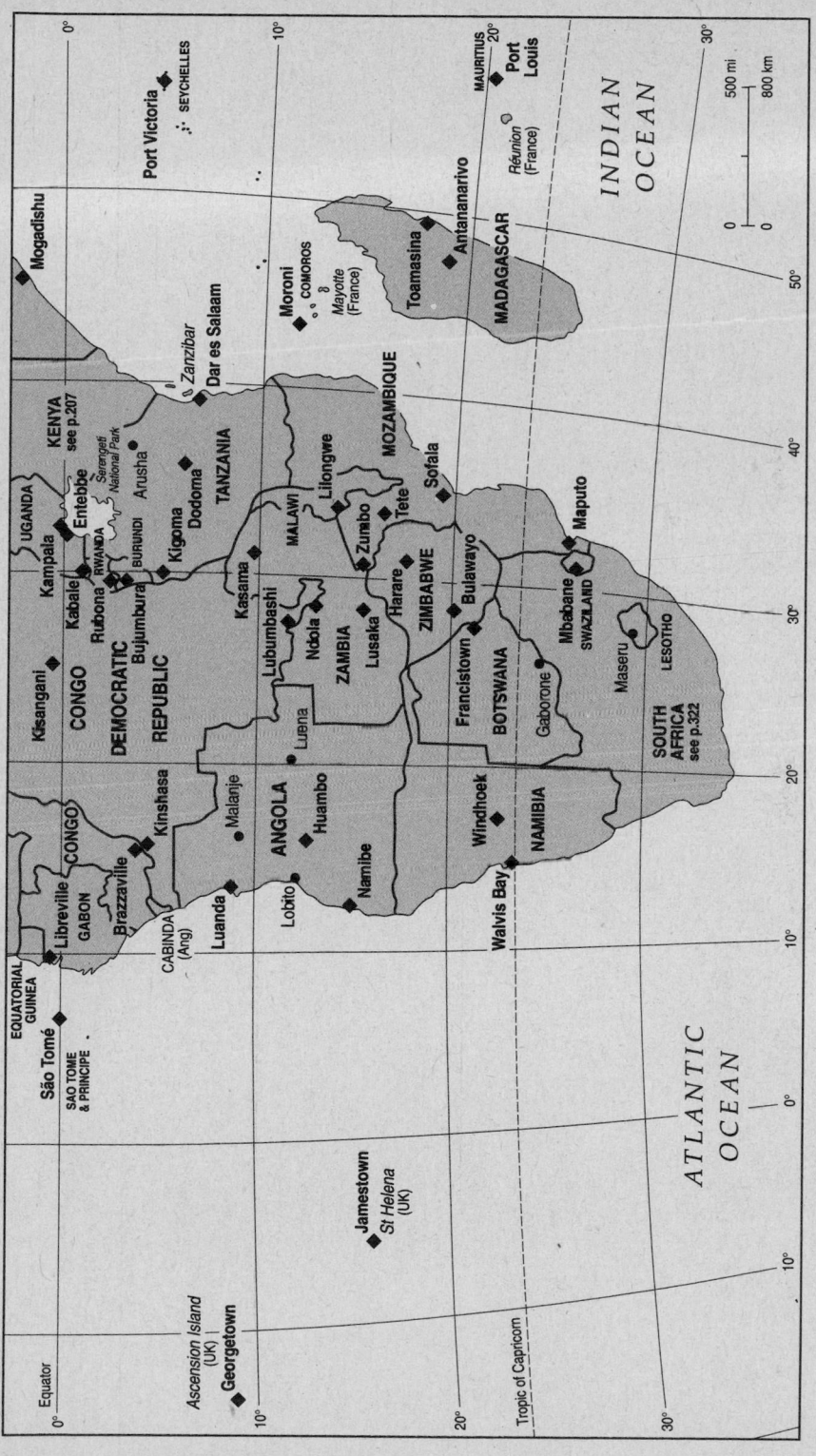

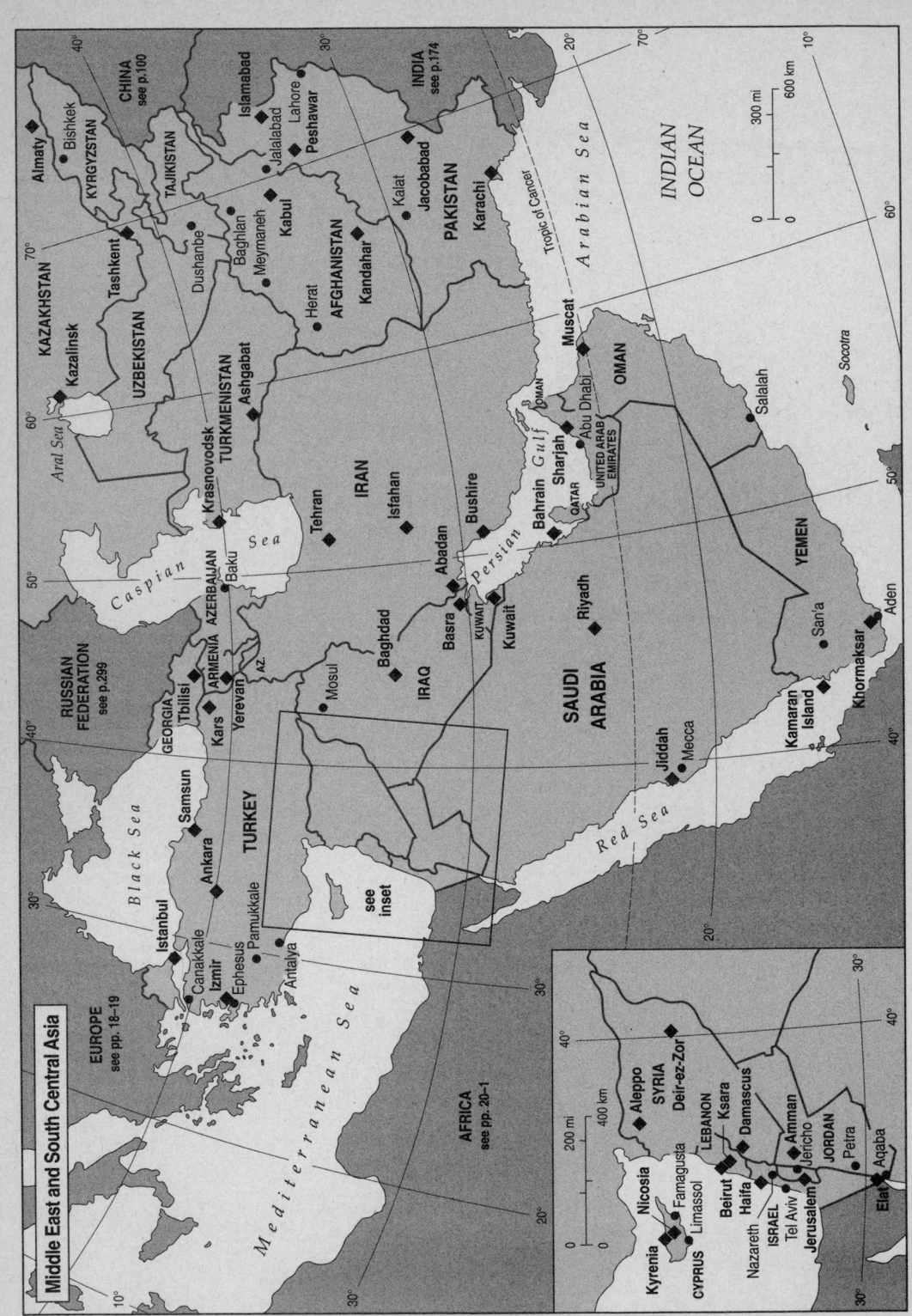

Middle East and South Central Asia

ASIA

KAZAKHSTAN

CHINA see p.100

KYRGYZSTAN

Almaty

Bishkek

TAJIKISTAN

Islamabad

INDIA see p.174

Kazalinsk

UZBEKISTAN

Tashkent

Jalalabad

Lahore

Peshawar

Kalat

Jacobabad

Dushanbe

Baghlan

Meymaneh

Kabul

AFGHANISTAN

Kandahar

PAKISTAN

Karachi

TURKMENISTAN

Ashgabat

Herat

Aral Sea

Krasnovodsk

IRAN

Isfahan

Tehran

INDIAN OCEAN

Arabian Sea

Socotra

Tropic of Cancer

Muscat

OMAN

Salalah

Abu Dhabi

Sharjah

UNITED ARAB EMIRATES

QATAR

Bahrain

Bushire

Abadan

Persian Gulf

OMAN

Caspian Sea

Baku

AZERBAIJAN

ARMENIA

Yerevan

AZ.

Kars

Tbilisi

GEORGIA

RUSSIAN FEDERATION see p.299

Baghdad

Basra

KUWAIT

Kuwait

Riyadh

SAUDI ARABIA

YEMEN

San'a

Aden

Khormaksar

Kamaran Island

Mosul

IRAQ

Jiddah

Mecca

Red Sea

Black Sea

Samsun

Ankara

TURKEY

Istanbul

Canakkale

Izmir

Ephesus

Pamukkale

Antalya

EUROPE see pp.18-19

Mediterranean Sea

AFRICA see pp.20-1

see inset

600 km

300 mi

Middle East and South Central Asia

Inset:

Aleppo

SYRIA

Deir-ez-Zor

LEBANON

Ksara

Damascus

Amman

Jericho

JORDAN

Petra

Aqaba

Elat

Nicosia

Kyrenia

Famagusta

Limassol

CYPRUS

Beirut

Haifa

Nazareth

Tel Aviv

ISRAEL

Jerusalem

400 km

200 mi

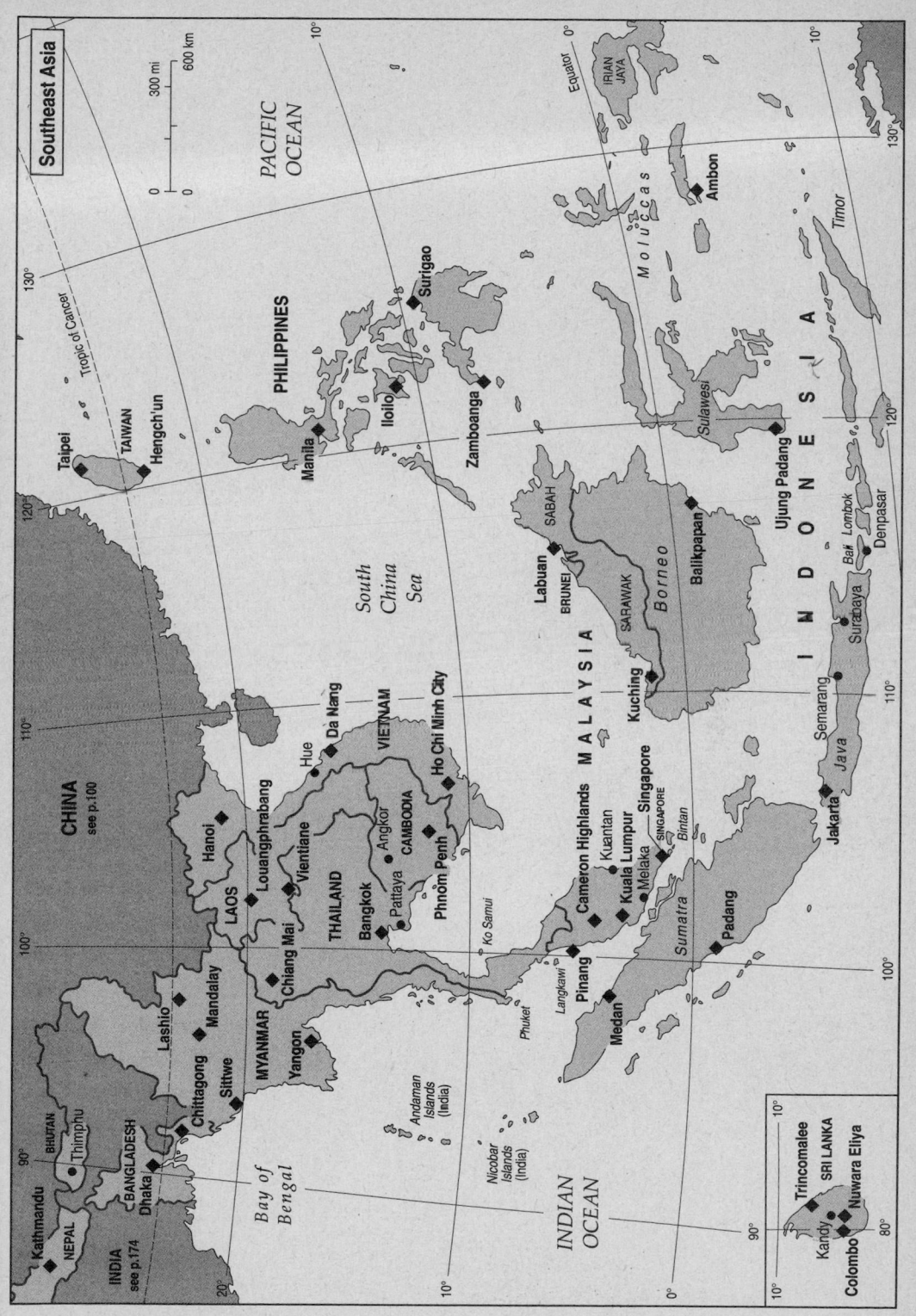

Southeast Asia

PACIFIC
OCEAN

600 km
300 mi

Tropic of Cancer

PHILIPPINES

Taipei
TAIWAN
Hengch'un

Manila
Iloilo
Zamboanga
Surigao

Equator

IRIAN
JAYA

Ambon

M o l u c c a s

Sulawesi

Ujung Padang

I N D O N E S I A

Timor

Balikpapan

Denpasar

Bali Lombok

Surabaya

Borneo

SABAH

BRUNEI
Labuan

SARAWAK

Kuching

Semarang

Java

Jakarta

South
China
Sea

MALAYSIA

Cameron Highlands

Kuantan

Kuala Lumpur

Singapore
SINGAPORE
Bintan

Meleka

Padang

Sumatra

Pinang

Medan

Langkawi

Ko Samui

Phuket

CHINA
see p.100

Hanoi

Louangphrabang

Vientiane

LAOS

Chiang Mai

MYANMAR

Yangon

Mandalay

Lashio

Chittagong

Sittwe

Da Nang

Hue

VIETNAM

Ho Chi Minh City

Angkor

CAMBODIA

Phnôm Penh

Pattaya

Bangkok

THAILAND

Andaman
Islands
(India)

Nicobar
Islands
(India)

Bay of
Bengal

INDIAN
OCEAN

Kathmandu

NEPAL

BHUTAN

Thimphu

BANGLADESH

Dhaka

INDIA
see p.174

Trincomalee

SRI LANKA

Nuwara Eliya

Kandy

Colombo

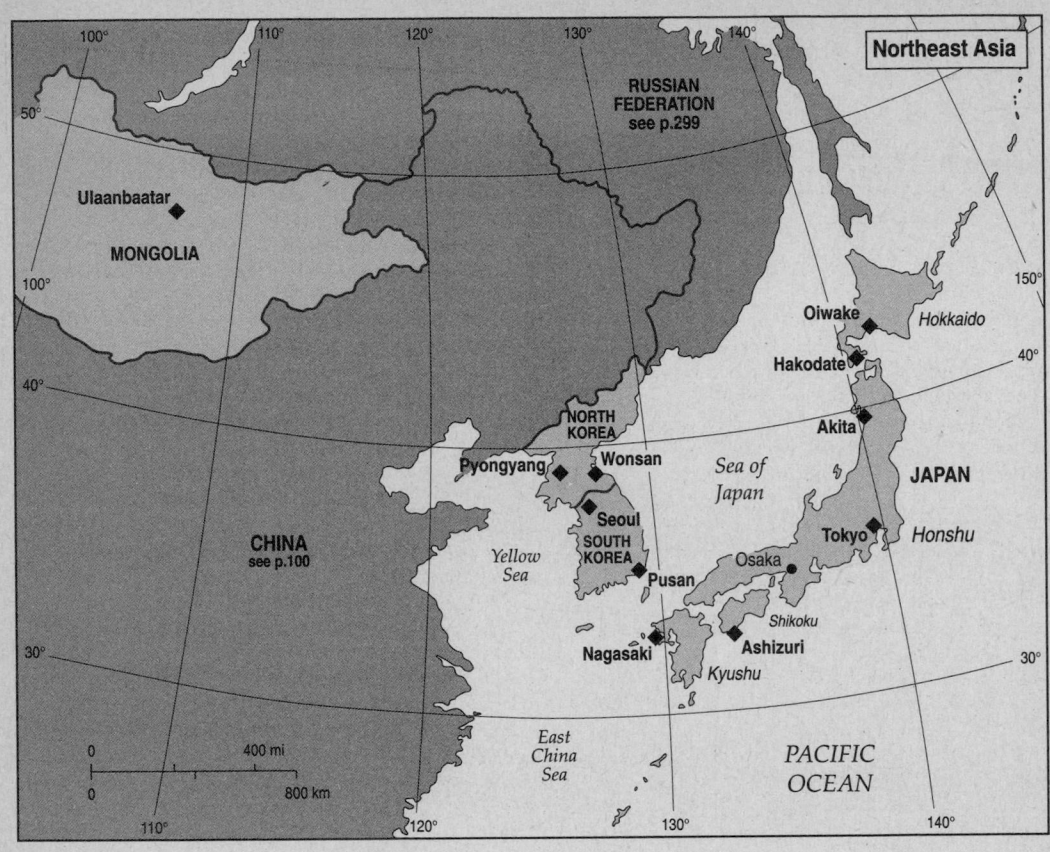

Northeast Asia

RUSSIAN
FEDERATION
see p.299

Ulaanbaatar

MONGOLIA

Oiwake

Hokkaido

Hakodate

Akita

NORTH
KOREA

Pyongyang   Wonsan

Sea of
Japan

JAPAN

Seoul
SOUTH
KOREA

CHINA
see p.100

Yellow
Sea

Pusan

Osaka

Tokyo   Honshu

Shikoku

Nagasaki   Ashizuri

Kyushu

East
China
Sea

PACIFIC
OCEAN

0   400 mi

0   800 km

Country by country weather

Use this A to Z to look up details about the weather in particular parts of the world. There is a separate entry for every country and for almost every overseas territory. In addition, there is a general entry for the Caribbean Islands. For selected countries with distinct weather zones, such as the USA, entries are divided by regional subheadings.

Most entries include at least one table showing information for a particular town or city that is representative of a region, if not the whole country. The latitude, longitude, and altitude of the weather station that recorded the information is given. The number of years over which figures have been recorded is also indicated.

Entries without tables cross-refer to tables that show almost identical weather in nearby countries. Each entry gives a concise description of the climate and most important seasonal differences. This includes a note of any weather hazards or dangerous features.

To help you apply the information in the tables to other locations nearby, all of the towns and cities that recorded information presented here are mapped – either in the **Weather station maps** on pp. 13–24 or on the country maps in selected entries. Most of the country maps in selected entries also show the country's climatic regions.

WHAT THE TABLES SHOW

Month by month, each table shows the figures recorded over a stated period of years for daily hours of sunshine, temperatures, relative humidity, and precipitation (rainfall and snow). Where applicable, the table also shows the degree of discomfort to be expected from the combined effects of heat and humidity. In all cases where a column is blank, this means that information either is not applicable or is not available.

Hours of sunshine The figures in the first column of each of the tables show month by month the average for bright sunshine each day. (For some locations these figures are not available.)

Temperature Average daily maximum and minimum temperatures are given for each month in Centigrade and Fahrenheit. These are shade temperatures. Maximum temperatures usually occur in early afternoon and minimum temperatures just before sunrise. The highest and lowest temperatures recorded in each month are also listed. These give an idea of the extremes that can occur.

Humidity Relative humidity is expressed as a percentage. A relative humidity of 100 percent means that air cannot hold any more water vapour at any given temperature. It is measured as a daily figure at one or more fixed hours during the day. Since relative humidity varies inversely with temperature, it is normally lowest in the early afternoon and highest just before sunrise. High humidity combined with high temperatures increases discomfort. See the Comfort Index on p. 1.

Precipitation Precipitation includes all forms of moisture falling on the earth, mainly rain and snow. The average monthly fall is shown in both millimetres and inches for each month. Also shown is the average number of days in each month on which a significant fall occurs. What is 'significant' varies from country to country so look closely at the heading for this column.

By dividing the monthly fall by the number of days with rain you can get an idea of the intensity of rainfall in each place. A large number of days with rain indicates a cloudy, changeable climate.

Heat and humidity The table warns of 'moderate' discomfort if some people would feel uncomfortable at the hottest time of the day in the afternoon humidity typical of the month. It warns of 'medium' discomfort if more than 50 percent of people would feel uncomfortable. It warns of 'high' discomfort if everyone would feel uncomfortable. It warns of 'extreme' discomfort in conditions likely to produce distinct stress and of 'danger' when conditions are so extreme that heatstroke is a serious possibility.

Afghanistan

See map page 22

This is a landlocked country, a little larger than France. It is bordered by Turkmenistan, Uzbekistan and Tajikistan on the north, Pakistan on the east and south, and Iran on the west. In the extreme east it has a very short boundary with China in the high Pamir Mountains.

Much of the country is mountainous; the highest peaks in the Pamirs and Hindu Kush rise to over 6,600 m/20,000 ft. The lowest areas are in the southwest along the Iranian border and in the north along the border with Turkmenistan and Uzbekistan.

Afghanistan has a harsh climate of the continental type and the severity of winter is accentuated by the high altitude of much of the country. Summers are warm, except in the highest areas, and at lower levels temperatures sometimes rise very high indeed. Winter and spring are the seasons of most changeable weather and most of the annual precipitation occurs at this time. Afghanistan is the most easterly country to experience the influence of the Mediterranean Sea, which is the source of most of the depressions that bring the winter precipitation. The high mountains to the south shield Afghanistan from the summer rains brought to India and parts of Pakistan by the southwest monsoon. Almost no rain falls from June to October. The lower parts of the country have a semi-arid or desert climate. In Seistan, along the Iranian border, hot, dry, dusty winds are among the most unpleasant features of the summer weather.

Summers are sunny and generally hot, except in the higher mountains. Sunshine lasts for six to seven hours a day in winter and as much as twelve to thirteen in summer.

Because of the large range of temperature conditions found in Afghanistan, there is both a danger of heat exhaustion or even heatstroke in the lower regions in summer, and of exposure, wind chill, and frostbite in the mountains in winter.

The table for **Kabul** (below) represents the climatic conditions over most of Afghanistan, particularly those in the mountainous centre and east. Compare the table for **Kandahar** (overleaf).

KABUL — EAST-CENTRAL AFGHANISTAN

	Sunshine average hours per day	Temperatures Average daily minimum °C	°F	Average daily maximum °C	°F	Highest recorded °C	°F	Lowest recorded °C	°F	Discomfort from heat and humidity	Relative humidity 8:00 %	Relative humidity 16:00 %	Average monthly precipitation mm	in	Wet days more than 2.5 mm/0.1 in	
Jan	6	−8	18	2	36	14	58	−21	−6		80	70	31	1.2	2.0	Jan
Feb	6	−6	22	4	40	23	74	−21	−5		79	62	36	1.4	3.0	Feb
March	6	1	34	12	53	25	77	−14	6		76	44	94	3.7	7.0	March
April	7	6	43	19	66	28	83	−3	27		69	35	102	4.0	6.0	April
May	10	11	51	26	78	35	95	1	34	Moderate	61	32	20	0.8	2.0	May
June	12	13	56	31	87	37	99	6	42	Medium	52	24	5	0.2	0.6	June
July	11	16	61	33	92	38	101	11	51	Medium	51	22	3	0.1	0.4	July
Aug	11	15	59	33	91	40	104	8	47	Medium	54	23	3	0.1	0.4	Aug
Sept	10	11	51	29	85	36	97	2	36	Moderate	58	18	0	0.0	0.1	Sept
Oct	9	6	42	23	73	32	89	−3	27		59	22	15	0.6	0.9	Oct
Nov	8	1	33	17	62	25	77	−15	5		67	31	20	0.8	2.0	Nov
Dec	6	−3	27	8	47	19	67	−15	5		76	53	10	0.4	1.0	Dec

Based on readings for 9 years at 34°30′ N, 69°13′ E, altitude 1827 m/5955 ft

KANDAHAR												SOUTHERN AFGHANISTAN			
Sunshine		Temperatures								Discomfort from heat and humidity	Precipitation and humidity				Wet days	
		Average daily				Highest recorded		Lowest recorded			Relative humidity		Average monthly precipitation			
		minimum		maximum							7:00	16:00				
average hours per day		°C	°F	°C	°F	°C	°F	°C	°F		%		mm	in	more than 2.5 mm/0.1 in	
Jan	7	−1	31	13	56	21	70	−10	14		83	51	79	3.1	5.0	Jan
Feb	7	2	36	17	62	27	80	−6	21		75	38	43	1.7	4.0	Feb
March	8	6	42	22	72	31	88	−6	21		74	31	20	0.8	2.0	March
April	9	10	50	28	83	36	97	1	33	Moderate	64	28	8	0.3	1.0	April
May	10	14	57	33	92	42	107	4	39	Medium	57	28	5	0.2	0.4	May
June	13	17	62	37	99	44	111	9	49	High	52	23	0	0.0	0.0	June
July	12	19	66	39	102	42	108	12	53	High	57	27	3	0.1	0.4	July
Aug	11	17	63	37	99	43	109	11	52	High	53	23	0	0.0	0.0	Aug
Sept	11	11	51	34	93	38	100	4	39	Medium	56	21	0	0.0	0.0	Sept
Oct	10	7	44	29	85	38	100	−1	30	Moderate	65	23	0	0.0	0.0	Oct
Nov	9	2	36	23	73	32	89	−9	16		76	29	0	0.0	0.4	Nov
Dec	7	−1	31	15	59	25	77	−9	15		81	43	20	0.8	2.0	Dec

Based on readings for 7 years at 31°36′ N, 65°40′ E, altitude 1055 m/3462 ft

The table for **Kandahar** (above) is representative of the lower and drier parts of the Afghanistan. Here winters are milder but there may be spells of very cold weather for a few days at a time.

Albania

See map page 19

Albania is a small, mountainous country about the same size as Wales or the state of Maryland. It has a coastline on the Mediterranean and its land frontier with Yugoslavia, Macedonia, and Greece traverses some of the wildest mountain scenery in Europe. The climate on the coast is typically Mediterranean with mild, wet winters and warm, sunny, and rather dry summers. Inland conditions vary depending on altitude but the higher areas above 1,500 m/ 5,000 ft are cold and frequently snowy in winter; here cold conditions with lying snow may linger into spring. For a Mediterranean country the precipitation is heavy; coastlands are quite wet in winter and mountain areas are among the wetter parts of Europe.

Midsummer months are generally sunny but the fine weather can be interrupted by occasional thundery downpours. The weather is rarely excessively hot on the coast and, although often rather humid, is made quite pleasant by the daily sea breezes. Winter conditions on the coast are generally mild but occasional cold winds from the north and east may bring an unwelcome chill for a few days when the mountains inland are covered with snow. When a warm humid wind – the sirocco – blows from the southwest or south, conditions may feel oppressive. This is particularly the case in autumn when Mediterranean Sea temperatures are at their highest. The sirocco then often precedes wet weather and a return to cooler temperatures. For conditions on the coast see the table for **Vlorë** (opposite and above).

Inland and in the mountains the annual sequence of weather is similar to that on the coast but the summers are cooler and less humid. See the table for **Tiranë** (opposite). During the stormier conditions of autumn and winter, rain may be heavy and cold and snow severe. Everywhere summer and early autumn are the most settled months. Sunshine amounts are quite high, averaging over eleven hours a day in July and four hours a day in January.

VLORE

COASTAL ALBANIA

Sunshine	Temperatures								Discomfort from heat and humidity	Precipitation and humidity				Wet days
	Average daily				Highest recorded		Lowest recorded			Relative humidity 7:30 14:30		Average monthly precipitation		
	minimum		maximum											
average hours per day	°C	°F	°C	°F	°C	°F	°C	°F		%		mm	in	more than 0.1 mm/0.004 in
Jan 4	6	42	13	56	22	72	−5	23		69	56	120	4.7	13 Jan
Feb 5	6	42	14	56	24	76	−5	23		68	54	106	4.2	12 Feb
March 6	8	46	16	60	27	81	−3	26		72	57	92	3.6	14 March
April 8	10	51	19	66	29	84	0	33		70	55	79	3.1	11 April
May 9	14	57	23	74	36	96	6	43		71	56	54	2.1	9 May
June 11	17	63	27	81	36	97	11	51	Medium	67	51	28	1.1	6 June
July 12	19	66	30	85	39	102	13	56	Medium	65	48	9	0.4	3 July
Aug 11	19	66	30	87	39	101	14	57	Medium	65	46	26	1.0	3 Aug
Sept 9	16	61	27	81	34	92	10	49	Medium	70	50	32	1.3	5 Sept
Oct 7	14	57	23	74	32	89	6	42		70	54	116	4.6	10 Oct
Nov 4	11	53	19	66	28	82	1	34		72	62	192	7.6	17 Nov
Dec 3	8	46	15	59	25	76	−4	25		69	60	141	5.6	17 Dec

Based on readings for 10 years at 40°28' N, 19°29' E, altitude 3 m/10 ft

TIRANE

CENTRAL ALBANIA

Sunshine	Temperatures								Discomfort from heat and humidity	Precipitation and humidity				Wet days
	Average daily				Highest recorded		Lowest recorded			Relative humidity 7:30 14:30		Average monthly precipitation		
	minimum		maximum											
average hours per day	°C	°F	°C	°F	°C	°F	°C	°F		%		mm	in	more than 0.1 mm/0.004 in
Jan 4	2	36	12	53	19	65	−8	18		83	58	135	5.3	13 Jan
Feb 4	2	36	12	54	22	71	−8	18		83	54	152	6.0	13 Feb
March 5	5	41	15	59	26	78	−4	25		83	53	128	5.0	14 March
April 7	8	47	18	65	28	82	−1	31		83	54	117	4.6	13 April
May 8	12	53	23	74	33	91	3	37		83	56	122	4.8	12 May
June 10	16	60	28	82	37	99	6	42	Medium	74	49	86	3.4	7 June
July 11	17	63	31	87	38	101	11	51	Medium	72	42	32	1.3	5 July
Aug 11	17	62	31	89	40	105	10	51	Medium	75	39	32	1.3	4 Aug
Sept 9	14	58	27	81	35	95	5	42	Moderate	82	45	60	2.4	6 Sept
Oct 7	10	50	23	73	31	87	1	35		85	59	105	4.1	9 Oct
Nov 3	8	47	17	63	25	78	−3	27		86	63	211	8.3	16 Nov
Dec 2	5	40	14	56	22	72	−7	20		83	63	173	6.8	16 Dec

Based on readings for 10 years at 41°20' N, 19°47' E, altitude 89 m/292 ft

Algeria

Algeria is a North African country four times as large as France. About one-sixth of the country, comprising the Mediterranean coastlands and the northern mountains, has a typical Mediterranean climate with winter rainfall. The rest of the country to the south of the Saharan Atlas Mountains is almost rainless and is part of the great Sahara desert.

Northern Algeria has two ranges of moderately high mountains: the Tell Atlas and the Saharan Atlas, separated by a region of elevated plains and interior basins, the Plateau of the Chotts. Climate and weather here vary locally depending on altitude.

MEDITERRANEAN ALGERIA

Rainfall is heaviest and most consitent along the Mediterranean coast and in the higher parts of the Tell Atlas where it varies from 400 mm/16 in to 800 mm/32 in per year. Most rainfall occurs between September and May with the heaviest and most consistent rains occurring from November to March.

The table for **Algiers** (below) is representative of coastal Algeria.

Above 900 m/3,000 ft precipitation often falls as snow and at the highest levels this may lie for several weeks. From May to September the weather is settled and hot with almost continuous sunshine. During the rest of the year it is more changeable, with an alternation from warm sunny days and cool nights to disturbed periods with rain and cloud. The mildest weather in winter is to be found on the coast; this area also tends to escape the fiercest summer heat, except when a hot dry sirocco from the south carries the heat of the Sahara northwards.

THE ALGERIAN PLATEAU

Inland the plateau of the Chotts and the Saharan Atlas have a rather more extreme continental type of climate with hotter summers and colder winters. Frost and snow occur here in winter and the nights can be very cold after quite warm days.

The heat in summer frequently reaches levels typical of the Sahara but is made more tolerable by the low humidity. Over much of the area rainfall is low and it has a tendency to a double maximum, one in the autumn and the other in spring.

ALGIERS											COASTAL ALGERIA		
Sunshine	Temperatures							Discomfort from heat and humidity	Precipitation and humidity			Wet days	
	Average daily				Highest recorded		Lowest recorded		Relative humidity		Average monthly precipitation		
	minimum		maximum						7:00	13:00			
average hours per day	°C	°F	°C	°F	°C	°F	°C	°F	%		mm	in	more than 1 mm/0.04 in
Jan	5	9	49	15	59	24	76	1	34		75	66	112	4.4	11.0	Jan
Feb	6	9	49	16	61	30	86	1	34		72	60	84	3.3	9.0	Feb
March	7	11	52	17	63	29	84	3	37		71	59	74	2.9	9.0	March
April	7	13	55	20	68	37	99	6	43		67	57	41	1.6	5.0	April
May	8	15	59	23	73	38	101	7	44	Moderate	72	60	46	1.8	5.0	May
June	9	18	65	26	78	38	101	13	55	Medium	72	60	15	0.6	2.0	June
July	10	21	70	28	83	41	106	17	62	Medium	73	60	0	0.0	0.4	July
Aug	10	22	71	29	85	42	107	18	64	Medium	70	60	5	0.2	0.5	Aug
Sept	8	21	69	27	81	39	103	12	53	Medium	74	62	41	1.6	4.0	Sept
Oct	6	17	63	23	74	38	100	7	45	Moderate	72	60	79	3.1	7.0	Oct
Nov	5	13	56	19	66	31	88	4	40		73	63	130	5.1	11.0	Nov
Dec	4	11	51	16	60	24	76	0	32		72	64	137	5.4	12.0	Dec

Based on readings for 25 years at 36°46′ S, 3°03′ E, altitude 59 m/194 ft

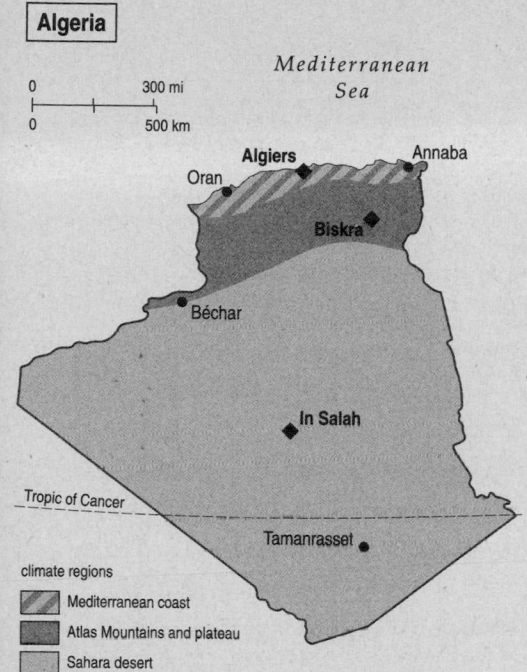

Algeria

Mediterranean
Sea

0 ——— 300 mi
0 ——— 500 km

Algiers   Annaba
Oran

Biskra

Béchar

In Salah

Tropic of Cancer

Tamanrasset

climate regions

Mediterranean coast
Atlas Mountains and plateau
Sahara desert

The table for **Biskra** (below) is typical of the Algerian plateau area on the fringe of the Sahara.

Immediately south of the Saharan Atlas, this narrow belt of steppe country, similar to that in southern Tunisia, has a definite wet season in winter but rainfall is low and unreliable.

Compare the table for **In Salah** – in the centre of the Sahara – overleaf.

THE ALGERIAN SAHARA

The Saharan desert region of Algeria has a climate that is virtually rainless. Occasional rain may fall in any month but the amounts are so small and unreliable as to make averages meaningless.

In the extreme south of Algeria sporadic rainfall is more probable in the period June to September as the intertropical rain-belt, which affects West Africa at this time, occasionally spreads this far north. In the southeast of Algeria the great mountain mass of the Hoggar, rising to nearly 2,700 m/9,000 ft, receives rather more rain which may fall at any season.

Algeria has a very sunny climate. In the north daily sunshine averages from five to six hours in winter and eleven to twelve in summer. In the Sahara they approach the maximum possible duration: nine to ten in winter and twelve to thirteen in summer.

BISKRA

ALGERIAN PLATEAU

	Sunshine	Temperatures								Discomfort from heat and humidity	Precipitation and humidity				Wet days	
		Average daily				Highest recorded		Lowest recorded			Relative humidity 7:30 13:30		Average monthly precipitation			
		minimum		maximum												
	average hours per day	°C	°F	°C	°F	°C	°F	°C	°F		%		mm	in	more than 0.1mm/0.004in	
Jan	7	7	44	16	61	24	75	−1	30		69	52	18	0.7	4	Jan
Feb	8	8	46	18	65	28	82	0	32		62	44	10	0.4	3	Feb
March	9	11	52	22	71	31	88	1	34		58	40	18	0.7	5	March
April	10	14	58	26	79	38	100	6	42	Moderate	47	32	10	0.4	2	April
May	10	18	65	31	87	40	104	8	47	Medium	47	32	15	0.6	3	May
June	11	24	75	36	97	46	115	17	62	High	42	27	8	0.3	2	June
July	12	27	80	42	107	47	117	20	68	Extreme	36	20	3	0.1	1	July
Aug	11	26	79	41	105	49	121	19	67	Extreme	38	25	3	0.1	1	Aug
Sept	9	23	73	34	94	43	110	12	54	Medium	50	34	18	0.7	3	Sept
Oct	8	17	63	28	82	38	101	8	47	Moderate	57	39	15	0.6	3	Oct
Nov	7	12	53	21	70	29	85	2	36		64	45	23	0.9	4	Nov
Dec	7	7	45	17	62	27	80	−1	30		69	49	18	0.7	3	Dec

Based on readings for 26 years at 34°51′ N, 5°44′ E, altitude 124 m/407 ft

IN SALAH												ALGERIAN SAHARA

Sunshine	Temperatures							Discomfort from heat and humidity	Precipitation and humidity				Wet days
	Average daily				Highest recorded		Lowest recorded			Relative humidity 7:00 13:00		Average monthly precipitation	
average hours per day	minimum		maximum										more than 0.1mm/0.004in
	°C	°F	°C	°F	°C	°F	°C	°F		%		mm	in
Jan	9	6	43	21	69	31	88	-3	26		63	37	3	0.1	0.4	Jan
Feb	10	8	47	24	75	35	95	-2	28		64	34	3	0.1	0.6	Feb
March	10	12	53	28	83	39	102	2	36	Moderate	51	35	0	0.0	0.4	March
April	11	17	62	33	92	42	107	9	48	Medium	40	27	0	0.0	0.6	April
May	11	21	69	37	99	46	114	12	54	High	37	23	0	0.0	0.9	May
June	11	27	80	43	110	50	122	16	61	Extreme	36	25	0	0.0	0.6	June
July	12	28	83	45	113	50	122	23	73	Extreme	29	16	0	0.0	0.0	July
Aug	11	28	82	44	111	50	122	22	72	Extreme	31	19	3	0.1	0.6	Aug
Sept	10	25	77	41	105	49	120	17	63	Extreme	38	24	0	0.0	0.7	Sept
Oct	9	19	66	34	94	44	111	9	48	Medium	44	28	0	0.0	0.8	Oct
Nov	9	12	53	27	80	36	97	3	38	Moderate	61	38	5	0.2	1.0	Nov
Dec	8	7	45	22	71	31	88	0	32		65	38	3	0.1	0.9	Dec

Based on readings for 15 years at 27°12′ N, 2°28′ E, altitude 277 m/919 ft

In the Sahara strong winds occasionally raise dust and sand which can be dangerous as well as most unpleasant. During the hottest weather there is some danger of heat exhaustion, or even heatstroke, unless proper precautions are taken.

The table for **In Salah** (above) is representative of the vast Saharan desert that encompasses most of Algeria and much of the territory of neighbouring countries. Summer temperatures are consistently high but temperatures at night fall low enough to be quite tolerable.

Winter nights in the Sahara can be chilly and frosty but the daytime is warm and sunny.

American Samoa

See map page 17

This American dependency in the South Pacific has a land area of only 197 sq km/76 sq miles distributed between seven rocky islands of volcanic origin.

The weather and climate are typical of a tropical, oceanic environment. Rainfall is heavy and the variations in temperature are small, with June and July coolest and most pleasant. The prevailing southeast trade winds are strong from May to November, when severe tropical storms may occur. The climate is generally healthy and pleasant; the moderately high temperature and humidity are tempered by brisk daytime winds, either as afternoon sea breezes or as predominant southeast trade winds.

The tables for **Papeete** on Tahiti and **Makatea** in the Tuamotu group (both on p. 149) show weather that is similar to that in American Samoa.

LES ESCALDES														ANDORRA
Sunshine	Temperatures								Discomfort from heat and humidity	Precipitation and humidity				Wet days
	Average daily				Highest recorded		Lowest recorded			Relative humidity		Average monthly precipitation		
	minimum		maximum											
average hours per day	°C	°F	°C	°F	°C	°F	°C	°F		%		mm	in	more than 0.1 mm/0.004 in
Jan	−1	30	6	43	15	59	−13	9				34	1.3	4	Jan
Feb	−1	30	7	45	17	63	−18	0				37	1.5	6	Feb
March	2	35	12	54	20	68	−9	16				46	1.8	6	March
April	4	39	14	58	25	77	−4	25				63	2.5	10	April
May	6	43	17	62	29	84	0	32				105	4.1	15	May
June	10	39	23	73	36	97	2	36				69	2.7	9	June
July	12	54	26	79	35	95	5	41				65	2.6	8	July
Aug	12	53	24	76	33	91	4	39				98	3.9	10	Aug
Sept	10	49	22	71	31	88	2	36				81	3.2	9	Sept
Oct	6	42	16	60	27	81	−5	23				73	2.9	8	Oct
Nov	2	35	10	51	20	68	−5	23				68	2.7	6	Nov
Dec	−1	31	6	42	13	55	−11	12				69	2.7	7	Dec

Based on readings for 9 years at 42°30′ N, 1°31′ E, altitude 1080 m/3545 ft

Andorra

See map page 18

This tiny independent principality is high in the eastern Pyrenees on the border between France and Spain. Lying on the southern or Spanish side of the crest line, it is rather sheltered and therefore drier than much of the French Pyrenees. The whole country lies above 840 m/2,750 ft. Winters are cold but dry and sunny. The midsummer months are slightly drier than spring and autumn and, with the cool temperatures, summer is a pleasant season.

The table for **Les Escaldes** (above) is representative of the valleys in this small state. Temperatures are lower in the higher mountainous area.

Angola

See map page 21

Angola is over twice the size of France. It lies between 6° and 18° S in southern Africa with a coastline on the Atlantic Ocean. It is bordered by the Congo Democratic Republic on the north, by Zambia on the east and by Namibia on the south. There is a steep rise inland from a narrow coastal plain to an extensive interior plateau with an average height of between 600 m/2,000 ft and 1,200 m/4,000 ft. The highest areas of the plateau rise to over 2,400 m/8,000 ft. To the north and east of these higher areas the land slopes gradually towards the basins of the Congo and Zambezi rivers.

Over most of Angola the weather and climate are typical of a tropical plateau, with a single wet season at the time of high sun between October and March and a long dry season. The table for **Huambo** (overleaf) shows this very clearly. Here both daytime and particularly night-time temperatures are reduced by altitude to produce a pleasant variety of tropical climate. Above 1,500 m/5,000 ft temperatures around the year are temperate rather than tropical

HUAMBO												INLAND ANGOLA	
Sunshine	Temperatures								Discomfort from heat and humidity	Precipitation and humidity			Wet days
☀ average hours per day	Average daily				Highest recorded		Lowest recorded			Relative humidity 9:00 15:00		Average monthly precipitation	🌧 more than 1 mm/0.04 in
	minimum		maximum										
	°C	°F	°C	°F	°C	°F	°C	°F		%		mm	in	
Jan	4	14	58	26	78	31	88	9	48	Medium	74	60	221	8.7	15.0	Jan
Feb	6	14	58	26	78	31	88	10	50	Medium	78	63	198	7.8	15.0	Feb
March	5	14	58	26	78	30	86	10	50	Medium	75	65	249	9.8	16.0	March
April	5	14	57	26	78	29	84	7	45	Moderate	68	54	145	5.7	9.0	April
May	8	11	51	26	78	29	84	6	42	Moderate	51	38	10	0.4	1.0	May
June	8	8	46	24	76	28	83	2	36		43	31	0	0.0	0.0	June
July	9	8	47	25	77	28	83	2	36		35	24	0	0.0	0.1	July
Aug	9	11	51	27	81	31	88	6	42	Moderate	34	25	0	0.0	0.2	Aug
Sept	7	13	55	29	84	32	90	8	46	Medium	47	33	15	0.6	3.0	Sept
Oct	6	14	58	27	81	32	90	11	51	Medium	67	54	140	5.5	14.0	Oct
Nov	5	14	58	26	78	31	87	8	47	Medium	73	65	244	9.6	18.0	Nov
Dec	5	14	58	26	78	31	87	9	49	Medium	75	64	226	8.9	18.0	Dec

Based on readings for 14 years at 12°48′ S, 15°45′ E, altitude 1700 m/5577 ft

and frost is not unknown. The dry season shortens by a month or two in the north of the country, as compared with Huambo, which has five virtually rainless months. Over most of the interior the mean annual rainfall is between 1,000 mm/40 in and 1,500 mm/60 in, being greater at higher levels.

The coastal region of Angola has a most unusual climate for the latitude. Temperature and rainfall are much reduced in a strip about fifty miles wide, as a direct consequence of the cold Benguela current, which flows from south to north along the shore. This current is responsible for the almost total absence of rain on the coast of Namibia to the south.

The same extreme dryness prevails in the southern coastal district of Angola as shown by the table for **Namibe** (opposite and above). The coastal region is desert or semi-desert as far north as **Luanda** (opposite) but there is a gradual increase of rainfall

northwards until, in the far north, it is more than 600 mm/24 in per year.

The coast experiences much low cloud and fog as a consequence of warm air moving over the cold ocean surface. Temperatures on the coast only rise to high levels when there is a pronounced offshore wind bringing heated air from the interior. The almost constant daytime sea breezes keep the temperatures on the coast low for a tropical region. Sunshine amounts are rather low on the coast, averaging from four to six hours per day. They are much higher inland, ranging from four to five hours per day in the wet season to as much as nine to ten hours in the dry season.

Because of the reduced temperatures inland, and the dry, cool nature of the coastal weather, Angola has a healthy and pleasant climate for a tropical country.

NAMIBE — SOUTH COASTAL ANGOLA

	Sunshine	Temperatures							Discomfort from heat and humidity	Precipitation and humidity				Wet days	
		Average daily				Highest recorded		Lowest recorded			Relative humidity		Average monthly precipitation			
		minimum		maximum							9:00	15:00				
	average hours per day	°C	°F	°C	°F	°C	°F	°C	°F		%		mm	in	more than 1 mm/0.04 in	
Jan	7	18	65	26	79	33	91	14	57	Medium	80	74	8	0.3	1.0	Jan
Feb	7	20	68	28	83	34	94	14	58	Medium	79	73	10	0.4	1.0	Feb
March	7	21	69	29	84	36	96	12	54	High	78	72	18	0.7	2.0	March
April	8	19	66	28	82	39	102	12	53	Medium	80	73	13	0.5	1.0	April
May	7	15	59	25	77	38	100	11	51	Medium	81	74	0	0.0	0.0	May
June	5	14	57	22	72	38	101	8	47		85	79	0	0.0	0.0	June
July	3	13	56	20	68	29	85	7	44		85	79	0	0.0	0.0	July
Aug	4	14	57	21	70	28	83	8	47		86	78	0	0.0	0.0	Aug
Sept	4	15	59	22	72	28	82	9	48		83	76	0	0.0	0.0	Sept
Oct	5	16	61	23	74	31	88	12	54	Moderate	82	77	0	0.0	0.2	Oct
Nov	7	17	63	26	78	32	90	11	52	Medium	79	75	3	0.1	0.5	Nov
Dec	7	18	64	26	79	33	92	12	54	Medium	79	73	3	0.1	0.5	Dec

Based on readings for 15 years at 15°12′ S, 12°09′ E, altitude 3 m/10 ft

LUANDA — NORTH COASTAL ANGOLA

	Sunshine	Temperatures							Discomfort from heat and humidity	Precipitation and humidity				Wet days	
		Average daily				Highest recorded		Lowest recorded			Relative humidity		Average monthly precipitation			
		minimum		maximum							9:00	15:00				
	average hours per day	°C	°F	°C	°F	°C	°F	°C	°F		%		mm	in	more than 1 mm/0.04 in	
Jan	7	23	74	28	83	33	91	21	69	Medium	79	76	25	1.0	3.0	Jan
Feb	7	24	75	29	85	35	95	21	70	High	77	74	36	1.4	3.0	Feb
March	7	24	75	30	86	35	95	21	70	High	79	75	76	3.0	6.0	March
April	6	24	75	29	85	34	94	21	70	High	82	77	117	4.6	8.0	April
May	7	23	73	28	82	36	97	18	64	Medium	81	78	13	0.5	2.0	May
June	7	20	68	25	77	32	89	15	59	Medium	81	76	0	0.0	0.1	June
July	5	18	65	23	74	29	85	14	58	Moderate	82	77	0	0.0	0.0	July
Aug	5	18	64	23	74	28	83	14	58	Moderate	84	78	0	0.0	0.4	Aug
Sept	5	19	67	24	76	29	84	17	62	Moderate	82	78	3	0.1	0.9	Sept
Oct	5	22	71	26	79	32	89	18	65	Medium	80	78	5	0.2	2.0	Oct
Nov	6	23	73	28	82	37	98	20	68	Medium	79	77	28	1.1	4.0	Nov
Dec	6	23	74	28	83	34	94	19	67	Medium	78	76	20	0.8	3.0	Dec

Based on readings for 27 years at 8°49′ S, 13°13′ E, altitude 59 m/194 ft

Antarctica

The continent of Antarctica is twice the size of the United States and is the largest area in the world with a permanent ice cap. Glaciers covered with snow extend to the coast which is fringed by large areas of pack and drift ice. Only the highest mountains in the interior project through this vast thickness of ice.

The table for **Stonington Island** (below), just within the Antarctic Circle off the peninsula of Graham Land, illustrates temperature conditions on the fringes of the continent. Inland conditions are even harsher and they are made more severe by the altitude of much of the interior and the frequent strong winds above gale force. The centre of the continent at the South Pole is over 2,800 m/9,200 ft. Virtually all precipitation in Antarctica is snow and this is frequently whipped up from the surface in fierce blizzards. The weather is changeable throughout the year. During the long Antarctic winter, conditions outdoors often reach or exceed the limits of human tolerance through the combination of low temperature and wind. This results in excessive wind chill and frostbite unless appropriate clothing is worn or shelter sought when conditions get too bad. During calm, sunny days in summer, particularly on the coast, temperatures rise above freezing point and with no wind the temperatures may feel quite warm.

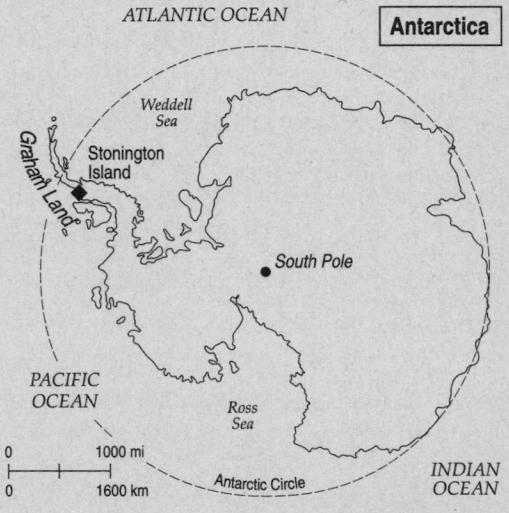

STONINGTON ISLAND													GRAHAM LAND
Sunshine	Temperatures							Discomfort from heat and humidity	Precipitation and humidity				Wet days
	Average daily				Highest recorded	Lowest recorded			Relative humidity		Average monthly precipitation		
	minimum		maximum						7:30	13:30			
average hours per day	°C	°F	°C	°F	°C	°F	°C	°F	%		mm	in	more than 1 mm/0.04 in
Jan	−3	27	3	37	6	43	−12	11	74	71	10	0.4	3	Jan
Feb	−4	25	1	34	7	45	−11	12	72	68	15	0.6	4	Feb
March	−8	18	−2	28	8	46	−35	−31	86	83	25	1.0	7	March
April	−10	14	−4	24	7	44	−27	−16	79	77	25	1.0	7	April
May	−14	7	−6	21	4	39	−36	−33	84	85	43	1.7	9	May
June	−17	2	−8	17	7	44	−37	−35	81	82	28	1.1	6	June
July	−16	3	−8	18	4	40	−36	−32	85	85	33	1.3	7	July
Aug	−19	−2	−9	16	4	40	−37	−35	85	84	25	1.0	7	Aug
Sept	−16	3	−8	17	5	41	−39	−39	79	80	41	1.6	7	Sept
Oct	−13	9	−4	24	6	42	−29	−20	80	79	43	1.7	8	Oct
Nov	−9	16	−3	27	8	47	−20	−4	75	73	23	0.9	5	Nov
Dec	−3	26	2	36	7	44	−13	9	69	67	5	0.2	1	Dec

Based on readings for 3 years at 68°11′ S, 67°01′ W, altitude 9 m/28 ft

Antigua and Barbuda

See map page 15

Antigua, the largest of the Leeward Islands, and its
sister island Barbuda make a two-island state whose
temperatures, sunshine, and humidity around the
year are very similar to those described in the general
entry for the Caribbean (pp. 92–3). The tables for
points on two other islands in the eastern Caribbean,
Roseau (p. 127) on Dominica and **Plymouth**
(p. 244) on Montserrat, show that near sea level, the
annual rainfall is about 1,250–2,000 mm/50–80 in,
well distributed throughout the year, with a wetter

season from July to November. The table for
Camp Jacob (p. 167) on the island of Guadeloupe,
also in the Leeward Islands, shows that rainfall
increases at higher elevations and on the windward
slopes exposed to the constant and moist, northeast
trade winds.

Antigua and Barbuda lie in the track of violent
tropical hurricanes which are most likely to develop
between August and October. Although the severest
of these storms may only strike every few years, these
are always the months of heaviest rainfall.

Argentina

The Argentine Republic is a large country with an
area exceeding 2.60 million sq km/1 million sq mi,
about one-third the size of the United States and
almost as large as India. It extends between 22° and
55° S and occupies the southern portion of South

climate regions

- Pampas
- northeast
- west
- Patagonia

America, east of the crest-line of the Andes, which
forms its border with Chile. On the north it is
bordered by Bolivia and Paraguay and on the east by
Brazil and Uruguay. From the estuary of the river
Plate to the southern tip of Tierra del Fuego its
coastline is on the Atlantic Ocean.

The centre and east of the country are mostly
flat and not very high; but the west has much
mountainous country rising to the higher peaks of
the Andes. These include Aconcagua, the highest
mountain in South America, at 7,000 m/22,800 ft;
north of here the range rarely falls below 3,000
m/10,000 ft. The northern Andes in Argentina have
surprisingly low precipitation, so that the snowline
may be as high as 6,000 m/20,000 ft.

The southern Andes have much more precipitation,
similar to that on the western slopes in southern
Chile, so that here there are glaciers and permanent
snowfields. The high Andean region of Argentina is
very sparsely populated.

Because of these great differences of latitude and
altitude there are many differences of weather and
climate within Argentina. The effect of the southern
Andes is to produce a sharp contrast between the
very cloudy and wet climate of southern Chile and
the dry, almost desert conditions of Argentine
Patagonia in the south, which is sheltered from the
persistent westerly winds which blow in these
latitudes. Argentina can be divided into four broad
climatic regions: east central Argentina or the
Pampas, the northeastern interior, western
Argentina, and Patagonia or southern Argentina,
to which should be added the distinctive mountain
climate of the high Andes.

BAHIA BLANCA										EAST-CENTRAL ARGENTINA		
Sunshine	Temperatures							Discomfort from heat and humidity	Precipitation and humidity		Wet days	
	Average daily		Highest recorded		Lowest recorded				Relative humidity	Average monthly precipitation		
average hours per day	minimum	maximum							7:00 14:00			more than 0.25 mm/0.01 in
	°C	°F	°C	°F	°C	°F	°C	°F		%	mm in	
Jan	9	17	62	31	88	42	107	6	42	Medium	63 41	43 1.7	5	Jan
Feb	9	16	60	29	84	43	109	2	36	Medium	70 41	56 2.2	5	Feb
March	7	14	57	26	79	38	100	4	39	Moderate	77 46	64 2.5	6	March
April	5	11	51	22	71	32	90	-1	30		80 50	58 2.3	5	April
May	3	7	45	17	63	29	85	-4	25		82 56	31 1.2	4	May
June	3	4	39	14	57	24	76	-8	18		86 64	23 0.9	3	June
July	3	4	39	14	57	26	79	-7	19		79 56	25 1.0	4	July
Aug	5	4	40	16	60	29	85	-8	18		80 54	25 1.0	4	Aug
Sept	6	7	44	18	65	33	91	-5	23		76 45	41 1.6	5	Sept
Oct	7	9	48	22	71	36	96	-4	25		68 40	56 2.2	6	Oct
Nov	8	12	54	26	78	38	101	-1	30	Moderate	63 38	53 2.1	6	Nov
Dec	8	15	59	29	85	41	105	3	37	Medium	58 35	48 1.9	5	Dec

Based on readings for 31 years at 38°43' S, 62°16' W, altitude 29 m/95 ft

EAST CENTRAL ARGENTINA

Including (with towns and cities in parentheses):
BUENOS AIRES (Bahía Blanca, Buenos Aires) and the
east of LA PAMPA (Victorica).

This area – the Pampas region – has a climate similar
to that of Uruguay. It is well outside the tropics and
has an adequate rainfall of between 500 mm/20 in
and 1,000 mm/40 in per year.

Winters are mild and summers warm, with more
rainfall during the summer months. The rain falls on
a few days so that wet, changeable weather is not
very frequent and rain is often heavy.

The annual rainfall decreases westwards and
southwards and this is illustrated by the tables for
Buenos Aires (opposite and above) and **Bahía
Blanca** (above) in the south of the Pampas,
and **Victorica** (opposite) in the west.

The weather here is moderately sunny with an
average of four to five hours sunshine a day in
winter and eight to nine hours in summer. The
region does not often experience extremes of heat or
cold. Frost may occur in most winter months but is
not prolonged or severe. The climate is generally
healthy and pleasant. This is the most important
agricultural region of the country and occasional
drought is the main economic hazard.

THE NORTHEASTERN INTERIOR

Including (with towns and cities in parentheses):
CHACO, CORRIENTES, ENTRE RIOS, FORMOSA,
MISIONES – Iguaçu falls, SANTA FE, SANTIAGO DEL
ESTERO (Santiago del Estero); the east of CORDOBA
and SALTA.

This region has a warmer climate than the Pampas
and, towards the north, where it includes part of the
Chaco region described for Paraguay, has a tropical
or near-tropical climate (see the table for **Asunción**
on p. 282). Temperatures remain quite high around
the year.

The combination of heat and humidity may at times
be uncomfortable in the summer months as this is
the cloudier, wetter season. For much of the time,
however, conditions are sunny and dry. Occasional
cold spells in winter may bring temperatures near or
below freezing for a few hours but the winters are
generally mild or even warm. Rainfall decreases
westwards in the northeastern interior of Argentina,
and the table for **Santiago del Estero** (p. 40) is
representative of the drier west.

BUENOS AIRES

EAST-CENTRAL ARGENTINA

	Sunshine average hours per day	Temperatures									Discomfort from heat and humidity	Precipitation and humidity				Wet days more than 0.25 mm/0.01 in	
		Average daily				Highest recorded		Lowest recorded				Relative humidity 7:00 14:00		Average monthly precipitation			
		minimum		maximum													
		°C	°F	°C	°F	°C	°F	°C	°F			%		mm	in		
Jan	9	17	63	29	85	40	104	6	43	Medium		81	61	79	3.1	7	Jan
Feb	9	17	63	28	83	39	103	4	40	Medium		83	63	71	2.8	6	Feb
March	7	16	60	26	79	37	99	4	39	Medium		87	69	109	4.3	7	March
April	7	12	53	22	72	36	97	-2	28			88	71	89	3.5	8	April
May	6	8	47	18	64	29	84	-4	25			90	74	76	3.0	7	May
June	4	5	41	14	57	25	77	-5	23			91	78	61	2.4	7	June
July	5	6	42	14	57	29	84	-6	22			92	79	56	2.2	8	July
Aug	6	6	43	16	60	31	87	-3	27			90	74	61	2.4	9	Aug
Sept	6	8	46	18	64	30	86	-2	28			86	68	79	3.1	8	Sept
Oct	8	10	50	21	69	33	91	-2	28			83	65	86	3.4	9	Oct
Nov	9	13	56	24	76	35	95	2	36	Moderate		79	60	84	3.3	9	Nov
Dec	9	16	61	28	82	39	102	4	39	Medium		79	62	99	3.9	8	Dec

Based on readings for 23 years at 34°35' S, 58°29' W, altitude 27 m/89 ft

VICTORICA

EAST-CENTRAL ARGENTINA

	Sunshine average hours per day	Temperatures									Discomfort from heat and humidity	Precipitation and humidity				Wet days more than 1 mm/0.04 in	
		Average daily				Highest recorded		Lowest recorded				Relative humidity 7:30 13:30		Average monthly precipitation			
		minimum		maximum													
		°C	°F	°C	°F	°C	°F	°C	°F			%		mm	in		
Jan	9	15	59	34	93	44	112	2	36	Medium		53	33	71	2.8	6	Jan
Feb	9	14	58	32	90	43	109	2	36	Medium		65	35	71	2.8	5	Feb
March	8	12	54	28	83	39	102	-1	30	Medium		73	44	71	2.8	5	March
April	7	8	46	24	75	37	98	-6	21			79	41	31	1.2	4	April
May	6	3	38	19	66	32	89	-9	16			88	47	25	1.0	3	May
June	5	0	32	15	59	26	78	-18	0			91	55	18	0.7	2	June
July	5	3	37	15	59	28	82	-11	12			88	52	15	0.6	2	July
Aug	6	1	34	18	64	29	85	-11	13			80	47	18	0.7	2	Aug
Sept	7	4	40	20	68	36	97	-7	20			62	33	28	1.1	4	Sept
Oct	8	8	46	24	75	41	106	-3	26			62	35	76	3.0	7	Oct
Nov	9	11	51	28	83	41	105	-2	28	Moderate		53	29	64	2.5	5	Nov
Dec	9	14	57	32	89	43	110	2	36	Medium		51	26	76	3.0	7	Dec

Based on readings for 24 years at 36°13' S, 65°26' W, altitude 312 m/1024 ft

SANTIAGO DEL ESTERO										NORTHEASTERN ARGENTINA		
Sunshine	Temperatures							Discomfort from heat and humidity	Precipitation and humidity		Wet days	
	Average daily				Highest recorded		Lowest recorded		Relative humidity	Average monthly precipitation		
	minimum		maximum						6:30 13:30			
average hours per day	°C	°F	°C	°F	°C	°F	°C	°F	%		mm	in	more than 0.25 mm/0.01 in
Jan	8	21	69	36	97	46	115	11	52	High	72	47	86	3.4	6	Jan
Feb	7	20	68	34	94	45	113	10	50	High	74	49	76	3.0	6	Feb
March	6	18	65	32	89	44	112	6	43	High	80	58	76	3.0	6	March
April	6	15	59	28	82	40	104	1	33	Medium	82	66	33	1.3	4	April
May	5	11	51	24	75	34	94	-3	27	Moderate	82	55	15	0.6	2	May
June	4	7	44	21	69	31	87	-7	20		80	56	8	0.3	2	June
July	6	7	44	21	70	36	96	-7	19		76	48	5	0.2	1	July
Aug	7	8	46	24	75	39	102	-7	19		70	39	5	0.2	1	Aug
Sept	7	12	53	28	82	42	108	-3	27	Medium	66	41	13	0.5	2	Sept
Oct	7	15	59	31	87	43	109	0	32	Medium	69	42	36	1.4	4	Oct
Nov	8	18	64	33	92	46	114	1	34	High	67	43	64	2.5	5	Nov
Dec	8	19	67	34	94	47	116	9	48	High	67	42	104	4.1	5	Dec

Based on readings for 23 years at 27°46' S, 64°18' W, altitude 199 m/653 ft

WESTERN ARGENTINA

Including (with towns and cities in parentheses): CATAMARCA, JUJUY, LA RIOJA, MENDOZA (Mendoza), NEUQUEN, SAN JUAN, SAN LUIS, TUCUMAN; the west of: CHUBUT, CORDOBA, LA PAMPA, RIO NEGRO, and SALTA.

Western Argentina, including the northern Andes, is a dry region. Even on the higher mountains snowfall is light and the dryness matches that of northern Chile on the western side of the Andes. The eastern slopes and foothills of the Andes as far south as 35° S is a semi-arid region and the lowlands are a virtual desert. In many places the annual rainfall is below 250 mm/10 in and very inconsistent.

Droughts in this area are frequent and often prolonged. Rainfall is more frequent during the summer months, which are generally hot and very sunny. Sunshine hours average as much as ten hours a day in summer and between seven and eight in winter. The table for **Mendoza** (opposite and above) is representative of this region.

SOUTHERN ARGENTINA

Including (with towns and cities in parentheses): most of: CHUBUT (Sarmiento, Trelew), Península

Valdés, and RIO NEGRO; SANTA CRUZ (Rio Gallegos), Tierra del Fuego (Ushuaia).

The table for **Sarmiento** (opposite) is representative of the coast and much of the interior of the southern third of Argentina, south of Bahía Blanca. It is a dry region compared with the very wet region of southern Chile on the other side of the Andes. In terms of temperature and changeable weather the region has a typical cool, temperate climate, similar to that of the British Isles; but the dryness is unusual for such a high latitude.

Towards the west, in the foothills of the Andes, rainfall is greater as cloud spills over from the western side of the range. The dryness of the eastern side continues to the cooler southern districts around the Strait of Magellan.

The table for **Punta Arenas**, in southern Chile (p. 98), is representative of the extreme south, where the summers are distinctly cool. The winters in the south are long with frequent frost and snow but, because of the influence of the ocean, the cold is never very severe or prolonged throughout the year. The summers are generally cool and cloudy with brief spells of fine, pleasant weather. Much of the winter precipitation is snow and autumn and winter are the wettest seasons.

MENDOZA — WESTERN ARGENTINA

	Sunshine average hours per day	Temperatures Average daily minimum °C	°F	Average daily maximum °C	°F	Highest recorded °C	°F	Lowest recorded °C	°F	Discomfort from heat and humidity	Precipitation and humidity Relative humidity 6:30 %	13:30	Average monthly precipitation mm	in	Wet days more than 0.25 mm/0.01 in	
Jan	10	16	60	32	90	43	109	5	41	Medium	59	42	23	0.9	5	Jan
Feb	9	15	59	31	87	41	105	5	41	Medium	63	44	31	1.2	5	Feb
March	8	13	55	28	82	37	99	-2	29	Medium	68	47	28	1.1	4	March
April	7	8	47	23	73	33	91	-1	30		73	50	13	0.5	3	April
May	6	5	41	18	65	30	86	-5	23		74	52	10	0.4	2	May
June	6	2	36	15	59	30	86	-9	15		73	50	8	0.3	2	June
July	6	2	35	15	59	28	83	-9	16		72	48	5	0.2	2	July
Aug	7	3	38	17	63	33	92	-5	23		67	42	8	0.3	2	Aug
Sept	8	7	44	21	69	34	93	-4	25		55	33	13	0.5	2	Sept
Oct	8	10	50	24	76	36	97	0	32		51	34	18	0.7	4	Oct
Nov	10	12	54	28	83	41	106	2	36	Moderate	52	34	18	0.7	4	Nov
Dec	10	14	58	31	88	42	108	2	36	Medium	54	37	18	0.7	5	Dec

Based on readings for 23 years at 32°53′ S, 68°49′ W, altitude 801 m/2625 ft

SARMIENTO — SOUTHERN ARGENTINA

	Sunshine average hours per day	Temperatures Average daily minimum °C	°F	Average daily maximum °C	°F	Highest recorded °C	°F	Lowest recorded °C	°F	Discomfort from heat and humidity	Precipitation and humidity Relative humidity 7:30 %	13:30	Average monthly precipitation mm	in	Wet days more than 1 mm/0.04 in	
Jan	9	11	52	26	78	37	99	1	34		52	29	5	0.2	1	Jan
Feb	8	11	51	25	77	36	96	1	34		59	32	8	0.3	1	Feb
March	7	8	47	21	70	34	93	-3	27		64	34	8	0.3	2	March
April	6	6	42	17	62	28	83	-8	18		72	45	10	0.4	3	April
May	4	2	36	12	54	22	71	-12	11		74	51	20	0.8	4	May
June	3	-1	31	8	46	18	64	-13	8		77	58	20	0.8	4	June
July	4	-2	29	7	45	20	68	-14	7		77	59	15	0.6	3	July
Aug	6	1	33	11	51	19	67	-16	3		76	49	13	0.5	3	Aug
Sept	6	2	36	14	57	24	76	-10	14		67	40	10	0.4	3	Sept
Oct	7	5	41	19	66	30	86	-7	19		56	31	8	0.3	2	Oct
Nov	8	8	46	21	70	33	92	-2	29		51	32	5	0.2	2	Nov
Dec	8	9	49	23	74	37	99	0	32		54	30	8	0.3	2	Dec

Based on readings for 8 years at 45°36′ S, 69°05′ W, altitude 268 m/879 ft

YEREVAN · ARMENIA

Sunshine average hours per day	Temperatures									Discomfort from heat and humidity	Precipitation and humidity				Wet days more than 0.1 mm/0.004 in
	Average daily				Highest recorded		Lowest recorded				Relative humidity 7:30 13:30		Average monthly precipitation		
	minimum		maximum												
	°C	°F	°C	°F	°C	°F	°C	°F		%		mm	in	
Jan 3	−9	15	−2	29	12	53	−27	−16		89	69	23	0.9	9 Jan
Feb 4	−8	18	1	34	16	61	−25	−13		87	64	25	1.0	8 Feb
March 6	−1	30	10	50	27	80	−18	0		81	56	28	1.1	7 March
April 7	6	42	19	66	29	84	−3	26		70	46	48	1.9	11 April
May 9	10	50	24	76	33	91	3	37	Moderate	74	52	53	2.1	12 May
June 11	14	57	31	87	36	97	6	43	Medium	65	39	23	0.9	6 June
July 12	17	63	34	93	40	104	9	48	High	62	36	15	0.6	4 July
Aug 11	18	64	33	92	39	102	10	50	Medium	66	36	8	0.3	2 Aug
Sept 10	13	55	28	83	34	93	2	35	Moderate	71	39	13	0.5	3 Sept
Oct 8	7	45	21	69	27	81	−2	29		84	47	23	0.9	5 Oct
Nov 5	1	34	10	50	20	68	−12	11		89	64	31	1.2	7 Nov
Dec 3	−3	26	3	38	16	61	−16	3		91	75	28	1.1	8 Dec

Based on readings for 17 years at 40°10′ N, 44°30′ E, altitude 990 m/3248 ft

GEORGETOWN · ASCENSION ISLAND

Sunshine average hours per day	Temperatures									Discomfort from heat and humidity	Precipitation and humidity				Wet days more than 1 mm/0.04 in
	Average daily				Highest recorded		Lowest recorded				Relative humidity 8:00 20:00		Average monthly precipitation		
	minimum		maximum												
	°C	°F	°C	°F	°C	°F	°C	°F		%		mm	in	
Jan 7	23	73	29	85	32	89	19	67	High	68	73	5	0.2	2 Jan
Feb 9	23	74	31	87	33	91	19	67	High	67	70	10	0.4	2 Feb
March 9	24	75	31	88	34	94	19	67	High	67	71	18	0.7	3 March
April 8	24	75	31	88	35	95	19	67	High	67	72	28	1.1	4 April
May 8	23	74	31	87	33	92	19	67	High	66	69	13	0.5	3 May
June 7	23	73	29	85	32	90	18	65	High	65	70	13	0.5	3 June
July 7	22	72	29	84	32	89	19	67	High	65	70	13	0.5	3 July
Aug 6	22	71	28	83	31	88	18	65	Medium	66	69	10	0.4	3 Aug
Sept 5	22	71	28	82	31	88	19	66	Medium	67	71	8	0.3	2 Sept
Oct 5	22	71	28	83	31	88	18	65	Medium	66	71	8	0.3	3 Oct
Nov 6	22	71	28	83	31	88	19	66	Medium	66	71	5	0.2	1 Nov
Dec 7	22	72	29	84	32	89	19	67	High	67	71	3	0.1	1 Dec

Based on readings for 29 years at 7°56′ S, 14°25′ W, altitude 17 m/55 ft

Armenia

See map page 22

Armenia occupies a high, landlocked plateau south of the Caucasus. Here the Tigris and Euphrates rivers both have their sources. The climate is almost tropical in summer but nights are chilly. Winters are cold and snowy.

The table for **Yerevan** (opposite) shows the weather that is typical of the country.

Ascension Island

See map page 21

Ascension Island is situated in latitude 8° S in the middle of the South Atlantic. It is remote and has no regular commercial air or steamer service. The climate is tropical although the island has a low annual rainfall for a tropical island.
Ascension amounts to a mere 88 sq km/34 sq mi and consists of a single mountain rising to 875 m/2,870 ft. Temperatures are warm to hot around the year. The ocean moderates the heat, however, throughout the year.

The table for **Georgetown** (opposite and below) shows the weather that is typical of the island.

Australia

See map overleaf

The Commonwealth of Australia consists of a large island continent lying between 11° and 39° S and the large offshore island of Tasmania between 41° and 44° S. The country is only a little smaller than the United States but its sparse population is comparable with that of Canada. Most of Australia's population lives in the climatically more favoured eastern, southern, and southwestern coastal areas. Between half and two-thirds of the country is desert or scrubland with a low and unreliable rainfall, and this region is almost uninhabited. Nearly half of Australia lies within the tropics.

The greater part of Australia consists of flat or gently undulating plains 150–600 m/500–2,000 ft above sea level. The east coast is backed by an almost continuous range of hills or mountains which are highest on the border between New South Wales and Victoria in the south. Here the Snowy Mountains include the highest peak in Australia at 2,225 m/7,300 ft. This is the only part of the country to experience significant snowfall, and even here the snow does not lie throughout the year.

For much of the year the east coast is exposed to the persistent and regular southeast trade winds blowing off the Pacific and this is the wettest part of the country. To the west of these eastern highlands rainfall decreases towards the interior desert.

Central Australia is situated in the latitude of the persistent subtropical anticyclonic belt and this is another reason for its dryness. In this respect it resembles the Sahara and Kalahari deserts of Africa, though it is not quite as rainless as the Sahara.

The wettest districts of Australia form a crescent around the 'dry heart' of the country. In the north and northeast, where temperatures are tropical, rainfall follows the sun and there is a very clear maximum fall at the time of high sun between November and April. Then winds on the north coast are from the northwest: the Australian monsoon, the counterpart of the outblowing Asiatic winter monsoon. These winds have become hot and humid as they cross the equatorial seas around Indonesia and the Philippines. The east and southeast coasts of Australia get rain at all seasons, with rather more in the summer. The south and southwest coasts of South and Western Australia are affected by westerly cyclonic disturbances during the cooler winter season and have their maximum rainfall at this time. The desert region reaches the coast between 18° and 30° S on the west coast and between 125° and 135° E on the south coast so that the wetter coastal fringe of the country is not continuous.

Much of Australia is warm or hot throughout the year, and even along the cooler southern coasts the winters are mild rather than cold. Only Tasmania, which is in the same latitude as New Zealand, has

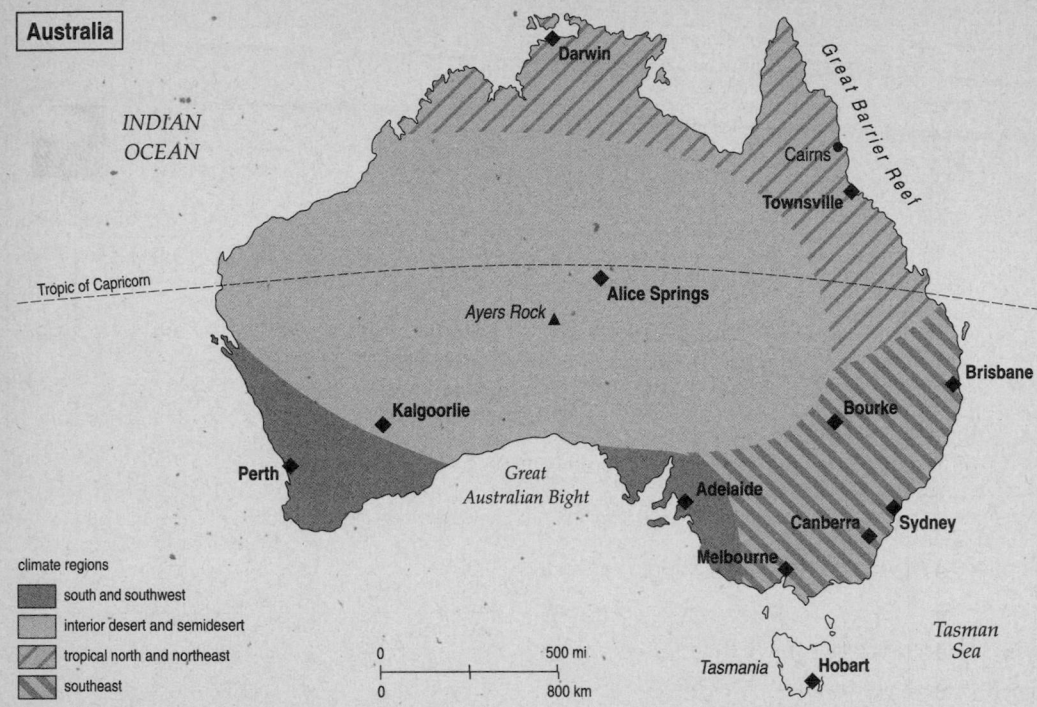

Australia

INDIAN
OCEAN

Darwin

Great Barrier Reef

Cairns

Townsville

Tropic of Capricorn

Ayers Rock ▲

Alice Springs

Brisbane

Bourke

Kalgoorlie

Perth

Great
Australian Bight

Adelaide

Canberra

Sydney

Melbourne

Tasman
Sea

Tasmania

Hobart

climate regions

- south and southwest
- interior desert and semidesert
- tropical north and northeast
- southeast

0   500 mi
0   800 km

a temperate climate comparable with that of Britain or northwest Europe. Very high temperatures may occasionally occur almost anywhere in Australia when winds blow out from the interior and 'import' the high temperatures and low humidity of the interior desert to the coastal regions. Only Tasmania escapes such extremes of heat; it also has abundant rain around the year. The combination of prolonged heat waves and drought is one of the main climatic hazards of much of Australia and is the main cause of the bush fires, which may rage for days.

Tropical cyclones, similar to the typhoons of the North Pacific and South China Sea, occur two or three times each year in the seas to the northeast and northwest of Australia. The northern part of the Queensland coast and the north and west coasts from Darwin southwards are affected by the torrential rain and sometimes by the very high winds near the storm centre. On the northwest coast of Australia these storms go by the Australian Aboriginal name of 'willy-willies'.

Because much of the country is fairly low and flat, contrasts of weather and climate are gradual and there are few sharp local changes. For a more detailed description the country can be divided into four climatic regions (in addition to Tasmania which is more temperate in climate): the tropical regional of the north and northeast, southeastern Australia,

southern and western Australia, and the desert and semi-arid regions of central Australia. These climatic regions rarely coincide with state boundaries. Only Victoria and Tasmania, the two smallest states, do not include part of the dry interior.

THE TROPICAL NORTH AND NORTHEAST

Including (with towns and cities in parentheses): the northern parts of WESTERN AUSTRALIA and the NORTHERN TERRITORY (Darwin); most of QUEENSLAND (Cairns, Townsville).

This region consists of the coastlands of Queensland, the Northern Territory and Western Australia, and the inland districts, which have more than 500 mm/20 in annual rainfall.

On the east coast the region's southern limit is to the north of Brisbane but, as the table for **Brisbane** on p. 46 shows, winter temperatures here are very close to those normally regarded as constituting a tropical climate. Brisbane differs from places farther north in that it gets some rain in all months, as distinct from **Townsville** (opposite and above) and **Darwin** (opposite), which are more typically tropical in having a virtual drought during the low sun period.

TOWNSVILLE, QUEENSLAND — NORTHERN AUSTRALIA

	Sunshine average hours per day	Average daily minimum °C	°F	Average daily maximum °C	°F	Highest recorded °C	°F	Lowest recorded °C	°F	Discomfort from heat and humidity	Relative humidity 9:00 %	15:00 %	Average monthly precipitation mm	in	Wet days more than 0.25mm/0.01in	
Jan	7	24	76	31	87	40	104	19	66	High	73	70	277	10.9	15	Jan
Feb	7	24	75	31	87	43	110	18	65	High	73	68	285	11.2	12	Feb
March	7	23	73	30	86	35	95	16	61	High	71	68	183	7.2	10	March
April	9	21	70	29	84	36	97	12	54	Medium	66	62	84	3.3	6	April
May	7	18	65	27	81	32	90	9	48	Medium	65	60	33	1.3	5	May
June	8	16	61	25	77	31	87	5	41	Moderate	66	60	36	1.4	4	June
July	9	15	59	24	75	29	85	6	42	Moderate	64	58	15	0.6	3	July
Aug	9	16	61	25	77	32	89	7	45	Moderate	63	59	15	0.5	3	Aug
Sept	9	19	66	27	80	34	94	11	52	Medium	63	61	18	0.7	2	Sept
Oct	9	22	71	28	83	34	94	12	53	Medium	64	64	33	1.3	4	Oct
Nov	9	23	74	29	85	38	101	17	63	Medium	65	66	48	1.9	5	Nov
Dec	8	24	76	31	87	38	101	18	65	High	70	69	137	5.4	12	Dec

Based on readings for 31 years at 19°14' S, 146°51' E, altitude 15 m/48 ft

DARWIN, NORTHERN TERRITORY — NORTHERN AUSTRALIA

	Sunshine average hours per day	Average daily minimum °C	°F	Average daily maximum °C	°F	Highest recorded °C	°F	Lowest recorded °C	°F	Discomfort from heat and humidity	Relative humidity 8:00 %	14:00 %	Average monthly precipitation mm	in	Wet days more than 0.25mm/0.01in	
Jan	6	25	77	32	90	38	100	20	68	High	78	71	386	15.2	20	Jan
Feb	6	25	77	32	90	38	101	21	69	High	79	72	312	12.3	18	Feb
March	7	25	77	33	91	39	102	20	68	Extreme	78	67	254	10.0	17	March
April	8	24	76	33	92	40	104	19	66	High	69	54	97	3.8	6	April
May	9	23	73	33	91	39	102	16	60	High	63	47	15	0.6	1	May
June	10	21	69	31	88	37	99	13	56	Medium	61	47	3	0.1	1	June
July	10	19	67	31	87	37	98	13	56	Medium	59	44	0	0.0	0	July
Aug	10	21	70	32	89	37	98	14	58	Medium	63	45	3	0.1	0	Aug
Sept	10	23	74	33	91	39	102	17	63	High	65	49	13	0.5	2	Sept
Oct	10	25	77	34	93	41	105	21	69	High	65	52	51	2.0	5	Oct
Nov	8	26	78	34	94	39	103	21	69	High	68	58	119	4.7	10	Nov
Dec	7	26	78	33	92	39	102	21	69	High	73	65	239	9.4	15	Dec

Based on readings for 58 years at 12°28' S, 130°51' E, altitude 30 m/97 ft

BRISBANE, QUEENSLAND									NORTHEASTERN AUSTRALIA				
Sunshine		Temperatures							Discomfort from heat and humidity	Precipitation and humidity				Wet days
		Average daily				Highest recorded		Lowest recorded			Relative humidity		Average monthly precipitation	
		minimum		maximum							9:00 15:00			
average hours per day		°C	°F	°C	°F	°C	°F	°C	°F		%		mm	in	more than 0.25 mm/0.01 in
Jan	8	21	69	29	85	43	110	15	59	Medium	66	59	163	6.4	13	Jan
Feb	7	20	68	29	85	41	106	14	58	Medium	69	60	160	6.3	14	Feb
March	7	19	66	28	82	37	99	11	52	Medium	72	60	145	5.7	15	March
April	7	16	61	26	79	35	95	7	44	Moderate	71	56	94	3.7	12	April
May	7	13	56	23	74	32	90	5	41		73	55	71	2.8	10	May
June	7	11	51	21	69	32	89	3	37		73	54	66	2.6	8	June
July	7	9	49	20	68	28	83	2	36		72	51	56	2.2	8	July
Aug	8	10	50	22	71	31	88	3	37		69	49	48	1.9	7	Aug
Sept	8	13	55	24	76	35	95	5	41	Moderate	64	51	48	1.9	8	Sept
Oct	8	16	60	27	80	38	101	6	43	Medium	60	53	64	2.5	9	Oct
Nov	8	18	64	28	82	41	106	9	48	Medium	60	57	94	3.7	10	Nov
Dec	9	19	67	29	85	41	106	13	56	Medium	62	56	127	5.0	12	Dec

Based on readings for 53 years at 27°28′ S, 153°02′ E, altitude 42 m/137 ft

The region is typically tropical in its combination of heat, rainfall, and high humidity during the summer or high sun period of November to March. At this time the weather can be distinctly sultry and oppressive. The higher temperatures and lower humidity experienced inland towards the dry interior are more bearable than the sticky heat of the coast. Like most of Australia, the north and northwest have a very sunny climate with daily sunshine averaging six to seven hours during the dry months. Annual sunshine hours are similar to those found in California or the European Mediterranean lands.

SOUTHEASTERN AUSTRALIA

Including (with towns and cities in parentheses): southeastern QUEENSLAND (Brisbane), VICTORIA (Melbourne), the FEDERAL CAPITAL TERRITORY (Canberra) and most of NEW SOUTH WALES (Bourke, Sydney), but excluding the drier western and northwestern part of this state.

This part of Australia has attracted the most extensive colonization by Europeans since the first settlement near Sydney in the late 18th century. It has a climate best described as warm-temperate with no real cold season, warm to hot summers, and rain well distributed throughout the year. The weather can be changeable at all times of the year and

summers are liable to prolonged heat waves and droughts. The hazard of drought is much greater inland as the average rainfall decreases; prolonged drought and unreliable rainfall have been persistent themes in the settlement history of Australia.

Cold spells are brief and never severe on the coast, as the tables for **Sydney** (opposite and above) and **Melbourne** (opposite) show. Temperatures can drop much lower inland (see the tables for **Canberra** and **Bourke** on p. 48).

The temperatures for Canberra also illustrate the effect of a moderate altitude in lowering the winter minimum temperatures. The low annual rainfall at Bourke illustrates the transition to the semi-arid conditions of the interior. The extreme maximum temperatures at Bourke are higher than those recorded in the tropical regions of the north. Both Sydney and Melbourne occasionally record temperatures well above 38°C/100°F.

Latitude here begins to affect the number of sunshine hours. Summer sunshine averages eight to nine hours a day in summer but only five to six in winter. At Melbourne, which gets more cloud and disturbed weather despite a lower rainfall, sunshine hours per day in winter are only three to four as against seven to eight in summer.

SYDNEY, NEW SOUTH WALES — SOUTHEASTERN AUSTRALIA

Sunshine average hours per day	Temperatures Average daily minimum		Average daily maximum		Highest recorded		Lowest recorded		Discomfort from heat and humidity	Precipitation and humidity Relative humidity 9:00	15:00	Average monthly precipitation mm	in	Wet days more than 0.25 mm/0.01 in	
	°C	°F	°C	°F	°C	°F	°C	°F		%		mm	in		
Jan	18	65	26	78	46	114	11	51	Medium	68	64	89	3.5	14	Jan
Feb	18	65	26	78	42	108	9	49	Medium	71	65	102	4.0	13	Feb
March	17	63	24	76	39	103	9	49	Moderate	73	65	127	5.0	14	March
April	14	58	22	71	33	91	7	45		76	64	135	5.3	14	April
May	11	52	19	66	30	86	4	40		77	63	127	5.0	13	May
June	9	48	16	61	27	80	2	36		77	62	117	4.6	12	June
July	8	46	16	60	26	78	2	36		76	60	117	4.6	12	July
Aug	9	48	17	63	28	82	3	37		72	56	76	3.0	11	Aug
Sept	11	51	19	67	33	92	5	41		67	55	74	2.9	12	Sept
Oct	13	56	22	71	37	99	6	42		65	57	71	2.8	12	Oct
Nov	16	60	23	74	39	103	8	46	Moderate	65	60	74	2.9	12	Nov
Dec	17	63	25	77	42	107	9	48	Moderate	66	62	74	2.9	13	Dec

Sunshine average hours per day: Jan 7, Feb 7, March 6, April 6, May 6, June 5, July 6, Aug 7, Sept 7, Oct 8, Nov 7, Dec 8

Based on readings for 87 years at 33°52′ S, 151°12′ E, altitude 42 m/138 ft

MELBOURNE, VICTORIA — SOUTHEASTERN AUSTRALIA

Sunshine average hours per day	Temperatures Average daily minimum		Average daily maximum		Highest recorded		Lowest recorded		Discomfort from heat and humidity	Precipitation and humidity Relative humidity 8:30	14:30	Average monthly precipitation mm	in	Wet days more than 0.25 mm/0.01 in	
	°C	°F	°C	°F	°C	°F	°C	°F		%		mm	in		
Jan	14	57	26	78	46	114	6	42	Moderate	58	48	48	1.9	9	Jan
Feb	14	57	26	78	43	110	4	40	Moderate	62	50	46	1.8	8	Feb
March	13	55	24	75	42	107	3	37	Moderate	64	51	56	2.2	9	March
April	11	51	20	68	35	95	2	35		72	56	58	2.3	13	April
May	8	47	17	62	29	84	-1	30		79	62	53	2.1	14	May
June	7	44	14	57	22	72	-2	28		83	67	53	2.1	16	June
July	6	42	13	56	21	69	-3	27		82	65	48	1.9	17	July
Aug	6	43	15	59	25	77	-2	28		76	60	48	1.9	17	Aug
Sept	8	46	17	63	32	89	-1	31		68	55	58	2.3	15	Sept
Oct	9	48	19	67	37	98	0	32		61	52	66	2.6	14	Oct
Nov	11	51	22	71	41	106	3	37		60	52	58	2.3	13	Nov
Dec	12	54	24	75	44	111	4	40	Moderate	59	51	58	2.3	11	Dec

Sunshine average hours per day: Jan 8, Feb 8, March 6, April 5, May 4, June 3, July 4, Aug 4, Sept 5, Oct 6, Nov 6, Dec 7

Based on readings for 88 years at 37°49′ S, 144°58′ E, altitude 35 m/115 ft

CANBERRA, AUSTRALIAN CAPITAL TERRITORY — SOUTHEASTERN AUSTRALIA

	Sunshine	Temperatures								Discomfort from heat and humidity	Precipitation and humidity				Wet days	
		Average daily				Highest recorded		Lowest recorded			Relative humidity 9:00 15:00		Average monthly precipitation			
		minimum		maximum												
	average hours per day	°C	°F	°C	°F	°C	°F	°C	°F		%		mm	in	more than 0.25 mm/0.01 in	
Jan	9	13	55	28	82	43	109	3	38	Moderate	56	35	48	1.9	7	Jan
Feb	8	13	55	28	82	39	103	1	33	Moderate	61	39	43	1.7	7	Feb
March	8	11	51	24	76	37	99	-1	31		69	42	56	2.2	7	March
April	7	7	44	19	67	33	91	-3	27		75	51	41	1.6	7	April
May	6	3	37	16	60	23	73	-7	19		82	57	46	1.8	7	May
June	5	1	34	12	53	19	66	-8	18		85	64	53	2.1	9	June
July	5	1	33	11	52	18	65	-10	14		85	63	46	1.8	10	July
Aug	6	2	35	13	55	23	73	-8	18		81	59	56	2.2	11	Aug
Sept	8	3	38	16	61	28	83	-4	24		72	50	41	1.6	9	Sept
Oct	8	6	43	20	68	34	94	-3	27		64	45	56	2.2	11	Oct
Nov	9	9	48	24	75	37	98	-2	28		59	41	48	1.9	8	Nov
Dec	9	12	53	27	80	39	103	0	32	Moderate	56	36	51	2.0	8	Dec

Based on readings for 23 years at 35°20′ S, 149°15′ E, altitude 560 m/1837 ft

BOURKE, NEW SOUTH WALES — SOUTHEASTERN AUSTRALIA

	Sunshine	Temperatures								Discomfort from heat and humidity	Precipitation and humidity				Wet days	
		Average daily				Highest recorded		Lowest recorded			Relative humidity 8:30 14:30		Average monthly precipitation			
		minimum		maximum												
	average hours per day	°C	°F	°C	°F	°C	°F	°C	°F		%		mm	in	more than 0.25 mm/0.01 in	
Jan		21	70	37	99	52	125	9	48	High	42	23	36	1.4	3	Jan
Feb		21	69	36	97	49	120	9	49	High	48	26	38	1.5	3	Feb
March		18	64	33	91	47	117	2	35	Medium	52	29	28	1.1	3	March
April		13	55	28	82	42	107	2	35	Moderate	57	35	28	1.1	3	April
May		8	47	23	73	35	95	-3	27		67	44	25	1.0	4	May
June		6	42	18	65	30	86	-4	25		76	51	28	1.1	4	June
July		4	40	18	65	29	84	-3	26		74	48	23	0.9	5	July
Aug		6	43	21	70	34	94	-3	27		64	38	20	0.8	3	Aug
Sept		9	49	25	77	38	100	-2	29		53	30	20	0.8	3	Sept
Oct		13	56	29	85	44	112	2	35	Moderate	45	26	23	0.9	4	Oct
Nov		17	63	34	93	46	115	3	38	Medium	43	25	31	1.2	4	Nov
Dec		19	67	36	97	49	121	5	41	High	42	25	36	1.4	5	Dec

Based on readings for 63 years at 30°05′ S, 145°58′ E, altitude 110 m/361 ft

SOUTHERN AND SOUTHWESTERN AUSTRALIA

Including (with towns and cities in parentheses): the area around Spencer Gulf in SOUTH AUSTRALIA (Adelaide), southwestern WESTERN AUSTRALIA (Perth), and parts of western VICTORIA.

This region consists of two small districts separated by the desert coast along the Great Australian Bight where the annual rainfall is below 250 mm/10 in. These regions are distinctive in that they have a Mediterranean climate. Rainfall is moderate and falls mainly in the winter. Summers are warm to hot with an almost complete drought. The winter season gets much changeable weather, associated with cyclonic disturbances in the westerly wind belt that affects the south of Australia during this season.

The tables for **Adelaide** (below) and **Perth** (overleaf) are representative of the wetter parts of these two districts. The mildness of the winter is illustrated by the fact that at neither place has the temperature ever fallen below freezing point. The winter maximum of rainfall is very clearly marked at both places, but Perth gets a much heavier rainfall than Adelaide. The extent of this wet winter climate is greater in Western Australia than it is in South Australia, where the transition to desert inland is

quite rapid. During the hot, dry summer, temperatures can occasionally rise very high: over 43°C/110°F. In summer these areas average between nine and ten hours of sunshine per day as compared with five to six in winter.

THE INTERIOR AND SEMI-DESERT

Including (with towns and cities in parentheses): the inland part of NORTHERN TERRITORY (Alice Springs), the greater part of WESTERN AUSTRALIA (Kalgoorlie) and SOUTH AUSTRALIA.

This is the most extensive climatic region of Australia and includes parts of each mainland state with the exception of Victoria. Its northern perimeter can be roughly defined by the 500 mm/20 in annual rainfall limit and in the south by the 300 mm/12 in annual rainfall line.

Rainfall is scanty and inconsistent everywhere. The cool-season rainfall of the south is much more effective than the hot-season rainfall of the tropical north of Australia. Compare the table for **Alice Springs** on p.50, which is almost in the centre of the continent, and that for **Kalgoorlie** on p. 51, which is on the desert margin of Western Australia.

ADELAIDE	Sunshine	Temperatures								Discomfort from heat and humidity	Precipitation and humidity				Wet days	
		Average daily				Highest recorded		Lowest recorded			Relative humidity 8:30 14:30		Average monthly precipitation			SOUTHERN AUSTRALIA
		minimum		maximum												
	average hours per day	°C	°F	°C	°F	°C	°F	°C	°F		%		mm	in	more than 0.25 mm/0.01 in	
Jan	10	16	61	30	86	48	118	7	45	Medium	38	31	20	0.8	5	Jan
Feb	9	17	62	30	86	46	114	7	45	Medium	41	32	18	0.7	5	Feb
March	8	15	59	27	81	44	111	7	44	Moderate	46	36	25	1.0	5	March
April	6	13	55	23	73	37	99	4	40		55	45	46	1.8	10	April
May	5	10	50	19	66	32	89	3	37		67	56	69	2.7	13	May
June	4	8	47	16	61	24	76	1	33		76	65	76	3.0	15	June
July	4	7	45	15	59	23	74	0	32		76	63	66	2.6	16	July
Aug	5	8	46	17	62	29	85	0	32		69	57	66	2.6	16	Aug
Sept	6	9	48	19	66	33	91	1	33		60	52	53	2.1	13	Sept
Oct	7	11	51	23	73	39	103	2	36		51	42	43	1.7	10	Oct
Nov	8	13	55	26	79	45	113	5	41	Moderate	43	36	28	1.1	8	Nov
Dec	9	15	59	28	83	46	115	6	43	Moderate	39	32	25	1.0	6	Dec

Based on readings for 86 years at 34°56′ S, 138°35′ E, altitude 43 m/140 ft

PERTH — WESTERN AUSTRALIA

	Sunshine	Temperatures							Discomfort from heat and humidity	Precipitation and humidity				Wet days	
	average hours per day	Average daily minimum		Average daily maximum		Highest recorded		Lowest recorded			Relative humidity 8:30	Relative humidity 14:30	Average monthly precipitation		more than 0.25 mm/0.01 in	
		°C	°F	°C	°F	°C	°F	°C	°F		%	%	mm	in		
Jan	10	17	63	29	85	43	110	9	49	Medium	51	44	8	0.3	3	Jan
Feb	10	17	63	29	85	44	112	9	48	Medium	53	43	10	0.4	3	Feb
March	9	16	61	27	81	41	106	8	46	Moderate	58	45	20	0.8	5	March
April	7	14	57	24	76	38	100	4	39		61	49	43	1.7	8	April
May	6	12	53	21	69	32	90	1	34		72	58	130	5.1	15	May
June	5	10	50	18	64	28	82	2	35		76	63	180	7.1	17	June
July	5	9	48	17	63	24	76	1	34		76	63	170	6.7	19	July
Aug	6	9	48	18	64	28	82	2	35		73	61	145	5.7	19	Aug
Sept	7	10	50	19	67	33	91	4	39		67	58	86	3.4	15	Sept
Oct	8	12	53	21	70	35	95	4	40		60	55	56	2.2	12	Oct
Nov	10	14	57	24	76	41	105	6	42		54	49	20	0.8	7	Nov
Dec	10	16	61	27	81	42	108	9	48	Moderate	50	47	13	0.5	5	Dec

Based on readings for 44 years at 31°57′ S, 115°51′ E, altitude 60 m/197 ft

ALICE SPRINGS, NORTHERN TERRITORY — CENTRAL AUSTRALIA

	Sunshine	Temperatures							Discomfort from heat and humidity	Precipitation and humidity				Wet days	
	average hours per day	Average daily minimum		Average daily maximum		Highest recorded		Lowest recorded			Relative humidity 8:00	Relative humidity 14:30	Average monthly precipitation		more than 0.25 mm/0.01 in	
		°C	°F	°C	°F	°C	°F	°C	°F		%	%	mm	in		
Jan	10	21	70	36	97	44	111	11	51	Medium	31	23	43	1.7	4	Jan
Feb	11	21	69	35	95	43	109	9	48	Medium	34	24	33	1.3	3	Feb
March	10	17	63	32	90	43	110	7	45	Medium	36	25	28	1.1	3	March
April	10	12	54	27	81	37	99	2	36	Moderate	40	28	10	0.4	2	April
May	8	8	46	23	73	36	96	-2	29		47	32	15	0.6	2	May
June	9	5	41	19	67	30	86	-6	22		54	35	13	0.5	2	June
July	9	4	39	19	67	30	86	-7	19		49	31	8	0.3	1	July
Aug	10	6	43	23	73	36	96	-4	25		39	25	8	0.3	2	Aug
Sept	10	9	49	27	81	38	100	-1	31	Moderate	31	22	8	0.3	1	Sept
Oct	10	14	58	31	88	41	106	4	39	Medium	27	21	18	0.7	3	Oct
Nov	11	18	64	34	93	42	108	6	42	Medium	27	21	31	1.2	4	Nov
Dec	10	20	68	36	96	44	111	10	50	Medium	29	22	38	1.5	4	Dec

Based on readings for 18 years at 23°38′ S, 133°58′ E, altitude 579 m/1901 ft

KALGOORLIE, WESTERN AUSTRALIA — CENTRAL AUSTRALIA

	Sunshine	Temperatures									Discomfort from heat and humidity	Precipitation and humidity				Wet days	
		Average daily				Highest recorded		Lowest recorded				Relative humidity		Average monthly precipitation			
		minimum		maximum								9:00	15:00				
average hours per day		°C	°F	°C	°F	°C	°F	°C	°F			%		mm	in	more than 0.25 mm/0.01 in	
Jan	11	18	64	34	93	46	114	8	47	Medium		44	25	10	0.4	3	Jan
Feb	11	18	64	33	92	46	115	9	48	Medium		49	30	20	0.8	2	Feb
March	9	16	61	30	86	42	107	6	43	Moderate		53	22	23	0.9	4	March
April	8	13	55	26	78	39	102	3	37	Moderate		58	38	23	0.9	4	April
May	7	9	49	21	69	33	92	2	35			65	46	31	1.2	5	May
June	6	7	45	17	63	28	82	-1	31			74	52	31	1.2	6	June
July	7	6	43	17	62	27	81	-1	30			73	45	23	0.9	7	July
Aug	7	7	44	18	65	31	87	-2	29			64	42	23	0.9	6	Aug
Sept	8	9	48	23	73	36	96	0	32			53	33	13	0.5	3	Sept
Oct	9	11	52	26	78	39	103	1	33			46	28	18	0.7	4	Oct
Nov	11	14	58	31	87	44	111	3	38	Medium		42	25	15	0.6	3	Nov
Dec	12	17	62	33	92	45	113	8	46	Medium		42	25	18	0.7	2	Dec

Based on readings for 30 years at 30°45′ S, 121°30′ E, altitude 370 m/1247 ft

HOBART — TASMANIA

	Sunshine	Temperatures									Discomfort from heat and humidity	Precipitation and humidity				Wet days	
		Average daily				Highest recorded		Lowest recorded				Relative humidity		Average monthly precipitation			
		minimum		maximum								9:00	15:00				
average hours per day		°C	°F	°C	°F	°C	°F	°C	°F			%		mm	in	more than 0.25 mm/0.01 in	
Jan	8	12	53	22	71	41	105	4	40			58	53	48	1.9	13	Jan
Feb	7	12	53	22	71	40	104	4	39			62	56	38	1.5	10	Feb
March	6	11	51	20	68	37	99	2	35			66	56	46	1.8	13	March
April	5	9	48	17	63	31	87	1	33			72	61	48	1.9	14	April
May	4	7	44	14	58	26	78	-2	29			77	63	46	1.8	14	May
June	4	5	41	12	53	21	69	-2	29			79	70	56	2.2	16	June
July	4	4	40	11	52	19	66	-2	28			80	69	53	2.1	17	July
Aug	5	5	41	13	55	22	72	-1	30			75	61	48	1.9	18	Aug
Sept	6	6	43	15	59	28	82	-1	30			67	58	53	2.1	17	Sept
Oct	6	8	46	17	63	33	92	0	32			63	56	58	2.3	18	Oct
Nov	7	9	48	19	66	37	98	2	35			59	54	61	2.4	16	Nov
Dec	7	11	51	21	69	41	105	3	38			58	54	53	2.1	14	Dec

Based on readings for 70 years at 42°53′ S, 147°20′ E, altitude 54 m/177 ft

As in most other continental interiors there is a considerable daily and seasonal change of temperature in the interior desert of Australia. Both Alice Springs and Kalgoorlie have experienced temperatures below freezing, and at Alice Springs, which is almost within the tropics, temperatures have been recorded below the freezing point in several winter months.

These desert areas are the sunniest part of Australia. Daily sunshine hours average from nine to ten around the year. The high temperatures are to some extent mitigated by low humidity. The occasional dust storms that arise during strong winds are a minor climatic hazard.

TASMANIA

This rugged island, a little smaller than Scotland, is mountainous so there are quite big differences in weather and climate between the coastal regions and the interior. The highest mountains in Tasmania rise to over 1,500 m/2,500 ft and, on the west, are fully exposed to the stormy westerly winds which bring heavy rainfall – over 2,500 mm/100 in a year in certain places.

The eastern lowlands, represented by the table for **Hobart** on p. 51, have a much lower rainfall of between 500 mm/20 in and 750 mm/30 in a year. The weather is changeable and often disturbed around the year.

Tasmania's climate is strongly influenced by the relative warmth of the southern ocean – winters are mild at sea level and summers are rarely excessively hot. Climate conditions and weather throughout the year are rather similar to that of northwest Europe, particularly Brittany or northwest Spain. Daily sunshine hours range from four to five in winter to seven or eight in summer, sunnier than much of northwest Europe.

The occasional high temperatures in summer (over 38°C/100°F) occur when very warm air is drawn southwards from the central region of Australia. Although snow is often heavy in winter on the mountains, it does not lie throughout the summer.

Austria

Austria is one of the most mountainous countries in Europe. Most of the west, centre, and south of the country is made up of the eastern Alps, which extend uninterrupted from Switzerland and Italy. In Austria the higher peaks rise to over 3,700 m/12,000 ft and are snow-covered throughout the year. The Alps are dissected by deep valleys, however, so that very different climatic and weather conditions occur over quite short distances.

The most extensive lowland in Austria is found in the north and east along the Danube valley from Linz to Vienna and east of Vienna, where the land becomes almost flat along the Hungarian border. The southeast of the country lies south of the main Alpine ranges, and here in the lower valleys and around the lakes it is not unusual for the summer weather to have an almost Mediterranean warmth and dryness.

The sequence of weather around the year varies little from one part of the country to another. The weather can be changeable at all times of the year. Everywhere the summer months are the wettest but summer rainfall is more likely to be heavy and thundery and therefore of shorter duration.

Winters are rather cold and during prolonged cold spells temperatures may be lowest in the valleys and lowlands. The coldest conditions in winter usually occur with east to northeast winds bringing very low temperatures from eastern Europe and Russia.

The character of summer or winter may differ from year to year. On average, sunshine is greater than in northwest Europe but lower than in Mediterranean countries. They range from nine to ten hours a day in July to between two to three in January.

Austria can be divided into three broad climatic regions: the Alps, the Danube valley and the Vienna basin, and the southeast including Styria and Carinthia.

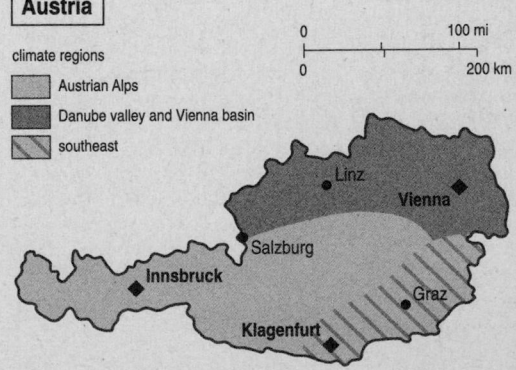

Austria

climate regions

- Austrian Alps
- Danube valley and Vienna basin
- southeast

0   100 mi

0   200 km

Linz

Vienna

Salzburg

Innsbruck

Graz

Klagenfurt

INNSBRUCK

AUSTRIAN ALPS

Sunshine	Temperatures								Discomfort from heat and humidity	Precipitation and humidity				Wet days
	Average daily		Highest recorded		Lowest recorded					Relative humidity 7:00 14:00		Average monthly precipitation		
average hours per day	minimum	maximum												more than 0.1 mm/0.004 in
	°C	°F	°C	°F	°C	°F	°C	°F		%		mm	in	
Jan	2	−7	20	1	34	19	65	−27	−16		86	67	54	2.1	13	Jan
Feb	4	−5	24	4	40	18	64	−27	−16		85	58	49	1.9	13	Feb
March	5	0	0	11	51	25	77	−17	2		83	46	41	1.6	11	March
April	5	4	39	16	60	29	83	−5	23		82	43	52	2.1	14	April
May	6	8	46	20	68	33	91	−2	28		81	43	73	2.9	15	May
June	6	11	52	24	74	36	97	1	34		84	48	110	4.3	19	June
July	7	13	55	25	77	37	98	4	40	Moderate	86	52	134	5.3	19	July
Aug	6	12	54	24	75	35	94	3	38	Moderate	88	52	108	4.3	17	Aug
Sept	6	10	49	21	69	31	87	−1	30		90	53	81	3.2	14	Sept
Oct	5	5	40	15	58	25	76	−5	24		90	55	67	2.6	12	Oct
Nov	3	0	0	8	46	23	73	−15	5		88	65	53	2.1	12	Nov
Dec	2	−4	24	2	36	18	64	−25	−13		87	70	46	1.8	13	Dec

Based on readings for 30 years at 47°16′ N, 11°24′ E, altitude 582 m/1910 ft

THE AUSTRIAN ALPS

Including (with towns and cities in parentheses): TIROL (Innsbruck) and SALZBURG (Salzburg).

In winter the higher Alpine winter sports resorts are much sunnier than the valleys, where conditions are often cloudy and foggy with low temperatures persisting for several days. Although temperatures may be lower on the mountains it may feel warmer in calm and sunny conditions. The reverse is the case in summer when the mountains may become cloudy during the hotter part of the day while the valleys stay sunny.

Certain Alpine valleys, particularly those running from south to north, experience a very warm, dry wind – the föhn. This may blow from twenty to forty days a year. The föhn is most frequent in autumn and spring, when it can melt snow with prodigious speed. It is then dangerous as it can trigger off avalanches on the mountain slopes. The air may become so dry during the föhn that there is a serious fire risk to wooden buildings. The source of the warm air is to the south of the Alps, but it is warmed and dried as it crosses the mountains and descends on the northern side. For details of climate and weather in this area see the table for **Innsbruck** (above).

THE DANUBE VALLEY

Including (with towns and cities in parentheses): the upper Danube valley (Linz) and the Vienna basin (Vienna).

This is the driest part of the country. Winter snowfall is rarely deep but snow may last for some weeks during cold winters. In general, conditions here are very similar to those in southern Germany throughout the year (see the table for **Vienna** on p. 54).

SOUTHEAST AUSTRIA

Including (with towns and cities in parentheses): STYRIA (Graz) and CARINTHIA (Klagenfurt).

In some of the sheltered valleys in this part of Austria the summers are notably warmer and sunnier than north of the Alps. During settled weather the almost uninterrupted sunshine appears to bring a touch of the Mediterranean to the area, but heavy thunderstorms and more unsettled weather are rarely absent for long. Although spring may be a little earlier here, the winters can be as cold and severe as farther north (see the table for **Klagenfurt** on p. 54).

VIENNA — DANUBE VALLEY

	Sunshine average hours per day	Temperatures Average daily minimum °C	°F	Average daily maximum °C	°F	Highest recorded °C	°F	Lowest recorded °C	°F	Discomfort from heat and humidity	Relative humidity 7:00 %	14:00 %	Average monthly precipitation mm	in	Wet days more than 0.1 mm/0.004 in	
Jan	2	-4	25	1	34	13	56	-22	7		81	72	39	1.5	15	Jan
Feb	3	-3	28	3	38	19	65	-23	9		80	66	44	1.7	14	Feb
March	4	-1	30	8	47	24	75	-11	12		78	57	44	1.7	13	March
April	6	6	42	15	58	27	81	-3	26		72	49	45	1.8	13	April
May	8	10	50	19	67	33	91	0	32		74	52	70	2.8	13	May
June	8	14	56	23	73	36	97	4	39		74	55	67	2.6	14	June
July	9	15	60	25	76	38	101	9	48	Moderate	74	54	84	3.3	13	July
Aug	8	15	59	24	75	34	94	8	46	Moderate	78	54	72	2.8	13	Aug
Sept	6	11	53	20	68	32	89	0	32		83	56	42	1.7	10	Sept
Oct	4	7	44	14	56	28	82	-3	26		86	64	56	2.2	13	Oct
Nov	2	3	37	7	45	20	67	-9	16		84	74	52	2.1	14	Nov
Dec	1	-1	30	3	37	17	62	-15	5		84	76	45	1.8	15	Dec

Based on readings for 30 years at 48°15′ N, 16°22′ E, altitude 203 m/666 ft

KLAGENFURT — SOUTHEASTERN AUSTRIA

	Sunshine average hours per day	Temperatures Average daily minimum °C	°F	Average daily maximum °C	°F	Highest recorded °C	°F	Lowest recorded °C	°F	Discomfort from heat and humidity	Relative humidity 7:00 %	14:00 %	Average monthly precipitation mm	in	Wet days more than 0.1 mm/0.004 in	
Jan	2	-9	17	-1	30	12	53	-27	-17		92	77	41	1.6	9	Jan
Feb	4	-7	20	3	38	16	61	-26	-15		91	65	45	1.8	8	Feb
March	5	-2	28	9	49	22	72	-19	-2		90	52	39	1.5	8	March
April	6	3	37	15	59	28	82	-7	19		89	49	71	2.8	11	April
May	7	7	45	20	67	31	87	-5	24		88	53	88	3.5	14	May
June	8	11	52	23	73	35	94	2	35		87	53	125	4.9	15	June
July	8	13	55	25	77	37	99	4	39	Moderate	89	54	125	4.9	14	July
Aug	7	12	54	24	76	34	94	3	38	Moderate	93	56	104	4.1	13	Aug
Sept	6	10	49	20	69	32	90	-1	30		95	59	83	3.3	10	Sept
Oct	4	5	40	14	56	24	74	-8	18		96	67	89	3.5	13	Oct
Nov	2	0	32	6	42	18	64	-12	11		95	77	75	3.0	12	Nov
Dec	1	-4	24	1	33	15	59	-23	-9		94	83	52	2.1	10	Dec

Based on readings for 30 years at 46°39′ N, 14°20′ E, altitude 448 m/1470 ft

Azerbaijan

See map page 22

This Caspian Sea republic has lowlands along its shores and a low central plain inland. The rest of the country rises sharply to high mountains with deep, enclosed valleys. The climate of Azerbaijan is almost tropical in summer in the lowlands, where the winters are warm but with cold spells. In the mountains winters are cold and snowy. The tables for **Tbilisi** in Georgia (p. 152) and for **Yerevan** in neighbouring Armenia (p. 42) illustrate the range of conditions found in the mountains of this region at different altitudes. The table for **Krasnovodsk** (p. 365) in Turkmenistan shows weather on the coast of the Caspian Sea.

Bahamas

See map page 15

The Bahamas are the most northerly group in the Caribbean Islands. They extend from 21° to 27° N in a southeast to northwest direction and stand between the open waters of the Atlantic and the enclosed Caribbean Sea.

There are about a dozen large islands and numerous small islands or coral reefs (called cays). Most are low-lying and for this reason their annual rainfall is lower than what is typical of many other islands in the West Indies (see the general entry for the Caribbean on pp. 92–3).

The climatic table for **Nassau** (below) on New Providence Island in the north of the group shows that winter temperatures in the Bahamas are occasionally rather low when cold air blows out of the North American continent in winter or spring.

Otherwise average temperatures are similar to the rest of the Caribbean Islands.

NASSAU — NEW PROVIDENCE ISLAND

	Sunshine	Temperatures								Discomfort from heat and humidity	Precipitation and humidity				Wet days	
		Average daily				Highest recorded		Lowest recorded			Relative humidity 7:00 13:00		Average monthly precipitation			
		minimum		maximum												
	average hours per day	°C	°F	°C	°F	°C	°F	°C	°F		%		mm	in	more than 1 mm/0.04 in	
Jan	7	18	65	25	77	29	85	5	41	Moderate	84	64	36	1.4	6	Jan
Feb	8	18	64	25	77	30	86	6	43	Moderate	82	62	38	1.5	5	Feb
March	9	19	66	26	79	31	88	8	46	Medium	81	64	36	1.4	5	March
April	9	21	69	27	81	33	91	12	53	Medium	79	65	64	2.5	6	April
May	9	22	71	29	84	33	92	12	53	Medium	79	65	117	4.6	9	May
June	8	23	74	31	87	34	94	17	62	High	81	68	163	6.4	12	June
July	9	24	75	31	88	34	94	19	67	High	80	69	147	5.8	14	July
Aug	9	24	76	32	89	34	94	19	67	High	82	70	135	5.3	14	Aug
Sept	7	24	75	31	88	33	92	18	65	High	84	73	175	6.9	15	Sept
Oct	7	23	73	29	85	33	92	12	54	High	83	71	165	6.5	13	Oct
Nov	7	21	70	27	81	32	89	9	49	Medium	83	68	71	2.8	9	Nov
Dec	7	19	67	26	79	30	86	7	45	Medium	84	66	33	1.3	6	Dec

Based on readings for 35 years at 25°05′ N, 72°21′ W, altitude 4 m/12 ft

BAHRAIN																	BAHRAIN
Sunshine	Temperatures								Discomfort from heat and humidity	Precipitation and humidity						Wet days	
	Average daily				Highest recorded		Lowest recorded			Relative humidity 7:30 15:30			Average monthly precipitation				
	minimum		maximum														
average hours per day	°C	°F	°C	°F	°C	°F	°C	°F		%			mm		in	more than 2.5 mm/0.1 in	
Jan	7	14	57	20	68	29	85	5	41		85	71	8	0.3	1	Jan
Feb	8	15	59	21	70	34	94	7	45		83	70	18	0.7	2	Feb
March	8	17	63	24	75	35	95	11	51	Moderate	80	70	13	0.5	1	March
April	9	21	70	29	84	41	105	13	56	Medium	75	66	8	0.3	1	April
May	10	26	78	33	92	42	108	19	66	High	71	63	0	0.0	0	May
June	11	28	82	36	96	44	111	21	70	Extreme	69	64	0	0.0	0	June
July	11	29	85	37	99	44	112	24	75	Extreme	69	67	0	0.0	0	July
Aug	11	29	85	38	100	45	113	24	75	Extreme	74	65	0	0.0	0	Aug
Sept	11	27	81	36	96	44	112	22	71	Extreme	75	64	0	0.0	0	Sept
Oct	10	24	75	32	90	39	103	19	66	High	80	66	0	0.0	0	Oct
Nov	9	21	69	28	82	36	97	14	58	Medium	80	70	18	0.7	1	Nov
Dec	7	16	60	22	71	31	88	9	48		85	77	18	0.7	2	Dec

Based on readings for 16 years at 26°12´ N, 50°30´ E, altitude 6 m/18 ft

Bahrain

See map page 22

Bahrain consists of one large island and a number of smaller ones lying off the coast of Saudi Arabia and west of the Quitter peninsula. The weather and climate here are similar to that of the Gulf coast of Arabia but are somewhat modified by Bahrain's insular nature.

Humidity is high throughout the year except when hot, dry winds blow off the mainland. The high temperatures between April and October are rendered particularly uncomfortable by the humidity.

Annual rainfall is low and mainly falls between November and March. Winter temperatures are mild and only chilly on the rare occasions when cold northerly winds blow from Iran. During the hottest weather in summer there is some danger of heat exhaustion or heatstroke, particularly for visitors not yet acclimatized. For more detail see the description for Saudi Arabia on p. 312.

DHAKA

COASTAL BANGLADESH

Sunshine	Temperatures								Discomfort from heat and humidity	Precipitation and humidity			Wet days	
	Average daily				Highest recorded		Lowest recorded			Relative humidity 12:00	Average monthly precipitation			
average hours per day	minimum		maximum										more than 2.5 mm/0.1 in	
	°C	°F	°C	°F	°C	°F	°C	°F		%	mm	in		
Jan	9	12	54	25	77	31	88	7	45	Moderate	46	18	0.7	1	Jan
Feb	8	13	55	28	82	34	93	8	46	Moderate	37	31	1.2	1	Feb
March	7	16	61	33	91	39	102	13	55	Medium	38	58	2.3	3	March
April	6	23	73	35	95	42	108	18	64	High	42	103	4.1	6	April
May	5	25	77	34	93	42	108	19	66	High	59	194	7.6	11	May
June	3	26	79	32	90	36	97	22	72	High	72	321	12.6	16	June
July	2	26	79	31	88	34	93	24	75	High	72	437	17.2	12	July
Aug	2	26	79	31	88	36	97	23	73	High	74	305	12.0	16	Aug
Sept	3	26	79	31	88	35	95	23	73	High	71	254	10.0	12	Sept
Oct	6	24	75	31	88	34	93	17	63	High	65	169	6.7	7	Oct
Nov	8	18	64	29	84	31	88	12	54	Medium	53	28	1.1	1	Nov
Dec	9	13	55	26	79	29	84	7	45	Moderate	50	2	0.1	0	Dec

Based on readings for 30 years at 23°46′ N, 90°23′ E, altitude 8 m/26 ft

Bangladesh

See map page 23

Bangladesh is a very low-lying country at the head of the Bay of Bengal. Most of the land boundary is with India. In the southeast there is a border with Myanmar.

Apart from the Chittagong hill district in the extreme southeast on the border with Myanmar, most of the country lies below 180 m/600 ft. Most of it consists of the swampy plains of the great delta of the rivers Brahmaputra and Ganges. The table for **Dhaka** (above) is typical of the country.

Bangladesh has a tropical monsoon climate with the same threefold division of the year as occurs in India (see p. 174). The cool season from November to February is here warmer than in much of India. During the hot season from March until early June some rainstorms occur and these are often thundery.

During the main rainy season of the southwest monsoon from June to September the rainfall is heavy and frequent. Most of the country receives between 1,500–2,500 mm/60–100 in of rain a year

and near the eastern border this rises to as much as 3,750 mm/150 in or more. The rainfall is most reliable and frequent during the season of the southwest monsoon and is brought by shallow depressions in the northern Bay of Bengal.

Rainfall in the period September to November is less reliable but is occasionally very heavy and is usually associated with violent tropical cyclones. These severe storms, which bring very strong winds and torrential rain, develop at this time in the Bay of Bengal and are the most dangerous feature of the climate of Bangladesh.

The storm waves and sea surges raise the water level along the coast and in the branching water courses of the delta so that widespread flooding of the low-lying areas occurs, adding to the devastation produced by the strong wind. Such storms have caused great loss of life and destruction of crops several times this century.

Although temperatures during the hot season are lower in Bangladesh than in some parts of India, the heat is made uncomfortable by the high humidity.

CHITTAGONG

INLAND BANGLADESH

Sunshine	Temperatures								Discomfort from heat and humidity	Precipitation and humidity				Wet days	
average hours per day	Average daily				Highest recorded		Lowest recorded			Relative humidity 8:00 17:30		Average monthly precipitation		more than 2.5 mm/0.1 in	
	minimum		maximum												
	°C	°F	°C	°F	°C	°F	°C	°F		%		mm	in		
Jan	13	55	26	79	32	89	7	45	Moderate	81	58	5	0.2	0.4	Jan
Feb	15	59	28	82	34	93	8	46	Medium	76	58	28	1.1	1.0	Feb
March	19	67	31	87	37	99	11	51	High	76	65	64	2.5	2.0	March
April	23	73	32	89	39	102	15	59	High	78	71	150	5.9	6.0	April
May	24	75	32	89	37	98	18	65	Extreme	79	77	264	10.4	11.0	May
June	25	77	31	87	37	98	20	68	Extreme	84	83	533	21.0	17.0	June
July	25	77	30	86	34	94	19	67	High	87	85	597	23.5	19.0	July
Aug	24	76	30	86	34	93	22	72	High	87	86	518	20.4	17.0	Aug
Sept	24	76	31	87	35	95	22	71	Extreme	86	84	320	12.6	13.0	Sept
Oct	23	73	31	87	34	94	17	62	High	85	78	180	7.1	7.0	Oct
Nov	18	65	29	84	34	93	11	52	High	84	71	56	2.2	2.0	Nov
Dec	14	57	26	79	31	88	8	47	Medium	85	68	15	0.6	0.7	Dec

Based on readings for 60 years at 22°21' N, 91°50' E, altitude 27 m/87 ft

This muggy, damp heat persists throughout the main rainy season.

The heat is rarely dangerous but is certainly unpleasant to the unacclimatized visitor. There is no great difference in temperature conditions around the year from one part of the country to another. During the hot season temperatures are a little lower on the coast than inland. See the table for **Chittagong** (above).

Because of the greater cloudiness during the rainy season, average daily hours of sunshine are least between June and September, about four hours a day. During the rest of the year they average from six to eight hours.

BRIDGETOWN															WEST COAST BARBADOS	
Sunshine		Temperatures								Discomfort from heat and humidity	Precipitation and humidity					Wet days	
		Average daily				Highest recorded		Lowest recorded			Relative humidity 8:00 17:00		Average monthly precipitation				
		minimum		maximum													
average hours per day		°C	°F	°C	°F	°C	°F	°C	°F		%		mm	in		more than 1 mm/0.04 in	
Jan	9	21	70	28	83	31	87	16	61	Medium	75	71	66	2.6		13	Jan
Feb	9	21	69	28	83	31	87	16	61	Medium	72	66	28	1.1		8	Feb
March	9	21	70	29	85	32	89	17	62	Medium	69	64	33	1.3		8	March
April	9	22	72	30	86	32	89	18	64	High	67	65	36	1.4		7	April
May	9	23	73	31	87	33	91	19	66	High	69	67	58	2.3		9	May
June	8	23	74	31	87	32	90	19	67	High	72	70	112	4.4		14	June
July	9	23	74	30	86	32	90	20	68	High	75	71	147	5.8		18	July
Aug	9	23	74	31	87	35	95	21	69	High	76	72	147	5.8		16	Aug
Sept	8	23	74	31	87	33	91	19	67	High	76	73	170	6.7		15	Sept
Oct	8	23	73	30	86	33	92	19	67	High	78	76	178	7.0		15	Oct
Nov	8	23	73	29	85	32	89	19	66	High	79	78	206	8.1		16	Nov
Dec	8	22	71	28	83	31	88	18	64	Medium	77	73	97	3.8		14	Dec

Based on readings for 35 years at 13°08′ N, 59°36′ W, altitude 55 m/181 ft

Barbados

See map page 15

The small island of Barbados is one of the largest, along with Martinique, St Lucia, Grenada, and St Vincent, of the Windward Islands. The Windward Islands, making up the southern segment of the Lesser Antilles, lie between 15° N and the coast of the South American continent.

Although still small, the larger islands of the Windward group are hilly or mountainous, and this tends to increase the rainfall above that of the small, flat islands in the group. However, Barbados does not rise as high as Martinique or St Lucia, and its climate is less wet than theirs.

The table for **Bridgetown** (above) shows conditions on the west coast of Barbados, which is somewhat sheltered from the prevailing winds.

All months receive appreciable rain but the heaviest rain is more likely to occur from July to November. This is the hurricane season and, although the most violent of these tropical storms may only strike a particular island every few years, less severe ones cause appreciable rainfall over quite a wide area.

Temperature, humidity, and sunshine throughout the year are typical of the Caribbean area. (See also the general entry for the Caribbean on pp. 92–3.)

Belarus

See map page 19

This former Soviet republic is bordered on the east by Russia, on the south by Ukraine, on the west by Poland and Lithuania and on the north by Latvia.

Like Lithuania and Latvia, the country shares much the same weather as northern European Russia (see pp. 300–2) The tables for **Vilnius** (p. 220) in southern Lithuania and **Kiev** (p. 369) in northern Ukraine are indicative of conditions in Belarus.

OSTEND												NORTHERN BELGIUM	
Sunshine		Temperatures							Discomfort from heat and humidity	Precipitation and humidity				Wet days
		Average daily				Highest recorded		Lowest recorded		Relative humidity 6:00 12:00		Average monthly precipitation		
		minimum		maximum										
average hours per day		°C	°F	°C	°F	°C	°F	°C	°F		%		mm	in	more than 0.1 mm/0.004 in
Jan	2	1	33	5	41	13	56	-13	9		91	90	41	1.6	13	Jan
Feb	3	2	35	6	44	17	63	-10	14		92	86	38	1.5	12	Feb
March	5	3	37	9	48	19	66	-6	22		91	82	31	1.2	11	March
April	7	6	42	11	53	23	73	-1	29		91	80	38	1.5	12	April
May	7	10	49	15	59	28	83	3	38		89	78	34	1.3	11	May
June	8	12	53	18	65	32	90	6	42		89	79	38	1.5	10	June
July	7	13	56	20	67	32	90	8	46		90	80	62	2.4	12	July
Aug	7	13	56	20	68	31	88	10	49		91	80	58	2.3	13	Aug
Sept	6	12	53	19	66	29	84	5	41		92	80	56	2.2	10	Sept
Oct	4	9	47	15	59	25	77	1	35		93	83	68	2.7	13	Oct
Nov	2	5	40	10	50	17	63	-5	22		93	89	74	2.9	15	Nov
Dec	1	2	36	6	43	14	57	-9	17		94	91	60	2.4	16	Dec

Based on readings for 10 years at 51°14' N, 2°55' E, altitude 10 m/33 ft

Belgium

See map page 18

Belgium is a small country about the same size as the Netherlands, which borders it on the north. It has a short coastline on the North Sea and is bordered on the west by France and on the east by Germany and Luxembourg. The general character of the climate is similar to that of the Netherlands with considerable variation from day to day and from one year to another.

The northern part of Belgium is low-lying and similar to the adjoining Netherlands. The climate of this area is well represented by the table for **Ostend** (above) and is similar to that of the Netherlands.

The central part of the country is of moderate elevation and consists of gently rolling countryside. Here the climate is a little colder in winter and warmer in summer than along the coast. It is also rather wetter in summer and thunderstorms are more frequent – see the table for **Brussels** (opposite and above).

The north and centre of the country contain the most productive agricultural districts and the largest towns.

The southern third of the country is sparsely populated. This is the Ardennes region which consists of forested hills with an average elevation of 300–500 m/1,000–1,600 ft. Here the winters are distinctly colder and, in an average year, snow may lie for as many as fifty days in the higher parts as compared with an average of ten days in the north of the country. Winters here are also wetter than farther north and hill fog occurs frequently. Summer in the Ardennes is only a little cooler than in the north and not very much wetter. The table for **Virton** (opposite) is representative of conditions in the valleys and lower parts of the Ardennes.

Except during severe winter weather in the Ardennes, the weather and climate of Belgium are rarely unpleasant or uncomfortable. Average daily sunshine amounts range from about two hours a day in January to between seven and eight hours in June.

BRUSSELS

CENTRAL BELGIUM

Sunshine		Temperatures								Discomfort from heat and humidity	Precipitation and humidity				Wet days
		Average daily				Highest recorded		Lowest recorded			Relative humidity		Average monthly precipitation		
		minimum		maximum							6:30	12:30			
average hours per day		°C	°F	°C	°F	°C	°F	°C	°F		%		mm	in	more than 0.1 mm/0.004 in
Jan	2	−1	30	4	40	13	56	−17	2		92	86	66	2.6	21	Jan
Feb	3	0	32	7	44	20	68	−11	12		92	81	61	2.4	17	Feb
March	4	2	36	10	51	22	72	−7	20		91	74	53	2.1	17	March
April	5	5	41	14	58	24	76	−2	29		91	71	60	2.4	18	April
May	6	8	46	18	65	29	84	−2	29		90	65	55	2.2	16	May
June	7	11	52	22	72	33	91	1	34		87	65	76	3.0	15	June
July	6	12	54	23	73	37	98	5	41	Moderate	91	68	95	3.7	17	July
Aug	6	12	54	22	72	34	93	6	42		93	69	80	3.2	18	Aug
Sept	5	11	51	21	69	31	88	3	38		94	69	63	2.5	13	Sept
Oct	4	7	45	15	60	26	79	−2	28		93	77	83	3.3	17	Oct
Nov	2	3	38	9	48	19	66	−7	20		93	85	75	3.0	20	Nov
Dec	1	0	32	6	42	15	59	−12	10		92	86	88	3.5	19	Dec

Based on readings for 10 years at 50°48′ N, 4°21′ E, altitude 100 m/328 ft

VIRTON

SOUTHERN BELGIUM

Sunshine		Temperatures								Discomfort from heat and humidity	Precipitation and humidity				Wet days
		Average daily				Highest recorded		Lowest recorded			Relative humidity		Average monthly precipitation		
		minimum		maximum							6:30	12:30			
average hours per day		°C	°F	°C	°F	°C	°F	°C	°F		%		mm	in	more than 0.1 mm/0.004 in
Jan	1	−2	28	3	38	13	55	−18	0		96	89	75	3.0	18	Jan
Feb	2	−1	30	6	43	19	65	−16	3		95	84	72	2.8	17	Feb
March	4	0	32	10	49	22	72	−12	10		95	72	61	2.4	16	March
April	5	3	38	14	57	26	78	−4	25		90	63	66	2.6	17	April
May	6	6	42	18	64	28	83	−4	25		89	61	61	2.4	16	May
June	6	10	49	22	71	33	91	0	32		87	62	62	2.4	14	June
July	6	11	51	22	72	36	97	2	36		90	64	74	2.9	14	July
Aug	6	11	51	22	72	32	90	3	37		93	68	88	3.5	17	Aug
Sept	5	8	47	20	68	31	88	0	32		95	69	74	2.9	15	Sept
Oct	4	5	40	15	58	25	76	−4	25		95	77	67	2.6	16	Oct
Nov	1	2	36	8	46	18	64	−9	16		94	85	85	3.4	19	Nov
Dec	1	−1	30	4	40	15	58	−13	9		96	90	103	4.1	18	Dec

Based on readings for 10 years at 49°33′ N, 5°34′ E, altitude 242 m/794 ft

BELIZE												BELIZE
Sunshine	Temperatures						Discomfort from heat and humidity	Precipitation and humidity				Wet days
	Average daily		Highest recorded		Lowest recorded			Relative humidity	Average monthly precipitation			
	minimum	maximum						7:00 19:00				
average hours per day	°C	°F	°C	°F	°C	°F	°C	°F		%	mm	in	more than 1 mm/0.04 in
Jan	4	19	67	27	81	32	90	9	49	Medium	92	89	137	5.4	12	Jan
Feb	5	21	69	28	82	34	93	9	49	High	91	87	61	2.4	6	Feb
March	5	22	71	29	84	35	95	12	54	High	90	87	38	1.5	4	March
April	4	23	74	30	86	36	97	15	59	High	91	87	56	2.2	5	April
May	3	24	75	31	87	36	96	16	60	Extreme	91	87	109	4.3	7	May
June	3	24	75	31	87	36	97	18	64	Extreme	93	87	196	7.7	13	June
July	3	24	75	31	87	35	95	17	62	Extreme	93	86	163	6.4	15	July
Aug	3	24	75	31	88	36	96	16	60	Extreme	92	87	170	6.7	14	Aug
Sept	3	23	74	31	87	36	97	16	60	Extreme	94	87	244	9.6	15	Sept
Oct	3	22	72	30	86	36	96	14	58	High	94	88	305	12.0	16	Oct
Nov	3	20	68	28	83	35	95	11	52	High	94	91	226	8.9	12	Nov
Dec	3	20	68	27	81	33	92	9	49	High	93	90	185	7.3	14	Dec

Based on readings for 27 years at 17°31′ N, 88°11′ W, altitude 5 m/17 ft

Belize

See map page 14

Belize is one of the smaller countries of Central America. Its weather and climate are described in more detail for Panama (pp. 278–80).

It is situated between 16° and 18° N and is bordered by Guatemala on the south and west and by Mexico on the north. It has a long coastline on the Caribbean Sea.

A large part of the country is low-lying (see the table for **Belize City** above) so that it has weather and climate typical of the *tierra caliente* (see p. 66), except in the southwest where some hills rise to more than 1,200 m/3,800 ft.

Annual rainfall is heavy on the coast and, although there is a wetter season between May and November, some rain occurs throughout the year.

The country is occasionally affected by very heavy rains brought by tropical storms or hurricanes which can cause severe damage to both dwellings and crops. The weather is hot and humid throughout the year.

Benin

See map page 20

Benin is a West African country with a short coastline on the Gulf of Guinea. It is situated between Nigeria to the east and Togo to the west and extends between 6° and 12° N. It is very narrow from east to west.

It shares the same climatic belts and sequence of weather around the year as those described on p. 266 for Nigeria and adjacent countries.

The coastal region has two rainy seasons, one peaking in May or June, the other in October, but in the north there is a single rainy season starting in

COTONOU										COASTAL BENIN		
Sunshine	Temperatures							Discomfort from heat and humidity	Precipitation and humidity			Wet days
	Average daily				Highest recorded		Lowest recorded		Relative humidity 8:00 13:00		Average monthly precipitation	
average hours per day	minimum		maximum									more than 1 mm/0.04 in
	°C	°F	°C	°F	°C	°F	°C	°F		%		mm	in	
Jan	7	23	74	27	80	32	90	19	66	Medium	90	68	33	1.3	2	Jan
Feb	8	25	77	28	82	34	93	21	70	Medium	88	70	33	1.3	2	Feb
March	7	26	79	28	83	34	94	21	70	Medium	85	69	117	4.6	5	March
April	7	26	78	28	83	35	95	21	70	Medium	83	70	125	4.9	7	April
May	7	24	76	27	81	34	94	21	70	Medium	86	74	254	10.0	11	May
June	5	23	74	26	78	33	91	18	65	Medium	90	78	366	14.4	13	June
July	4	23	74	26	78	32	89	20	68	Medium	88	77	89	3.5	7	July
Aug	5	23	73	25	77	31	87	21	69	Medium	88	76	38	1.5	3	Aug
Sept	5	23	74	26	78	32	89	20	68	Medium	88	76	66	2.6	6	Sept
Oct	6	24	75	27	80	33	91	22	71	Medium	87	75	135	5.3	9	Oct
Nov	8	24	76	28	82	33	92	22	71	Medium	88	74	58	2.3	6	Nov
Dec	7	24	76	27	81	33	91	19	67	Medium	91	71	13	0.5	1	Dec

Based on readings for 5 years at 6°12' N, 2°26' E, altitude 7 m/23 ft

May or June. In the north there is a single long dry season between October and April. At this time temperatures are warm to hot with a very low relative humidity and the dust-laden harmattan wind blows from the northeast.

From December to February the harmattan affects the whole country, except a strip along the coast. The coast has southwesterly winds, the dry harmattan reaching right to the coast on only a few days.

The table for **Cotonou** (above), which is on the coast, is representative of the south of the country. On the coast the period from December to February is least likely to experience rainy days. The coast of

Benin is a little drier round the year than the districts immediately inland. This is thought to be a consequence of two local features that apply to this part of the West African coastline. First, at the time when rainfall is heaviest in much of West Africa the waters offshore are unusually cool for near-equatorial latitudes; a cool current appears on the ocean surface. Second, the coast here follows a direction from west-southwest to east-northeast and is parallel with the prevailing winds.

For the centre and north of the country the climatic conditions round the year are well represented by the tables for **Ibadan** (p. 267) and **Kano** (p. 266) respectively; both these places are in Nigeria.

Bermuda

See map page 13

The island of Bermuda, an area of only 52 sq km/20 sq mi, lies in the North Atlantic in latitude 32° N at a distance of 1,125 km/700 mi from New York.

It has a subtropical climate which is much influenced by the warmth of the North Atlantic

waters, for it is fully in the path of the warm Gulf Stream current. The summers are consequently warm to hot and the winters mild with occasional warm, sunny days.

An abundant rainfall is well distributed throughout the year but falls on fewer days than in drier places in North America or Britain.

HAMILTON																BERMUDA
Sunshine		Temperatures								Discomfort from heat and humidity	Precipitation and humidity				Wet days	
average hours per day		Average daily minimum		Average daily maximum		Highest recorded		Lowest recorded			Relative humidity		Average monthly precipitation		more than 1 mm/0.04 in	
		°C	°F	°C	°F	°C	°F	°C	°F		% 7:30	% 14:30	mm	in		
Jan	5	14	58	20	68	27	81	5	41		78	70	112	4.4	14	Jan
Feb	5	14	57	20	68	27	81	4	40		76	69	119	4.7	13	Feb
March	6	14	57	20	68	29	84	5	41		77	69	122	4.8	12	March
April	8	15	59	22	71	31	87	6	42		78	70	104	4.1	9	April
May	8	18	64	24	76	31	88	9	49	Moderate	81	75	117	4.6	9	May
June	8	21	69	27	81	33	92	14	58	Medium	82	74	112	4.4	9	June
July	10	23	73	29	85	37	98	17	62	High	81	73	114	4.5	10	July
Aug	9	23	74	30	86	37	99	17	62	High	79	69	137	5.4	13	Aug
Sept	8	22	72	29	84	37	98	15	59	High	81	73	132	5.2	10	Sept
Oct	6	21	69	26	79	33	92	12	53	Medium	79	72	147	5.8	12	Oct
Nov	6	17	63	23	74	31	87	9	49	Moderate	76	70	127	5.0	13	Nov
Dec	5	16	60	21	70	27	81	7	45		77	70	119	4.7	15	Dec

Based on readings for 57 years at 32°17′ N, 64°46′ W, altitude 46 m/151 ft

Bermuda has a sunny climate with daily sunshine hours ranging from five to six in winter to nine to ten in summer and is a popular tourist spot for visitors from North America.

The main island, and a series of smaller ones which are all part of a coral reef, are low-lying, with no land higher than 75 m/250 ft. The table for **Hamilton** (above) is representative of the island.

Bermuda is occasionally affected by hurricanes that have moved north from the Caribbean, but these violent tropical storms are usually in the decaying stage by the time they reach this latitude.

Bhutan

See map page 23

Bhutan is a small independent state in treaty relationship with its larger neighbour, India, to the south. It is bordered by Sikkim on the west and China on the north. It is a mountainous country, extending from the highest parts of the Himalayas to the foothill region on the Indian border. The climate and weather of Bhutan are similar to those described for Nepal (pp. 254-5). The table for Darjeeling in India (p. 176) is representative of conditions in the lower part of the country.

Bolivia

See map page 16

Bolivia, a landlocked country twice the size of France or Texas, lies between 10° and 23° S. It is bordered on the north by Brazil, east by Paraguay, south by Argentina, and west by Chile and Peru.

The country has two very contrasting climatic regions. In the west the great mountain range of the Andes, here at its broadest, rises to peaks of over 6,100 m/20,000 ft, and between the western and eastern ranges of the Andes there is an extensive highland plateau, the *páramos* or *altiplano*, at

LA PAZ											ANDEAN PLATEAU OF BOLIVIA		
Sunshine		Temperatures							Discomfort from heat and humidity	Precipitation and humidity			Wet days	
		Average daily				Highest recorded		Lowest recorded		Relative humidity	Average monthly precipitation			
average hours per day		minimum		maximum									more than 1 mm/0.04 in	
		°C	°F	°C	°F	°C	°F	°C	°F	%	mm	in		
Jan	6	6	43	17	63	25	77	1	33		114	4.5	21	Jan
Feb	5	6	43	17	63	24	76	2	36		107	4.2	18	Feb
March	5	6	42	18	64	24	76	2	36		66	2.6	16	March
April	6	4	40	18	65	24	75	-1	30		33	1.3	9	April
May	8	3	37	18	64	22	72	-1	30		13	0.5	5	May
June	9	1	34	17	62	21	70	-3	27		8	0.3	2	June
July	9	1	33	17	62	22	71	-3	26		10	0.4	2	July
Aug	8	2	35	17	63	22	72	-3	27		13	0.5	4	Aug
Sept	7	3	38	18	64	27	80	-1	30		28	1.1	9	Sept
Oct	6	4	40	19	66	24	76	-1	30		41	1.6	9	Oct
Nov	6	6	42	19	67	25	77	-1	30		48	1.9	11	Nov
Dec	6	6	42	18	65	24	76	2	35		94	3.7	18	Dec

Based on readings for 31 years at 16°30′ S, 68°08′ W, altitude 3658 m/12,001 ft

3,000–4,000 m/10,000–13,000 ft. However, east of the Andes the land drops sharply to the forested lowlands of the Amazon basin on the Brazilian border and the lowland of the Chaco region on the border with Paraguay.

The climate of the Andean plateau is represented by the table for **La Paz** (above). This is an extreme type of tropical highland climate. Precipitation is low and occurs mostly between December and March during the high sun period when there are many rainy days. Temperatures are much reduced by altitude with only small differences from month to month. The daily range is large, so the nights are quite cold, particularly during the dry winter or low sun period when frost is almost a nightly occurrence. In some parts annual precipitation is as low as 250 mm/10 in, particularly in the western mountains and valleys; consequently the permanent snowline may be as high as 6,100 m/20,000 ft.

At 3,000 m/10,000 ft atmospheric pressure is only about two-thirds that at sea level and at 5,200 m/17,000 ft it is only about half. This reduced pressure causes problems for visitors, who may suffer from mountain sickness, called here the *soroche*. For a fit person acclimatization takes a few days to a week or so. The area is not recommended for those with weak hearts or lung complaints.

Sunshine ranges from about six hours a day in the rainy season, when there is usually cloud in the afternoon, to as much as eight hours a day in the dry season. The sun's rays are particularly powerful because of the thin atmosphere at this height, and sunburn can be a hazard. Temperature drops very rapidly after sunset and the nights feel distinctly chilly. The greatest differences of weather and climate in this high mountain region are those experienced during the course of the day and those arising from sudden changes of altitude.

The lowlands east of the Andes – more than half the country – lie mostly between 230 m/750 ft and 900 m/3,000 ft. Their climate is similar to the equatorial regions of the Amazon basin in Brazil or the Chaco region of Paraguay. Temperatures are warm to hot around the year, with a single rainy season at the time of high sun. This region is much wetter than the Andean plateau, with the annual precipitation being everywhere more than 1,000 mm/40 in, rising to 1,500 mm/60 in towards the north. Combined heat and humidity can cause discomfort and heat stress in October to March (see the table for **Concepción** overleaf). During the dry period of low sun, occasional bursts of colder air reach these lowlands as a result of outbreaks of polar air from Antarctica. Temperatures may fall to a few degrees above freezing for a night or so. Such extreme events

CONCEPCION													LOWLAND BOLIVIA
Sunshine	Temperatures							Discomfort from heat and humidity	Precipitation and humidity				Wet days	
	Average daily				Highest recorded		Lowest recorded		Relative humidity 8:00 14:00		Average monthly precipitation			
	minimum		maximum											
average hours per day	°C	°F	°C	°F	°C	°F	°C	°F		%		mm	in	more than 1 mm/0.04 in	
Jan	19	66	29	85	36	96	13	55	Medium	93	63	193	7.6	15	Jan
Feb	19	66	30	86	34	93	9	49	High	93	74	155	6.1	13	Feb
March	18	65	29	85	34	93	12	54	High	91	71	117	4.6	12	March
April	17	62	30	86	34	93	9	48	High	91	65	61	2.4	5	April
May	15	59	28	83	34	93	6	43	Medium	88	61	79	3.1	6	May
June	13	56	27	80	32	90	7	45	Medium	93	61	23	0.9	4	June
July	12	54	27	81	34	94	2	36	Medium	87	55	28	1.1	2	July
Aug	13	56	31	87	36	97	4	39	Medium	81	47	15	0.6	4	Aug
Sept	16	61	33	91	38	100	4	40	High	80	49	58	2.3	4	Sept
Oct	17	62	31	88	37	98	7	45	High	77	58	76	3.0	8	Oct
Nov	19	66	31	88	38	101	11	52	High	81	61	206	8.1	11	Nov
Dec	18	65	30	86	34	94	8	47	High	87	69	132	5.2	15	Dec

Based on readings for 5 years at 16°15′ S, 62°03′ W, altitude 490 m/1607 ft

are rare, however. In the Andean region of Bolivia, as elsewhere in Central and northern South America, the inhabitants distinguish three or four climatic zones depending on altitude: *tierra caliente*, from sea level to about 900 m/3,000 ft; *tierra templada*, between 900–1,800 m/3,000–6,000 ft; and *tierra fria*, from 1,800–3,000 m/6,000 –10,000 ft, above which is the *páramos* or *altiplano*.

Bosnia-Herzegovina

See map page 19

Even though the Adriatic is not far away, this landlocked country has weather typical of inland eastern Europe, with cold winters and warm summers. Summer is the wettest season. Much of the country is mountainous or hilly, and winter snow lies for long periods in the higher regions.

The table for **Sarajevo** (opposite and above) is typical of conditions in the more mountainous parts of Bosnia-Herzegovina.

Botswana

See map page 21

This large but very sparsely populated country lies in the centre of southern Africa and is surrounded by Namibia and Zimbabwe on the north and by South Africa on the east and south. Botswana's weather and climate are like the western interior of South Africa. Being a part of the great Kalahari desert, it is a region of low and unreliable rainfall. What rain there is tends to come in the summer or warm season. Winters can be quite chilly with occasional frost. Annual rainfall decreases westwards and southwards.

The climatic table for **Francistown** (opposite) is representative of the wetter north and east. Here mean annual rainfall is usually over 400 mm/16 in but in the west and south it falls below 200 mm/8 in.

SARAJEVO

CENTRAL BOSNIA

	Sunshine average hours per day	Temperatures										Discomfort from heat and humidity	Precipitation and humidity				Wet days more than 0.1 mm/0.004 in
		Average daily				Highest recorded		Lowest recorded					Relative humidity 7:00 14:00		Average monthly precipitation			
		minimum		maximum														
		°C	°F	°C	°F	°C	°F	°C	°F				%		mm	in		
Jan	2	−4	25	3	37	15	59	−22	−8				84	75	66	2.6	16	Jan
Feb	3	−3	27	5	41	19	66	−21	−6				81	67	64	2.5	14	Feb
March	4	0	32	10	50	25	77	−15	5				82	58	62	2.4	13	March
April	5	5	41	15	59	30	86	−6	21				77	54	64	2.5	13	April
May	6	8	46	19	66	31	88	−2	28				79	55	90	3.5	16	May
June	8	12	54	23	73	33	91	5	41				78	53	88	3.5	14	June
July	9	13	55	26	79	37	99	6	43		Moderate		78	49	71	2.8	12	July
Aug	9	13	55	27	81	38	100	4	39		Moderate		76	45	70	2.8	8	Aug
Sept	7	10	50	23	73	34	93	2	36				82	52	78	3.1	9	Sept
Oct	4	6	43	16	61	26	79	−2	28				85	62	103	4.1	12	Oct
Nov	2	3	37	9	48	21	70	−12	10				85	71	91	3.6	15	Nov
Dec	2	−1	30	6	43	17	63	−16	3				84	75	85	3.3	15	Dec

Based on readings for 12 years at 43°52′ N, 18°62′ E, altitude 630 m/2067 ft

FRANCISTOWN

NORTHERN AND EASTERN BOTSWANA

	Sunshine average hours per day	Temperatures									Discomfort from heat and humidity	Precipitation and humidity				Wet days more than 1 mm/0.04 in
		Average daily				Highest recorded		Lowest recorded				Relative humidity 8:00		Average monthly precipitation		
		minimum		maximum												
		°C	°F	°C	°F	°C	°F	°C	°F			%		mm	in	
Jan	7	18	65	31	88	40	104	9	48		High	69		107	4.2	8.0	Jan
Feb	8	18	64	30	86	39	103	9	48		High	73		79	3.1	7.0	Feb
March	8	16	61	29	85	38	100	9	48		High	74		71	2.8	5.0	March
April	9	13	56	28	83	36	96	0	32		Medium	70		18	0.7	2.0	April
May	9	9	48	26	79	34	94	−2	28		Medium	68		5	0.2	0.7	May
June	10	5	41	23	74	31	88	−4	24		Moderate	70		3	0.1	0.3	June
July	9	5	41	24	75	32	89	−3	27		Moderate	63		0	0.0	0.1	July
Aug	10	7	45	26	79	35	95	−3	27		Medium	60		0	0.0	0.1	Aug
Sept	10	12	54	30	86	38	100	−1	31		Medium	55		0	0.0	0.5	Sept
Oct	9	16	61	32	90	41	105	5	41		High	56		23	0.9	3.0	Oct
Nov	8	18	64	32	89	42	107	7	44		High	63		56	2.2	5.0	Nov
Dec	8	18	65	31	88	41	105	10	50		High	65		86	3.4	7.0	Dec

Based on readings for 20 years at 21°13′ S, 27°30′ E, altitude 1004 m/3294 ft

Brazil

Brazil is a little larger than the United States, and it contains almost half of South America within its borders. Extending from 5° N to 34° S, it is broadest at about 7° S, the greater part of the country lying within the tropics.

Unlike most other South American countries, it does not include any part of the Andes mountains, so no area of the country has permanent snowfields. The highest areas within Brazil just fail to reach 3,000 m/10,000 ft and there are no large areas above 1,800 m/6,000 ft.

The two largest physical regions of the country are the Amazon basin and the Brazilian plateau.

The first of these is the Amazon basin, which occupies the whole north and centre of the country. Everywhere the basin is below 300 m/1,000 ft. It has the climate of an equatorial lowland with few differences from place to place.

The second large region is the Brazilian plateau, which lies to the south and east of the Amazon basin and is highest in the east near the Atlantic coast. Most of the plateau has an average height of 600–900 m/2,000–3,000 ft, and it decreases in height northwards and westwards towards the basins of the Amazon and Paraguay rivers.

From Recife in the north to Pôrto Alegre in the south, the Atlantic coastlands of Brazil are narrow and are overlooked by the hills forming the high edge of the plateau. Only around the mouth of the Amazon in the north are there extensive lowlands on the Atlantic coast.

This geography makes for a simple division of the country into four climatic regions: the Amazon basin, the Brazilian plateau, the coastlands within the tropics and the southern states of Paraná, Rio Grande do Sul, and Santa Catarina.

This last division is distinctive because it is outside the tropics and has a temperate climate similar to that of Uruguay, but modified by the greater height of the interior.

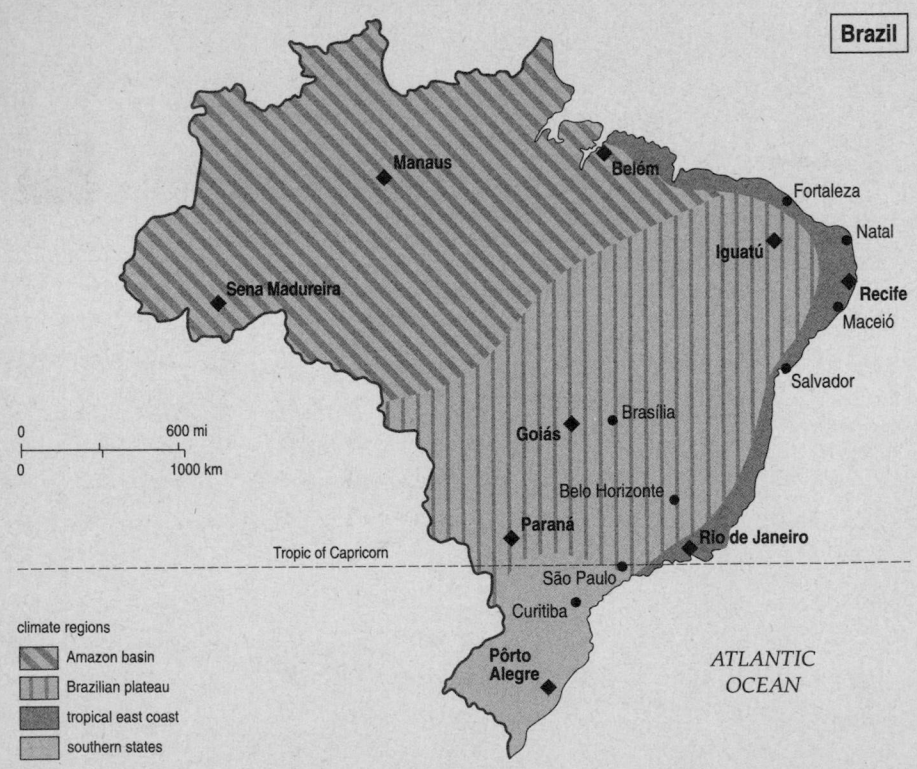

Brazil

climate regions

Amazon basin

Brazilian plateau

tropical east coast

southern states

THE AMAZON BASIN

Including (with towns and cities in parentheses): ACRE (Sena Madureira), AMAPA, AMAZONAS SELVAS (Manaus), RORAIMA; northern inland parts of MARANHAO; the northern and central parts of PARA and the Amazon delta (Belém); and northern and western parts of RONDONIA.

This is the largest area in the world with a typical equatorial climate. Rainfall is everywhere above 1,500 mm/60 in a year and in much of the region over 2,000 mm/80 in. There is no real dry season but there are some variations in the period of the year when most rain falls.

Temperatures are typically tropical in all months with averages midday of 27–32° C/80°–90° F. Frost is unknown, although in the southern parts of the region occasional cold spells, lasting a day or two and known as *friagem*, cause night temperatures to fall below 10° C/50° F. These spells are most uncomfortable for the local inhabitants, who then stay indoors and light fires. The cold spells are most likely to occur at the time of low sun between May and September. They are caused by invasions of cold air, originating from Antarctica and the southern oceans, which track northwards across Argentina and Paraguay into central Brazil.

Excessively high temperatures are almost unknown in the Amazon basin; daytime temperatures of 38° C/100° F are very rare. The high humidity and the monotony of the temperature from day to day make this area unpleasant for those unfamiliar with, or unacclimatized to, the hot, wet tropics, but conditions are not physically dangerous.

The tables for **Belém** (below), **Manaus** (overleaf), and **Sena Madureira** (overleaf) are representative of this vast region. These tables show that there is little difference in terms of temperature and humidity from place to place.

Belém at the mouth of the Amazon is the wettest place, and the heaviest rainfall comes in the months January to May, but all months have many days with rain. Manaus in the central part of the region is not quite so set, and the period June to September is drier than at Belém.

Sena Madureira in the extreme southwest of the Amazon basin is nearer the Andes and so wetter. Being farther south, it has a greater concentration of rain in the period of high sun from December to March and a distinct drier season at the time of low sun. Hours of sunshine a day range from three to four in the wetter months to seven to eight in the drier season.

BELEM

AMAZON BASIN

	Sunshine	Temperatures								Discomfort from heat and humidity	Precipitation and humidity				Wet days	
		Average daily				Highest recorded		Lowest recorded			Relative humidity		Average monthly precipitation			
		minimum		maximum							7:00	12:00				
	average hours per day	°C	°F	°C	°F	°C	°F	°C	°F		%		mm	in	more than 0.25 mm/0.01 in	
Jan	5	22	72	31	87	35	95	19	66	Extreme	96	88	318	12.5	27	Jan
Feb	4	22	72	30	86	34	94	20	68	Extreme	98	91	358	14.1	26	Feb
March	3	23	73	31	87	35	95	19	66	Extreme	98	90	358	14.1	28	March
April	4	23	73	31	87	35	95	21	69	Extreme	98	89	320	12.6	27	April
May	6	23	73	31	88	34	94	20	68	Extreme	98	87	259	10.2	24	May
June	8	22	72	31	88	34	93	20	68	Extreme	98	85	170	6.7	22	June
July	9	22	71	31	88	34	94	18	64	Extreme	97	86	150	5.9	19	July
Aug	9	22	71	31	88	35	95	19	67	Extreme	97	85	112	4.4	16	Aug
Sept	8	22	71	32	89	36	96	18	65	Extreme	97	83	89	3.5	16	Sept
Oct	8	22	71	32	89	37	98	19	67	Extreme	97	80	84	3.3	15	Oct
Nov	7	22	71	32	90	36	97	19	67	Extreme	97	81	66	2.6	12	Nov
Dec	7	22	72	32	89	36	97	19	66	Extreme	98	84	155	6.1	19	Dec

Based on readings for 16 years at 1°27' S, 48°29' W, altitude 13 m/42 ft

MANAUS

AMAZON BASIN

Sunshine	Temperatures								Discomfort from heat and humidity	Precipitation and humidity				Wet days
	Average daily				Highest recorded		Lowest recorded			Relative humidity 6:00 13:00		Average monthly precipitation		
	minimum		maximum											
average hours per day	°C	°F	°C	°F	°C	°F	°C	°F		%		mm	in	more than 0.25 mm/0.01 in
Jan 4	24	75	31	88	37	99	18	65	High	89	70	249	9.8	20 Jan
Feb 4	24	75	31	88	38	100	20	68	High	89	71	231	9.1	19 Feb
March 4	24	75	31	88	36	97	19	67	High	89	72	262	10.3	20 March
April 4	24	75	31	87	34	94	20	68	High	90	73	221	8.7	19 April
May 5	24	75	31	88	35	95	20	68	High	89	72	170	6.7	18 May
June 7	24	75	31	88	35	95	18	65	High	87	68	84	3.3	11 June
July 8	24	75	32	89	35	95	18	64	High	87	64	58	2.3	8 July
Aug 8	24	75	33	91	37	98	19	67	High	85	59	38	1.5	6 Aug
Sept 8	24	75	33	92	37	99	20	68	High	84	57	46	1.8	7 Sept
Oct 7	24	76	33	92	38	100	20	68	High	85	59	107	4.2	11 Oct
Nov 6	24	76	33	91	37	99	20	68	High	86	63	142	5.6	12 Nov
Dec 5	24	75	32	90	38	101	19	67	High	88	68	203	8.0	16 Dec

Based on readings for 11 years at 3°08′ S, 60°01′ W, altitude 44 m/144 ft

SENA MADUREIRA

AMAZON BASIN

Sunshine	Temperatures								Discomfort from heat and humidity	Precipitation and humidity				Wet days
	Average daily				Highest recorded		Lowest recorded			Relative humidity 5:30 19:30		Average monthly precipitation		
	minimum		maximum											
average hours per day	°C	°F	°C	°F	°C	°F	°C	°F		%		mm	in	more than 0.25 mm/0.01 in
Jan	21	69	33	92	37	99	16	61	Extreme	98	98	285	11.2	18 Jan
Feb	21	69	33	92	37	99	15	59	Extreme	98	98	287	11.3	16 Feb
March	21	69	33	91	37	99	16	60	Extreme	98	98	259	10.2	17 March
April	20	68	33	91	37	99	14	57	Extreme	98	99	239	9.4	15 April
May	19	67	32	90	37	98	12	54	Extreme	98	99	104	4.1	8 May
June	18	65	33	90	37	98	7	45	Extreme	98	98	56	2.2	7 June
July	17	63	33	91	37	99	8	47	Extreme	97	98	28	1.1	5 July
Aug	18	65	34	93	37	99	5	41	Dangerous	97	99	38	1.5	5 Aug
Sept	20	68	34	93	37	99	8	46	Dangerous	98	98	102	4.0	8 Sept
Oct	21	69	34	93	37	99	14	57	Dangerous	98	98	178	7.0	11 Oct
Nov	21	69	34	93	38	100	14	57	Dangerous	98	98	191	7.5	12 Nov
Dec	21	70	34	93	37	99	17	63	Dangerous	98	98	297	11.7	16 Dec

Based on readings for 12 years at 9°04′ S, 68°39′ W, altitude 135 m/443 ft

THE BRAZILIAN PLATEAU

Including (with towns and cities in parentheses):
BRASILIA (Brasília), GOIAS (Goiás), MATO GROSSO,
MATO GROSSO DO SUL (Paraná) and MINAS GERAIS
(Belo Horizonte); all but the coast of: BAHIA, CEARA
(Iguatú), PARAIBA, PERNAMBUCO, PIAUI and SAO
PAULO (São Paulo); inland parts of ALGOAS,
ESPIRITO SANTO, and RIO GRANDE DO NORTE; and
southern MARANHAO.

This region is as large and extensive as the Amazon
basin but, lying farther south and being at a
moderate altitude, it has a very different climate.
There is a much more distinct wet and dry season,
and both the daily and annual temperature ranges are
quite marked.

With the exception of the northeast of this region,
in the valley of the river São Francisco and the
province of Ceará, annual rainfall is about 1,250–
1,500 mm/50–60 in. There is a very distinct wet
season at the time of high sun, with almost all the
rain falling between October and April. The
remaining months are almost dry.

The dry region in the northeast not only has a much
lower average rainfall, with many places receiving less
than 750 mm/30 in, but the rainfall is most irregular

from year to year. This district suffers many
prolonged droughts, which cause great distress and
damage to both agriculture and cattle rearing.

Average conditions in this dry region are represented
by the table for **Iguatú** (below).

The table for **Goiás** (overleaf) is representative of
conditions in the area of the new capital of the
country, Brasília, which has not been established
long enough for reliable weather statistics to be
collected.

The table for Goiás and that for **Paraná** (overleaf)
both show conditions over the wetter parts of this
region. There is not a great variation in average
monthly temperatures around the year but during
the drier months of low sun the daily range of
temperature is greater because the nights are
generally clear and the days sunnier. These months
are the most comfortable because midday humidity is
lower. The wet season has more cloud, higher
humidity, and higher night temperatures.

Average daily sunshine hours in this region range
from five to six during the wetter months to as much
as nine to ten during the dry season. Frost is virtually
unknown except in some valleys in the extreme south
or on the higher parts near the east coast.

IGUATU

BRAZILIAN PLATEAU

	Sunshine	Temperatures								Discomfort from heat and humidity	Precipitation and humidity				Wet days
	average hours per day	Average daily				Highest recorded		Lowest recorded			Relative humidity 7:30 14:30		Average monthly precipitation		more than 0.25 mm/0.01 in	
		minimum		maximum												
		°C	°F	°C	°F	°C	°F	°C	°F		%		mm	in		
Jan		23	74	34	94	38	101	17	63	High	83	44	89	3.5	7	Jan
Feb		23	73	33	91	39	102	17	63	High	89	52	173	6.8	12	Feb
March		23	73	32	90	37	99	17	63	High	93	60	185	7.3	13	March
April		23	73	31	88	37	99	17	63	High	93	62	160	6.3	13	April
May		22	71	31	88	36	97	15	59	High	91	61	61	2.4	7	May
June		21	70	32	89	35	95	10	50	High	87	59	36	1.4	3	June
July		21	69	32	90	36	96	9	49	Medium	81	44	5	0.2	2	July
Aug		21	69	34	93	37	99	11	51	High	77	35	3	0.1	0	Aug
Sept		22	72	35	95	38	101	16	61	High	78	32	18	0.7	2	Sept
Oct		23	73	36	96	38	101	15	59	High	75	31	18	0.7	2	Oct
Nov		23	74	36	96	38	101	16	61	High	77	36	10	0.4	1	Nov
Dec		23	74	36	96	38	101	16	61	High	82	38	33	1.3	3	Dec

Based on readings for 12 years at 6°24′ S, 39°35′ W, altitude 209 m/685 ft

GOIAS

BRAZILIAN PLATEAU

Sunshine	Temperatures								Discomfort from heat and humidity	Precipitation and humidity				Wet days
	Average daily				Highest recorded		Lowest recorded			Relative humidity 6:30 13:30		Average monthly precipitation		
	minimum		maximum											
average hours per day	°C	°F	°C	°F	°C	°F	°C	°F		%		mm	in	more than 0.25 mm/0.01 in
Jan	17	63	30	86	37	99	13	55	High	88	73	317	12.5	16	Jan
Feb	17	63	32	89	38	100	13	55	High	87	69	251	9.9	14	Feb
March	17	63	32	89	37	98	13	56	High	85	65	259	10.2	15	March
April	17	63	33	91	37	99	13	55	High	82	60	117	4.6	7	April
May	16	60	33	91	36	96	11	52	High	77	51	10	0.4	1	May
June	13	55	32	90	35	95	6	43	High	74	50	8	0.3	0	June
July	13	56	32	89	36	96	5	41	High	67	48	0	0.0	0	July
Aug	15	59	34	93	38	101	9	49	High	64	40	8	0.3	1	Aug
Sept	18	64	34	94	40	104	12	53	High	66	42	58	2.3	4	Sept
Oct	17	63	34	94	40	104	10	50	High	77	51	135	5.3	8	Oct
Nov	17	63	32	90	39	102	12	54	High	86	65	239	9.4	13	Nov
Dec	17	62	31	87	38	101	11	52	High	90	73	241	9.5	13	Dec

Based on readings for 8 years at 15°58′ S, 50°04′ W, altitude 520 m/1706 ft

PARANA

BRAZILIAN PLATEAU

Sunshine	Temperatures								Discomfort from heat and humidity	Precipitation and humidity				Wet days
	Average daily				Highest recorded		Lowest recorded			Relative humidity 7:00 14:00		Average monthly precipitation		
	minimum		maximum											
average hours per day	°C	°F	°C	°F	°C	°F	°C	°F		%		mm	in	more than 0.25 mm/0.01 in
Jan	14	58	32	90	38	101	9	49	High	93	69	287	11.3	14	Jan
Feb	15	59	32	89	36	97	9	49	High	94	69	236	9.3	13	Feb
March	15	59	32	89	37	98	9	49	High	94	69	239	9.4	13	March
April	14	58	32	90	37	99	9	49	High	93	64	102	4.0	7	April
May	12	54	33	91	37	98	6	43	High	92	58	13	0.5	1	May
June	9	49	33	91	36	97	5	41	High	89	50	0	0	0	June
July	9	48	33	91	36	97	3	37	High	89	51	3	0.1	0	July
Aug	10	50	34	93	38	100	3	37	High	81	48	5	0.2	1	Aug
Sept	13	55	35	95	41	105	6	42	High	87	51	28	1.1	3	Sept
Oct	14	58	34	94	40	104	7	45	High	88	53	127	5.0	8	Oct
Nov	14	58	33	91	38	100	10	50	Extreme	93	67	231	9.1	13	Nov
Dec	14	58	32	90	39	103	10	50	High	93	66	310	12.2	15	Dec

Based on readings for 19 years at 12°26′ S, 48°06′ W, altitude 260 m/853 ft

RECIFE											EASTERN TROPICAL BRAZIL	
Sunshine	Temperatures						Discomfort from heat and humidity	Precipitation and humidity				Wet days
	Average daily				Highest recorded	Lowest recorded		Relative humidity 7:30 14:30		Average monthly precipitation		
	minimum		maximum									
average hours per day	°C	°F	°C	°F	°C	°F	°C	°F		%	mm	in	more than 0.25 mm/0.01 in
Jan 7	25	77	30	86	34	94	22	71	High	77	69	53	2.1	10 Jan
Feb 7	25	77	30	86	34	93	21	69	High	81	70	84	3.3	12 Feb
March 8	24	76	30	86	34	94	21	69	High	81	71	160	6.3	14 March
April 8	24	75	29	85	34	93	21	69	High	83	73	221	8.7	17 April
May 7	23	74	28	83	32	90	21	69	Medium	84	74	267	10.5	21 May
June 5	23	73	28	82	32	89	19	66	Medium	84	75	277	10.9	21 June
July 6	22	71	27	80	31	87	18	64	Medium	83	75	254	10.0	22 July
Aug 7	22	71	27	81	31	88	18	64	Medium	82	73	152	6.0	19 Aug
Sept 7	23	73	28	82	32	90	19	66	Medium	78	70	64	2.5	11 Sept
Oct 9	24	75	29	84	33	91	20	68	Medium	75	67	25	1.0	8 Oct
Nov 9	24	76	29	85	33	91	21	69	Medium	74	68	25	1.0	7 Nov
Dec 8	25	77	29	85	33	92	21	70	Medium	76	67	28	1.1	6 Dec

Based on readings for 26 years at 8°04' S, 34°53' W, altitude 30 m/97 ft

THE TROPICAL EAST COAST

Including (with towns and cities in parentheses): the southern coast of PARA; the coasts of: ALGOAS (Maceió), BAHIA (Salvador), CEARA (Fortaleza), ESPIRITO SANTO (Rio de Janeiro), MARANHAO, PARAIBA, PERNAMBUCO (Recife), PIAUI, RIO GRANDE DO NORTE (Natal), and SAO PAULO.

This long, narrow region extends from south of the mouth of the Amazon to Santos, and has a typically hot, tropical climate. There are, however, some important differences in the season of greatest rainfall from north to south.

Near the mouth of the Amazon all months are wet but rainfall is greater in the months December to May, as shown by the table for **Belém** (p. 69). From about 3° S to Bahía at 14° S the wettest months are from May to August and the rest of the year is comparatively dry (see the table for **Recife** above). This unusual regime of rainfall only applies to the coastal lowlands; inland on the plateau the rainfall is less and the wet season is the period of high sun.

South of Bahía the distribution of rainfall changes and the table for **Rio de Janeiro** (overleaf) shows that the wettest period is from November to April. Here some appreciable rainfall occurs in all months.

Nowhere on this coast do maximum temperatures rise so high as to be uncomfortable, though the combination of warmth and humidity can be uncomfortable at night.

Daytime heat is often tempered by the sea breeze. Along this coast, from Recife southwards, cloudy and cool weather with some rain or drizzle may last for a few days at the period of low sun. As the tables show, temperatures never drop very low and frost is unknown on the coast but in the hills, behind Santos, occasional frosts may damage the valuable coffee crop. Hours of sunshine on the coast are less round the year than at similar latitudes inland on the plateau. They average from five to six hours in the wetter season to six to seven in the drier months.

THE SOUTHERN STATES OF BRAZIL

Including (with towns and cities in parentheses): PARANA (Curitiba), SANTA CATARINA, and RIO GRANDE DO SUL (Pôrto Alegre).

This region comprises Brazil south of the tropics. Both along the coast and in the plateau districts inland the climate is warm-temperate, and is similar to that found in Uruguay and northern Argentina. As

RIO DE JANEIRO

EASTERN TROPICAL BRAZIL

	Sunshine	Temperatures								Discomfort from heat and humidity	Precipitation and humidity				Wet days	
		Average daily				Highest recorded		Lowest recorded			Relative humidity		Average monthly precipitation			
		minimum		maximum							7:00	14:00				
average hours per day		°C	°F	°C	°F	°C	°F	°C	°F		%		mm	in	more than 0.25 mm/0.01 in	
Jan	7	23	73	29	84	39	102	16	60	High	82	70	125	4.9	13	Jan
Feb	7	23	73	29	85	37	98	17	63	High	84	71	122	4.8	11	Feb
March	7	22	72	28	83	36	97	18	64	Medium	87	74	130	5.1	12	March
April	6	21	69	27	80	34	94	16	60	Medium	87	73	107	4.2	10	April
May	6	19	66	25	77	35	95	13	56	Medium	87	70	79	3.1	10	May
June	6	18	64	24	76	32	90	11	52	Moderate	87	69	53	2.1	7	June
July	6	17	63	24	75	33	91	11	52	Moderate	86	68	41	1.6	7	July
Aug	7	18	64	24	76	34	93	12	53	Moderate	84	66	43	1.7	7	Aug
Sept	5	18	65	24	75	38	100	10	50	Moderate	84	72	66	2.6	11	Sept
Oct	5	19	66	25	77	39	102	14	57	Medium	83	72	79	3.1	13	Oct
Nov	6	20	68	26	79	38	100	15	59	Medium	82	72	104	4.1	13	Nov
Dec	6	22	71	28	82	39	102	13	56	Medium	82	72	137	5.4	14	Dec

Based on readings for 38 years at 22°55′ S, 43°12′ W, altitude 61 m/201 ft

PORTO ALEGRE

SOUTHERN BRAZIL

	Sunshine	Temperatures								Discomfort from heat and humidity	Precipitation and humidity				Wet days	
		Average daily				Highest recorded		Lowest recorded			Relative humidity		Average monthly precipitation			
		minimum		maximum							6:30	13:30				
average hours per day		°C	°F	°C	°F	°C	°F	°C	°F		%		mm	in	more than 0.25 mm/0.01 in	
Jan	8	19	67	31	87	39	103	11	51	High	79	55	89	3.5	8	Jan
Feb	8	20	68	31	87	41	105	11	52	High	84	56	81	3.2	9	Feb
March	7	18	65	28	83	39	102	9	48	Medium	87	57	99	3.9	8	March
April	6	16	60	26	78	36	97	5	41	Medium	91	61	104	4.1	9	April
May	6	12	54	22	71	33	91	−1	30		92	64	114	4.5	9	May
June	5	9	49	19	66	32	89	−2	28		92	66	130	5.1	10	June
July	5	9	49	19	66	32	89	−4	25		92	66	114	4.5	9	July
Aug	6	10	50	20	68	33	92	−1	30		92	65	127	5.0	11	Aug
Sept	5	12	54	21	70	36	97	0	32		89	63	132	5.2	10	Sept
Oct	7	14	57	23	74	38	100	4	39	Moderate	84	60	86	3.4	10	Oct
Nov	8	16	60	27	80	38	100	6	43	Medium	79	55	79	3.1	8	Nov
Dec	9	18	64	29	85	39	103	8	46	Medium	77	54	89	3.5	7	Dec

Based on readings for 22 years at 30°02′ S, 51°13′ W, altitude 10 m/33 ft

the table for **Pôrto Alegre** (opposite and below) shows, even on the coast there is a distinct cooler season when frost can be expected in the winter months. Here winter has a real significance and the difference between the seasons is determined by temperature rather than rainfall. On the coast rainfall is well distributed throughout the year but the cooler months are also slightly wetter. This area is affected by travelling depressions that form in the disturbed region of the westerlies farther south, and by more frequent invasions of cold air from the Antarctic.

During the warmer summer months temperatures reach similar levels to those found farther north in the tropical regions of Brazil. This region has a generally healthy and pleasant climate with an average of eight to nine hours of sunshine a day in the summer months.

Inland where the land is higher, frosts are quite common in winter but snow is very rare. Inland the wettest months are during the summer, in contrast to the coastal district.

Brunei

See map page 23

Brunei is a small independent country, a little smaller than the county of Devon in England. It is situated on the north coast of Borneo between the Malaysia territories of Sabah and Sarawak. Its weather and climate are well represented by the table for **Labuan** in Sabah (p. 226).

Bulgaria

See map page 19

Bulgaria is in southeast Europe, where the climate is transitional between that of the Mediterranean and that of the plains of southern Russia. It has a coastline on the Black Sea and in the north the Danube forms the boundary with Romania. The western and southern borders with Yugoslavia and

PLOVDIV																	LOWLAND BULGARIA
Sunshine		Temperatures									Discomfort from heat and humidity	Precipitation and humidity					Wet days
		Average daily				Highest recorded		Lowest recorded				Relative humidity		Average monthly precipitation			
		minimum		maximum								6:30	13:30				
average hours per day		°C	°F	°C	°F	°C	°F	°C	°F			%		mm	in		more than 0.2 mm/0.008 in
Jan	3	–3	26	5	40	16	60	–23	–9			91	76	39	1.5		8	Jan
Feb	4	–2	28	7	45	23	73	–25	–13			88	67	33	1.3		8	Feb
March	5	1	34	12	54	25	77	–18	1			88	60	37	1.5		8	March
April	7	5	43	18	65	31	87	–4	25			83	53	36	1.4		9	April
May	8	10	50	23	74	32	89	0	32			81	53	51	2.0		11	May
June	9	14	57	28	82	36	97	6	43	Medium		76	50	65	2.6		9	June
July	11	16	61	31	87	40	104	8	47	Medium		73	45	37	1.5		8	July
Aug	10	15	59	30	86	38	101	8	47	Medium		76	46	28	1.1		6	Aug
Sept	8	11	52	26	78	35	94	0	32	Moderate		85	48	32	1.3		5	Sept
Oct	5	8	46	21	69	33	91	–3	28			91	59	41	1.6		9	Oct
Nov	3	3	37	12	54	23	74	–8	18			92	69	49	1.9		8	Nov
Dec	2	–2	29	6	43	19	66	–17	1			90	76	44	1.7		10	Dec

Based on readings for 9 years at 42°29′ N, 24°45′ E, altitude 160 m/525 ft

VARNA

LOWLAND BULGARIA

Sunshine	Temperatures								Discomfort from heat and humidity	Precipitation and humidity				Wet days	
	Average daily				Highest recorded		Lowest recorded			Relative humidity		Average monthly precipitation			
	minimum		maximum							7:00	14:00				
average hours per day	°C	°F	°C	°F	°C	°F	°C	°F		%		mm	in	more than 0.2 mm/0.008 in	
Jan	2	−1	30	6	42	20	69	−16	4		89	80	28	1.1	8	Jan
Feb	3	−1	30	6	43	21	71	−13	9		86	75	30	1.2	9	Feb
March	4	2	36	11	51	24	75	−8	17		86	70	26	1.0	7	March
April	6	7	44	16	60	30	85	−2	28		83	68	37	1.5	8	April
May	8	12	53	22	71	34	93	2	36		83	69	26	1.0	8	May
June	9	16	61	26	79	35	96	9	48	Medium	78	67	64	2.5	9	June
July	11	19	65	30	86	39	102	10	50	High	75	61	45	1.8	6	July
Aug	10	18	64	29	85	36	98	11	52	Medium	79	60	37	1.5	6	Aug
Sept	8	14	58	26	78	34	93	3	37	Medium	83	62	27	1.1	5	Sept
Oct	6	11	52	21	69	32	90	1	34		88	68	58	2.3	8	Oct
Nov	3	6	43	13	55	24	76	−6	22		87	72	35	1.4	9	Nov
Dec	2	1	34	7	45	21	70	−14	8		88	79	63	2.5	11	Dec

Based on readings for 9 years at 43°12′ N, 27°55′ E, altitude 35 m/115 ft

SOFIA

HIGHLAND BULGARIA

Sunshine	Temperatures								Discomfort from heat and humidity	Precipitation and humidity				Wet days	
	Average daily				Highest recorded		Lowest recorded			Relative humidity		Average monthly precipitation			
	minimum		maximum							6:30	13:30				
average hours per day	°C	°F	°C	°F	°C	°F	°C	°F		%		mm	in	more than 0.2 mm/0.008 in	
Jan	2	−4	25	2	35	16	61	−21	−6		88	78	36	1.4	9	Jan
Feb	3	−3	27	4	39	17	63	−19	−2		85	69	28	1.1	10	Feb
March	4	1	33	10	50	24	75	−15	5		82	56	41	1.6	10	March
April	6	5	42	16	60	28	83	−5	23		77	50	61	2.4	12	April
May	7	10	50	21	69	29	85	0	32		75	52	87	3.4	13	May
June	9	14	56	24	76	32	90	4	40	Moderate	72	51	73	2.9	12	June
July	10	16	60	27	81	37	98	7	44	Moderate	71	46	68	2.7	10	July
Aug	10	15	59	26	79	34	93	8	46	Moderate	75	46	64	2.5	9	Aug
Sept	7	11	52	22	70	34	93	−2	29		82	51	41	1.6	7	Sept
Oct	5	8	46	17	63	30	86	−2	28		86	59	65	2.6	11	Oct
Nov	3	3	37	9	48	24	76	−7	20		90	72	48	1.9	10	Nov
Dec	1	−2	28	4	38	17	62	−16	3		87	77	49	1.9	12	Dec

Based on readings for 9 years at 42°42′ N, 23°20′ E, altitude 550 m/1805 ft

Greece respectively pass through mountainous country rising to 1,800–2,750 m/6,000–9,000 ft. The largest areas of lowland are along the coast and in the valley of the river Maritsa in the centre of the country. Here the summers are warm and occasionally rather hot, while winters are fairly cold – see the tables for **Plovdiv** (p. 75) and **Varna** (opposite). Rainfall is moderate and well distributed throughout the year with a slight summer maximum.

On the coast (Varna) the winters are slightly warmer, but even here spells of bitterly cold weather can occur when winds blow from the northeast carrying cold air from Russia. During such cold spells the Danube and other rivers may freeze over. Hot spells in summer are associated with winds from both the northeast and the southeast. During settled spells of weather in summer, conditions on the Black Sea coast may resemble those around the Mediterranean, and this area has developed some summer tourist

resorts. Such fine, hot spells, however, may be interrupted by thunderstorms with hail and heavy rain. The total number of wet days is not large throughout the whole country but snow is frequent in winter and even occasionally in spring.

In the higher parts of the country (see the table for **Sofia**, opposite and below) winters are colder and the summers pleasant and fresh. Snow may lie until June on the highest mountains. There are opportunities for winter sports in such mountains.

Although the climate is generally temperate and pleasant, its variability throughout the year means that it may at times be uncomfortably cold in winter and rather warm and sultry in summer. Spring can be a very changeable season with rapid alternations between warm and cold days. Daily hours of sunshine range from about two in January to as much as ten in midsummer.

Burkina Faso

See map page 20

This is a small landlocked country about the size of the United Kingdom. Situated in the interior of

West Africa it is bordered by Mali and Niger on the north and by the Côte d'Ivoire and Ghana on the south. It has a typical tropical climate, similar to that of southern Mali, with a single rainy season and a

OUAGADOUGOU

BURKINA FASO

Sunshine		Temperatures								Discomfort from heat and humidity	Precipitation and humidity				Wet days
		Average daily				Highest recorded		Lowest recorded				Relative humidity 7:00 14:00		Average monthly precipitation		
		minimum		maximum												
average hours per day		°C	°F	°C	°F	°C	°F	°C	°F		%			mm	in	more than 1 mm/0.04 in
Jan	9	16	60	33	92	45	113	9	40	Medium	42	19		0	0.0	0.1	Jan
Feb	9	20	68	37	98	45	113	12	54	Medium	38	19		3	0.1	0.3	Feb
March	9	23	73	40	104	45	113	15	60	High	39	20		13	0.5	0.7	March
April	8	26	79	39	103	47	116	15	60	High	51	28		15	0.6	2.0	April
May	9	26	78	38	101	48	118	19	68	Extreme	65	40		84	3.3	6.0	May
June	8	24	76	36	96	44	111	17	64	High	73	49		122	4.8	9.0	June
July	7	23	74	33	91	41	106	18	66	High	78	62		203	8.0	12.0	July
Aug	6	22	72	31	87	38	101	14	58	High	81	67		277	10.9	14.0	Aug
Sept	7	23	73	32	89	39	102	19	68	High	79	60		145	5.7	11.0	Sept
Oct	9	23	74	35	95	41	106	18	66	High	72	44		33	1.3	3.0	Oct
Nov	9	22	71	36	96	42	107	16	62	High	58	30		0	0.0	0.2	Nov
Dec	8	17	62	35	95	45	113	11	52	Medium	46	23		0	0.0	0.0	Dec

Based on readings for 10 years at 12°22′ N, 1°31′ W, altitude 302 m/991 ft

long dry season. The general features of the weather and climate of this part of Africa are described for Mali on pp. 230–1. The table for **Ouagadougou** (p. 77) is representative of the whole country and a brief comparison between this and the climatic table for **Bamako** in Mali on p. 231 will show that on the whole there is little difference between these two West African localities.

The climate is hot around the year, and the heat is most uncomfortable during the period May to October, when humidity and cloud are greatest. During the low sun period from November to March, drier air is brought by the northeasterly harmattan, although on occasions this also brings unpleasant conditions with dust-laden air.

Hours of sunshine are greatest during the dry season, when they average eight to nine hours a day as compared with six to seven hours a day during the rainy season.

Burundi

See map page 21.

This small country in central Africa is about the size of Wales or Israel and is densely populated. It lies between 2° and 4° S and is bordered by Rwanda to the north, Tanzania to the east, and the Congo Democratic Republic to the west.

It is a hilly and mountainous country, with its highest point rising to over 4,600 m/15,000 ft. Climate and weather are similar to that found in the eastern Congo and southwestern Uganda. Rainfall is equatorial but temperatures are much reduced because of the altitude. The months June to September are predominantly dry but the rest of the year is moderately wet. By equatorial standards the climate is quite healthy and not unpleasant.

The climatic table for **Bujumbura** (below) on the northern shores of Lake Tanganyika is representative of the lower regions of the country.

The climatic table for **Rubona** in Rwanda (p. 307) illustrates conditions in some of the higher areas. The mountains are much wetter with more cloud.

BUJUMBURA										LOWER REGIONS OF BURUNDI		
Sunshine		Temperatures							Discomfort from heat and humidity	Precipitation and humidity		Wet days
		Average daily				Highest recorded		Lowest recorded		Relative humidity	Average monthly precipitation	
		minimum		maximum						all hours		
average hours per day		°C	°F	°C	°F	°C	°F	°C	°F	%	mm in	more than 0.1 mm/0.004 in
Jan	5	19	66	28	82	34	93	14	58	Medium	79	94 3.7	15	Jan
Feb	5	19	66	28	82	32	90	15	59	Medium	79	109 4.3	14	Feb
March	6	19	66	28	82	32	90	14	58	High	81	121 4.8	17	March
April	5	19	66	28	82	31	87	15	59	High	82	125 4.9	18	April
May	7	19	66	28	82	31	87	16	60	Medium	78	57 2.2	10	May
June	8	18	64	29	84	31	87	13	55	Medium	67	11 0.4	3	June
July	9	17	63	29	84	31	87	11	52	Medium	62	5 0.2	1	July
Aug	8	18	64	30	86	33	91	13	55	Medium	55	11 0.4	2	Aug
Sept	7	19	66	31	88	33	91	14	58	High	59	37 1.5	8	Sept
Oct	6	20	68	30	86	33	91	14	58	High	65	64 2.5	12	Oct
Nov	5	19	66	28	82	33	91	15	59	Medium	75	100 3.9	19	Nov
Dec	5	19	66	28	82	34	93	16	60	Medium	78	114 4.5	19	Dec

Based on readings for 10 years at 3°23′ S, 29°21′ E, altitude 805 m/2640 ft

PHNOM PENH												CAMBODIA
Sunshine	Temperatures						Discomfort from heat and humidity	Precipitation and humidity				Wet days
	Average daily				Highest recorded	Lowest recorded		Relative humidity	Average monthly precipitation			
	minimum		maximum					all hours				
average hours per day	°C	°F	°C	°F	°C	°F	°C	°F		%	mm	in	more than 2.5 mm/0.1 in

		°C	°F	°C	°F	°C	°F	°C	°F		%	mm	in		
Jan	9	21	70	31	87	35	96	14	57	High	71	7	0.3	1	Jan
Feb	9	22	72	32	90	37	98	15	59	High	71	10	0.4	1	Feb
March	9	23	74	34	92	39	102	19	66	Extreme	70	40	1.6	3	March
April	8	24	76	35	94	41	105	20	68	Extreme	73	77	3.0	6	April
May	7	24	76	34	92	38	100	21	69	Extreme	81	134	5.3	14	May
June	6	24	76	33	91	38	101	21	70	Extreme	81	155	6.0	15	June
July	6	24	75	32	89	37	98	20	68	Extreme	83	171	6.7	16	July
Aug	6	26	76	32	89	36	97	22	72	Extreme	83	160	6.3	16	Aug
Sept	5	25	76	31	88	36	96	22	72	Extreme	85	224	8.8	19	Sept
Oct	7	24	76	30	87	34	93	21	70	High	83	257	10.1	17	Oct
Nov	8	23	74	30	86	34	93	18	64	High	79	127	5.0	9	Nov
Dec	9	22	71	30	86	35	96	14	58	High	74	45	1.8	4	Dec

Based on readings for x years at 10°33′ N, 104°55′ E, altitude 12 m/39 ft

Cambodia

See map page 23

Cambodia is a small country in Indo-China, about the same size as England. It has a short southwest coastline on the Gulf of Siam. It has land borders with Thailand, Laos, and Vietnam on the west, north, and east respectively. The general features of the climate of the country are similar to those described for Vietnam on p. 419.

There is a small, hilly region in the southwest and the slopes facing the Gulf of Siam have a heavy rainfall.

Elsewhere the country is low-lying and rainfall is lower than in much of Vietnam.

The dry season from December to April is hot and sunshine averages about eight hours a day. The main rainy season is much more cloudy; humidity is higher; and the weather is then sultry and oppressive. Temperatures remain quite high in the lowlands throughout the year. There may be frequent heat stress as a result of the high temperatures and humidity during the rainy season, but this is not usually severe.

Cameroon

See map page 20

Cameroon is a central African country about the size of France, situated between 2° and 12° N. It has a short coastline on the Gulf of Guinea but has land borders with Nigeria on the west, with Chad on the north, with the Central African Republic on the east, and with Congo and Gabon on the south. The

climate and weather of the northern part of the country are similar to those described for northern Nigeria on p. 266 and for Chad on p. 94.

There is a single wet season between April and September at the time of high sun and a pronounced dry season during the rest of the year. Rainfall is between 1,000 mm/40 in and 1,750 mm/70 in

YAOUNDE

SOUTHERN CAMEROON

Sunshine	Temperatures								Discomfort from heat and humidity	Precipitation and humidity				Wet days	
	Average daily				Highest recorded		Lowest recorded			Relative humidity 7:00 13:00		Average monthly precipitation			
	minimum		maximum												
average hours per day	°C	°F	°C	°F	°C	°F	°C	°F		%		mm	in	more than 0.1 mm/0.004 in	
Jan 6	19	67	29	85	33	91	14	57	Medium	97	62	23	0.9	3	Jan
Feb 6	19	67	29	85	33	92	15	59	Medium	97	62	66	2.6	5	Feb
March 5	19	67	29	85	33	91	16	60	Medium	97	65	147	5.8	13	March
April 5	19	66	29	85	36	96	15	59	Medium	97	67	170	6.7	15	April
May 5	19	67	28	83	34	94	16	60	Medium	98	70	196	7.7	18	May
June 4	19	66	27	81	32	90	15	59	Medium	97	73	152	6.0	17	June
July 3	19	66	27	80	31	87	16	60	Medium	97	74	74	2.9	11	July
Aug 3	18	65	27	80	34	93	16	60	Medium	97	75	79	3.1	10	Aug
Sept 3	19	66	27	81	31	88	15	59	Medium	98	73	213	8.4	20	Sept
Oct 4	18	65	27	81	33	91	15	59	Medium	98	72	295	11.6	24	Oct
Nov 5	19	66	28	83	32	89	17	62	Medium	98	66	117	4.6	14	Nov
Dec 6	19	66	28	83	32	90	16	60	Medium	98	60	23	0.9	4	Dec

Based on readings for 7 years at 3°53′ N, 11°32′ E, altitude 770 m/2526 ft

DOUALA

COASTAL CAMEROON

Sunshine	Temperatures								Discomfort from heat and humidity	Precipitation and humidity				Wet days	
	Average daily				Highest recorded		Lowest recorded			Relative humidity 7:00 14:00		Average monthly precipitation			
	minimum		maximum												
average hours per day	°C	°F	°C	°F	°C	°F	°C	°F		%		mm	in	more than 1 mm/0.04 in	
Jan 5	23	73	30	86	34	93	20	68	High	95	74	46	1.8	4	Jan
Feb 6	23	74	30	86	33	91	20	68	High	96	75	94	3.7	6	Feb
March 5	23	73	30	86	33	91	19	66	High	95	76	203	8.0	12	March
April 5	23	73	30	86	33	92	19	66	High	94	76	231	9.1	12	April
May 5	23	73	30	86	35	95	19	66	High	95	79	300	11.8	16	May
June 3	22	72	28	83	32	90	19	66	High	95	82	539	21.2	19	June
July 2	22	71	27	80	32	89	19	66	Medium	96	86	742	29.2	24	July
Aug 1	22	71	27	80	30	86	19	67	Medium	96	84	693	27.3	24	Aug
Sept 2	22	72	27	81	31	87	19	67	Medium	95	84	531	20.9	21	Sept
Oct 4	22	71	27	81	31	88	18	65	Medium	95	83	429	16.9	20	Oct
Nov 5	23	73	29	84	33	91	19	66	High	95	80	155	6.1	10	Nov
Dec 5	23	73	29	85	32	90	19	67	High	95	78	64	2.5	6	Dec

Based on readings for 17 years at 4°03′ N, 9°41′ E, altitude 8 m/26 ft

annually. In the south of the country rainfall occurs in all months with an equatorial pattern of distribution: two wet seasons and two dry seasons, similar to that described in the more detailed account of this region for the Congo Democratic Republic.

The table for **Yaoundé** (opposite) is typical of the southern part of the country. That for **Douala** (opposite and below), situated on the coast, shows the much heavier annual rainfall here and the particularly wet period between June and September. This is a consequence of the exposure to the moist southwesterly winds of the Guinea monsoon which are uplifted as they strike the high mountain, the Cameroon Peak. A small area of the Peak is one of the three places in the world experiencing an average annual rainfall in excess of 10,000 mm/400 in! The other places are in the Hawaiian Islands and Assam in India.

Canada

Canada is a vast country, about as large as China, situated between 42° and 83° N. A large part of Canada lies within the Arctic Circle, and only a narrow strip close to the southern border with the United States has a temperate climate.

Much of this more favoured area has a severe winter with prolonged frost and snow. With the exception of Hudson Bay, which is frozen over for about nine months of the year, the northern coast of Canada on the Arctic Ocean is permanently ice-bound or severely obstructed for most of the year by ice floes. Only the Pacific coast of British Columbia and the Atlantic coasts of Newfoundland and the maritime provinces south of the Gulf of St Lawrence have harbours that do not regularly freeze in winter.

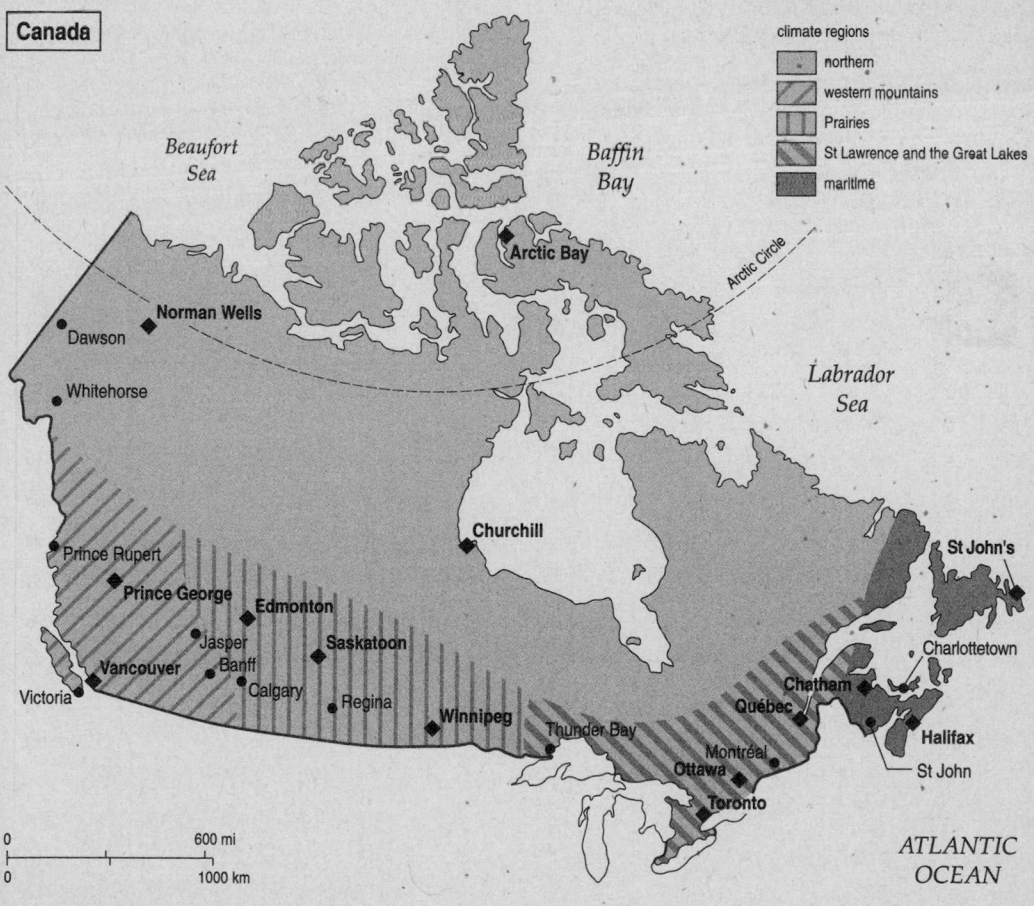

Canada

climate regions
- northern
- western mountains
- Prairies
- St Lawrence and the Great Lakes
- maritime

Beaufort Sea

Baffin Bay

Arctic Bay

Arctic Circle

Labrador Sea

Dawson
Norman Wells
Whitehorse

Churchill

St John's

Prince Rupert
Prince George
Edmonton
Jasper
Banff
Vancouver
Calgary
Victoria
Saskatoon
Regina
Winnipeg
Thunder Bay
Charlottetown
Chatham
Québec
Montréal
Ottawa
Toronto
Halifax
St John

0   600 mi
0   1000 km

ATLANTIC OCEAN

The reasons for the very cold winters over most of Canada are the high latitude of much of the country and the generally flat and low-lying land east of the Rocky Mountains. Cold air from the Canadian Arctic has virtually no obstruction as it sweeps south and east in winter and spring, thus importing very cold conditions to most of the country.

Southern Canada also lies in one of the most frequented tracts of cyclonic depressions in North America; many of these cross the region of the Great Lakes and the St Lawrence valley before moving out into the Atlantic. The cold air involved in the circulation of these depressions frequently has its origin far to the north.

The influence of the warmer maritime air of Pacific Ocean origin is mainly confined to the small area of Canada west of the Rockies in British Columbia. The coast and some inland valleys in this province have a very different climate to the rest of the country, resembling that of the British Isles and other parts of northwest Europe. Here winters are mild and summers warm with rain falling all through the year but with a maximum fall in winter.

Winter temperatures on the Atlantic shores are warmer than those in the interior of the continent, particularly where the sea does not freeze, but the summer temperatures are kept lower than in the interior because of the cold Labrador current, which flows southwards close to the coast.

Much of the interior of Canada has a very continental climate with surprisingly high summer temperatures, in spite of the shortness of the summer, and a long, very cold winter. Even the barren northlands of Canada have quite warm summers and in this there is a close parallel with much of Siberia.

For a more detailed description of the weather and climate of Canada it is convenient to divide the country into the following climatic regions: eastern Canada, the St Lawrence and Great Lakes region, the Prairies, western Canada including the Rockies, and northern Canada.

MARITIME EASTERN CANADA

Including (with towns and cities in parentheses): NEWFOUNDLAND (St John's), NOVA SCOTIA (Halifax), NEW BRUNSWICK (Chatham, St John) and PRINCE EDWARD ISLAND (Charlottetown); and eastern LABRADOR and eastern parts of QUEBEC.

This region includes those areas where the influence of the Atlantic Ocean modifies the harshness of

ST JOHN'S, NEWFOUNDLAND												MARITIME EASTERN CANADA		
Sunshine		Temperatures								Discomfort from heat and humidity	Precipitation and humidity				Wet days
		Average daily				Highest recorded		Lowest recorded			Relative humidity		Average monthly precipitation		
		minimum		maximum							all hours				
average hours per day		°C	°F	°C	°F	°C	°F	°C	°F		%		mm	in	more than 0.25mm/0.0 in
Jan	2	−8	18	−2	29	15	59	−28	−19		76		135	5.3	15	Jan
Feb	3	−9	16	−2	28	13	56	−29	−21		77		125	4.9	15	Feb
March	3	−6	22	1	33	19	67	−26	−14		79		117	4.6	15	March
April	4	−1	30	5	41	22	72	−18	−1		81		107	4.2	15	April
May	5	2	35	10	50	27	81	−7	20		79		91	3.6	15	May
June	6	7	44	16	61	31	87	−3	27		77		89	3.5	13	June
July	7	11	51	20	68	32	90	1	33		79		89	3.5	13	July
Aug	6	12	53	21	69	34	93	0	32		80		94	3.7	13	Aug
Sept	5	8	47	17	62	29	84	−2	29		80		97	3.8	14	Sept
Oct	4	4	40	12	53	31	87	−6	22		78		135	5.3	16	Oct
Nov	2	0	32	6	42	20	68	−14	6		80		150	5.9	17	Nov
Dec	2	−4	24	1	34	16	60	−20	−4		79		140	5.5	17	Dec

Based on readings for 68 years at 47°34′ N, 52°42′ W, altitude 74 m/243 ft

winter to some extent and makes the summers more cool and changeable than farther inland. It has the most changeable weather around the year because of the large number of cyclonic depressions, which follow a track from the Great Lakes to Newfoundland. Frequent changes of weather from day to day are the rule in all months, and cloud and rain are well distributed around the year. Much of the winter precipitation is in the form of snow which, except on the coast, may lie for long periods.

The tables for **St John's** (opposite and below) and **Halifax** (below) show the influence of the open sea in keeping winter temperatures a little higher and summer temperatures slightly lower than at places farther inland. The table for **Chatham** (overleaf), which is only a little way inland from the Gulf of St Lawrence, shows how the annual range of temperature increases away from the sea.

This area is very liable to sea fog, and this can be persistent offshore during the summer months. The Grand Banks area south of Newfoundland and the Gulf of St Lawrence are among the foggiest sea areas in the world and lie across an important shipping route. Another navigational hazard in this sea area is the frequent occurrence of icebergs in summer, which drift south in the cold waters of the Labrador current. The temperature contrast between the warm waters of the Gulf Stream and the cold Labrador current is the principal cause of the fogs. This is one of the least sunny regions of Canada. Hours of sunshine a day range from two to three in winter to seven or eight in summer.

THE ST LAWRENCE AND GREAT LAKES REGION

Including (with towns and cities in parentheses): southern and central parts of QUEBEC (Québec, Montréal) and of ONTARIO (Ottawa, Toronto, Thunder Bay).

This area is bordered by the Great Lakes and the United States on the south and is the most southerly part of Canada. It is the most densely settled and developed region. The southerly latitude and the warmth of the waters of the lakes, which do not usually freeze over completely until December, help to make this one of the warmest parts of Canada.

As the tables for **Ottawa** (overleaf), **Québec** (p. 85), and **Toronto** (p. 85) show, however, winters here are severe. Toronto, on the shore of Lake Ontario, has appreciably higher winter temperatures than Ottawa and Québec. Summers are quite warm with considerable amounts of sunshine, averaging eight to

HALIFAX, NOVA SCOTIA														MARITIME EASTERN CANADA	
Sunshine	Temperatures								Discomfort from heat and humidity	Precipitation and humidity				Wet days	
	Average daily				Highest recorded		Lowest recorded			Relative humidity 8:30 14:30		Average monthly precipitation			
	minimum		maximum												
average hours per day	°C	°F	°C	°F	°C	°F	°C	°F		%		mm	in	more than 0.25 mm/0.01 in	
Jan	3	−9	15	0	13	14	58	−27	−17		82	69	137	5.4	17	Jan
Feb	4	−9	15	−1	31	11	52	−29	−21		81	63	109	4.3	14	Feb
March	5	−5	23	3	38	21	70	−23	−10		77	60	125	4.9	15	March
April	5	−1	31	8	47	28	83	−14	7		76	60	114	4.5	14	April
May	6	4	40	15	59	32	90	−4	24		76	62	104	4.1	14	May
June	7	9	48	20	68	34	94	0	32		77	63	102	4.0	14	June
July	8	13	55	23	74	37	99	4	39	Moderate	81	64	97	3.8	13	July
Aug	7	13	56	23	74	34	94	4	39	Moderate	82	65	112	4.4	12	Aug
Sept	6	10	50	19	67	34	94	−2	29		82	65	104	4.1	12	Sept
Oct	5	5	41	14	57	31	88	−6	21		82	63	137	5.4	13	Oct
Nov	3	0	32	8	46	21	69	−16	4		84	71	135	5.3	14	Nov
Dec	3	−6	21	2	35	17	62	−26	−14		80	68	137	5.4	15	Dec

Based on readings for 72 years at 44°39' N, 63°36' W, altitude 30 m/99 ft

CHATHAM, NEW BRUNSWICK

MARITIME EASTERN CANADA

	Sunshine average hours per day	Temperatures									Discomfort from heat and humidity	Precipitation and humidity				Wet days more than 0.25 mm/0.01 in	
		Average daily				Highest recorded		Lowest recorded				Relative humidity 8:00 20:00		Average monthly precipitation			
		minimum		maximum													
		°C	°F	°C	°F	°C	°F	°C	°F			%		mm	in		
Jan	3	–17	2	–5	23	11	52	–42	–43			89	83	86	3.4	11	Jan
Feb	4	–17	2	–4	25	13	55	–39	–39			89	83	69	2.7	13	Feb
March	5	–9	15	2	35	19	67	–32	–25			80	73	84	3.3	13	March
April	6	–2	28	8	47	29	85	–20	–4			76	73	76	3.0	12	April
May	7	4	39	16	60	33	92	–7	20			72	69	81	3.2	13	May
June	7	9	49	22	71	36	96	–1	30			75	72	91	3.6	13	June
July	8	13	56	25	77	37	98	3	38	Medium		79	73	99	3.9	12	July
Aug	8	12	54	24	75	39	102	1	33	Moderate		81	76	102	4.0	13	Aug
Sept	6	8	46	19	66	33	92	–5	23			84	83	79	3.1	13	Sept
Oct	5	3	37	13	55	29	84	–11	12			87	80	102	4.0	12	Oct
Nov	3	–4	25	4	40	21	70	–24	–12			90	87	86	3.4	14	Nov
Dec	3	–12	10	–3	27	14	58	–34	–30			87	82	81	3.2	12	Dec

Based on readings for 50 years at 47°02′ N, 65°27′ W, altitude 30 m/98 ft

OTTAWA, ONTARIO

CENTRAL CANADA

	Sunshine average hours per day	Temperatures									Discomfort from heat and humidity	Precipitation and humidity				Wet days more than 0.25 mm/0.01 in	
		Average daily				Highest recorded		Lowest recorded				Relative humidity 7:30 13:30		Average monthly precipitation			
		minimum		maximum													
		°C	°F	°C	°F	°C	°F	°C	°F			%		mm	in		
Jan	3	–16	3	–6	21	12	54	–36	–32			83	76	74	2.9	13	Jan
Feb	4	–16	3	–6	22	12	54	–37	–35			88	73	56	2.2	12	Feb
March	5	–9	16	1	33	26	78	–37	–34			84	66	71	2.8	12	March
April	6	–1	31	11	51	30	86	–19	–2			76	58	69	2.7	11	April
May	7	7	44	19	66	34	94	–6	21			77	55	64	2.5	11	May
June	8	12	54	24	76	36	97	1	33	Moderate		80	56	89	3.5	10	June
July	9	14	58	27	81	38	101	3	38	Medium		80	53	86	3.4	11	July
Aug	8	13	55	25	77	38	100	2	35	Moderate		84	54	66	2.6	10	Aug
Sept	6	9	48	20	68	39	102	–4	24			90	59	81	3.2	11	Sept
Oct	4	3	37	12	54	31	87	–10	14			86	63	74	2.9	12	Oct
Nov	3	–3	26	4	39	22	71	–23	–10			84	68	76	3.0	12	Nov
Dec	2	–13	9	–4	24	13	55	–37	–34			83	75	66	2.6	14	Dec

Based on readings for 65 years at 45°20′ N, 75°41′ W, altitude 103 m/339 ft

QUEBEC

CENTRAL CANADA

Sunshine	Temperatures								Discomfort from heat and humidity	Precipitation and humidity				Wet days	
average hours per day	Average daily				Highest recorded		Lowest recorded			Relative humidity 8:00 20:00		Average monthly precipitation		more than 0.25 mm/0.01 in	
	minimum		maximum												
	°C	°F	°C	°F	°C	°F	°C	°F		%		mm	in		
Jan	2	-17	2	-8	18	11	52	-37	-34		80	78	89	3.5	14	Jan
Feb	3	-16	4	-7	20	9	49	-36	-32		80	64	69	2.7	14	Feb
March	4	-9	15	-1	31	18	64	-30	-22		79	75	76	3.0	14	March
April	5	-2	29	7	45	27	80	-18	-1		75	67	58	2.3	12	April
May	6	5	41	16	61	33	91	-7	20		73	63	79	3.1	13	May
June	6	11	52	22	72	34	94	-1	31		79	68	94	3.7	14	June
July	7	14	57	24	76	36	96	4	39	Moderate	79	70	102	4.0	13	July
Aug	7	12	54	23	73	36	97	3	37	Moderate	83	73	102	4.0	12	Aug
Sept	5	8	47	18	64	31	88	-3	27		85	77	91	3.6	13	Sept
Oct	4	3	37	11	51	25	77	-10	14		81	75	86	3.4	13	Oct
Nov	2	-4	24	2	36	22	71	-29	-20		81	79	81	3.2	14	Nov
Dec	2	-13	9	-6	22	12	54	-36	-32		81	80	81	3.2	17	Dec

Based on readings for 68 years at 46°48′ N, 71°13′ W, altitude 90 m/296 ft

TORONTO, ONTARIO

CENTRAL CANADA

Sunshine	Temperatures								Discomfort from heat and humidity	Precipitation and humidity				Wet days	
average hours per day	Average daily				Highest recorded		Lowest recorded			Relative humidity 6:30 12:30		Average monthly precipitation		more than 0.25 mm/0.01 in	
	minimum		maximum												
	°C	°F	°C	°F	°C	°F	°C	°F		%		mm	in		
Jan	2	-9	16	-1	30	14	58	-32	-26		78	70	69	2.7	16	Jan
Feb	4	-9	15	-1	30	13	55	-32	-25		78	67	61	2.4	12	Feb
March	4	-5	23	3	37	27	80	-27	-16		76	62	66	2.6	13	March
April	6	1	34	10	50	32	90	-15	5		74	56	64	2.5	12	April
May	7	7	44	17	63	34	93	-4	25		73	55	74	2.9	13	May
June	9	12	54	23	73	36	97	-2	28		78	58	69	2.7	11	June
July	9	15	59	26	79	41	105	4	39	Moderate	79	56	74	2.9	10	July
Aug	8	14	58	25	77	39	102	4	40	Moderate	83	58	69	2.7	9	Aug
Sept	7	11	51	21	69	36	96	-2	28		87	60	74	2.9	12	Sept
Oct	5	4	40	13	56	29	85	-9	16		87	62	61	2.4	11	Oct
Nov	3	-1	31	6	43	21	70	-21	-5		82	68	71	2.8	13	Nov
Dec	2	-6	21	1	33	16	61	-30	-22		80	71	66	2.6	13	Dec

Based on readings for 105 years at 43°40′ N, 79°24′ W, altitude 116 m/379 ft

nine hours a day. Most of the winter precipitation is snow and the ground is usually snow-covered from mid-December to mid-March. This is one of the snowiest regions of North America, except for parts of the western Rockies. In an average winter 2.5–3 m/8–10 ft of snow may fall, but it does not necessarily accumulate to this depth because of periodic thaws and evaporation.

Like maritime eastern Canada, the weather here can be very variable at all times of the year, so that in some years there may be early or late cold spells and midwinter thaws. This variability of weather and the relatively high precipitation around the year are a consequence of this region's position in the track of numerous cyclonic storms.

THE CANADIAN PRAIRIES

Including (with towns and cities in parentheses): the southern and central parts of MANITOBA (Winnipeg), SASKATCHEWAN (Saskatoon, Regina) and ALBERTA (Edmonton, Calgary).

This region lies between the western shores of Lake Superior and the Rocky Mountains. It is the most continental climate of any part of Canada. Winters are long and severe, with minimum temperatures not much higher than those recorded farther north in the Canadian Arctic. The relatively short summers are warm with a moderate rainfall, much of which falls in heavy showers. The summers are warm enough, and just long enough, to make this an important wheat-growing region. Like the Midwest region of the United States, which borders it on the south, it has much fine, sunny weather. Sunshine averages three to four hours a day in winter and nine to ten in summer. Winter snowfall is comparatively light and the ground is often swept bare of snow by strong winds before the next fall occurs.

The transition from summer to winter and from winter to summer often occurs very quickly, so that the concept of spring and autumn as understood in more temperate or maritime climates is misleading.

The tables for **Winnipeg** (below), **Saskatoon** (opposite) and **Edmonton** (opposite and below) are representative of this region. Edmonton has experienced higher temperatures in the midwinter months of January and February than the other two places. This shows the effect of the chinook wind, which can suddenly raise winter temperatures for a day or two at the foot of the Rockies. It is a föhn-type wind and occurs when air is drawn from the west across the mountains and is warmed as it descends on the eastern side. It can be very effective in melting snow quickly.

WINNIPEG, MANITOBA															CANADIAN PRAIRIES
Sunshine		Temperatures								Discomfort from heat and humidity	Precipitation and humidity				Wet days	
		Average daily				Highest recorded		Lowest recorded			Relative humidity		Average monthly precipitation			
		minimum		maximum							6:00	12:00				
average hours per day		°C	°F	°C	°F	°C	°F	°C	°F		%		mm	in	more than 0.25 mm/0.01 in	
Jan	4	−25	−13	−14	7	8	46	−44	−48		89	83	23	0.9	12	Jan
Feb	5	−23	−9	−11	12	8	47	−44	−47		92	83	23	0.9	11	Feb
March	5	−15	5	−3	27	23	74	−39	−38		89	78	31	1.2	9	March
April	7	−3	27	9	48	32	90	−28	−18		82	57	36	1.4	9	April
May	8	4	39	18	65	38	100	−12	11		80	52	58	2.3	10	May
June	8	10	50	23	74	38	101	−6	21	Moderate	85	60	79	3.1	12	June
July	10	13	55	26	79	42	108	2	35	Moderate	85	53	79	3.1	10	July
Aug	9	11	51	24	76	39	103	−1	30	Moderate	88	53	64	2.5	10	Aug
Sept	6	6	43	18	65	37	99	−8	17		90	61	58	2.3	9	Sept
Oct	5	−1	31	11	51	30	86	−21	−5		86	62	38	1.5	6	Oct
Nov	3	−11	13	−1	30	22	71	−37	−34		89	79	28	1.1	9	Nov
Dec	3	−19	−3	−9	15	12	53	−48	−54		92	85	23	0.9	11	Dec

Based on readings for 66 years at 49°54' N, 97°14' W, altitude 240 m/786 ft

SASKATOON, SASKATCHEWAN

CANADIAN PRAIRIES

	Sunshine average hours per day	Temperatures Average daily minimum °C	°F	Average daily maximum °C	°F	Highest recorded °C	°F	Lowest recorded °C	°F	Discomfort from heat and humidity	Relative humidity 5:30 %	17:30 %	Average monthly precipitation mm	in	Wet days more than 0.25 mm/0.01 in	
Jan	3	−24	−11	−13	9	10	50	−49	−55		98	86	23	0.9	9	Jan
Feb	5	−22	−8	−11	13	13	55	−45	−49		94	89	13	0.5	10	Feb
March	6	−14	6	−3	27	23	73	−37	−34		93	75	18	0.7	6	March
April	8	−3	26	9	49	33	91	−23	−9		84	52	18	0.7	7	April
May	9	3	38	18	64	37	99	−13	9		83	47	36	1.4	10	May
June	9	9	48	22	71	40	104	−3	26		85	50	66	2.6	12	June
July	11	11	52	25	77	40	104	−1	31	Moderate	87	47	61	2.4	9	July
Aug	9	9	48	24	75	38	100	−2	28		89	46	48	1.9	9	Aug
Sept	7	3	38	17	63	33	92	−11	12		86	53	38	1.5	8	Sept
Oct	5	−3	27	11	51	32	90	−26	−14		86	62	23	0.9	7	Oct
Nov	3	−11	12	−1	31	20	68	−35	−31		90	83	13	0.5	9	Nov
Dec	3	−19	−2	−9	16	14	58	−41	−41		92	88	15	0.6	7	Dec

Based on readings for 38 years at 52°08′ N, 106°38′ W, altitude 515 m/1690 ft

EDMONTON, ALBERTA

CANADIAN PRAIRIES

	Sunshine average hours per day	Temperatures Average daily minimum °C	°F	Average daily maximum °C	°F	Highest recorded °C	°F	Lowest recorded °C	°F	Discomfort from heat and humidity	Relative humidity 5:00 %	11:00 %	Average monthly precipitation mm	in	Wet days more than 0.25 mm/0.01 in	
Jan	3	−20	−4	−9	15	14	57	−50	−57		86	78	23	0.9	12	Jan
Feb	4	−17	1	−6	22	17	62	−50	−57		86	75	15	0.6	9	Feb
March	5	−11	12	1	34	22	72	−40	−40		85	68	20	0.8	10	March
April	7	−2	28	11	52	31	88	−26	−15		79	50	23	0.9	8	April
May	9	3	38	18	64	34	94	−23	10		81	47	48	1.9	12	May
June	8	7	45	21	70	37	99	−4	25		88	65	79	3.1	15	June
July	10	9	49	23	74	37	98	−2	29		89	58	84	3.3	14	July
Aug	8	8	47	22	72	36	96	−3	26		91	58	58	2.3	12	Aug
Sept	6	3	38	17	62	32	90	−11	12		90	61	33	1.3	9	Sept
Oct	5	−1	30	11	52	28	83	−27	−15		84	62	18	0.7	9	Oct
Nov	4	−9	16	1	34	23	74	−42	−44		88	74	18	0.7	11	Nov
Dec	3	−15	5	−6	21	16	61	−43	−46		87	78	20	0.8	12	Dec

Based on readings for 56 years at 53°35′ N, 113°30′ W, altitude 677 m/2199 ft

VANCOUVER, BRITISH COLUMBIA — WEST COAST CANADA

	Sunshine average hours per day	Temperatures								Discomfort from heat and humidity	Precipitation and humidity				Wet days more than 0.25 mm/0.01 in	
		Average daily minimum		Average daily maximum		Highest recorded		Lowest recorded			Relative humidity 4:30 16:30		Average monthly precipitation			
		°C	°F	°C	°F	°C	°F	°C	°F		%		mm	in		
Jan	2	0	32	5	41	15	59	-17	2		93	85	218	8.6	20	Jan
Feb	3	1	34	7	44	16	61	-13	8		91	78	147	5.8	17	Feb
March	4	3	37	10	50	20	68	-9	15		91	70	127	5.0	17	March
April	6	4	40	14	58	26	79	-3	27		89	67	84	3.3	14	April
May	8	8	46	18	64	28	83	1	33		88	63	71	2.8	12	May
June	7	11	52	21	69	33	92	2	35		87	65	64	2.5	11	June
July	9	12	54	23	74	33	91	4	40	Moderate	89	62	31	1.2	7	July
Aug	8	12	54	23	73	33	92	4	39	Moderate	90	62	43	1.7	8	Aug
Sept	6	9	49	18	65	29	85	-1	30		92	72	91	3.6	9	Sept
Oct	4	7	44	14	57	25	77	-6	21		92	80	147	5.8	16	Oct
Nov	3	4	39	9	48	23	74	-12	10		91	84	211	8.3	19	Nov
Dec	2	2	35	6	43	16	60	-13	8		91	88	224	8.8	22	Dec

Based on readings for 43 years at 49°17′ N, 123°05′ W, altitude 14 m/45 ft

PRINCE GEORGE, BRITISH COLUMBIA — WESTERN CANADA

	Sunshine average hours per day	Temperatures								Discomfort from heat and humidity	Precipitation and humidity				Wet days more than 0.25 mm/0.01 in	
		Average daily minimum		Average daily maximum		Highest recorded		Lowest recorded			Relative humidity 4:30 16:30		Average monthly precipitation			
		°C	°F	°C	°F	°C	°F	°C	°F		%		mm	in		
Jan	2	-16	3	-5	23	12	54	-49	-57		89	86	46	1.8	14	Jan
Feb	3	-14	6	-1	31	14	58	-47	-52		92	77	31	1.2	12	Feb
March	4	-8	18	6	42	20	68	-37	-35		82	59	36	1.4	13	March
April	6	-3	27	12	54	30	86	-25	-13		84	49	20	0.8	12	April
May	8	1	34	18	64	35	95	-11	12		83	41	33	1.3	11	May
June	8	6	42	21	70	34	93	-4	24		88	55	53	2.1	15	June
July	9	7	44	24	75	39	102	-2	28	Moderate	93	52	41	1.6	15	July
Aug	8	6	43	23	74	36	96	-4	25		92	48	48	1.9	14	Aug
Sept	6	2	36	18	65	33	92	-14	6		92	58	51	2.0	13	Sept
Oct	3	-1	30	11	52	29	84	-20	-4		91	68	51	2.0	16	Oct
Nov	2	-6	21	3	38	17	62	-33	-28		93	86	48	1.9	14	Nov
Dec	1	-13	8	-4	25	13	55	-48	-56		93	89	48	1.9	13	Dec

Based on readings for 27 years at 53°53′ N, 122°40′ W, altitude 677 m/2218 ft

THE WESTERN MOUNTAINS

Including (with towns and cities in parentheses): ALBERTA within the Rocky Mountains (Banff, Jasper) and the southern and central parts of BRITISH COLUMBIA (Vancouver, Victoria, Prince George, Prince Rupert).

This is a mountainous region with a very indented coastline on the Pacific Ocean. The highest mountains rise to between 3,000–4,000 m/10,000–13,000 ft and are found in two chains: the western or Coast Mountains and the eastern or main chain of the Rockies.

The area between consists of deep valleys and high plateaux. Because of this varied relief and wide range of altitude, there are many local differences of weather and climate.

The Coast Mountains have a very heavy precipitation and above 1,200 m/4,000 ft much of this is snow. Some of the valleys have a very low annual precipitation; as little as 375 mm/15 in.

The coastal region of British Columbia, which includes numerous islands, has a very mild winter climate with much rainfall at this season. It has the warmest winters in any part of Canada. Weather and climate around the year are very similar to that found in the British Isles, but the summers are a little warmer and sunnier.

These mild winters quickly give way to severe conditions inland with frequent snowfalls in the mountains and quite low temperatures in the valleys where winter frosts are hard and frequent.

This difference is well illustrated by the two tables for **Vancouver** (opposite and above), on the coast, and **Prince George** (opposite), which is well inland in the valley of the Fraser river. The winter minimum temperatures at Prince George are almost as low as those in the Prairies. The winter precipitation at Prince George is very much less than on the coast.

This region is less sunny than much of central Canada. Winter sunshine is reduced by the more frequent cloudy days, and on the coast fog is a frequent occurrence. The summers are fairly sunny with an average eight to nine hours a day, compared with only two to three in winter. Although the weather is often changeable this is perhaps the most climatically favourable region of Canada; the coastal districts escape the harsh Canadian winter and the summers are warm and rarely too hot or oppressive.

NORTHERN CANADA

Including (with towns and cities in parentheses): the YUKON (Whitehorse, Dawson), the NORTHWEST TERRITORIES (Norman Wells, Arctic Bay) and most of LABRADOR; and the northern parts of BRITISH COLUMBIA, ALBERTA, SASKATCHEWAN, MANITOBA (Churchill), ONTARIO and QUEBEC.

This region comprises at least two-thirds of Canada but is very sparsely populated because it has such a harsh climate which is quite unsuitable for any form of agriculture. It resembles the climate of northern European Russia and Siberia.

In the south it consists of a vast area of coniferous forest, to the north of which lies the Atlantic tundra region, covered with snow for eight to nine months of the year. In the far north the islands of the Arctic archipelago to the west of Greenland are covered with snow and ice throughout the year.

The harsh conditions during the long winter are well illustrated by the temperatures in the tables for **Churchill** (overleaf), on the shores of Hudson Bay, for **Norman Wells** (overleaf), on the Mackenzie river just south of the Arctic Circle, and for **Arctic Bay** (p. 91), on the northern shore of Baffin Island.

The tables show that at Churchill and Norman Wells temperatures can rise to quite high levels during the short summer. For much of the summer, however, the weather can be changeable and disturbed. Snow and frost may occur in any month when cold air is drawn down from the polar regions.

In the north of this region the phenomenon of permafrost is widespread. The top two or three feet of ground thaw during the summer, but below this the earth is frozen for tens or even hundreds of feet.

This poses particular problems for building and construction works which involve any foundations, whether housing, roads, or oil and gas pipelines. The line marking the approximate southern limit of permafrost runs from northwest to southeast from the Yukon and Great Slave Lake to the southern shore of Hudson Bay and then eastwards to the coast of Labrador.

Wind chill (see p. 2) is a frequent, and probably the most dangerous, weather hazard in northern Canada. During severe weather in winter it can be a serious problem in almost any part of the country, except on the west coast.

CHURCHILL, MANITOBA

NORTHERN CANADA

	Sunshine	Temperatures							Discomfort from heat and humidity	Precipitation and humidity				Wet days	
		Average daily				Highest recorded		Lowest recorded			Relative humidity		Average monthly precipitation			
		minimum		maximum							6:00	12:00				
	average hours per day	°C	°F	°C	°F	°C	°F	°C	°F		%		mm	in	more than 0.25 mm/0.01 in	
Jan	3	−33	−27	−24	−11	4	39	−49	−57		—	—	13	0.5	5	Jan
Feb	5	−32	−25	−22	−8	−1	31	−48	−52		—	—	15	0.6	6	Feb
March	6	−27	−16	−16	4	5	41	−48	−52		—	—	23	0.9	6	March
April	6	−16	4	−4	24	17	62	−32	−26		93	88	23	0.9	6	April
May	6	−6	22	3	38	31	87	−26	−14		92	86	23	0.9	7	May
June	7	1	34	11	52	31	88	−11	13		88	73	48	1.9	9	June
July	9	6	43	18	64	36	96	−6	22		88	71	56	2.2	10	July
Aug	8	6	43	17	62	32	90	−4	25		93	74	69	2.7	12	Aug
Sept	3	1	34	9	49	29	84	−9	15		94	84	58	2.3	11	Sept
Oct	2	−7	20	1	34	18	65	−27	−17		95	89	36	1.4	12	Oct
Nov	2	−19	−2	−11	13	7	45	−47	−53		94	91	25	1.0	9	Nov
Dec	2	−28	19	−19	−3	1	34	−44	−47		97	93	18	0.7	8	Dec

Based on readings for 30 years at 58°47′ N, 94°11′ W, altitude 13 m/43 ft

NORMAN WELLS, NORTHWEST TERRITORIES

NORTHERN CANADA

	Sunshine	Temperatures							Discomfort from heat and humidity	Precipitation and humidity				Wet days	
		Average daily				Highest recorded		Lowest recorded			Relative humidity		Average monthly precipitation			
		minimum		maximum							4:00	10:00				
	average hours per day	°C	°F	°C	°F	°C	°F	°C	°F		%		mm	in	more than 0.25 mm/0.01 in	
Jan		−32	−26	−24	−11	−3	27	−53	−63		90	88	18	0.7	14	Jan
Feb		−31	−23	−22	−7	−6	22	−54	−66		85	81	15	0.6	11	Feb
March		−24	−12	−12	10	11	52	−46	−51		85	84	8	0.3	8	March
April		−14	7	−1	31	14	58	−32	−25		85	71	13	0.5	8	April
May		0	32	12	53	31	88	−13	8		81	65	18	0.7	6	May
June		8	46	20	68	31	88	−1	30		77	59	36	1.4	10	June
July		10	50	22	72	32	89	−1	30		81	63	51	2.0	10	July
Aug		7	45	18	65	32	89	−6	21		88	71	69	2.7	13	Aug
Sept		2	35	10	50	26	78	−14	7		89	81	43	1.7	13	Sept
Oct		−7	20	0	32	15	59	−27	−17		90	87	20	0.8	11	Oct
Nov		−20	−4	−13	9	2	35	−43	−45		94	94	20	0.8	14	Nov
Dec		−29	−21	−21	−6	2	35	−47	−53		90	89	18	0.7	12	Dec

Based on readings for 7 years at 65°15′ N, 126°38′ W, altitude 88 m/290 ft

ARCTIC BAY, NORTHWEST TERRITORIES

NORTHERN CANADA

Sunshine	Temperatures								Discomfort from heat and humidity	Precipitation and humidity				Wet days	
	Average daily				Highest recorded		Lowest recorded			Relative humidity 7:00 19:00		Average monthly precipitation		more than 0.25 mm/0.01 in	
	minimum		maximum												
average hours per day	°C	°F	°C	°F	°C	°F	°C	°F		%		mm	in		
Jan	−33	−28	−26	−14	−2	28	−46	−51		80	80	8	0.3	6	Jan
Feb	−36	−33	−28	−19	2	36	−50	−57		79	79	5	0.2	3	Feb
March	−32	−25	−22	−7	−3	27	−45	−49		81	80	8	0.3	6	March
April	−26	−14	−14	6	1	34	−38	−37		82	80	5	0.2	6	April
May	−11	12	−3	27	11	51	−26	−14		86	80	8	0.3	6	May
June	−1	30	6	42	17	63	−12	11		81	75	13	0.5	6	June
July	2	36	11	51	24	75	−6	22		82	75	18	0.7	7	July
Aug	2	35	8	47	18	64	−4	24		87	81	33	1.3	10	Aug
Sept	−3	26	1	34	13	56	−13	9		85	82	23	0.9	8	Sept
Oct	−12	10	−7	20	7	44	−24	−12		83	82	18	0.7	8	Oct
Nov	−23	−10	−17	2	1	34	−41	−42		80	79	8	0.3	6	Nov
Dec	−30	−22	−23	−10	1	34	−41	−41		80	79	5	0.2	5	Dec

Based on readings for 12 years at 73°16′ N, 84°17′ W, altitude 11 m/36 ft

PRAIA													SAO TIAGO ISLAND, CAPE VERDE	
Sunshine		Temperatures							Discomfort from heat and humidity	Precipitation and humidity				Wet days
average hours per day		Average daily				Highest recorded		Lowest recorded		Relative humidity 9:30 15:30		Average monthly precipitation		more than 1 mm/0.04 in
		minimum		maximum										
		°C	°F	°C	°F	°C	°F	°C	°F	%		mm	in	
Jan	7	20	68	25	77	30	86	17	63	Moderate	63 59		3.0	0.1	0.9	Jan
Feb	8	19	67	25	77	31	87	13	56	Moderate	59 57		0.0	0.0	0.3	Feb
March	9	20	68	26	78	33	91	17	62	Moderate	58 55		0.0	0.0	0.1	March
April	10	21	69	26	79	34	93	18	64	Moderate	58 54		0.0	0.0	0.0	April
May	10	21	70	27	81	33	92	18	65	Medium	59 55		0.0	0.0	0.0	May
June	9	22	72	28	82	34	93	19	67	Medium	62 59		0.0	0.0	0.0	June
July	7	24	75	28	83	33	91	19	66	Medium	68 66		5.0	0.2	0.5	July
Aug	6	24	76	29	84	32	90	22	72	High	73 71		97.0	3.8	8.0	Aug
Sept	7	25	77	29	84	34	94	22	72	High	74 73		114.0	4.5	7.0	Sept
Oct	8	24	76	29	85	33	91	22	72	Medium	69 65		31.0	1.2	3.0	Oct
Nov	8	23	74	28	82	32	90	20	68	Medium	64 63		8.0	0.3	0.9	Nov
Dec	7	22	71	26	79	31	87	18	64	Medium	63 62		3.0	0.1	0.5	Dec

Based on readings for 25 years at 14°54´ N, 23°31´ W, altitude 35 m/112 ft

Cape Verde

See map page 20

The Cape Verde Islands consist of a group of ten main islands and a number of smaller islets with a total land area of 4,040 sq km/1,560 sq mi. They are situated between 14° to 16° N about 480 km/300 mi off the west coast of Africa.

The islands are volcanic and hilly. They have a low and irregular rainfall, being at the northern limit of the tropical rain-belt. Most of the rain falls between August and October. The rainfall is very low at sea level but increases in the hills.

The temperature is typically tropical with no cool season, although there is a small range of temperature around the year; the coolest months are December to March. The combination of moderately high temperature and high humidity can be unpleasant, except when this is tempered by the daily sea breeze. Daily hours of sunshine average from seven to ten and are highest in the months February to June. There is more cloud during the rainier months.

The table for **Praia** (above) is representative of weather conditions on the islands.

Caribbean Islands

See map page 15

Situated between 10° and 26° N, and therefore almost entirely within the tropics, all the West Indian islands have a distinctly oceanic variety of tropical climate. Because of the similarity of weather and climate over this whole area, the Caribbean Islands are described together. Short notes only appear under the separate headings for each political unit or group of small islands.

The islands form a large arc extending eastwards from the Yucatán peninsula of Mexico and the Florida peninsula of the United States. The larger islands are, from west to east: Cuba, Jamaica, Hispaniola (divided into the two separate political units of Haiti and the Dominican Republic), and Puerto Rico.

To the north of these larger islands lies a group of small scattered islands: the Bahamas and the Turks and Caicos Islands. The chain of islands east of Puerto Rico, known as the Lesser Antilles, curves southwards, terminating in Trinidad, which is close to the coast of Venezuela. The Lesser Antilles are often divided into the Leeward Islands group in the north and the Windward Islands group in the south.

Despite the large area over which these islands are scattered, there is a strong similarity of weather and climate everywhere. The waters of the Atlantic Ocean and the Caribbean Sea are warm at all times of the year, being influenced by ocean currents from equatorial latitudes, which unite to form the Gulf Stream to the north of the Caribbean. The area lies for the whole year under the influence of the northeast trade winds, or the North Atlantic anticyclone, which lies farthest south in the winter period.

Almost everywhere the wettest months are from May to October and the winter period is relatively, but by no means completely, dry. The area experiences no great extremes of temperature; winters are warm and sunny and summers are hot, but without excessively high temperatures so that heat stress is rarely felt.

Almost nowhere in the Caribbean have maximum temperatures above 38°C/100°F been experienced, and only in Cuba and the northern islands of the Bahamas do winter temperatures occasionally fall much below 15°C/60°F. This equability of temperature is a consequence of the strong influence of the warm sea. Waves of cold air from North America in winter and spring affect only western Cuba and the northern Bahamas for a few days, and the air arriving in the islands may be as much as 5°–8°C/10°–15°F warmer than when it left the coast of the mainland.

Most of the larger and many of the smaller islands are mountainous, and this gives rise to numerous local differences of weather and climate. Apart from the fall of temperature with altitude, there is often a big increase of rainfall on the mountains; and the northern and eastern slopes and coasts of the islands are usually considerably wetter than the southern and western sides, which are sheltered from the persistent northeast trade winds.

Unfortunately most of the climatic data available for the West Indian islands is from places at or near sea level, but a good example of the increase of rainfall with altitude can be seen by comparing the table for **Camp Jacob** (p. 167) on the islands of Guadeloupe with that for **Plymouth** (p. 244) on the nearby island of Montserrat – both in the Leeward Islands. Camp Jacob, at an altitude of 530 m/1,750 ft, has more than twice the annual rainfall of Plymouth.

Annual rainfall on the highest mountains in Cuba and Jamaica is two or three times that of the places at sea level for which tables are given in this book. In these wetter mountain areas cloud is more frequent than at sea level at all times of the year.

The Caribbean Islands have developed an important tourist trade, and one reason for this is the large number of hours of sunshine around the year. Daily sunshine hours average from seven to nine, with more in the driest months. The winter months are the driest and sunniest and the slightly lower temperatures are made more pleasant by frequent sea breezes and lower humidity. Even in the warmest months the combination of temperature and humidity is rarely very uncomfortable if moderated by a strong breeze.

The tables show that some places have a large number of days with rain; as many as one in two or one in three. This should not be taken to imply that it rains all day; on many days cloud builds up in the afternoon to give short thundery showers in the late afternoon and evening. Prolonged spells of rain are rare and are usually associated with hurricanes or tropical storms, which are the worst features of the weather and climate of the Caribbean.

Hurricanes occur between June and November and are most frequent in the months of August and September. During the worst of these storms 250–500 mm/10–20 in of rain may fall over a period of two or three days and the very violent winds may cause damage. Individual islands may go several years without experiencing a severe hurricane and, on the larger islands, their worst effects may be confined to only one area. Over the area as a whole, however, some two to three hurricanes may occur each year. They develop east of the Caribbean and move westwards before curving north and east close to the North American mainland.

A significant proportion of the rainfall in the months August to October may be caused by hurricanes since places which escape the centre of the storm with its damaging winds may be affected by the cloud and heavy rainfall on the fringe. Tropical storms that do not develop to full hurricane intensity may bring a period of two or three days of cloud and rain.

Cayman Islands

See map page 15

These low-lying islands south of Cuba have typical Caribbean weather. They are hot throughout the year, and rain, in the form of brief, heavy showers, falls mainly from May to November. The greatest risk of tropical storms or hurricanes is between August and October. For details of a similar Caribbean climate see the table for **Kingston** (p. 201) in Jamaica. For a more detailed description of this type of climate, see the general entry for the Caribbean region (pp. 92–3).

Central African Republic

See map page 20

This is a landlocked state situated between 2° and 10° N. Rather larger than France, it is very sparsely populated.

The northern part of the country has weather and climate similar to that described for northern Nigeria and illustrated by the table for **Kano** (p. 266). There is a single rainy season and a moderate annual rainfall of 875–1,000 mm/ 35–40 in. Daytime temperatures rise quite high in the period preceding the main rainy season between May and September. During the rest of the year rainfall is light and sparse.

The southern half of the country has a more equatorial type of climate as described in more detail on p. 112 for the Congo Democratic Republic. The annual rainfall is between 1,500 mm/60 in and 2,000 mm/80 in, falling in all months but with a relatively drier period from December to February at the time of low sun. The table for **Bangui** (opposite) illustrates conditions in the south of the Central African Republic.

Chad

See map page 20

Chad is a country slightly larger than Egypt, situated in interior West Africa between 10° and 23° N. It is rather sparsely populated as the northern part of the country includes part of the Sahara desert. The general features of the climate of this part of Africa are described for Mali on p. 230. Chad borders Niger on the west and the Sudan on the east and includes the same climatic belts.

The northern half of the country, the Sahara desert, is virtually rainless. Here the climate is hot around the year with abundant sunshine. The table for **Faya** (opposite), which lies beyond the northern limit of the summer rain-belt, is representative of this area. The southern half of the country, roughly south of 15° N, is part of the Sahel belt, where rain occurs during the period of high sun between May and September.

The table for **N'djamena** (p. 96) is representative of this wetter Sahel region. Here sunshine amounts are lower during the rainy season from July to September, averaging six to seven hours a day as compared with nine to ten during the dry season.

BANGUI

CENTRAL AFRICAN REPUBLIC

	Sunshine average hours per day	Temperatures										Discomfort from heat and humidity	Precipitation and humidity				Wet days more than 0.1 mm/0.004 in	
		Average daily				Highest recorded		Lowest recorded					Relative humidity 7:00 13:00		Average monthly precipitation			
		minimum		maximum														
		°C	°F	°C	°F	°C	°F	°C	°F				%		mm	in		
Jan	7	20	68	32	90	37	98	14	57		High		92	49	25	1.0	3	Jan
Feb	7	21	70	34	93	38	101	14	57		High		90	49	43	1.7	5	Feb
March	6	22	71	33	91	38	100	18	64		High		91	57	127	5.0	11	March
April	6	22	71	33	91	37	99	18	65		High		92	59	135	5.3	10	April
May	6	21	70	32	89	36	96	18	65		High		94	64	188	7.4	15	May
June	6	21	70	31	87	35	95	18	65		High		95	67	114	4.5	12	June
July	4	21	69	29	85	34	94	18	64		High		96	71	226	8.9	17	July
Aug	4	21	69	29	85	34	93	17	62		High		96	72	206	8.1	19	Aug
Sept	5	21	69	31	87	34	94	18	65		High		95	68	150	5.9	16	Sept
Oct	5	21	69	31	87	34	94	18	64		High		94	66	201	7.9	19	Oct
Nov	6	20	68	31	88	34	94	17	63		High		94	63	125	4.9	11	Nov
Dec	7	19	66	32	90	36	96	14	57		Medium		92	47	5	0.2	2	Dec

Based on readings for 5 years at 4°22′ N, 18°34′ E, altitude 387 m/1270 ft

FAYA

SAHARAN CHAD

	Sunshine average hours per day	Temperatures										Discomfort from heat and humidity	Precipitation and humidity				Wet days more than 0.1 mm/0.004 in	
		Average daily				Highest recorded		Lowest recorded					Relative humidity 7:30 13:30		Average monthly precipitation			
		minimum		maximum														
		°C	°F	°C	°F	°C	°F	°C	°F				%		mm	in		
Jan		12	54	29	84	39	103	4	40		Moderate		47	26	0	0.0	0.0	Jan
Feb		14	57	32	89	43	109	7	44		Medium		44	23	0	0.0	0.0	Feb
March		18	65	36	97	44	111	11	52		Medium		35	18	0	0.0	0.0	March
April		21	69	40	104	49	121	14	57		High		35	17	0	0.0	0.0	April
May		24	76	44	112	49	121	17	63		Extreme		39	21	0	0.0	0.4	May
June		24	76	43	110	49	120	17	62		Extreme		39	23	0	0.0	0.0	June
July		24	76	43	109	47	116	16	61		Extreme		54	29	0	0.0	0.2	July
Aug		24	75	40	104	46	114	16	60		Extreme		66	36	18	0.7	4.0	Aug
Sept		24	76	39	103	46	115	17	63		Extreme		46	30	0	0.0	0.4	Sept
Oct		22	72	39	103	47	116	12	54		High		37	21	0	0.0	0.0	Oct
Nov		18	65	33	91	39	102	9	48		Medium		45	22	0	0.0	0.0	Nov
Dec		13	55	28	82	36	97	3	37		Moderate		50	28	0	0.0	0.0	Dec

Based on readings for 5 years at 18°00′ N, 19°10′ E, altitude 225 m/837 ft

N'DJAMENA								SAHELIAN CHAD					
Sunshine	Temperatures						Discomfort from heat and humidity	Precipitation and humidity					Wet days
	Average daily				Highest recorded	Lowest recorded		Relative humidity 7:00 13:00		Average monthly precipitation			
average hours per day	minimum		maximum										more than 0.1 mm/0.004 in
	°C	°F	°C	°F	°C	°F	°C	°F		%	mm	in	
Jan	11	14	57	34	93	42 107	8 47	Medium	51	13	0	0.0	0	Jan
Feb	10	16	61	37	98	43 109	11 51	Medium	39	10	0	0.0	0	Feb
March	9	21	70	40 104		44 111	13 56	High	32	10	0	0.0	0	March
April	9	23	74	42 107		46 114	16 61	High	37	13	3	0.1	1	April
May	9	25	77	40 104		44 112	17 62	Extreme	62	30	31	1.2	6	May
June	8	24	76	38 100		43 109	18 65	Extreme	74	40	66	2.6	10	June
July	7	22	72	33	92	41 106	18 65	High	85	59	170	6.7	15	July
Aug	6	22	72	31	87	36 96	19 66	High	93	72	320	12.6	22	Aug
Sept	7	22	72	33	91	37 98	19 66	High	91	63	119	4.7	13	Sept
Oct	9	21	70	36	97	39 103	14 57	High	83	41	36	1.4	4	Oct
Nov	10	17	63	36	97	40 104	11 52	Medium	46	17	0	0.0	0	Nov
Dec	11	14	57	33	92	38 101	8 47	Medium	50	16	0	0.0	0	Dec

Based on readings for 5 years at 12°07′ N, 15°02′ E, altitude 295 m/968 ft

Chile

See map page 99

Chile has a remarkable shape. It extends over 4,200 km/2,600 mi, between 22° and 55° S, on the Pacific coast of South America, yet has an average breadth of only 160–320 km/100–200 mi.

Its eastern border with Bolivia and Argentina follows the crest-line of the main Andes mountain chain, so that the eastern part of this narrow country is very mountainous with the higher parts rising to over 5,000 m/16,000 ft.

South of Santiago the mountains are lower and more broken, but the country is rugged with hundreds of small islands offshore from Puerto Montt to Tierra del Fuego.

Much of Chile, therefore, has a mountain climate with perpetual snow and glaciers in the higher parts. The height of the snowline gradually decreases from north to south as temperature decreases and precipitation increases. Precipitation is light on the mountains in the north, so the snowline is high. Most people live in the lowlands of central Chile

between Valparaíso and Valdivia. The north of the country is a desert. The southern third, rugged and densely forested, has a changeable, cool, wet climate.

NORTHERN CHILE

Including (with towns and cities in parentheses):the lowlands of northern Chile (Antofagasta, Iquique), from the border with Peru southwards to about Coquimbo at 30° S.

This is one of the driest regions in the world. This is a typical 'cold-water-coast desert' where, in spite of being virtually rainless, the weather is often cloudy and relatively cool for the latitude. The coastal strip has much fog and frequent light drizzle with low amounts of sunshine. The cloud usually breaks up by day inland in summer and temperatures here are a little higher.

There is a small difference of temperature from summer to winter and the weather is remarkably constant from one day to another. The table for **Antofagasta** (opposite and above) illustrates conditions in this coastal desert.

ANTOFAGASTA

NORTHERN COASTAL CHILE

	Sunshine	Temperatures								Discomfort from heat and humidity	Precipitation and humidity				Wet days
		Average daily				Highest recorded		Lowest recorded			Relative humidity 7:30 13:30		Average monthly precipitation		
		minimum		maximum											
	average hours per day	°C	°F	°C	°F	°C	°F	°C	°F		%		mm	in	more than 0.01 mm/0.04 in
Jan	11	17	63	24	76	28	83	11	52	Moderate	77	71	0	0.0	0.0
Feb	10	17	63	24	76	29	85	14	57	Moderate	78	70	0	0.0	0.0
March	8	16	61	28	74	28	83	13	55	Medium	80	71	0	0.0	0.0
April	4	14	58	21	70	27	80	10	50		78	72	0	0.0	0.1
May	6	13	55	19	67	24	75	8	47		79	73	0	0.0	0.1
June	6	11	52	18	65	26	78	6	43		78	71	3	0.1	0.2
July	6	11	51	17	63	26	79	6	43		80	73	5	0.2	0.5
Aug	6	11	52	17	62	24	75	5	41		79	73	3	0.1	0.4
Sept	6	12	53	18	64	22	72	7	45		77	71	0	0.0	0.5
Oct	6	13	55	19	66	23	73	8	47		75	71	3	0.1	0.2
Nov	7	14	58	21	69	24	76	11	51		74	71	0	0.0	0.3
Dec	9	16	60	22	72	27	80	11	51		75	70	0	0.0	0.0

Based on readings for 22 years at 23°42' S, 70°24' W, altitude 94 m/308 ft

SANTIAGO

CENTRAL CHILE

	Sunshine	Temperatures								Discomfort from heat and humidity	Precipitation and humidity				Wet days
		Average daily				Highest recorded		Lowest recorded			Relative humidity 7:30 14:30		Average monthly precipitation		
		minimum		maximum											
	average hours per day	°C	°F	°C	°F	°C	°F	°C	°F		%		mm	in	more than 1 mm/0.04 in
Jan	11	12	53	29	85	36	96	6	43	Medium	70	38	3	0.1	0
Feb	9	11	52	29	84	37	98	6	43	Medium	78	40	3	0.1	0
March	9	9	49	27	80	34	94	3	38	Moderate	86	41	5	0.2	1
April	6	7	45	23	74	31	88	1	33		89	46	13	0.5	1
May	4	5	41	18	65	31	87	-3	27		92	58	64	2.5	5
June	3	3	37	14	58	27	80	-3	26		93	64	84	3.3	6
July	3	3	37	15	59	27	81	-4	24		91	60	76	3.0	6
Aug	4	4	39	17	62	29	85	-3	26		91	58	56	2.2	5
Sept	5	6	42	19	66	31	88	-1	31		89	55	31	1.2	3
Oct	6	7	45	22	72	33	92	0	32		83	50	15	0.6	3
Nov	9	9	48	26	78	36	97	3	37	Moderate	73	41	8	0.3	1
Dec	10	11	51	28	83	37	99	2	36	Moderate	69	38	5	0.2	0

Based on readings for 14 years at 33°27' S, 70°42' W, altitude 520 m/1706 ft

VALDIVIA · SOUTHERN CHILE

	Sunshine average hours per day	Temperatures Average daily minimum °C	°F	Average daily maximum °C	°F	Highest recorded °C	°F	Lowest recorded °C	°F	Discomfort from heat and humidity	Relative humidity 7:00 %	13:00 %	Average monthly precipitation mm	in	Wet days more than 1 mm/0.04 in	
Jan	8	11	52	23	73	36	97	3	37	Moderate	87	64	66	2.6	7	Jan
Feb	8	11	51	23	73	35	95	2	35	Moderate	90	67	74	2.9	7	Feb
March	7	9	49	21	69	33	91	2	36		93	70	132	5.2	11	March
April	4	8	46	17	62	28	82	-2	29		94	77	234	9.2	12	April
May	2	6	43	13	56	22	71	-3	26		95	87	361	14.2	21	May
June	2	6	42	11	52	17	63	-4	25		95	89	550	17.7	21	June
July	2	5	41	11	52	19	66	-4	24		95	89	394	15.5	20	July
Aug	3	4	40	12	54	20	68	-4	25		95	83	328	12.9	18	Aug
Sept	4	5	41	14	58	26	79	-3	27		94	74	208	8.2	13	Sept
Oct	4	7	44	17	63	29	84	-1	31		93	71	127	5.0	13	Oct
Nov	6	8	46	18	65	32	90	0	32		89	68	125	4.9	10	Nov
Dec	7	10	50	21	69	33	92	3	37		89	67	104	4.1	10	Dec

Based on readings for 29 years at 39°48′ S, 73°14′ W, altitude 5 m/16 ft

PUNTA ARENAS · SOUTHERN CHILE

	Sunshine average hours per day	Temperatures Average daily minimum °C	°F	Average daily maximum °C	°F	Highest recorded °C	°F	Lowest recorded °C	°F	Discomfort from heat and humidity	Relative humidity 7:30 %	13:30 %	Average monthly precipitation mm	in	Wet days more than 1 mm/0.04 in	
Jan		7	45	14	58	30	86	-3	26		74	68	38	1.5	6	Jan
Feb		7	44	14	58	26	79	-2	28		74	64	23	0.9	5	Feb
March		5	41	12	54	24	75	-4	24		78	69	33	1.3	7	March
April		4	39	10	50	21	69	-5	23		82	73	36	1.4	9	April
May		2	35	7	45	17	63	-9	16		83	76	33	1.3	6	May
June		1	33	5	41	11	52	-12	11		84	80	41	1.6	8	June
July		-1	31	4	40	12	53	-11	12		83	79	28	1.1	6	July
Aug		1	33	6	42	13	55	-9	15		83	77	31	1.2	5	Aug
Sept		2	35	8	46	16	61	-7	19		81	71	23	0.9	5	Sept
Oct		3	38	11	51	19	67	-4	25		75	65	28	1.1	5	Oct
Nov		4	40	12	54	24	76	-5	23		73	65	18	0.7	5	Nov
Dec		6	43	14	57	24	75	-5	23		74	67	36	1.4	8	Dec

Based on readings for 15 years at 53°10′ S, 70°54′ W, altitude 8 m/26 ft

CENTRAL CHILE

Including (with towns and cities in parentheses): all of Chile between about 32° and 38° S (Concepción, Santiago, Valparaíso).

Central Chile has a Mediterranean climate. The summers are virtually rainless and quite warm, while the winter months from April to September are mild and moderately wet with changeable weather. Frost and snow occasionally occur inland but are rare on the coast.

Daily hours of sunshine on the coast average from two to three in winter to eight or nine in summer. Inland, where there is less cloud, this increases to three to four in winter and nine to ten in summer.

The table for **Santiago** (p. 97) is typical of this central portion of Chile.

SOUTHERN CHILE

Including (with towns and cities in parentheses): all of Chile south of about 38° S (Puerto Montt, Puerto Natáles, Punta Arenas, Valdivia) and Tierra del Fuego.

The table for **Valdivia** (opposite) is representative of the north of this area while that for **Punta Arenas** (opposite), on the Strait of Magellan, is representative of the extreme south of the country.

Much of this area is very wet all the year round with much cloud and frequent disturbed, changeable weather. Annual precipitation is 2,500–5,000 mm/ 100–200 in, much of which falls as snow farther south and on the higher mountains. Winters are rarely very cold on the coast but the summers are cool and cloudy. The weather and climate here are very similar to that on the coasts of British Columbia, Alaska, or Norway. Punta Arenas is exceptional in having a very low annual rainfall because it is sheltered from the wet, westerly winds by the southern Andes. The weather and climate here are similar to that of southern Argentina.

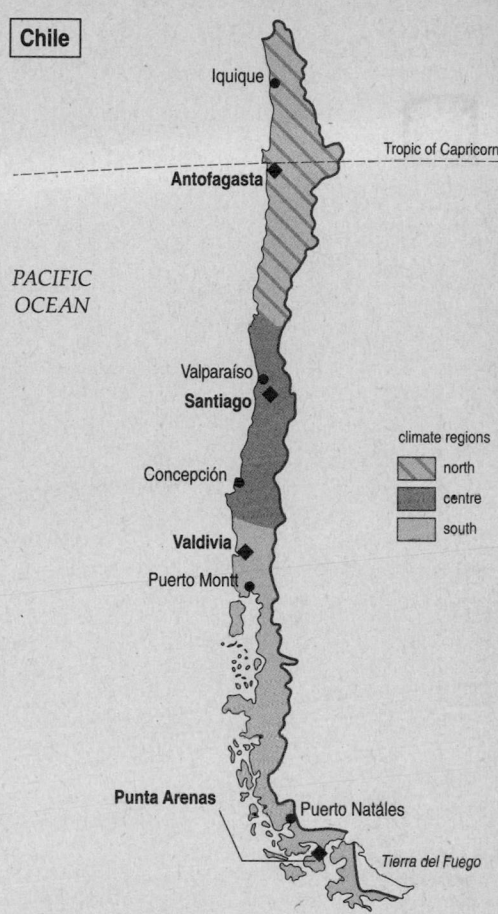

Chile

Iquique

Tropic of Capricorn

Antofagasta

PACIFIC OCEAN

Valparaíso
Santiago

Concepción

climate regions

Valdivia
Puerto Montt

Punta Arenas
Puerto Natáles

Tierra del Fuego

north
centre
south

China

See map overleaf

The vast area of China extends from 53° to 18° N and from 73° to 134° E in central and eastern Asia. It has a range of climates varying from tropical to cold temperate, and from high mountain to desert.

The country is often divided into China proper and the outer territories. China proper consists of the coastal regions fronting the Pacific and the valleys of the three great rivers: Huang He, Chiang Jiang, and Xi Jiang. This is the most productive and populated part of the country. The outer territories consist of Manchuria in the northeast, Inner Mongolia in the north, Xinjiang Uygur in the west, and Tibet in the southwest.

China has a long land border with Kazakhstan and Kyrgyzstan in the north and west, and on the south is bordered by Pakistan, India, Nepal, Myanmar, Laos, and Vietnam. Except in Inner Mongolia and Manchuria, these land borders traverse some of the most mountainous country in the world. This helps to make the climate of most parts of China very

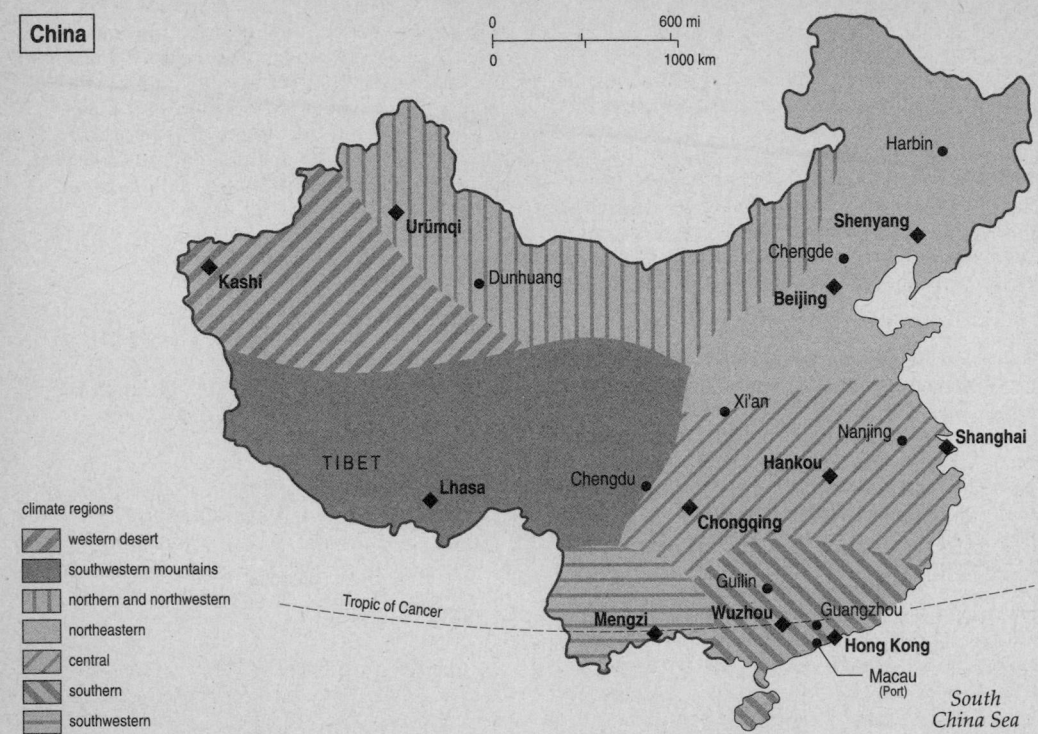

China

climate regions
- western desert
- southwestern mountains
- northern and northwestern
- northeastern
- central
- southern
- southwestern

distinctive and throughout history has also tended to isolate China from outside influences of other kinds.

The climate of China proper and Manchuria is dominated by the great seasonal wind reversal called the Asiatic monsoon. From October until April winds tend to blow out from China and the heart of Asia under the influence of the great high-pressure system which develops in Siberia and central Asia at this time. From May until September or October, as the continent of Asia heats up, this area becomes one of low atmospheric pressure and winds are drawn into much of China, both from the Indian Ocean and the Pacific. These warm, moist winds bring most of the annual rainfall to Manchuria and China proper at this time. Tibet, Xinjiang Uygur, and Inner Mongolia, furthest removed from the influence of the sea, receive much less rain.

The second important control over the climate of China is latitude. While most of the country has warm to hot summers, there is a great difference in winter temperature both from north to south and from the western provinces to the coastal regions. North China, including Manchuria, has extremely cold winters of almost Siberian severity, while Inner Mongolia and Xinjiang Uygur share in this winter cold. Tibet, being a great upland plateau rimmed by

some of the highest mountains in the world, has cool summers and very cold winters.

This monsoonal climate is so characteristic and dominant over most of the country that some climatologists have referred to the 'Chinese type of climate' to indicate a large seasonal range of temperature, a wet summer, and a dry winter. It has been a factor in the cultural unity of China proper. Except in the far north of China and in the outer territories, this warm, wet summer results in rice being the dominant food crop of the country.

This similarity of both cause and effect, however, should not be allowed to hide the fact that there are important differences of weather and climate, both from north to south and from the lowlands and river valleys of China proper to the desert and mountainous regions of the outer provinces. South and central China have a tropical or subtropical climate with no real winter cold, while north China, Manchuria, and the western provinces have a severe winter. Eastern China has abundant summer rain while the northern and western regions contain much desert and semi-desert.

For a more detailed description of the weather and climate, the country is divided into the following major climatic regions: northeast China including Manchuria, central China, south China, southwest China (Yunnan), the southwestern mountains, the western desert, and the north and northwest.

NORTHEASTERN CHINA

Including (with towns and cities in parentheses): the eastern part of INNER MONGOLIA; HEBEI (Beijing, Chengde), MANCHURIA (Shenyang, Harbin), SHANDONG, SHANXI, SHAANXI (Xi'an); and northern HENAN.

The tables for **Shenyang** (below) in Manchuria and for **Beijing** (overleaf) are representative of conditions here. This region broadly consists of the great lowland area of the Huang He valley, part of Inner Mongolia, and the whole of Manchuria. Winters are very cold with frequent light snow and much frost. The strong outblowing winds often raise clouds of dust which are a troublesome feature of the weather.

There is a rapid decrease in both winter and summer temperatures northwards so that in northern Manchuria rivers are frozen for four to six months. The extreme north of Manchuria has a significantly colder summer than Shenyang or Beijing and snow lies for between 100 and 150 days.

Summers are warm and humid over much of north China and may be rather uncomfortable. Summer rainfall is almost everywhere sufficient for cultivation but tends to be unreliable; in some years drought may be a problem. The most unpleasant features of the climate are the summer humidity and the cold, increased by wind chill in winter, so that warm winter clothing is very necessary.

CENTRAL CHINA

Including (with towns and cities in parentheses): southern HENAN; ANHUI (Nanjing), HUBEI (Hankou), JHEJIANG, JIANGSU, SHANGHAI SHI (Shanghai), SHANXI, ZHEJIANG; northern FUJIAN and northern JIANGXI; eastern SICHUAN (Chongqing); and western GUIZHOU.

The tables for **Shanghai** (overleaf) on the Coast and for **Hankou** (p. 103), about 640 km/400 mi inland in the valley of the Chiang Jiang, are representative of the central China region, which has warmer summers and milder winters than northern China.

Although the main rainy season is summer, there is some rain throughout the year and the winter weather is more changeable than in north China. There are periods of wet weather, alternating with

SHENYANG																MANCHURIA
Sunshine		Temperatures							Discomfort from heat and humidity	Precipitation and humidity				Wet days	
		Average daily				Highest recorded		Lowest recorded			Relative humidity		Average monthly precipitation			
		minimum		maximum							6:00	14:00				
average hours per day		°C	°F	°C	°F	°C	°F	°C	°F		%		mm	in	more than 1 mm/0.04 in	
Jan	6	–18	–1	–6	22	7	45	–31	–24		75	48	8	0.3	2	Jan
Feb	7	–14	6	–2	28	11	51	–33	–27		74	44	8	0.3	2	Feb
March	8	–6	21	6	43	19	66	–20	–4		69	37	18	0.7	3	March
April	8	3	37	16	61	30	86	–8	18		64	34	28	1.1	5	April
May	8	10	50	23	74	33	91	1	33		71	40	69	2.7	7	May
June	9	16	61	29	84	39	103	8	46	Medium	75	41	84	3.3	8	June
July	7	21	69	31	87	39	102	14	58	High	87	59	183	7.2	11	July
Aug	7	19	67	29	85	36	96	9	49	Medium	91	57	170	6.7	8	Aug
Sept	8	11	52	24	75	34	93	0	32		88	47	64	2.5	7	Sept
Oct	7	3	38	16	61	27	80	–8	18		81	44	36	1.4	5	Oct
Nov	6	–6	22	5	41	26	78	–26	–15		75	46	28	1.1	4	Nov
Dec	6	–15	5	–4	25	11	52	–29	–20		76	51	15	0.6	3	Dec

Based on readings for 10 years at 41°48′ N, 123°23′ E, altitude 43 m/141 ft

BEIJING

NORTHEASTERN CHINA

	Sunshine average hours per day	Temperatures								Discomfort from heat and humidity	Precipitation and humidity			Wet days more than 0.1 mm/0.004 in	
		Average daily				Highest recorded		Lowest recorded			Relative humidity all hours	Average monthly precipitation			
		minimum		maximum											
		°C	°F	°C	°F	°C	°F	°C	°F		%	mm	in		
Jan	7	−10	14	1	34	14	57	−23	−9		50	4	0.2	3	Jan
Feb	7	−8	18	4	39	19	66	−18	0		50	5	0.2	3	Feb
March	8	−1	30	11	52	28	82	−14	7		48	8	0.3	3	March
April	8	7	45	21	70	36	97	−3	27		46	17	0.7	4	April
May	9	13	55	27	81	38	100	3	37	Moderate	49	35	1.4	6	May
June	9	18	64	31	88	43	109	10	50	High	56	78	3.1	8	June
July	7	21	70	31	88	41	106	15	59	High	72	243	9.6	13	July
Aug	7	20	68	30	86	38	100	11	52	High	74	141	5.6	11	Aug
Sept	8	14	57	26	79	34	93	2	36	Medium	67	58	2.3	7	Sept
Oct	8	6	43	20	68	31	88	−5	23		59	16	0.6	3	Oct
Nov	6	−2	28	9	48	24	75	−13	9		56	11	0.4	3	Nov
Dec	6	−8	18	3	37	13	55	−20	−4		51	3	0.1	2	Dec

Based on readings for 35 years at 39°57′ N, 116°19′ E, altitude 52 m/171 ft

SHANGHAI

CENTRAL CHINA

	Sunshine average hours per day	Temperatures								Discomfort from heat and humidity	Precipitation and humidity				Wet days more than 1 mm/0.04 in	
		Average daily				Highest recorded		Lowest recorded			Relative humidity 6:00 14:00		Average monthly precipitation			
		minimum		maximum												
		°C	°F	°C	°F	°C	°F	°C	°F		%		mm	in		
Jan	4	1	33	8	46	23	74	−12	10		87	58	48	1.9	6	Jan
Feb	4	1	34	8	47	28	83	−8	17		89	60	58	2.3	9	Feb
March	4	4	40	13	55	30	86	−6	21		89	53	84	3.3	9	March
April	5	10	50	19	66	34	93	−1	30		91	58	94	3.7	9	April
May	5	15	59	25	77	36	96	3	37	Moderate	92	56	94	3.7	9	May
June	5	19	67	28	82	39	103	11	51	Medium	94	66	180	7.1	11	June
July	7	23	74	32	90	40	104	16	61	High	93	66	147	5.8	9	July
Aug	7	23	74	32	90	40	104	16	61	High	94	65	142	5.6	9	Aug
Sept	5	19	66	28	82	38	100	7	44	Medium	94	64	130	5.1	11	Sept
Oct	6	14	57	23	74	33	92	1	34		92	53	71	2.8	4	Oct
Nov	5	7	45	17	63	30	86	−5	23		90	55	51	2.0	6	Nov
Dec	5	2	36	12	53	24	75	−10	14		89	62	36	1.4	6	Dec

Based on readings for 38 years at 31°12′ N, 121°26′ E, altitude 7 m/23 ft

HANKOU

CENTRAL CHINA

	Sunshine	Temperatures								Discomfort from heat and humidity	Precipitation and humidity				Wet days	
		Average daily				Highest recorded		Lowest recorded			Relative humidity		Average monthly precipitation			
	average hours per day	minimum		maximum							4:30	12:30				more than
		°C	°F	°C	°F	°C	°F	°C	°F		%		mm	in		1 mm/0.04 in
Jan		1	34	8	46	24	76	–11	13		83	64	46	1.8	6	Jan
Feb		2	36	9	49	22	71	–11	13		85	65	48	1.9	6	Feb
March		6	43	14	57	32	90	–4	24		86	65	97	3.8	10	March
April		13	55	21	69	36	97	0	32		87	61	152	6.0	7	April
May		18	64	26	79	36	96	4	40	Medium	88	61	165	6.5	11	May
June		23	73	31	87	38	100	14	58	High	88	62	244	9.6	10	June
July		26	79	34	93	41	106	16	61	Extreme	88	62	180	7.1	9	July
Aug		26	79	34	93	41	106	16	60	Extreme	86	60	97	3.8	6	Aug
Sept		21	69	29	84	38	101	12	54	Medium	84	57	71	2.8	5	Sept
Oct		16	60	23	73	32	90	2	35		84	55	81	3.2	5	Oct
Nov		9	48	17	62	26	79	–2	28		83	57	48	1.9	5	Nov
Dec		3	38	11	51	22	72	–7	20		82	61	28	1.1	5	Dec

Based on readings for 28 years at 30°35′ N, 114°17′ E, altitude 37 m/121 ft

CHONGQING

CENTRAL CHINA

	Sunshine	Temperatures								Discomfort from heat and humidity	Precipitation and humidity			Wet days	
		Average daily				Highest recorded		Lowest recorded			Relative humidity	Average monthly precipitation			
	average hours per day	minimum		maximum							all hours				more than
		°C	°F	°C	°F	°C	°F	°C	°F		%	mm	in		1 mm/0.04 in
Jan	1	5	41	9	49	20	68	–2	29		87	15	0.6	4	Jan
Feb	2	7	45	13	55	26	79	–1	30		88	20	0.8	4	Feb
March	3	11	52	18	65	40	104	3	37		87	38	1.5	7	March
April	4	16	60	23	73	40	104	7	44	Moderate	86	99	3.9	9	April
May	5	19	67	27	80	40	104	12	54	Medium	87	142	5.6	13	May
June	4	22	72	29	85	39	103	14	58	High	86	180	7.1	11	June
July	7	24	76	34	93	43	110	15	59	Extreme	80	142	5.6	6	July
Aug	6	25	77	35	95	44	111	17	62	Extreme	76	122	4.8	6	Aug
Sept	4	22	71	28	82	40	104	14	57	High	84	150	5.9	11	Sept
Oct	2	16	61	22	71	34	94	8	46	Moderate	88	112	4.4	13	Oct
Nov	2	12	53	16	61	28	83	5	41		91	48	1.9	9	Nov
Dec	2	8	46	13	55	22	72	–1	31		91	20	0.8	6	Dec

Based on readings for 8 years at 29°33′ N, 106°33′ E, altitude 230 m/755 ft

cold spells during which frost and snow occur; snow falls on about five to ten days a year. This variable winter weather is not unlike that experienced in parts of western Europe and the mid-Atlantic states of the USA. It is a consequence of frontal systems and depressions moving from west to east along a zone of convergence between cold Siberian air and warm air from the Pacific.

Summer weather is warm and usually humid because warm, damp air moves in from the Pacific; the heat and humidity are occasionally uncomfortable.

The coastal regions occasionally receive very heavy rainfall from typhoons, or tropical cyclones, which intensify in the South China Sea and move northeastwards along the coast. The very strong winds associated with these disturbances are most severe in the coastal belt.

Farther inland in central China there is a region in the middle and upper Chiang Jiang valley, the basin of Sichuwan, where winters are distinctly milder and summers receive less rain.

This area has a more pleasant climate as winter snow and frost are less frequent and summer humidity is less uncomfortable. The table for **Chongqing** (p. 103) is representative of this mild region.

SOUTHERN CHINA

Including (with towns and cities in parentheses): southern FUJIAN and southern JIANGXI; GUANDONG (Guangzhou), GUANXI ZHUANGZU (Guilin, Wuzhou), HONG KONG, HUNAN, MACAU; and eastern GUIZHOU.

This region is partly within the tropics and is the warmest and wettest part of the country in summer. Between May and September rainfall is very heavy along the coast and abundant inland. Winters are mild and frost almost unknown. The summer heat and humidity can be uncomfortable. Conditions are represented by the table for **Hong Kong** (below) and **Wuzhou** inland (opposite and below). Conditions at Guangzhou and Macau are very similar.

Typhoons are more frequent here and at their most violent and bring very heavy rain and strong winds for a few days at a time to the coastal regions. Typhoons are most frequent from July to October.

Hong Kong consists of one major island, a number of smaller inhabited islands, and a portion of the mainland. Its total area is only 1,013 sq km/391 sq mi. Situated in 22° N, it is just within the tropics and has a similar monsoon climate to that of southern China. Rainfall is particularly heavy from early May

HONG KONG										Discomfort from heat and humidity	Precipitation and humidity				Wet days	
Sunshine		Temperatures									Relative humidity 6:30 12:30		Average monthly precipitation		more than 1 mm/0.04 in	
		Average daily				Highest recorded		Lowest recorded								
		minimum		maximum												
average hours per day		°C	°F	°C	°F	°C	°F	°C	°F		%		mm	in		
Jan	5	13	56	18	64	26	79	0	32		77	66	33	1.3	4	Jan
Feb	4	13	55	17	63	26	79	3	38		82	73	46	1.8	5	Feb
March	3	16	60	19	67	28	83	7	45		84	74	74	2.9	7	March
April	4	19	67	24	75	32	89	11	52	Medium	87	77	137	5.4	8	April
May	5	23	74	28	82	33	91	16	60	Medium	87	78	292	11.5	13	May
June	5	26	78	29	85	34	94	19	67	High	86	77	394	15.5	18	June
July	8	26	78	31	87	34	94	22	72	High	87	77	381	15.0	17	July
Aug	6	26	78	31	87	36	97	22	72	High	87	77	367	14.2	15	Aug
Sept	6	25	77	29	85	34	94	18	65	High	83	72	257	10.1	12	Sept
Oct	7	23	73	27	81	34	94	13	57	Medium	75	63	114	4.5	6	Oct
Nov	7	18	65	23	74	30	86	7	44	Moderate	73	60	43	1.7	2	Nov
Dec	6	15	59	20	68	28	82	5	41		74	63	31	1.2	3	Dec

SOUTHERN CHINA

Based on readings for 50 years at 22°18′ N, 114°10′ E, altitude 33 m/109 ft

until late September, but some rain occurs in all months. Although occasional cold spells, lasting a few days, occur in winter, snow and frost are virtually unknown and the period from October to March is generally warm and dry.

Humidity is high during the hot, wet summer and the weather is often very sultry and oppressive. Particularly between July and September, typhoons, moving northwards from the South China Sea, bring heavy rain and very violent winds which can cause damage to property and loss of life.

Although mainly dry, the months from February to April are cloudy and sunshine then averages only three or four hours a day, as compared with an average of six to eight hours a day during the months July to December.

SOUTHWEST CHINA: YUNNAN

This inland region along the border with Myanmar, Vietnam, and Laos is hilly and mountainous. Summer temperatures are somewhat moderated by altitude. Winters are generally warm to mild with much sunshine and very little rain. Only occasionally does cold air penetrate here from the north, bringing occasional frost at higher levels. Summers are wet at higher levels but in sheltered valleys the rainfall is

not excessive. This region has the most pleasant weather and climate in China around the year (see the table for **Mengzi** overleaf).

THE SOUTHWESTERN MOUNTAINS

Including (with towns and cities in parentheses): western SICHUAN (Chengdu); QUINGHAI and TIBET (Lhasa); and southern and western fringes of XINJIANG UYGUR.

This is a region of high plateaux and encircling mountains, situated in south central China. Its southern boundary includes the highest peaks of the Himalayas, such as Everest. Most of it lies above 3,700 m/12,000 ft, and some extensive areas rise above 4,900 m/16,000 ft. Winters are severe with frequent light snow and hard frost. Considering the altitude, summer temperatures are surprisingly warm in the daytime, but there is a very sharp drop in temperature at night.

Most of the precipitation is rain during the summer, when moist air is drawn into Tibet by the Asian monsoon winds. In the west and north of Tibet some winter precipitation falls as snow; but the permanent snowline is surprisingly high at about

WUZHOU													SOUTHERN CHINA
Sunshine	Temperatures						Discomfort from heat and humidity	Precipitation and humidity				Wet days	
	Average daily		Highest recorded		Lowest recorded			Relative humidity 5:30 13:30		Average monthly precipitation			
	minimum	maximum											
average hours per day	°C °F	°C °F	°C °F		°C °F			%		mm	in	more than 1 mm/0.04 in	
Jan	8 47	16 60	28 83		1 33			79	65	33	1.3	7	Jan
Feb	10 50	17 62	31 87		0 32			83	65	56	2.2	10	Feb
March	14 57	20 68	32 89		4 39			85	69	97	3.8	13	March
April	19 67	25 77	33 92		9 48		Medium	87	77	160	6.3	14	April
May	23 74	29 84	36 96		15 59		High	87	70	206	8.1	16	May
June	25 77	31 87	36 96		19 67		High	89	73	193	7.6	17	June
July	26 78	32 89	38 100		22 72		High	87	69	160	6.3	15	July
Aug	26 79	32 89	38 101		22 72		High	88	66	178	7.0	15	Aug
Sept	24 76	31 87	36 96		17 62		High	83	61	84	3.3	10	Sept
Oct	19 67	27 80	34 94		10 50		Medium	83	62	43	1.7	5	Oct
Nov	15 59	23 74	33 91		6 43		Moderate	81	68	38	1.5	6	Nov
Dec	12 54	19 66	28 83		2 35			78	59	38	1.5	7	Dec

Based on readings for 6 years at 23°38′ N, 111°17′ E, altitude 11 m/35 ft

MENGZI

SOUTHWESTERN CHINA

Sunshine	Temperatures								Discomfort from heat and humidity	Precipitation and humidity			Wet days	
	Average daily				Highest recorded		Lowest recorded			Relative humidity	Average monthly precipitation			
	minimum		maximum							all hours				
average hours per day	°C	°F	°C	°F	°C	°F	°C	°F		%	mm	in	more than 0.25 mm/0.01 in	
Jan	8	46	20	68	29	84	-2	29		55	8	0.3	2	Jan
Feb	9	49	22	71	30	86	0	32		53	18	0.7	5	Feb
March	12	54	25	77	34	93	1	33	Moderate	48	28	1.1	5	March
April	16	60	28	82	36	97	4	39	Medium	50	41	1.6	8	April
May	18	65	29	84	37	98	11	51	Medium	57	127	5.0	12	May
June	19	67	29	84	35	95	13	56	Medium	64	132	5.2	15	June
July	19	67	28	83	35	95	15	59	Medium	69	196	7.7	18	July
Aug	19	67	28	83	37	98	13	56	Medium	70	198	7.8	20	Aug
Sept	18	64	28	82	34	93	10	50	Medium	66	97	3.8	12	Sept
Oct	15	59	24	76	32	90	4	40	Moderate	67	51	2.0	10	Oct
Nov	12	53	22	71	32	89	1	34		67	56	2.2	7	Nov
Dec	8	46	20	68	28	82	-3	26		56	15	0.6	2	Dec

Based on readings for 23 years at 23°30′ N, 103°30′ E, altitude 1250 m/4100 ft

LHASA

TIBET

Sunshine	Temperatures								Discomfort from heat and humidity	Precipitation and humidity			Wet days	
	Average daily				Highest recorded		Lowest recorded			Relative humidity	Average monthly precipitation			
	minimum		maximum							08:30				
average hours per day	°C	°F	°C	°F	°C	°F	°C	°F		%	mm	in	more than 2.5 mm/0.1 in	
Jan	6	-10	14	7	44	16	61	-16	3		71	0	0.0	0.0	Jan
Feb	6	-7	20	9	48	22	72	-15	5		71	13	0.5	0.4	Feb
March	8	-2	28	12	53	21	69	-10	14		72	8	0.3	1.0	March
April	6	1	33	16	60	24	76	-8	18		67	5	0.2	0.4	April
May	5	5	41	19	67	26	79	-3	27		59	25	1.0	3.0	May
June	2	9	49	24	75	32	89	2	36	Moderate	64	64	2.5	8.0	June
July	2	9	49	23	74	29	84	2	35	Moderate	71	122	4.8	13.0	July
Aug	3	9	48	22	72	27	81	3	37		72	89	3.5	10.0	Aug
Sept	5	7	45	21	70	26	78	0	32		71	66	2.6	7.0	Sept
Oct	10	1	34	17	62	23	74	-8	18		64	13	0.5	2.0	Oct
Nov	10	-5	23	13	55	21	69	-12	10		71	3	0.1	0.1	Nov
Dec	9	-9	16	9	48	16	61	-15	5		71	0	0.0	0.0	Dec

Based on readings for 7 years at 29°40′ N, 91°07′ E, altitude 3685 m/12,090 ft

KASHI

WESTERN SINKIANG

Sunshine	Temperatures								Discomfort from heat and humidity	Precipitation and humidity			Wet days
average hours per day	Average daily				Highest recorded		Lowest recorded			Relative humidity 8:00	Average monthly precipitation		more than 2.5 mm/0.1 in
	minimum		maximum										
	°C	°F	°C	°F	°C	°F	°C	°F		%	mm	in	
Jan	−11	12	1	33	11	51	−22	−7		76	15	0.6	1.0	Jan
Feb	−7	19	6	43	17	62	−20	−4		71	3	0.1	0.5	Feb
March	2	35	13	56	26	78	−13	8		57	13	0.5	1.0	March
April	9	48	22	71	34	93	−3	27		47	5	0.2	1.0	April
May	14	58	27	81	36	97	4	39	Moderate	46	8	0.3	1.0	May
June	18	64	32	89	39	102	6	42	Medium	44	5	0.2	1.0	June
July	20	68	33	92	41	106	12	53	High	49	10	0.4	1.0	July
Aug	19	66	32	90	38	101	12	54	High	54	8	0.3	2.0	Aug
Sept	14	57	28	83	37	98	4	39	Medium	55	3	0.1	1.0	Sept
Oct	6	43	22	71	32	89	−2	29		57	3	0.1	0.1	Oct
Nov	−2	29	12	54	21	70	−17	1		67	5	0.2	1.0	Nov
Dec	−8	17	3	38	17	62	−26	−15		79	8	0.3	0.4	Dec

Based on readings for 10 years at 39°24′ N, 76°07′ E, altitude 1309 m/4296 ft

URUMQI

INNER MONGOLIA

Sunshine	Temperatures								Discomfort from heat and humidity	Precipitation and humidity			Wet days
average hours per day	Average daily				Highest recorded		Lowest recorded			Relative humidity	Average monthly precipitation		more than 0.1 mm/0.004 in
	minimum		maximum										
	°C	°F	°C	°F	°C	°F	°C	°F		%	mm	in	
Jan	6	−22	−7	−11	13	1	33	−34	−30			15	0.6	17	Jan
Feb	5	−19	−3	−8	17	1	34	−31	−25			8	0.3	14	Feb
March	6	−11	12	−1	31	19	66	−24	−11			13	0.5	14	March
April	7	2	36	16	60	28	82	−10	14			38	1.5	9	April
May	10	8	47	22	72	32	90	−10	15			28	1.1	5	May
June	9	12	54	26	78	39	103	1	33			38	1.5	11	June
July	9	14	58	28	82	39	103	9	49			18	0.7	5	July
Aug	9	13	56	27	80	44	112	6	42			25	1.0	4	Aug
Sept	9	8	47	21	69	34	93	2	35			15	0.6	4	Sept
Oct	7	−1	31	10	50	26	79	−15	5			43	1.7	10	Oct
Nov	5	−11	13	−1	30	16	60	−33	−27			41	1.6	14	Nov
Dec	5	−13	8	−8	17	3	37	−32	−25			10	0.4	18	Dec

Based on readings for 6 years at 43°45′ N, 87°40′ E, altitude 906 m/2972 ft

6,600 m/20,000 ft. Apart from the low temperatures, strong winds, which accentuate wind chill, are the worst feature of the climate. The table for **Lhasa** (p. 106) shows conditions in the valleys and lower southeastern part of Tibet. For much of the year the air is very clear and sunshine is abundant.

THE WESTERN DESERT

Including (with towns and cities in parentheses): central and southern XINJIANG UYGUR (Kashi).

This remote and sparsely populated region of Central Asia is almost entirely desert. It has a continental type of climate with cold winters and hot summers. The very sparse precipitation is well distributed around the year, with a winter maximum in some places; this is brought by weak depressions moving in from the west. Humidity is low throughout the year and the climate is generally healthy; the principal hazards are very low temperatures accompanied by strong winds in winter and occasional very high temperatures in summer.

Climate varies locally depending on altitude; there are high mountains on the border with Kyrgyzstan and Tibet, but extensive areas of interior lowland. The table for **Kashi** (p. 107) illustrates conditions in the west of Xinjiang Uygur at medium levels.

NORTH AND NORTHWEST CHINA

Including (with towns and cities in parentheses): Western and central INNER MONGOLIA; and GANSU (Dunhuang) and northern XINJIANG UYGUR (Urümqi).

Situated to the north and east of Xinjiang Uygur, this is a region of mountain ranges and extensive semi-desert lowlands. It adjoins central Siberia (see p. 303) and Mongolia (see p. 242). It has an extreme continental type of climate with very cold winters and warm summers. The sparse precipitation is well distributed around the year. The summers are somewhat cooler than Xinjiang Uygur, but winters are even colder, resembling those of Manchuria. The ground is snow-covered for 100–150 days a year. See the table for **Urümqi** (p. 107) and the description of Mongolia on p. 242.

Strong winds in winter and spring often raise great clouds of dust which are blown eastwards into north China. This is one of the more unpleasant features of the climate. The severe winters make warm clothing very necessary and wind chill may increase the feeling of cold. Sunshine amounts vary from five to six hours a day in winter to about nine hours a day in summer.

Colombia

See map page 16

Colombia has a coastline both on the Pacific Ocean and on the Caribbean Sea. It borders Panama on the northwest, Venezuela and Brazil on the east, and Peru and Ecuador on the south. It is about twice as large as France or Texas. Extending between 12° N and 4° S, it experiences a tropical climate, but in the higher parts of the country this is much modified by altitude. There are narrow plains along the coast but inland altitude rises sharply to the high ranges of the Andes. In the east of the country there are extensive lowlands in the forested Amazon basin.

On the Pacific coast, and on the lower slopes of the western Andes, rainfall is almost everywhere over 2,500 mm/100 in and in many places it is more than 5,000 mm/200 in. All months are wet. Temperatures and humidity remain high throughout the year and the climate is generally sultry and oppressive. An unusual feature of this area is the fact that the heaviest rainfall occurs during the night, which is rare for equatorial regions, although there are frequent afternoon thunderstorms.

The table for **Andagoya** (opposite and above) is typical of the lower slopes of the western Andes.

On the Caribbean coast it is not so wet. There is a drier period from December to March. The area is also hot and humid. In the east, near the Venezuelan border, annual rainfall is low for a tropical coastland.

Most of central Colombia is mountainous; the higher Andean peaks rise to over 5,500 m/18,000 ft. Large rivers, the Magdelena and the Cauca, flow northwards in wide valleys between a series of mountain ranges. There are considerable differences of temperature depending on altitude. The mountains above 4,500 m/15,000 ft receive most of their precipitation as snow. The whole region receives abundant precipitation of between 1,000–2,500 mm/40–100 in a year, and this is well distributed throughout the year with no real dry season. The western ranges are wetter than those to the east. The threefold division into *tierra caliente*, *tierra templada*, and *tierra fria*, as described for Bolivia on p. 66, is equally true for Colombia. The table for **Bogotá** (opposite) is typical of conditions

ANDAGOYA

PACIFIC COLOMBIA

	Sunshine	Temperatures								Discomfort from heat and humidity	Precipitation and humidity			Wet days	
	average hours per day	Average daily				Highest recorded		Lowest recorded			Relative humidity	Average monthly precipitation		more than 0.25 mm/0.01 in	
		minimum		maximum											
		°C	°F	°C	°F	°C	°F	°C	°F		%	mm	in		
Jan		24	75	32	90	35	95	20	68			635	25.0	26	Jan
Feb		24	75	32	89	36	96	21	69			544	21.4	21	Feb
March		24	75	32	90	36	96	21	69			495	19.5	23	March
April		24	75	32	90	36	96	21	69			663	26.1	25	April
May		24	75	32	89	36	96	21	70			647	25.5	26	May
June		23	74	32	89	34	94	20	68			655	25.8	25	June
July		23	74	32	89	36	96	21	69			592	23.3	27	July
Aug		23	74	32	89	35	95	21	70			592	23.3	27	Aug
Sept		23	74	32	90	35	95	21	70			625	24.6	27	Sept
Oct		23	74	32	90	36	97	17	62			577	22.7	25	Oct
Nov		23	74	31	88	35	95	19	66			569	22.4	27	Nov
Dec		23	74	31	88	35	95	21	70			495	19.5	27	Dec

Based on readings for 8 years at 5°06′ N, 74°40′ W, altitude 60 m/197 ft

BOGOTA

CENTRAL HIGHLAND COLOMBIA

	Sunshine	Temperatures								Discomfort from heat and humidity	Precipitation and humidity				Wet days	
	average hours per day	Average daily				Highest recorded		Lowest recorded			Relative humidity		Average monthly precipitation		more than 0.25 mm/0.01 in	
		minimum		maximum							6:00	14:00				
		°C	°F	°C	°F	°C	°F	°C	°F		%		mm	in		
Jan	6	9	48	19	67	23	74	4	40		84	51	58	2.3	6	Jan
Feb	5	9	49	20	68	24	75	6	42		83	53	66	2.6	7	Feb
March	4	10	50	19	67	24	75	6	42		83	54	102	4.0	13	March
April	3	11	51	19	67	24	75	7	45		84	57	147	5.8	20	April
May	3	11	51	19	66	23	74	7	45		85	58	114	4.5	17	May
June	4	11	51	18	65	22	72	7	44		85	56	61	2.4	16	June
July	4	10	50	18	64	22	72	7	44		83	56	51	2.0	18	July
Aug	4	10	50	18	65	22	72	7	44		83	54	56	2.2	16	Aug
Sept	4	9	49	19	66	23	73	7	44		82	54	61	2.4	13	Sept
Oct	3	10	50	19	66	23	73	6	43		86	61	160	6.3	20	Oct
Nov	4	10	50	19	66	23	73	7	44		88	64	119	4.7	16	Nov
Dec	5	9	49	19	66	23	73	4	40		85	56	66	2.6	15	Dec

Based on readings for 10 years at 4°36′ N, 74°05′ W, altitude 2645 m/8678 ft

in the higher *tierra fria* zone. Here the weather and climate are truly those of 'perpetual spring', as understood in temperate latitudes.

Nights are cool but never really cold, and at this height frost is unknown. The days feel warm in the sun but are never really hot. Rain and afternoon cloud are frequent. Sunshine averages from three to five hours a day throughout the year. At lower levels, and in the drier valleys, sunshine is rather more, from six to seven hours a day.

The lowland in the east of the country is sparsely populated and as yet largely undeveloped. Climate here is hot throughout the year and wet weather is frequent, with an annual rainfall of 2,000–2,500 mm/80–100 in.

As in other parts of the northern Amazon basin, there are two relatively wetter periods: December to January and April to May. The table for **Manaus** in Brazil (p. 80) is representative of this wet equatorial lowland.

Comoros

See map page 21

This Indian Ocean republic is a group of volcanic islands lying at the northern end of the Mozambique

channel between Madagascar and Africa. The climate is warm but not excessively hot. A dry season occurs from May to October, the other months being rainy. The table for **Moroni** (opposite) shows weather typical of the Comoros.

Congo Republic

See map page 21

The Congo Republic, formerly a French colony, should not be confused with the larger neighbouring country of the Congo Democratic Republic (formerly Zaïre). The Congo Republic lies between 4° N and 5° S in central Africa and has the river Congo and its tributary the Ubangui as its southeastern border with the Congo Democratic Republic. It is a little larger than the United Kingdom but sparsely populated. Most of the country is a low plateau between 200 m/650 ft and 1,000 m/3,250 ft above sea level. There is a low coastal plain on the Atlantic coast. The weather and

climate of the country are similar to those described in more detail for the Congo Democratic Republic on p. 112.

Annual rainfall is almost everywhere between 1,250 mm/50 in and 1,750 mm/70 in and is well distributed around the year. Rainfall is least in the south of the country and along the coast. The table for **Brazzaville** (opposite) is representative of the south of the country. This shows a distinct dry season between June and September when the sun and the intertropical rain-belt are farthest north; there is a second but brief drier period in January when the rain-belt is farthest south.

MORONI — THE COMOROS

Sunshine	Temperatures								Discomfort from heat and humidity	Precipitation and humidity		Wet days	
average hours per day	Average daily				Highest recorded		Lowest recorded			Relative humidity	Average monthly precipitation	more than 0.1 mm/0.04 in	
	minimum		maximum										
	°C	°F	°C	°F	°C	°F	°C	°F		%	mm	in	
Jan 6	23	73	30	86	34	93	20	68			345	13.6	18 Jan
Feb 6	23	73	30	87	34	93	20	68			311	12.2	17 Feb
March 7	23	73	31	87	35	94	20	68			300	11.8	17 March
April 6	23	73	30	87	34	93	20	68			296	11.7	19 April
May 7	21	70	29	85	33	92	17	63			233	9.2	13 May
June 8	20	68	28	83	32	89	14	57			215	8.5	12 June
July 8	19	66	28	82	31	88	14	56			194	7.6	12 July
Aug 7	19	66	27	81	31	88	14	57			118	4.6	11 Aug
Sept 7	19	66	28	82	31	88	15	59			117	4.6	11 Sept
Oct 8	20	68	29	84	33	92	16	60			91	3.6	12 Oct
Nov 8	22	72	31	87	34	94	18	65			102	4	12 Nov
Dec 7	23	73	31	87	36	96	19	66			220	8.7	16 Dec

Based on readings for 29 years at 11°42′ S, 43°14′ E, altitude 12 m/39 ft

BRAZZAVILLE — SOUTHERN CONGO REPUBLIC

Sunshine	Temperatures								Discomfort from heat and humidity	Precipitation and humidity			Wet days	
average hours per day	Average daily				Highest recorded		Lowest recorded			Relative humidity		Average monthly precipitation	more than 10 mm/0.4 in	
	minimum		maximum							8:00	16:00			
	°C	°F	°C	°F	°C	°F	°C	°F		%		mm	in	
Jan 5	21	69	31	88	34	94	18	64	High	86	65	160	6.3	2 Jan
Feb 5	21	70	32	89	35	95	17	63	High	86	66	125	4.9	5 Feb
March 5	21	70	33	91	37	98	18	65	High	86	65	188	7.4	6 March
April 6	22	71	33	91	35	95	19	67	High	87	65	178	7.0	6 April
May 5	21	70	32	89	36	96	17	63	High	89	69	109	4.3	4 May
June 5	18	65	29	84	34	93	13	56	Medium	88	67	15	0.6	0 June
July 4	17	63	28	82	32	89	12	54	Medium	86	60	0	0.0	0 July
Aug 5	18	65	29	85	34	93	13	55	Medium	79	56	0	0.0	0 Aug
Sept 4	20	68	31	88	35	95	16	61	Medium	77	54	56	2.2	1 Sept
Oct 5	21	70	32	89	36	97	17	63	High	80	61	137	5.4	5 Oct
Nov 5	21	70	31	88	36	97	18	65	High	87	69	292	11.5	9 Nov
Dec 5	21	70	31	87	35	95	18	64	High	87	71	213	8.4	5 Dec

Based on readings for 7 years at 4°15′ S, 15°15′ E, altitude 318 m/1043 ft

Congo Democratic Republic

See map page 21

Including a description of the climate and weather of central Africa: Cameroon, Central African Republic, Congo, Gabon, and Equatorial Guinea.

These six countries occupy an area of about 3.9 million sq km/1.5 million sq mi – almost half the area of Brazil or the United States. The countries extend almost equal distances on either side of the equator from 13° N to 13° S. A large part of the region consists of the basin of the Congo river and its numerous tributaries, and lies 300–600 m/1,000–3,000 ft above sea level.

The land rises on the Congo Democratic Republic's southern border with Angola; along its northeastern border with Uganda, Rwanda, and Burundi there is a mountain range with peaks such as Ruwenzori rising to between 4,500 m/14,500 ft and 5,100 m/16,500 ft. There are also some high, isolated mountain peaks in Cameroon. Only in these high mountain regions are temperatures significantly below tropical levels; snow may fall on the summits of the mountains.

With the exception of the high mountains, the region has an equatorial or tropical climate. The central part of the region, roughly between 4° N and the equator, has rain around the year with two periods when rain is heaviest and most probable. On either side of this typical equatorial rainfall area there are districts where rainfall is concentrated into a single rainy season at the time of high sun; there is a marked dry season at the time of low sun.

The double wet season with some rain in all months is well illustrated by the table for **Kisangani** (below) in the north-central part of the Congo Democratic Republic; it is almost on the equator. The single wet season with a pronounced dry season is illustrated by the table for **Lubumbashi** (opposite and below) at 12° S in the south of the Congo Democratic Republic. In the northern parts of Cameroon and the Central African Republic there is also a single rainy season, as found in northern Nigeria and Chad, when the sun is north of the equator between March and September.

The annual rainfall is moderately high over the whole of this large area, ranging from 1,200 mm/

KISANGANI										EQUATORIAL CONGO DEMOCRATIC REPUBLIC					
Sunshine		Temperatures								Discomfort from heat and humidity	Precipitation and humidity				Wet days
		Average daily				Highest recorded		Lowest recorded			Relative humidity 5:30 11:30		Average monthly precipitation		
		minimum		maximum											
average hours per day		°C	°F	°C	°F	°C	°F	°C	°F		%		mm	in	more than 0.1 mm/0.004 in
Jan	6	21	69	31	88	36	97	17	63	High	97	66	53	2.1	6	Jan
Feb	6	21	69	31	88	36	97	18	65	High	97	63	84	3.3	9	Feb
March	6	21	69	31	88	36	96	17	62	High	96	64	178	7.0	11	March
April	6	21	70	31	88	35	95	18	64	High	97	68	158	6.2	10	April
May	6	21	69	31	87	34	94	18	65	High	97	69	137	5.4	10	May
June	5	21	69	30	86	34	93	18	64	High	97	71	114	4.5	9	June
July	4	19	67	29	84	33	92	17	63	High	97	72	132	5.2	10	July
Aug	4	20	68	28	83	33	92	17	63	Medium	97	75	165	6.5	11	Aug
Sept	5	20	68	29	85	34	93	17	62	Medium	97	69	183	7.2	13	Sept
Oct	6	20	68	30	86	34	93	18	64	High	97	70	218	8.6	14	Oct
Nov	5	20	68	29	85	35	95	18	64	Medium	97	67	198	7.8	15	Nov
Dec	5	20	68	30	86	35	95	16	61	High	95	60	84	3.3	10	Dec

Based on readings for 9 years at 0°26′ N, 25°14′ E, altitude 418 m/1370 ft

48 in to 2,000 mm/80 in. The only districts where rainfall is less than this is on the coast near the mouth of the Congo river and in the extreme northern and southern fringes of the region. In small parts of the region, on the western side of the Cameroon mountains and on the mountains near the eastern border of the Congo Democratic Republic, annual rainfall is significantly greater.

This is a region where temperatures remain high throughout the year. At lower levels near the equator they rarely fall below 18° C/64° F, even at night. Daytime maximum temperatures, however, rarely rise above 35° C/95° F. Humidity remains high throughout the year and rarely falls very low during the hottest part of the day, so that the weather feels sultry and oppressive most of the time. Except during occasional thunder squalls, winds are light so that the temperature feels higher than the thermometer might suggest. Temperatures rise higher during the daytime in those areas where there is a pronounced dry season; at this time humidity is also lower and these higher temperatures may not feel so oppressive as the lower temperatures during the wet season when there is higher humidity, much cloud, and little sunshine.

Temperatures are reduced by the effect of altitude in the mountain areas of Cameroon and the eastern

Congo Democratic Republic, but these areas have much cloud, high humidity, less sun, and frequent heavy rain so that the climate is rather monotonous and unpleasant except during the brief spells of dry, clear, and sunny weather. Over much of this region of central Africa the very monotony of the weather and the absence of any great seasonal contrast have an enervating and depressing effect. It has been said that 'night is the winter of the Tropics' and that in these areas 'there is no weather only climate'. While these are perhaps overstatements, there is certainly truth in them.

The Congo Democratic Republic is the largest country in the region and amounts to over half the total area. It is almost entirely landlocked, with only a very short coastal strip on the Atlantic around the mouth of the Congo, between the Congo Republic (Brazzaville) and Angola. This small area is affected by the same relative dryness that is typical of coastal Angola. Rainfall increases inland. The climate of much of the central Congo Democratic Republic are represented by the table for **Kisangani** (opposite). The table for **Kinshasa** (overleaf) at 4° S shows a distribution of rainfall around the year more typical of the districts south of the equator; there is a single, long wet season with a short dry season from June to September when the sun is north of the equator. The table for **Lubumbashi** (below) situated at 12°

LUBUMBASHI										SOUTHERN CONGO DEMOCRATIC REPUBLIC				
Sunshine	Temperatures								Discomfort from heat and humidity	Precipitation and humidity				Wet days
	Average daily				Highest recorded		Lowest recorded			Relative humidity		Average monthly precipitation		
	minimum		maximum							8:00 12:00				
average hours per day	°C	°F	°C	°F	°C	°F	°C	°F		%		mm	in	more than 0.1 mm/0.004 in
Jan	4	16	61	28	82	33	91	10	50	Medium	91	50	267	10.5	25.0	Jan
Feb	4	17	62	28	82	32	90	12	54	Medium	90	54	244	9.6	24.0	Feb
March	5	16	61	28	82	34	93	8	46	Medium	93	46	213	8.4	22.0	March
April	8	14	57	28	82	32	90	5	41	Medium	90	41	56	2.2	12.0	April
May	9	10	50	27	81	32	89	3	38	Moderate	89	38	5	0.2	2.0	May
June	10	7	44	26	79	30	86	1	34	Moderate	86	34	0	0.0	0.0	June
July	10	6	43	26	79	32	89	1	33	Moderate	89	33	0	0.0	0.0	July
Aug	10	8	46	28	83	34	94	1	33	Moderate	94	33	0	0.0	0.3	Aug
Sept	10	11	52	32	89	37	99	3	37	Medium	99	37	3	0.1	1.0	Sept
Oct	9	14	58	33	91	37	98	7	45	High	98	45	31	1.2	6.0	Oct
Nov	6	16	61	31	87	36	97	10	50	Medium	97	50	150	5.9	18.0	Nov
Dec	4	17	62	28	82	34	93	12	54	Medium	93	54	269	10.6	25.0	Dec

Based on readings for 13 years at 11°39′ S, 27°28′ E, altitude 1230 m/4035 ft

KINSHASA										WESTERN CONGO DEMOCRATIC REPUBLIC			
Sunshine		Temperatures						Discomfort from heat and humidity	Precipitation and humidity				Wet days
		Average daily		Highest recorded		Lowest recorded			Relative humidity 6:00 12:00		Average monthly precipitation		
average hours per day		minimum	maximum										more than 0.1 mm/0.004 in
		°C	°F	°C	°F	°C	°F	°C	°F		%	mm	in	
Jan	4	21	70	31	87	36	96	18	64	High	94	72	135	5.3	11.0	Jan
Feb	5	22	71	31	88	36	97	18	64	High	94	71	145	5.7	11.0	Feb
March	5	22	71	32	89	36	97	18	64	High	94	71	196	7.7	12.0	March
April	5	22	71	32	89	36	97	19	67	High	95	70	196	7.7	16.0	April
May	5	22	71	31	88	35	95	18	64	High	95	73	159	6.2	12.0	May
June	4	19	67	29	84	34	93	15	59	High	94	71	8	0.3	1.0	June
July	4	18	64	27	81	32	90	14	58	Medium	93	67	3	0.1	0.1	July
Aug	5	18	65	29	84	35	95	14	58	Medium	89	61	3	0.1	0.6	Aug
Sept	4	20	68	31	87	36	96	16	61	High	88	61	30	1.2	5.0	Sept
Oct	5	21	70	31	88	36	97	15	59	High	92	66	119	4.7	11.0	Oct
Nov	5	22	71	31	87	34	94	17	62	High	94	71	222	8.7	16.0	Nov
Dec	4	21	70	30	86	36	97	17	63	High	94	73	142	5.6	15.0	Dec

Based on readings for 8 years at 4°20′ S, 15°18′ E, altitude 322 m/1066 ft

S and at an altitude of 1,300 m/4,260 ft shows a prolonged dry season between May and October during which the night-time temperatures fall much lower then elsewhere. There is rather more sunshine here, particularly during the dry season. Rainfall is lower during the rainy season, so that the climate is more like that found in the neighbouring regions of Zambia and Angola. Here the average number of sunshine hours a day ranges from four to five in the wet season to nine to ten in the dry season. This is a greater variation and a larger number of hours of sunshine a year than occurs almost anywhere else in the Congo Democratic Republic, and much more than in the consistently wet regions.

Cook Islands

See map page 17

This South Pacific territory – self-governing in association with New Zealand – comprises 15 islands scattered through an expanse of ocean between Samoa in the west and French Polynesia in the east.

The weather and climate are typical of a tropical oceanic environment. Very similar conditions prevail throughout the year, with high temperatures and humidity. The daily range of temperature is quite small – about 4°–5° C/10° F. There is abundant rainfall. Being south of the equator, the Cook Islands have their season of maximum rainfall between November and March or April. Rainfall is moderate to heavy and occurs in all months.

Tropical storms of the cyclone or typhoon type are less frequent here than in the western Pacific, but do occur occasionally. Weather can be quite variable from day to day. Periods of continuous rain lasting a day or more are not unusual, but much rain comes in heavy afternoon or evening downpours after an otherwise fine, sunny day.

The climate is generally healthy and pleasant; the moderately high temperature and humidity are tempered by brisk daytime winds, either as afternoon sea breezes or as predominant southeast trade winds.

The tables for **Papeete** (p. 149) on Tahiti and **Apia** (p. 309) in Samoa are representative of weather in the Cook Islands.

SAN JOSE

INLAND COSTA RICA

	Sunshine	Temperatures								Discomfort from heat and humidity	Precipitation and humidity				Wet days	
		Average daily				Highest recorded		Lowest recorded			Relative humidity 6:30 13:30		Average monthly precipitation			
		minimum		maximum												
	average hours per day	°C	°F	°C	°F	°C	°F	°C	°F		%		mm	in	more than 0.1 mm/0.004 in	
Jan	7	14	58	24	75	31	87	9	49	Moderate	83	63	15	0.6	3	Jan
Feb	8	14	58	24	76	31	88	11	51	Moderate	82	57	5	0.2	1	Feb
March	8	15	59	26	79	33	91	10	50	Moderate	81	55	20	0.8	2	March
April	7	17	62	26	79	32	89	12	53	Medium	80	60	46	1.8	7	April
May	5	17	62	27	80	31	88	12	54	Medium	85	70	229	9.0	19	May
June	4	17	62	26	79	33	92	14	57	Medium	91	74	241	9.5	22	June
July	4	17	62	25	77	29	84	12	54	Medium	89	74	211	8.3	23	July
Aug	4	16	61	26	78	29	85	13	56	Medium	89	73	241	9.5	24	Aug
Sept	5	16	61	26	79	30	86	13	56	Medium	91	76	305	12.0	24	Sept
Oct	4	16	60	25	77	29	85	13	55	Medium	92	78	300	11.8	25	Oct
Nov	5	16	60	25	77	29	84	11	52	Medium	87	71	145	5.7	14	Nov
Dec	6	14	58	24	75	31	87	9	49	Moderate	85	67	41	1.6	6	Dec

Based on readings for 8 years at 9°56′ N, 84°08′ W, altitude 1146 m/3760 ft

Costa Rica

See map page 14

This small Central American country is situated between 8° and 11° N and has a border with Panama on the south and with Nicaragua on the north. It is about twice the size of Wales or the state of Massachusetts.

The general conditions of weather and climate in this region are described in detail for Panama (pp. 278–80). Like other countries of Central America, Costa Rica is mountainous with the highest peaks exceeding 3,700 m/12,000 ft. It has a coastline on both the Pacific and the Caribbean.

The table for the capital, **San José** (above), illustrates conditions in the *tierra templada*, where the nights are much cooler than at sea level and the days less hot and humid. Conditions at sea level on the Pacific shore are similar to those shown in the table for **Balboe Heights** (p. 279) in Panama. The Caribbean shore to the east is equally hot and rather wetter.

ABIDJAN												COASTAL COTE D'IVOIRE	
Sunshine		Temperatures						Discomfort from heat and humidity	Precipitation and humidity				Wet days
		Average daily		Highest recorded		Lowest recorded			Relative humidity 5:30 11:30		Average monthly precipitation		
average hours per day		minimum	maximum										more than 1 mm/0.04 in
		°C	°F	°C	°F	°C	°F	°C	°F		%	mm	in	
Jan	6	23	73	31	88	34	94	15	59	High	96	73	41	1.6	3	Jan
Feb	7	24	75	32	90	35	95	18	64	High	94	71	53	2.1	4	Feb
March	7	24	75	32	90	36	96	19	67	High	94	72	99	3.9	6	March
April	7	24	75	32	90	35	95	20	68	High	93	72	125	4.9	9	April
May	6	24	75	31	88	34	94	20	68	High	94	76	361	14.2	16	May
June	4	23	73	29	85	34	93	20	68	High	95	82	495	19.5	18	June
July	4	23	73	28	83	33	91	18	64	Medium	93	78	213	8.4	8	July
Aug	4	22	71	28	82	31	88	17	63	Medium	95	79	53	2.1	7	Aug
Sept	4	23	73	28	83	32	90	18	65	High	95	80	71	2.8	8	Sept
Oct	6	23	74	29	85	33	92	19	67	High	94	79	168	6.6	13	Oct
Nov	7	23	74	31	87	34	94	19	67	High	94	73	201	7.9	13	Nov
Dec	7	23	74	31	88	35	95	17	62	High	96	72	79	3.1	6	Dec

Based on readings for 13 years at 5°19' N, 4°01' W, altitude 20 m/65 ft

Côte d'Ivoire

See map page 20

Côte d'Ivoire is situated in West Africa with a coastline on the Gulf of Guinea between Liberia on the west and Ghana on the east. It extends between 4° and 10° N. It shares the same climatic belts and sequence of weather around the year as that described on p. 266 for Nigeria. The coastal region has two rainy seasons, one peaking in May or June, the other in October, but in the north there is a single rainy season starting in May or June.

The climate of the coastal region is represented by the table for **Abidjan** (above) which is wetter than **Accra** (p. 161) in Ghana. Abidjan has a climate very similar to that of **Lagos** (p. 267) in Nigeria. On the coast the period from December to February is least likely to experience rainy days.

Rainfall becomes progressively less inland and there the two separate rainy seasons of the coast merge into a single wet season; there is a much longer dry season at the time of low sun. At this time temperatures are warm to hot with a very low relative humidity, and the dust-laden harmattan wind blows from the northeast. From December to February the harmattan affects the whole country, except a strip along the coast. These dry southwesterly winds reach right to the coast on only a few days.

Conditions in the north of the country are well represented by the climatic tables for **Tamale** (p. 161) in Ghana or **Kano** (p. 266) in Nigeria.

DUBROVNIK

CROATIA

Sunshine	Temperatures								Discomfort from heat and humidity	Precipitation and humidity				Wet days
	Average daily				Highest recorded		Lowest recorded			Relative humidity		Average monthly precipitation		
	minimum		maximum							7:00	14:00			
average hours per day	°C	°F	°C	°F	°C	°F	°C	°F		%		mm	in	more than 0.1 mm/0.004 in
Jan 4	6	42	12	53	19	66	-7	19		63	59	139	5.5	13 Jan
Feb 5	6	43	13	55	21	69	-5	24		65	63	125	4.9	13 Feb
March 5	8	47	14	58	23	73	-2	29		64	63	104	4.1	11 March
April 6	11	52	17	63	26	80	3	37		67	66	104	4.1	10 April
May 8	14	58	21	70	29	84	6	44		69	69	75	3.0	10 May
June 10	18	65	25	78	34	93	11	52	Moderate	64	66	48	1.9	6 June
July 12	21	69	29	83	37	99	15	58	Medium	67	61	26	1.0	4 July
Aug 11	21	69	28	82	37	98	11	52	Medium	57	61	38	1.5	3 Aug
Sept 9	18	64	25	77	34	94	9	49	Moderate	63	63	101	4.0	7 Sept
Oct 7	14	57	21	69	28	82	6	42		64	63	162	6.4	11 Oct
Nov 4	10	51	17	62	24	76	-3	27		67	65	198	7.8	16 Nov
Dec 3	8	46	14	56	19	67	-4	26		67	65	178	7.0	15 Dec

Based on readings for 19 years at 42°39′ N, 18°06′ E, altitude 49 m/161 ft

Croatia

See map page 18–19

The part of Croatia that is best known and most visited by tourists is the Dalmatian coast and its offshore islands in the Adriatic Sea. This region has a Mediterranean type of climate with mild winters and warm, sunny summers. The coast is backed by the high mountains of the Dinaric Alps, rising to 1,200–1,800 m/4,000–6,000 ft. Winter rainfall here is heavy. The table for **Dubrovnik** (above) is characteristic of weather on the Dalmatian coast of Croatia.

An unpleasant feature of the winter weather is a cold gusty wind, the *bora*, which brings cold air from central and eastern Europe down to the coast for a few days at a time; it blows particularly violently in the north of the Adriatic. Summers on this coast are not entirely rainless, and the fine, sunny weather is often interrupted by thunderstorms. Sunshine averages some four hours a day in winter and from ten to twelve hours a day in summer.

Inland climatic conditions rapidly become more typical of eastern Europe with cold winters and warm summers; summer here is the wettest season. Much of inland Croatia is mountainous or hilly, and winter snow lies for long periods in the higher regions. The table for **Sarajevo** (p. 67) in Bosnia-Herzegovina shows conditions that are also typical of the more mountainous parts of Croatia. Eastern Croatia includes much low-lying land in the valleys of the Danube, Drave, and Save; winters are rather cold and rainfall lower. The table for **Belgrade** (p. 424) in Serbia represents similar conditions.

HAVANA										NORTHERN CUBA	
Sunshine	Temperatures						Discomfort from heat and humidity	Precipitation and humidity			Wet days
average hours per day	Average daily		Highest recorded		Lowest recorded			Relative humidity 5:30 11:30		Average monthly precipitation	more than 1 mm/0.04 in
	minimum	maximum									
	°C	°F	°C	°F	°C	°F	°C	°F		%	mm	in	
Jan	6	18	65	26	79	32	89	10	50	Medium	85	64	71	2.8	6	Jan
Feb	6	18	65	26	79	33	91	10	50	Medium	85	61	46	1.8	4	Feb
March	7	19	67	27	81	33	91	12	53	Medium	84	58	46	1.8	4	March
April	7	21	69	29	84	34	94	13	55	Medium	83	58	58	2.3	4	April
May	8	22	72	30	86	34	94	15	59	High	85	62	119	4.7	7	May
June	6	23	74	31	88	36	96	19	66	High	87	65	165	6.5	10	June
July	6	24	75	32	89	34	93	19	66	High	87	62	125	4.9	9	July
Aug	6	24	75	32	89	35	95	20	68	High	88	64	135	5.3	10	Aug
Sept	5	24	75	31	88	34	94	19	67	High	89	66	150	5.9	11	Sept
Oct	5	23	73	29	85	34	94	17	63	Medium	87	68	173	6.8	11	Oct
Nov	5	21	69	27	81	33	91	13	55	Medium	85	65	79	3.1	7	Nov
Dec	5	19	67	26	79	32	89	11	51	Medium	84	64	58	2.3	6	Dec

Based on readings for 25 years at 23°08′ N, 82°21′ W, altitude 24 m/80 ft

Cuba

See map page 15

Cuba is the largest of the islands of the Caribbean. It is about as large as the state of Pennsylvania and a little smaller than England. It extends for a distance of almost 110 km/700 mi. Although there are mountains rising to 900–1,800 m/3,000–6,000 ft, much of the island is low-lying. The table for **Havana** (above) is representative of the low-lying parts on the north of the island. Rainfall on the north coast is rather more than in the south and the hills may receive over 2,500 mm/100 in a year.

The drier region of the island is in the southeast around Guantánamo, where rain is as low as 500 mm/20 in a year. Western Cuba is occasionally affected in winter and spring by waves of cold air from the interior of North America. Temperatures can drop below 10° C/50° F for a day or two. Such low temperatures are unusual for the Caribbean.

Cyprus

See map page 22

Cyprus is the largest island in the eastern Mediterranean. It has a typical Mediterranean climate but its proximity to the land-mass of southwest Asia makes it one of the hottest parts of the Mediterranean in midsummer. This applies particularly to the central plain and the coastal regions. The island is mountainous and the two main mountain masses, the Kyrenia range in the north and the Troödos Mountains rising to nearly 2,000 m/over 6,000 ft, have a cooler and wetter climate which supports excellent pine forests.

Summers are hot or warm, depending on altitude, and almost completely rainless from late May to mid-September. During this period the weather is constant from day to day and almost completely cloudless. The rest of the year is more changeable, with the heaviest rainfall and greatest chance of

KYRENIA — COASTAL CYPRUS

	Sunshine average hours per day	Average daily minimum °C	°F	Average daily maximum °C	°F	Highest recorded °C	°F	Lowest recorded °C	°F	Discomfort from heat and humidity	Relative humidity 8:00 %	14:00 %	Average monthly precipitation mm	in	Wet days more than 0.2mm/0.008in	
Jan		9	48	16	62	24	76	-4	25		75	70	117	4.6	13	Jan
Feb		9	48	17	62	23	73	-1	31		74	67	79	3.1	10	Feb
March		10	49	19	65	27	81	2	35		70	67	60	2.4	7	March
April		12	53	22	71	31	87	3	37		70	68	20	0.8	4	April
May		16	60	26	78	36	97	6	43	Medium	68	68	13	0.5	2	May
June		20	67	30	86	41	106	11	52	High	68	65	2	0.1	0	June
July		22	72	33	91	41	105	13	55	High	64	62	0	0.0	0	July
Aug		23	73	33	92	42	107	14	57	High	65	60	0	0.0	0	Aug
Sept		21	69	31	87	39	103	13	56	High	65	60	5	0.2	1	Sept
Oct		17	63	27	81	36	97	11	51	Medium	67	62	37	1.5	3	Oct
Nov		14	58	23	73	32	90	4	40	Moderate	73	66	68	2.7	7	Nov
Dec		11	52	18	65	24	75	1	34		75	69	133	5.2	11	Dec

Based on readings for 26 years at 35°20' N, 33°19' E, altitude 20 m/66 ft

NICOSIA — LOWLAND INTERIOR CYPRUS

	Sunshine average hours per day	Average daily minimum °C	°F	Average daily maximum °C	°F	Highest recorded °C	°F	Lowest recorded °C	°F	Discomfort from heat and humidity	Relative humidity 8:00 %	14:00 %	Average monthly precipitation mm	in	Wet days more than 0.2mm/0.008in	
Jan	5	5	42	15	59	22	71	-3	26		83	66	76	3.0	14	Jan
Feb	7	5	42	16	61	26	79	-6	22		80	61	45	1.8	10	Feb
March	7	7	44	19	66	30	86	-2	29		73	55	36	1.4	8	March
April	9	10	50	24	75	35	95	1	34		64	46	18	0.7	4	April
May	11	14	58	29	85	43	109	7	45	Medium	55	41	22	0.9	3	May
June	13	18	65	34	92	44	111	11	51	High	52	37	9	0.4	1	June
July	13	21	70	37	98	44	111	15	59	High	51	34	1	0.0	0	July
Aug	12	21	69	37	98	44	112	14	58	High	57	35	2	0.1	0	Aug
Sept	11	18	65	33	92	42	107	12	53	Medium	60	38	10	0.4	1	Sept
Oct	9	14	58	28	83	41	105	6	42	Medium	65	45	25	1.0	4	Oct
Nov	7	10	51	22	72	33	91	-1	30		75	53	33	1.3	6	Nov
Dec	5	7	45	17	63	24	75	-3	27		82	63	68	2.7	11	Dec

Based on readings for 30 years at 35°09' N, 33°21' E, altitude 175 m/574 ft

disturbed weather in the midwinter months. Temperatures in winter are generally mild except in the mountains where, above 1,000 m/3,300 ft, snow becomes frequent and on the summit of Troödos it may lie for four to five months. During this time skiing is possible. Disturbed winter weather rarely lasts more than a few days. During spring and autumn settled weather may last for two or three weeks, with brief interruptions of stormy wet weather.

Conditions around the coast are represented by the table for **Kyrenia** (p. 119). In summer the high daytime temperatures on the coast are tempered by cooling sea breezes but the nights may feel rather warm and sultry. The table for **Nicosia** (p. 119) is representative of conditions at low levels inland where daytime temperatures are very high in midsummer. The evenings and nights, however,

feel cooler than on the coast. In the higher parts of the mountains summer conditions feel delightfully cool and fresh after the heat of the lowlands. There are numerous hill resorts for tourists.

Cyprus is a very sunny island even in winter. The average number of daily hours of sunshine ranges from six in midwinter to twelve or thirteen in midsummer. For those who find high temperatures unpleasant, the best time to visit Cyprus is in the spring, when the weather is generally sunny and warm and the island is colourful with flowering plants. In late summer and autumn the island appears scorched and dry after the long summer drought. Although hardy northerners may be tempted to swim on a sunny day in winter, they will find the sea around Cyprus to be rather chilly from December until early May.

Czech Republic

See map on page 29

The Czech Republic consists of the ancient provinces of Bohemia and Moravia with a mountainous rim on the German border. It is completely landlocked within Central Europe, with a climate that is transitional between the milder and wetter conditions of Atlantic Europe and the more extreme conditions (severe winters and warm summers) found in Russia.

The country is hilly with much of its area rising over 1,000 m/3,250 ft. There is little difference of weather from one area to another and everywhere it can be changeable at all times of the year. The longest spells of settled weather occur during calm but cold days in winter. The most unpleasant weather occurs in winter when easterly winds from

Russia may bring very low temperatures for several days on end. Spring and summer are the wettest seasons. Summers are moderately warm, but fine weather is often broken by thunderstorms; extreme heat is rare. Spells of disturbed summer weather are often brought by disturbances originating over the northern Mediterranean.

Conditions in Bohemia are illustrated in the table for **Prague** (opposite and above). Conditions in Moravia are illustrated in the table for **Brno** (opposite).

The number of wet days is rather less than in western Europe and the number of hours of sunshine rather more. Summer sunshine averages as much as eight hours per day.

PRAGUE

BOHEMIA

Sunshine	Temperatures									Discomfort from heat and humidity	Precipitation and humidity				Wet days
	Average daily				Highest recorded		Lowest recorded				Relative humidity		Average monthly precipitation		
	minimum		maximum								7:00	14:00			
average hours per day	°C	°F	°C	°F	°C	°F	°C	°F			%		mm	in	more than 0.1 mm/0.004 in
Jan	2	−5	23	0	31	13	55	−23	−9		84	73	18	0.7	13	Jan
Feb	3	−4	24	1	34	18	64	−28	−18		83	67	18	0.7	11	Feb
March	5	−1	30	7	44	22	71	−14	6		82	55	18	0.7	10	March
April	6	3	38	12	54	29	84	−6	21		77	47	27	1.1	11	April
May	8	8	46	18	64	32	90	−2	29		75	45	48	1.9	13	May
June	9	11	52	21	70	36	98	5	41		74	46	54	2.1	12	June
July	8	13	55	23	73	38	100	6	43		77	49	68	2.7	13	July
Aug	8	13	55	22	72	36	97	5	41		81	48	55	2.1	12	Aug
Sept	6	9	49	18	65	33	92	0	32		84	51	31	1.2	10	Sept
Oct	4	5	41	12	53	26	79	−6	21		87	60	33	1.3	13	Oct
Nov	2	1	33	5	42	18	63	−10	14		87	73	20	0.8	12	Nov
Dec	1	−3	27	1	34	13	56	−21	−6		87	78	21	0.8	13	Dec

Based on readings for 23 years at 50°04' N, 14°26' E, altitude 262 m/860 ft

BRNO

MORAVIA

Sunshine	Temperatures									Discomfort from heat and humidity	Precipitation and humidity				Wet days
	Average daily				Highest recorded		Lowest recorded				Relative humidity		Average monthly precipitation		
	minimum		maximum								7:00	14:00			
average hours per day	°C	°F	°C	°F	°C	°F	°C	°F			%		mm	in	more than 0.1 mm/0.004 in
Jan	2	−5	24	1	34	14	58	−20	−4		88	77	30	1.2	12	Jan
Feb	3	−5	24	3	37	16	60	−25	−12		88	69	32	1.3	11	Feb
March	5	−1	30	8	47	23	73	−14	6		87	58	22	0.9	8	March
April	7	4	39	15	59	27	81	−6	21		82	49	36	1.4	12	April
May	9	9	47	20	68	32	89	−3	27		77	49	49	1.9	11	May
June	9	12	53	23	74	35	96	3	37		77	52	67	2.6	13	June
July	9	14	57	25	77	37	98	5	40	Moderate	81	52	81	3.2	14	July
Aug	8	13	55	25	76	36	97	5	41	Moderate	85	53	73	2.9	13	Aug
Sept	7	9	49	21	70	32	90	0	32		90	55	42	1.7	10	Sept
Oct	5	4	40	14	58	26	79	−7	19		91	63	36	1.4	10	Oct
Nov	2	2	35	7	45	18	64	−10	13		91	77	38	1.5	12	Nov
Dec	2	−1	30	3	38	14	57	−19	−1		91	82	40	1.6	14	Dec

Based on readings for 14 years at 49°12' N, 16°34' E, altitude 223 m/732 ft

Denmark

Denmark consists of the peninsula of Jutland and a group of islands at the entrance to the Baltic Sea, between Sweden and Germany. It has two self-governing dependencies – Greenland and the Faeroe Islands.

GREENLAND

See map page 12

Greenland has an area four times as large as France or the state of Texas, and is situated between 60° and 83° N so that three-quarters of the country lies within the Arctic Circle. Only about 16 percent of its area is free from permanent snow and ice. These ice-free areas consist of high mountains around the coast through which great glaciers descend to deposit masses of ice in the surrounding seas. The Greenland glaciers are main source of icebergs in the North Atlantic.

The northern shores of Greenland are permanently blocked by sea ice. Baffin Bay on the west generally has more open water in winter than the Greenland Sea to the east.

The table for **Nuuk** (below) on the west coast is representative of the coasts of Greenland. Winters are long and severe and summers very short and cool. Precipitation, mostly snow, is moderately heavy around the coasts so that the icecap is continuously replenished.

The interior of the country consists of a great icecap up to 3,000 m/10,000 ft thick – it is the largest accumulation of snow and ice in the northern hemisphere. The table for **Qaanaaq** (opposite) in the north of Greenland is representative of most of the interior icecap.

This has a true Arctic climate. Temperatures are above freezing for brief periods in the summer only. There are occasional relatively warm summer days when the weather may feel quite pleasant if the wind is light or calm and the sun is shining. The low precipitation at Thule is probably typical of much of the interior icecap.

Conditions are most hazardous when there is a combination of low temperature and strong wind and, consequently, a high wind chill (see pp. 2–3).

NUUK												WEST COAST GREENLAND	
Sunshine		Temperatures						Discomfort from heat and humidity	Precipitation and humidity				Wet days
		Average daily		Highest recorded		Lowest recorded			Relative humidity	Average monthly precipitation			
		minimum	maximum						all hours				
average hours per day		°C	°F	°C	°F	°C	°F	°C	°F		%	mm	in	more than .01 mm/.004 in
Jan	1	–12	10	–7	19	11	52	–29	–20		85	36	1.4	13	Jan
Feb	3	–13	9	–7	20	11	51	–27	–17		86	43	1.7	12	Feb
March	6	–11	13	–4	24	12	53	–28	–19		87	41	1.6	13	March
April	8	–7	20	–1	31	13	56	–21	–6		85	31	1.2	11	April
May	6	–2	29	4	40	16	61	–12	11		83	43	1.7	10	May
June	5	1	34	8	47	23	74	–6	22		92	36	1.4	10	June
July	6	3	38	11	52	24	76	–2	29		85	56	2.2	10	July
Aug	4	3	38	11	51	22	71	–3	27		86	79	3.1	12	Aug
Sept	3	1	34	6	43	17	62	–8	18		85	84	3.3	13	Sept
Oct	2	–3	26	2	35	18	65	–14	6		84	64	2.5	13	Oct
Nov	1	–7	19	–2	28	14	58	–18	–1		85	48	1.9	13	Nov
Dec	0	–10	14	–5	23	15	59	–26	–14		85	38	1.5	12	Dec

Based on readings for 40 years at 64°11' N, 51°43' W, altitude 20 m/66 ft

QAANAAQ — NORTHERN GREENLAND

	Sunshine average hours per day	Temperatures								Discomfort from heat and humidity	Precipitation and humidity				Wet days more than 0.25 mm/0.01 in	
		Average daily				Highest recorded		Lowest recorded			Relative humidity 3:30 15:30		Average monthly precipitation			
		minimum		maximum												
		°C	°F	°C	°F	°C	°F	°C	°F		%		mm	in		
Jan		−27	−16	−17	1	2	36	−38	−37		76	76	3	0.1	0	Jan
Feb		−29	−21	−20	−4	2	36	−41	−41		76	76	3	0.1	0	Feb
March		−28	−19	−19	−2	1	34	−39	−38		75	73	3	0.1	0	March
April		−23	−10	−13	9	3	37	−32	−26		88	71	3	0.1	0	April
May		−9	16	−2	28	7	44	−22	−8		77	74	3	0.1	0	May
June		−1	30	5	41	15	59	−6	22		81	78	5	0.2	1	June
July		2	36	8	46	15	59	−2	28		84	80	13	0.5	2	July
Aug		1	33	6	43	14	57	−4	24		77	71	13	0.5	2	Aug
Sept		−6	21	1	33	7	45	−14	6		80	76	10	0.4	1	Sept
Oct		−13	8	−5	23	10	50	−24	−11		80	78	3	0.1	0	Oct
Nov		−19	−3	−11	13	3	38	−33	−28		79	81	3	0.1	0	Nov
Dec		−27	−17	−18	−1	2	35	−38	−37		75	76	5	0.2	0	Dec

Based on readings for 3 years at 76°33′ N, 68°49′ W, altitude 37 m/121 ft

HOYVIK — FAEROE ISLANDS

	Sunshine average hours per day	Temperatures								Discomfort from heat and humidity	Precipitation and humidity				Wet days more than 0.1 mm/0.004 in	
		Average daily				Highest recorded		Lowest recorded			Relative humidity 8:30 14:30		Average monthly precipitation			
		minimum		maximum												
		°C	°F	°C	°F	°C	°F	°C	°F		%		mm	in		
Jan	1	2	35	6	43	15	59	−10	14		81	82	149	5.9	25	Jan
Feb	1	1	34	6	42	12	53	−10	13		82	82	136	5.4	22	Feb
March	2	2	36	7	44	13	55	−9	17		82	81	114	4.5	23	March
April	4	3	37	8	46	13	56	−7	20		81	80	106	4.2	22	April
May	5	5	41	10	49	19	66	−5	24		82	82	67	2.6	16	May
June	5	7	45	12	53	19	66	1	33		83	83	74	2.9	16	June
July	4	9	48	13	56	22	72	2	36		86	84	79	3.1	18	July
Aug	3	9	49	14	56	22	71	3	38		87	84	96	3.8	20	Aug
Sept	3	8	46	12	54	18	65	0	32		85	84	132	5.2	12	Sept
Oct	2	5	42	10	50	17	62	−4	24		83	82	157	6.2	24	Oct
Nov	1	4	39	8	47	15	58	−5	23		83	84	156	6.1	24	Nov
Dec	0	3	37	7	45	12	54	−10	14		82	83	167	6.6	26	Dec

Based on readings for 27 years at 62°02′ N, 6°45′ W, altitude 20 m/66 ft

FANO

WEST COAST DENMARK

Sunshine	Temperatures								Discomfort from heat and humidity	Precipitation and humidity				Wet days
	Average daily				Highest recorded		Lowest recorded			Relative humidity 7:30 13:30		Average monthly precipitation		
	minimum		maximum											
average hours per day	°C	°F	°C	°F	°C	°F	°C	°F		%		mm	in	more than 0.1 mm/0.004 in
Jan 1	-2	29	3	37	10	49	-22	-8		90	89	60	2.4	17 Jan
Feb 2	-2	28	3	37	10	49	-21	-6		89	88	45	1.8	13 Feb
March 4	-1	31	6	42	18	64	-18	0		89	83	38	1.5	12 March
April 6	3	37	10	51	25	77	-5	23		86	75	39	1.5	12 April
May 8	7	45	16	60	30	86	-2	29		80	67	43	1.7	11 May
June 9	11	51	19	66	33	91	1	35		78	66	43	1.7	12 June
July 8	13	56	21	70	35	95	5	41		81	69	74	2.9	14 July
Aug 7	13	56	21	69	33	91	4	38		83	69	85	3.4	15 Aug
Sept 6	11	51	18	64	29	84	1	34		86	73	88	3.5	16 Sept
Oct 3	7	44	13	55	21	69	-6	21		89	80	82	3.2	17 Oct
Nov 2	3	38	8	46	14	57	-7	20		91	88	68	2.7	19 Nov
Dec 1	1	33	5	41	15	58	-13	8		92	91	64	2.5	19 Dec

Based on readings for 30 years at 55°27′ N, 8°24′ E, altitude 3 m/10 ft

COPENHAGEN

EAST COAST DENMARK

Sunshine	Temperatures								Discomfort from heat and humidity	Precipitation and humidity				Wet days
	Average daily				Highest recorded		Lowest recorded			Relative humidity 8:00 14:00		Average monthly precipitation		
	minimum		maximum											
average hours per day	°C	°F	°C	°F	°C	°F	°C	°F		%		mm	in	more than 0.1 mm/0.004 in
Jan 1	-2	28	2	36	10	50	-24	-12		88	85	49	1.9	17 Jan
Feb 2	-3	28	2	36	14	57	-20	-3		86	83	39	1.5	13 Feb
March 4	-1	31	5	41	19	65	-18	0		85	78	32	1.3	12 March
April 5	3	38	10	51	22	70	-9	16		79	68	38	1.5	13 April
May 8	8	46	16	61	28	82	-2	29		70	59	43	1.7	11 May
June 8	11	52	19	67	33	91	3	37		70	60	47	1.9	13 June
July 8	14	57	22	71	31	87	8	46		74	62	71	2.8	14 July
Aug 7	14	56	21	70	31	87	6	42		78	64	66	2.6	14 Aug
Sept 5	11	51	18	64	27	80	1	34		83	69	62	2.4	15 Sept
Oct 3	7	44	12	54	20	68	-4	25		86	76	59	2.3	16 Oct
Nov 1	3	38	7	45	14	58	-7	20		88	83	48	1.9	16 Nov
Dec 1	1	34	4	40	12	54	-11	12		89	87	49	1.9	17 Dec

Based on readings for 30 years at 55°41′ N, 12°33′ E, altitude 9 m/33 ft

Strong winds are often a feature of the winter weather on the coast as very cold air from the interior is funnelled down the glaciated valleys when a North Atlantic depression passes near the coast. The Greenland icecap is the source of some of the coldest air to affect northwest Europe.

THE FAEROE ISLANDS

See map page 18

This small group of islands is situated in the stormiest part of the North Atlantic, midway between Scotland and Iceland. Under the influence of the warm ocean current of the Gulf Stream, the climate is very mild for the latitude. The table for **Hoyvik** (p. 123) is representative of the Faeroes.

Winters in the Faeroes are warmer than those in Denmark, 6° of latitude to the south. The islands are cloudy, wet, and windy throughout the year, for they lie in the path of the majority of Atlantic depressions. They are never very cold for long in winter and the summers are cool and sunless. Daily sunshine in the summer months averages only about four hours.

MAINLAND DENMARK

See map page 18

Denmark's cool maritime climate is rather similar to that of Britain or the state of Washington. Because of its small size and low elevation – no part of Denmark

is higher than 180 m/600 ft – weather and climate do not vary much throughout the country.

Spells of cold weather occur in most winters when the waters of the Baltic freeze in whole or in part. In some winters such spells may be prolonged. If this happens the waters of the Sound between Zeeland and south Sweden may freeze. The average duration of winter snow cover is about thirty days but in some winters there may be little snow.

Conditions in summer are variable from year to year and from day to day. Although spells of warm, settled weather may last for a few weeks in some years, it rarely becomes unpleasantly hot. Precipitation occurs all the year round, but summer and autumn are the wettest seasons.

The west coast (see the table for **Fanø** opposite) is a little wetter than the east (see the table for **Copenhagen** opposite and below).

When Atlantic storms cross the country or move into the North Sea, quite severe gales may affect Denmark, and the west coast has the reputation of being particularly exposed and windswept. Such gales may occur at all times of the year but are less frequent and less severe in summer.

Denmark has a generally pleasant climate the year round and, apart from the occasional cold winter, rarely suffers extremes of weather. Daily sunshine hours range from between one and two in winter to about eight in summer.

DJIBOUTI											COASTAL DJIBOUTI			
Sunshine	Temperatures							Discomfort from heat and humidity	Precipitation and humidity				Wet days	
	Average daily				Highest recorded		Lowest recorded		Relative humidity 6:00 12:00		Average monthly precipitation		more than 1 mm/0.04 in	
average hours per day	minimum		maximum											
	°C	°F	°C	°F	°C	°F	°C	°F		%	mm	in		
Jan	8	23	73	29	84	34	93	19	66	Medium	82	69	10	0.4	3.0	Jan
Feb	8	24	75	29	84	34	93	18	65	High	82	71	13	0.5	2.0	Feb
March	9	25	77	31	87	37	98	21	69	High	83	73	25	1.0	2.0	March
April	9	26	79	32	90	38	101	21	70	Extreme	84	74	13	0.5	1.0	April
May	10	28	82	34	93	44	112	21	70	Extreme	83	70	5	0.2	1.0	May
June	8	30	86	37	99	47	117	23	73	Extreme	62	53	0	0.0	0.3	June
July	8	31	87	41	106	47	117	22	72	Extreme	57	43	3	0.1	1.0	July
Aug	9	29	85	39	103	47	116	22	72	Extreme	62	44	8	0.3	1.0	Aug
Sept	9	29	85	36	96	44	112	23	73	Extreme	73	60	8	0.3	1.0	Sept
Oct	10	27	80	33	92	39	102	21	70	High	77	65	10	0.4	1.0	Oct
Nov	10	25	77	31	88	36	96	18	65	High	79	67	23	0.9	2.0	Nov
Dec	8	23	73	29	85	34	94	17	63	High	82	71	13	0.5	2.0	Dec

Based on readings for 11 years at 11°36′ N, 43°09′ E, altitude 7 m/23 ft

Djibouti

See map page 20

This small country was formerly known as French Somaliland and later as the French Territory of the Afars and the Issas. It is at the entrance to the Red Sea with a coastline on the southern shores of the Gulf of Aden. It is about as big as Wales or the state of Vermont. It is bordered by Ethiopia on the west and Somalia on the south.

There is a low-lying coastal plain which is very hot all the year round but has lower temperatures at the period of low sun (see the table for the captal city, **Djibouti**, above). Inland there are extensive areas above 600 m/2,000 ft, where temperatures and humidity are a little lower than on the coast.

Annual rainfall is almost everywhere below 500 mm/20 in and is much less in many places. The scanty rainfall on the coast is more likely to come in the period November to March, but inland the rains are more probable during the period of high sun from April to October. Hours of sunshine average from eight to nine hours a day around the year.

ROSEAU

SOUTHERN DOMINICA

	Sunshine average hours per day	Temperatures								Discomfort from heat and humidity	Precipitation and humidity				Wet days more than 1 mm/0.04 in	
		Average daily				Highest recorded		Lowest recorded			Relative humidity 9:00 15:00		Average monthly precipitation			
		minimum		maximum												
		°C	°F	°C	°F	°C	°F	°C	°F		%		mm	in		
Jan	8	20	68	29	84	33	91	16	60	Medium	76	65	132	5.2	16	Jan
Feb	8	19	67	29	85	34	93	16	61	Medium	73	62	74	2.9	10	Feb
March	9	20	68	31	87	36	96	16	61	High	70	59	74	2.9	13	March
April	8	21	69	31	88	36	97	17	63	High	66	61	61	2.4	10	April
May	8	22	71	32	90	36	97	18	64	High	67	61	97	3.8	11	May
June	7	23	73	32	90	36	96	20	68	High	69	65	196	7.7	15	June
July	8	22	72	32	89	35	95	18	65	High	75	69	274	10.8	22	July
Aug	8	23	73	32	89	35	95	19	67	High	76	69	262	10.3	22	Aug
Sept	8	23	73	32	90	35	95	18	65	High	74	67	226	8.9	16	Sept
Oct	7	22	72	32	89	37	98	18	65	High	75	70	198	7.8	16	Oct
Nov	8	22	71	31	87	35	95	18	64	High	78	70	224	8.8	18	Nov
Dec	8	21	69	30	86	34	93	17	62	High	77	67	163	6.4	16	Dec

Based on readings for 17 years at 15°18′ N, 61°23′ W, altitude 18 m/60 ft

Dominica

See map page 15

The island of Dominica is the most northerly of the Windward Islands, the southern segment of the Lesser Antilles. These islands lie between 15° N and the coast of the South American continent.

The table for **Roseau** (above) shows that near sea level the annual rainfall is about 1,250–2,000 mm/50–80 in, well distributed throughout the year, with a wetter season from July to November.

All months receive appreciable rain, but July to November is the hurricane season and, although the most violent of these tropical storms may only strike Dominica every few years, less severe ones cause appreciable rainfall over quite a wide area. Temperature, humidity, and sunshine throughout the year are typical of those described in the general entry for the Caribbean (pp. 92–3).

SANTO DOMINGO													COASTAL DOMINICAN REPUBLIC			
Sunshine		Temperatures							Discomfort from heat and humidity	Precipitation and humidity					Wet days	
		Average daily				Highest recorded		Lowest recorded		Relative humidity 9:00 15:00			Average monthly precipitation			
		minimum		maximum												
average hours per day		°C	°F	°C	°F	°C	°F	°C	°F		%		mm	in	more than 1 mm/0.04 in	
Jan	8	19	66	29	84	33	92	15	59	Medium	91	64	61	2.4	7	Jan
Feb	8	19	66	29	85	34	93	16	60	Medium	88	58	36	1.4	6	Feb
March	8	19	67	29	84	34	94	16	60	Medium	90	60	48	1.9	5	March
April	8	21	69	29	85	35	95	17	62	Medium	90	62	99	3.9	7	April
May	7	22	71	30	86	34	94	18	65	High	89	65	173	6.8	11	May
June	8	22	72	31	87	36	96	19	67	High	90	66	158	6.2	12	June
July	9	22	72	31	88	37	98	20	68	High	90	66	163	6.4	11	July
Aug	9	23	73	31	88	37	98	18	64	High	90	66	160	6.3	11	Aug
Sept	8	22	72	31	88	37	98	20	68	High	91	66	185	7.3	11	Sept
Oct	8	22	72	31	87	35	95	19	66	High	92	66	152	6.0	11	Oct
Nov	7	21	70	30	86	36	97	16	61	High	92	66	122	4.8	10	Nov
Dec	7	19	67	29	85	35	95	17	62	Medium	91	66	61	2.4	8	Dec

Based on readings for 25 years at 18°29′ N, 69°54′ W, altitude 17 m/57 ft

Dominican Republic

See map page 15

The Dominican Republic occupies the eastern two-thirds of the large Caribbean island of Hispaniola and has a land border with Haiti on the west. The country has an area of nearly 49,000 sq km/ 19,000 sq mi, twice as large as the state of Vermont or Wales. It is the most mountainous of the Caribbean Islands, with the highest peaks rising over 3,000 m/10,000 ft, but there are also considerable areas of lowland. Apart from the mountains, which are cooler and wetter, the weather and climate are represented by the table for **Santo Domingo** (above) on the south coast. The north coast is almost twice as wet throughout the year and has more rain in the winter season than is usual in the Caribbean.

SEYMOUR ISLAND — GALAPAGOS ISLANDS

	Sunshine: average hours per day	Temperatures: Average daily minimum °C	°F	Average daily maximum °C	°F	Highest recorded °C	°F	Lowest recorded °C	°F	Discomfort from heat and humidity	Precipitation and humidity: Relative humidity %	Average monthly precipitation mm	in	Wet days: trace or more	
Jan	6	22	72	30	86	32	90	19	66			20	0.8	8	Jan
Feb	8	24	75	30	86	32	90	21	70			36	1.4	9	Feb
March	8	24	75	31	88	34	93	21	70			28	1.1	6	March
April	8	24	75	31	87	32	90	22	71			18	0.7	6	April
May	8	23	73	30	86	32	89	21	69			0	0.0	4	May
June	8	22	71	28	83	31	87	20	68			0	0.0	4	June
July	6	21	69	27	81	31	88	19	67			0	0.0	9	July
Aug	6	19	67	27	81	31	87	16	60			0	0.0	8	Aug
Sept	5	19	66	27	80	30	86	15	59			0	0.0	7	Sept
Oct	5	19	67	27	81	30	86	14	58			0	0.0	2	Oct
Nov	6	20	68	27	81	30	86	17	62			0	0.0	4	Nov
Dec	6	21	70	28	83	31	88	16	61			0	0.0	6	Dec

Based on readings for 3 years at 0°28′ S, 90°18′ W, altitude 11 m/36 ft

Ecuador

See map page 16

Ecuador, as its name implies, lies across the equator between 1° N and 5° S on the west coast of South America. It is a small country, a little larger than the United Kingdom and about the size of the state of Arizona.

Mainland Ecuador includes three types of country, which form three different and distinctive climatic regions: a narrow coastal plain, a high mountainous central region including the main Andean mountain ranges, and a forested lowland region in the east which is part of the Amazon basin. The Galápagos Islands, 1,050 km/650 mi west of the coast of Ecuador, constitute a fourth climatic region.

GALAPAGOS ISLANDS

This island group lies almost on the equator. There are some fifteen large, and hundreds of smaller, islands with a total area of about 7,770 sq km/3,000 sq mi. They are famous for their unusual flora and fauna and are now a nature reserve. The islands have an unusual climate in view of their proximity to the equator; rainfall is low and temperatures are lower than would be expected. There are no extremes of heat or cold. This is a consequence of their location in the Pacific Ocean, where the cooler waters of the Humboldt current have a marked effect on the weather (see pp. 96 and 238 for Chile and Peru respectively).

There is more rain on the large islands that are hilly, as the table for **Seymour Island** (above) shows. Rainfall is low at sea level and it falls in the period from January to April. Light drizzle and even fog, however, are not uncommon at other times of the year.

COASTAL ECUADOR

The climate of the coastlands of Ecuador is indicated by the table for **Guayaquil** (overleaf). Temperature and humidity are high here throughout the year. Guayaquil has a single main rainy season from December to April. Towards the north the total annual rainfall increases to as much as 2,000 mm/80 in or more and some rain falls in all months; this is a typical equatorial pattern of rainfall. In the extreme

GUAYAQUIL

COASTAL ECUADOR

Sunshine	Temperatures								Discomfort from heat and humidity	Precipitation and humidity			Wet days
	Average daily				Highest recorded		Lowest recorded			Relative humidity	Average monthly precipitation		
	minimum		maximum										
average hours per day	°C	°F	°C	°F	°C	°F	°C	°F		%	mm	in	more than 10 mm/0.4 in
Jan 3	21	70	31	88	36	96	19	67			239	9.4	20 Jan
Feb 4	22	71	31	87	34	93	19	66			249	9.8	25 Feb
March 5	22	72	31	88	33	92	18	64			277	10.9	24 March
April 5	22	71	32	89	34	93	21	69			117	4.6	14 April
May 5	20	68	31	88	35	95	18	65			28	1.1	9 May
June 4	20	68	31	87	34	94	18	64			8	0.3	4 June
July 4	19	67	29	84	33	91	17	62			5	0.2	2 July
Aug 4	18	65	30	86	33	92	17	62			0	0.0	0 Aug
Sept 5	19	66	31	87	34	93	14	57			3	0.1	2 Sept
Oct 4	20	68	30	86	34	94	17	62			8	0.3	3 Oct
Nov 4	20	68	31	88	34	94	16	61			3	0.1	4 Nov
Dec 4	21	70	31	88	37	98	19	66			51	2.0	10 Dec

Based on readings for 3 years at 2°10´ S, 79°53´ W, altitude 6 m/20 ft

QUITO

INLAND HIGHLAND ECUADOR

Sunshine	Temperatures								Discomfort from heat and humidity	Precipitation and humidity				Wet days
	Average daily				Highest recorded		Lowest recorded			Relative humidity		Average monthly precipitation		
	minimum		maximum							5:00	13:00			
average hours per day	°C	°F	°C	°F	°C	°F	°C	°F		%		mm	in	more than 10 mm/0.4 in
Jan 5	8	46	22	72	26	79	3	37		93	54	99	3.9	16 Jan
Feb 5	8	47	22	71	27	80	1	34		93	59	112	4.4	17 Feb
March 4	8	47	22	71	27	80	4	40		93	59	142	5.6	20 March
April 5	8	47	21	70	26	78	4	40		93	60	175	6.9	22 April
May 5	8	47	21	70	26	79	2	35		93	60	137	5.4	21 May
June 6	7	45	22	71	26	78	2	36		88	51	43	1.7	12 June
July 7	7	44	22	72	26	79	1	33		81	43	20	0.8	7 July
Aug 7	7	45	23	73	28	82	2	36		80	40	31	1.2	9 Aug
Sept 8	7	45	23	73	28	83	2	35		85	44	69	2.7	14 Sept
Oct 5	8	46	22	72	30	86	0	32		92	53	112	4.4	18 Oct
Nov 6	7	45	22	72	27	80	1	33		92	53	97	3.8	14 Nov
Dec 6	8	46	22	72	27	81	1	34		94	54	79	3.1	16 Dec

Based on readings for 13 years at 0°13´ S, 78°32´ W, altitude 2879 m/9446 ft

south of the coastal district, rainfall decreases sharply and is as low as 200 mm/8 in a year as the dry coastal belt of Peru is approached.

ANDEAN ECUADOR

In the central Andean region temperatures are much reduced by altitude, and the division into *tierra caliente*, *tierra templada*, and *tierra fria* described on p. 66 for Bolivia is appropriate. Because of heavier precipitation as compared with Peru and Bolivia, the snowline is near 5,000 m/16,000 ft. The risk of mountain sickness at altitudes above 3,000 m/ 10,000 ft is something that the visitor should take into account. The table for **Quito** (opposite and below) in the Andean region shows a climate often described as one of 'perpetual spring' with warm

days and chilly nights and little variation of temperature around the year. Much of the rainfall in this mountainous region comes in the afternoon and evening as clouds build up over the mountains and thunderstorms develop. Sunshine hours are least at Quito in the rainy season when they average four to five a day and greatest in the dry season when there are as many as seven to eight.

EASTERN ECUADOR

The eastern foot of the Andes is low-lying and has a typical hot, wet, equatorial type of climate with rainfall well distributed throughout the year. It is similar to that described on p. 69 for the extensive Amazon forest region of Brazil.

Egypt

See map page 20

Egypt, almost twice the size of France, is situated in northeastern Africa. It has long coastlines on the Mediterranean and on the Red Sea. A small part of the country, the Sinai desert, lies east of the Suez Canal and is, strictly speaking, in Asia. Egypt has

land boundaries with Libya on the west, with the Sudan on the south, and a shorter boundary with Israel on the east.

Egypt is one of the hottest and sunniest countries in the world. With the exception of a strip about 80 km/50 mi wide along the Mediterranean coast,

ALEXANDRIA															NORTHERN EGYPT	
Sunshine		Temperatures								Discomfort from heat and humidity	Precipitation and humidity				Wet days	
		Average daily				Highest recorded		Lowest recorded			Relative humidity		Average monthly precipitation			
		minimum		maximum							8:00	14:00				
average hours per day		°C	°F	°C	°F	°C	°F	°C	°F		%		mm	in	more than 1 mm/0.04 in	
Jan	7	11	51	18	65	28	82	3	38		71	61	48	1.9	7.0	Jan
Feb	8	11	52	19	66	33	91	3	37		70	59	23	0.9	5.0	Feb
March	9	13	55	21	70	40	103	7	44		67	57	10	0.4	3.0	March
April	10	15	59	23	74	42	108	9	49	Moderate	67	60	3	0.1	1.0	April
May	11	18	64	26	79	44	111	12	54	Medium	70	64	0	0.0	0.5	May
June	12	21	69	28	83	44	111	15	59	Medium	72	68	0	0.0	0.0	June
July	12	23	73	29	85	40	103	17	63	High	76	70	0	0.0	0.0	July
Aug	12	23	74	31	87	41	105	18	64	High	72	68	0	0.0	0.0	Aug
Sept	11	23	73	30	86	41	106	16	60	High	68	63	0	0.0	0.1	Sept
Oct	9	20	68	28	83	40	104	12	54	Medium	68	61	5	0.2	1.0	Oct
Nov	8	17	62	25	77	35	95	8	46	Moderate	69	60	33	1.3	4.0	Nov
Dec	7	13	55	21	69	31	88	3	37		72	60	56	2.2	7.0	Dec

Based on readings for 45 years at 31°12′ N, 29°53′ E, altitude 32 m/105 ft

CAIRO

NORTHERN EGYPT

Sunshine	Temperatures									Discomfort from heat and humidity	Precipitation and humidity				Wet days
	Average daily				Highest recorded		Lowest recorded				Relative humidity		Average monthly precipitation		
	minimum		maximum								8:00	14:00			
average hours per day	°C	°F	°C	°F	°C	°F	°C	°F			%		mm	in	more than 1 mm/0.04 in
Jan 7	8	47	18	65	31	88	2	35			69	40	5	0.2	1.0 Jan
Feb 8	9	48	21	69	33	92	2	35			64	33	5	0.2	1.0 Feb
March 9	11	52	24	75	38	101	3	38			63	27	5	0.2	0.8 March
April 10	14	57	28	83	45	113	6	42	Moderate		55	21	3	0.1	0.4 April
May 10	17	63	33	91	47	116	9	49	Medium		50	18	3	0.1	0.2 May
June 12	20	68	35	95	47	117	13	55	Medium		55	20	0	0.0	0.0 June
July 12	21	70	36	96	43	109	16	61	Medium		65	24	0	0.0	0.0 July
Aug 11	22	71	35	95	43	109	17	63	Medium		69	28	0	0.0	0.0 Aug
Sept 10	20	68	32	90	42	108	14	58	Medium		68	31	0	0.0	0.0 Sept
Oct 9	18	65	30	86	43	109	11	51	Medium		67	31	0	0.0	0.3 Oct
Nov 8	14	58	26	78	38	100	6	42	Moderate		68	38	3	0.1	0.8 Nov
Dec 6	10	50	20	68	31	87	1	34			70	41	5	0.2	1.0 Dec

Based on readings for 42 years at 29°52' N, 31°20' E, altitude 116 m/381 ft

ASWAN

SOUTHERN EGYPT

Sunshine	Temperatures									Discomfort from heat and humidity	Precipitation and humidity				Wet days
	Average daily				Highest recorded		Lowest recorded				Relative humidity		Average monthly precipitation		
	minimum		maximum								8:00	14:00			
average hours per day	°C	°F	°C	°F	°C	°F	°C	°F			%		mm	in	more than 1 mm/0.04 in
Jan 7	10	50	23	74	38	100	3	38			52	29	0	0.0	0.0 Jan
Feb 7	11	52	26	78	39	102	2	35			46	22	0	0.0	0.0 Feb
March 8	14	58	31	87	43	110	6	43	Moderate		36	17	0	0.0	0.0 March
April 9	19	66	36	96	46	115	9	49	Medium		29	15	0	0.0	0.1 April
May 9	23	74	39	103	48	118	11	52	High		29	15	0	0.0	0.5 May
June 10	26	78	42	107	51	123	20	68	High		26	16	0	0.0	0.0 June
July 10	26	79	41	106	51	124	21	70	High		31	16	0	0.0	0.0 July
Aug 10	26	79	41	106	49	120	19	67	High		34	18	0	0.0	0.0 Aug
Sept 9	24	75	39	103	47	117	17	63	High		37	19	0	0.0	0.0 Sept
Oct 8	22	71	37	98	44	112	14	57	High		40	21	0	0.0	0.0 Oct
Nov 8	17	62	31	87	42	107	6	43	Medium		46	26	0	0.0	0.0 Nov
Dec 7	12	53	25	77	37	99	4	40			50	31	0	0.0	0.0 Dec

Based on readings for 20 years at 24°02' N, 32°53' E, altitude 112 m/366 ft

Egypt has a desert climate, being entirely within the Sahara. The legendary fertility of Egypt is a consequence of the fact that about 3 percent of the country consists of the Nile valley and delta. The river Nile has no tributaries within Egypt but is nourished by the heavy rains that fall far to the south in Ethiopia and East Africa. The Nile valley and delta are intensively cultivated by irrigation and contain about 95 percent of Egypt's population.

The Mediterranean coastal strip has an average annual rainfall of 100–200 mm/4–8 in, which is not sufficient to support crops. Over the rest of Egypt, roughly south of Cairo, the annual rainfall is a mere 25–50 mm/1–2 in. In central and southern Egypt several years may pass without any significant rain. When rain does fall it is usually in the form of a brief and sometimes damaging downpour which may cause a local flood.

The climate of the Mediterranean coastal strip is represented by the table for **Alexandria** (p. 131). Here the weather in the winter period from November to March may be quite variable with some cloudy days when rain and disturbed weather are brought by depressions moving from west to east in the Mediterranean.

For much of the time, however, the winter weather is warm and sunny; but some cold days occur when northerly winds are strong. Summers are sunny and hot, but the daytime temperature is modified by strong sea breezes on the coast.

The most unpleasant weather near the coast occurs between March and early June, when a weak depression draws very hot air from the Sahara towards the coast. These hot dry khamsin winds are often dust-laden and may raise sand particles in the desert which obscure visibility and irritate eyes, nose, and mouth. Virtually any part of Egypt can experience such winds, and a severe khamsin is most unpleasant and even dangerous. The very high temperatures occasionally experienced at Alexandria and **Cairo** (see table opposite and above) almost always occur during the khamsin season. Otherwise northern Egypt does not experience the high temperatures regularly recorded in the south of the country.

Winters are generally warm in the south of Egypt, but temperatures fall abruptly at night so that desert evenings in winter can be quite chilly (see the table for **Aswan** opposite and below). Farther north the nights can be distinctly chilly and occasional ground frost is not unknown.

In the Nile valley the humidity from the large irrigated areas causes local morning mist and fog, particularly in winter, but this quickly clears as the sun becomes powerful. On the higher hills of Sinai behind the Red Sea coast, which rise to 2,000–2,400 m/7,000–8,000 ft, snow may fall in winter but it rarely lies for more than a day or so.

The heat of southern Egypt in summer is fierce and there is almost no relief from one day to another. The very low humidity, however, makes the heat more bearable and it is rarely dangerous to the acclimatized visitor.

Visitors should allow a period of acclimatization before engaging in vigorous activity during the heat of the day and should also take precautions against sunburn. Shade temperatures are misleading in Egypt, where the sun is ubiquitous, and there is no shade in the desert! Visitors are more likely to suffer minor sickness and stomach disorders in Egypt from unhygienic food and drink rather than from the direct effect of the climate.

From what has been said above it is clear that Egypt has a very sunny climate; daily sunshine hours average about twelve a day in summer to between eight and ten a day in winter. There are occasional completely cloudy days in winter in the north, but very few in the south.

Places such as Luxor and Aswan and the few oases in the Sahara desert have an almost perfect winter climate: dry, sunny, and not excessively hot.

SAN SALVADOR												INLAND EL SALVADOR	
Sunshine	Temperatures								Discomfort from heat and humidity	Precipitation and humidity				Wet days
	Average daily				Highest recorded		Lowest recorded			Relative humidity 7:00 14:00		Average monthly precipitation		
average hours per day	minimum		maximum											with trace or more
	°C	°F	°C	°F	°C	°F	°C	°F		%		mm	in	
Jan	10	16	60	32	90	38	101	7	45	Medium	81	45	8	0.3	1	Jan
Feb	10	16	60	33	92	39	103	9	49	High	80	43	5	0.2	1	Feb
March	10	17	62	34	94	41	105	7	45	High	79	44	10	0.4	1	March
April	8	18	65	34	93	40	104	12	54	High	79	50	43	1.7	4	April
May	8	19	67	33	91	39	103	14	58	High	86	60	196	7.7	13	May
June	6	19	66	31	87	37	98	13	56	High	89	66	328	12.9	19	June
July	8	18	65	32	89	37	98	14	58	High	88	61	292	11.5	19	July
Aug	8	19	66	32	89	37	98	16	60	High	89	62	297	11.7	19	Aug
Sept	6	19	66	31	87	37	99	12	53	High	91	69	307	12.1	20	Sept
Oct	7	18	65	31	87	38	101	12	54	High	88	66	241	9.5	16	Oct
Nov	9	17	63	31	87	39	102	9	49	High	80	56	41	1.6	4	Nov
Dec	10	16	61	32	89	38	101	8	47	High	81	50	10	0.4	2	Dec

Based on readings for 33 years at 13°42´ N, 89°13´ W, altitude 682 m/2238 ft

El Salvador

See map page 14

This is one of the smallest countries of Central America, whose weather and climate are described in more detail on pp. 278–80 for Panama. It is about as large as Wales or the state of Massachusetts and is situated between 13° and 14° N. It is a mountainous country with the highest points reaching over 1,800 m/6,000 ft. It is the only country in this region with no coastline on the Caribbean Sea.

There is a narrow coastal plain on the Pacific shore and this forms the most extensive region of *tierra caliente* (lowlands – see p. 66), with a typical hot, tropical climate and a single rainy season between May and October.

Annual rainfall in this lowland is similar to that shown in the table for **San Salvador** (above), which is in the lower part of the hill country; here daytime temperatures are similar to the lowlands but nights are much cooler.

In the higher areas of the *tierra templada* (middle elevations – see p. 66) climatic conditions are similar to those shown for **Guatemala City** on p. 167.

MALABO											FERNANDO PO, EQUATORIAL GUINEA		
Sunshine		Temperatures							Discomfort from heat and humidity	Precipitation and humidity			Wet days
		Average daily				Highest recorded		Lowest recorded		Relative humidity	Average monthly precipitation		
		minimum		maximum						all hours			more than
average hours per day		°C	°F	°C	°F	°C	°F	°C	°F	%	mm	in	0.1 mm/0.004 in
Jan	4	19	67	31	87	32	89	18	64	Extreme	86	5	0.2	3	Jan
Feb	5	21	69	32	89	33	91	19	66	Extreme	85	31	1.2	5	Feb
March	3	21	69	31	88	32	90	19	66	Extreme	90	193	7.6	13	March
April	4	21	70	32	89	32	90	19	67	Extreme	89	163	6.4	15	April
May	4	22	71	31	87	32	89	19	66	Extreme	87	262	10.3	23	May
June	3	21	69	29	85	31	87	18	65	High	90	302	11.9	23	June
July	2	21	69	29	84	29	85	18	64	High	90	160	6.3	17	July
Aug	2	21	69	29	85	30	86	17	63	High	92	114	4.5	14	Aug
Sept	2	21	69	30	86	31	87	18	64	Extreme	95	201	7.9	24	Sept
Oct	2	21	70	30	86	31	87	18	65	Extreme	94	231	9.1	23	Oct
Nov	3	22	71	30	86	31	88	19	66	Extreme	93	117	4.6	12	Nov
Dec	4	21	70	31	87	31	88	17	63	Extreme	91	20	0.8	4	Dec

Based on readings for 2 years at 3°46′ N, 8°46′ E, altitude not known

Equatorial Guinea

See map page 21

Formerly the Spanish colony of Rio Muni, Equatorial Guinea is about the size of Wales or Israel. It lies on the coast of the Gulf of Guinea between Cameroon to the north and Gabon to the south. The country includes the offshore island of Fernando Po, which is mountainous and therefore particularly wet, and a number of smaller islands.

Both the mainland and the islands have a typical equatorial climate with high temperatures, high humidity, heavy rainfall, and much cloud around the year. Annual rainfall is almost everywhere around 2,000 mm/80 in. Weather and climate are similar to those described for the Congo Democratic Republic. Conditions are represented by the table for **Malabo** (above) on Fernando Po.

Eritrea

See map page 20

This republic on the Red Sea coast lies between the Sudan in the northwest and Djibouti in the southeast. Ethiopia borders it on the south. To the west of the coastal plain rises an inland plateau, the most densely populated region of the country. The climate here is invigorating with cool breezes, about 1,150 mm/46 in of rainfall annually, almost constant sunshine, and little change in seasonal temperature. By contrast, much of the coast and a broad reach of

the south of the country belongs to the Danakil desert, one of the hottest places on earth. It has virtually no rainfall. The scrubby, rocky hill country in the very north of the country is another dry wilderness area, as are the western lowlands bordering the Sudan and Ethiopia. For weather similar to that in the inland plateau of Eritrea see the tables for **Addis Ababa** and **Harer** both in the neighbouring Ethiopian highlands (p. 137). For weather similar to that in the Danakil desert region of Eritrea, see the table for **Djibouti** (p. 126).

TALLINN										ESTONIAN REPUBLIC		
Sunshine		Temperatures						Discomfort from heat and humidity	Precipitation and humidity			Wet days	
		Average daily				Highest recorded	Lowest recorded		Relative humidity		Average monthly precipitation		
		minimum		maximum					7:30 13:00				
average hours per day		°C	°F	°C	°F	°C	°F	°C	°F		%	mm	in	more than 0.1 mm/0.004 in
Jan	1	-10	14	-4	25	5	41	-30	-22		87	86	39	1.5	19	Jan
Feb	2	-11	12	-4	25	3	37	-30	-22		87	83	30	1.2	16	Feb
March	4	-7	19	0	32	12	54	-25	-13		89	77	21	0.8	13	March
April	6	0	32	7	45	21	70	-13	9		84	66	31	1.2	11	April
May	7	5	41	14	57	27	81	-3	27		79	63	44	1.7	12	May
June	11	10	50	19	66	31	88	0	32		72	55	40	1.6	10	June
July	10	12	54	20	68	29	84	5	41		79	59	68	2.7	13	July
Aug	8	11	52	19	66	31	88	2	36		85	64	78	3.1	15	Aug
Sept	5	9	48	15	59	28	82	-3	27		87	69	71	2.8	16	Sept
Oct	2	4	39	10	50	19	66	-7	19		89	79	68	2.7	17	Oct
Nov	1	-1	30	3	37	11	52	-21	-6		90	86	56	2.2	18	Nov
Dec	0	-7	19	-1	30	7	45	-25	-13		88	87	39	1.5	19	Dec

Based on readings for 8 years at 59°25' N, 24°48' E, altitude 44 m/144 ft

Estonia

See map page 19

This small country on the northwestern boundary of Russia has a very similar climate to northern European Russia (see p. 300), but is a little milder in winter thanks to the moderating influence of the Baltic Sea, which does not freeze for prolonged periods. It is more open than Russia to weather influences coming from the Atlantic and northwest Europe. However, during severe spells of winter weather, it is dominated by cold winds from the interior of Russia.

The table for **Tallinn** (above) shows that conditions in Estonia do not differ much from the weather at **St Petersburg** (see table p. 302) in Russia.

Ethiopia

See map page 20

Ethiopia is a mountainous country in East Africa situated between 18° and 4° N. It is bordered by Sudan on the west, Kenya on the south, Somalia and Djibouti on the east, and Eritrea in the north. Large parts of the country lie between 1,800 m/6,000 ft and 2,400 m/8,000 ft and the highest mountain rises to over 4,600 m/15,000 ft. There are lowland regions in the east of the country. Most of Ethiopia has a tropical climate moderated by altitude with a marked wet season at the time of high sun. The eastern lowlands are much drier with a hot, semi-arid to desert climate. In the highlands of Ethiopia temperatures are reasonably warm around the year but rarely very hot. Above 1,800 m/6,000 ft the daily temperatures are rather similar to those in summer in northern France or New England. The tables for **Addis Ababa** (opposite and above) and **Harer** (opposite) are representative of conditions throughout the year in the highlands.

Most of the rain comes during the period April to September. In the west there tends to be a single

ADDIS ABABA · ETHIOPIAN HIGHLANDS

Month	Sunshine average hours per day	Temperatures Average daily minimum °C	°F	Average daily maximum °C	°F	Highest recorded °C	°F	Lowest recorded °C	°F	Discomfort from heat and humidity	Relative humidity 7:00 %	Relative humidity 13:00 %	Average monthly precipitation mm	in	Wet days more than 0.1 mm/0.004 in	Month
Jan	9	6	43	24	75	28	82	2	35		61	33	13	0.5	2	Jan
Feb	9	8	47	24	76	30	86	2	36		64	39	38	1.5	5	Feb
March	8	9	49	25	77	29	84	3	38		58	37	66	2.6	8	March
April	7	10	50	25	77	31	88	4	40	Moderate	65	44	86	3.4	10	April
May	8	10	50	25	77	33	91	4	39	Moderate	63	43	86	3.4	10	May
June	6	9	49	23	74	34	94	7	44		76	59	137	5.4	20	June
July	3	10	50	21	69	31	88	7	45		86	73	279	11.0	28	July
Aug	3	10	50	21	69	29	84	6	43		86	72	300	11.8	27	Aug
Sept	5	9	49	22	72	27	81	3	38		79	64	191	7.5	21	Sept
Oct	8	7	45	24	75	33	91	2	36		56	39	20	0.8	3	Oct
Nov	9	6	43	23	73	27	81	1	33		59	37	15	0.6	2	Nov
Dec	9	5	41	23	73	28	82	0	32		62	29	5	0.2	2	Dec

Based on readings for 12 years at 9°20′ N, 38°45′ E, altitude 2450 m/8038 ft

HARER · ETHIOPIAN HIGHLANDS

Month	Sunshine average hours per day	Temperatures Average daily minimum °C	°F	Average daily maximum °C	°F	Highest recorded °C	°F	Lowest recorded °C	°F	Discomfort from heat and humidity	Relative humidity 8:00 %	Average monthly precipitation mm	in	Wet days more than 1 mm/0.04 in	Month
Jan	8	13	55	25	77	28	82	7	45	Moderate	52	8	0.3	1.0	Jan
Feb	8	14	57	26	78	29	84	11	52	Moderate	50	33	1.3	3.0	Feb
March	7	14	58	27	80	32	90	11	52	Medium	56	76	3.0	7.0	March
April	8	15	59	27	80	30	86	13	55	Medium	59	119	4.7	11.0	April
May	7	15	59	27	80	31	88	13	55	Medium	76	127	5.0	10.0	May
June	7	14	58	26	78	31	88	12	54	Medium	73	89	3.5	9.0	June
July	4	14	57	24	75	29	84	11	52	Moderate	76	130	5.1	12.0	July
Aug	4	14	57	23	74	28	82	11	52	Moderate	76	160	6.3	15.0	Aug
Sept	6	14	58	24	76	29	84	12	54	Moderate	74	94	3.7	13.0	Sept
Oct	7	14	58	26	78	29	84	10	50	Moderate	55	36	1.4	5.0	Oct
Nov	10	13	56	26	78	28	82	8	46	Moderate	49	15	0.6	1.0	Nov
Dec	10	13	56	26	78	29	84	7	45	Moderate	52	10	0.4	0.9	Dec

Based on readings for 10 years at 9°42′ N, 42°30′ E, altitude 1851 m/6071 ft

maximum of rainfall in July and August, but towards the east there is often a brief wetter period in April and May then a pause before the heavier rains in July and August. The rainy season is often called the monsoon in Ethiopia because it is associated with a change in the predominant wind direction; northeast winds prevail during the dry season and westerly to southwesterly winds during the rains. Rainfall is above 1,000 mm/40 in a year almost everywhere in the highlands and it rises to as much as 1,500–2,000 mm/60–80 in in the wetter western parts.

Night-time temperatures may fall to near or below freezing in the mountains, particularly during the dry season. Occasional snow may fall on the highest peaks but there are no permanent snowfields.

In the northeastern lowlands, the Danakil desert, and in the southeastern lowlands, the Ogaden region, rainfall is low and temperatures are high around the year. The weather and climate are similar to that in the neighbouring countries of Somalia and Djibouti (see the table for **Djibouti** on p. 126). The scanty rainfall, usually below 500 mm/20 in a year, is very unreliable and severe droughts often occur.

Over most of Ethiopia sunshine is much reduced during the wet season when there is an average of two to four hours a day in July and August as compared with eight to nine hours during November to February. Thunderstorms are very frequent in the wetter parts of the country, occurring almost daily during the wet season; in many places there are over a hundred thunderstorms a year. Except in the hot lowlands, the climate of Ethiopia is generally healthy and pleasant, although the constant cloud and rain during the height of the wet season can be rather depressing for the visitor.

Falkland Islands

See map page 16

The Falklands consist of two main islands with a number of smaller islands, most of which are uninhabited. They are situated between 51° and 52° S, some 650 km/400 mi from the coast of South America. The total land area of the islands is about half the size of Wales or the size of the state of Connecticut. The islands have a number of hills or low mountains rising to 450–600 m/1,500–2,000 ft but much of the area is low-lying.

The weather and climate of the Falklands are similar to those of the Hebrides or Shetland Islands, but with a longer and slightly more severe winter. The Falklands are situated in the very stormy latitudes of the southern westerly winds or 'Roaring Forties' and gales are very frequent, particularly during the winter months. The weather is very changeable throughout the year with much cloud and rain but the total annual rainfall is not large.

The number of days with rain is similar to that in Britain and the number of days with snow is greater than that in the Shetland Islands. Sleet and snow are frequent in the winter months but the snow does not lie very deep or very long, since the weather is so frequently changing. The summers are cool and during the brief, fine, settled spells temperatures never rise very high. The average number of hours of sunshine a day ranges from two to three in winter to about six in summer. The table for **Stanley** (opposite and above) is representative of conditions at or near sea level.

Fiji

See map page 17

This southwest Pacific republic occupies 840 islands and islets to the east of Vanuatu and west of Tonga. They share with neighbouring countries the features of a typical tropical oceanic climate. The table for **Suva** (opposite), Fiji's capital, shows weather that is typical of the country.

Very similar conditions prevail throughout the year, with high temperatures and humidity. The daily range of temperature is quite small – about 4°–5° C/10° F. There is abundant rainfall. Being south of the equator, Fiji has its season of maximum rainfall between November and April. On some islands there is no great difference between the amount of rain from month to month. Tropical cyclones are less frequent than in the Pacific north of the equator. Much of the rainfall comes in short, heavy showers, often after a sunny morning, but longer periods of heavy rain lasting a day or so occur in the wetter months. Except in the wettest places, where cloud is more frequent, the country has moderately large amounts of sunshine, from six to eight hours a day.

STANLEY

EAST FALKLAND ISLAND

	Sunshine	Temperatures							Discomfort from heat and humidity	Precipitation and humidity			Wet days	
		Average daily				Highest recorded		Lowest recorded			Relative humidity 9:00	Average monthly precipitation			
		minimum		maximum											
	average hours per day	°C	°F	°C	°F	°C	°F	°C	°F		%	mm	in	more than 1 mm/0.04 in	
Jan	7	6	42	13	56	24	76	−1	30		78	71	2.8	17	Jan
Feb	6	5	41	13	55	23	74	−1	30		79	58	2.3	12	Feb
March	5	4	40	12	53	21	70	−3	27		82	64	2.5	15	March
April	3	3	37	9	49	17	63	−6	21		86	66	2.6	14	April
May	2	1	34	7	44	14	58	−7	20		88	66	2.6	15	May
June	2	−1	31	5	41	11	51	−11	12		89	53	2.1	13	June
July	2	−1	31	4	40	10	50	−9	16		89	51	2.0	13	July
Aug	3	−1	31	5	41	11	52	−11	12		87	51	2.0	13	Aug
Sept	4	1	33	7	45	15	59	−11	13		84	38	1.5	12	Sept
Oct	5	2	35	9	48	18	64	−6	22		80	41	1.6	11	Oct
Nov	7	3	37	11	52	22	71	−3	26		75	51	2.0	12	Nov
Dec	7	4	39	12	54	22	71	−2	29		77	71	2.8	15	Dec

Based on readings for 25 years at 51°42′ S, 57°51′ W, altitude 2 m/6 ft

SUVA

VITI LEVU ISLAND, FIJI

	Sunshine	Temperatures							Discomfort from heat and humidity	Precipitation and humidity				Wet days	
		Average daily				Highest recorded		Lowest recorded			Relative humidity 8:00 14:00		Average monthly precipitation			
		minimum		maximum												
	average hours per day	°C	°F	°C	°F	°C	°F	°C	°F		%		mm	in	more than 1 mm/0.04 in	
Jan	7	23	74	29	86	35	95	19	67	High	78	74	290	11.4	18	Jan
Feb	6	23	74	29	86	36	97	19	67	High	80	76	272	10.7	18	Feb
March	6	23	74	29	86	37	98	19	66	High	81	76	368	14.5	21	March
April	7	23	73	29	84	34	94	16	61	High	81	77	310	12.2	19	April
May	7	22	71	28	82	34	93	16	61	Medium	82	79	257	10.1	16	May
June	7	21	69	27	80	32	90	14	58	Medium	81	74	170	6.7	13	June
July	7	20	68	26	79	32	90	13	55	Medium	80	73	125	4.9	14	July
Aug	8	20	68	26	79	32	90	14	57	Medium	80	74	211	8.3	15	Aug
Sept	7	21	69	27	80	32	90	14	57	Medium	78	73	196	7.7	16	Sept
Oct	7	21	70	27	81	34	93	14	57	Medium	76	73	211	8.3	15	Oct
Nov	7	22	71	28	83	34	93	13	55	Medium	76	74	249	9.8	15	Nov
Dec	7	23	73	29	85	36	97	17	62	High	77	74	318	12.5	18	Dec

Based on readings for 43 years at 18°08′ S, 178°26′ E, altitude 6 m/20 ft

In this area of the Pacific the principal difference in the weather and climate is the amount of rainfall per month. Temperature and humidity are very similar from one island to another. The climate may generally be described as pleasant and healthy, although the combination of high temperature and humidity can be a little oppressive when not tempered by sea breezes or a brisk wind.

Finland

See map page 19

Finland, between 60° and 70° N, has a severe winter resembling that of Alaska or the Yukon. By contrast, the summers can be surprisingly warm, particularly in the south. In the north, above the Arctic Circle, the long midsummer sunshine compensates, to some extent, for the northerly latitude.

The south and centre of Finland are low-lying. It is a land of pine forests and innumerable lakes. The north, or Finnish Lapland, is higher, but only along the northwestern border with Norway do hills rise above 900 m/3,000 ft. The southwest coast is the mildest part of the country in winter, since the more open waters of the Baltic do not freeze as often as the Gulfs of Bothnia and Finland. Summers in the south and centre are as warm as those of Denmark and south Sweden. See the tables for **Helsinki** (below) on the coast and **Tampere** (opposite) which

lies inland. The winters are long and cold, with snow lying for an average of 90–120 days. Summer precipitation is nowhere very heavy and in winter it is mostly snow.

In the north the snow cover lasts from mid-October until late April or mid-May. Here, in the brief Arctic summer, daytime temperatures may rise almost as high as in the south and sunshine may average as much as nine to ten hours a day (see the table for **Inari** opposite and below). Weather is changeable from day to day at all seasons, however, for Finland is influenced by weather disturbances originating over the Atlantic. The longest spells of settled weather are in winter. Warm clothing is essential in winter and in severe weather there is a danger of frostbite, particularly in Arctic Finland, if suitable clothing is not worn. One irritant, an indirect result of the summer climate, is the swarms of mosquitoes and gnats which appear during the warm weather.

HELSINKI											SOUTHERN COASTAL FINLAND		
Sunshine	Temperatures							Discomfort from heat and humidity	Precipitation and humidity				Wet days
	Average daily				Highest recorded		Lowest recorded		Relative humidity		Average monthly precipitation		
average hours per day	minimum		maximum						7:30 13:30				more than 0.1 mm/0.004 in
	°C	°F	°C	°F	°C	°F	°C	°F		%	mm	in	
Jan	1	−9	17	−3	26	7	44	−33 −28		89	87	56	2.2	20	Jan
Feb	3	−10	15	−4	25	12	53	−30 −22		89	82	42	1.7	18	Feb
March	4	−7	20	0	32	15	59	−26 −15		86	70	36	1.4	14	March
April	6	−1	30	6	44	21	69	−14 8		81	66	44	1.7	13	April
May	9	4	40	14	56	26	79	−6 22		70	58	41	1.6	12	May
June	10	9	49	19	66	31	88	0 32		72	59	51	2.0	13	June
July	9	13	55	22	71	33	92	5 42		76	63	68	2.7	14	July
Aug	8	12	53	20	68	30	86	4 38		83	67	72	2.8	15	Aug
Sept	5	8	46	15	59	24	76	−4 25		89	72	71	2.8	15	Sept
Oct	3	3	37	8	47	18	64	−10 14		91	79	73	2.9	18	Oct
Nov	1	−1	30	3	37	11	51	−16 3		90	86	68	2.7	19	Nov
Dec	1	−5	23	−1	31	9	49	−28 −18		90	89	66	2.6	20	Dec

Based on readings for 30 years at 60°12′ N, 24°55′ E, altitude 46 m/151 ft

TAMPERE

SOUTHERN FINLAND

Sunshine	Temperatures											Discomfort from heat and humidity	Precipitation and humidity				Wet days
	Average daily				Highest recorded		Lowest recorded						Relative humidity 7:30 13:30		Average monthly precipitation		
average hours per day	minimum		maximum														more than 0.1 mm/0.004 in
	°C	°F	°C	°F	°C	°F	°C	°F					%		mm	in	
Jan 1	−11	12	−5	24	7	45	−36	−33					87	86	38	1.5	17 Jan
Feb 2	−11	12	−4	24	9	48	−36	−33					86	81	30	1.2	14 Feb
March 4	−9	16	0	31	12	54	−31	−23					86	69	25	1.0	11 March
April 6	−2	28	7	45	22	71	−22	−7					83	63	35	1.4	12 April
May 9	3	38	14	58	28	83	−7	19					74	54	42	1.7	11 May
June 9	9	48	19	67	31	88	−2	28					73	56	48	1.9	12 June
July 8	12	54	22	72	33	91	1	34					78	59	76	3.0	14 July
Aug 7	11	51	20	69	32	89	−1	31					86	63	75	3.0	14 Aug
Sept 4	7	44	14	57	27	80	−6	22					90	69	57	2.2	15 Sept
Oct 3	2	35	7	45	17	63	−14	7					90	79	57	2.2	16 Oct
Nov 1	−2	28	2	35	10	51	−22	−7					90	87	49	1.9	18 Nov
Dec 1	−6	20	−2	29	9	48	−32	−27					89	88	41	1.6	18 Dec

Based on readings for 30 years at 61°28´ N, 23°46´ E, altitude 84 m/276 ft

INARI

NORTHERN FINLAND

Sunshine	Temperatures											Discomfort from heat and humidity	Precipitation and humidity				Wet days
	Average daily				Highest recorded		Lowest recorded						Relative humidity		Average monthly precipitation		
average hours per day	minimum		maximum														more than 0.1 mm/0.004 in
	°C	°F	°C	°F	°C	°F	°C	°F					%		mm	in	
Jan 0	−18	−1	−9	17	4	38	−41	−43							22	0.9	14 Jan
Feb 1	−17	2	−9	16	6	42	−42	−43							19	0.8	13 Feb
March 5	−14	7	−3	26	8	46	−38	−37							15	0.6	10 March
April 6	−9	17	2	35	13	56	−29	−19							20	0.8	9 April
May 6	0	31	8	47	24	75	−12	11							29	1.1	13 May
June 7	6	42	14	57	28	82	−2	28							54	2.1	16 June
July 7	9	48	17	63	31	88	2	35							53	2.1	15 July
Aug 4	7	45	15	59	26	79	0	32							66	2.6	16 Aug
Sept 3	3	38	9	47	24	75	−6	22							44	1.7	15 Sept
Oct 2	−3	26	1	34	14	56	−18	−1							28	1.1	13 Oct
Nov 0	−10	13	−4	24	7	44	−36	−32							25	1.0	13 Nov
Dec 0	−18	0	−8	18	2	36	−40	−40							30	1.2	15 Dec

Based on readings for 10 years at 69°04´ N, 27°06´ E, altitude 149 m/489 ft

France

France is a large country, two and a half times as big as Great Britain, extending for some 1,000 km/ 600 mi from north to south and from east to west. Although much of northern and western France is low-lying and rather flat, there are some high mountain regions in the south and east: part of the western Alps, the Pyrenees which form the border with Spain, and the Massif Central which rises to over 1,800 m/6,000 ft in its southern and central parts. Consequently, there are considerable variations of climate within France.

Northern and northwestern France is most affected by the changeable weather brought in by Atlantic disturbances and its climate is rather similar to that of the UK. Southern France has a Mediterranean type of climate and is warmer than the north, particularly in summer. Central and eastern France, roughly east of a line through Dunkirk, Paris, and Lyon, has a more continental climate which bears some resemblance to that found in western Germany and Switzerland.

The high mountain areas have their own distinctive climates with heavier precipitation, much of it snow in winter; these areas are colder all the year round. Only along the Mediterranean coast and in the adjacent mountain regions is summer generally settled, sunny, and warm. Everywhere else the weather can be changeable at all times of the year.

It is most convenient for purposes of description to divide France into five climatic regions and to describe briefly the weather found in each.

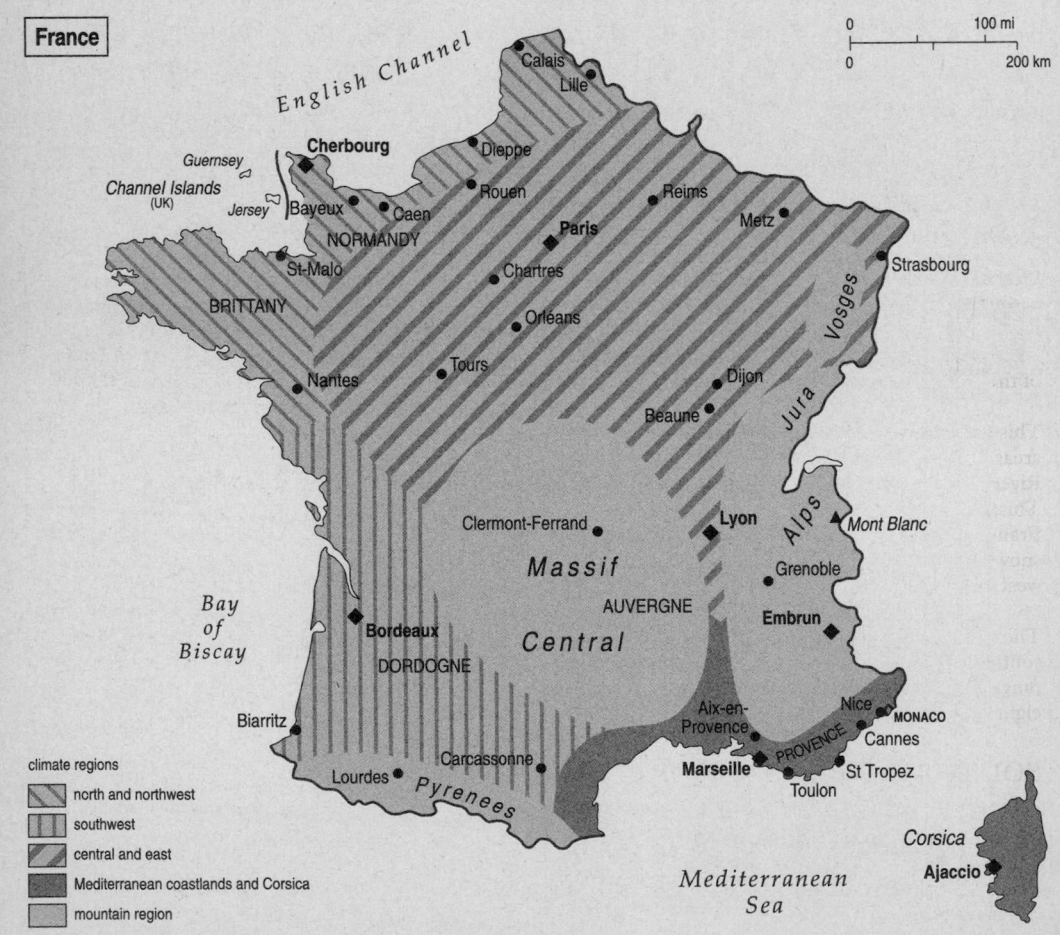

France

English Channel
Calais
Lille
Cherbourg
Dieppe
Guernsey
Channel Islands (UK)
Jersey Bayeux Caen
Rouen
Reims
Metz
Paris
NORMANDY
St-Malo
Chartres
Strasbourg
BRITTANY
Orléans
Vosges
Nantes
Tours
Dijon
Beaune
Jura
Clermont-Ferrand
Lyon
Alps
Mont Blanc
Massif
Grenoble
Bay of Biscay
AUVERGNE
Embrun
Bordeaux
Central
DORDOGNE
Biarritz
Aix-en-Provence
Nice
MONACO
Cannes
PROVENCE
Carcassonne
Marseille
St Tropez
Lourdes
Pyrenees
Toulon
Corsica
Ajaccio
Mediterranean Sea

climate regions
north and northwest
southwest
central and east
Mediterranean coastlands and Corsica
mountain region

0   100 mi
0   200 km

CHERBOURG										NORTHWESTERN FRANCE		
Sunshine	Temperatures						Discomfort from heat and humidity	Precipitation and humidity			Wet days	
average hours per day	Average daily			Highest recorded		Lowest recorded		Relative humidity 6:00 12:00		Average monthly precipitation	more than 0.1 mm/0.004 in	
	minimum		maximum									
	°C	°F	°C	°F	°C	°F	°C	°F	%	mm	in	
Jan	2	4	40	8	47	14	58	-6	21	83 79	109	4.3	19	Jan
Feb	2	4	39	8	47	18	65	-10	14	82 76	75	3.0	15	Feb
March	5	5	41	10	51	23	73	-4	25	83 74	62	2.4	13	March
April	5	7	45	12	54	24	75	0	31	83 73	49	1.9	12	April
May	7	9	49	15	59	30	86	4	38	85 73	41	1.6	11	May
June	7	12	54	18	64	31	89	6	43	86 74	39	1.5	10	June
July	8	14	57	19	67	32	89	8	46	86 74	55	2.2	12	July
Aug	7	14	57	20	67	33	91	9	48	88 75	71	2.8	12	Aug
Sept	5	13	56	19	65	30	87	6	43	86 74	79	3.1	15	Sept
Oct	2	10	51	15	60	26	78	3	38	84 73	99	3.9	16	Oct
Nov	2	8	46	12	53	19	66	-1	31	83 77	133	5.2	17	Nov
Dec	2	5	42	10	49	17	62	-6	22	84 79	119	4.7	19	Dec

Based on readings for 30 years at 49°39′ N, 1°38′ W, altitude 8 m/26 ft

NORTHERN AND NORTHWESTERN FRANCE

Including (with towns and cities in parentheses): LE NORD (Lille, Calais); most of PICARDY and NORMANDY (Dieppe, Rouen, Caen, Bayeux, Cherbourg); and BRITTANY (St Malo) and the mouth of the Loire (Nantes).

This area comprises the coasts and adjacent inland areas from the Belgian border to the mouth of the River Loire (see the table for **Cherbourg** above). This area has the most maritime climate in all France. Winters are generally mild and frost and snow are not too frequent, becoming less so in the west. Rain occurs at all times of the year.

The summers are a little warmer than those found in southern Britain. Average daily hours of sunshine range from two in midwinter to between seven and eight in midsummer.

SOUTHWESTERN FRANCE

Including (with towns and cities in parentheses): CHARENTES, DORDOGNE, GIRONDE (Bordeaux), NAVARRE (Biarritz), central MIDI-PYRENEES and western parts of LANGUEDOC-ROUSSILLON (Carcassonne).

This is mainly a lowland region, often called by its historic name of Aquitaine (see the table for **Bordeaux** overleaf). The summers are much warmer and sunnier than in northwest France. Winters are mild and cold spells do not last long. Summers can be rather wet, particularly towards the Pyrenees and the Spanish border, but the rain tends to be heavy and brief. Summers have more sunshine and longer spells of settled weather than farther north.

CENTRAL AND EASTERN FRANCE

Including (with towns and cities in parentheses): ALSACE (Strasbourg) and LORRAINE (Metz), excluding the mountain areas of the Vosges BURGUNDY (Beaune, Dijon), LE CENTER (Chartres, Orléans), CHAMPAGNE (Reims), ILE DE FRANCE (Paris), TOURAINE (Tours), and the northern Rhône valley (Lyon).

This area is marked by rather colder winters with a greater chance of frost and snow than in the northwest. Summers also tend to be a little warmer. Rainfall is generally low and tends to fall in summer when it is often associated with thunderstorms. Winters become colder towards the east and they are not any warmer farther south. In winter occasional

BORDEAUX

SOUTHWESTERN FRANCE

average hours per day		Average daily °C minimum	Average daily °F	Average daily °C maximum	Average daily °F	Highest recorded °C	Highest recorded °F	Lowest recorded °C	Lowest recorded °F	Discomfort from heat and humidity	Relative humidity 6:00 %	Relative humidity 12:00 %	Average monthly precipitation mm	Average monthly precipitation in	more than 0.1 mm/0.004 in	
Jan	3	2	35	9	49	18	65	-12	10		93	80	90	3.5	16	Jan
Feb	4	2	36	11	51	22	72	-15	5		91	73	75	3.0	13	Feb
March	5	4	40	15	59	26	78	-6	21		91	64	63	2.5	13	March
April	7	6	43	17	63	31	88	-5	23		91	60	48	1.9	13	April
May	7	9	48	20	69	34	92	-3	26		91	60	61	2.4	14	May
June	8	12	54	24	75	38	101	3	37	Moderate	91	62	65	2.6	11	June
July	9	14	57	25	78	39	101	5	41	Moderate	91	61	56	2.2	11	July
Aug	8	14	56	26	78	37	99	6	42	Medium	93	60	70	2.8	12	Aug
Sept	7	12	54	23	74	36	97	-2	29	Moderate	96	67	84	3.3	13	Sept
Oct	5	8	47	18	65	30	87	-5	22		96	71	83	3.3	14	Oct
Nov	3	5	40	13	55	24	75	-6	21		95	80	96	3.8	15	Nov
Dec	2	3	37	9	49	21	70	-12	11		94	83	109	4.3	17	Dec

Based on readings for 30 years at 44°50′ N, 0°42′ W, altitude 46 m/151 ft

PARIS

NORTH-CENTRAL FRANCE

average hours per day		Average daily °C minimum	Average daily °F	Average daily °C maximum	Average daily °F	Highest recorded °C	Highest recorded °F	Lowest recorded °C	Lowest recorded °F	Discomfort from heat and humidity	Relative humidity 6:00 %	Relative humidity 12:00 %	Average monthly precipitation mm	Average monthly precipitation in	more than 0.1 mm/0.004 in	
Jan	2	1	34	6	43	15	58	-12	10		88	80	56	2.2	17	Jan
Feb	3	1	34	7	45	21	71	-15	6		87	73	46	1.8	14	Feb
March	5	4	39	12	54	26	78	-4	24		85	63	35	1.4	12	March
April	6	6	43	16	60	30	86	0	32		82	54	42	1.7	13	April
May	7	10	49	20	68	33	91	2	36		83	55	57	2.2	12	May
June	8	13	55	23	73	38	100	6	42		83	58	54	2.1	12	June
July	8	15	58	25	76	40	104	9	48	Moderate	83	57	59	2.3	12	July
Aug	7	14	58	24	75	35	95	8	46	Moderate	87	61	64	2.5	13	Aug
Sept	6	12	53	21	70	33	92	3	37		90	65	55	2.2	13	Sept
Oct	4	8	46	16	60	28	83	-3	27		91	71	50	2.0	13	Oct
Nov	2	5	40	10	50	21	69	-5	23		91	79	51	2.0	15	Nov
Dec	2	2	36	7	44	17	62	-13	9		90	82	50	2.0	16	Dec

Based on readings for 30 years at 48°49′ N, 2°20′ E, altitude 75 m/246 ft

very cold spells can occur. There is a definite increase in summer warmth in the south and an increase in sunshine from an average of seven to nine hours a day. Compare the tables for **Paris** (opposite and below) and **Lyon** (below).

THE MEDITERRANEAN COAST AND CORSICA

Including (with towns and cities in parentheses): the southern Rhône valley and most of LANGUEDOC-ROUSSILLON; coastal PROVENCE (Aix-en-Provence, Cannes, Marseille, Nice, St Tropez, Toulon); and CORSICA (Ajaccio).

Apart from the island of Corsica (represented by the table for **Ajaccio** overleaf), a Mediterranean climate is confined to the Rhône valley south of Valence and the coastal areas of Languedoc and Provence at the foot of the Cevennes and southern Alps. Here summers are warm, or even hot, with a three-month period when rain rarely falls. When it does rain at this season it is heavy and often associated with thunder. Sunshine is abundant, as much as eleven to twelve hours a day in summer and five in midwinter. Winters are generally mild and sunny but this pleasant weather is often interrupted by very

changeable cold and blustery weather brought by a northerly wind called the mistral. This blows with particular strength in the Rhône valley and around **Marseille** (overleaf). The mistral can bring unseasonably cold weather for a few days in spring. The Côte d'Azur from Toulon to the Italian border, including the small independent principality of Monaco, is much less exposed to the cold blasts of the mistral and in Corsica the cold is moderated by the warm waters of the Mediterranean.

Corsica, which is particularly popular as a holiday resort because of its mild winters at sea level and hot sunny summers, is a mountainous island. In the interior altitudes exceed 2,000 m/6,500 ft and here winter snowfall can be heavy and snow cover may last well into spring.

THE MOUNTAINOUS REGIONS

Including (with towns and cities in parentheses): the Pyrenees (Lourdes); the Massif Central: AUVERGNE (Clermont-Ferrand), LIMOUSIN, western parts of RHONE-ALPES and northern parts of MIDI-PYRENEES and LANGUEDOC-ROUSSILLON; and the Vosges, the Jura, and the Alps (Embrun, Grenoble).

The principal mountain regions of France are the Vosges in Alsace and Lorraine, the Jura and Alps

LYON													EASTERN FRANCE	
Sunshine	Temperatures							Discomfort from heat and humidity	Precipitation and humidity				Wet days	
	Average daily		Highest recorded		Lowest recorded				Relative humidity		Average monthly precipitation			
	minimum	maximum							6:30 12:30					
average hours per day	°C	°F	°C	°F	°C	°F	°C	°F		%		mm	in	more than 0.1 mm/0.004 in	
Jan	2	–1	30	5	42	18	64	–17	2		89	80	52	2.1	15	Jan
Feb	3	0	31	7	45	22	71	–21	–7		87	72	46	1.8	12	Feb
March	5	3	37	13	55	23	73	–10	14		87	60	53	2.1	11	March
April	6	6	42	16	61	30	86	–4	24		84	56	56	2.2	11	April
May	8	9	49	20	69	32	90	1	33		83	56	69	2.7	13	May
June	8	13	55	24	75	37	98	2	36	Moderate	82	55	85	3.4	11	June
July	9	15	59	27	80	40	103	6	44	Medium	79	50	56	2.2	10	July
Aug	8	14	58	26	79	40	103	6	44	Moderate	85	54	89	3.5	11	Aug
Sept	7	12	53	23	73	36	96	1	33	Moderate	89	60	93	3.7	11	Sept
Oct	4	7	45	16	61	28	82	–5	24		92	69	77	3.0	12	Oct
Nov	2	4	38	10	50	23	73	–8	18		91	78	80	3.2	14	Nov
Dec	2	0	33	6	43	19	66	–20	–3		90	80	57	2.2	14	Dec

Based on readings for 30 years at 45°43′ N, 4°57′ E, altitude 200 m/656 ft

AJACCIO — CORSICA

Sunshine	Temperatures									Discomfort from heat and humidity	Precipitation and humidity				Wet days	
	Average daily				Highest recorded		Lowest recorded				Relative humidity 6:30 12:30		Average monthly precipitation			
	minimum		maximum													
average hours per day	°C	°F	°C	°F	°C	°F	°C	°F			%		mm	in	more than 0.01 mm/.004 in	
Jan 4	3	38	13	55	21	69	−5	23			84	66	76	3.0	12	Jan
Feb 5	4	39	14	56	23	74	−6	21			85	67	65	2.6	10	Feb
March 6	5	41	16	60	26	79	−4	25			85	67	53	2.1	9	March
April 8	7	45	18	64	29	85	−2	29			85	66	48	1.9	9	April
May 10	10	50	21	70	33	91	3	37			83	69	50	2.0	8	May
June 11	14	56	25	77	37	99	7	45	Moderate		78	65	21	0.8	4	June
July 12	16	60	27	81	37	98	9	49	Medium		75	65	10	0.4	1	July
Aug 11	16	60	28	82	39	101	9	48	Medium		78	64	16	0.6	2	Aug
Sept 9	15	58	26	78	36	97	8	46	Medium		83	64	50	2.0	6	Sept
Oct 7	11	52	22	71	31	88	2	36			84	63	88	3.5	10	Oct
Nov 5	7	45	18	63	26	79	−2	28			87	66	97	3.8	11	Nov
Dec 4	4	40	15	58	22	72	−4	26			85	66	98	3.9	13	Dec

Based on readings for 30 years at 41°55′ n, 8°48′ e, altitude 4 m/12 ft

MARSEILLE — SOUTHERN FRANCE

Sunshine	Temperatures									Discomfort from heat and humidity	Precipitation and humidity				Wet days	
	Average daily				Highest recorded		Lowest recorded				Relative humidity 6:30 12:30		Average monthly precipitation			
	minimum		maximum													
average hours per day	°C	°F	°C	°F	°C	°F	°C	°F			%		mm	in	more than 0.1 mm/0.004 in	
Jan 4	2	35	10	50	18	65	−11	13			82	68	43	1.7	8	Jan
Feb 6	2	36	12	53	22	71	−17	2			81	60	32	1.3	6	Feb
March 6	5	41	15	59	24	75	−10	14			80	57	43	1.7	7	March
April 8	8	46	18	64	29	83	−2	28			79	54	42	1.7	7	April
May 9	11	52	22	71	31	89	0	32			78	54	46	1.8	8	May
June 10	15	58	26	79	37	99	5	42	Moderate		72	50	24	0.9	4	June
July 11	17	63	29	84	39	102	8	46	Medium		69	45	11	0.4	2	July
Aug 10	17	63	28	83	37	99	9	47	Medium		75	49	34	1.3	5	Aug
Sept 8	15	58	25	77	34	94	1	34	Moderate		81	54	60	2.4	6	Sept
Oct 6	10	51	20	68	29	84	−1	30			84	61	76	3.0	8	Oct
Nov 5	6	43	15	58	23	73	−5	22			85	66	69	2.7	9	Nov
Dec 4	3	37	11	52	20	68	−11	13			83	68	66	2.6	10	Dec

Based on readings for 30 years at 43°27′ N, 5°13′ E, altitude 4 m/13 ft

EMBRUN														ALPINE FRANCE	
Sunshine	Temperatures								Discomfort from heat and humidity	Precipitation and humidity				Wet days	
	Average daily				Highest recorded		Lowest recorded			Relative humidity 6:30 12:30		Average monthly precipitation			
	minimum		maximum												
average hours per day	°C	°F	°C	°F	°C	°F	°C	°F		%		mm	in	more than 0.1 mm/0.004 in	
Jan	5	−5	24	5	41	17	62	−16	3		69	54	49	1.9	9	Jan
Feb	6	−3	26	7	45	20	68	−19	−2		69	49	43	1.7	8	Feb
March	7	0	33	12	53	24	74	−12	11		68	41	48	1.9	8	March
April	8	3	38	15	60	26	80	−5	22		72	39	51	2.0	9	April
May	8	7	45	19	67	29	85	−3	28		76	43	61	2.4	11	May
June	9	10	50	23	73	33	91	−1	31		78	45	62	2.4	10	June
July	10	12	54	26	79	34	93	3	38	Moderate	75	40	48	1.9	7	July
Aug	9	12	53	25	77	34	93	4	39	Moderate	77	42	65	2.6	8	Aug
Sept	8	10	49	22	71	31	89	0	32		80	49	70	2.8	8	Sept
Oct	7	5	42	16	61	23	74	−5	22		77	51	70	2.8	9	Oct
Nov	5	1	33	10	50	20	67	−9	16		75	54	68	2.7	10	Nov
Dec	4	−3	26	6	42	15	59	−15	6		71	57	65	2.6	10	Dec

Based on readings for 30 years at 44°34′ N, 6°30′ E, altitude 871 m/2858 ft

along the borders with Switzerland and Italy, the Pyrenees in the extreme south, and the higher parts of the Massif Central. These areas are the wettest and coldest regions of France and much of the winter precipitation is snow. Winter sports are best developed in the Alps and Pyrenees but can be pursued for a shorter period in the other mountain regions. The weather and climate of the French Alps and Jura is very similar to that found in the Swiss Alps (see p. 355).

The table for **Embrun** (above) illustrates conditions at medium levels in the heart of the French Alps. In the Pyrenees precipitation tends to be greatest in winter and autumn but in the Vosges, Jura, and the northern Alps, summer and autumn are the wettest seasons. The southern Alps, Pyrenees, and parts of the Massif Central have relatively fine and warm summer weather, considering their height, but this may be briefly interrupted by cloud, rain, and thunder.

The most unpleasant aspect of the summer weather in these mountain areas is the frequent and sudden onset of cloud towards midday which may obscure the peaks but leave the valleys clear. In winter conditions are often reversed with the mountains rising into clear blue skies and the valleys enveloped in low cloud and fog. Severe frosts may occur in settled calm weather in all valley regions in winter.

French Guiana

See map page 16

This is a small country on the north coast of South America, bordered on the west by Surinam and on the south and east by Brazil. Situated between 2° and 6° N, it has an equatorial type of climate which is described in more detail on p. 168 for Guyana. French Guiana has a large area of lowland. Here the main rainy season is from December to June and the months August to October are almost dry. This is the principal climatic difference between French Guiana and Surinam and Guyana.

Otherwise temperature and humidity remain high through the year and there is little difference between the lowlands in all these countries. Cayenne is rather wetter, taking the year as a whole, than Georgetown in Guyana and Paramaribo in Surinam. The table for

CAYENNE											COASTAL FRENCH GUIANA		
Sunshine		Temperatures						Discomfort from heat and humidity	Precipitation and humidity				Wet days
		Average daily				Highest recorded		Lowest recorded		Relative humidity		Average monthly precipitation	
average hours per day		minimum		maximum						9:00 15:00			more than 1 mm/0.04 in
		°C	°F	°C	°F	°C	°F	°C	°F		%	mm	in
Jan	5	23	74	29	84	33	91	19	67	High	83	80	366	14.4	20	Jan
Feb	4	23	74	29	85	34	93	20	68	High	81	78	312	12.3	16	Feb
March	4	23	74	29	85	33	92	19	66	High	83	80	401	15.8	22	March
April	4	24	75	30	86	33	92	18	65	High	84	81	480	18.9	21	April
May	4	23	74	29	85	33	92	20	68	High	86	83	551	21.7	26	May
June	6	23	73	31	87	34	93	21	69	High	85	79	394	15.5	23	June
July	7	23	73	31	88	34	93	20	68	High	82	75	175	6.9	18	July
Aug	8	23	73	32	90	36	96	20	68	High	77	71	71	2.8	9	Aug
Sept	9	23	74	33	91	36	97	21	70	Extreme	73	69	31	1.2	4	Sept
Oct	9	23	74	33	91	36	97	20	68	Extreme	73	69	33	1.3	4	Oct
Nov	8	23	74	32	89	35	95	20	68	Extreme	78	74	117	4.6	11	Nov
Dec	6	23	74	30	86	34	93	20	68	High	83	79	272	10.7	18	Dec

Based on readings for 23 years at 4°56′ N, 52°27′ W, altitude 6 m/20 ft

Cayenne (above) on the coast is representative of a large part of the country. Only a small area in the south of the country consists of upland plateau where climatic conditions are better represented by the table for **Santa Elena** (p. 418) in Venezuela.

French Polynesia

See map page 17

This overseas French territory in the South Pacific comprises the Gambier, Marquesas, Society, Tuamotu, Tubuai, and Austral Islands. Although Tahiti, in the Society Islands, is large and well known for its mountainous landscapes, many of the other islands in French Polynesia are merely flat coral reefs and atolls.

The weather and climate are typical of a tropical oceanic environment. Very similar conditions prevail throughout the year with high temperatures and humidity. The daily range of temperature is quite small, about 4°–5° C/10° F.

There is abundant rainfall. Being south of the equator, French Polynesia has its season of maximum rainfall between November and March or April. Rainfall is moderate to heavy and occurs in all months. Tropical storms of the cyclone or typhoon type are less frequent here than in the western Pacific but do occur occasionally. Weather can be quite variable from day to day. Periods of continuous rain lasting a day or more are not unusual but much rain comes in the afternoon or in evening downpours after an otherwise fine, sunny day.

The climate is generally healthy and pleasant; the moderately high temperature and humidity are tempered by brisk daytime winds, either as afternoon sea breezes or as predominant southeast trade winds.

The tables for **Makatea** (opposite and above), in the Tuamotu group of islands, and **Papeete** (opposite), on Tahiti, are representative of the weather in French Polynesia.

MAKATEA
TUAMOTU ISLANDS

Sunshine	Temperatures								Discomfort from heat and humidity	Precipitation and humidity				Wet days
	Average daily				Highest recorded		Lowest recorded			Relative humidity 6:00 18:00		Average monthly precipitation		
	minimum		maximum											
average hours per day	°C	°F	°C	°F	°C	°F	°C	°F		%		mm	in	more than 0.25 mm/0.01 in
Jan	24	75	32	89	34	94	21	69	Extreme	87	80	170	6.7	16	Jan
Feb	23	74	31	88	34	94	20	68	Extreme	88	83	234	8.8	18	Feb
March	23	74	32	89	34	93	20	68	Extreme	89	82	155	6.1	17	March
April	23	74	31	87	34	93	19	67	Extreme	89	85	180	7.1	17	April
May	23	73	30	86	33	91	18	64	High	85	82	91	3.6	14	May
June	22	72	29	85	32	90	16	60	High	85	82	122	4.8	10	June
July	22	71	29	84	32	89	17	62	High	84	80	81	3.2	10	July
Aug	22	71	29	84	32	89	17	62	High	84	80	109	4.3	16	Aug
Sept	22	71	29	85	32	90	18	64	High	82	80	94	3.7	13	Sept
Oct	23	73	30	86	34	93	19	66	High	82	80	84	3.3	10	Oct
Nov	23	74	31	88	35	95	19	66	Extreme	84	81	130	5.1	17	Nov
Dec	23	74	32	89	34	94	20	68	Extreme	87	82	140	5.5	17	Dec

Based on readings for 6 years at 15°47′ S, 148°14′ W, altitude 47 m/154 ft

PAPEETE
TAHITI

Sunshine	Temperatures								Discomfort from heat and humidity	Precipitation and humidity				Wet days
	Average daily				Highest recorded		Lowest recorded			Relative humidity 8:00 16:00		Average monthly precipitation		
	minimum		maximum											
average hours per day	°C	°F	°C	°F	°C	°F	°C	°F		%		mm	in	more than 2.5 mm/0.1 in
Jan	5	22	72	32	89	35	95	19	67	Extreme	82	77	252	9.9	16	Jan
Feb	6	22	72	32	89	33	92	19	67	Extreme	82	77	244	9.6	16	Feb
March	7	22	72	32	89	33	92	19	67	Extreme	84	78	429	16.9	17	March
April	7	22	72	32	89	33	92	19	67	Extreme	85	78	142	5.6	10	April
May	7	21	70	31	87	33	91	18	65	High	84	78	102	4.0	10	May
June	7	21	69	30	86	32	90	16	61	High	85	79	76	3.0	8	June
July	7	20	68	30	86	32	89	16	61	High	83	77	53	2.1	5	July
Aug	7	20	68	30	86	30	86	16	61	High	83	78	43	1.7	6	Aug
Sept	8	21	69	30	86	31	87	17	62	High	81	76	53	2.1	6	Sept
Oct	7	21	70	31	87	32	89	17	62	High	79	76	89	3.5	9	Oct
Nov	7	22	71	31	88	32	90	18	64	High	80	77	150	5.9	13	Nov
Dec	6	22	72	31	88	33	91	19	66	High	81	78	249	9.8	14	Dec

Based on readings for 9 years at 17°32′ S, 149°34′ W, altitude 92 m/302 ft

	Sunshine	Temperatures											Discomfort from heat and humidity	Precipitation and humidity				Wet days
		Average daily				Highest recorded		Lowest recorded						Relative humidity		Average monthly precipitation		
		minimum		maximum										6:30	12:30			
	average hours per day	°C	°F	°C	°F	°C	°F	°C	°F					%		mm	in	more than 0.1 mm/0.004 in
Jan	5	23	73	31	87	34	94	17	63				High	93	76	249	9.8	13.0	Jan
Feb	6	22	72	31	88	34	94	17	63				High	94	75	236	9.3	11.0	Feb
March	5	23	73	32	89	36	96	17	63				Extreme	94	74	335	13.2	15.0	March
April	5	23	73	32	89	35	95	18	64				Extreme	95	75	340	13.4	14.0	April
May	5	22	72	31	88	37	99	18	64				High	93	75	244	9.6	11.0	May
June	4	21	70	29	85	35	95	17	63				High	85	71	13	0.5	1.0	June
July	4	20	68	28	83	33	92	17	62				Medium	85	69	3	0.1	0.7	July
Aug	3	21	69	29	84	33	92	17	63				High	86	70	18	0.7	3.0	Aug
Sept	3	22	71	29	85	33	92	19	66				High	88	74	104	4.1	11.0	Sept
Oct	4	22	71	30	86	33	92	19	67				High	92	79	345	13.6	19.0	Oct
Nov	4	22	71	30	86	35	95	19	67				High	94	79	373	14.7	19.0	Nov
Dec	5	22	72	31	87	33	92	19	66				High	92	76	249	9.8	13.0	Dec

Based on readings for 11 years at 0°23' N, 9°26' E, altitude 35 m/115 ft

Gabon

See map page 21

Gabon is one of the four territories which formerly made up the French colony of Equatorial Africa; the others are the Congo Republic (Brazzaville), Cameroon, and the Central African Republic. Gabon is bordered on the north by Cameroon and on the south by the Congo Republic. It has a coastline on the South Atlantic and lies between 2° N and 4° S.

It is part of the same major climatic region described in more detail for the Congo Democratic Republic.

The whole country has a typical equatorial climate: hot, wet, and humid around the year with much cloud.

Annual rainfall is almost everywhere between 1,250 mm/50 in and 2,000 mm/80 in, rising to 2,500 mm/120 in near the coast and in the higher districts.

The table for **Libreville** (above) illustrates conditions over most of the country. The driest months are almost everywhere June to August when the intertropical rain-belt has moved to its farthest position north.

BANJUL														GAMBIA
Sunshine		Temperatures							Discomfort from heat and humidity	Precipitation and humidity				Wet days
average hours per day		Average daily				Highest recorded		Lowest recorded		Relative humidity 5:00 14:00		Average monthly precipitation		more than 1 mm/0.04 in
		minimum		maximum										
		°C	°F	°C	°F	°C	°F	°C	°F	%		mm	in	
Jan	9	15	59	31	88	37	99	7	45	Medium	67	27	3	0.1	0.1	Jan
Feb	10	16	61	32	90	39	102	10	50	Medium	66	26	3	0.1	0.3	Feb
March	10	17	63	34	94	40	104	12	53	Medium	76	29	0	0.0	0.0	March
April	10	18	65	33	91	41	106	12	54	High	82	41	0	0.0	0.0	April
May	10	19	67	32	89	41	106	14	57	High	88	49	10	0.4	0.9	May
June	9	23	73	32	89	38	100	18	65	High	91	61	58	2.3	5.0	June
July	6	23	74	30	86	34	93	21	69	High	94	72	282	11.1	16.0	July
Aug	6	23	73	29	85	33	92	20	68	High	95	78	500	19.7	19.0	Aug
Sept	6	23	73	31	87	34	94	17	63	High	95	73	310	12.2	19.0	Sept
Oct	8	22	72	32	89	37	99	16	61	High	95	65	109	4.3	8.0	Oct
Nov	8	18	65	32	89	36	96	12	54	Medium	90	47	18	0.7	0.8	Nov
Dec	9	16	61	31	88	36	96	9	48	Medium	77	36	3	0.1	0.2	Dec

Based on readings for 9 years at 13°21' N, 16°40' W, altitude 27 m/90 ft

Gambia

See map page 20

The Gambia is a tiny country situated on the west coast of Africa on 13° N. It is entirely surrounded by Senegal and extends in a narrow strip inland on either side of the Gambia river. It is about the same size as the county of Yorkshire or the state of Connecticut. It has climate and weather similar to that of central Senegal. The table for **Banjul** (above) is representative of the whole country and shows conditions very similar to those in the table for **Dakar** (p. 314).

TBILISI													GEORGIA
Sunshine		Temperatures						Discomfort from heat and humidity	Precipitation and humidity				Wet days
		Average daily				Highest recorded	Lowest recorded		Relative humidity		Average monthly precipitation		
		minimum		maximum					9:00	15:00			
average hours per day		°C	°F	°C	°F	°C	°F	°C	°F		%	mm	in	more than 0.1 mm/0.004 in
Jan	3	-1	30	7	45	20	67	-13	9		79	60	17	0.7	6	Jan
Feb	4	0	31	9	47	22	72	-15	5		75	53	15	0.6	7	Feb
March	5	3	38	13	56	24	76	-6	21		69	50	27	1.1	8	March
April	5	8	46	17	63	29	84	-4	25		66	49	61	2.4	13	April
May	7	12	54	24	75	32	90	3	36		61	47	75	3.0	12	May
June	9	16	61	28	82	35	95	6	42	Medium	57	42	54	2.1	11	June
July	9	19	67	31	87	40	103	12	54	Medium	57	40	46	1.8	8	July
Aug	8	19	65	30	86	37	99	14	57	Medium	60	42	46	1.8	9	Aug
Sept	7	15	59	26	78	36	96	5	41	Moderate	66	49	45	1.8	8	Sept
Oct	6	10	49	20	68	29	85	-2	28		71	53	30	1.2	7	Oct
Nov	3	5	41	14	57	23	73	-4	25		78	60	27	1.1	7	Nov
Dec	3	1	34	9	48	22	72	-11	13		80	65	19	0.8	7	Dec

Based on readings for 8 years at 41°41′ N, 44°57′ E, altitude 490 m/1608 ft

Georgia

See map page 22

The climate of this mountainous country on the eastern shore of the Black Sea is almost tropical in summer, while the winters are warmer even than in the mild southern Russian regions to the north.

Cold spells, however, do occur and low temperatures are frequent in winter, both on the high mountains and in the deep, enclosed valleys. The western part of the country is wet throughout the year.

There are lowlands along the shores of the Black Sea. Here conditions are milder in winter and quite hot in summer.

The table for **Tbilisi** (above) in southeastern Georgia illustrates the conditions inland.

Germany

Germany has an area of about 355,000 sq km/ 137,000 sq mi. Occupying a central position in Europe, it extends from Denmark in the north to Switzerland and Austria in the south.

It is bordered on the west by the Benelux Countries and France and on the east by Poland and the Czech Republic. Germany has coastlines both on the North Sea and on the Baltic.

Northern Germany is part of the North European Plain and is generally low-lying and rather flat. Central and southern Germany is hilly and rises southwards towards the Alps on the Austrian border.

This increasing altitude in the centre and south of the country compensates for the decreasing latitude

so that in summer temperatures do not differ significantly from north to south.

However, in winter temperatures decrease and the number of days with frost and snow increase both southwards and eastwards. This is a consequence of increasing distance from the sea, higher altitude, and the effect of cold easterly winds from Russia.

Germany has a variable climate with frequent changes of weather from day to day. The character of individual summers and winters may also be very different from year to year, depending on whether oceanic or continental influences dominate. During severe winters, rivers and canals may freeze and snow may lie for long periods. Over most of the country the summers are marginally wetter than the

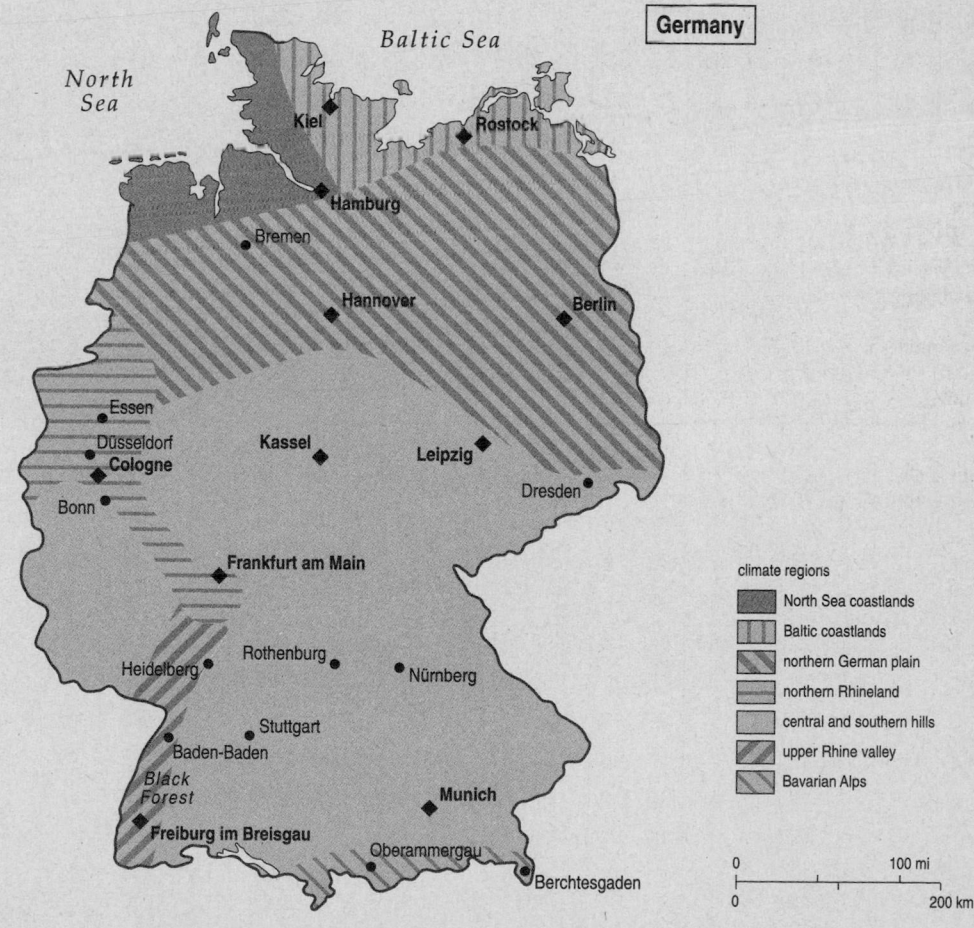

climate regions

North Sea coastlands

Baltic coastlands

northern German plain

northern Rhineland

central and southern hills

upper Rhine valley

Bavarian Alps

HAMBURG

NORTH SEA COASTLANDS

Month	Sunshine average hours per day	Temperatures Average daily minimum °C	minimum °F	maximum °C	maximum °F	Highest recorded °C	Highest recorded °F	Lowest recorded °C	Lowest recorded °F	Discomfort from heat and humidity	Precipitation and humidity Relative humidity 6:30 %	13:30 %	Average monthly precipitation mm	in	Wet days more than 0.1 mm/0.004 in	Month
Jan	2	-2	28	2	36	14	57	-23	-9		89	84	58	2.3	18	Jan
Feb	2	-2	28	3	37	19	65	-29	-20		89	80	48	1.9	16	Feb
March	4	-1	31	7	44	21	70	-14	6		88	68	39	1.5	13	March
April	6	3	38	13	55	27	81	-7	19		85	61	52	2.1	14	April
May	7	7	45	18	64	32	90	-5	23		81	57	56	2.2	14	May
June	8	11	51	21	69	35	94	1	34		81	59	63	2.5	14	June
July	7	13	55	22	73	35	95	3	38		85	63	83	3.3	17	July
Aug	7	12	54	22	72	36	96	3	37		89	63	81	3.2	16	Aug
Sept	6	10	49	19	66	32	90	-1	30		91	65	62	2.4	15	Sept
Oct	3	6	43	13	55	25	77	-6	21		92	74	59	2.3	17	Oct
Nov	1	3	37	7	45	17	63	-8	18		92	83	57	2.2	18	Nov
Dec	1	0	31	4	39	17	62	-16	2		91	86	57	2.2	18	Dec

Based on readings for 30 years at 53°38′ N, 10°00′ E, altitude 22 m/72 ft

KIEL

BALTIC COAST

Month	Sunshine average hours per day	Temperatures Average daily minimum °C	minimum °F	maximum °C	maximum °F	Highest recorded °C	Highest recorded °F	Lowest recorded °C	Lowest recorded °F	Discomfort from heat and humidity	Precipitation and humidity Relative humidity 6:30 %	13:30 %	Average monthly precipitation mm	in	Wet days more than 0.1 mm/0.004 in	Month
Jan	1	-2	28	2	36	12	54	-21	-6		88	84	63	2.5	18	Jan
Feb	2	-2	28	3	37	16	61	-25	-13		89	81	55	2.2	16	Feb
March	4	0	32	6	43	21	70	-14	7		88	74	40	1.6	13	March
April	6	3	37	11	52	26	79	-5	23		86	66	45	1.8	13	April
May	8	7	45	15	59	30	86	-2	28		82	62	47	1.9	12	May
June	8	11	52	19	66	34	93	2	36		82	63	60	2.4	14	June
July	7	13	55	21	70	33	91	6	43		85	65	75	2.9	15	July
Aug	7	13	55	21	70	32	90	6	43		89	67	88	3.5	15	Aug
Sept	6	11	52	18	64	30	86	1	34		90	69	67	2.6	15	Sept
Oct	3	7	45	13	55	22	72	-3	27		90	75	67	2.6	17	Oct
Nov	2	3	37	7	45	15	59	-6	21		90	83	59	2.3	19	Nov
Dec	1	0	32	4	39	12	54	-13	9		90	86	59	2.3	19	Dec

Based on readings for 25 years at 51°20′ N, 9°31′ E, altitude 3 m/10 ft

winters but in the west the autumn may be the wettest season. Summer rain is often thundery. The annual range of temperature is least in the northwest and increases southwards and eastwards.

For a more detailed description of weather and climate the country can be divided into seven regions: the North Sea coast, the Baltic coast, the North German Plain, the North Rhineland, the central and southern hills, the upper Rhine, and the Bavarian Alps.

THE NORTH SEA COASTLANDS

Including (with towns and cities in parentheses): HAMBURG (Hamburg), western SCHLESWIG-HOLSTEIN, coastal NIEDERSACHSEN, and the East Frisian Islands.

This is the mildest area of Germany in winter but the weather can be cold when east winds prevail. Autumn tends to be the wettest season. Weather can be variable at all seasons and the region is open to the influence of Atlantic storms.

The average daily sunshine ranges from about two hours in winter to six in summer. Conditions are represented by the table for **Hamburg** (opposite).

THE BALTIC COAST

Including (with towns and cities in parentheses): the east coast of SCHLESWIG-HOLSTEIN (Kiel) and the north coast of MECKLENBURG (Rostock).

This region has a more severe winter than the North Sea coast, particularly in winters when there is much sea ice in the Baltic. Summers are rather more settled than on the North Sea coast with more sunshine. However, it is often thundery when it rains. See the tables for **Kiel** (opposite and below) and **Rostock** (below).

THE NORTH GERMAN PLAIN

Including (with towns and cities in parentheses): notheastern NORTH RHINE-WESTPHALIA; BRANDENBURG (Berlin), BREMEN (Bremen), SAXONY-ANHALT; and most of MECKLENBURG and NIEDERSACHSEN (Hannover).

This low-lying, gently undulating area is a western extension of the great North European Plain. From the Dutch border to Poland there is no great difference in climate or weather except that winters become colder eastwards and summers more settled and slightly warmer. During severe cold spells in winter, canals and navigable rivers may freeze.

ROSTOCK												BALTIC COAST	
Sunshine	Temperatures							Discomfort from heat and humidity	Precipitation and humidity				Wet days
	Average daily			Highest recorded		Lowest recorded			Relative humidity	Average monthly precipitation			
average hours per day	minimum		maximum						7:00 14:00				more than
	°C	°F	°C	°F	°C	°F	°C	°F		%	mm	in	0.1 mm/0.004 in
Jan	1	−2	28	2	36	11	52	−18	−1	91	86	46	1.8	18	Jan
Feb	2	−3	26	2	36	15	60	−20	−3	91	84	36	1.4	16	Feb
March	4	−1	31	7	44	21	69	−18	1	90	72	30	1.2	12	March
April	6	3	37	11	52	26	79	−5	24	86	65	42	1.7	15	April
May	7	7	44	17	62	31	88	−3	27	80	60	48	1.9	12	May
June	8	10	51	20	68	33	92	2	36	79	61	60	2.4	12	June
July	7	13	55	22	72	34	92	6	43	83	63	79	3.1	15	July
Aug	7	13	55	21	71	32	89	5	42	88	65	71	2.8	14	Aug
Sept	6	9	49	18	64	29	84	1	33	90	66	69	2.7	13	Sept
Oct	3	6	43	12	54	22	72	−5	24	92	76	65	2.6	18	Oct
Nov	2	2	36	7	44	15	60	−9	16	93	86	39	1.5	15	Nov
Dec	1	−1	30	3	38	14	57	−16	2	93	88	45	1.8	17	Dec

Based on readings for 17 years at 54°05′ N, 12°06′ E, altitude 20 m/66 ft

HANNOVER

NORTH GERMAN PLAIN

Sunshine	Temperatures									Discomfort from heat and humidity	Precipitation and humidity				Wet days	
	Average daily				Highest recorded		Lowest recorded				Relative humidity		Average monthly precipitation				
	minimum		maximum								6:30	13:30					
average hours per day	°C	°F	°C	°F	°C	°F	°C	°F			%		mm	in		more than 0.1 mm/0.004 in	
Jan 2	−3	28	3	37	14	57	−29	−19			88	81	46	1.8		18	Jan
Feb 2	−2	28	4	38	16	61	−24	−12			89	77	44	1.7		17	Feb
March 4	0	32	8	46	22	72	−17	2			89	67	36	1.4		13	March
April 6	3	38	13	56	27	81	−6	21			86	59	47	1.9		15	April
May 7	7	45	18	64	33	91	−3	27			82	55	51	2.0		14	May
June 8	10	51	21	70	34	93	2	35			81	57	63	2.5		14	June
July 7	13	55	23	73	35	95	5	42		Moderate	85	61	79	3.1		16	July
Aug 7	12	54	23	73	38	100	4	39			88	59	69	2.7		15	Aug
Sept 5	9	49	19	67	33	91	−1	30			91	64	52	2.1		14	Sept
Oct 3	6	42	13	56	26	79	−8	18			92	73	56	2.2		15	Oct
Nov 2	2	36	8	46	18	65	−11	12			91	81	54	2.1		17	Nov
Dec 1	−1	31	4	39	15	59	−21	−6			90	84	46	1.8		17	Dec

Based on readings for 30 years at 52°20′ N, 9°43′ E, altitude 52 m/171 ft

BERLIN

NORTH GERMAN PLAIN

Sunshine	Temperatures									Discomfort from heat and humidity	Precipitation and humidity				Wet days	
	Average daily				Highest recorded		Lowest recorded				Relative humidity		Average monthly precipitation				
	minimum		maximum								7:00	14:00					
average hours per day	°C	°F	°C	°F	°C	°F	°C	°F			%		mm	in		more than 0.1 mm/0.004 in	
Jan 2	−3	26	2	35	13	55	−21	−6			89	82	46	1.8		17	Jan
Feb 2	−3	26	3	37	17	62	−22	−8			89	78	40	1.6		15	Feb
March 5	0	31	8	46	22	71	−14	6			88	67	33	1.3		12	March
April 6	4	39	13	56	30	86	−6	21			84	60	42	1.7		13	April
May 8	8	47	19	66	32	90	−3	27			80	57	49	1.9		12	May
June 8	12	53	22	72	35	95	3	38			80	58	65	2.6		13	June
July 8	14	57	24	75	37	99	5	42		Moderate	84	61	73	2.9		14	July
Aug 7	13	56	23	74	37	98	6	43		Moderate	88	61	69	2.7		14	Aug
Sept 6	10	50	20	68	34	93	1	34			92	65	48	1.9		12	Sept
Oct 4	6	42	13	56	25	77	−4	24			93	73	49	1.9		14	Oct
Nov 2	2	36	7	45	17	63	−9	17			92	83	46	1.8		16	Nov
Dec 1	−1	29	3	38	15	59	−18	0			91	86	43	1.7		15	Dec

Based on readings for 29 years at 52°27′ N, 13°18′ E, altitude 55 m/180 ft

LEIPZIG

CENTRAL GERMANY

	Sunshine	Temperatures								Discomfort from heat and humidity	Precipitation and humidity				Wet days	
	average hours per day	Average daily				Highest recorded		Lowest recorded			Relative humidity 7:00 14:00		Average monthly precipitation		more than 0.1 mm/0.004 in	
		minimum		maximum												
		°C	°F	°C	°F	°C	°F	°C	°F		%		mm	in		
Jan	2	–3	27	2	36	13	55	–24	–10		86	78	41	1.6	17	Jan
Feb	2	–3	26	3	38	17	62	–23	–9		87	75	39	1.5	15	Feb
March	4	0	32	8	47	22	71	–15	6		86	66	38	1.5	14	March
April	6	4	40	14	57	29	85	–6	22		82	57	41	1.6	14	April
May	7	8	47	19	66	31	88	–3	26		80	55	52	2.1	13	May
June	8	12	51	22	72	36	98	5	40		79	56	69	2.7	13	June
July	7	14	57	24	75	38	100	7	45	Moderate	82	58	83	3.3	15	July
Aug	7	13	56	24	74	38	100	6	42	Moderate	85	57	62	2.4	13	Aug
Sept	6	10	50	20	68	35	94	1	34		89	61	42	1.7	13	Sept
Oct	4	6	42	14	57	27	81	–5	23		90	68	49	1.9	14	Oct
Nov	2	2	36	8	46	20	67	–8	18		89	78	41	1.6	15	Nov
Dec	1	–1	30	4	39	17	62	–21	–5		88	81	38	1.5	15	Dec

Based on readings for 27 years at 51°19′ N, 12°25′ E, altitude 141 m/463 ft

KASSEL

CENTRAL GERMANY

	Sunshine	Temperatures								Discomfort from heat and humidity	Precipitation and humidity				Wet days	
	average hours per day	Average daily				Highest recorded		Lowest recorded			Relative humidity 6:30 13:20		Average monthly precipitation		more than 0.1 mm/0.004 in	
		minimum		maximum												
		°C	°F	°C	°F	°C	°F	°C	°F		%		mm	in		
Jan	1	–3	27	2	36	13	55	–26	–15		87	81	48	1.9	17	Jan
Feb	2	–3	27	3	38	16	61	–23	–9		87	75	40	1.6	15	Feb
March	4	0	32	8	47	21	70	–15	6		87	64	34	1.3	13	March
April	5	4	39	13	55	28	82	–5	23		83	58	47	1.9	15	April
May	7	7	45	18	64	32	90	–3	27		82	55	59	2.3	13	May
June	7	11	51	21	70	33	91	–3	27		82	56	62	2.4	14	June
July	7	13	55	23	73	35	95	6	42		85	58	73	2.9	16	July
Aug	6	12	54	22	72	36	96	5	41		88	57	63	2.5	14	Aug
Sept	5	9	49	19	66	33	91	–1	31		91	62	52	2.1	13	Sept
Oct	3	5	42	13	55	24	74	–5	24		92	70	53	2.1	15	Oct
Nov	1	2	36	7	45	18	65	–8	18		89	79	51	2.0	16	Nov
Dec	1	–1	30	3	38	16	60	–18	–1		89	84	49	1.9	16	Dec

Based on readings for 28 years at 51°20′ N, 9°31′ E, altitude 198 m/650 ft

MUNICH

SOUTHERN GERMANY

Sunshine	Temperatures								Discomfort from heat and humidity	Precipitation and humidity				Wet days	
	Average daily				Highest recorded		Lowest recorded			Relative humidity 7:00 14:00		Average monthly precipitation		more than 0.1 mm/0.004 in	
	minimum		maximum												
average hours per day	°C	°F	°C	°F	°C	°F	°C	°F		%		mm	in		
Jan	−5	23	1	35	16	62	−29	−20		87	77	59	2.3	16	Jan
Feb	−5	23	3	38	20	68	−30	−21		87	71	53	2.1	16	Feb
March	−1	30	9	48	24	74	−18	0		86	61	48	1.9	13	March
April	3	38	14	56	29	84	−16	3		82	55	62	2.4	15	April
May	7	45	18	64	31	87	−6	22		81	57	109	4.3	15	May
June	11	51	21	70	35	94	3	37		80	58	125	4.9	17	June
July	13	55	23	74	35	95	5	40		81	57	139	5.5	16	July
Aug	12	54	23	73	36	96	3	38		85	58	107	4.2	16	Aug
Sept	9	48	20	67	32	90	−3	28		89	61	85	3.4	13	Sept
Oct	4	40	13	56	28	82	−6	21		91	68	66	2.6	13	Oct
Nov	0	33	7	44	20	67	−12	10		92	78	57	2.2	15	Nov
Dec	−4	26	2	36	16	60	−22	−8		90	82	47	1.9	15	Dec

Based on readings for 29 years at 48°08′ N, 11°42′ E, altitude 524 m/1719 ft

COLOGNE

NORTHERN RHINELAND

Sunshine	Temperatures								Discomfort from heat and humidity	Precipitation and humidity				Wet days	
	Average daily				Highest recorded		Lowest recorded			Relative humidity 6:30 13:30		Average monthly precipitation		more than 0.1 mm/0.004 in	
	minimum		maximum												
average hours per day	°C	°F	°C	°F	°C	°F	°C	°F		%		mm	in		
Jan	−1	30	4	39	15	59	−25	−13		85	77	60	2.4	18	Jan
Feb	0	32	6	43	16	61	−20	−4		87	73	44	1.7	15	Feb
March	2	36	10	50	21	70	−8	18		84	61	42	1.7	13	March
April	5	41	14	57	27	81	−4	25		83	59	60	2.4	17	April
May	8	46	19	66	33	91	−3	27		80	55	51	2.0	13	May
June	12	54	22	72	34	93	3	37		79	54	75	2.9	13	June
July	14	57	24	75	38	100	7	45	Moderate	82	56	69	2.7	14	July
Aug	14	57	24	75	37	99	5	41	Moderate	85	56	73	2.9	14	Aug
Sept	11	52	20	68	31	88	−1	30		88	61	55	2.2	14	Sept
Oct	7	45	14	57	26	79	−3	27		89	69	53	2.1	16	Oct
Nov	4	39	9	48	19	66	−5	23		87	77	65	2.6	18	Nov
Dec	0	32	5	41	14	57	−19	−2		87	81	52	2.1	17	Dec

Based on readings for 16 years at 50°58′ N, 6°58′ E, altitude 45 m/148 ft

FRANKFURT AM MAIN

NORTHERN RHINELAND

	Sunshine	Temperatures								Discomfort from heat and humidity	Precipitation and humidity				Wet days
		Average daily				Highest recorded		Lowest recorded			Relative humidity 6:30 13:30		Average monthly precipitation		more than 0.1 mm/0.004 in
		minimum		maximum											
	average hours per day	°C	°F	°C	°F	°C	°F	°C	°F		%		mm	in	
Jan	1	-2	29	3	38	14	57	-24	-11		86	77	58	2.3	17	Jan
Feb	2	-1	30	5	41	18	65	-19	-3		86	70	44	1.7	15	Feb
March	4	2	35	11	51	24	75	-8	17		84	57	38	1.5	12	March
April	5	6	42	16	60	31	87	-4	26		79	51	44	1.7	14	April
May	7	9	49	20	69	34	94	-2	29		78	50	55	2.2	14	May
June	8	13	55	23	74	38	101	4	39		78	52	73	2.9	14	June
July	7	15	58	25	77	38	101	8	46	Moderate	81	53	70	2.8	14	July
Aug	7	14	57	24	76	38	100	7	44	Moderate	85	54	76	3.0	14	Aug
Sept	5	11	52	21	69	34	94	1	33		89	60	57	2.2	13	Sept
Oct	3	7	44	14	58	26	78	-4	25		91	68	52	2.1	14	Oct
Nov	1	3	38	8	47	19	65	-7	19		89	77	55	2.2	16	Nov
Dec	1	0	32	4	39	14	56	-18	0		88	81	54	2.1	16	Dec

Based on readings for 29 years at 50°07′ N, 8°39′ E, altitude 103 m/338 ft

Such cold spells are caused by persistent easterly winds blowing from Russia. However, in some winters such spells are short and infrequent. Summers are generally more settled than in the coastal regions to the north. Although summer is the wettest season, the rain is often thundery and shortlived, so that summer sunshine amounts are moderately high. See the climatic tables for **Hannover** and **Berlin** (both on p. 156).

THE CENTRAL AND SOUTHERN HILLS

Including (with towns and cities in parentheses): BADEN-WURTTEMBURG (Stuttgart), BAVARIA (Munich, Nürnberg, Rothenburg), SAXONY (Dresden, Leipzig), THURINGEN, most of HESSEN (Kassel) SAARLAND, and most of RHINELAND-PALATINATE.

This extensive region of central and southern Germany includes all the higher ground south of the North German Plain up to the Alpine foothills of Bavaria as well as the hills west of the Rhine gorge. As the tables for **Kassel** and **Leipzig** (both on p. 157) and **Munich** (opposite and above) show, there is not a very great difference in weather and climate over this extensive region. Temperature varies mainly as a result of altitude so that the higher

parts of Bavaria and the Harz Mountains have the coldest winters and the longest duration of snow cover. Summers are generally warm with much sunshine, despite the heavier summer rainfall. Frosts may be severe in some valleys in winter despite the lower altitude. As in much of central Europe, summers may vary from one year to another, some being warm and dry, others cloudy and wet.

THE NORTHERN RHINELAND

Including (with towns and cities in parentheses): western NORTH RHINE-WESTPHALIA (Bonn, Cologne, Düsseldorf, Essen), northeastern and eastern RHINELAND-PALATINATE, southwestern HESSEN (Frankfurt am Main).

This northwestern district of Germany includes the Ruhr industrial region and the gorge section of the Rhine valley from Mannheim to Bonn. On either side of the Rhine gorge are uplands such as the Eifel and Westerwald, where the climate is similar to that of the Central and Southern Hills. The climatic tables for **Cologne** (opposite) and **Frankfurt am Main** (above) are representative of the lowland section of this region which contains many large and important towns. The hill slopes along the Rhine and Moselle valleys have a climate particularly suitable to the cultivation of the vine. Winters can be

FREIBURG IM BREISGAU										UPPER RHINE VALLEY	

Sunshine	Temperatures							Discomfort from heat and humidity	Precipitation and humidity			Wet days
	Average daily				Highest recorded		Lowest recorded			Relative humidity	Average monthly precipitation	
average hours per day	minimum		maximum							6:30 13:30		more than 0.1 mm/0.004 in
	°C	°F	°C	°F	°C	°F	°C	°F		%	mm	in	
Jan	2	-2	29	4	39	18	64	-23	-9		85 78	61 2.4	17	Jan
Feb	3	-2	28	5	41	21	70	-22	-8		85 72	53 2.1	14	Feb
March	5	1	34	11	51	24	74	-13	9		83 60	52 2.1	13	March
April	6	5	41	15	59	29	85	-6	21		80 56	68 2.7	15	April
May	7	9	48	20	67	32	89	-2	28		81 57	79 3.1	14	May
June	8	12	53	22	72	36	97	3	38		81 60	117 4.6	15	June
July	8	14	57	24	76	39	101	5	40	Moderate	80 58	106 4.2	15	July
Aug	8	13	56	24	75	37	99	3	38	Moderate	84 59	100 3.9	14	Aug
Sept	6	11	51	21	69	34	93	0	32		88 63	98 3.9	14	Sept
Oct	4	6	43	14	58	27	81	-5	23		90 70	67 2.6	14	Oct
Nov	2	2	36	8	47	21	69	-9	17		88 76	69 2.7	15	Nov
Dec	2	-1	31	5	40	16	61	-21	-5		86 79	52 2.1	17	Dec

Based on readings for 27 years at 48°01′ N, 7°50′ E, altitude 259 m/850 ft

quite cold and the summer weather is often disturbed and variable but is generally sufficiently warm and sunny to make this a notable area for wine.

THE UPPER RHINE VALLEY

Including (with towns and cities in parentheses): southwestern RHINELAND-PALATINATE and western BADEN-WURTTEMBURG (Baden-Baden, Freiburg im Breisgau, Heidelberg), including the Black Forest.

This small district of southwest Germany includes the German portion of the Upper Rhine valley as far as the Swiss frontier. In spring and summer it is the warmest part of the country and produces a variety of crops including vines and tobacco. It is a sunny region in summer with up to eight hours sunshine per day. However, winters are quite cold because of

proximity to the Alps and distance from the ocean. See the table for **Freiburg im Breisgau** (above).

THE BAVARIAN ALPS

Including (with towns and cities in parentheses): the southernmost part of BAVARIA (Oberammergau, Berchtesgaden).

This small mountain region extends along the border with the Austrian Tyrol; it contains the highest mountains in Germany and is a popular area for winter sports. It has a number of lake resorts which are popular in summer. Weather and climate are similar to that found in the Austrian Tyrol (see the table for **Innsbruck** on p. 53). Winters are cold and snowy but the summers are moderately warm despite being rather wet.

Ghana

See page 30

Ghana is situated in West Africa with a coastline on the Gulf of Guinea. In area it is about the size of the United Kingdom and extends between 5° and 11° N. It is bordered on the west by the Côte d'Ivoire, on

the north by Burkina Faso, and on the east by Togo. Ghana experiences the same sequence of weather and climate around the year as that described for Nigeria (p. 266) and adjacent countries: the coastal region has two rainy seasons, one peaking in May or June, the other in October, but in the north there is a

ACCRA

COASTAL GHANA

	Sunshine	Temperatures								Discomfort from heat and humidity	Precipitation and humidity				Wet days	
		Average daily				Highest recorded		Lowest recorded			Relative humidity 6:00 12:00		Average monthly precipitation			
		minimum		maximum												
	average hours per day	°C	°F	°C	°F	°C	°F	°C	°F		%		mm	in	more than 0.25 mm/0.01 in	
Jan	7	23	73	31	87	34	94	15	59	High	95	61	15	0.6	1	Jan
Feb	8	24	75	31	88	38	100	17	62	High	96	61	33	1.3	2	Feb
March	7	24	76	31	88	38	100	20	68	High	95	63	56	2.2	4	March
April	7	24	76	31	88	34	93	19	67	High	96	65	81	3.2	6	April
May	7	24	75	31	87	35	95	21	69	High	96	68	142	5.6	9	May
June	5	23	74	29	84	33	92	20	68	High	97	74	178	7.0	10	June
July	5	23	73	27	81	32	90	19	66	Medium	97	76	46	1.8	4	July
Aug	5	22	71	27	80	32	89	18	64	Medium	97	77	15	0.6	3	Aug
Sept	6	23	73	27	81	32	89	20	68	Medium	96	72	36	1.4	4	Sept
Oct	7	23	74	29	85	32	90	19	67	High	97	71	64	2.5	6	Oct
Nov	8	24	75	31	87	33	91	21	69	High	97	66	36	1.4	3	Nov
Dec	8	24	75	31	88	34	94	17	63	High	97	64	23	0.9	2	Dec

Based on readings for 17 years at 5°33′ N, 0°12′ W, altitude 27 m/88 ft

TAMALE

NORTHERN GHANA

	Sunshine	Temperatures								Discomfort from heat and humidity	Precipitation and humidity				Wet days	
		Average daily				Highest recorded		Lowest recorded			Relative humidity 6:00 12:00		Average monthly precipitation			
		minimum		maximum												
	average hours per day	°C	°F	°C	°F	°C	°F	°C	°F		%		mm	in	more than 0.25 mm/0.01 in	
Jan	8	21	69	36	96	39	103	15	59	Medium	36	20	3	0.1	0.6	Jan
Feb	9	23	73	37	99	40	104	17	63	High	56	33	3	0.1	0.4	Feb
March	8	24	76	37	99	41	105	19	66	High	62	37	53	2.1	0.4	March
April	8	24	76	36	97	41	106	20	68	Extreme	80	52	69	2.7	6.0	April
May	8	24	75	33	92	39	102	19	66	High	88	62	104	4.1	10.0	May
June	7	22	72	31	88	36	97	19	66	High	92	69	142	5.6	12.0	June
July	5	22	72	29	85	34	94	18	65	High	94	72	135	5.3	14.0	July
Aug	4	22	71	29	84	33	92	19	67	High	95	74	196	7.7	16.0	Aug
Sept	5	22	71	30	86	33	92	19	66	High	95	74	226	8.9	19.0	Sept
Oct	8	22	71	32	90	36	96	19	66	High	94	66	99	3.9	13.0	Oct
Nov	10	22	71	34	94	37	99	16	61	High	78	42	10	0.4	1.0	Nov
Dec	9	20	68	35	95	38	100	15	59	Medium	54	27	5	0.2	0.8	Dec

Based on readings for 13 years at 9°24′ N, 0°50′ W, altitude 194 m/635 ft

single rainy season starting in May or June. There is, however, one local peculiarity about the distribution of rainfall in Ghana. Rainfall is lower on the coast than it is a short distance inland. This is thought to be a consequence of two local features which apply to this part of the West African coastline.

First, at the time when rainfall is heaviest in much of West Africa the waters offshore are unusually cool for near-equatorial latitudes; a cool current appears on the ocean surface. Second, the coast here follows a direction from west-southwest to east-northeast and is parallel with the prevailing winds. The table for **Accra** (p. 161) is representative of this drier coastal strip. Farther inland rainfall increases.

In the northern half of the country there is an increasing tendency for a single rainy season and the table for **Tamale** (p. 161) is representative of this region. Annual rainfall is lower here as also in the northern part of Nigeria.

As a consequence of the lower rainfall and less cloud, Accra is rather sunnier than many other places on this coast; hours of sunshine average about five a day during the rainy season and as much as seven to eight hours during the drier months.

Sunshine hours are reduced in the wetter districts inland but increase again in the drier regions of northern Ghana.

Gibraltar

See map page 18

Gibraltar has an area of only 10 sq km/4 sq mi and is a British Crown Colony at the extreme south of Spain, commanding the strait at the entrance to the Mediterranean. It consists of a rocky peninsula rising to over 300 m/1,000 ft. Gibraltar has a Mediterranean climate with a very dry summer. The winters are considerably wetter than much of

southern Spain due to exposure to Atlantic storms. Winters are rather warmer and the summers not quite so hot as the adjoining regions of Spain. Because of the shape of the rocky mountain which obstructs the flow of easterly and westerly winds in the strait, the winds around Gibraltar are often particularly gusty. Both the airfield and the port can be affected by these turbulent winds on occasions. See the table for **North Front** (below).

NORTH FRONT
GIBRALTAR

	Sunshine average hours per day	Temperatures									Discomfort from heat and humidity	Precipitation and humidity				Wet days more than 1 mm/0.04 in	
		Average daily				Highest recorded		Lowest recorded				Relative humidity 8:30 14:30		Average monthly precipitation			
		minimum		maximum													
		°C	°F	°C	°F	°C	°F	°C	°F			%		mm	in		
Jan	6	10	50	16	60	23	74	3	37			81	70	152	6.0	10	Jan
Feb	7	11	51	17	62	24	75	1	33			79	67	98	3.9	7	Feb
March	7	12	54	18	65	27	81	3	38			78	66	106	4.2	10	March
April	8	13	56	20	68	28	82	7	45			74	64	59	2.3	6	April
May	10	15	60	23	73	31	87	8	47		Moderate	72	62	25	1.0	4	May
June	11	18	64	25	78	33	91	14	57		Moderate	73	62	4	0.2	1	June
July	11	20	68	28	83	38	101	14	58		Medium	72	60	1	0.0	0	July
Aug	11	21	69	29	83	37	99	14	57		Medium	73	60	3	0.1	1	Aug
Sept	9	19	67	26	79	33	92	14	57		Medium	76	65	23	0.9	2	Sept
Oct	7	17	62	23	73	33	92	10	50		Moderate	78	69	55	2.2	5	Oct
Nov	6	14	57	19	66	29	84	8	46			81	72	114	4.5	7	Nov
Dec	6	11	53	17	62	24	75	2	36			80	70	127	5.0	10	Dec

Based on readings for 15 years at 36°09' N, 5°21' W, altitude 2 m/7 ft

Greece

See map page 19

Greece is situated in the extreme southeast of Europe. It is a mountainous country with a very indented coastline and it includes numerous islands in the Aegean Sea, the Ionian Islands in the west, of which Corfu is the best known, and the large island of Crete, which lies in the middle of the eastern Mediterranean.

As a result of this intermingling of mountain, island, and sea, there are many local differences in the weather and climate within the country but the general features of weather throughout the year are much the same.

In the north the climate bears some resemblance to that found in Bulgaria and Macedonia; elsewhere the influence of the Mediterranean is dominant. Summers are warm or even hot with almost no cloud or rain for three months.

The wettest season is winter, when the weather is generally mild at sea level although occasional spells of cold weather occur. Snow may fall almost anywhere in Greece in winter but is rare in the islands and does not lie for long at sea level. Spring and autumn are short seasons of transition from winter rain to summer heat and sun, when the weather may be very changeable from day to day. For those who dislike heat, April and May or September or October may be the most enjoyable seasons in Greece.

An outstanding feature of the Greek climate is the large amount of sunshine. This varies from four to five hours a day in midwinter to as much as twelve to fourteen hours a day in midsummer. These amounts may be rather reduced in the mountains and in the extreme north. Rain tends to be heavy when it occurs and rarely lasts for very long except in the mountains or along the wetter west coast.

Around the coasts and on the islands the summer heat is greatly tempered by strong to fresh daytime breezes. On a few occasions, however, when the air is calm, the daytime heat can be oppressive inland or in a large town such as Athens. During the three summer months a persistent northerly wind, known as the etesian, blows in the Aegean, on occasions

TRIKALA															CENTRAL GREECE	
Sunshine	Temperatures								Discomfort from heat and humidity	Precipitation and humidity					Wet days	
	Average daily				Highest recorded		Lowest recorded			Relative humidity 7:30 13:30		Average monthly precipitation				
	minimum		maximum													
average hours per day	°C	°F	°C	°F	°C	°F	°C	°F		%		mm	in		more than 0.1 mm/0.004 in	
Jan	3	0	33	9	48	20	68	-12	11		84	72	84	3.3	13	Jan
Feb	4	2	35	13	55	22	71	-8	18		80	60	69	2.7	11	Feb
March	5	4	40	16	61	26	79	-2	28		76	54	59	2.3	10	March
April	5	8	47	21	70	31	88	-1	30		73	51	80	3.2	9	April
May	7	12	54	25	78	35	94	4	39	Moderate	70	48	61	2.4	9	May
June	8	16	61	31	87	41	105	10	49	Medium	61	40	51	2.0	7	June
July	11	19	67	35	94	44	110	10	50	High	53	34	19	0.8	4	July
Aug	11	19	66	34	93	42	107	12	53	Medium	56	33	12	0.5	3	Aug
Sept	8	15	60	30	86	40	104	8	47	Medium	67	42	27	1.1	5	Sept
Oct	5	12	54	25	76	37	98	2	36	Moderate	77	53	80	3.2	9	Oct
Nov	3	7	45	17	62	26	78	-2	29		84	66	90	0.4	11	Nov
Dec	3	4	38	11	51	21	69	-8	18		87	75	125	4.9	17	Dec

Based on readings for 6 years at 39°33′ N, 21°46′ E, altitude 149 m/489 ft

ATHENS
EASTERN COASTAL GREECE

	Sunshine	Temperatures									Discomfort from heat and humidity	Precipitation and humidity				Wet days
		Average daily				Highest recorded		Lowest recorded				Relative humidity 7:30 13:30		Average monthly precipitation		
		minimum		maximum												
	average hours per day	°C	°F	°C	°F	°C	°F	°C	°F			%		mm	in	more than 0.1 mm/0.004 in
Jan	4	6	44	13	55	21	70	-4	24			77	62	62	2.4	16	Jan
Feb	5	7	44	14	57	23	73	-6	22			74	57	37	1.5	11	Feb
March	6	8	46	16	60	28	82	-1	31			71	54	37	1.5	11	March
April	8	11	52	20	68	32	90	0	32			65	48	23	1.0	9	April
May	9	16	61	25	77	36	97	6	43	Moderate		60	47	23	1.0	8	May
June	11	20	68	30	86	42	107	14	57	Medium		50	39	14	0.6	4	June
July	12	23	73	33	92	42	108	16	61	Medium		47	34	6	0.2	2	July
Aug	12	23	73	33	92	43	109	16	60	Medium		48	34	7	0.3	3	Aug
Sept	9	19	67	29	84	38	101	12	53	Medium		58	42	15	0.6	4	Sept
Oct	7	15	60	24	75	37	98	7	45	Moderate		70	52	51	2.0	8	Oct
Nov	5	12	53	19	66	28	82	-1	30			78	61	56	2.2	12	Nov
Dec	4	8	47	15	58	22	72	-4	25			78	63	71	2.8	15	Dec

Based on readings for 30 years at 37°58′ N, 24°43′ E, altitude 107 m/351 ft

THESSALONIKI
NORTHERN GREECE

	Sunshine	Temperatures									Discomfort from heat and humidity	Precipitation and humidity				Wet days
		Average daily				Highest recorded		Lowest recorded				Relative humidity 7:30 13:30		Average monthly precipitation		
		minimum		maximum												
	average hours per day	°C	°F	°C	°F	°C	°F	°C	°F			%		mm	in	more than 0.1 mm/0.004 in
Jan	4	2	35	9	49	20	67	-10	13			85	71	44	1.7	11	Jan
Feb	5	3	37	12	53	24	76	-9	16			80	61	34	1.3	8	Feb
March	5	5	41	14	58	30	86	-5	24			79	61	38	1.5	9	March
April	8	10	49	20	67	30	86	-1	30			75	58	41	1.6	9	April
May	9	14	58	25	77	38	100	5	41	Moderate		73	57	40	1.6	10	May
June	10	18	65	29	85	38	100	10	49	Medium		66	50	40	1.6	7	June
July	12	21	70	32	90	42	107	14	58	High		63	48	22	0.9	4	July
Aug	11	21	69	32	90	40	104	10	51	High		65	48	14	0.6	3	Aug
Sept	8	17	63	28	82	37	99	8	47	Medium		73	54	29	1.1	5	Sept
Oct	6	13	55	22	71	33	91	4	39			81	62	57	2.2	8	Oct
Nov	4	9	47	16	61	24	76	-3	27			85	70	55	2.2	11	Nov
Dec	4	4	39	11	53	21	70	-7	19			86	73	56	2.2	11	Dec

Based on readings for 27 years at 40°37′ N, 22°57′ E, altitude 25 m/82 ft

NAXOS								AEGEAN ISLANDS				
Sunshine	Temperatures						Discomfort from heat and humidity	Precipitation and humidity				Wet days	
	Average daily			Highest recorded		Lowest recorded		Relative humidity 7:30 13:30		Average monthly precipitation			
	minimum		maximum										
average hours per day	°C	°F	°C	°F	°C	°F	°C	°F		%	mm	in	more than 0.1 mm/0.004 in
Jan	3	10	50	15	58	21	70	3	37		75	69	91	3.6	12	Jan
Feb	3	10	49	15	59	25	76	0	32		75	68	73	2.9	9	Feb
March	5	11	51	16	61	27	81	3	38		75	67	69	2.7	8	March
April	6	13	56	20	67	30	86	8	46		74	65	19	0.8	4	April
May	8	16	61	23	73	33	91	11	52	Moderate	73	65	12	0.5	3	May
June	11	20	68	26	78	35	94	15	59	Medium	72	65	11	0.4	1	June
July	13	22	72	27	81	38	100	17	63	Medium	72	66	2	0.1	0	July
Aug	12	22	72	28	82	35	94	17	62	Medium	74	67	1	0.0	0	Aug
Sept	10	20	69	26	78	34	94	12	54	Medium	74	66	11	0.4	1	Sept
Oct	6	18	64	24	75	32	90	11	52	Moderate	76	67	45	1.8	4	Oct
Nov	3	15	58	20	68	28	82	8	47		75	67	48	1.9	6	Nov
Dec	3	12	53	17	62	22	72	1	34		75	69	93	3.7	12	Dec

Based on readings for 10 years at 37°06' N, 25°24' E, altitude 3 m/10 ft

reaching near gale force. It is strongest by day and drops to a near calm at night.

In the mountain regions of Greece, where many areas rise above 2,000 m/6,500 ft, the weather in winter and even early spring can be severe with frequent and heavy falls of snow and prolonged frost. Here summers are very pleasant as the days are sunny and often warm. The table for **Trikala** (p. 163) illustrates weather conditions inland at moderate elevation and within the mountains.

Eastern Greece is the driest part of the country and the table for **Athens** (opposite and above) is representative of much of eastern Greece at low levels. The table for **Thessaloniki** (opposite) shows that in northern Greece the winters are a little colder and the summers are not quite so rainless; summer thunderstorms occur here. Conditions in the Aegean Islands and Crete are illustrated by the table for **Naxos** (above); here the winters are the mildest in the countryside and the summer heat is tempered by sea breezes and the persistent etesian wind.

Visitors to Greece may find the sea rather too chilly for bathing in April or even early May, despite the high air temperature on sunny days. On the other hand, in October or even November the sea still retains much of its summer warmth.

Grenada

See map page 15

This island state is part of the Windward Islands, the southern islands of the Lesser Antilles. The Windward Islands lie between 15° N and the coast of the South American continent. The largest islands of this group are Barbados, Martinique, St Lucia, Grenada, and St Vincent. Although still small, these larger islands of the Windward group are hilly or mountainous and this tends to increase the rainfall above that of the small, flat islands in this group. As their climatic tables show, **Barbados** (p. 59) is less wet around the year than **Martinique** (p. 234) and **St Lucia** (p. 308), both of which have higher mountains.

All months receive appreciable rain but the heaviest rain is more likely to occur from July to November.

This is the hurricane season and, although the most violent of these tropical storms may only strike a particular island every few years, less severe ones cause appreciable rainfall over quite a wide area of Grenada.

Temperature, humidity, and sunshine throughout the year are typical of the Caribbean area. The climatic tables for Barbados, Martinique, and St Lucia reflect conditions on the west coasts of the islands which are more sheltered from the prevailing winds.

Guadeloupe

See map page 15

The islands that make up this overseas département of France are the most southerly of the Leeward Islands, the northerly islands of the Lesser Antilles.

Temperature and humidity around the year in the Leeward Islands are very similar to those described in general for the Caribbean (p. 92), as are the amount and distribution of sunshine.

The tables for **Roseau** (p. 127) on Dominica and **Plymouth** (p. 244) on Montserrat show that, near sea level and on the low-lying islands, the annual rainfall in the Leeward Islands is about 1,250–2,000 mm/50–80 in, well distributed throughout the year,

and with a wetter season from July to November. The table for **Camp Jacob** (opposite), in the interior of the island of Guadeloupe at an altitude of 530 m/1,750 ft, shows that rainfall increases on the more mountainous of the Leeward Islands and on the windward slopes exposed to the constant and moist northeast trade winds.

Guadeloupe lies in the track of violent tropical hurricanes which are most likely to develop between August and October. The severest of these storms may only strike Guadeloupe every few years but the appreciable rainfall they, and less violent disturbances, bring to a wider area accounts for the heavier rainfall during these months.

Guam

See map page 17

The American territory of Guam is the largest of the Marianas Islands. The weather described in the entry for Northern Marianas is similar to that on

Guam, and the tables for **Saipan** (p. 269) in the Northern Marianas and for **Ujelang** (p. 233) in the Marshall Islands illustrate the conditions that are typical on the island.

Guatemala

See map page 14

Guatemala is one of the larger countries of Central America, an area described in more detail on pp. 278–80 under Panama. Lying between 14° and 18° N, Guatemala is bordered on the north by Mexico, on the east by Belize, and on the south by Honduras and El Salvador. It has a very short coastline on the Caribbean Sea and a longer west coast on the Pacific. In area it is about the size of the state of Pennsylvania and a little smaller than England.

The northern part of the country is a low plain and forms part of the *tierra caliente* (lowlands – see

p. 66), an area of typical hot, tropical climate with some rain all the year round and maximum rainfall between May and September. The west and south of the country are very mountainous with some volcanic peaks rising to over 4,000 m/13,000 ft. A large part of the hilly country is typical *tierra templada* (middle altitudes – see p. 66), and its very pleasant climate is well represented by the table for **Guatemala City** (opposite). Rainfall here is moderate with a distinct dry season from November to April. Conditions on the Pacific coast, where there is a narrow strip of *tierra caliente*, have similar dry and wet seasons but rainfall is heavier and there is little relief from the high temperatures at night.

CAMP JACOB

GUADELOUPE ISLAND

Sunshine	Temperatures								Discomfort from heat and humidity	Precipitation and humidity				Wet days	
	Average daily				Highest recorded		Lowest recorded			Relative humidity		Average monthly precipitation			
	minimum		maximum							7:00	17:00				
average hours per day	°C	°F	°C	°F	°C	°F	°C	°F		%		mm	in	more than 1 mm/0.04 in	
Jan	7	18	64	25	77	30	86	13	56	Medium	83	80	234	9.2	23	Jan
Feb	8	17	63	24	76	31	88	12	54	Moderate	82	77	155	6.1	18	Feb
March	8	17	63	25	77	29	85	13	56	Medium	82	75	206	8.1	20	March
April	8	18	65	26	79	29	85	14	58	Medium	82	76	185	7.3	20	April
May	7	19	67	27	80	31	87	16	60	Medium	85	77	292	11.5	23	May
June	8	21	69	27	80	30	86	14	57	Medium	83	76	358	14.1	25	June
July	7	20	68	27	81	30	86	14	57	Medium	83	76	447	17.6	27	July
Aug	7	21	69	28	82	31	88	14	57	Medium	82	75	389	15.3	26	Aug
Sept	7	21	69	28	82	32	89	17	63	Medium	84	78	417	16.4	23	Sept
Oct	7	20	68	27	81	33	92	15	59	Medium	84	81	315	12.4	24	Oct
Nov	7	19	67	27	80	33	91	16	60	Medium	84	79	312	12.3	22	Nov
Dec	7	18	65	26	78	31	88	14	58	Medium	85	81	257	10.1	23	Dec

Based on readings for 10 years at 16°01′ N, 61°42′ W, altitude 533 m/1750 ft

GUATEMALA

MID-ALTITUDE GUATEMALA

Sunshine	Temperatures								Discomfort from heat and humidity	Precipitation and humidity				Wet days	
	Average daily				Highest recorded		Lowest recorded			Relative humidity		Average monthly precipitation			
	minimum		maximum							7:00	14:00				
average hours per day	°C	°F	°C	°F	°C	°F	°C	°F		%		mm	in	more than 0.25 mm/0.01 in	
Jan	5	12	53	23	73	30	86	5	41	Moderate	91	69	8	0.3	4	Jan
Feb	5	12	54	25	77	29	85	6	43	Moderate	89	62	3	0.1	2	Feb
March	5	14	57	27	81	30	86	5	41	Medium	86	51	13	0.5	3	March
April	4	14	58	28	82	32	90	8	47	Medium	81	51	31	1.2	5	April
May	3	16	60	29	84	32	89	11	52	Medium	83	55	152	6.0	15	May
June	1	16	61	27	81	30	86	11	52	Medium	89	70	274	10.8	23	June
July	2	16	60	26	78	29	84	11	51	Medium	91	67	203	8.0	21	July
Aug	1	16	60	26	79	28	83	11	52	Medium	90	72	198	7.8	21	Aug
Sept	2	16	60	26	79	28	82	12	54	Medium	92	71	231	9.1	22	Sept
Oct	2	16	60	24	76	28	82	10	50	Moderate	92	72	173	6.8	18	Oct
Nov	3	14	57	23	74	28	83	7	44	Moderate	89	71	23	0.9	7	Nov
Dec	5	13	55	22	72	28	83	5	41		89	70	8	0.3	4	Dec

Based on readings for 6 years at 14°37′ N, 90°31′ W, altitude 1480 m/4855 ft

Guinea

See map on page 20

Guinea is a West African country with a coastline on the Atlantic. In area it is about as large as the United Kingdom. It has an extensive coastal plain and inland the country rises to a plateau which slopes gradually eastwards towards the upper Niger valley. The climate of Guinea is similar to that of Sierra

Leone and is described on p. 316. The climate of the coastal region is represented by the table for **Conakry** (opposite). Rainfall is particularly heavy at Conakry, which is situated on a headland. The driest part of Guinea is in the northeast along the border with Mali. Here the climate is better illustrated by the table for **Bamako** (p. 231) in Mali.

Guinea-Bissau

See map on page 20

This small country is situated on the west coast of Africa at about 12° N. In area it is a little larger that Israel. It has a climate similar to that of southern Senegal, which it borders on the north, and northern Guinea, which it borders on the south.

The description of the climate and weather of Senegal and the Gambia are equally appropriate for Guinea-Bissau. The climatic tables for **Dakar** (p. 314) and **Banjul** (p. 151) give a good idea of conditions around the year. Guinea-Bissau being farther south than most of Senegal, its annual rainfall in is marginally greater.

Guyana

See map page 16

Including a description of the weather and climate of Surinam and French Guiana.

Guyana is situated on the Atlantic coast of South America between 1° and 8° N. It is about as large as Britain. It is bordered by Venezuela on the west, by Brazil on the south, and by Surinam on the east.

The weather and climate of Guyana are similar to those of neighbouring Surinam and French Guiana to the east. All three countries have coastlines on the Atlantic, open for most of the year to the moist northeast trade winds. Inland the country rises, towards the Venezuelan and Brazilian borders, to a plateau which is surmounted by isolated hills. Twice a year the whole area comes under the influence of the intertropical belt of cloud and rain which meteorologists call the intertropical convergence.

The lowlands have a typical hot, wet, equatorial type of climate with constant, high humidity. This area is often very sultry and oppressive as well as having a very monotonous weather regime, for there is little change from day to day. Wet days alternate almost equally with dry days. The nights are particularly oppressive but during the day the regular sea breeze brings some relief on the coast. Temperatures never

rise to very high levels and so are not dangerous but the heat and humidity are enervating to the unacclimatized visitor. Sunshine amounts are moderately large; from four to five hours a day in the wetter months and as much as eight hours a day during the drier seasons.

Inland in the higher plateaux areas rainfall may be slightly less and there is a tendency for a single rainy season from April to September, although all months get some rain. Daytime temperatures are here a little lower than on the coast and night temperatures are much cooler, so that the climate is less uncomfortable. Humidity is also lower during the drier months. Climatic conditions here are well represented by the table for **Santa Elena** (p. 418) which is just across the border in western Venezuela.

Guyana is the most northerly and the largest of the three countries. It has the largest area of upland plateau with the highest mountain rising to over 2,750 m/9,000 ft. The table for **Georgetown** (opposite) shows weather typical of the coastal area and the lowlands. The rainiest months are May to July and November to January, as the intertropical convergence brings the heaviest and most reliable rains. These are the months with most cloud and least sun. Note the constant high humidity and the remarkably constant temperature around the year.

CONAKRY — COASTAL GUINEA

	Sunshine average hours per day	Temperatures Average daily minimum °C	°F	Average daily maximum °C	°F	Highest recorded °C	°F	Lowest recorded °C	°F	Discomfort from heat and humidity	Relative humidity 7:00 %	12:00 %	Average monthly precipitation mm	in	Wet days more than 1 mm/0.04 in	
Jan	5	22	72	31	88	34	94	18	64	High	89	65	3	0.1	0.1	Jan
Feb	7	23	73	31	88	34	94	17	63	High	90	65	3	0.1	0.3	Feb
March	9	23	73	32	89	36	96	21	69	High	85	63	10	0.4	0.6	March
April	7	23	73	32	90	35	95	20	68	High	83	64	23	0.9	2.0	April
May	5	24	75	32	89	35	95	19	66	High	85	70	158	6.2	11.0	May
June	3	23	73	30	86	33	92	18	65	High	89	77	559	22.0	22.0	June
July	2	22	72	28	83	32	89	19	67	High	93	84	1298	51.1	29.0	July
Aug	2	22	72	28	82	31	87	20	68	High	94	87	1054	41.5	27.0	Aug
Sept	4	23	73	29	85	32	90	19	66	High	94	82	683	26.9	24.0	Sept
Oct	5	23	73	31	87	33	91	18	64	High	92	77	371	14.6	19.0	Oct
Nov	6	24	75	31	87	33	91	21	69	High	91	74	122	4.8	8.0	Nov
Dec	3	23	74	31	88	34	93	19	66	High	88	67	10	0.4	0.5	Dec

Based on readings for 7 years at 9°31′ N, 13°43′ W, altitude 7 m/23 ft

GEORGETOWN — COASTAL GUYANA

	Sunshine average hours per day	Temperatures Average daily minimum °C	°F	Average daily maximum °C	°F	Highest recorded °C	°F	Lowest recorded °C	°F	Discomfort from heat and humidity	Relative humidity 7:00 %	13:00 %	Average monthly precipitation mm	in	Wet days more than 1 mm/0.04 in	
Jan	6	23	74	29	84	31	88	20	68	High	87	75	203	8.0	17	Jan
Feb	7	23	74	29	84	32	89	21	69	High	85	72	114	4.5	13	Feb
March	7	24	75	29	84	32	89	21	69	High	83	71	175	6.9	12	March
April	7	24	76	29	85	32	90	22	71	High	84	71	140	5.5	12	April
May	6	24	75	29	85	32	90	21	70	High	88	75	290	11.4	20	May
June	6	24	75	29	85	32	89	21	69	High	92	77	302	11.9	24	June
July	7	24	75	29	85	32	90	21	70	High	93	74	254	10.0	21	July
Aug	8	24	75	30	86	32	90	22	71	High	92	73	175	6.9	16	Aug
Sept	8	24	76	31	87	34	93	21	69	High	90	69	81	3.2	7	Sept
Oct	7	24	76	31	87	34	93	21	70	High	88	69	76	3.0	9	Oct
Nov	7	24	76	30	86	33	91	21	69	High	88	69	155	6.1	10	Nov
Dec	6	24	75	29	84	32	90	21	70	High	89	75	287	11.3	20	Dec

Based on readings for 45 years at 6°50′ N, 58°12′ W, altitude 2 m/6 ft

PORT-AU-PRINCE													LOWLAND HAITI	
Sunshine		Temperatures						Discomfort from heat and humidity	Precipitation and humidity				Wet days	
		Average daily				Highest recorded			Relative humidity 7:00 13:00		Average monthly precipitation			
		minimum		maximum				Lowest recorded						
average hours per day		°C	°F	°C	°F	°C	°F	°C °F		%		mm	in	more than 1 mm/0.04 in
Jan	9	20	68	31	87	34	93	17 62	Medium	71	44	33	1.3	3	Jan
Feb	9	20	68	31	88	35	95	16 61	Medium	71	44	58	2.3	5	Feb
March	9	21	69	32	89	37	98	16 60	Medium	70	45	86	3.4	7	March
April	9	22	71	32	89	37	98	16 61	High	71	49	160	6.3	11	April
May	8	22	72	32 · 90		37	99	19 66	High	75	54	231	9.1	13	May
June	8	23	73	33	92	37	99	19 66	High	71	50	102	4.0	8	June
July	9	23	74	34	94	38	101	19 67	High	68	43	74	2.9	7	July
Aug	9	23	73	34	93	38	101	20 68	High	72	49	145	5.7	11	Aug
Sept	8	23	73	33	91	37	99	19 67	High	76	54	175	6.9	12	Sept
Oct	8	22	72	32	90	37	98	19 66	High	79	56	170	6.7	12	Oct
Nov	7	22	71	31	88	36	96	18 64	Medium	77	54	86	3.4	7	Nov
Dec	7	21	69	31	87	34	93	16 60	Medium	73	48	33	1.3	3	Dec

Based on readings for 42 years at 18°33' N, 72°20' W, altitude 37 m/121 ft

Haiti

See map page 15

Haiti occupies the western third of the Caribbean island of Hispaniola; it has a land border with the Dominican Republic.

With an area of 28,000 sq km/10,700 sq mi it is a little larger than Wales or the state of Maryland and lies east of Cuba and Jamaica in the central Caribbean. The country is mountainous and there

are may local variations in rainfall depending on relief and aspect; the north coast is wetter than the south. The table for **Port-au-Prince** (above) is representative of the temperature and rainfall in the lower districts of the island.

Afternoon humidity is rather lower than is usual on the coast in the Caribbean. This may be caused by a föhn effect as the moist northeast trade winds are drawn across the mountains in the interior.

Honduras

See map page 14

Honduras is one of the largest countries of Central America whose weather and climate are described in more detail on pp. 278–80 for Panama. It is situated between 13° and 16° N, between Nicaragua to the south and Guatemala to the north.

It has a western border with El Salvador and a very short coastline on the Pacific. In size it is similar to

Pennsylvania and a little smaller than England. Much of the country is mountainous and the only extensive lowland is in the extreme east. Reliable climatic data for Honduras is sparse.

The table for **Tegucigalpa** (opposite and above) is representative of the hilly country of the *tierra templada* (middle altitudes – see p. 66), where there is a larger daily temperature range and cooler nights than is found in the low-lying *tierra caliente* (lowlands

TEGUCIGALPA										MID-ALTITUDE HONDURAS		
Sunshine	Temperatures							Discomfort from heat and humidity	Precipitation and humidity		Wet days	
	Average daily				Highest recorded		Lowest recorded		Relative humidity	Average monthly precipitation		
	minimum		maximum									
average hours per day	°C	°F	°C	°F	°C	°F	°C	°F	%	mm	in	more than 0.25 mm/0.01 in
Jan	9	14	57	25	77						12	0.5	5	Jan
Feb	9	14	57	27	80						2	0.1	3	Feb
March	9	15	59	29	84						1	0.0	2	March
April	8	17	62	30	86						26	1.0	2	April
May	8	18	64	30	85						180	7.1	9	May
June	6	18	65	28	82						177	7.0	13	June
July	8	18	64	27	81						70	2.8	11	July
Aug	8	17	63	28	83						74	2.9	11	Aug
Sept	6	17	63	28	83						151	5.9	16	Sept
Oct	7	17	63	27	80						87	3.4	13	Oct
Nov	7	16	60	26	78						38	1.5	8	Nov
Dec	8	15	59	25	77						14	0.5	7	Dec

Based on readings for 10 years at 14°04′ N, 87°13′ W, altitude 1007 m/3304 ft

– see p. 66). The Caribbean coast of Honduras mostly faces north and has a much lower annual rainfall than Nicaragua to the south or Belize to the north. It appears that annual rainfall here is no more than on the Pacific shore and, unusually for this region, most rain falls in the winter period of low sun. During the low sun period the northeast trade winds are blowing more directly onshore.

Hungary

See map page 19

Hungary is a completely landlocked country situated well inland in central part of the European continent. Surrounded by the Alps and Carpathian Mountains, it is cut off from the moderating influence of the Atlantic Ocean.

Most of the country is low-lying and flat, consisting of the broad valleys of the rivers Danube and Tisza. Only small areas in the north and west, such as the Bakony Forest, rise above 600 m/ 2,000 ft.

Hungary's inland situation gives it a rather extreme type of climate compared with western Europe; there is a considerable difference between summer and winter. Spells of weather tend to persist for longer than in more oceanic climates. Summers or winters, however, may differ considerably from one year to another. Summer drought or wetness may persist for a whole season, while some winters may be particularly cold and snowy.

Spring and early summer are generally the wetter time of year but much of the rain comes in heavy thundery downpours; in early summer almost one day in three may have a thunderstorm. Daily hours of sunshine in summer are between nine and ten. Much of the time, the summer weather is pleasantly warm or even hot.

Winters are, in general, cold and snow lies on the ground for between thirty and forty days on average – longer in severe winters. Fog is frequent during settled weather in winter.

The Danube is often completely frozen over during severe cold spells and floating ice is usually a hazard to navigation from January to March. The severest

BUDAPEST

CENTRAL HUNGARY

Sunshine	Temperatures									Discomfort from heat and humidity	Precipitation and humidity				Wet days
	Average daily				Highest recorded		Lowest recorded				Relative humidity 7:30 14:30		Average monthly precipitation			
	minimum		maximum													
average hours per day	°C	°F	°C	°F	°C	°F	°C	°F			%		mm	in	more than 0.1 mm/0.004 in
Jan	2	-4	25	1	34	14	57	-23	-9		85	76	37	1.5	13	Jan
Feb	3	-2	28	4	39	17	63	-20	-4		83	68	44	1.7	12	Feb
March	5	2	35	10	50	23	74	-9	15		79	55	38	1.5	11	March
April	7	7	44	17	62	29	85	-3	26		72	48	45	1.8	11	April
May	8	11	52	22	71	33	91	1	34		72	49	72	2.8	13	May
June	9	15	58	26	78	39	103	4	39	Moderate	72	49	69	2.7	13	June
July	10	16	62	28	82	38	101	6	43	Medium	71	47	56	2.2	10	July
Aug	9	16	60	27	81	39	102	8	47	Moderate	74	47	47	1.9	9	Aug
Sept	7	12	53	23	74	35	95	2	36		79	49	33	1.3	7	Sept
Oct	5	7	44	16	61	32	90	-5	24		86	60	57	2.2	10	Oct
Nov	2	3	38	8	47	21	70	-8	17		88	76	70	2.8	14	Nov
Dec	1	-1	30	4	39	15	58	-13	8		87	81	46	1.8	13	Dec

Based on readings for 26 years at 47°26′ N, 19°11′ E, altitude 139 m/456 ft

DEBRECEN

EASTERN HUNGARY

Sunshine	Temperatures									Discomfort from heat and humidity	Precipitation and humidity				Wet days
	Average daily				Highest recorded		Lowest recorded				Relative humidity 7:30 14:30		Average monthly precipitation			
	minimum		maximum													
average hours per day	°C	°F	°C	°F	°C	°F	°C	°F			%		mm	in	more than 0.1 mm/0.004 in
Jan	2	-6	21	0	33	14	58	-28	-18		89	78	34	1.3	13	Jan
Feb	3	-4	25	3	38	18	64	-26	-14		88	71	35	1.4	11	Feb
March	5	0	32	10	50	25	78	-18	0		85	59	30	1.2	11	March
April	6	5	41	16	62	31	87	-6	21		80	51	37	1.5	11	April
May	8	10	50	22	71	33	91	-3	28		78	52	60	2.4	13	May
June	9	13	56	25	77	38	100	4	38	Moderate	78	53	80	3.2	13	June
July	10	15	59	27	81	38	101	6	42	Medium	78	50	56	2.2	11	July
Aug	9	14	57	27	80	39	103	5	41	Medium	82	50	64	2.5	10	Aug
Sept	7	10	50	23	73	36	98	-2	29		87	50	40	1.6	8	Sept
Oct	5	5	41	16	61	31	88	-9	16		90	59	49	1.9	10	Oct
Nov	2	2	36	9	47	22	71	-12	11		91	75	53	2.1	12	Nov
Dec	2	-2	28	3	38	17	63	-20	-3		91	80	39	1.5	13	Dec

Based on readings for 28 years at 47°30′ N, 21°38′ E, altitude 111 m/364 ft

and most unpleasant winter weather comes when bitterly cold, easterly winds blow from Ukraine.

The transition from winter to summer and vice versa often comes rather quickly so that spring and autumn are not the well-defined seasons of western Europe. At these times of the year there may be

abrupt and unpleasant changes of temperature from day to day.

There are no great differences of weather and climate within Hungary. The tables for **Budapest** (opposite) and **Debrecen** (opposite and below) show very similar features throughout the year.

Iceland

See map page 18

Iceland is an island in the stormiest region of the North Atlantic, lying between Norway and Greenland. Two features of this location control its weather and climate.

First, it lies in the weather-system track most frequented by meteorological depressions throughout the year.

Second, it also lies in the path of the current of warm oceanic water called the Gulf Stream. Consequently, the weather is disturbed and changeable throughout the year but in winter the temperatures at sea level are surprisingly mild for the latitude.

The Arctic Circle just touches the north coast of the island. Inland Iceland is mountainous with several volcanic peaks rising above 1,500 m/5,000 ft. These higher areas of the country are covered with snow throughout the year and there are extensive ice fields at higher levels.

Although very cold air from the Arctic occasionally affects the island in winter and spring, and drifting ice may block inlets on the north coast, the main port and capital, **Reykjavik** (see table below), is ice free throughout the year.

The summers are generally cool and cloudy with brief spells of fine, pleasant weather. Much of the winter precipitation is snow and autumn and winter are the wettest seasons.

REYKJAVIK												SOUTHWESTERN ICELAND		
Sunshine		Temperatures							Discomfort from heat and humidity	Precipitation and humidity				Wet days
		Average daily				Highest recorded		Lowest recorded		Relative humidity		Average monthly precipitation		
average hours per day		minimum		maximum						8:30 14:30				more than 0.1 mm/0.004 in
		°C	°F	°C	°F	°C	°F	°C	°F	%		mm	in	0.1 mm/0.004 in
Jan	1	–2	28	2	35	10	50	–17	1	81	79	89	3.5	20	Jan
Feb	2	–2	28	3	37	10	50	–14	8	78	75	64	2.5	17	Feb
March	4	–1	30	4	39	14	58	–14	6	78	72	62	2.4	18	March
April	5	1	33	6	43	15	59	–13	9	80	73	56	2.2	18	April
May	6	4	39	10	50	21	69	–7	19	75	67	42	1.7	16	May
June	6	7	45	12	54	21	69	0	32	78	72	42	1.7	15	June
July	6	9	48	14	57	23	74	1	35	81	72	50	2.0	15	July
Aug	5	8	47	14	56	21	70	0	32	81	71	56	2.2	16	Aug
Sept	4	6	43	11	52	20	68	–4	26	82	73	67	2.6	19	Sept
Oct	2	3	38	7	45	16	60	–10	14	83	78	94	3.7	21	Oct
Nov	1	0	32	4	39	12	53	–12	11	80	80	78	3.1	18	Nov
Dec	0	–2	29	2	36	11	53	–17	2	81	80	79	3.1	20	Dec

Based on readings for 30 years at 64°08′ N, 21°56′ W, altitude 18 m/59 ft

India

India is a large country, nearly half the size of the United States. It extends from 8° to 33° N, and includes vast plains such as the Ganges valley and high mountains like the Himalayas – the highest in the world.

The wide variety in the terrain makes for a wide variety of climatic conditions. These range from permanent snowfields to tropical coastlands; from areas of virtual desert in the northwest plains to fertile, intensively cultivated rice fields in Assam.

The climate of India is dominated by the great wind system known as the Asiatic monsoon. This is completely unlike the prevailing wind system that operates in many countries, that is, a wind that prevails from the same direction throughout the year. The monsoon reverses direction at certain times of the year. For some months it will blow steadily from the southwest; for other months, from the northeast.

From June to October the country is influenced by the moist, rain-bearing monsoon from the southwest. On some mountain ranges, facing the sea, rainfall can be very heavy indeed.

The coolest, driest time over most of the country is from December to February, when light northerly winds bring clear skies and little rain. From March to May the climate becomes hotter and hotter and the drought continues. The rains only come when the wind turns again to the southwest.

On average, the arrival of the rains – the 'burst of the monsoon' as it is called – comes to the south of India during late May or early June. It will reach the north about six weeks later. In some years the rains will be torrential; in other years they may be light or locally variable, in which case the monsoon will be said to have 'failed'. Results for food crops can, of course, be disastrous.

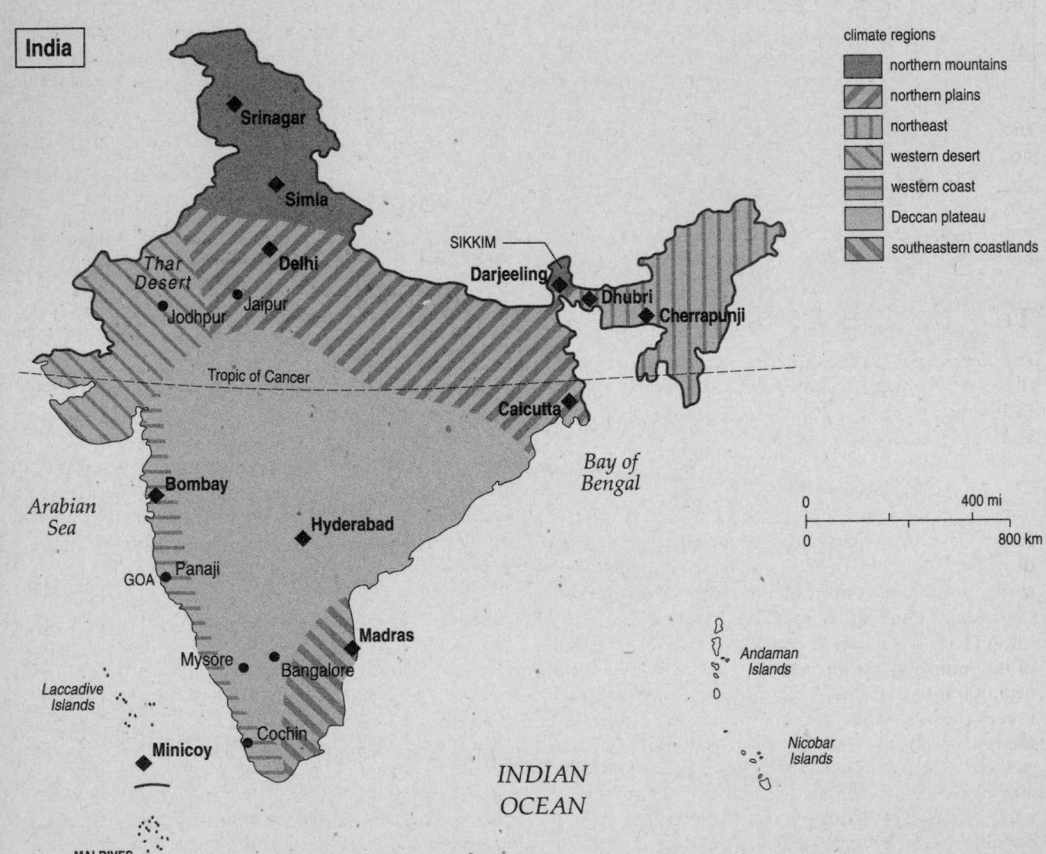

India

climate regions
- northern mountains
- northern plains
- northeast
- western desert
- western coast
- Deccan plateau
- southeastern coastlands

SRINAGAR															KASHMIR
Sunshine	Temperatures								Discomfort from heat and humidity	Precipitation and humidity				Wet days	
	Average daily				Highest recorded		Lowest recorded			Relative humidity 8:00 16:30		Average monthly precipitation			
	minimum		maximum												
average hours per day	°C	°F	°C	°F	°C	°F	°C	°F		%		mm	in	more than 2.5 mm/0.1 in	
Jan	3	-2	28	5	41	13	56	-13	8		90	76	74	2.9	6	Jan
Feb	4	-1	30	7	45	21	69	-14	6		88	68	71	2.8	6	Feb
March	4	3	38	14	57	26	78	-5	23		84	57	91	3.6	7	March
April	6	7	45	19	66	31	88	1	33		79	52	94	3.7	8	April
May	8	11	52	24	76	36	96	3	37		71	43	61	2.4	5	May
June	8	14	58	29	85	37	99	7	45	Medium	67	40	36	1.4	3	June
July	8	18	65	31	88	37	99	11	52	Medium	73	46	58	2.3	5	July
Aug	8	18	64	31	87	36	97	11	51	Medium	78	49	61	2.4	5	Aug
Sept	8	12	54	28	82	35	95	4	40	Medium	76	43	38	1.5	3	Sept
Oct	8	5	41	22	72	34	93	-2	29		78	48	31	1.2	3	Oct
Nov	7	-1	31	16	60	23	74	-8	18		82	51	10	0.4	1	Nov
Dec	5	-2	28	9	48	17	63	-11	13		88	63	33	1.3	3	Dec

Based on readings for 30 years at 34°05' N, 74°50' E, altitude 1587 m/5205 ft

India can be divided into seven climatic regions: the northern mountains or Himalayas, the northern plains from the Ganges delta to just northwest of Delhi, the western desert, the Deccan plateau, the west coast, the southeast coastlands, and the extreme northeast of the country.

THE NORTHERN MOUNTAINS

Including (with towns and cities in parentheses): HIMACHAL PRADESH (Simla), JAMMU AND KASHMIR (Srinagar), SIKKIM; northwestern ASSAM (Darjeeling) and northwestern UTTAR PRADESH.

This region includes the Himalayas and their foothills. Here some rain can occur all the year round. In winter light rain or snow is brought by disturbances travelling from the west. The main rainy season, however, is from July to October during the southwest monsoon. Winters are pleasant and cool at lower levels but it can get quite hot before the 'burst' of the monsoon. At intermediate levels, from 1,800 m/6,000 ft to 2,450 m/8,000 ft, the summer climate is very pleasant and cool. Sikkim has a range of climate which varies with altitude as described on p. 254 for Nepal. Kashmir (see table for **Srinagar** above) and hill stations such as **Simla** (see table overleaf) and **Darjeeling** (see table overleaf) are popular refuges from the heat of the plains.

THE NORTHERN PLAINS

Including (with towns and cities in parentheses): BIHAR, DELHI, HARYANA, PUNJAB, WEST BENGAL (Calcutta); central and southern UTTAR PRADESH; northern MADHYA PRADESH and northern ORISSA.

Extending from the Punjab to the Ganges delta, this low-lying region is everywhere hot and generally dry from March until June. Some occasional thunderstorms occur at this season, more particularly in the east.

With the arrival of the main monsoon rains in July, temperatures drop a little in the more cloudy weather but the high humidity causes this season to be almost as unpleasant as the preceding hot season and the nights are particularly sticky.

Rainfall decreases from east to west and to the west and northwest of Delhi conditions verge on desert. During the winter from December to February, the weather is generally sunny and dry. The nights and early mornings can feel quite chilly but the days are warm and pleasant. Some light rain may occur in the west and no part of the region is completely dry at this time. The contrast between the wetter east and drier west is well shown by comparing the climatic tables for **Calcutta** and **Delhi** (both on p. 177).

SIMLA

NORTHERN MOUNTAINS OF INDIA

Sunshine	Temperatures								Discomfort from heat and humidity	Precipitation and humidity				Wet days
	Average daily				Highest recorded		Lowest recorded			Relative humidity 8:00 16:30		Average monthly precipitation		
	minimum		maximum											
average hours per day	°C	°F	°C	°F	°C	°F	°C	°F		%		mm	in	more than 2.5 mm/0.1 in
Jan	2	36	8	47	17	63	-9	15		49	59	61	2.4	4	Jan
Feb	3	37	9	48	19	67	-8	18		49	61	69	2.7	5	Feb
March	7	44	14	57	24	75	-6	22		38	43	61	2.4	5	March
April	11	52	18	65	28	83	0	32		36	35	53	2.1	4	April
May	14	58	22	72	30	86	4	40		40	35	66	2.6	5	May
June	16	61	23	73	31	87	8	46		60	59	175	6.9	10	June
July	16	60	21	69	28	82	10	50		88	87	424	16.7	20	July
Aug	15	59	19	67	26	78	11	52		91	91	434	17.1	19	Aug
Sept	14	57	19	67	24	76	5	41		75	77	160	6.3	9	Sept
Oct	11	51	17	63	24	75	4	39		47	52	33	1.3	2	Oct
Nov	7	45	14	57	19	67	0	32		36	44	13	0.5	1	Nov
Dec	4	40	11	51	20	68	-6	21		38	55	28	1.1	2	Dec

Based on readings for 30 years at 31°06' N, 77°10' E, altitude 2202 m/7224 ft

DARJEELING

NORTHERN MOUNTAINS OF INDIA

Sunshine	Temperatures								Discomfort from heat and humidity	Precipitation and humidity				Wet days
	Average daily				Highest recorded		Lowest recorded			Relative humidity 8:00 16:30		Average monthly precipitation		
	minimum		maximum											
average hours per day	°C	°F	°C	°F	°C	°F	°C	°F		%		mm	in	more than 2.5 mm/0.1 in
Jan	2	35	8	47	16	61	-3	27		82	84	13	0.5	1	Jan
Feb	2	36	9	48	17	62	-2	28		84	80	28	1.1	3	Feb
March	6	42	14	57	23	74	-1	31		75	70	43	1.7	4	March
April	9	49	17	62	24	75	1	34		81	75	104	4.1	7	April
May	12	53	18	64	25	77	6	42		90	85	216	8.5	14	May
June	13	56	18	65	24	76	8	47		95	91	589	23.2	21	June
July	14	58	19	66	25	77	9	48		97	92	798	31.4	26	July
Aug	14	57	18	65	25	77	11	51		96	93	638	25.1	24	Aug
Sept	13	55	18	64	25	77	10	50		94	92	447	17.6	17	Sept
Oct	10	50	16	61	23	74	4	40		89	85	130	5.1	5	Oct
Nov	6	42	12	54	19	67	2	36		79	79	23	0.9	1	Nov
Dec	3	37	9	49	17	62	-1	30		78	78	8	0.3	1	Dec

Based on readings for 25 years at 27°03' N, 88°16' E, altitude 2265 m/7431 ft

CALCUTTA

NORTHERN PLAINS OF INDIA

	Sunshine	Temperatures								Discomfort from heat and humidity	Precipitation and humidity				Wet days	
		Average daily				Highest recorded		Lowest recorded			Relative humidity 8:00 17:30		Average monthly precipitation			
		minimum		maximum												
	average hours per day	°C	°F	°C	°F	°C	°F	°C	°F		%		mm	in	more than 2.5 mm/0.1 in	
Jan	8	13	55	27	80	32	89	7	44	Medium	85	52	10	0.4	0.8	Jan
Feb	9	15	59	29	84	37	98	8	46	Medium	82	45	31	1.2	2.0	Feb
March	9	21	69	34	93	40	104	10	50	High	79	46	36	1.4	2.0	March
April	9	24	75	36	97	42	107	16	61	Extreme	76	56	43	1.7	3.0	April
May	8	25	77	36	96	42	108	18	65	Extreme	77	62	140	5.5	7.0	May
June	5	26	79	33	92	44	111	21	70	Extreme	82	75	297	11.7	13.0	June
July	4	26	79	32	89	37	98	23	73	Extreme	86	80	325	12.8	18.0	July
Aug	4	26	78	32	89	36	96	23	74	Extreme	88	82	328	12.9	18.0	Aug
Sept	5	26	78	32	90	36	97	22	72	Extreme	86	81	252	9.9	13.0	Sept
Oct	7	24	74	32	89	36	96	17	63	High	85	72	114	4.5	6.0	Oct
Nov	8	18	64	29	84	33	92	11	51	Medium	79	63	20	0.8	1.0	Nov
Dec	8	13	55	26	79	31	87	7	45	Moderate	80	55	5	0.2	0.3	Dec

Based on readings for 60 years at 22°32′ N, 88°20′ E, altitude 6 m/21 ft

DELHI

NORTHERN PLAINS OF INDIA

	Sunshine	Temperatures								Discomfort from heat and humidity	Precipitation and humidity				Wet days	
		Average daily				Highest recorded		Lowest recorded			Relative humidity 8:00 16:30		Average monthly precipitation			
		minimum		maximum												
	average hours per day	°C	°F	°C	°F	°C	°F	°C	°F		%		mm	in	more than 2.5 mm/0.1 in	
Jan	7	7	44	21	70	29	84	-1	31		72	41	23	0.9	2.0	Jan
Feb	9	9	49	24	75	32	89	0	32		67	35	18	0.7	2.0	Feb
March	8	14	58	31	87	39	103	7	45	Medium	49	23	13	0.5	1.0	March
April	9	20	68	36	97	46	114	12	53	Medium	35	19	8	0.3	1.0	April
May	8	26	79	41	105	46	115	18	65	High	35	20	13	0.5	2.0	May
June	6	28	83	39	102	46	115	19	66	Extreme	53	36	74	2.9	4.0	June
July	6	27	81	36	96	45	113	22	71	Extreme	75	59	180	7.1	8.0	July
Aug	6	26	79	34	93	40	104	22	72	Extreme	80	64	173	6.8	8.0	Aug
Sept	7	24	75	34	93	41	105	18	64	High	72	51	117	4.6	4.0	Sept
Oct	9	18	65	34	93	39	103	11	51	Medium	56	32	10	0.4	1.0	Oct
Nov	10	11	52	29	84	34	93	5	41	Medium	51	31	3	0.1	0.2	Nov
Dec	9	8	46	23	73	28	83	1	34		69	42	10	0.4	1.0	Dec

Based on readings for 10 years at 28°35′ N, 77°12′ E, altitude 218 m/714 ft

THE WESTERN DESERT

Including (with towns and cities in parentheses): RAJASTHAN (Jaipur, Jodhpur) and most of GUJARAT.

This is the eastern part of what used to be called the Thar or Great Indian Desert before the partition of India. The climate is similar to that of the Sind province of Pakistan, the conditions are illustrated by the climatic table for **Jacobabad** (p. 275) in Pakistan. Annual rainfall is almost everywhere below 500 mm/20 in per year and in many places only half this. This area is one of the hottest parts of the world from May to July and the arrival of the monsoon with some light rain and more cloud makes very little difference to temperatures, so that July, August, and September are hot and humid. The cool season from November to March is warm, sunny, and dry.

THE DECCAN PLATEAU

Including (with towns and cities in parentheses): most of ANDHRA PRADESH (Hyderabad), KARNATAKA (Bangalore, Mysore), MADHYA PRADESH, MAHARASHTRA and ORISSA; east central TAMIL NADU.

The interior of the centre and south is a low plateau with a different climate from that of the coastlands. The three main seasonal divisions of the year apply equally well here, but rainfall is moderate compared with the coastlands and, in the northwest, rather low. During the hot season, temperatures can approach those of the northern plains. Altitude is the main control on temperature but towards the south even the cool season is tropical with warm sunny days moderated by dry heat and pleasant cool evenings (see the table for **Hyderabad** below).

THE WESTERN COAST

Including (with towns and cities in parentheses): southeastern GUJARAT; the coasts of KARNATAKA and MAHARASHTRA (Bombay); DAMAN, GOA (Panaji) and KERALA (Cochin).

This is a narrow coastal plain backed by a steep mountain barrier, the Western Ghats. Rainfall is abundant and heavy during the southwest monsoon season. The heat can be very oppressive because of the humidity throughout the year, particularly in the hot season. Some hill stations in the Western Ghats have a pleasant climate during the hot season but are very cloudy and wet during the monsoon. Towards the south some rain can occur at any time of the year and the monsoon arrives earlier.

The table for **Bombay** (opposite) is representative of conditions at sea level.

HYDERABAD — DECCAN PENINSULA

	Sunshine average hours per day	Temperatures Average daily min °C	min °F	Average daily max °C	max °F	Highest recorded °C	°F	Lowest recorded °C	°F	Discomfort from heat and humidity	Relative humidity 8:00 %	Relative humidity 16:30 %	Average monthly precipitation mm	in	Wet days more than 2.5 mm/0.1 in	
Jan	10	16	60	29	84	35	95	8	47	Medium	73	41	8	0.3	0.5	Jan
Feb	10	18	64	32	89	37	99	11	52	Medium	64	34	10	0.4	1.0	Feb
March	9	21	70	36	97	41	106	16	60	High	54	27	13	0.5	1.0	March
April	9	24	76	38	101	43	110	16	61	High	53	34	31	1.2	2.0	April
May	9	27	80	40	104	44	112	19	67	Extreme	52	35	28	1.1	2.0	May
June	7	24	76	35	95	44	111	18	64	Extreme	70	55	112	4.4	7.0	June
July	7	23	73	31	87	37	99	19	67	High	81	65	152	6.0	11.0	July
Aug	4	23	73	31	87	36	97	19	67	High	80	68	135	5.3	10.0	Aug
Sept	5	22	72	31	87	36	97	18	64	High	81	70	165	6.5	9.0	Sept
Oct	6	21	69	31	88	36	97	14	57	Medium	72	53	64	2.5	4.0	Oct
Nov	9	17	63	29	84	33	92	8	46	Medium	71	45	28	1.1	2.0	Nov
Dec	10	15	59	28	83	33	92	8	46	Medium	73	41	8	0.3	0.4	Dec

Based on readings for 30 years at 17°26' N, 78°27' E, altitude 541 m/1778 ft

BOMBAY
WESTERN COAST OF INDIA

Sunshine		Temperatures								Discomfort from heat and humidity	Precipitation and humidity				Wet days	
		Average daily				Highest recorded		Lowest recorded			Relative humidity 8:00 16:00		Average monthly precipitation			
		minimum		maximum												
average hours per day		°C	°F	°C	°F	°C	°F	°C	°F		%		mm	in	more than 2.5 mm/0.1 in	
Jan	9	19	67	28	83	34	94	12	53	Medium	70	61	2.5	0.1	0.2	Jan
Feb	10	19	67	28	83	36	97	12	53	Medium	71	62	2.5	0.1	0.2	Feb
March	9	22	72	30	86	38	101	17	62	High	73	65	2.5	0.1	0.1	March
April	10	24	76	32	89	38	100	20	68	High	75	67	0.0	0.0	0.1	April
May	10	27	80	33	91	36	96	23	73	Extreme	74	68	18.0	0.7	1.0	May
June	5	26	79	32	89	37	99	21	70	Extreme	79	77	485.0	19.1	14.0	June
July	2	25	77	29	85	36	96	22	72	High	83	83	617.0	24.3	21.0	July
Aug	3	24	76	29	85	32	90	22	72	High	83	81	340.0	13.4	19.0	Aug
Sept	5	24	76	29	85	35	95	22	71	High	85	78	264.0	10.4	13.0	Sept
Oct	8	24	76	32	89	36	97	21	70	High	81	71	64.0	2.5	3.0	Oct
Nov	9	23	73	32	89	36	96	18	64	High	73	64	13.0	0.5	1.0	Nov
Dec	9	21	69	31	87	34	94	13	55	High	70	62	2.5	0.1	0.1	Dec

Based on readings for 60 years at 18°54′ N, 72°49′ E, altitude 11 m/37 ft

MADRAS
SOUTHEASTERN COASTLANDS OF INDIA

Sunshine		Temperatures								Discomfort from heat and humidity	Precipitation and humidity				Wet days	
		Average daily				Highest recorded		Lowest recorded			Relative humidity 8:00 17:00		Average monthly precipitation			
		minimum		maximum												
average hours per day		°C	°F	°C	°F	°C	°F	°C	°F		%		mm	in	more than 2.5 mm/0.1 in	
Jan	9	19	67	29	85	33	91	14	57	Medium	87	67	36	1.4	2.0	Jan
Feb	10	20	68	31	88	37	98	15	59	High	83	66	10	0.4	0.7	Feb
March	10	22	72	33	91	39	102	17	62	Extreme	80	67	8	0.3	0.4	March
April	10	26	78	35	95	43	109	20	68	Extreme	74	72	15	0.6	0.9	April
May	9	28	82	38	101	45	113	21	70	Extreme	63	67	25	1.0	1.0	May
June	7	27	81	38	100	43	110	21	69	Extreme	59	61	48	1.9	4.0	June
July	5	26	79	36	96	41	106	22	71	Extreme	65	62	91	3.6	7.0	July
Aug	6	26	78	35	95	40	104	21	69	Extreme	71	66	117	4.6	8.0	Aug
Sept	7	25	77	34	94	39	102	21	69	Extreme	75	70	119	4.7	7.0	Sept
Oct	7	24	75	32	90	39	102	17	62	Extreme	83	75	305	12.0	11.0	Oct
Nov	7	22	72	29	85	34	94	15	59	High	86	75	356	14.0	11.0	Nov
Dec	7	21	69	29	84	33	91	14	57	High	87	72	140	5.5	5.0	Dec

Based on readings for 60 years at 13°04′ N, 80°15′ E, altitude 16 m/51 ft

CHERRAPUNJI

NORTHEASTERN INDIA

Sunshine	Temperatures								Discomfort from heat and humidity	Precipitation and humidity				Wet days
	Average daily				Highest recorded		Lowest recorded			Relative humidity 8:30 17:30		Average monthly precipitation		
	minimum		maximum											
average hours per day	°C	°F	°C	°F	°C	°F	°C	°F		%		mm	in	more than 2.5 mm/0.1 in
Jan	8	46	16	60	27	80	1	34		66	72	18	0.7	1.0	Jan
Feb	9	49	17	62	29	84	1	33		63	70	53	2.1	3.0	Feb
March	13	55	21	69	31	87	1	33		61	62	185	7.3	7.0	March
April	15	59	22	71	28	83	4	39		77	69	666	26.2	16.0	April
May	16	61	22	72	28	82	3	38	Moderate	82	84	1280	50.4	22.0	May
June	18	64	22	72	28	82	12	53	Moderate	91	90	2695	106.1	25.0	June
July	18	65	22	72	28	83	12	53	Moderate	93	92	2446	96.3	27.0	July
Aug	18	65	23	73	28	83	13	56	Moderate	92	91	1781	70.1	26.0	Aug
Sept	18	65	23	73	29	84	13	55	Moderate	87	87	1100	43.3	19.0	Sept
Oct	16	61	22	72	29	85	11	51	Moderate	76	84	493	19.4	9.0	Oct
Nov	12	54	19	67	27	80	7	44		64	80	69	2.7	2.0	Nov
Dec	9	48	17	62	23	74	4	39		63	79	13	0.5	0.7	Dec

Based on readings for 35 years at 25°15′ N, 91°44′ E, altitude 1313 m/4309 ft

DHUBRI

NORTHEASTERN INDIA

Sunshine	Temperatures								Discomfort from heat and humidity	Precipitation and humidity				Wet days
	Average daily				Highest recorded		Lowest recorded			Relative humidity 8:00 17:30		Average monthly precipitation		
	minimum		maximum											
average hours per day	°C	°F	°C	°F	°C	°F	°C	°F		%		mm	in	more than 2.5 mm/0.1 in
Jan	12	53	23	74	27	81	6	43		90	59	8	0.3	1	Jan
Feb	13	56	26	78	32	90	3	37	Moderate	84	54	18	0.7	1	Feb
March	17	63	30	86	38	101	10	50	Medium	75	41	46	1.8	3	March
April	21	70	31	87	39	103	12	54	Medium	79	49	130	5.1	8	April
May	23	73	30	86	39	103	17	63	High	86	75	373	14.7	15	May
June	24	76	30	86	36	96	21	69	High	91	83	605	23.8	18	June
July	26	78	30	86	35	95	23	73	High	91	83	434	17.1	16	July
Aug	26	79	30	86	34	94	22	72	High	90	83	343	13.5	15	Aug
Sept	25	77	29	85	35	95	21	69	High	91	83	368	14.5	13	Sept
Oct	23	73	29	85	33	92	17	62	High	88	75	117	4.6	5	Oct
Nov	18	64	27	80	31	88	12	53	Medium	86	71	8	0.3	1	Nov
Dec	13	55	23	74	27	80	8	46	Moderate	89	67	3	0.1	0	Dec

Based on readings for 32 years at 26°01′ N, 89°59′ E, altitude 35 m/115 ft

THE SOUTHEASTERN COASTLANDS

Including (with towns and cities in parentheses): southeastern ANDRHA PRADESH and most of TAMIL NADU (Madras).

Here the main rains do not occur until October to December and they are often associated with tropical storms or cyclones developing in the Bay of Bengal. Because of the lack of cloud, the period of southwest monsoon from June to September can be unpleasant with high temperatures and humidity.

The east coast north of Banda has its main rainy season at the time of the southwest monsoon, but this area is occasionally affected by heavy rain and strong winds caused by tropical cyclones between July to November (see the table for **Madras**, p. 179).

NORTHEASTERN INDIA

Including (with towns and cities in parentheses): ARUNACHAL PRADESH, ASSAM (Dhubri), MEGHALAYA (Cherrapunji), MIZORAM, NAGALAND, and TRIPURA.

This area is almost detached from the rest of India by Bangladesh. It is a region of plains and mountainous tracts. Its climate is similar to that of the northern plains and Himalayas, depending on altitude. Here some significant rainfall can occur in the period March to May but the main rainy season from June to October is, in places, very wet indeed. **Cherrapunji** (see table opposite) at an altitude of 1,300 m/4,300 ft has the distinction of being one of the three wettest places in the world with an annual rainfall averaging 10,800 mm/425in! The table for **Dhubri** (opposite and below) is representative of the lowlands.

Indonesia

See map page 23

Indonesia is about half the size of India, and consists of a large number of islands between 5° N and 10° S of the equator, extending over 45° of longitude. The largest islands from west to east are Sumatra, Java, Borneo, and Celebes but there are over 3,000 smaller islands, of which Bali and the Moluccas are the best known. Indonesia also includes the western portion (Irian Jaya) of the large island of New Guinea. The climate of Irian Jaya is described under Papua New Guinea on p. 280.

Most of the islands are very mountainous with numerous volcanic peaks and other mountain ranges exceeding 3,000 m/10,000 ft. There are consequently many sharp local differences of climate within Indonesia; not only are temperatures much lower in the hills, but the amount and season of maximum rainfall vary with the different exposure of the islands to the two main seasonal wind systems. The whole archipelago is alternately dominated by the north monsoon, blowing from China and the north Pacific between November and March, and the south monsoon, blowing from the Indian Ocean and the Australian continent between May and September. For a few weeks around April and October the winds are light and variable in direction; this is the period of transition when the Doldrum belt, or intertropical convergence, moves north or south across the islands.

Apart from the reduced temperatures on the higher mountains, the weather and climate of Indonesia are typical of equatorial regions. Rainfall is almost everywhere heavy and well distributed around the year. Most places receive 1,500–4,000 mm/60–160 in of rain a year. Many places have two wetter periods during the passing of the Doldrum belt; but south-facing coasts and islands south of the equator tend to be wetter during the period of the south monsoon, and north-facing coasts and the northern islands are wetter during the period of the north monsoon. Compare the climatic tables for **Jakarta** (overleaf) on the north coast of Java with those for **Ambon** (overleaf) in the Moluccas and **Balikpapan** (p. 183) on the southeast coast of Borneo. The table for **Ujung Padang** (p. 183) represents conditions in the south of the Celebes.

Much of the rainfall is heavy and accompanied by thunder. Some parts of Indonesia have more thunderstorms than anywhere else in the world. In spite of the heavy rainfall, sunshine hours are abundant in Indonesia. During the wetter months, sunshine averages four to five hours a day, rising to eight or nine hours a day during drier periods. Jakarta, one of the drier places in the country, receives three times as much rain as London but it falls on fewer days per year and for only half the number of hours.

Temperatures remain high throughout the year and there is little difference from month to month. There are only two types of weather in Indonesia: fine and sunny or cloudy and wet. Only the extreme southern islands, such as Timor, are occasionally affected by strong winds associated with tropical cyclones;

JAKARTA   JAVA

Sunshine	Temperatures								Discomfort from heat and humidity	Precipitation and humidity				Wet days
	Average daily		Highest recorded		Lowest recorded					Relative humidity 6:00 14:00		Average monthly precipitation		
	minimum	maximum												
average hours per day	°C	°F	°C	°F	°C	°F	°C	°F		%		mm	in	more than 1 mm/0.04 in
Jan	5	23	74	29	84	34	93	21	69	High	95	75	300	11.8	18	Jan
Feb	5	23	74	29	84	33	92	21	69	High	95	75	300	11.8	17	Feb
March	6	23	74	30	86	33	92	21	69	High	94	73	211	8.3	15	March
April	7	24	75	31	87	34	94	21	69	High	94	71	147	5.8	11	April
May	7	24	75	31	87	34	93	21	70	High	94	69	114	4.5	9	May
June	7	23	74	31	87	34	93	19	67	High	93	67	97	3.8	7	June
July	7	23	73	31	87	33	92	19	67	High	92	64	64	2.5	5	July
Aug	8	23	73	31	87	34	94	19	67	High	90	61	43	1.7	4	Aug
Sept	8	23	74	31	88	36	96	19	66	High	90	62	66	2.6	5	Sept
Oct	7	23	74	31	87	37	98	21	69	High	90	64	112	4.4	8	Oct
Nov	6	23	74	30	86	36	96	20	68	High	92	68	142	5.6	12	Nov
Dec	5	23	74	29	85	34	93	19	67	High	92	71	203	8.0	14	Dec

Based on readings for 80 years at 6°11′ S, 106°50′ E, altitude 8 m/26 ft

AMBON   MOLUCCAS

Sunshine	Temperatures								Discomfort from heat and humidity	Precipitation and humidity				Wet days
	Average daily		Highest recorded		Lowest recorded					Relative humidity 6:00 14:00		Average monthly precipitation		
	minimum	maximum												
average hours per day	°C	°F	°C	°F	°C	°F	°C	°F		%		mm	in	more than 0.1 mm/0.004 in
Jan	6	24	76	31	88	36	96	22	72	High	89	66	127	5.0	13	Jan
Feb	7	24	76	31	88	36	96	23	73	High	89	64	119	4.7	13	Feb
March	7	24	76	31	88	35	95	22	72	High	90	67	135	5.3	15	March
April	6	24	76	30	86	34	93	22	71	High	92	72	279	11.0	19	April
May	5	24	75	29	84	32	90	21	70	High	92	74	516	20.3	22	May
June	4	23	74	28	82	31	87	21	69	Medium	91	76	638	25.1	24	June
July	4	23	74	27	81	30	86	20	68	Medium	90	76	602	23.7	23	July
Aug	4	23	74	27	81	31	87	19	67	Medium	89	75	401	15.8	20	Aug
Sept	5	23	74	28	83	31	88	19	66	Medium	91	71	241	9.5	15	Sept
Oct	6	23	74	29	85	33	91	19	66	Medium	91	68	155	6.1	13	Oct
Nov	7	24	75	31	88	34	94	21	70	High	92	66	114	4.5	11	Nov
Dec	7	24	76	31	88	36	96	20	68	High	91	64	132	5.2	13	Dec

Based on readings for 18 years at 3°42′ S, 128°10′ E, altitude 4 m/14 ft

BALIKPAPAN

BORNEO

Sunshine	Temperatures									Discomfort from heat and humidity	Precipitation and humidity				Wet days
	Average daily				Highest recorded		Lowest recorded				Relative humidity		Average monthly precipitation		
	minimum		maximum								8:00	14:00			
average hours per day	°C	°F	°C	°F	°C	°F	°C	°F			%		mm	in	more than 0.5 mm/0.02 in
Jan	23	73	29	85	33	92	21	70	High		89	74	201	7.9	14	Jan
Feb	23	73	30	86	33	92	22	71	High		89	72	175	6.9	13	Feb
March	23	73	30	86	33	92	21	70	High		90	72	231	9.1	15	March
April	23	73	29	85	32	90	21	70	High		89	74	208	8.2	13	April
May	23	74	29	85	33	91	22	71	High		89	76	231	9.1	13	May
June	23	74	29	84	32	90	16	60	High		89	75	193	7.6	12	June
July	23	73	28	83	29	85	20	68	Medium		89	75	180	7.1	11	July
Aug	23	74	29	84	30	86	21	69	High		87	72	163	6.4	11	Aug
Sept	23	74	29	84	31	88	19	67	High		84	70	140	5.5	9	Sept
Oct	23	74	29	85	33	91	21	69	High		84	71	132	5.2	9	Oct
Nov	23	73	29	85	33	92	21	70	High		87	73	168	6.6	12	Nov
Dec	23	73	29	85	33	92	21	70	High		87	70	206	8.1	15	Dec

Based on readings for 6 years at 1°17′ S, 116°51′ E, altitude 7 m/23 ft

UJUNG PADANG

SULAWESI

Sunshine	Temperatures									Discomfort from heat and humidity	Precipitation and humidity				Wet days
	Average daily				Highest recorded		Lowest recorded				Relative humidity		Average monthly precipitation		
	minimum		maximum								6:00	14:00			
average hours per day	°C	°F	°C	°F	°C	°F	°C	°F			%		mm	in	more than 0.5 mm/0.02 in
Jan	5	23	74	29	84	31	88	21	70	High		90	80	686	27.0	25	Jan
Feb	6	24	75	29	84	32	89	21	70	High		90	77	536	21.1	20	Feb
March	6	23	74	29	85	32	89	21	70	High		91	77	424	16.7	18	March
April	8	23	74	30	86	33	91	21	69	High		91	72	150	5.9	10	April
May	8	23	74	31	87	33	91	17	63	High		91	70	89	3.5	8	May
June	8	22	72	30	86	33	91	17	63	High		90	67	74	2.9	6	June
July	9	21	70	30	86	33	92	17	63	High		89	65	36	1.4	4	July
Aug	10	21	69	31	87	34	94	17	62	High		87	65	10	0.4	2	Aug
Sept	10	21	70	31	87	35	95	14	58	High		83	66	15	0.6	2	Sept
Oct	10	22	72	31	87	33	92	18	65	High		85	71	43	1.7	5	Oct
Nov	9	23	74	30	86	33	91	19	66	High		89	73	178	7.0	11	Nov
Dec	5	23	74	29	84	32	89	21	69	High		90	79	610	24.0	22	Dec

Based on readings for 10 years at 5°08′ S, 119°28′ E, altitude 2 m/6 ft.

MEDAN   SUMATRA

Sunshine	Temperatures								Discomfort from heat and humidity	Precipitation and humidity				Wet days
	Average daily				Highest recorded		Lowest recorded			Relative humidity 6:00 12:00		Average monthly precipitation		
	minimum		maximum											
average hours per day	°C	°F	°C	°F	°C	°F	°C	°F		%		mm	in	more than 0.5 mm/0.02 in
Jan	4	22	71	29	85	34	93	18	65	Medium	94	66	137	5.4	11	Jan
Feb	3	22	71	31	87	34	94	18	65	High	93	61	91	3.6	7	Feb
March	4	22	72	31	88	35	95	18	65	High	93	61	104	4.1	8	March
April	5	23	73	32	89	35	95	19	67	High	93	62	132	5.2	10	April
May	8	23	73	32	89	36	96	18	65	High	93	63	175	6.9	12	May
June	5	22	72	32	89	35	95	17	63	High	93	63	132	5.2	9	June
July	6	22	72	32	89	36	96	18	64	High	92	59	135	5.3	9	July
Aug	6	22	72	32	89	35	95	18	65	High	93	61	178	7.0	13	Aug
Sept	7	22	72	31	88	36	96	19	66	High	94	66	211	8.3	14	Sept
Oct	9	22	72	30	86	34	93	18	64	High	94	69	259	10.2	17	Oct
Nov	8	22	72	30	86	34	93	16	60	High	88	69	246	9.7	17	Nov
Dec	5	22	72	29	85	34	94	18	65	Medium	88	68	229	9.0	15	Dec

Based on readings for 16 years at 3°35′ N, 98°41′ E, altitude 24 m/77 ft

PADANG   SUMATRA

Sunshine	Temperatures								Discomfort from heat and humidity	Precipitation and humidity				Wet days
	Average daily				Highest recorded		Lowest recorded			Relative humidity 6:00 12:00		Average monthly precipitation		
	minimum		maximum											
average hours per day	°C	°F	°C	°F	°C	°F	°C	°F		%		mm	in	more than 0.5 mm/0.02 in
Jan	7	23	74	31	87	34	93	21	70	High	88	67	351	13.8	16	Jan
Feb	8	23	74	31	87	34	94	21	69	High	88	66	259	10.2	13	Feb
March	7	23	74	31	87	34	93	21	70	High	88	66	307	12.1	15	March
April	8	24	75	31	87	33	92	22	71	High	89	66	363	14.3	17	April
May	8	24	75	31	88	34	93	22	71	High	87	65	315	12.4	14	May
June	8	23	74	31	87	34	93	20	68	High	86	63	307	12.1	12	June
July	7	23	74	31	87	33	92	21	70	High	85	62	277	10.9	12	July
Aug	7	23	74	31	87	33	92	21	69	High	86	64	348	13.7	14	Aug
Sept	7	23	74	30	86	33	91	21	70	High	87	65	152	6.0	16	Sept
Oct	7	23	74	30	86	33	92	21	70	High	88	68	495	19.5	20	Oct
Nov	6	23	74	30	86	33	91	21	70	High	89	68	518	20.4	21	Nov
Dec	6	23	74	30	86	33	91	21	70	High	89	69	480	18.9	20	Dec

Based on readings for 17 years at 0°56′ S, 100°22′ E, altitude 7 m/22 ft

but wind squalls may occur during thunderstorms. On the coast the daily range of temperature is small but this increases inland and in the hills.

The cooler nights inland and the daytime sea breezes and strong monsoon winds afford the main relief from the heat and humidity on the coast. The weather may often feel muggy and oppressive to the visitor but heat stress is not severe. Dampness and humidity are the worst features of the climate and this may trouble the elderly or those not in good health.

The tables for **Medan** (opposite) and **Padang** (opposite and below) represent conditions on the island of Sumatra.

Iran

See map page 22

Iran is a large country three times the size of France. It is bordered by Turkmenistan and the Caspian Sea on the north, Afghanistan and Pakistan on the east, the Persian (Arabian) Gulf on the south, and Iraq and Turkey on the west.

Much of the interior consists of a high plateau between 900–1,500 m/3,000–5,000 ft above sea level. The Iranian plateau is surrounded on all sides by mountains: the Elburz ranges on the north and the Zagros on the west and south. In the higher parts these mountains rise to between 3,000 m/10,000 ft and 4,600 m/15,000 ft, so that winter snowfall feeds many of the country's rivers.

Much of Iran has a very harsh climate with great extremes of heat and cold between summer and winter. Large portions of central, southern, and eastern Iran consist of desert and steppe with annual precipitation below 300 mm/12 in.

With the exception of the northern slopes of the Elburz Mountains and the Caspian coastlands, rainfall is confined to the winter and spring months. In the extreme north of the country some rainfall occurs throughout the year.

Summers are everywhere warm to hot with almost continuous sunshine. Winter weather is changeable with a mixture of mild, wet spells and some very cold weather with frost and snow when cold air

ABADAN

COASTAL IRAN

	Sunshine	Temperatures								Discomfort from heat and humidity	Precipitation and humidity				Wet days	
		Average daily				Highest recorded		Lowest recorded			Relative humidity 9:00	Average monthly precipitation				
		minimum		maximum												
	average hours per day	°C	°F	°C	°F	°C	°F	°C	°F		%	mm	in		more than 1 mm/0.04 in	
Jan	7	7	44	17	63	25	77	-3	26		77	38	1.5		6.0	Jan
Feb	7	9	49	20	68	28	83	-3	27		75	43	1.7		5.0	Feb
March	8	13	55	24	76	34	93	2	36	Moderate	59	15	0.6		3.0	March
April	8	18	64	31	88	43	109	7	45	Medium	45	20	0.8		3.0	April
May	8	23	74	38	101	47	116	16	60	High	33	3	0.1		1.0	May
June	10	26	78	42	108	48	118	19	67	Extreme	25	0	0.0		0.0	June
July	10	28	82	44	112	50	122	23	73	Extreme	25	0	0.0		0.0	July
Aug	9	27	81	45	113	51	123	22	71	Extreme	29	0	0.0		0.0	Aug
Sept	9	23	73	42	107	48	118	16	60	Extreme	33	0	0.0		0.0	Sept
Oct	8	18	65	36	97	43	110	12	53	High	39	3	0.1		0.4	Oct
Nov	7	14	57	27	81	36	97	1	33	Medium	60	25	1.0		3.0	Nov
Dec	7	9	48	20	68	29	84	-4	24		75	46	1.8		4.0	Dec

Based on readings for 10 years at 30°21′ N, 48°16′ E, altitude 2 m/7 ft

BUSHIRE

COASTAL IRAN

Sunshine	Temperatures									Discomfort from heat and humidity	Precipitation and humidity				Wet days
	Average daily				Highest recorded		Lowest recorded				Relative humidity 7:30 15:30		Average monthly precipitation		
	minimum		maximum												
average hours per day	°C	°F	°C	°F	°C	°F	°C	°F			%		mm	in	more than 0.25 mm/0.01 in
Jan	7	11	51	18	64	27	80	0	32		82	78	74	2.9	5.0	Jan
Feb	7	12	53	18	65	29	85	3	37		82	76	46	1.8	3.0	Feb
March	7	15	59	23	73	41	105	6	42	Moderate	76	71	20	0.8	2.0	March
April	8	19	67	27	81	39	103	8	47	Medium	72	72	10	0.4	1.0	April
May	9	24	76	32	89	42	107	14	58	Extreme	73	74	0	0.0	0.0	May
June	11	27	81	33	92	44	112	19	67	Extreme	74	72	0	0.0	0.0	June
July	10	29	84	35	95	44	112	23	74	Extreme	75	73	0	0.0	0.0	July
Aug	10	29	84	36	97	46	115	21	69	Extreme	72	71	0	0.0	0.0	Aug
Sept	10	26	79	34	94	42	107	17	63	Extreme	71	69	0	0.0	0.0	Sept
Oct	9	22	72	31	88	38	101	13	55	High	68	68	3	0.1	0.2	Oct
Nov	8	17	63	26	78	34	93	6	42	Medium	74	71	41	1.6	3.0	Nov
Dec	7	13	55	20	68	31	87	3	37		82	77	81	3.2	4.0	Dec

Based on readings for 53 years at 28°59′ N, 50°49′ E, altitude 4 m/14 ft

ISFAHAN

INTERIOR IRAN

Sunshine	Temperatures									Discomfort from heat and humidity	Precipitation and humidity				Wet days
	Average daily				Highest recorded		Lowest recorded				Relative humidity 7:30 15:30		Average monthly precipitation		
	minimum		maximum												
average hours per day	°C	°F	°C	°F	°C	°F	°C	°F			%		mm	in	more than 2.5 mm/0.1 in
Jan	7	–4	24	8	47	18	65	–19	–3		74	53	15	0.6	3.0	Jan
Feb	7	–2	29	12	53	23	74	–14	7		68	40	10	0.4	3.0	Feb
March	9	3	37	16	61	28	82	–11	12		57	33	25	1.0	2.0	March
April	8	8	46	22	72	31	88	–3	26		55	25	15	0.6	2.0	April
May	10	12	54	28	83	36	96	3	37	Moderate	50	27	5	0.2	1.0	May
June	12	17	62	33	92	43	110	9	48	Medium	42	18	0	0.0	0.1	June
July	11	19	67	37	98	42	107	9	48	Medium	41	15	0	0.0	0.2	July
Aug	11	18	64	36	96	42	108	12	53	Medium	42	15	0	0.0	0.1	Aug
Sept	10	13	56	32	90	38	100	6	42	Medium	44	19	0	0.0	0.1	Sept
Oct	8	8	46	25	77	33	92	–1	30		51	24	3	0.1	0.3	Oct
Nov	8	3	37	17	63	25	77	–9	16		64	35	15	0.6	2.0	Nov
Dec	7	–2	29	11	52	23	73	–13	9		72	45	20	0.8	1.0	Dec

Based on readings for 22 years at 32°34′ N, 51°44′ E, altitude 1773 m/5817 ft

TEHRAN												INTERIOR IRAN	
Sunshine		Temperatures						Discomfort from heat and humidity	Precipitation and humidity				Wet days
average hours per day		Average daily				Highest recorded	Lowest recorded		Relative humidity 7:30 17:30		Average monthly precipitation		more than 2.5 mm/0.1 in
		minimum		maximum									
		°C	°F	°C	°F	°C	°F	°C	°F		%	mm	in	
Jan	6	-3	27	7	45	18	65	-21	-5		77	75	46	1.8	4.0	Jan
Feb	7	0	32	10	50	19	67	-16	4		73	59	38	1.5	4.0	Feb
March	7	4	39	15	59	29	85	-9	16		61	39	46	1.8	5.0	March
April	7	9	49	22	71	33	91	-2	28		54	40	36	1.4	3.0	April
May	9	14	58	28	82	37	99	4	39	Medium	55	47	13	0.5	2.0	May
June	12	19	66	34	93	42	107	11	51	High	50	49	3	0.1	1.0	June
July	11	22	72	37	99	43	109	15	59	High	51	41	3	0.1	0.5	July
Aug	11	22	71	36	97	43	109	14	57	High	47	46	3	0.1	0.2	Aug
Sept	10	18	64	32	90	38	101	8	47	High	49	49	3	0.1	0.3	Sept
Oct	8	12	53	24	76	32	90	3	38	Moderate	53	54	8	0.3	1.0	Oct
Nov	7	6	43	17	63	29	84	-7	19		63	66	20	0.8	3.0	Nov
Dec	6	1	33	11	51	20	68	-12	10		76	75	31	1.2	4.0	Dec

Based on readings for 22 years at 35°41′ N, 51°25′ E, altitude 1220 m/4002 ft

blows from Siberia. Along the shore of the Persian Gulf and Arabian Sea winters are much milder as shown by the tables for **Abadan** (p. 185) and **Bushire** (opposite and above).

The very high temperatures experienced here in summer are similar to those in lowland Iraq and there is a danger of heat exhaustion and even heatstroke.

Temperatures in the interior plateau are considerably lower in winter but are very high during the long sunny summer (see the tables for **Tehran** above and **Isfahan** opposite).

In the southern coastlands the high humidity makes the high temperatures even more unpleasant in summer. In the interior daytime humidities are usually quite low in summer and the most dangerous conditions arise when high temperatures are combined with occasional strong, dusty winds.

The small area of Iran along the Caspian coast has a very different climate from the rest of the country. Here precipitation is heaviest from late summer until midwinter and occurs around the year.

This region is much wetter and cloudier than the interior and the annual precipitation ranges from 800 mm/35 in to 2,000 mm/80 in. It is a fertile, well-forested region and contrasts in a startling way with the arid landscape of interior Iran, where most cultivation is dependent upon irrigation from underground water resources, streams fed by rain, and snow falling on the surrounding mountains.

Spring and autumn are quite short seasons in Iran between the heat of summer and the more changeable and often cold weather of winter. These seasons are the best time to visit Iran even if the weather may, on occasions, be a little uncertain with short lapses into either the cold of winter or the heat of summer.

BAGHDAD

LOWLAND IRAQ

	Sunshine	Temperatures								Discomfort from heat and humidity	Precipitation and humidity				Wet days
		Average daily				Highest recorded		Lowest recorded			Relative humidity		Average monthly precipitation		
		minimum		maximum							6:00	15:00			
	average hours per day	°C	°F	°C	°F	°C	°F	°C	°F		%		mm	in	more than 1 mm/0.04 in
Jan	6	4	39	16	60	25	77	-8	18		84	51	23	0.9	4	Jan
Feb	7	6	42	18	64	30	86	-5	23		78	42	25	1.0	3	Feb
March	8	9	48	22	71	32	90	-3	27		73	36	28	1.1	4	March
April	9	14	57	29	85	40	104	3	37	Medium	64	34	13	0.5	3	April
May	10	19	67	36	97	44	112	11	51	Medium	47	19	3	0.1	1	May
June	12	23	73	41	105	48	119	14	58	High	34	13	0	0.0	0	June
July	11	24	76	43	110	49	121	17	62	High	32	12	0	0.0	0	July
Aug	11	24	76	43	110	49	120	18	64	High	33	13	0	0.0	0	Aug
Sept	11	21	70	40	104	47	116	11	51	High	38	15	0	0.0	0	Sept
Oct	9	16	61	33	92	42	107	4	39	Medium	49	22	3	0.1	1	Oct
Nov	7	11	51	25	77	34	94	-2	29		70	39	20	0.8	3	Nov
Dec	6	6	42	18	64	26	79	-7	20		84	52	25	1.0	5	Dec

Based on readings for 15 years at 33°20′ N, 44°24′ E, altitude 34 m/111 ft

BASRA

SOUTHERN IRAQ

	Sunshine	Temperatures								Discomfort from heat and humidity	Precipitation and humidity				Wet days
		Average daily				Highest recorded		Lowest recorded			Relative humidity		Average monthly precipitation		
		minimum		maximum							5:00	16:00			
	average hours per day	°C	°F	°C	°F	°C	°F	°C	°F		%		mm	in	more than 1 mm/0.04 in
Jan	7	7	45	18	64	27	81	-4	24		89	62	36	1.4	5.0	Jan
Feb	8	9	48	20	68	31	87	-2	28		87	55	28	1.1	4.0	Feb
March	9	13	55	24	75	35	95	2	36		81	49	31	1.2	3.0	March
April	8	17	63	29	85	41	105	8	47	Medium	76	43	31	1.2	3.0	April
May	10	24	76	35	95	46	114	9	48	High	65	40	5	0.2	0.7	May
June	11	27	81	38	100	46	115	21	69	Extreme	60	41	0	0.0	0.0	June
July	10	27	81	40	104	51	123	22	72	Extreme	58	35	0	0.0	0.0	July
Aug	11	26	78	41	105	49	120	20	68	Extreme	56	32	0	0.0	0.0	Aug
Sept	10	22	72	39	102	47	116	14	58	Extreme	62	32	0	0.0	0.0	Sept
Oct	9	18	64	34	94	46	114	7	45	High	67	36	0	0.0	0.0	Oct
Nov	8	14	57	27	80	37	98	3	38	Medium	83	52	36	1.4	2.0	Nov
Dec	7	9	48	21	69	29	85	-2	29		89	62	20	0.8	3.0	Dec

Based on readings for 10 years at 30°34′ N, 47°47′ E, altitude 2.5 m/8 ft

Iraq

See map page 22

Iraq is an almost landlocked country lying between
Turkey on the north, Iran on the east, Saudi Arabia
and Kuwait on the south, and Jordan and Syria on
the west. It has a very short coastline on the Persian
(Arabian) Gulf.

Most of the country is flat and low-lying and consists
of the low plateau of the Syrian and Arabian deserts
to the west and, in central Iraq, the broad valleys
of the rivers Tigris and Euphrates (ancient
Mesopotamia). These rivers enter the Gulf in a
combined stream, the Shatt-al-Arab, near Basra. The
northeast of Iraq (Kurdistan) is mountainous and the
climate is similar to that found in the mountains of
western Iran (see p. 185).

The western desert region and Mesopotamia have a
very harsh climate with a marked contrast between
the extremely hot, sunny, and dry summers and a
cooler winter during which some rain falls. Iraq
experiences some of the highest temperatures
anywhere in the world. These scorching conditions
are often accompanied by a persistent dusty,
northwesterly wind, the *shamal*, which adds to the
unpleasantness. Heat exhaustion and even heatstroke
are hazards.

There is no great difference in summer temperatures
from north to south but temperatures are distinctly
lower and more pleasant at this time in the Kurdistan
mountains. Winters are very mild in the south, but
become cooler towards the north. Frost and snow
occasionally occur at low levels in the north and
snowfall may be heavy in Kurdistan.

Most of the country has a desert or steppe climate
with annual rainfall below 200 mm/8 in. Only in the
northern plains around Mosul and Kirkuk and in the
Kurdistan mountains is precipitation heavier. The
summer months from May to September are virtually
rainless and the heaviest precipitation comes between
December and March.

Melting snow in spring in the mountains of Turkey,
Iran, and Kurdistan causes the rivers Tigris and
Euphrates to flood in a spectacular manner between
March and May at a time when the long, hot, dry
summer in Iraq is beginning.

The climatic table for **Baghdad** is representative of
conditions around the year in most of lowland Iraq.

That for **Basra** shows the higher summer humidity
in the south where the summer heat is even more
oppressive.

Conditions in the northern plains are similar to those
illustrated by the climatic table for **Deir ez Zor**
(p. 348) in Syria.

Ireland

The Republic of Ireland, often called Eire, is the largest portion of the island lying to the west of Britain. It shares with the rest of the British Isles a mild, changeable climate with very rare extremes of heat or cold.

Ireland is even more influenced by the warm waters of the North Atlantic than England. Consequently, its climate is a little wetter the year round, being milder in winter and cooler and cloudier in summer. This mild, rainy climate is particularly favourable to the growth of grass and moss and for this reason Ireland has been called the Emerald Isle.

The driest parts of the country are the east and south (see the tables for **Dublin** opposite and **Cork** opposite and below). The east and the interior (see the table for **Mullingar** p. 192) have slightly warmer summers and cooler winters.

The west coast is more influenced by the Atlantic and is both wetter and cloudier with particularly mild winters (see the table for **Valentia** on p. 192). Differences of weather and climate, however, are relatively small throughout the country.

Snow is very rare along the west and south coasts but occurs on a few days a year in the east and on the mountains. Although there are numerous mountain ranges in Ireland, few of these exceed 800 m/2,600 ft and even at these heights snow does not lie for long.

In the wetter west of the country rain is frequent but on many days it is very light and in the form of drizzle. The sunniest parts of the country are the east and south coasts with sunshine hours averaging from two a day in winter to six in midsummer.

Over most of Ireland spring is the driest time of the year and May is the sunniest month. Except in the extreme east around Dublin, autumn and winter are the wettest seasons.

Occasional severe weather in winter takes two forms: storms and gales which particularly affect the west; and rare spells with frost and snow when cold easterly or northerly winds bring severe weather to the whole British Isles.

For weather conditions in Northern Ireland, see the table for **Belfast** (p. 373).

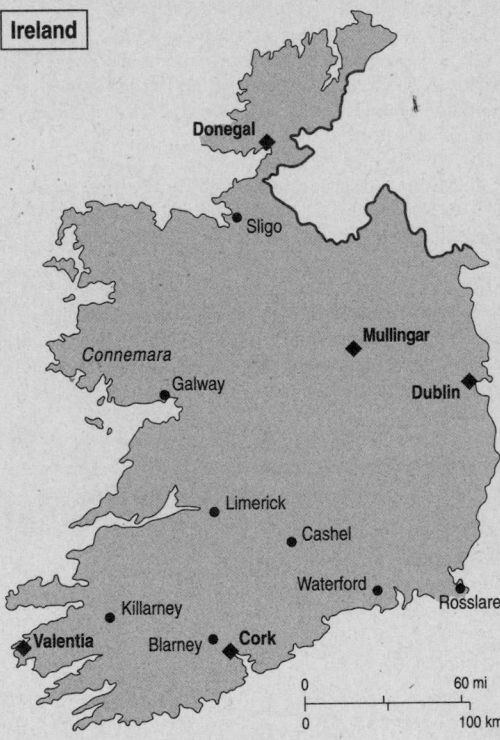

Ireland

DUBLIN

SOUTHEASTERN IRELAND

Sunshine	Temperatures								Discomfort from heat and humidity	Precipitation and humidity			Wet days
	Average daily				Highest recorded		Lowest recorded			Relative humidity 09:30	Average monthly precipitation		
	minimum		maximum										
average hours per day	°C	°F	°C	°F	°C	°F	°C	°F		%	mm	in	more than 1 mm/0.04 in
Jan 2	1	34	8	46	14	58	−12	10		88	67	2.6	13 Jan
Feb 3	2	35	8	47	17	62	−10	14		86	55	2.2	10 Feb
March 3	3	37	10	51	21	69	−9	15		82	51	2.0	10 March
April 5	4	39	13	55	22	72	−5	23		76	45	1.8	11 April
May 6	6	43	15	60	25	77	−6	22		75	60	2.4	10 May
June 6	9	48	18	65	29	84	1	33		76	57	2.2	11 June
July 5	11	52	20	67	30	86	3	38		78	70	2.8	13 July
Aug 5	11	51	19	67	27	81	2	36		80	74	2.9	12 Aug
Sept 4	9	48	17	63	25	78	−1	30		83	72	2.8	12 Sept
Oct 3	6	43	14	57	24	76	−4	24		85	70	2.8	11 Oct
Nov 2	4	39	10	51	18	65	−7	20		88	67	2.6	12 Nov
Dec 2	3	37	8	47	17	63	−9	15		88	74	2.9	14 Dec

Based on readings for 30 years at 53°22′ N, 6°21′ W, altitude 47 m/154 ft

CORK

EAST COAST IRELAND

Sunshine	Temperatures								Discomfort from heat and humidity	Precipitation and humidity			Wet days
	Average daily				Highest recorded		Lowest recorded			Relative humidity 09:30	Average monthly precipitation		
	minimum		maximum										
average hours per day	°C	°F	°C	°F	°C	°F	°C	°F		%	mm	in	more than 1 mm/0.04 in
Jan 2	2	36	9	47	14	58	−9	15		89	119	4.7	15 Jan
Feb 3	3	37	9	48	15	59	−7	20		88	79	3.1	11 Feb
March 3	4	39	11	52	18	64	−5	23		87	94	3.7	12 March
April 5	5	42	13	56	22	72	−2	28		81	57	2.2	11 April
May 6	7	45	16	61	26	79	−1	30		78	71	2.8	11 May
June 6	10	51	19	66	29	84	3	37		79	57	2.2	10 June
July 5	12	54	20	68	28	82	5	41		80	70	2.8	11 July
Aug 5	12	53	20	68	29	85	3	37		83	71	2.8	11 Aug
Sept 4	10	50	18	64	26	79	1	34		86	94	3.7	12 Sept
Oct 3	7	45	14	58	21	70	−5	23		90	99	3.9	12 Oct
Nov 2	4	40	11	52	18	64	−6	21		90	116	4.6	14 Nov
Dec 2	3	38	9	49	16	60	−7	19		89	122	4.8	16 Dec

Based on readings for 30 years at 51°54′ N, 8°29′ W, altitude 15 m/49 ft

MULLINGAR

INLAND IRELAND

	Sunshine	Temperatures								Discomfort from heat and humidity	Precipitation and humidity				Wet days	
		Average daily				Highest recorded		Lowest recorded			Relative humidity 9:30 14:30		Average monthly precipitation			
		minimum		maximum												
	average hours per day	°C	°F	°C	°F	°C	°F	°C	°F		%		mm	in	more than 1 mm/0.04 in	
Jan	2	1	34	7	44	13	56	–9	16		93	85	88	3.5	14	Jan
Feb	3	1	34	7	45	15	58	–12	10		92	79	63	2.5	12	Feb
March	3	3	37	10	50	21	69	–9	15		89	72	59	2.3	11	March
April	5	4	39	13	55	22	71	–3	26		82	68	55	2.2	12	April
May	6	6	43	16	60	26	78	–1	30		78	66	61	2.4	11	May
June	6	9	48	18	64	30	86	2	35		80	69	75	3.0	12	June
July	4	11	51	19	66	29	83	5	40		84	73	89	3.5	14	July
Aug	5	10	51	19	67	30	85	4	39		87	73	87	3.4	13	Aug
Sept	4	9	48	17	62	26	78	0	32		90	75	99	3.9	15	Sept
Oct	3	6	44	13	56	23	73	–3	27		92	78	94	3.7	13	Oct
Nov	2	4	39	10	49	17	63	–5	24		94	84	86	3.4	14	Nov
Dec	1	2	36	8	46	14	58	–9	16		94	88	111	4.4	18	Dec

Based on readings for 17 years at 53°31′ N, 7°21′ W, altitude 108 m/354 ft

VALENTIA

SOUTHWESTERN IRELAND

	Sunshine	Temperatures								Discomfort from heat and humidity	Precipitation and humidity				Wet days	
		Average daily				Highest recorded		Lowest recorded			Relative humidity 9:30 14:30		Average monthly precipitation			
		minimum		maximum												
	average hours per day	°C	°F	°C	°F	°C	°F	°C	°F		%		mm	in	more than 1 mm/0.04 in	
Jan	2	5	40	9	49	14	57	–7	19		84	79	165	6.5	20	Jan
Feb	3	4	40	9	49	17	62	–5	22		83	76	107	4.2	15	Feb
March	4	5	42	11	52	20	68	–3	26		81	73	103	4.1	14	March
April	5	6	43	13	55	24	75	–2	29		77	71	75	3.0	13	April
May	7	8	47	15	59	26	79	0	32		76	72	86	3.4	13	May
June	6	11	51	17	62	27	81	2	36		80	77	81	3.2	13	June
July	5	12	54	18	64	30	85	6	43		83	79	107	4.2	15	July
Aug	5	13	55	18	65	30	86	4	40		84	78	95	3.7	15	Aug
Sept	4	11	52	17	62	27	80	2	35		84	78	122	4.8	16	Sept
Oct	3	9	48	14	58	24	74	–2	28		85	78	140	5.5	17	Oct
Nov	2	7	44	12	53	18	65	–2	28		84	79	151	5.9	18	Nov
Dec	1	6	42	10	50	16	60	–5	23		84	81	168	6.6	21	Dec

Based on readings for 30 years at 51°56′ N, 10°15′ W, altitude 9 m/30 ft

Israel

See map page 22

Israel is a small country on the eastern shores of the Mediterranean with land borders with Lebanon and Syria on the north, Jordan on the east, and Egypt on the south. About 60 percent of the country's 25,000 sq km/10,000 sq mi consists of the Negev desert. The Negev lies south of Beersheba and extends to Elat on the Gulf of Aqaba.

The weather and climate of Israel are very similar to those described for Syria on p. 348. The main contrast of weather and climate within Israel is between that of the Negev and the northern part of the country.

The northern part of Israel has a typical Mediterranean climate with abundant sunshine, mild, wet winters, and long, hot, dry summers. Winter rainfall can be quite heavy but falls on a small number of days.

On the coast the summer heat is at times rather oppressive and humid but is tempered by afternoon sea breezes. The winters here are mild, and frost and snow are very rare events. For weather conditions on the coast see the table for **Haifa** below).

Inland in Galilee and in the occupied West Bank territory of Samaria and Judea, the country is hilly, with heights ranging from 500 m/1,650 ft to 1,000 m/3,300 ft. Rainfall is rather heavier here and snow may occasionally fall. Nights are chilly in winter and fresh and cool in summer.

The summer heat in the hills is drier and less oppressive than on the coast (see the table for **Jerusalem** overleaf).

In the southern desert of Negev annual rainfall is low, decreasing from about 200 mm/8 in in the north to as little as 50 mm/2 in at **Elat** (see table overleaf) on the Gulf of Aqaba.

The scanty rainfall in the Negev region comes as short but heavy local showers. These may occur at any time during the period from September to April. Cloudy skies are rare here even in midwinter. Winter nights may be quite cold with frost and occasional snow or sleet.

HAIFA

COASTAL ISRAEL

	Sunshine	Temperatures								Discomfort from heat and humidity	Precipitation and humidity				Wet days	
		Average daily				Highest recorded		Lowest recorded			Relative humidity 8:30 14:30		Average monthly precipitation			
		minimum		maximum												
	average hours per day	°C	°F	°C	°F	°C	°F	°C	°F		%		mm	in	more than 1 mm/0.04 in	
Jan	6	9	49	18	65	26	79	-2	29		66	56	175	6.9	13.0	Jan
Feb	6	10	50	19	67	31	87	-3	27		65	56	109	4.3	11.0	Feb
March	9	12	53	22	71	40	104	1	33		62	56	41	1.6	7.0	March
April	10	14	58	25	77	43	109	4	40	Moderate	60	57	25	1.0	4.0	April
May	12	18	65	28	83	44	112	10	50	Medium	62	59	5	0.2	1.0	May
June	12	22	71	29	85	43	109	13	56	Medium	67	66	0	0.0	0.0	June
July	12	24	75	31	88	36	96	17	63	High	70	68	0	0.0	0.0	July
Aug	12	24	76	32	90	37	99	18	65	High	70	69	0	0.0	0.0	Aug
Sept	11	23	74	31	88	42	107	16	61	High	67	66	3	0.1	0.2	Sept
Oct	10	20	68	29	85	41	106	8	47	Medium	66	66	25	1.0	2.0	Oct
Nov	8	16	60	26	78	36	97	7	44	Moderate	61	56	94	3.7	7.0	Nov
Dec	7	12	53	20	68	29	85	1	33		66	56	185	7.3	11.0	Dec

Based on readings for 16 years at 32°48' N, 34°59' E, altitude 10 m/33 ft

JERUSALEM
INLAND ISRAEL

Sunshine	Temperatures								Discomfort from heat and humidity	Precipitation and humidity				Wet days	
	Average daily				Highest recorded		Lowest recorded			Relative humidity 8:30 13:30		Average monthly precipitation			
	minimum		maximum												
average hours per day	°C	°F	°C	°F	°C	°F	°C	°F		%		mm	in	more than 1 mm/0.04 in	
Jan	6	5	41	13	55	25	77	-3	26		77	66	132	5.2	9.0	Jan
Feb	7	6	42	13	56	27	80	-3	27		74	58	132	5.2	11.0	Feb
March	7	8	46	18	65	31	87	-1	30		61	57	64	2.5	3.0	March
April	10	10	50	23	73	39	102	2	36		56	42	28	1.1	3.0	April
May	11	14	57	27	81	39	103	6	42	Moderate	47	33	3	0.1	0.6	May
June	14	16	60	29	85	42	107	8	47	Medium	48	32	0	0.0	0.1	June
July	13	17	63	31	87	38	100	10	50	Medium	52	35	0	0.0	0.0	July
Aug	13	18	64	31	87	39	103	11	52	Medium	58	36	0	0.0	0.0	Aug
Sept	11	17	62	29	85	39	103	10	50	Medium	61	36	0	0.0	0.1	Sept
Oct	7	15	59	27	81	36	97	8	47	Moderate	60	36	13	0.5	1.0	Oct
Nov	7	12	53	21	70	31	88	4	39		65	50	71	2.8	4.0	Nov
Dec	6	7	45	15	59	26	79	-3	27		73	60	86	3.4	7.0	Dec

Based on readings for 19 years at 31°47′ N, 35°13′ E, altitude 557 m/1485 ft

ELAT
SOUTHERN ISRAEL

Sunshine	Temperatures								Discomfort from heat and humidity	Precipitation and humidity				Wet days	
	Average daily				Highest recorded		Lowest recorded			Relative humidity 8:30 14:30		Average monthly precipitation			
	minimum		maximum												
average hours per day	°C	°F	°C	°F	°C	°F	°C	°F		%		mm	in	more than 1 mm/0.04 in	
Jan	7	10	50	21	70	27	81	3	37		60	39	0	0.0	1.0	Jan
Feb	8	11	52	23	73	31	87	3	37		62	40	8	0.3	1.0	Feb
March	8	14	57	26	79	34	93	8	47	Moderate	56	38	8	0.3	2.0	March
April	9	18	64	31	87	41	105	11	51	Medium	46	30	5	0.2	1.0	April
May	10	17	62	36	96	44	112	16	60	High	41	28	0	0.0	0.1	May
June	11	24	75	38	101	44	112	21	69	High	38	20	0	0.0	0.0	June
July	11	26	79	39	103	47	116	22	72	High	36	13	0	0.0	0.0	July
Aug	11	26	79	40	104	46	114	23	74	High	40	24	0	0.0	0.0	Aug
Sept	10	25	77	37	99	43	110	21	70	High	52	27	0	0.0	0.0	Sept
Oct	9	21	70	33	92	39	103	16	60	Medium	55	34	0	0.0	0.0	Oct
Nov	8	16	61	28	82	37	98	8	46	Moderate	56	38	0	0.0	1.0	Nov
Dec	7	12	53	23	74	31	88	5	41		58	42	8	0.3	1.0	Dec

Based on readings for 4 years at 29°33′ N, 34°57′ E, altitude 2 m/7 ft

Except under khamsin conditions, nights in the desert are rarely very hot and may feel pleasantly fresh after the dry heat of the day.

The most unpleasant weather in Israel, as in neighbouring countries, occurs when hot dry winds import high temperatures from the Arabian desert. These khamsin winds go under the Hebrew name *sharav* in Israel. They are most frequent and most severe at the beginning and end of the hot, dry summer period.

Israel has a very sunny climate with an average of six to seven hours of sunshine a day in winter and twelve to thirteen in summer. It is one of the few countries to have exploited its sunshine for solar heating of domestic hot water. A great many homes make use of rooftop solar heating panels for this purpose.

Italy

Italy can be divided into three distinct geographical regions: the southern side of the Alps where Italy borders France, Switzerland, Austria, and Yugoslavia; the great plain of the Po valley from Turin to Venice; and the long and mountainous peninsula of central and southern Italy together with the large islands of Sardinia and Sicily.

Each of these regions has a distinctive and different type of weather and climate.

Occasionally all parts of Italy experience very high temperatures in summer and even autumn when the sirocco blows. This is a warm, humid wind from North Africa that acquires its humidity over the Mediterranean. A spell of sirocco weather in autumn often ends with very heavy rain accompanied by thunder. Sea temperatures around Italy are usually sufficiently warm to make bathing pleasant from mid-May until October but the water can be surprisingly cold on warm sunny days in spring.

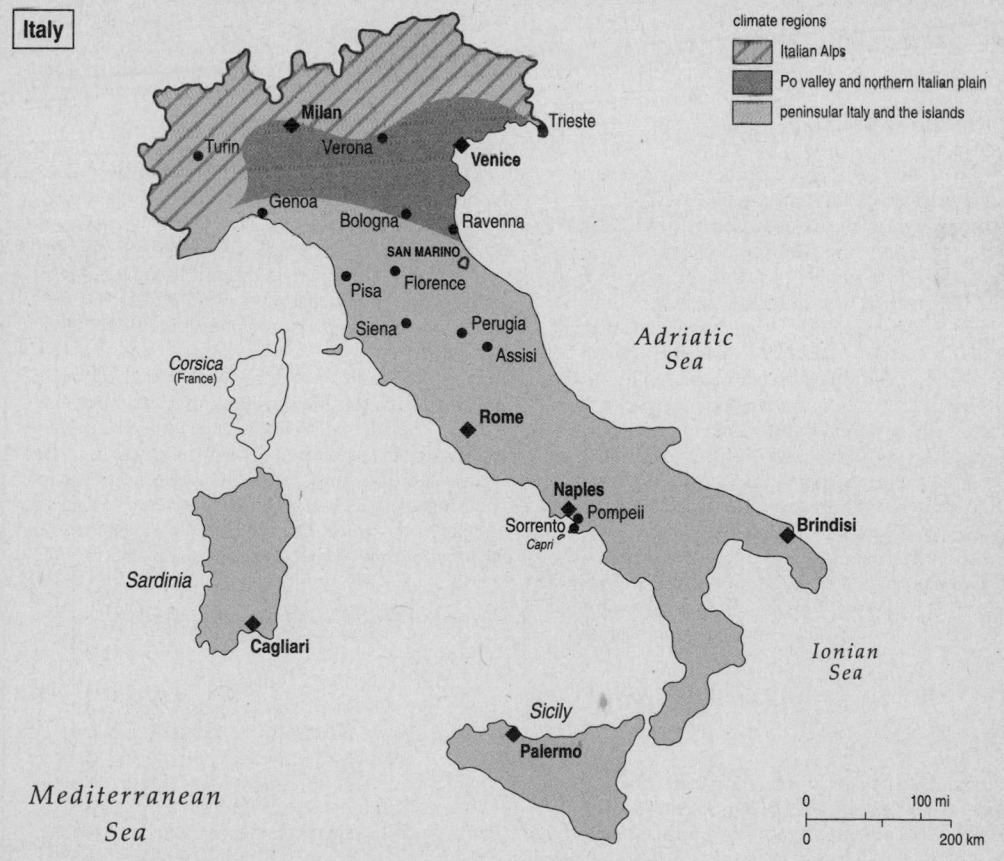

MILAN													NORTHERN ITALY
Sunshine	Temperatures								Discomfort from heat and humidity	Precipitation and humidity			Wet days
average hours per day	Average daily				Highest recorded		Lowest recorded			Relative humidity 6:30 12:30		Average monthly precipitation	more than 1 mm/0.04 in
	minimum		maximum										
	°C	°F	°C	°F	°C	°F	°C	°F		%		mm in	
Jan	2	0	32	5	40	15	60	–10	14		90	82	44 1.6	6	Jan
Feb	3	2	35	8	46	20	68	–11	13		87	73	60 2.4	7	Feb
March	5	6	43	13	56	22	72	–2	28		88	65	77 3.0	7	March
April	6	10	49	18	65	29	84	0	33		86	57	94 3.7	8	April
May	7	14	57	23	74	33	92	6	42		86	59	76 3.0	8	May
June	8	17	63	27	80	35	96	9	49	Medium	84	56	118 4.7	9	June
July	9	20	67	29	84	38	101	10	51	Medium	85	61	64 2.5	6	July
Aug	8	19	66	28	82	36	97	12	54	Medium	89	58	91 3.6	7	Aug
Sept	6	16	61	24	75	33	91	7	45	Moderate	91	63	69 2.7	5	Sept
Oct	4	11	52	17	63	26	79	1	35		94	73	125 4.9	8	Oct
Nov	2	6	43	10	51	21	69	–1	29		92	80	122 4.8	10	Nov
Dec	2	2	35	6	43	18	64	–7	19		94	89	77 3.0	7	Dec

Based on readings for 16 years at 45°28′ N, 9°11′ E, altitude 121 m/397 ft

ALPINE ITALY

Including (with towns and cities in parentheses): PIEMONTE (Turin), TRENTINO ALTO-ADIGE, VALLE D'AOSTA; northern LOMBARDY, northeastern VENETO and most of FRIULI-VENEZIA GIULIA (Trieste).

In the Italian Alps, where the higher mountains rise to above 3,000 m/10,000 ft, the climate is similar to that of the Swiss and Austrian Alps (pp. 345 and 53). Precipitation, however, is rather heavier. The lower slopes and valleys of the Italian Alps are also a little warmer both in summer and winter. Summer tends to be the rainiest season and thunderstorms are frequent in spring, summer, and autumn. The mildest winters and warmest and sunniest summers are found in the region of lakes Maggiore, Como, and Garda. Here sunshine averages from three to four hours a day in winter and up to nine hours in summer. A föhn wind sometimes blows from the north, raising temperatures and lowering humidity.

THE PO VALLEY AND NORTH ITALIAN PLAIN

Including (with towns and cities in parentheses): most of EMILIA-ROMAGNA (Bologna, Ravenna), LOMBARDY (Milan) and VENETO (Venice, Verona).

This is a remarkably flat and low-lying region of dense population and great agricultural productivity. It extends from Turin to Venice and almost as far as the port of Trieste. It has a distinctive climate with rain well distributed around the year. The summers are as hot and almost as sunny as those in southern Italy. Winters are surprisingly cold for about three months. Fog, frost, and snow are frequent and this area is colder than Paris or London in midwinter.

Summer and autumn rainfall is often in the form of thunderstorms but the rain falls on a small number of days. The sun shines an average of two to three hours a day in winter and nine in summer. In winter the small area around Trieste is sometimes affected by strong and gusty winds, the *bora*, which bring very cold air from central Europe (see the tables for **Milan** above and **Venice** opposite and above).

PENINSULAR ITALY AND THE ISLANDS

Including (with towns and cities in parentheses): ABRUZZI, APULIA (Brindisi), BASILICATA, CALABRIA, CAMPANIA (Naples, Pompeii, Sorrento) and Capri, LAZIO (Rome), LIGURIA (Genoa), MARCHE, MOLISE, SARDINIA (Cagliari), SICILY (Palermo), TUSCANY (Florence, Pisa, Siena), UMBRIA (Perugia, Assisi).

VENICE — NORTHERN ITALY

	Sunshine average hours per day	Temperatures Average daily minimum °C	°F	Average daily maximum °C	°F	Highest recorded °C	°F	Lowest recorded °C	°F	Discomfort from heat and humidity	Relative humidity 7:00 %	Relative humidity 13:00 %	Average monthly precipitation mm	in	Wet days more than 1 mm/0.04 in	
Jan	3	1	33	6	42	14	57	−8	18		86	76	37	1.5	6	Jan
Feb	4	2	35	8	46	18	64	−9	15		80	76	48	1.9	6	Feb
March	5	5	41	12	53	22	72	−5	24		86	68	61	2.4	7	March
April	6	10	49	17	62	27	81	2	35		86	67	78	3.1	9	April
May	8	14	56	21	70	33	91	5	41		85	69	65	2.6	8	May
June	9	17	63	25	76	33	91	8	47	Moderate	83	65	69	2.7	8	June
July	10	19	66	27	81	34	94	12	53	Medium	82	64	52	2.1	7	July
Aug	8	18	65	27	80	34	93	13	55	Medium	84	63	69	2.7	7	Aug
Sept	7	16	61	24	75	31	87	9	49	Moderate	87	64	59	2.3	5	Sept
Oct	5	11	53	19	65	27	80	3	38		88	68	77	3.0	7	Oct
Nov	2	7	44	12	53	21	69	−2	28		88	75	94	3.7	9	Nov
Dec	3	3	37	8	46	15	59	−4	24		88	79	61	2.4	8	Dec

Based on readings for 16 years at 45°27′ N, 12°19′ E, altitude 1 m/3 ft

ROME — COASTAL ITALY

	Sunshine average hours per day	Temperatures Average daily minimum °C	°F	Average daily maximum °C	°F	Highest recorded °C	°F	Lowest recorded °C	°F	Discomfort from heat and humidity	Relative humidity 7:00 %	Relative humidity 13:00 %	Average monthly precipitation mm	in	Wet days more than 1 mm/0.04 in	
Jan	4	5	40	11	52	19	66	−5	24		85	68	71	2.8	8	Jan
Feb	4	5	42	13	55	20	68	−6	21		86	64	62	2.4	9	Feb
March	6	7	45	15	59	23	74	−2	28		83	56	57	2.2	8	March
April	7	10	50	19	66	26	78	1	35		83	54	51	2.0	6	April
May	8	13	56	23	74	31	89	3	38		77	54	46	1.8	5	May
June	9	17	63	28	82	36	98	10	50	Medium	74	48	37	1.5	4	June
July	11	20	67	30	87	36	98	12	54	Medium	70	42	15	0.6	1	July
Aug	10	20	67	30	86	40	104	12	53	Medium	73	43	21	0.8	2	Aug
Sept	8	17	62	26	79	33	92	11	51	Moderate	83	50	63	2.5	5	Sept
Oct	6	13	55	22	71	29	84	4	39		86	59	99	3.9	8	Oct
Nov	4	9	49	16	61	23	74	−1	30		87	66	129	5.9	11	Nov
Dec	4	6	44	13	55	19	65	−3	27		85	70	93	3.7	10	Dec

Based on readings for 16 years at 41°54′ N, 12°29′ E, altitude 17 m/56 ft

NAPLES

COASTAL ITALY

Sunshine	Temperatures									Discomfort from heat and humidity	Precipitation and humidity				Wet days
	Average daily				Highest recorded		Lowest recorded				Relative humidity		Average monthly precipitation		
	minimum		maximum								7:00 13:00				
average hours per day	°C	°F	°C	°F	°C	°F	°C	°F			%		mm	in	more than 1 mm/0.04 in
Jan 4	4	40	12	53	20	69	-4	24			77	68	116	4.6	11 Jan
Feb 4	5	41	13	55	20	69	-4	25			78	67	85	3.4	10 Feb
March 5	6	44	15	59	25	77	-4	25			77	62	73	2.9	9 March
April 7	9	48	18	65	27	80	1	34			79	61	62	2.4	8 April
May 8	12	54	22	72	32	90	3	37			85	63	44	1.7	7 May
June 9	16	61	26	79	35	95	7	45	Moderate		75	58	31	1.2	4 June
July 10	18	65	29	84	36	96	11	52	Medium		73	53	19	0.8	2 July
Aug 10	18	65	29	84	37	99	13	55	Medium		74	53	32	1.3	3 Aug
Sept 8	16	61	26	79	34	93	8	46	Moderate		78	59	64	2.5	5 Sept
Oct 6	12	54	22	71	29	84	3	38			79	63	107	4.2	9 Oct
Nov 4	9	48	17	63	26	79	-2	29			81	68	147	5.8	11 Nov
Dec 3	6	44	14	56	20	67	-4	24			80	70	135	5.3	12 Dec

Based on readings for 16 years at 40°53′ N, 14°17′ E, altitude 110 m/361 ft

BRINDISI

COASTAL ITALY

Sunshine	Temperatures									Discomfort from heat and humidity	Precipitation and humidity				Wet days
	Average daily				Highest recorded		Lowest recorded				Relative humidity		Average monthly precipitation		
	minimum		maximum								7:00 13:00				
average hours per day	°C	°F	°C	°F	°C	°F	°C	°F			%		mm	in	more than 1 mm/0.04 in
Jan 4	6	43	12	54	19	66	-2	28			82	73	77	3.0	11 Jan
Feb 5	7	44	13	56	22	72	-2	29			81	68	57	2.2	7 Feb
March 6	8	47	15	58	22	72	-4	25			82	67	59	2.3	8 March
April 7	11	51	18	65	27	81	3	37			81	67	47	1.9	7 April
May 9	14	58	22	72	34	92	6	43			80	67	39	1.5	5 May
June 10	18	65	26	79	38	100	12	54	Medium		75	65	25	1.0	3 June
July 12	21	70	29	84	39	103	12	53	Medium		75	64	14	0.6	1 July
Aug 10	21	70	29	84	40	104	15	59	Medium		75	62	30	1.2	2 Aug
Sept 8	18	65	26	79	34	93	10	49	Medium		80	66	38	1.5	4 Sept
Oct 7	15	59	22	71	30	85	7	44			83	70	79	3.1	6 Oct
Nov 5	11	53	18	64	26	78	3	38			83	72	96	3.8	10 Nov
Dec 4	8	47	14	58	24	76	-1	30			84	73	83	3.3	9 Dec

Based on readings for 16 years at 40°38′ N, 17°56′ E, altitude 28 m/84 ft

PALERMO
SICILY

Sunshine	Temperatures									Discomfort from heat and humidity	Precipitation and humidity				Wet days
	Average daily				Highest recorded		Lowest recorded				Relative humidity		Average monthly precipitation		
	minimum		maximum								7:00	13:00			
average hours per day	°C	°F	°C	°F	°C	°F	°C	°F			%		mm	in	more than 1 mm/0.04 in
Jan	4	8	46	16	60	30	87	0	33		76	67	71	2.8	12	Jan
Feb	5	8	47	16	62	27	80	0	32		72	63	43	1.7	8	Feb
March	6	9	48	17	63	30	85	1	34		72	60	50	2.0	8	March
April	7	11	52	20	68	34	93	4	38		70	60	49	1.9	6	April
May	8	14	58	24	74	36	97	8	46	Moderate	71	58	19	0.8	3	May
June	10	18	64	27	81	40	103	11	52	Medium	68	54	9	0.4	2	June
July	10	21	69	30	85	41	106	14	56	Medium	64	52	2	0.1	0	July
Aug	9	21	70	30	86	42	107	16	61	Medium	64	52	18	0.7	2	Aug
Sept	8	19	66	28	83	41	106	11	52	Medium	66	53	41	1.6	4	Sept
Oct	6	16	60	25	77	35	95	9	49	Moderate	72	61	77	3.0	8	Oct
Nov	6	12	54	21	71	32	89	5	40		74	64	71	2.8	8	Nov
Dec	4	10	49	18	64	26	78	2	36		74	65	62	2.4	10	Dec

Based on readings for 16 years at 38°06′ N, 13°19′ E, altitude 31 m/102 ft

CAGLIARI
SARDINIA

Sunshine	Temperatures									Discomfort from heat and humidity	Precipitation and humidity				Wet days
	Average daily				Highest recorded		Lowest recorded				Relative humidity		Average monthly precipitation		
	minimum		maximum								6:30	12:30			
average hours per day	°C	°F	°C	°F	°C	°F	°C	°F			%		mm	in	more than 1 mm/0.04 in
Jan	4	7	44	14	58	21	70	-2	28		87	73	50	2.0	8	Jan
Feb	4	7	45	15	58	21	70	-1	30		87	69	50	2.0	7	Feb
March	6	9	47	17	62	25	76	1	33		88	66	45	1.8	7	March
April	7	11	51	19	66	28	83	4	40		86	65	31	1.2	5	April
May	9	14	57	23	74	35	95	7	44	Moderate	85	65	26	1.0	4	May
June	9	18	64	27	81	37	99	10	50	Medium	82	58	13	0.5	1	June
July	11	21	69	30	87	40	104	14	58	Medium	81	58	1	0.0	0	July
Aug	10	21	69	30	86	38	100	15	60	High	82	61	10	0.4	1	Aug
Sept	8	19	66	27	81	35	95	12	53	Medium	86	61	32	1.3	3	Sept
Oct	6	15	59	23	74	29	84	8	46	Moderate	89	64	54	2.1	6	Oct
Nov	4	11	52	19	66	26	79	4	40		87	67	72	2.8	9	Nov
Dec	3	9	48	16	60	24	76	-1	30		87	73	67	2.6	9	Dec

Based on readings for 16 years at 39°12′ N, 9°05′ E, altitude 7 m/23 ft

The long Italian peninsula, from Genoa and Rimini in the north to Reggio di Calabria and Brindisi in the south, has a mountainous interior where the Appennines rise to over 1,800 m/6,000 ft. The climate of the coastal areas is thus very different from that of the interior, particularly in winter.

The higher areas are cold, wet, and often snowy. The coastal regions, where most of the large towns are located, have a typical Mediterranean climate with mild winters and hot, generally dry, summers. The length and intensity of the summer dry season increases southwards. Compare the tables for **Rome** (p. 197), **Naples** (p.198), and **Brindisi** (p. 198).

There is no great difference in the temperatures at sea level from north to south. The east coast of the peninsula is not as wet as the west coast. The east coast north of Pescara is occasionally affected by the cold *bora* winds in winter and spring but the wind is less strong here than around Trieste.

The whole of peninsular Italy and the large islands of Sicily and Sardinia have very changeable weather in autumn, winter, and spring in marked contrast to the settled sunny weather of summer.

Disturbed weather can continue into late May and may commence any time after early September. Throughout the winter, however, cloudy, rainy days alternate with spells of mild, sunny weather.

The least number of rainy days and the highest number of hours of sunshine occur in the extreme south of the mainland and in Sicily and Sardinia. Here sunshine averages from four to five hours a day in winter and up to ten or eleven hours in summer.

The heat of summer is usually moderated on the coast by daytime sea breezes but the nights can occasionally be warm and even humid. See the tables for **Palermo** and **Cagliari** (both p. 199).

Jamaica

See map page 15

Jamaica is one of the larger of the West Indian islands. It is situated west of Haiti and south of Cuba, and has an area of 11,500 sq km/4,400 sq mi, about the size of the state of Connecticut. It is one of the more mountains islands of the Caribbean with the highest peaks of the Blue Mountains reaching

over 2,300 m/7,500 ft. The northern slopes of these mountains may have up to 5,000 mm/200 in of rain a year as compared with about 750 mm/30 in on the drier, sheltered south coast (see the table for **Kingston** opposite). In spite of the low annual rainfall, the south coast has experienced as much as 250 mm/10 in or more in 24 hours during the passage of a hurricane.

Japan

See map page 24

Japan comprises a group of islands between 45° and 32° N off the east coast of Asia. The total area of the country is about one-and-a-half times that of the United Kingdom.

From north to south the main islands are Hokkaido, Honshu (the largest island and sometimes called 'the mainland'), Shikoku, and Kyushu.

All the islands are hilly or even mountainous, particularly Honshu, where the highest peaks such as Fujiyama rise to over 3,600 m/12,000 ft. There are numerous other peaks rising to over 2,000 m/6,500 ft, many of which are extinct or even active volcanoes. The higher mountains in Hokkaido and Honshu are snow-covered throughout the year and there are many opportunities for winter sports.

The climate of Japan around the year is much influenced by the great seasonal wind reversal of the Asian monsoon but there are important differences between Korea or north China and Japan. The relatively narrow Sea of Japan separates the mainland from Japan. The Japanese islands have a climate modified and moderated by the sea; winters are less cold than in the same latitude on the continent and precipitation is much heavier.

Winter precipitation is particularly heavy on the west coast of northern Honshu and in Hokkaido. Here snowfall is heavy as the cold, outblowing winter monsoon from Siberia and Manchuria is warmed and picks up moisture over the sea. In parts of this area precipitation is greater in winter than in summer. Elsewhere in Japan winter is a relatively dry season. Much of the cloud and precipitation is associated with depressions which develop where

KINGSTON

SOUTH-COAST JAMAICA

Sunshine	Temperatures								Discomfort from heat and humidity	Precipitation and humidity				Wet days
	Average daily				Highest recorded		Lowest recorded			Relative humidity 7:00 15:00		Average monthly precipitation		
average hours per day	minimum		maximum											more than 1 mm/0.04 in
	°C	°F	°C	°F	°C	°F	°C	°F		%		mm	in	
Jan	8	19	67	30	86	34	93	14	57	High	84	61	23	0.9	3	Jan
Feb	9	19	67	30	86	33	92	15	59	High	84	62	15	0.6	3	Feb
March	9	20	68	30	86	34	93	14	58	High	81	62	23	0.9	2	March
April	9	21	70	31	87	34	93	17	63	High	79	66	31	1.2	3	April
May	8	22	72	31	87	34	94	19	66	High	77	68	102	4.0	4	May
June	8	23	74	32	89	35	95	20	68	High	78	68	89	3.5	5	June
July	9	23	73	32	90	36	96	19	66	High	77	65	89	3.5	4	July
Aug	8	23	73	32	90	36	97	20	68	High	82	70	91	3.6	7	Aug
Sept	8	23	73	32	89	36	96	20	68	High	85	70	99	3.9	6	Sept
Oct	7	23	73	31	88	36	96	18	65	High	88	73	180	7.1	9	Oct
Nov	8	22	71	31	87	36	96	17	62	High	87	68	74	2.9	5	Nov
Dec	8	21	69	31	87	36	96	14	57	High	85	62	36	1.4	4	Dec

Based on readings for 33 years at 17°58′ N, 76°48′ W, altitude 34 m/110 ft

HAKODATE

SOUTHERN HOKKAIDO ISLAND

Sunshine	Temperatures								Discomfort from heat and humidity	Precipitation and humidity				Wet days
	Average daily				Highest recorded		Lowest recorded			Relative humidity 6:30 14:30		Average monthly precipitation		
average hours per day	minimum		maximum											more than 1 mm/0.04 in
	°C	°F	°C	°F	°C	°F	°C	°F		%		mm	in	
Jan	4	–7	19	0	32	13	55	–22	–7		81	71	66	2.6	13	Jan
Feb	4	–7	19	1	34	11	51	–21	–5		81	69	58	2.3	11	Feb
March	5	–3	26	4	40	17	62	–19	–2		80	67	66	2.6	11	March
April	7	2	35	11	51	22	71	–7	19		81	62	71	2.8	9	April
May	7	6	43	15	59	27	80	–1	30		85	67	84	3.3	9	May
June	6	11	51	18	65	28	82	2	36		90	76	89	3.5	9	June
July	5	16	61	23	73	32	90	6	43	Moderate	93	79	137	5.4	10	July
Aug	6	18	64	26	78	33	92	9	48	Medium	93	76	130	5.1	9	Aug
Sept	6	13	56	23	72	31	88	2	35	Moderate	90	69	178	7.0	13	Sept
Oct	6	7	44	17	62	27	80	–4	25		85	64	119	4.7	11	Oct
Nov	4	1	34	9	49	22	71	–12	11		79	62	104	4.1	13	Nov
Dec	3	–4	24	3	37	16	61	–19	–3		81	72	81	3.2	15	Dec

Based on readings for 65 years at 41°49′ N, 140°45′ E, altitude 33 m/109 ft

warm, humid air from the Pacific meets colder continental air along the North Pacific polar front. Winter weather is variable and changeable over the whole of Japan but this is particularly so in the north and west of the country.

In summer and early autumn much of the heavy rain is brought by typhoons, or tropical cyclones, which move north from the South China Sea or the region east of the Philippines. In some parts of central and southern Japan there is a double rainfall maximum; one in early summer, the so-called *Bai-U* or plum rains, and a second brought by typhoons in late summer or early autumn.

Winters in northern Japan, particularly in Hokkaido, are severe with heavy falls of snow. At sea level the climate is much like that of Newfoundland or northern New England. See the tables for **Hakodate** (p. 201) in southern Hokkaido and **Akita** (below) in northern Honshu.

In southern Honshu and in Kyushu and Shikoku the winters are mild and almost subtropical. This is particularly so around the coasts of the Inland Sea, the narrow stretch of water which separates these islands. Winter rainfall is light here and snow and frost very rare (see the tables for **Nagasaki** opposite and above and **Ashizuri** opposite).

In northern Japan the summers are short but quite warm and on the eastern coasts the summers are wetter than the winters. In central and southern Japan the summers are very warm but excessively hot days are rare. Because the country is dominated by moist maritime air at this time with frequent cold, the summer heat is often sultry and oppressive, particularly in Japan's great cities.

In the mountains temperatures are sufficiently reduced by altitude as to be quite pleasant in summer. Here on sunny days in spring and summer, conditions can be quite delightful. Compare the climatic table for **Oiwake** (p. 204), inland in the hills at 1,006 m/3,300 ft, with that for **Tokyo** (p. 204), which is on the coast of central Honshu and is representative of some of the major cities of Japan.

In most places in Japan the daily sunshine is limited by the humid atmosphere and abundant rain. Hours of sunshine are lowest in Hokkaido and northern Honshu, where they average from two to three a day in winter and five or six a day in summer. Farther south there is more sunshine with an average of six to seven hours a day around the year. Summer sunshine is often less than that in spring, which is a drier season. Spring is perhaps the most pleasant season in Japan; the weather is usually warm and sunny, but fresher and drier than in summer or autumn.

AKITA — NORTHERN HONSHU ISLAND

	Sunshine average hours per day	Temperatures Average daily minimum		Average daily maximum		Highest recorded		Lowest recorded		Discomfort from heat and humidity	Relative humidity 6:30	Relative humidity 14:30	Average monthly precipitation mm	Average monthly precipitation in	Wet days more than 1 mm/0.04 in	
		°C	°F	°C	°F	°C	°F	°C	°F		%	%	mm	in		
Jan	2	−5	23	2	35	14	57	−19	−3		81	73	142	5.6	22	Jan
Feb	2	−5	23	3	37	13	56	−24	−12		82	71	104	4.1	20	Feb
March	4	−2	28	6	42	21	70	−19	−3		81	67	104	4.1	18	March
April	6	4	39	13	55	25	77	−7	19		84	63	109	4.3	12	April
May	7	8	47	18	64	30	86	−2	29		88	68	112	4.4	11	May
June	7	14	57	23	73	34	93	4	39	Moderate	91	71	127	5.0	8	June
July	6	18	65	26	79	35	95	10	50	Medium	95	78	198	7.8	12	July
Aug	7	19	67	28	83	36	96	9	48	Medium	94	71	188	7.4	9	Aug
Sept	6	15	59	24	76	34	93	3	38	Moderate	94	71	211	8.3	14	Sept
Oct	5	8	47	18	64	27	80	−2	29		90	65	188	7.4	15	Oct
Nov	4	3	37	11	52	23	74	−4	24		87	70	191	7.5	21	Nov
Dec	1	−2	28	4	40	22	71	−19	−2		80	72	178	7.0	21	Dec

Based on readings for 30 years at 39°41′ N, 140°06′ E, altitude 10 m/33 ft

NAGASAKI

KYUSHU ISLAND

	Sunshine average hours per day	Temperatures										Discomfort from heat and humidity	Precipitation and humidity				Wet days more than 1 mm/0.04 in	
		Average daily				Highest recorded		Lowest recorded					Relative humidity 5:30 13:30		Average monthly precipitation			
		minimum		maximum														
		°C	°F	°C	°F	°C	°F	°C	°F				%		mm	in		
Jan	4	2	36	9	49	21	70	-6	22				74	59	71	2.8	11	Jan
Feb	5	2	36	10	50	23	73	-4	24				75	60	84	3.3	9	Feb
March	6	5	41	14	57	24	76	-3	26				74	56	125	4.9	11	March
April	7	10	50	19	66	28	82	1	34				79	60	185	7.3	11	April
May	7	14	57	23	73	29	85	6	42		Moderate		84	65	170	6.7	10	May
June	6	18	65	26	78	34	94	12	53		Medium		88	70	312	12.3	13	June
July	7	23	73	29	85	36	96	15	59		High		91	72	257	10.1	10	July
Aug	8	23	74	31	88	37	98	17	63		High		86	65	175	6.9	9	Aug
Sept	6	20	68	27	81	34	94	11	52		Medium		83	67	249	9.8	11	Sept
Oct	6	14	58	22	72	31	87	5	41				75	55	114	4.5	6	Oct
Nov	6	9	49	17	63	27	81	1	33				75	59	94	3.7	8	Nov
Dec	4	4	40	12	53	24	75	-3	26				76	63	81	3.2	10	Dec

Based on readings for 59 years at 33°44′ N, 129°53′ E, altitude 133 m/436 ft

ASHIZURI

SHIKOKU ISLAND

	Sunshine average hours per day	Temperatures										Discomfort from heat and humidity	Precipitation and humidity				Wet days more than 1 mm/0.04 in	
		Average daily				Highest recorded		Lowest recorded					Relative humidity 6:00 14:00		Average monthly precipitation			
		minimum		maximum														
		°C	°F	°C	°F	°C	°F	°C	°F				%		mm	in		
Jan	6	4	40	12	53	21	69	-4	24				68	57	64	2.5	6	Jan
Feb	6	4	40	12	53	21	70	-3	26				69	57	142	5.6	7	Feb
March	6	7	45	15	59	23	73	-1	30				70	58	160	6.3	9	March
April	7	12	54	19	66	24	75	4	39				75	63	188	7.4	8	April
May	6	17	62	22	72	28	82	9	49				83	71	244	9.6	11	May
June	5	19	67	24	76	29	84	14	57		Moderate		89	79	323	12.7	13	June
July	7	24	75	28	83	33	92	19	67		High		91	80	257	10.1	13	July
Aug	9	25	77	29	85	34	94	20	68		High		89	77	213	8.4	11	Aug
Sept	6	22	72	28	82	32	90	16	61		Medium		85	75	323	12.7	13	Sept
Oct	6	17	63	23	73	28	83	9	48		Moderate		76	65	279	11.0	9	Oct
Nov	6	12	54	19	66	26	79	3	38				74	63	175	6.9	8	Nov
Dec	6	7	45	14	58	23	74	-1	30				71	61	107	4.2	7	Dec

Based on readings for 12 years at 32°44′ N, 133°01′ E, altitude 65 m/213 ft

OIWAKE

INLAND HONSHU ISLAND

	Sunshine	Temperatures								Discomfort from heat and humidity	Precipitation and humidity				Wet days	
	average hours per day	Average daily				Highest recorded		Lowest recorded			Relative humidity 6:00 14:00		Average monthly precipitation		more than 1 mm/0.04 in	
		minimum		maximum												
		°C	°F	°C	°F	°C	°F	°C	°F		%		mm	in		
Jan	4	−10	14	2	35	14	58	−21	−5		88	49	25	1.0	5	Jan
Feb	4	−10	14	2	35	15	59	−18	−1		91	51	43	1.7	6	Feb
March	5	−7	19	6	43	22	71	−19	−2		89	50	61	2.4	7	March
April	7	−1	31	13	55	27	80	−11	13		90	54	84	3.3	10	April
May	7	3	37	18	65	28	83	−6	21		88	56	102	4.0	9	May
June	6	10	50	21	69	29	84	2	35		95	68	160	6.3	13	June
July	6	16	60	24	76	33	91	7	45	Moderate	97	72	188	7.4	15	July
Aug	6	18	64	26	78	34	93	8	46	Medium	96	70	155	6.1	12	Aug
Sept	6	12	54	22	71	31	87	3	38		97	74	160	6.3	14	Sept
Oct	5	6	42	17	63	26	78	−3	26		97	67	147	5.8	10	Oct
Nov	4	−1	30	11	52	21	70	−7	19		92	61	56	2.2	6	Nov
Dec	3	−6	21	5	41	21	69	−17	2		91	59	38	1.5	6	Dec

Based on readings for 10 years at 36°20′ N, 138°33′ E, altitude 1006 m/3300 ft

TOKYO

CENTRAL COASTAL HONSHU ISLAND

	Sunshine	Temperatures								Discomfort from heat and humidity	Precipitation and humidity				Wet days	
	average hours per day	Average daily				Highest recorded		Lowest recorded			Relative humidity 6:30 14:30		Average monthly precipitation		more than 1 mm/0.04 in	
		minimum		maximum												
		°C	°F	°C	°F	°C	°F	°C	°F		%		mm	in		
Jan	6	−2	29	8	47	22	72	−8	17		73	48	48	1.9	5	Jan
Feb	6	−1	31	9	48	25	77	−8	18		71	48	74	2.9	6	Feb
March	6	2	36	12	54	25	77	−6	22		75	53	107	4.2	10	March
April	7	8	46	17	63	29	85	−1	30		81	59	135	5.3	10	April
May	6	12	54	22	71	31	88	2	36		85	62	147	5.8	10	May
June	5	17	63	24	76	34	93	8	47	Moderate	89	68	165	6.5	12	June
July	6	21	70	28	83	37	99	13	55	Medium	91	69	142	5.6	10	July
Aug	7	22	72	30	86	38	101	16	60	High	92	66	152	6.0	9	Aug
Sept	5	19	66	26	79	36	96	11	51	Medium	91	68	234	9.2	12	Sept
Oct	4	13	55	21	69	32	90	2	36		88	64	208	8.2	11	Oct
Nov	5	6	43	16	60	27	81	−3	26		83	58	97	3.8	7	Nov
Dec	5	1	33	11	52	23	74	−7	20		77	51	56	2.2	5	Dec

Based on readings for 60 years at 35°41′ N, 139°46′ E, altitude 6 m/19 ft

Jordan

See map page 22

Jordan is a small, almost landlocked country with an area of about 90,000 sq km/35,000 sq mi. It is bordered by Syria on the north, Iraq and Saudi Arabia on the east and south, and Israel on the west. In the extreme south at Aqaba it has a short coastline on the Gulf of Aqaba branch of the Red Sea.

Climate and weather around the year are similar to those described for Syria on p. 348. About 90 percent of Jordan is desert, with an annual rainfall below 200 mm/8 in and falling as low as 25–50 mm/1–2 in in places. This is part of the great desert of Arabia and Syria. Summers are uniformly hot and sunny but winter weather can be cold, occasionalaly with snow on high ground. The scanty rainfall occurs in winter and spring, usually as heavy showers.

The northwestern part of the country is hilly, with some areas rising to over 1,000 m/3,300 ft. The altitude and proximity to the Mediterranean make this the wettest and most fertile part of Jordan. Here the annual rainfall varies from as much as 800 mm/32 in in the higher parts to as little as 300 mm/12 in. The rain mostly falls between November and March (see the table for **Amman** below).

On the western side of these mountains there is a long north to south valley, much of which is well below Mediterranean level. In this valley the river Jordan flows south to the Dead Sea, the lowest spot on the face of the earth. Winters are very mild and summers particularly hot, while the whole area has a very low rainfall. To the west of the Jordan valley are the hills of Samaria and Judea, described for Israel (see the table for **Jerusalem** on p. 194).

Jordan is a very sunny country with average daily sunshine hours ranging from six to seven in winter and as much as twelve to thirteen in summer. Although summer temperatures are high in the desert, the heat is usually moderated by low humidity and a stiff daytime breeze. The nights are cool and pleasant.

The worst weather is brought by hot, dry winds from Arabia (the khamsin). These are most likely to blow in early or late summer and last for a day or two at a time. Under these conditions heat stress may be felt.

AMMAN — NORTHWESTERN JORDAN

Sunshine average hours per day	Temperatures										Discomfort from heat and humidity	Precipitation and humidity				Wet days more than 1 mm/0.04 in
	Average daily				Highest recorded		Lowest recorded					Relative humidity 8:30 14:30		Average monthly precipitation		
	minimum		maximum													
	°C	°F	°C	°F	°C	°F	°C	°F				%		mm	in	
Jan	7	4	39	12	54	24	76	-6	21			80	56	69	2.7	8.0	Jan
Feb	7	4	40	13	56	29	85	-5	23			78	52	74	2.9	8.0	Feb
March	8	6	43	16	60	32	90	-3	26			57	44	31	1.2	4.0	March
April	10	9	49	23	73	39	103	1	34			53	34	15	0.6	3.0	April
May	11	14	57	28	83	41	105	5	41	Moderate		39	28	5	0.2	0.8	May
June	13	16	61	31	87	43	109	8	46	Medium		40	28	0	0.0	0.0	June
July	13	18	65	32	89	40	104	13	56	Medium		41	30	0	0.0	0.0	July
Aug	13	18	65	32	90	43	109	13	55	Medium		45	30	0	0.0	0.0	Aug
Sept	11	17	62	31	88	39	103	11	52	Medium		53	31	0	0.0	0.0	Sept
Oct	10	14	57	27	81	37	99	7	44	Moderate		53	31	5	0.2	1.0	Oct
Nov	8	10	50	21	70	33	91	2	35			66	40	33	1.3	4.0	Nov
Dec	6	6	42	15	59	25	77	-4	25			77	53	46	1.8	5.0	Dec

Based on readings for 25 years at 31°57′ N, 35°57′ E, altitude 777 m/2548 ft

KAZALINSK

CENTRAL KAZAKHSTAN

	Sunshine	Temperatures							Discomfort from heat and humidity	Precipitation and humidity				Wet days	
		Average daily				Highest recorded		Lowest recorded			Relative humidity 7:00 13:00		Average monthly precipitation			
		minimum		maximum												
	average hours per day	°C	°F	°C	°F	°C	°F	°C	°F		%		mm	in	more than 0.1 mm/0.004 in	
Jan		–15	5	–9	16	5	41	–33	–27		88	80	10	0.4	7	Jan
Feb		–15	5	–6	21	11	51	–32	–26		88	75	10	0.4	5	Feb
March		–8	17	2	35	23	73	–30	–22		88	68	13	0.5	4	March
April		–3	27	14	58	31	87	–12	11		74	48	13	0.5	4	April
May		11	52	24	76	39	102	–3	27		59	37	15	0.6	4	May
June		16	61	30	86	42	108	7	45	Medium	58	37	5	0.2	2	June
July		18	65	32	90	41	106	10	50	Medium	59	34	5	0.2	2	July
Aug		16	61	29	85	41	106	8	47	Medium	63	37	8	0.3	2	Aug
Sept		9	49	23	74	37	98	2	36		70	41	8	0.3	2	Sept
Oct		2	35	14	57	29	85	–11	13		79	48	10	0.4	3	Oct
Nov		–5	23	3	37	19	67	–11	13		90	72	13	0.5	5	Nov
Dec		–9	15	–4	24	12	53	–31	–23		91	80	15	0.6	6	Dec

Based on readings for 10 years at 45°46′ N, 62°06′ E, altitude 63 m/207 ft

ALMATY

EASTERN KAZAKHSTAN

	Sunshine	Temperatures							Discomfort from heat and humidity	Precipitation and humidity				Wet days	
		Average daily				Highest recorded		Lowest recorded			Relative humidity 7:00 13:00		Average monthly precipitation			
		minimum		maximum												
	average hours per day	°C	°F	°C	°F	°C	°F	°C	°F		%		mm	in	more than 0.01 mm/.004 in	
Jan	4	–14	7	–5	23	12	53	–34	–30		87	72	33	1.3	9	Jan
Feb	4	–13	9	–3	26	14	57	–32	–25		86	69	23	0.9	6	Feb
March	5	–6	22	4	39	24	76	–28	–18		85	66	56	2.2	10	March
April	7	3	38	13	56	29	84	–11	13		72	53	102	4.0	12	April
May	8	10	50	20	68	36	96	–1	31		66	49	94	3.7	11	May
June	9	14	57	24	76	38	100	4	39		66	48	66	2.6	10	June
July	10	16	60	27	81	38	100	7	45	Moderate	65	43	36	1.4	9	July
Aug	10	14	57	27	80	37	98	4	39	Moderate	66	39	31	1.2	6	Aug
Sept	8	8	47	22	71	34	94	–3	27		72	39	25	1.0	4	Sept
Oct	6	2	35	13	55	29	85	–17	2		80	49	51	2.0	7	Oct
Nov	4	–5	23	4	39	23	74	–27	–17		85	67	48	1.9	8	Nov
Dec	4	–9	15	–2	29	15	59	–32	–25		86	72	33	1.3	7	Dec

Based on readings for 19 years at 43°16′ N, 76°53′ E, altitude 775 m/2543 ft

Kazakhstan

See map page 22

This central Asian republic includes extensive deserts as well as semi-arid steppes. Part of eastern Kazakhstan belongs to the mountainous region on the borders of Afghanistan and China.

In the steppes and deserts the summers are warm to hot but the heat is made more bearable by the low humidity. The winters are cold but generally dry and sunny. The table for **Kazalinsk** is representative of weather in western Kazakhstan.

The highest mountains of the east carry snow the year round. However, the east is a rather dry region considering its height. Winters are cold but spring comes earlier than farther north.

The table for **Almaty** illustrates conditions in the valleys of eastern Kazakhstan.

Kenya

Kenya is a country about as large as France and is situated in East Africa between 5° N and 5° S. It has a very diverse relief with a low coastal plain on the Indian Ocean shore, extensive inland plateaux regions between 915 m/3,000 ft and 1,500 m/5,000 ft and several mountain ranges and isolated peaks such as Mount Kenya, which rises to 5,200 m/17,000 ft and has a permanent snow-cap. It is bordered on the north by Ethiopia and Somalia, on the south by Tanzania, and on the west by Uganda and the shores of Lake Victoria.

Although Kenya lies across the equator, annual rainfall over most of the country is surprisingly low and variable from year to year. This is because the intertropical belt of cloud and rain passes quickly across Kenya in April and October and because the predominant seasonal winds, the north and south monsoons as they are called in East Africa, have a track parallel to the coast and have already passed over large areas of land before reaching Kenya.

Because of the reduction of temperature with altitude, temperatures over much of Kenya are subtropical or temperate, reminiscent of California, and of summer in France or southern Britain, rather than of other countries in equatorial Africa.

Only the coastal lowlands of the country experience the constant high temperatures and humidity associated with equatorial latitudes. Even here they are less oppressive than one might expect, because of the regular daytime sea breezes and longer hours of sunshine. It is not surprising that with such a favourable climate – sunny, only moderately wet, and not too hot – and a great variety of scenery, wildlife, game parks, and good communications, Kenya has many attractions for the tourist.

The variety of relief and the range of altitude in Kenya produce a considerable number of distinctive local climates and local weather too numerous to be detailed here. The country can be divided broadly into three climatic regions – the coast, the drylands of the northern frontier district and lower inland plateau, and the Kenya highlands – each with certain features of equatorial climates.

There is a double rainy season between March and May and between November and December, with two intervening dry seasons. There is a small difference of temperature from month to month through the year. Both these features can be seen in the three tables for Kenya included overleaf.

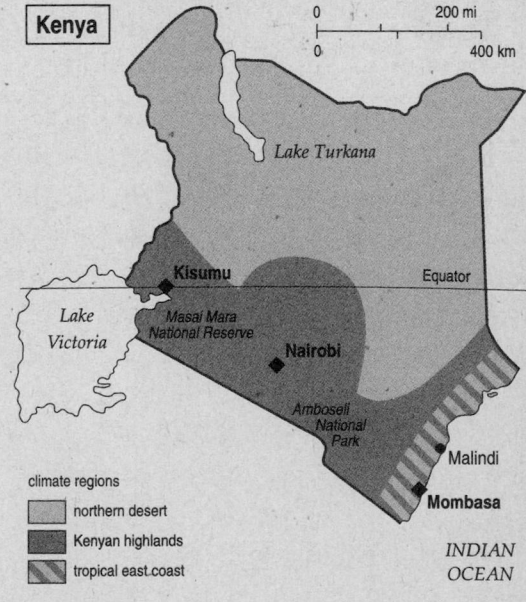

Kenya

0 — 200 mi
0 — 400 km

Lake Turkana

Kisumu

Lake Victoria

Masai Mara National Reserve

Nairobi

Amboseli National Park

Equator

Malindi

Mombasa

INDIAN OCEAN

climate regions
- northern desert
- Kenyan highlands
- tropical east coast

MOMBASA

COASTAL KENYA

Sunshine average hours per day		Temperatures								Discomfort from heat and humidity	Precipitation and humidity				Wet days more than 0.25 mm/0.01 in	
		Average daily				Highest recorded		Lowest recorded			Relative humidity 8:00 14:00		Average monthly precipitation			
		minimum		maximum												
		°C	°F	°C	°F	°C	°F	°C	°F		%		mm	in		
Jan	8	24	75	31	87	35	95	21	69	High	76	66	25	1.0	6	Jan
Feb	9	24	76	31	87	35	95	21	70	High	75	63	18	0.7	3	Feb
March	9	25	77	31	88	36	96	22	71	High	77	63	64	2.5	7	March
April	8	24	76	30	86	36	96	21	69	High	81	71	196	7.7	15	April
May	6	23	74	28	83	33	92	19	67	Medium	85	76	320	12.6	20	May
June	8	23	73	28	82	32	89	16	61	Medium	82	72	119	4.7	15	June
July	7	22	71	27	81	33	92	18	64	Medium	82	72	89	3.5	14	July
Aug	8	22	71	27	81	31	88	17	63	Medium	76	72	64	2.5	16	Aug
Sept	9	22	72	28	82	32	90	18	64	Medium	81	70	64	2.5	14	Sept
Oct	9	23	74	29	84	32	90	18	64	Medium	79	69	86	3.4	10	Oct
Nov	9	24	75	29	85	34	93	20	68	Medium	78	69	97	3.8	10	Nov
Dec	9	24	75	30	86	36	96	21	69	High	78	69	61	2.4	9	Dec

Based on readings for 45 years at 4°03′ S, 39°39′ E, altitude 16 m/52 ft

NAIROBI

KENYAN HIGHLANDS

Sunshine average hours per day		Temperatures								Discomfort from heat and humidity	Precipitation and humidity				Wet days more than 0.25 mm/0.01 in	
		Average daily				Highest recorded		Lowest recorded			Relative humidity 8:00 14:00		Average monthly precipitation			
		minimum		maximum												
		°C	°F	°C	°F	°C	°F	°C	°F		%		mm	in		
Jan	9	12	54	25	77	29	84	8	47	Moderate	74	44	38	1.5	5	Jan
Feb	9	13	55	26	79	31	87	9	48	Moderate	74	40	64	2.5	6	Feb
March	9	14	57	25	77	30	86	9	49	Moderate	81	45	125	4.9	11	March
April	7	14	58	24	75	28	82	11	52	Moderate	88	56	211	8.3	16	April
May	6	13	56	22	72	28	82	9	48	Moderate	88	62	158	6.2	17	May
June	6	12	53	21	70	27	80	7	45		89	60	46	1.8	9	June
July	4	11	51	21	69	26	79	6	43		86	58	15	0.6	6	July
Aug	4	11	52	21	70	27	80	7	44		86	56	23	0.9	7	Aug
Sept	6	11	52	24	75	28	82	5	41		82	45	31	1.2	6	Sept
Oct	7	13	55	24	76	30	86	7	45		82	43	53	2.1	8	Oct
Nov	7	13	56	23	74	28	82	6	43		86	53	109	4.3	15	Nov
Dec	8	13	55	23	74	28	82	8	47		81	53	86	3.4	11	Dec

Based on readings for 15 years at 1°16′ S, 36°48′ E, altitude 1820 m/5971 ft

KISUMU														KENYAN HIGHLANDS
Sunshine		Temperatures								Discomfort from heat and humidity	Precipitation and humidity				Wet days
		Average daily				Highest recorded		Lowest recorded			Relative humidity		Average monthly precipitation		
		minimum		maximum							8:00	14:00			
average hours per day		°C	°F	°C	°F	°C	°F	°C	°F		%		mm	in	more than 0.25 mm/0.01 in
Jan	9	18	65	29	85	36	97	14	57	Medium	60	41	48	1.9	6	Jan
Feb	9	19	66	29	84	37	98	14	57	Medium	62	41	81	3.2	8	Feb
March	8	19	66	28	83	37	98	16	60	Medium	68	46	140	5.5	12	March
April	8	18	65	28	82	37	98	16	60	Medium	74	52	191	7.5	14	April
May	8	18	65	27	81	34	93	16	60	Medium	77	57	155	6.1	14	May
June	8	17	63	27	80	32	89	13	55	Medium	76	53	84	3.3	9	June
July	7	17	63	27	80	33	91	13	56	Medium	76	52	58	2.3	8	July
Aug	7	17	63	27	81	36	97	12	54	Medium	73	50	76	3.0	10	Aug
Sept	8	17	63	28	83	34	93	12	54	Medium	66	47	64	2.5	8	Sept
Oct	8	18	64	29	85	34	94	13	55	Medium	61	41	56	2.2	7	Oct
Nov	7	18	65	29	85	35	95	13	56	Medium	62	43	86	3.4	9	Nov
Dec	8	18	64	29	84	37	98	13	56	Medium	61	41	102	4.0	8	Dec

Based on readings for 20 years at 0°06' S, 34°45' E, altitude 1148 m/3769 ft

THE COASTAL REGION

Along the coast of Kenya the average annual rainfall is over 1,000 mm/40 in, except in the north where it is rather less. The wettest season occurs as the intertropical rain-belt moves north in April and May. The second rainy season in October and November, sometimes called the 'little rains' in Kenya, is less conspicuous. Some rain, often in the form of night or early morning showers, occurs in all months.

Temperatures remain quite high around the year as does humidity. However, the weather is less oppressive than might be thought because of the regular and strong onshore winds in the daytime and the greater number of sunshine hours which average seven to eight a day in all months. The weather, however, can feel sultry, particularly at night.

The table for **Mombasa** (opposite and above) is representative of this region.

THE NORTHERN DRYLANDS

Much of this region has a very low annual rainfall for an equatorial region. Rainfall is generally below 500 mm/20 in and in the far north is often below 250 mm/10 in. In the lower districts temperatures are high round the year, there is much sunshine, and the

region is a typical hot desert like the adjoining southern parts of Somalia and Ethiopia. Humidity is low and, apart from occasional excessive heat, it is a healthy climate.

THE KENYAN HIGHLANDS

Most of this region lies between 1,220 m/4,000 ft and 2,150 m/7,000 ft and occupies the centre and west of the country on either side of the eastern Rift valley, extending to the Ugandan border. It is the most densely populated part of the country and contains the most productive agricultural land.

There is a double rainy season but rainfall is moderate and only exceeds 1,250 mm/50 in a year on the higher parts. Over most of the region the sunniest time of the year is from December to March. The cloudiest period is from June to September when there is much drizzle but little heavy rain. This period is often called 'winter' in the Kenyan Highlands and the evenings may feel chilly compared with the sunnier months.

The table for **Nairobi** (opposite) is representative of much of the region. The table for **Kisumu** (above) on the shores of Lake Victoria, which is virtually an inland sea, shows that there is rather more rainfall in each month here. This is a consequence of the greater humidity picked up by winds crossing the lake and of thunderstorms which are liable to break out during the night. In the Kenyan Highlands there are small regions above 2,500 m/8,000 ft and isolated higher mountains such as Mount Elgon and Mount Kenya. Here temperatures fall low enough for frost to occur and at higher levels some precipitation may be snow. Mount Kenya has permanent snowfields.

Kiribati

See map page 17

This scattered equatorial republic reaches across three island groups in the Western and Central Pacific – the Gilbert, Phoenix, and Line Islands. Almost all of the islands are low-lying coral atolls.

They all experience very similar conditions of temperature and humidity throughout the year. They have a typical tropical oceanic climate with moderately high temperatures and humidity which vary little from month to month. The daily range of temperature is quite small – about 4°–5° C/10° F. All have abundant or moderately heavy rainfall.

Islands north of the equator have a wetter season from June to November. Those near the equator have rainfall more evenly spread throughout the year. South of the equator there is more rainfall from November to April. Average rainfall in the country as a whole ranges from an annual fall of 3,000 mm/120 in in the north to only 500 mm/20 in in the south.

All the islands have moderately large amounts of sunshine, averaging between six and eight hours a day in spite of a large number of days on which some rain falls. Much of the rainfall is in the form of short, heavy showers but days with continuous rain are more frequent in the wetter months.

Although the combination of temperature and humidity is often rather muggy and oppressive, particularly at night, the daytime temperatures are usually moderate and feel more comfortable because of the brisk winds, both the daytime sea breezes and the predominant and regular trade winds.

The table for **Yaren** (p. 255) on Nauru is typical of the Gilbert Islands on or near the equator.

KUWAIT																**KUWAIT**

Sunshine	Temperatures								Discomfort from heat and humidity	Precipitation and humidity					Wet days	
	Average daily				Highest recorded		Lowest recorded			Relative humidity 5:30 14:30		Average monthly precipitation				
	minimum		maximum													
average hours per day	°C	°F	°C	°F	°C	°F	°C	°F		%		mm	in		more than 2.5 mm/0.1 in	
Jan	8	9	49	16	61	28	82	1	33		77	61	23	0.9	2.0	Jan
Feb	9	11	51	18	65	26	78	2	36		68	61	23	0.9	2.0	Feb
March	9	15	59	22	72	32	90	4	40		72	61	28	1.1	2.0	March
April	8	20	68	28	83	39	103	12	54	Medium	67	55	5	0.2	0.9	April
May	10	25	77	34	94	43	109	16	60	High	67	55	0	0.0	0.3	May
June	10	28	82	37	98	48	119	22	72	Extreme	62	49	0	0.0	0.0	June
July	10	30	86	39	103	48	118	26	78	Extreme	45	41	0	0.0	0.0	July
Aug	11	30	86	40	104	46	115	20	68	Extreme	50	46	0	0.0	0.0	Aug
Sept	10	27	81	38	100	47	117	19	67	Extreme	52	51	0	0.0	0.0	Sept
Oct	10	23	73	33	91	41	105	14	57	High	64	60	3	0.1	0.0	Oct
Nov	8	17	62	25	77	38	100	6	43	Moderate	66	59	15	0.6	1.0	Nov
Dec	7	12	53	18	65	26	79	2	36		76	65	28	1.1	3.0	Dec

Based on readings for 14 years at 29°21′ N, 48°00′ E, altitude 5 m/16 ft

Kuwait

See map page 22

Kuwait is one of the largest of the smaller states of the Arabian peninsula. It has land borders with Iraq and Saudi Arabia and a coastline on the Persian Gulf. It is a low-lying desert country where the average annual rainfall is about 125 mm/5 in. Most rain falls between November and March and there are very few rainy days.

Winter temperatures are mild and only occasionally does it feel cold when northerly or northwesterly winds bring cold air from Iran or Iraq. Summers are uniformly hot and temperatures can rise very high when hot winds blow from the heart of Arabia.

On the coast temperatures are a little lower than inland but the heat is rendered even more uncomfortable by the high humidity.

Another unpleasant feature of the weather is the occasional sandstorm when strong winds blow from the interior. As in other parts of Arabia there is some danger of heat exhaustion or even heatstroke during the hottest weather, and visitors should take sensible precautions until they have become acclimatized.

The table for **Kuwait** (above) shows weather that is typical of this country. For more detail see the description for Saudi Arabia on p. 312.

Kyrgyzstan

See map page 22

Kyrgyzstan is part of a mountainous region on the borders of Afghanistan and China. It includes peaks rising to over 6,000 m/20,000 ft. These mountains carry snow the year round. However, because of the distance from the sea and the shelter of the Pamir and Himalayan ranges to the south and southeast, it is a rather dry region considering its height. Winters are cold but spring comes earlier than farther north.

The tables for **Almaty** (p. 216) in Kazakhstan and **Tashkent** (p. 415) in Uzbekistan illustrate conditions in the valleys of this region.

Laos

See map page 23

Laos is a completely landlocked country of Indo-China, bordered by Myanmar and China on the north, Vietnam on the east, Cambodia on the south, and Thailand on the west. It is about as large as the United Kingdom and much of the country is rather hilly and mountainous.

The general features of the weather and climate of Laos are similar to those described for Vietnam on p. 419. It has a single rainy season with a maximum rainfall between May and September or October. The rest of the year is dry and sunny. Temperatures remain high the year round but in the northern mountains occasional cooler days may come during the winter season of the north monsoon. As in northern Vietnam, cooler, cloudier weather at this time is associated with outbreaks of colder continental air from China.

The humidity is significantly lower during the dry season and, in spite of the warmth, the weather is more comfortable and pleasant than during the rather muggy and sultry days of the main monsoon rains. See the tables for **Louangphrabang** (opposite) and **Vientiane** (opposite and below) which are representative of the lower parts of Laos.

LOUANGPHRABANG
LOWLAND LAOS

	Sunshine average hours per day	Average daily min °C	Average daily min °F	Average daily max °C	Average daily max °F	Highest recorded °C	Highest recorded °F	Lowest recorded °C	Lowest recorded °F	Discomfort from heat and humidity	Relative humidity 10:00 %	Relative humidity 16:00 %	Average monthly precipitation mm	Average monthly precipitation in	Wet days more than 1 mm/0.04 in	
Jan	5	13	56	28	82	39	103	1	33	Medium	80	59	15	0.6	2	Jan
Feb	6	14	58	32	89	39	102	8	46	High	75	49	18	0.7	2	Feb
March	6	17	63	34	93	41	106	10	50	High	68	48	31	1.2	4	March
April	5	21	69	36	96	45	113	14	57	High	67	49	109	4.3	8	April
May	5	23	73	35	95	44	111	17	63	Extreme	67	57	163	6.4	13	May
June	5	23	74	34	93	40	104	14	57	Extreme	71	71	155	6.1	12	June
July	4	23	74	32	90	39	102	19	67	High	71	71	231	9.1	17	July
Aug	4	23	74	32	90	40	104	14	57	Extreme	80	76	300	11.8	19	Aug
Sept	6	23	73	33	91	38	100	11	51	Extreme	73	70	165	6.5	12	Sept
Oct	7	21	69	32	89	38	101	13	55	High	72	69	79	3.1	7	Oct
Nov	5	18	64	29	85	36	97	6	43	Medium	73	67	31	1.2	3	Nov
Dec	4	15	59	27	81	33	91	4	40	Medium	79	62	13	0.5	1	Dec

Based on readings for 28 years at 19°53′ N, 102°08′ E, altitude 287 m/942 ft

VIENTIANE
LOWLAND LAOS

	Sunshine average hours per day	Average daily min °C	Average daily min °F	Average daily max °C	Average daily max °F	Highest recorded °C	Highest recorded °F	Lowest recorded °C	Lowest recorded °F	Discomfort from heat and humidity	Relative humidity all hours %	Average monthly precipitation mm	Average monthly precipitation in	Wet days more than 1 mm/0.04 in	
Jan	8	14	57	28	83	35	95	4	39	Medium	77	5	0.2	1	Jan
Feb	8	17	63	30	86	37	98	8	46	High	75	15	0.6	2	Feb
March	7	19	67	33	91	40	104	12	54	Extreme	71	38	1.5	4	March
April	8	23	73	34	93	39	103	17	63	Extreme	74	99	3.9	7	April
May	7	23	73	32	90	39	102	21	69	Extreme	82	267	10.5	15	May
June	5	24	75	32	89	36	96	21	70	Extreme	85	302	11.9	17	June
July	5	24	75	31	87	34	94	21	70	Extreme	87	267	10.5	18	July
Aug	5	24	75	31	88	37	98	21	70	Extreme	86	292	11.5	18	Aug
Sept	8	24	75	31	87	35	95	21	70	Extreme	86	302	11.9	16	Sept
Oct	8	21	70	31	87	34	94	13	55	Extreme	82	109	4.3	7	Oct
Nov	8	18	65	29	85	34	94	11	51	High	79	15	0.6	1	Nov
Dec	8	16	60	28	83	33	92	5	41	Medium	78	3	0.1	1	Dec

Based on readings for 9 years at 17°58′ N, 102°36′ E, altitude 162 m/531 ft

RIGA												LATVIA
Sunshine	Temperatures						Discomfort from heat and humidity	Precipitation and humidity				Wet days
	Average daily		Highest recorded		Lowest recorded			Relative humidity		Average monthly precipitation		
average hours per day	minimum	maximum						7:30 13:30				more than 0.1 mm/0.004 in
	°C °F	°C °F	°C °F		°C °F			%		mm in		
Jan	1	−10 14	−4 25	4 39	−28 −19			83	79	31	1.2	19	Jan
Feb	2	−10 15	−3 27	5 40	−28 −19			83	74	29	1.1	18	Feb
March	4	−7 20	2 35	21 69	−23 −9			85	69	27	1.1	16	March
April	6	1 34	10 50	24 75	−11 12			81	61	33	1.3	13	April
May	7	6 42	16 61	29 83	−5 23			77	59	44	1.7	13	May
June	11	9 49	21 69	32 90	−1 30			69	53	45	1.8	11	June
July	10	11 52	22 71	33 91	4 39			76	55	53	2.1	12	July
Aug	9	11 52	21 70	32 89	0 32			81	59	70	2.8	16	Aug
Sept	6	8 47	17 63	29 85	−1 30			84	64	64	2.5	17	Sept
Oct	3	4 40	11 52	23 74	−7 19			88	75	62	2.4	19	Oct
Nov	1	−1 30	4 39	17 63	−16 3			87	78	62	2.4	19	Nov
Dec	1	−7 20	−2 29	7 45	−27 −17			88	84	47	1.9	21	Dec

Based on readings for 8 years at 56°58′ N, 24°04′ E, altitude 3 m/10 ft

Latvia

See map page 19

This small country on the northwestern boundary of Russia has a very similar climate to the adjacent parts of Russia (see p. 299), but is a little milder in winter thanks to the moderating influence of the Baltic Sea, which does not freeze for prolonged periods. It is more open than Russia to the weather influences coming from the Atlantic and northwestern Europe. However, during severe spells of winter weather Latvia is dominated by cold winds from the interior of Russia. The table for **Riga** (above) shows that conditions in Latvia do not differ much from those at **St Petersburg** (see p. 302) in Russia.

Lebanon

See map page 22

This small, mountainous country lies at the eastern end of the Mediterranean. It is bordered by Syria on the north and east and by Israel on the south. With an area of some 8,000 sq km/3,400 sq mi, it is about the size of Yorkshire or a little smaller than the state of Connecticut.

The general weather and climatic conditions of Lebanon are similar to those described for Syria on p. 348. Temperature and precipitation, however, vary greatly from place to place because of the large differences of altitude. Snow lies on the higher mountains until mid-June and some small patches survive throughout the dry, sunny summer.

The country consists of two parallel mountain ranges running from north to south: the Lebanon Mountains on the west and the Anti-Lebanon range with Mount Hermon on the east. These mountains rise to an average height of over 1,800 m/6,000 ft but with summits exceeding 3,000 m/10,000 ft.

These ranges are separated by a narrow north to south valley, the Bekaa, which is everywhere above

BEIRUT

COASTAL LEBANON

Sunshine	Temperatures									Discomfort from heat and humidity	Precipitation and humidity				Wet days	
	Average daily				Highest recorded		Lowest recorded				Relative humidity 9:00 15:00		Average monthly precipitation				
	minimum		maximum														
average hours per day	°C	°F	°C	°F	°C	°F	°C	°F			%		mm	in		more than 1 mm/0.04 in	
Jan	5	11	51	17	62	25	77	−1	31		72	70	191	7.5	15.0	Jan
Feb	5	11	51	17	63	31	87	−1	30		72	70	158	6.2	12.0	Feb
March	6	12	54	19	66	36	97	2	36		72	69	94	3.7	9.0	March
April	8	14	58	22	72	37	99	6	43		72	67	56	2.2	5.0	April
May	10	18	64	26	78	42	107	10	50	Medium	69	64	18	0.7	2.0	May
June	12	21	69	28	83	40	104	13	56	Medium	67	61	3	0.1	0.4	June
July	12	23	73	31	87	37	98	18	64	High	66	58	0	0.0	0.0	July
Aug	11	23	74	32	89	37	99	17	62	High	65	57	0	0.0	0.0	Aug
Sept	9	23	73	30	86	37	99	16	60	Medium	64	57	5	0.2	1.0	Sept
Oct	8	21	69	27	81	38	101	11	52	Medium	65	62	51	2.0	4.0	Oct
Nov	7	16	61	23	73	33	91	5	41	Moderate	67	61	132	5.2	8.0	Nov
Dec	5	13	55	18	65	29	84	−1	30		70	69	185	7.3	12.0	Dec

Based on readings for 62 years at 33°54′ N, 35°28′ E, altitude 34 m/111 ft

KSARA

INLAND LEBANON

Sunshine	Temperatures									Discomfort from heat and humidity	Precipitation and humidity				Wet days	
	Average daily				Highest recorded		Lowest recorded				Relative humidity all hours	Average monthly precipitation				
	minimum		maximum													
average hours per day	°C	°F	°C	°F	°C	°F	°C	°F			%	mm	in		more than 1 mm/0.04 in	
Jan	4	1	34	11	51	20	68	−8	17		78	122	4.8	15.0	Jan
Feb	5	3	37	12	53	22	71	−7	19		75	165	6.5	12.0	Feb
March	6	4	40	16	61	28	82	−3	26		62	48	1.9	10.0	March
April	8	8	46	21	69	33	91	−1	31		55	43	1.7	5.0	April
May	10	11	52	26	78	36	97	3	38	Moderate	50	13	0.5	2.0	May
June	12	14	57	29	84	36	97	7	45	Medium	45	0	0.0	0.3	June
July	13	16	61	31	87	38	101	10	50	Medium	44	0	0.0	0.0	July
Aug	12	16	61	32	90	40	104	10	50	Medium	45	0	0.0	0.1	Aug
Sept	11	14	57	30	86	39	103	7	44	Medium	49	0	0.0	0.5	Sept
Oct	8	11	52	26	79	34	93	4	39	Moderate	52	18	0.7	4.0	Oct
Nov	6	7	45	19	66	30	86	−1	30		65	69	2.7	7.0	Nov
Dec	4	3	38	13	55	21	70	−7	20		76	107	4.2	12.0	Dec

Based on readings for 9 years at 33°49′ N, 35°35′ E, altitude 920 m/3018 ft

1,000 m/3,300 ft. There is a very narrow plain along the Mediterranean coast.

Summers are warm to hot with a high humidity on the coast so that the nights may be muggy and a little unpleasant. The daytime heat is usually tempered by an afternoon sea breeze. Winters are very mild along the coast (see the table for **Beirut** on p. 215). Winter rainfall can be heavy on the coast and snow falls on the Lebanon Mountains.

Inland the Bekaa valley and the eastern mountains are much drier; but no part of Lebanon is a desert such as is found extensively in Syria and Jordan. Summers are delightfully sunny, fresh, and cool in the mountains, where there are numerous summer resorts.

From the higher mountain resorts skiing is possible from late December until April or May. It is often said that, in winter and spring, one can ski in the morning and swim in the Mediterranean in the afternoon. Visitors may find the Mediterranean a little cool for swimming before May, however, and to do both in one day requires fairly rapid transit by car on mountain roads!

Conditions inland and in the Bekaa valley are shown by the table for **Ksara** on p. 215. Winters are drier but cooler than on the coast with frequent snow and frost.

On the coast and in the Lebanon Mountains the winter rain and snow may be very heavy and disturbed weather brought by Mediterranean depressions may last for several days at a time. In between these unsettled spells of weather there are long periods when it is fine, mild, and sunny.

In early and late summer Lebanon is often affected, for a few days at a time, by the hot, dry khamsin which blows out of Arabia. These winds bring the hottest days and conditions may then be distinctly unpleasant with danger of heat stress.

Lesotho

See map page 21

This small country lies entirely surrounded by South Africa. It is about as large as Wales or Israel and lies in the eastern part of the high veld. Most of the country is above 1,800 m/6,000 ft and includes the highest land in southern Africa, which rises to 3,300 m/11,000 ft.

Lesotho's weather and climate are similar to the high veld of South Africa but temperatures are significantly lower at higher levels and snow is quite frequent in winter. At lower elevations the winters are dry and mild but with frequent cold nights. Summers are warm with more frequent rain but temperatures are rarely excessively high. The low humidity and large number of sunshine hours make for a pleasant and healthy climate for most of the year.

The table for **Bloemfontein** (p. 325) in South Africa is representative of the warmer temperatures at lower levels.

MONROVIA												LIBERIA	
Sunshine	Temperatures							Discomfort from heat and humidity	Precipitation and humidity				Wet days
	Average daily				Highest recorded		Lowest recorded		Relative humidity 7:30 11:30		Average monthly precipitation		
average hours per day	minimum		maximum										more than 0.25mm/0.01in
	°C	°F	°C	°F	°C	°F	°C	°F		%		mm	in
Jan	6	23 73	30	86	32	90	13	55	High	95	78	31	1.2	5	Jan
Feb	6	23 73	29	85	33	91	20	68	High	94	76	56	2.2	5	Feb
March	7	23 74	31	87	32	90	19	67	High	92	77	97	3.8	10	March
April	6	23 73	31	87	33	91	16	60	Extreme	91	80	216	8.5	17	April
May	5	22 72	30	86	34	93	16	60	High	89	79	516	20.3	21	May
June	4	23 73	27	81	31	87	18	65	Medium	89	82	973	38.3	26	June
July	3	22 72	27	80	29	85	16	61	Medium	88	83	996	39.2	24	July
Aug	3	23 73	27	80	30	86	18	65	Medium	87	84	373	14.7	20	Aug
Sept	4	22 72	27	81	29	85	18	65	Medium	92	86	744	29.3	26	Sept
Oct	4	22 72	28	83	30	86	19	66	High	92	84	772	30.4	22	Oct
Nov	6	23 73	29	85	32	89	16	61	High	91	80	236	9.3	19	Nov
Dec	5	23 73	30	86	32	89	14	57	High	93	79	130	5.1	12	Dec

Based on readings for 3 years at 6°18' N, 10°48' W, altitude 23 m/75 ft

Liberia

See map page 20

Liberia is about as large as England and is situated on the west coast of Africa between 4° and 10° N. It has an extensive coastal plain and inland rises to a plateau with a maximum altitude of about 1,000 m/3,300 ft. The climate of the country is similar to that of Sierra Leone (p. 316).

The climatic table for **Monrovia** (above), on the coast of Liberia, illustrates conditions in most of the country.

In parts of Liberia the rainy season lasts a little longer than in Sierra Leone, with a brief drier season in August so that the summer rains may have a double maximum.

TRIPOLI

WESTERN COASTAL LIBYA

Sunshine	Temperatures								Discomfort from heat and humidity	Precipitation and humidity				Wet days
	Average daily				Highest recorded		Lowest recorded			Relative humidity 7:00 12:00		Average monthly precipitation		
	minimum		maximum											
average hours per day	°C	°F	°C	°F	°C	°F	°C	°F		%		mm	in	more than 0.1 mm/.004 in
Jan 5	8	47	16	61	28	83	1	34		68	59	81	3.2	11.0 Jan
Feb 6	9	49	17	63	33	91	3	37		71	60	46	1.8	7.0 Feb
March 6	11	52	19	67	38	101	4	39		65	57	28	1.1	5.0 March
April 7	14	57	22	72	41	105	6	43		62	57	10	0.4	2.0 April
May 8	16	61	24	76	43	109	6	43	Moderate	58	62	5	0.2	3.0 May
June 10	19	67	27	81	44	112	10	50	Medium	57	70	3	0.1	1.0 June
July 11	22	71	29	85	46	114	16	60	High	54	72	0	0.0	0.2 July
Aug 11	22	72	30	86	44	112	17	62	High	72	69	0	0.0	0.3 Aug
Sept 8	22	71	29	85	45	113	15	59	Medium	67	67	10	0.4	2.0 Sept
Oct 7	18	65	27	80	41	106	10	50	Medium	65	59	41	1.6	5.0 Oct
Nov 5	14	57	23	73	36	96	6	42		66	53	66	2.6	7.0 Nov
Dec 5	9	49	18	64	30	86	1	33		65	55	94	3.7	11.0 Dec

Based on readings for 47 years at 32°54' N, 13°11' E, altitude 22 m/72 ft

BENGHAZI

EASTERN COASTAL LIBYA

Sunshine	Temperatures								Discomfort from heat and humidity	Precipitation and humidity				Wet days
	Average daily				Highest recorded		Lowest recorded			Relative humidity 9:30 15:30		Average monthly precipitation		
	minimum		maximum											
average hours per day	°C	°F	°C	°F	°C	°F	°C	°F		%		mm	in	more than 0.1 mm/.004 in
Jan 5	10	50	17	63	24	76	3	38		69	60	66	2.6	13.0 Jan
Feb 6	11	51	18	64	28	82	3	38		63	58	41	1.6	9.0 Feb
March 7	12	54	21	69	38	101	3	37		51	49	20	0.8	6.0 March
April 9	14	58	23	74	41	105	5	41		49	50	5	0.2	2.0 April
May 9	17	63	26	79	42	108	9	48	Moderate	49	51	3	0.1	1.0 May
June 11	20	68	28	83	43	109	13	55	Medium	53	56	0	0.0	0.2 June
July 11	22	71	29	84	41	105	14	57	Medium	59	61	0	0.0	0.1 July
Aug 11	22	72	29	85	41	105	16	60	Medium	61	61	0	0.0	0.1 Aug
Sept 10	21	69	28	83	41	106	11	52	Medium	55	56	3	0.1	1.0 Sept
Oct 8	19	66	27	80	38	100	11	51	Medium	49	51	18	0.7	4.0 Oct
Nov 7	16	60	23	74	35	95	7	45		57	54	46	1.8	8.0 Nov
Dec 5	12	53	19	66	26	78	4	40		65	59	66	2.6	12.0 Dec

Based on readings for 40 years at 32°06' N, 20°04' E, altitude 25 m/82 ft

Libya

See map page 20

Libya is a large country in North Africa. It has a long coastline on the Mediterranean but the greater part consists of the central Sahara desert. The Mediterranean coastal fringes have a Mediterranean climate with some rain between October and March, but the vast area of desert inland has very little rain at all and here some of the highest temperatures in the world have been recorded.

The general climatic and weather conditions over Libya are similar to those described for coastal and interior Egypt (p. 131) and Algeria (p. 30). The climatic tables for **Tripoli** (opposite) in western Libya (Tripolitania) and **Benghazi** (opposite and below) in eastern Libya (Cyrenaica) show conditions around the year in the coastal regions.

Mediterranean depressions bring the scanty winter rain. The amounts are variable from year to year. Along the coast of the Gulf of Sidra, between Misurata and Benghazi, rainfall is rather less, so that the desert reaches the coast. The wettest area of the country is in the hill and plateau region of the Jebel Akhdar (the Green Mountains) between Benghazi and Derna, where the land rises to over 500 m/1,600 ft and rainfall is as much as 600 mm/24 in per year.

Beyond a distance of 160 km/100 mi or less from the coast, annual rainfall drops below 100 mm/4 in and is often very much less. Indeed, over much of the Sahara rainfall is so slight and irregular as to make any average figure almost meaningless.

As elsewhere on the coasts of the southern Mediterranean, winter weather can be changeable from day to day with cool, cloudy, rainy spells interrupting the generally warm, sunny, and settled weather. Inland, in the desert, conditions are almost uniformly settled and sunny with very high temperatures in summer and warm days in winter. The climate here is similar to that shown by the tables for **Aswan** in Egypt on p. 132 or **Biskra** and **In Salah** in Algeria on pp. 31–2.

The coastal districts of Libya are affected from March to June by very hot, dusty winds from the desert which bring very high temperatures, often exceeding 50° C/122° F for a day or two. They are similar in origin to the khamsin winds of Egypt. They go under the local name of *ghibli*.

Liechtenstein

See map page 18

Situated in the central Alps between Switzerland and Austria, this small independent principality has an area of about 158 sq km/62 sq mi. It contains part of the upper Rhine valley and mountains rising to 2,600 m/8,500 ft. It has a similar climate to that described on pp. 345 and 53 for the Swiss and Austrian Alps. See the tables for **Innsbruck** (p. 53) in Austria and **Zürich** (p. 346) in Switzerland.

VILNIUS															LITHUANIA
Sunshine		Temperatures							Discomfort from heat and humidity	Precipitation and humidity					Wet days
		Average daily				Highest recorded		Lowest recorded		Relative humidity 7:30 13:30			Average monthly precipitation		
		minimum		maximum											
average hours per day		°C	°F	°C	°F	°C	°F	°C	°F		%		mm	in	more than 0.1 mm/0.004 in
Jan	1	-11	12	-5	23	4	39	-28	-18		87	84	30	1.2	20	Jan
Feb	2	-10	14	-3	27	6	43	-29	-20		87	79	39	1.5	17	Feb
March	4	-7	19	1	34	19	66	-30	-22		89	73	38	1.5	15	March
April	6	2	36	12	54	25	77	-12	10		85	63	41	1.6	13	April
May	7	7	45	18	64	28	82	-3	27		80	59	85	3.3	17	May
June	10	11	52	21	70	30	86	3	37		75	56	67	2.6	12	June
July	10	12	54	23	73	35	95	5	41		80	56	51	2.0	11	July
Aug	9	11	52	22	72	34	93	1	34		83	57	97	3.8	13	Aug
Sept	6	8	46	17	63	29	84	-1	30		89	62	61	2.4	13	Sept
Oct	3	4	39	11	52	24	75	-8	18		93	78	49	1.9	15	Oct
Nov	1	-1	30	4	39	15	59	-15	5		91	85	65	2.6	17	Nov
Dec	1	-7	19	-3	27	5	41	-26	-15		91	88	39	1.5	21	Dec

Based on readings for 8 years at 54°38′ N, 25°17′ E, altitude 189 m/620 ft

Lithuania

See map page 19

This small country on the northwestern boundary of Russia has a very similar climate to the adjacent parts of Russia (see p. 299), but is a little milder in winter thanks to the moderating influence of the Baltic Sea, which does not freeze for prolonged periods. It is more open than Russia to the weather influences coming from the Atlantic and from northwestern Europe. However, during severe spells of winter weather it is dominated by cold winds from the interior of Russia.

The table for **Vilnius** (above) shows that conditions in Estonia do not differ much from the weather at **St Petersburg** (p. 302) in Russia.

LUXEMBOURG										SOUTHERN LUXEMBOURG			
Sunshine		Temperatures						Discomfort from heat and humidity	Precipitation and humidity				Wet days
		Average daily				Highest recorded		Lowest recorded		Relative humidity	Average monthly precipitation		
average hours per day		minimum		maximum						6:30 12:30			more than 0.1 mm/0.004 in
		°C	°F	°C	°F	°C	°F	°C	°F		%	mm	in	
Jan	1	-1	29	3	37	11	52	-15	5		92 86	61	2.4	20	Jan
Feb	2	-1	31	4	40	17	63	-20	-3		91 78	65	2.6	16	Feb
March	5	1	35	10	49	23	73	-11	13		88 64	42	1.7	14	March
April	6	4	40	14	57	29	85	-4	25		85 58	47	1.9	13	April
May	6	8	46	18	65	30	86	-2	29		87 59	64	2.5	15	May
June	6	11	52	21	70	34	92	4	39		88 61	64	2.5	14	June
July	6	13	55	23	73	37	98	5	42	Moderate	89 61	60	2.4	14	July
Aug	6	12	54	22	71	33	92	4	40		91 63	84	3.3	15	Aug
Sept	5	10	50	19	66	33	91	1	34		93 67	72	2.8	16	Sept
Oct	3	6	43	13	56	22	72	-5	24		95 76	53	2.1	15	Oct
Nov	1	3	37	7	44	17	63	-7	19		93 86	67	2.6	19	Nov
Dec	1	0	33	4	39	14	57	-14	8		95 91	81	3.2	20	Dec

Based on readings for 12 years at 49°37′ N, 6°03′ E, altitude 330 m/1083 ft

Luxembourg

See map page 18

Luxembourg is only about as large as an average British or American county. The north of the country consists of part of the forested Ardennes hills and has a similar climate to the neighbouring area of Belgium (see the description for this area of Belgium and the table for **Virton** on p. 60–1).

Southern Luxembourg borders France on the southwest and Germany on the east. It is the most populous area and contains the capital of the same name. In the extreme southeast is part of the sheltered Moselle valley, where summers and autumns are warm enough for vines to be cultivated for wine-making.

The south of the country is drier and sunnier than the north. On occasions winters can be quite severe with snow cover lasting for some weeks. Its inland position and the shelter of the Ardennes exclude the milder influence of the sea which is more evident in the Netherlands and northern Belgium.

SKOPJE													MACEDONIA
Sunshine	Temperatures							Discomfort from heat and humidity	Precipitation and humidity				Wet days
average hours per day	Average daily				Highest recorded		Lowest recorded		Relative humidity 7:30 14:30		Average monthly precipitation		more than 0.1 mm/0.004 in
	minimum		maximum										
	°C	°F	°C	°F	°C	°F	°C	°F		%	mm	in	
Jan	2	-3	27	5	40	20	67	-21	-6		91	76	39	1.5	11	Jan
Feb	4	-3	28	8	47	24	75	-22	-8		90	65	32	1.3	8	Feb
March	4	1	33	12	53	34	94	-19	-2		88	58	37	1.5	9	March
April	7	5	42	19	67	30	85	-3	26		81	48	38	1.5	8	April
May	7	10	50	23	74	36	96	-2	29		80	52	54	2.1	12	May
June	9	13	56	28	82	39	102	6	42	Medium	75	47	47	1.9	8	June
July	10	15	59	31	87	41	105	7	44	Medium	70	42	29	1.1	7	July
Aug	10	14	58	31	88	41	105	4	40	Medium	72	39	28	1.1	4	Aug
Sept	7	11	52	26	79	37	98	1	33	Moderate	84	46	35	1.4	7	Sept
Oct	5	6	43	19	65	34	92	-4	25		93	59	61	2.4	9	Oct
Nov	2	3	37	12	53	21	70	-11	12		94	72	55	2.2	12	Nov
Dec	2	-1	30	7	45	21	70	-17	1		94	76	53	2.1	9	Dec

Based on readings for 12 years at 41°59′ N, 21°28′ E, altitude 240 m/787 ft

Macedonia

See map page 19

This landlocked Balkan state has cold winters and warm summers. Summer is the wettest season but it is sunnier and drier than the summer in Serbia, Macedonia's northern neighbour.

Much of the country is mountainous or hilly and winter snow lies for long periods in the higher regions.

The table for **Skopje** (above) is representative of weather conditions in Macedonia.

Madagascar

See map page 21

This large island, the size of France, is situated in the Indian Ocean between 12° and 26° S at an average distance of 640 km/400 mi from the coast of Africa.

The eastern side of the island is exposed to the moisture-laden southeast trade winds of the Indian Ocean for much of the year.

Between November and February, at the time of high sun, the whole island is affected by the belt of cloud and rain associated with the intertropical

convergence (the doldrums – the area of light winds between the trade winds and the monsoon blowing from the opposite direction).

Madagascar is a mountainous island with a steep escarpment rising to 1,200–1,800 m/4,000–6,000 ft behind the east coast. Much of the interior is a plateau above which some isolated, extinct volcanoes rise to heights of 2,100–2,900 m/7,000–9,500 ft. The island slopes down more gradually to the south and west, where there are wider coastal plains.

The whole island has a tropical climate, but at elevations above 900 m/3,000 ft temperatures are

TOAMASINA

EAST COAST OF MADAGASCAR

Sunshine	Temperatures								Discomfort from heat and humidity	Precipitation and humidity				Wet days	
	Average daily				Highest recorded		Lowest recorded			Relative humidity 7:30 13:30		Average monthly precipitation			
	minimum		maximum												
average hours per day	°C	°F	°C	°F	°C	°F	°C	°F		%		mm	in	more than 1 mm/0.04 in	
Jan 7	23	74	30	86	37	98	21	69	High	89	75	366	14.4	20	Jan
Feb 7	23	74	30	86	35	95	21	70	High	90	75	376	14.8	19	Feb
March 6	23	73	29	85	36	96	20	68	High	92	77	452	17.8	20	March
April 7	22	72	28	83	33	91	19	67	Medium	93	79	399	15.7	19	April
May 7	21	69	27	80	30	86	17	63	Medium	94	78	264	10.4	18	May
June 6	19	66	25	77	28	83	14	57	Medium	92	79	282	11.1	20	June
July 6	18	65	24	75	28	83	15	59	Medium	92	80	302	11.9	20	July
Aug 6	18	64	24	76	27	81	13	56	Moderate	92	78	203	8.0	19	Aug
Sept 7	18	65	26	78	29	84	15	59	Medium	89	73	132	5.2	15	Sept
Oct 8	19	67	27	81	30	86	16	60	Medium	85	68	99	3.9	12	Oct
Nov 8	21	70	29	84	32	89	17	62	High	87	70	117	4.6	12	Nov
Dec 7	23	73	29	85	35	92	19	66	High	87	72	262	10.3	18	Dec

Based on readings for 20 years at 18°07' S, 49°24' E, altitude 6 m/20 ft

sufficiently reduced by altitude as to be very rarely oppressive or uncomfortable.

The lowlands are hot and rather humid, particularly during the rainy season. The east coast is wet for much of the year as it is exposed to trade winds off the Indian Ocean which are forced to rise and shed their moisture as they meet the steep eastward-facing escarpment

The table for **Toamasina** (above) is representative of the east coast of Madagascar. It has an annual rainfall of 3,500 mm/140 in falling on 240 days of the year.

Most of the east coast receives over 2,000 mm/80 in annual rainfall as does another small area in the northwest around Diego Suarez. Rainfall is lower on the plateau in the interior of the country and decreases to the west and south.

The lowlands in the southwest of the island only receive between 400–800 mm/16 –32 in of rain in the course of the year, mostly falling between December and March.

The central plateau areas receive an annual rainfall intermediate between these extremes, varying between 1,000 mm/40 in and 1,500 mm/60 in.

Most rain here falls between November and March, much of it in heavy downpours associated with hail and thunder.

The rainfall during the rest of the year is mostly very light and sporadic (see the table for **Antananarivo** overleaf).

On the plateau temperatures fall to moderate levels during the dry season and the nights may be chilly but frost only occurs on the highest mountains.

Hours of sunshine are quite high around the year even on the wetter east coast. At Toamasina sunshine ranges from an average of six hours a day during the cloudier wet months to an average of eight hours a day during the drier months. In the drier parts of the island sunshine hours range from eight to ten hours a day.

Apart from the combination of heat and humidity which affects the lower districts of the island during the wet season, the weather and climate of much of the island is sunny, warm, and pleasant for much of the year and this is particularly the case on the inland plateau.

Two or three times a year some part of Madagascar is affected by torrential rain and high winds

ANTANANARIVO													CENTRAL MADAGASCAR

Sunshine		Temperatures								Discomfort from heat and humidity	Precipitation and humidity				Wet days

		Average daily				Highest recorded		Lowest recorded			Relative humidity 7:00 13:00		Average monthly precipitation		
		minimum		maximum											
average hours per day		°C	°F	°C	°F	°C	°F	°C	°F		%		mm	in	more than 1 mm/0.04 in
Jan	7	16	61	26	79	33	91	12	53	Medium	91	70	300	11.8	21	Jan
Feb	8	16	61	26	78	32	90	11	52	Medium	92	71	279	11.0	20	Feb
March	7	16	60	26	79	31	87	11	51	Medium	93	68	178	7.0	17	March
April	8	14	58	24	76	31	87	7	45	Moderate	93	66	53	2.1	11	April
May	7	12	54	23	73	29	85	4	40	Moderate	94	63	18	0.7	9	May
June	7	10	50	21	69	27	80	1	34		93	62	8	0.3	9	June
July	7	9	48	20	68	27	80	3	37		93	61	8	0.3	10	July
Aug	7	9	48	21	70	29	85	2	35		92	57	10	0.4	9	Aug
Sept	9	11	51	23	74	33	92	3	38		88	53	18	0.7	7	Sept
Oct	9	12	54	27	80	35	95	6	42	Moderate	85	49	61	2.4	9	Oct
Nov	8	14	58	27	81	34	94	6	42	Medium	86	54	135	5.3	13	Nov
Dec	6	16	60	27	80	33	91	11	52	Medium	89	64	287	11.3	20	Dec

Based on readings for 44 years at 18°55′ S, 47°33′ E, altitude 1372 m/4500 ft

associated with tropical cyclones which develop in the Indian Ocean north of the island. These weather disturbances may move southwards either on the western or eastern side of the island and the most damaging effects of their strong winds are felt in the coastal districts.

Malawi

See map page 21

Malawi is about as large as England and is situated in south-central Africa. It is bordered on the north by Tanzania, on the east and south by Mozambique, and on the west by Zambia. The general features of the weather and climate of Malawi are similar to those of Zambia and Zimbabwe and are described on p. 425 for Zambia.

Malawi is a long, narrow country extending from north to south and containing within its borders the large Lake Malawi (formerly Lake Nyasa). It also has a rather diverse relief with mountains rising above 3,000 m/10,000 ft and land in the lower Shire valley lying below 180 m/600 ft. It thus has a greater range of weather and climate than either Zambia or Zimbabwe.

Conditions in the Shire valley are typically tropical with high temperatures around the year and a most unpleasant combination of high temperature and high humidity during the rainy season. Frost is unknown here.

The table for **Zumbo** (p. 249) in Mozambique is representative of conditions in these tropical lowlands.

Lilongwe (see table opposite and above) has a range of weather and climate throughout the year similar to that of the uplands of much of Zambia and Zimbabwe. Daytime temperatures here rarely rise to very high or uncomfortable levels and there is abundant sunshine during the dry season when occasional frosts occur.

The mountainous regions of southern Malawi, and in the north overlooking Lake Malawi, are amongst the wettest districts in this part of Africa with an annual rainfall of between 1,500 mm/60 in and 2,000 mm/80 in.

LILONGWE															MALAWI
Sunshine	Temperatures								Discomfort from heat and humidity	Precipitation and humidity					Wet days
	Average daily				Highest recorded		Lowest recorded			Relative humidity 8:00 14:00		Average monthly precipitation			
	minimum		maximum												
average hours per day	°C	°F	°C	°F	°C	°F	°C	°F		%		mm	in		more than 0.25 mm/0.01 in
Jan	5	17	63	27	80	32	90	13	55	Medium	85	64	208	8.2	19.0	Jan
Feb	5	17	63	27	80	31	88	12	54	Medium	89	66	218	8.6	18.0	Feb
March	6	16	61	27	80	32	89	11	52	Medium	86	60	125	4.9	13.0	March
April	8	14	57	27	80	30	86	10	50	Medium	84	50	43	1.7	5.0	April
May	8	11	51	25	77	30	86	4	39	Moderate	82	41	3	0.1	1.0	May
June	8	8	47	23	74	28	82	2	36		79	38	0	0.0	0.1	June
July	8	7	45	23	74	28	82	-1	31		77	33	0	0.0	0.1	July
Aug	8	8	47	25	77	31	88	-1	31		68	31	0	0.0	1.0	Aug
Sept	9	12	53	27	81	32	89	4	39	Moderate	55	30	0	0.0	0.6	Sept
Oct	10	15	59	30	86	34	93	9	48	Medium	50	28	0	0.0	1.0	Oct
Nov	7	17	63	29	85	34	94	12	54	Medium	60	42	53	2.1	7.0	Nov
Dec	5	18	64	28	82	33	92	13	56	Medium	76	58	125	4.9	15.0	Dec

Based on readings for 8 years at 13°59' S, 33°45' E, altitude 1100 m/3610 ft

Unusually for this area the heaviest rains are delayed until March of April and some rain may fall in all months. Over most of the country an annual rainfall of between 875–1,250 mm/35–50 in is more usual. Apart from the lowlands in the south, which are unhealthy, sultry, and oppressive, the weather and climate over the rest of the country are generally healthy and pleasant. At times the weather can be surprisingly cold during the dry season, particularly above 1,500 m/5,000 ft.

Malaysia

See map page 23

The Federation of Malaysia consists of three separate territories: Malaya, Sarawak, and Sabah. Malaya is a narrow mountainous peninsula south of Thailand; Sarawak and Sabah, which occupy the northern portion of the large island of Borneo, have a land border with Indonesia. In all three territories the highest mountains rise to over 2,000 m/6,500 ft.

Situated between 1° and 6° N, the whole of Malaysia has an equatorial climate with high temperatures and wet months round the year. The principal differences of climate within the country are those arising from difference of altitude and the exposure of the coastal lowlands to the alternating southwest and northeast monsoon winds. The former blow from April to September and the latter from November to February. There is a brief period of light variable winds during the changeover in March and October. Coasts exposed to the northeast monsoon in Malaysia tend to be wetter than those exposed to the southwest monsoon. Rainfall is well distributed throughout the year and falls on as many as 150 to 200 days almost everywhere.

In most places there is a definite double rainy season with the heaviest rains falling in two periods: March to May and September to November. The tables for **Kuching** (overleaf) in Sarawak and **Labuan** (overleaf) in Sabah show that here the period November to March, when the northeast monsoon is blowing, is the wettest period.

Temperatures vary little from month to month, humidity is high, and there is no large daily range of temperature so night-time temperatures are oppressive. Temperatures are distinctly lower in the

KUCHING

SARAWAK

Sunshine	Temperatures								Discomfort from heat and humidity	Precipitation and humidity			Wet days
	Average daily				Highest recorded		Lowest recorded			Relative humidity 14:00	Average monthly precipitation		
	minimum		maximum										
average hours per day	°C	°F	°C	°F	°C	°F	°C	°F		%	mm	in	more than 0.1 mm/0.004 in
Jan	4	22	72	29	85	34	93	19	66	High	75	610	24.0	24	Jan
Feb	4	22	72	30	86	34	93	18	64	High	74	510	20.1	21	Feb
March	5	23	73	31	88	34	93	21	69	High	73	328	12.9	22	March
April	6	23	73	32	90	36	96	21	69	High	71	279	11.0	20	April
May	6	23	73	32	90	35	95	21	70	High	70	262	10.3	21	May
June	6	23	73	33	91	36	96	19	67	High	66	180	7.1	15	June
July	6	22	72	32	90	36	97	19	67	High	66	196	7.7	18	July
Aug	5	22	72	33	91	36	96	18	65	Extreme	68	234	9.2	19	Aug
Sept	5	22	72	32	89	34	94	19	66	High	70	218	8.6	20	Sept
Oct	4	23	73	32	89	34	94	21	69	High	71	267	10.5	24	Oct
Nov	5	22	72	31	88	34	93	21	69	High	74	358	14.1	26	Nov
Dec	4	22	72	31	87	33	92	21	69	High	75	462	18.2	25	Dec

Based on readings for 5 years at 1°29′ N, 110°20′ E, altitude 26 m/85 ft

LABUAN

SABAH

Sunshine	Temperatures								Discomfort from heat and humidity	Precipitation and humidity				Wet days
	Average daily				Highest recorded		Lowest recorded			Relative humidity 9:30 15:30		Average monthly precipitation		
	minimum		maximum											
average hours per day	°C	°F	°C	°F	°C	°F	°C	°F		%		mm	in	more than 0.25 mm/0.01 in
Jan	7	24	76	30	86	33	92	20	68	High	85	81	112	4.4	9	Jan
Feb	8	24	76	30	86	33	92	20	68	High	86	81	117	4.6	11	Feb
March	8	24	76	31	87	34	93	17	63	Extreme	85	80	150	5.9	10	March
April	9	24	76	32	89	35	95	16	60	Extreme	85	78	297	11.7	15	April
May	7	24	76	32	89	36	96	15	59	Extreme	85	79	345	13.6	19	May
June	7	24	76	31	88	34	94	16	60	High	85	78	351	13.8	16	June
July	7	25	77	31	88	34	93	20	68	High	85	78	318	12.5	15	July
Aug	7	24	76	31	88	34	94	20	68	High	82	76	297	11.7	17	Aug
Sept	6	24	76	31	87	33	92	18	64	High	83	77	417	16.4	18	Sept
Oct	7	24	76	31	87	34	94	17	63	High	83	79	465	18.3	21	Oct
Nov	7	24	76	31	87	34	93	21	69	High	83	78	419	16.5	21	Nov
Dec	7	24	76	30	86	34	93	21	69	High	84	79	285	11.2	19	Dec

Based on readings for 20 years at 5°17′ N, 115°16′ E, altitude 18 m/58 ft

KUALA LUMPUR

INLAND MALAYAN PENINSULA

Sunshine	Temperatures									Discomfort from heat and humidity	Precipitation and humidity				Wet days	
	Average daily				Highest recorded		Lowest recorded				Relative humidity 7:00 13:00		Average monthly precipitation			
	minimum		maximum													
average hours per day	°C	°F	°C	°F	°C	°F	°C	°F			%		mm	in	more than 0.25 mm/0.01 in	
Jan 6	22	72	32	90	36	96	18	64	High		97	60	158	6.2	14	Jan
Feb 7	22	72	33	92	37	98	20	68	High		97	60	201	7.9	14	Feb
March 7	23	73	33	92	37	98	20	68	High		97	58	259	10.2	17	March
April 6	23	74	33	91	36	96	21	70	High		97	63	292	11.5	20	April
May 6	23	73	33	91	36	97	21	69	High		97	66	224	8.8	16	May
June 7	22	72	33	91	36	96	20	68	High		96	63	130	5.1	13	June
July 7	23	73	32	90	36	96	19	67	High		95	63	99	3.9	12	July
Aug 6	23	73	32	90	36	96	20	68	High		96	62	163	6.4	14	Aug
Sept 6	23	73	32	90	35	95	20	68	High		96	64	218	8.6	17	Sept
Oct 5	23	73	32	89	35	95	21	69	High		96	65	249	9.8	20	Oct
Nov 5	23	73	32	89	35	95	21	69	High		97	66	259	10.2	20	Nov
Dec 5	22	72	32	89	35	95	19	66	High		97	61	191	7.5	18	Dec

Based on readings for 19 years at 3°07´ N, 101°42´ E, altitude 39 m/127 ft

PINANG

WESTERN COAST OF THE MALAYAN PENINSULA

Sunshine	Temperatures									Discomfort from heat and humidity	Precipitation and humidity				Wet days	
	Average daily				Highest recorded		Lowest recorded				Relative humidity 8:30 14:30		Average monthly precipitation			
	minimum		maximum													
average hours per day	°C	°F	°C	°F	°C	°F	°C	°F			%		mm	in	more than 0.25 mm/0.01 in	
Jan 8	23	73	32	90	37	98	19	66	High		75	68	94	3.7	8	Jan
Feb 8	23	73	33	91	36	97	19	66	High		74	64	79	3.1	7	Feb
March 8	23	74	33	92	37	98	19	67	High		75	64	142	5.6	11	March
April 8	24	75	33	91	37	98	19	67	High		79	66	188	7.4	14	April
May 7	23	74	32	90	36	96	19	67	High		78	66	272	10.7	16	May
June 7	23	74	32	90	36	97	20	68	High		77	67	196	7.7	12	June
July 7	23	74	32	90	35	95	21	69	High		77	67	191	7.5	12	July
Aug 6	23	73	32	89	36	96	21	69	High		78	67	295	11.6	15	Aug
Sept 5	23	73	31	88	37	98	20	68	High		80	69	401	15.8	18	Sept
Oct 5	23	73	32	89	34	94	19	67	High		81	70	429	16.9	21	Oct
Nov 6	23	73	31	88	35	95	18	65	High		79	71	302	11.9	19	Nov
Dec 7	23	73	32	89	35	95	19	67	High		76	68	147	5.8	11	Dec

Based on readings for 48 years at 5°25´ N, 100°19´ E, altitude 5 m/17 ft

CAMERON HIGHLANDS											HIGHLANDS OF THE MALAYAN PENINSULA		
Sunshine		Temperatures							Discomfort from heat and humidity	Precipitation and humidity			Wet days
		Average daily				Highest recorded		Lowest recorded		Relative humidity 7:00 13:00		Average monthly precipitation	
average hours per day		minimum		maximum									more than 0.25 mm/0.01 in
		°C	°F	°C	°F	°C	°F	°C	°F		%	mm in	
Jan	5	13	56	22	71	25	77	2	36		95	76	168	6.6	17	Jan
Feb	5	13	55	22	72	26	79	4	40		95	73	132	5.2	14	Feb
March	6	13	55	23	73	26	79	6	43	Moderate	97	75	216	8.5	19	March
April	5	14	57	23	74	27	80	8	47	Moderate	97	78	297	11.7	23	April
May	5	14	58	23	74	26	79	7	45	Moderate	98	79	246	9.7	22	May
June	5	13	56	23	74	27	80	5	41	Moderate	97	73	140	5.5	16	June
July	5	13	55	23	73	26	79	7	44	Moderate	98	73	122	4.8	15	July
Aug	4	13	56	22	72	26	78	7	45		98	76	163	6.4	19	Aug
Sept	4	14	57	22	72	26	78	8	46		98	78	262	10.3	22	Sept
Oct	4	14	57	22	72	25	77	7	44	Moderate	98	80	340	13.4	26	Oct
Nov	3	14	57	22	71	26	78	7	44	Moderate	97	81	330	13.0	24	Nov
Dec	4	13	56	22	71	25	77	6	42		96	79	229	9.0	21	Dec

Based on readings for 26 years at 4°28′ N, 101°23′ E, altitude 1448 m/4750 ft

hills where there are a number of resorts but, although there is little stress from temperature in the hills, the higher humidity, greater rain, and less sunshine offset this benefit.

The tables for **Kuala Lumpur** (p. 227), which is situated inland at a low altitude, and **Pinang** (p. 227) on the west coast are representative of the lowland areas of Malaysia.

The table for **Cameron Highlands** (above) shows the cooler, wetter conditions in the mountains.

More representative of the east coast of the Malayan peninsula is the table for **Singapore** (p. 317).

The climate of Malaysia is rather oppressive and humid for the unacclimatized visitor but severe heat stress is rare. The worst months are March, April, and October when winds are light during the changeover from the southwest to northeast monsoons. During the afternoons conditions on the coast are relieved by sea breezes. Wind speed is the most important influence in Malaysia in mitigating the oppressive sultry heat.

Daily hours of sunshine are inversely proportional to amount of rain. They average from four to five hours during the wettest months to eight or nine during the drier periods. Much of the rain is heavy and accompanied by thunder.

MINICOY ISLAND — INDIAN OCEAN

	Sunshine	Temperatures							Discomfort from heat and humidity	Precipitation and humidity				Wet days
	average hours per day	Average daily				Highest recorded		Lowest recorded			Relative humidity 8:00 17:00		Average monthly precipitation		more than 2.5 mm/0.01 in
		minimum		maximum											
		°C	°F	°C	°F	°C	°F	°C	°F		%		mm	in	
Jan		23	73	29	85	32	90	17	63	High	74	73	46	1.8	3
Feb		24	75	29	85	32	90	17	63	High	74	75	18	0.7	1
March		25	77	30	86	33	92	22	71	High	72	74	23	0.9	1
April		27	80	31	87	37	98	22	72	High	72	74	58	2.3	3
May		26	79	31	88	37	98	22	71	High	76	77	178	7.0	9
June		25	77	30	86	34	93	22	72	High	81	81	295	11.6	17
July		24	76	29	85	32	90	21	69	High	79	82	226	8.9	14
Aug		25	77	29	85	32	90	21	70	High	79	79	198	7.8	12
Sept		25	77	29	85	32	90	22	72	High	79	79	160	6.3	10
Oct		24	76	29	85	33	92	21	70	High	77	78	185	7.3	11
Nov		23	74	29	85	33	91	20	68	High	78	79	140	5.5	8
Dec		23	74	29	85	32	90	21	69	High	74	80	86	3.4	4

Based on readings for 20 years at 8°18' N, 73°00' E, altitude 3 m/9 ft

Maldives

See map page 174

This island nation extends in a long chain 1,900 km/1,200 mi from north to south in the Arabian Sea and Indian Ocean between 12° N and 6° S.

There are over 7,000 islands, many of them merely low-lying coral reefs; only about 200 islands are inhabited. The Maldives have a tropical climate with abundant rainfall and moderately high temperatures around the year.

The table for **Minicoy Island** (above), which is actually in India, shows weather similar to that of the northern Maldives. The islands near or south of the equator have rain more evenly distributed through the year or a maximum fall in the period November to March.

Daily hours of sunshine average three to four in the wetter months and as much as eight to nine in the drier season.

The northern islands of the Maldives group are very occasionally affected by violent storms as tropical cyclones develop in the Arabian Sea between August and November. These bring very strong winds and torrential rain.

TIMBUKTU

CENTRAL MALI

Sunshine	Temperatures								Discomfort from heat and humidity	Precipitation and humidity				Wet days
	Average daily				Highest recorded		Lowest recorded			Relative humidity 6:00 12:00		Average monthly precipitation		
	minimum		maximum											
average hours per day	°C	°F	°C	°F	°C	°F	°C	°F		%		mm	in	more than 1 mm/0.04 in
Jan	9	13	55	31	87	39	102	5	41	Medium	39	22	0	0.0	0.1	Jan
Feb	10	14	58	34	93	42	107	6	42	Medium	33	19	0	0.0	0.2	Feb
March	10	19	66	38	100	46	115	9	48	High	34	18	3	0.1	1.0	March
April	10	22	72	42	107	48	118	14	57	High	27	15	0	0.0	0.3	April
May	10	26	78	43	110	48	118	19	66	Extreme	34	18	5	0.2	2.0	May
June	9	27	80	43	109	48	119	20	68	Extreme	55	31	23	0.9	5.0	June
July	10	25	77	39	103	48	119	19	66	Extreme	74	45	79	3.1	9.0	July
Aug	9	24	75	36	97	44	111	19	67	Extreme	83	57	81	3.2	9.0	Aug
Sept	9	24	76	39	103	46	115	20	68	Extreme	76	45	38	1.5	5.0	Sept
Oct	9	23	73	40	104	45	113	17	63	High	50	23	3	0.1	2.0	Oct
Nov	10	18	65	37	98	43	109	8	47	Medium	36	17	0	0.0	0.0	Nov
Dec	9	13	56	32	89	39	102	6	42	Medium	35	19	0	0.0	0.0	Dec

Based on readings for 13 years at 16°46′ N, 3°01′ W, altitude 301 m/988 ft

Mali

See map page 20

Including a description of the climate and weather of Burkina Faso, Niger, and Chad in the Sahel belt of interior West Africa.

Mali has a climate which is very similar to that found in three other countries of interior West Africa: Burkina Faso, Niger, and Chad. These four countries all lie on the southern side of the Sahara desert, in what is called the Sahel belt or the Soudan region. Only Burkina Faso does not extend far enough north to include part of the Sahara desert within its borders. The general features of the weather and climate of all four countries are described here.

These countries are landlocked and lie in a belt between 25° and 10° N. In the south of this belt annual rainfall is about 1,000 mm/40 in a year and this decreases northwards to virtually nil in the Sahara. Effectively, the desert border is at about 15° N, where annual rainfall is about 400 mm/16 in. The length of the rainy season and the reliability of the rain also decrease from south to north. The rainy season here is the period of high sun from May until September, with the heaviest and most reliable rains coming in July and August.

The period from November until March is virtually rainless everywhere. This is the dry season with warm to hot, sunny days and persistent northeasterly winds (the harmattan). The arrival of the rains is heralded by light to variable winds and then, when the rains arrive, the winds become persistently west to southwest. These winds following the harmattan period bring cloudy and more humid air from the equatorial regions of the South Atlantic.

Temperatures are highest from March to May before the change of wind direction. Much of the rain in this part of the world occurs in heavy downpours associated with thunder squalls which are more likely to occur in the afternoon or evening and to die out at night. Some longer spells of light rain or drizzle occur, however.

Humidity is low during the very hot period before the arrival of the rains. Although the heat can be fierce and impose some stress at this time, it is no

BAMAKO											SOUTHERN MALI	
Sunshine		Temperatures						Discomfort from heat and humidity	Precipitation and humidity			Wet days
		Average daily		Highest recorded		Lowest recorded			Relative humidity	Average monthly precipitation		
		minimum	maximum						5:30 11:30			
average hours per day		°C °F	°C °F	°C °F		°C °F			%	mm	in	more than 1 mm/0.04 in
Jan	9	16 61	33 91	42 107		9 48		Medium	38 19	0	0.0	0.1	Jan
Feb	9	19 66	36 97	47 117		11 51		Medium	33 18	0	0.0	0.0	Feb
March	9	22 71	39 102	43 109		14 58		High	41 23	3	0.1	0.7	March
April	8	24 76	39 103	44 111		18 65		Extreme	63 36	15	0.6	2.0	April
May	8	24 76	39 102	46 115		19 66		Extreme	70 40	74	2.9	5.0	May
June	8	23 73	34 94	41 105		18 64		High	74 49	137	5.4	10.0	June
July	7	22 71	32 89	39 102		18 64		High	91 70	279	11.0	16.0	July
Aug	5	22 71	31 87	36 96		17 63		High	94 73	348	13.7	17.0	Aug
Sept	7	22 71	32 89	36 97		17 63		High	93 68	206	8.1	12.0	Sept
Oct	8	22 71	34 93	40 104		15 59		High	73 41	43	1.7	6.0	Oct
Nov	8	18 65	34 94	43 110		12 53		Medium	70 34	15	0.6	1.0	Nov
Dec	8	17 62	33 92	40 104		8 47		High	69 40	0	0.0	0.1	Dec

Based on readings for 11 years at 12°39' N, 7°58' W, altitude 340 m/1116 ft

more unpleasant than the slightly cooler but more humid conditions during the rainy season.

The weather and climate of the northern part of this region are typical of the Sahara desert: very hot and dry during the period of high sun from May until September; and rather cooler but still very warm and persistently sunny during the period of low sun. Any rare and sporadic rainfall that reaches the region is likely to occur during the hottest season as occasional thunderstorms break out when the rain-belt is at its most northerly position.

Mali is the most westerly of these four countries. It has an area larger than Egypt and is sparsely populated except in the south. About half of Mali lies in the southern Sahara and is virtually rainless. Climate and weather here are represented by the table for **Faya** (p. 95) in Chad.

The table for **Timbuktu** (opposite and above) shows conditions in central Mali at the northern limit of the summer rain-belt. This table shows the reduction in temperature and the increase of humidity in July after the arrival of the rains.

The table for **Bamako** (above) shows the heavier rainfall and longer rainy season experienced in the south of the country. When the harmattan is strong it is often dust-laden and this, combined with high temperatures and very low humidity, can be unpleasant.

VALLETTA												MALTA
Sunshine	Temperatures							Discomfort from heat and humidity	Precipitation and humidity				Wet days
average hours per day	Average daily				Highest recorded		Lowest recorded			Relative humidity	Average monthly precipitation		more than 1 mm/0.04 in
	minimum		maximum							8:00 14:00			
	°C	°F	°C	°F	°C	°F	°C	°F		%	mm	in	
Jan	5	10	50	14	58	23	73	5	41		76	67	90	3.5	12	Jan
Feb	6	10	51	15	59	24	76	5	41		76	66	60	2.4	8	Feb
March	7	11	52	16	61	26	79	5	41		78	65	39	1.5	5	March
April	9	13	56	18	65	28	82	7	45		78	64	15	0.6	2	April
May	10	16	61	22	71	34	94	12	53		75	63	12	0.5	2	May
June	11	19	67	26	79	39	103	14	57	Medium	72	60	2	0.1	0	June
July	12	22	72	29	84	39	103	18	64	Medium	71	59	0	0.0	0	July
Aug	11	23	73	29	85	40	104	17	62	Medium	76	62	8	0.3	1	Aug
Sept	9	22	71	27	81	37	98	16	61	Medium	76	64	29	1.1	3	Sept
Oct	7	19	66	24	75	33	91	16	61	Moderate	77	65	63	2.5	6	Oct
Nov	6	16	60	20	67	26	79	9	49		78	67	91	3.6	9	Nov
Dec	5	12	54	16	61	22	72	6	42		77	68	110	4.3	13	Dec

Based on readings for 17 years at 35°54′ N, 14°31′ E, altitude 70 m/230 ft

Malta

See map page 18

The Maltese islands of Malta and Gozo lie in the central Mediterranean, midway between Sicily and North Africa. The area is small, only 316 sq km/ 122 sq mi, and is low-lying and flat. The weather is strongly influenced by the sea and has a very characteristic Mediterranean flavour, similar to that found in southern Italy or southern Greece.

Winters are mild, with only rare occurrences of cold weather brought by north and northeast winds from central Europe. Summers are warm, dry, and very sunny. Daytime temperatures in summer are usually mitigated by cooling sea breezes but in spring and autumn a very hot wind from Africa occasionally brings unpleasantly high temperatures. This is the sirocco, which also affects Italy and Greece; in Malta the air is usually rather drier because of the short sea track from the African coast.

Annual rainfall in Malta is low and the length of the dry season in summer is longer than in southern Italy. Malta has a very sunny climate with an average of five to six hours of sunshine a day in midwinter and over twelve hours a day in summer.

The table for **Valletta** (above) shows weather that is characteristic of Malta.

UJELANG												MARSHALL ISLANDS	
Sunshine	Temperatures							Discomfort from heat and humidity	Precipitation and humidity				Wet days	
	Average daily				Highest recorded		Lowest recorded		Relative humidity		Average monthly precipitation			
	minimum		maximum						7:00	14:00				
average hours per day	°C	°F	°C	°F	°C	°F	°C	°F		%		mm	in	more than 0.25 mm/0.01 in
Jan	25	77	29	84	32	90	22	72	High	81	77	53	2.1	13	Jan
Feb	25	77	29	85	33	91	22	72	High	82	76	46	1.8	13	Feb
March	25	77	30	86	33	91	23	73	High	82	76	66	2.6	12	March
April	25	77	30	86	33	91	23	73	High	84	78	135	5.3	17	April
May	26	78	31	87	32	90	23	73	High	85	79	168	6.6	19	May
June	26	78	31	87	32	90	23	73	High	85	79	180	7.1	21	June
July	25	77	31	88	34	93	22	72	High	86	79	213	8.4	23	July
Aug	25	77	31	88	34	94	22	71	High	87	78	216	8.5	22	Aug
Sept	25	77	31	88	34	93	23	73	Extreme	87	80	262	10.3	24	Sept
Oct	25	77	31	88	35	95	23	73	Extreme	87	80	264	10.4	23	Oct
Nov	26	78	31	87	33	92	23	73	Extreme	86	80	244	9.6	22	Nov
Dec	26	78	30	86	32	90	22	72	High	82	78	125	4.9	19	Dec

Based on readings for 4 years at 9°46′ N, 160°58′ E, altitude 10 m/33 ft

Marshall Islands

See map page 17

This Pacific republic shares a climate with three other groups of islands – the Caroline, Gilbert, and Marianas Islands – all located in the western Pacific north of the equator. The Marshalls consist of two chains of coral atolls about 1,300 km/800 mi long.

Like its neighbours, the country experiences very similar conditions of temperature and humidity throughout the year. There is a typical tropical oceanic climate with moderately high temperatures and humidity that vary little from month to month.

The daily temperature range is quite small – about 4°–5° C/10° F. There is abundant rainfall, but it is somewhat lighter than in neighbouring countries with islands that reach higher elevations. The wettest season is from June to November.

The Marshall Islands are liable to tropical cyclones (the typhoons of the South China Sea) with their heavy rainfall and very strong winds, which can do considerable damage. The main season for such storms is from July to November. The worst storms may only affect one particular island every two or three years but the much larger area of heavy rain associated with a cyclone contributes to the heavier rainfall of these months.

All the islands in the country have moderately large amounts of sunshine, averaging six to eight hours a day in spite of a large number of days on which some rain falls. Much of this rain is in the form of short, heavy showers, although whole days with continuous rain are more frequent in the wetter months.

Although the combination of temperature and humidity is often rather muggy and oppressive, particularly at night, the daytime temperatures are usually moderate and feel more comfortable because of the brisk winds, both daytime sea breezes and the predominant and regular trade winds.

The table for **Ujelang** (above) illustrates conditions that are typical of the Marshall Islands.

FORT-DE-FRANCE										WEST COAST MARTINIQUE		
Sunshine	Temperatures							Discomfort from heat and humidity	Precipitation and humidity		Wet days	
	Average daily				Highest recorded		Lowest recorded		Relative humidity	Average monthly precipitation		
average hours per day	minimum		maximum						6:00 16:00		more than 0.25 mm/0.01 in	
	°C	°F	°C	°F	°C	°F	°C	°F		%	mm in	
Jan	8	21	69	28	83	32	90	15	59	Medium	90	77	119	4.7	19	Jan
Feb	8	21	69	29	84	33	91	16	60	High	88	73	109	4.3	15	Feb
March	9	21	69	29	85	33	91	13	56	High	88	72	74	2.9	15	March
April	8	22	71	30	86	34	94	17	63	High	88	71	99	3.9	13	April
May	8	23	73	31	87	34	93	19	66	High	88	74	119	4.7	18	May
June	7	23	74	30	86	33	92	19	66	High	89	77	188	7.4	21	June
July	8	23	74	30	86	32	90	20	68	High	90	78	239	9.4	22	July
Aug	8	23	74	31	87	34	94	19	66	High	91	78	262	10.3	22	Aug
Sept	8	23	74	31	88	36	96	20	68	High	91	79	236	9.3	29	Sept
Oct	7	23	73	31	87	34	94	18	65	Extreme	92	80	246	9.7	19	Oct
Nov	8	22	72	30	86	33	92	18	64	High	92	81	201	7.9	20	Nov
Dec	8	22	71	29	84	32	89	16	61	High	91	79	150	5.9	19	Dec

Based on readings for 22 years at 14°37′ N, 61°05′ W, altitude 4 m/13 ft

Martinique

See map page 15

This overseas département of France is one of the largest, along with Barbados, St Lucia, Grenada, and St Vincent, of the Windward Islands, the southern islands of the Lesser Antilles, which lie between 15° N and the coast of South America.

Although still small, these larger members of the Windward chain are hilly or mountainous and this tends to increase the rainfall above that of the small, flat islands in the group.

The table for **Fort-de-France** (above) shows that Martinique, with its higher mountains, is wetter than Barbados (see p. 59) around the year. The tables for Barbados and Martinique reflect conditions on the west coasts of the islands, which are somewhat sheltered from the prevailing winds.

All months receive appreciable rain but the heaviest rain is more likely to occur from July to November. This is the hurricane season and, although the most violent of these tropical storms may only strike a particular island every few years, less severe ones cause appreciable rainfall over quite a wide area.

Temperature, humidity, and sunshine throughout the year are typical of those described in the general entry for the Caribbean (p. 92).

NOUAKCHOTT									COASTAL MAURITANIA			
Sunshine	Temperatures						Discomfort from heat and humidity	Precipitation and humidity				Wet days
	Average daily				Highest recorded	Lowest recorded		Relative humidity 5:00 11:00		Average monthly precipitation		
	minimum		maximum									
average hours per day	°C	°F	°C	°F	°C	°F	°C	°F		%	mm	in	more than 1 mm/0.04 in
Jan	8	14	57	29	85	36	96	7	45	Medium	51	31	0	0.0	0.1	Jan
Feb	9	15	59	31	87	39	103	9	49	Medium	54	30	3	0.1	0.2	Feb
March	10	17	63	32	89	41	106	11	51	Medium	65	30	0	0.0	0.1	March
April	10	18	64	32	90	43	109	12	54	Medium	68	32	0	0.0	0.1	April
May	10	21	69	34	93	46	115	14	58	High	73	35	0	0.0	0.1	May
June	10	23	73	33	92	46	114	18	64	High	79	48	3	0.1	0.3	June
July	9	23	74	32	89	43	109	21	70	High	85	63	13	0.5	1.0	July
Aug	9	24	75	32	90	42	108	20	68	High	88	69	104	4.1	3.0	Aug
Sept	9	24	75	34	93	44	111	22	71	High	85	59	23	0.9	3.0	Sept
Oct	9	22	71	33	91	43	109	17	63	High	73	41	10	0.4	1.0	Oct
Nov	9	18	65	32	89	42	107	13	56	Medium	64	35	3	0.1	0.2	Nov
Dec	8	13	56	28	83	37	98	7	44	Moderate	58	34	0	0.0	0.3	Dec

Based on readings for 5 years at 18°07′ N, 15°36′ W, altitude 21 m/69 ft

Mauritania

See map page 20

A large but very sparsely populated country of West Africa, Mauritania occupies the western part of the Sahara desert with a coastline on the Atlantic Ocean and land borders with Western Sahara (former Spanish Sahara) on the north, Algeria and Mali on the east, and Senegal on the south.

Situated between 15° and 27° N it has a very hot, dry climate for most of the year. The southern half of the country has some unreliable and sparse rainfall between June and October. During these months southwesterly winds (the West African monsoon) bring moisture-laden air from the South Atlantic. At this time of year there is more cloud and the air is rather humid.

During the rest of the year the prevailing winds are from the northeast, bringing very dry and sometimes dusty, hazy air from the northern part of the Sahara. This is the harmattan of West Africa, which has a very low humidity.

The north of the country is virtually rainless but occasional downpours can occur at any season. As the table for **Nouakchott** above shows, there is some rain between July and October; this table is representative of the Atlantic coast of Mauritania.

In the extreme south of the country annual rainfall averages between 300 mm/12 in and 375 mm/15 in but is very variable from year to year. This is insufficient for cultivation as it comes at the hottest time of the year.

Sunshine amounts are high throughout the year, averaging from eight to ten hours a day. They are least in midwinter when the days are shorter, but are also reduced in midsummer since this is the season when there is more cloud in the humid southwesterly winds.

For much of the year the climate is too hot and dry by day to be pleasant. The slightly cooler conditions on the coast are a result of daily sea breezes but this is partly offset by the higher humidity.

PORT LOUIS										LOWLAND MAURITIUS		
Sunshine	Temperatures							Discomfort from heat and humidity	Precipitation and humidity			Wet days
	Average daily				Highest recorded		Lowest recorded		Relative humidity		Average monthly precipitation	
	minimum		maximum						7:00	13:00		
average hours per day	°C	°F	°C	°F	°C	°F	°C	°F		%		mm	in	more than 2.5 mm/0.1 in
Jan	8	23	73	30	86	35	95	17	63	High	86	67	216	8.5	12	Jan
Feb	8	23	73	29	85	33	91	18	64	High	88	71	198	7.8	11	Feb
March	7	22	72	29	84	32	90	17	63	High	90	72	221	8.7	11	March
April	8	21	70	28	82	31	88	14	58	Medium	89	71	127	5.0	9	April
May	8	19	66	26	79	29	85	13	55	Medium	88	68	97	3.8	7	May
June	7	17	63	24	76	28	83	11	51	Moderate	87	65	66	2.6	6	June
July	7	17	62	24	75	27	80	11	51	Moderate	85	64	58	2.3	6	July
Aug	7	17	62	24	75	27	80	10	50	Moderate	85	61	64	2.5	6	Aug
Sept	8	17	63	25	77	28	83	11	51	Moderate	83	58	36	1.4	4	Sept
Oct	9	18	64	27	80	31	88	13	55	Medium	80	57	41	1.6	4	Oct
Nov	9	19	67	28	83	33	91	14	57	Medium	77	56	46	1.8	4	Nov
Dec	9	22	71	29	85	35	95	17	62	Medium	81	61	117	4.6	7	Dec

Based on readings for 40 years at 20°06′ S, 57°32′ E, altitude 55 m/181 ft

Mauritius

See map page 21

This small but densely populated island consists of a series of volcanic hills rising to a height of 600–800 m/2,000–2,600 ft with a fringing coastal plain. It is situated in latitude 20° S in the Indian Ocean about 800 km/500 mi east of Madagascar.

Mauritius has a tropical oceanic climate with moderately high temperatures and humidity throughout the year. Temperatures never rise to such high levels as to be really uncomfortable or dangerous, although on occasions the nights may be rather sticky and oppressive. Rain occurs in all months but the wettest period is from December to April. During these months tropical cyclones occasionally strike the island or pass near enough to give very heavy rainfall and violent damaging winds.

The table for **Port Louis** (above) illustrates conditions at lower levels on the island. The south and southeast coasts, being exposed to the dominant southeast trade winds, receive almost twice as much rain as Port Louis and rainfall is also heavier on the higher ground inland. Outside the main rainy season the weather is generally sunny and pleasant with slightly lower temperatures and a strong sea breeze.

Mexico

See map page 14

Mexico, the largest country of Central America, is bordered on the north by the United States and on the south by Guatemala and Belize. About three times as large as Texas, it is shaped roughly like a wedge, widest in the north and tapering to the narrow Isthmus of Tehuantepec in the south. It is situated between 14° and 32° N, the northern half of the country lying outside the tropics. Almost two-thirds of the country consists of plateaux and high mountains with a climate that is warm-temperate; other parts have a tropical climate with temperature reduced by altitude.

There are three important climatic influences which help to determine the character of the climate of different parts of Mexico. The cold Californian current, which sweeps southwards on the Pacific coast, has the effect of lowering temperatures and reducing rainfall on the west coast as far south as the tip of the peninsula of Lower California. This and the influence of the North Pacific anticyclone help to make much of northwestern Mexico desert or semi-desert; this is a continuation of the dry zone of the United States in southern California, New Mexico, and Arizona.

The warm waters of the Caribbean Sea, and the influence of the constant northeast trade winds, make the eastern coastal region a typical tropical coast with a marked single wet season in summer. The weather and climate of this region, particularly south of Tampico, have much in common with that of the Caribbean Islands described on pp. 92–3.

An important influence is the presence to the north of the great continental landmass of North America. This area becomes very cold in winter, particularly when cold air sweeps down from the Canadian Arctic, and very warm in summer. The northern part of Mexico shares these extreme temperature conditions. In winter cold waves, or 'northers', can bring near-freezing conditions for a few days to the east coast as far south as Tampico or Veracruz. Snow has fallen as far south as Tampico, which is within the tropics. The west coast is protected from such cold waves by the mountains and plateaux of central Mexico.

As in other mountainous South and Central American countries, the climatic zones are described on the basis of altitude, using Spanish terms: *tierra caliente*, the area below about 600 m/2,000 ft; *tierra templada*, the land between 600 m/2,000 ft and 1,800 m/6,000 ft; and *tierra fría*, the mountains and plateaux above this level. Only a very narrow coastal belt on the Pacific shore falls into the *tierra caliente* category, but there is a more extensive area on the Caribbean shore, including the whole Yucatán peninsula. The largest part of Mexico falls into *tierra templada* and *tierra fría*. This division takes little account of rainfall and is mainly on the basis of temperature. In most of the *tierra fría* frost is frequent at night in winter and snow can occur anywhere but only lies above 3,000–3,600 m/10,000–12,000 ft.

The rainy season over the whole country is the period of high sun from May to October. The rest of the year is not completely rainless but the amount and frequency of rain in the winter season is low. The wettest part of the country is the lowland on the Caribbean coast; the north coast of the Yucatán peninsula is relatively much drier than the east coast or the interior. Annual rainfall here is between 1,000 m/40 in and 1,500 m/60 in but some places in northern Yucatán get less than 500 mm/20 in.

The shores of the Pacific and Gulf of California, north of the Tropic of Cancer, get less than 250 mm/10 in of rain a year, but this increases southwards to between 1,000 mm/40 in and 1,500 mm/60 in. Rainfall is heaviest where the coast is backed by high mountains. On the plateau, where some of the winter precipitation may fall as snow, the annual rainfall is rather less than on the coast. Much of the plateau is sheltered from maritime influences by the high mountains of the eastern and western Sierra Madre so that it has a reduced rainfall. Annual amounts of 500 mm/20 in or less in the extreme north to 875 mm/35 in in the centre and south are typical of the central highland region.

Most of Mexico has sunny weather for a large part of the year. The cloudiest regions are the wetter parts of the east coast and the northern part of the Pacific coast, where low cloud and fog are formed over the cold ocean current. The drier regions of the interior and much of the *tierra templada* have high amounts of sunshine: as much as seven or eight hours a day in the drier months to five or six during the wetter season.

The table for **Guaymas** (overleaf) is representative of the drier northwest of the country. Conditions in the interior are represented by the tables for **Monterrey** (overleaf) and **Mexico City** (p. 239);

GUAYMAS

NORTHWESTERN MEXICO

Sunshine average hours per day	Temperatures Average daily minimum °C	°F	Average daily maximum °C	°F	Highest recorded °C	°F	Lowest recorded °C	°F	Discomfort from heat and humidity	Precipitation and humidity Relative humidity all hours %	Average monthly precipitation mm	in	Wet days with trace or more	
Jan	7	13	55	23	73	30	86	7	45		52	5	0.2	2	Jan
Feb	7	14	57	24	75	39	102	6	43	Moderate	53	0	0.0	1	Feb
March	8	16	60	26	79	35	95	9	49	Moderate	50	8	0.3	2	March
April	9	18	64	29	84	40	104	12	53	Medium	48	5	0.2	1	April
May	10	21	69	31	88	44	111	13	56	Medium	50	5	0.2	1	May
June	10	24	76	34	93	43	109	18	64	High	57	3	0.1	1	June
July	9	27	80	34	94	44	111	21	69	Extreme	63	43	1.7	7	July
Aug	8	27	80	35	95	47	117	21	69	Extreme	64	91	3.6	8	Aug
Sept	8	26	78	35	95	43	109	18	64	Extreme	66	61	2.4	6	Sept
Oct	9	22	72	21	70	43	109	13	55		67	10	0.4	2	Oct
Nov	8	18	64	28	82	37	99	9	48	Medium	70	15	0.6	3	Nov
Dec	6	13	56	23	74	38	100	8	46	Moderate	72	38	1.5	5	Dec

Based on readings for 6 years at 27°55′ N, 110°53′ W, altitude 8 m/26 ft

MONTERREY

MEXICAN INTERIOR

Sunshine average hours per day	Temperatures Average daily minimum °C	°F	Average daily maximum °C	°F	Highest recorded °C	°F	Lowest recorded °C	°F	Discomfort from heat and humidity	Precipitation and humidity Relative humidity 7:30	14:30 %	Average monthly precipitation mm	in	Wet days with trace or more	
Jan	5	9	48	20	68	34	94	-4	25		77	60	15	0.6	6	Jan
Feb	5	11	52	22	72	37	99	-3	26		78	59	18	0.7	5	Feb
March	6	14	57	24	76	38	100	-1	30		68	45	20	0.8	7	March
April	5	17	62	29	84	41	105	6	42	Medium	77	53	33	1.3	7	April
May	6	20	68	31	87	42	107	11	51	Medium	76	51	33	1.3	9	May
June	8	22	71	33	91	41	105	13	55	High	83	57	76	3.0	8	June
July	7	22	71	32	90	39	102	16	60	High	75	49	58	2.3	8	July
Aug	6	22	72	33	92	39	102	16	60	High	79	57	61	2.4	7	Aug
Sept	6	21	70	30	86	38	101	11	51	High	76	66	132	5.2	10	Sept
Oct	6	18	64	27	80	35	95	7	45	Medium	73	67	76	3.0	9	Oct
Nov	5	13	55	22	71	34	94	-1	30		65	60	38	1.5	8	Nov
Dec	4	10	50	18	65	34	94	-1	30		66	55	20	0.8	6	Dec

Based on readings for 11 years at 25°40′ N, 100°18′ W, altitude 528 m/1732 ft

MEXICO CITY

MEXICAN INTERIOR

	Sunshine average hours per day	Temperatures								Discomfort from heat and humidity	Precipitation and humidity				Wet days with trace or more	
		Average daily				Highest recorded		Lowest recorded			Relative humidity 6:30 13:30		Average monthly precipitation			
		minimum		maximum												
		°C	°F	°C	°F	°C	°F	°C	°F		%		mm	in		
Jan	7	6	42	19	66	23	74	-3	27		79	34	13	0.5	4	Jan
Feb	8	6	43	21	69	27	81	-2	29		72	28	5	0.2	5	Feb
March	8	8	47	24	75	29	84	1	34		68	26	10	0.4	9	March
April	8	11	51	25	77	32	90	1	33		66	29	20	0.8	14	April
May	7	12	54	26	78	32	89	6	43		69	29	53	2.1	17	May
June	7	13	55	24	76	31	87	9	49		82	48	119	4.7	21	June
July	6	12	53	23	73	28	83	8	47		84	50	170	6.7	27	July
Aug	6	12	54	23	73	27	81	9	49		85	50	152	6.0	27	Aug
Sept	6	12	53	23	74	26	78	1	34		86	54	130	5.1	23	Sept
Oct	6	10	50	21	70	26	78	2	35		83	47	51	2.0	13	Oct
Nov	7	8	46	20	68	25	77	2	36		82	41	18	0.7	6	Nov
Dec	7	6	43	19	66	23	73	0	32		81	37	8	0.3	4	Dec

Based on readings for 7 years at 19°24′ N, 99°12′ W, altitude 2309 m/7575 ft

MERIDA

NORTHERN YUCATAN

	Sunshine average hours per day	Temperatures								Discomfort from heat and humidity	Precipitation and humidity				Wet days with trace or more	
		Average daily				Highest recorded		Lowest recorded			Relative humidity 7:00 14:00		Average monthly precipitation			
		minimum		maximum												
		°C	°F	°C	°F	°C	°F	°C	°F		%		mm	in		
Jan	5	17	62	28	83	33	92	12	53	Medium	87	53	25	1.0	8	Jan
Feb	5	17	63	29	85	35	95	11	51	Medium	84	48	18	0.7	6	Feb
March	6	19	66	37	89	37	98	11	52	Extreme	84	46	28	1.1	6	March
April	6	21	69	41	92	41	106	14	58	Extreme	80	41	28	1.1	5	April
May	7	22	72	40	94	40	104	17	63	Extreme	81	45	79	3.1	10	May
June	6	23	73	33	92	39	103	21	69	High	87	58	173	6.8	19	June
July	6	23	73	33	92	36	97	18	64	High	88	56	122	4.8	20	July
Aug	6	23	73	33	91	38	100	19	67	High	89	58	135	5.3	19	Aug
Sept	5	23	73	32	90	36	96	20	68	High	90	62	155	6.1	20	Sept
Oct	5	22	71	31	87	34	94	17	63	High	87	62	102	4.0	17	Oct
Nov	5	19	67	29	85	33	91	13	56	Medium	86	55	33	1.3	12	Nov
Dec	5	18	64	28	82	33	92	13	55	Medium	87	53	31	1.2	9	Dec

Based on readings for 21 years at 20°58′ N, 89°38′ W, altitude 22 m/72 ft

ACAPULCO — WEST COAST MEXICO

	Sunshine average hours per day	Temperatures								Discomfort from heat and humidity	Precipitation and humidity			Wet days more than 0.25 mm/0.01 in	
		Average daily				Highest recorded		Lowest recorded			Relative humidity all hours	Average monthly precipitation			
		minimum		maximum											
		°C	°F	°C	°F	°C	°F	°C	°F		%	mm	in		
Jan	9	22	72	31	88	36	97	11	52	High	74	6	0.2	1	Jan
Feb	9	22	72	31	88	36	97	18	64	High	75	1	0.0	0	Feb
March	9	22	72	31	88	38	100	18	64	High	75	0	0.0	0	March
April	8	23	73	32	90	37	99	18	64	Extreme	73	1	0.0	0	April
May	7	25	77	32	90	41	106	20	68	Extreme	74	36	1.4	3	May
June	7	25	77	33	91	37	99	21	70	Extreme	76	281	11.1	13	June
July	7	25	77	32	90	38	100	21	70	Extreme	77	256	10.1	14	July
Aug	7	25	77	33	91	37	99	25	77	Extreme	75	252	9.9	13	Aug
Sept	6	24	75	32	90	37	99	20	68	Extreme	79	349	13.8	16	Sept
Oct	7	24	75	32	90	37	99	21	70	Extreme	79	159	6.3	9	Oct
Nov	9	23	73	32	90	37	99	19	66	Extreme	77	28	1.1	2	Nov
Dec	9	22	72	31	88	41	106	11	52	High	77	8	0.3	1	Dec

Based on readings for 30 years at 16°50′ N, 96°56′ W, altitude 3 m/10 ft

SALINA CRUZ — WEST COAST MEXICO

	Sunshine average hours per day	Temperatures								Discomfort from heat and humidity	Precipitation and humidity			Wet days with trace or more	
		Average daily				Highest recorded		Lowest recorded			Relative humidity all hours	Average monthly precipitation			
		minimum		maximum											
		°C	°F	°C	°F	°C	°F	°C	°F		%	mm	in		
Jan	9	22	72	29	85	33	91	17	62	Medium	60	3	0.1	0.3	Jan
Feb	9	22	72	29	85	33	92	17	63	Medium	62	5	0.2	0.5	Feb
March	9	23	74	30	86	35	95	17	63	High	63	0	0.0	0.6	March
April	8	24	76	31	88	36	97	18	65	High	64	0	0.0	0.5	April
May	8	26	78	33	91	37	98	21	70	High	64	51	2.0	3.0	May
June	6	25	77	31	88	36	97	19	66	High	72	241	9.5	12.0	June
July	7	24	76	32	89	35	95	20	68	High	70	165	6.5	11.0	July
Aug	7	25	77	32	89	36	97	20	68	High	69	188	7.4	9.0	Aug
Sept	6	24	75	31	87	35	95	20	68	High	74	297	11.7	12.0	Sept
Oct	8	24	75	31	87	34	93	19	66	High	65	61	2.4	4.0	Oct
Nov	9	23	74	30	86	34	94	17	62	Medium	58	13	0.5	1.0	Nov
Dec	9	22	72	29	85	34	93	17	63	Medium	59	3	0.1	0.6	Dec

Based on readings for 10 years at 16°12′ N, 95°12′ W, altitude 56 m/184 ft

these show a larger daily range of temperature. Monterrey is at the upper limit of the *tierra caliente*, while Mexico City is typical of the *tierra fria*.

The table for **Mérida** (p. 239), in northern Yucatán, **Acapulco** (opposite) and **Salina Cruz** (opposite and below), on the Pacific coast in the south, show the higher and typically tropical temperatures of the southern lowlands. Mérida is wetter than some parts of Yucatán.

The combination of heat and humidity can be uncomfortable during the wet season. Otherwise most of Mexico has a healthy and reasonably pleasant climate for most of the year.

At the altitude of Mexico City and above, sudden exertion can lead to breathlessness, as visitors may take a few days to adjust to the lower atmospheric pressure. On the higher parts of the plateau the sun may at times feel very powerful by day and the rapid drop of temperature at night may strike very chilly.

Both the east and west coasts of Mexico are occasionally affected by tropical storms which develop in the Caribbean or the Pacific and bring two or three days of heavy rain. These are most likely to occur in the months August to October. Very few of these reach the strength of fully developed hurricanes; if they do, the east-coast districts are more liable to severe damage.

Micronesia

See map page 17

The Federated States of Micronesia comprises more than 600 of the Caroline Islands. These islands experience much the same weather as three other groups in the western Pacific north of the equator – the Gilbert, Marianas, and Marshall Islands.

Micronesia has a typical tropical oceanic climate with moderately high temperatures and humidity which vary little from month to month. The daily range of temperature is quite small – about 4°–5° C/10° F. All of the country's islands have abundant or moderately heavy rainfall and most have a wetter season from June to November.

Islands near the equator have rainfall more evenly spread throughout the year. The actual amount of rainfall on each island depends both on the altitude of the land and on exposure to the dominant winds: the northeast trade winds in the low sun period and the southeast monsoon in the high sun period.

Islands more than 5° N of the equator are liable to experience tropical cyclones (the typhoons of the South China Sea) with their heavy rainfall and very strong winds, which can do considerable damage.

The main season for such storms is from July to November. The worst of such storms may only affect one particular island every two or three years, but the much larger area of heavy rain associated with a cyclone contributes to the heavier rainfall of these months.

Micronesia has moderately large amounts of sunshine, averaging between six and eight hours a day in spite of a large number of days on which some rain falls. Much of the rainfall is in the form of short, heavy showers but days with continuous rain are more frequent in the wetter months. Although the combination of temperature and humidity is often rather muggy and oppressive, particularly at night, the daytime temperatures are usually moderate and feel more comfortable because of the brisk winds, both the daytime sea breezes and the predominant and regular trade winds.

The tables for **Saipan** (p. 269) in the Marianas and for **Ujelang** (p. 233) in the Marshalls illustrate conditions that are reflected in most of Micronesia. That for **Yaren** (p. 255) on Nauru is more typical of Micronesian islands on or near the equator; here rainfall is more evenly distributed throughout the year and tropical cyclones are never experienced.

CHISINAU														MOLDOVA
Sunshine	Temperatures							Discomfort from heat and humidity	Precipitation and humidity				Wet days	
	Average daily				Highest recorded		Lowest recorded		Relative humidity		Average monthly precipitation			
	minimum		maximum						8:00 13:00					
average hours per day	°C	°F	°C	°F	°C	°F	°C	°F	%		mm	in	more than 0.1 mm/0.004 in	
Jan	2	-8	18	-1	30	13	55	-29	-20		83	76	56	2.2	15	Jan
Feb	2	-5	23	-1	30	19	66	-23	-9		87	75	50	2.0	17	Feb
March	4	-1	30	6	43	25	77	-15	5		82	62	42	1.7	12	March
April	7	5	41	16	61	29	84	-6	21		67	41	35	1.4	9	April
May	9	11	52	23	73	34	93	1	34		64	41	34	1.3	10	May
June	9	14	57	26	79	35	95	6	43	Moderate	67	47	68	2.7	12	June
July	9	16	61	27	81	36	97	10	50	Moderate	68	48	65	2.6	10	July
Aug	9	15	59	27	81	35	95	5	41	Moderate	73	46	38	1.5	7	Aug
Sept	7	11	52	23	73	36	97	2	36	Moderate	75	67	45	1.8	7	Sept
Oct	6	7	45	17	63	28	82	-4	25		84	52	22	0.9	6	Oct
Nov	2	3	37	10	50	24	75	-14	7		87	71	39	1.5	12	Nov
Dec	1	-4	25	2	36	16	61	-19	-2		84	76	45	1.8	14	Dec

Based on readings for 8 years at 47°01′ N, 28°52′ E, altitude 95 m/312 ft

Moldova

See map page 19

Although the winters are cold in Moldova and spells of extremely cold weather occur when easterly winds blow from Siberia, the winter is shorter than in northern areas of neighbouring Ukraine and Romania and the spring thaw comes earlier. The table for **Chisinau** (above) is representative of weather in Moldova.

Monaco

See map page 18

The tiny independent principality of Monaco, consisting almost entirely of the town of **Monte Carlo** (see table opposite and above), is situated on the Mediterranean coast of France. It is in the heart of the popular seaside resort area of the Côte d'Azur and enjoys a Mediterranean type of climate which is described on p. 145 for Mediterranean France. The area of Monaco is less than 1 sq mi.

Mongolia

See map page 24

Mongolia is a large but very sparsely populated country in the heart of Asia. It is bordered by Russia on the north and China on the south. With an area of 1,565,000 sq km/604,000 sq mi, it is almost three times the size of France yet it has a population of a little over a million. In the west and north there are mountains rising to over 3,000 m/10,000 ft but there are extensive areas of flat or undulating plains which

MONTE CARLO — MONACO

	Sunshine	Temperatures								Discomfort from heat and humidity	Precipitation and humidity				Wet days	
	average hours per day	Average daily				Highest recorded		Lowest recorded			Relative humidity 6:30 13:30		Average monthly precipitation		more than 0.1 mm/0.004 in	
		minimum		maximum												
		°C	°F	°C	°F	°C	°F	°C	°F		%		mm	in		
Jan	5	8	47	12	54	21	70	0	32		67	67	61	2.4	5	Jan
Feb	5	8	47	13	55	19	66	-1	30		70	69	58	2.3	5	Feb
March	5	10	50	14	57	20	68	1	34		74	73	71	2.8	7	March
April	6	12	54	16	61	25	77	4	39		77	72	65	2.6	5	April
May	7	15	59	19	66	29	84	8	46		78	75	64	2.5	5	May
June	8	19	66	23	73	34	93	12	54	Moderate	79	75	33	1.3	4	June
July	9	22	71	26	78	33	91	14	57	Medium	78	71	21	0.8	1	July
Aug	9	22	71	26	78	34	93	14	57	Medium	76	72	22	0.9	2	Aug
Sept	7	20	67	24	74	31	87	11	52	Moderate	77	71	66	2.6	4	Sept
Oct	6	16	61	20	68	27	80	7	45		73	71	113	4.5	7	Oct
Nov	5	12	54	16	61	22	72	5	41		72	72	123	4.8	7	Nov
Dec	4	10	49	14	56	20	68	1	33		71	72	99	3.9	6	Dec

Based on readings for 30 years at 43°43' N, 7°25' E, altitude 55 m/180 ft

ULAANBAATAR — NORTHERN MONGOLIA

	Sunshine	Temperatures								Discomfort from heat and humidity	Precipitation and humidity				Wet days	
	average hours per day	Average daily				Highest recorded		Lowest recorded			Relative humidity 7:00 13:00		Average monthly precipitation		more than 1 mm/0.04 in	
		minimum		maximum												
		°C	°F	°C	°F	°C	°F	°C	°F		%		mm	in		
Jan	3	-32	-26	-19	-2	-6	21	-44	-47		81	73	0	0.0	1	Jan
Feb	4	-29	-21	-13	9	2	35	-44	-48		78	66	0	0.0	1	Feb
March	5	-22	-7	-4	25	18	64	-39	-39		78	61	3	0.1	2	March
April	6	-8	17	7	44	24	76	-24	-11		64	42	5	0.2	2	April
May	8	-2	29	13	55	30	86	-12	10		64	40	10	0.4	4	May
June	7	7	44	21	69	36	97	-4	24		68	44	28	1.1	5	June
July	7	11	51	22	71	33	92	1	34		77	54	76	3.0	10	July
Aug	7	8	46	21	69	33	91	-7	20		76	49	51	2.0	8	Aug
Sept	6	2	35	14	58	28	83	-11	13		78	43	23	0.9	3	Sept
Oct	5	-8	18	6	43	23	73	-27	-16		77	48	5	0.2	2	Oct
Nov	3	-20	-4	-6	22	11	52	-36	-32		82	57	5	0.2	2	Nov
Dec	2	-28	-19	-16	3	0	32	-43	-45		88	75	3	0.1	1	Dec

Based on readings for 12 years at 47°55' N, 106°50' E, altitude 1325 m/4347 ft

are desert in the south and steppe grassland in the north and east.

Mongolia has an extreme continental type of climate similar to that of south-central Siberia or Manchuria. Winters are long and very cold. There is a swift transition in April to a short, warm summer and an equally rapid return to the winter cold in October. Rainfall is everywhere low; probably no more than 375 mm/15in–500 mm/20 in a year in the mountains and as little as 125 mm/5 in in the drier lowland parts. Winter is almost entirely dry with occasional light snow except in the western mountains where snow is heavier. The wetter parts receive almost all their precipitation between June and September when moist air is able to penetrate the interior under the influence of the Chinese summer monsoon.

The table for **Ulaanbaatar** (p. 243) shows conditions over much of the country but southern Mongolia receives even less rain. Conditions during the short summer are quite pleasant, but during the long, cold winter very warm clothing is required and, when strong winds arise, wind chill can be very severe. On many days during the winter, however, winds are light, the sky is clear, and there is abundant sunshine.

Montserrat

See map page 15

This British island colony lies in the Leeward Islands, the northerly islands of the Lesser Antilles. Temperature and humidity around the year in the Leeward Islands are very similar to those described in the general entry for the Caribbean (pp. 92–3), as are the amount and distribution of sunshine. The table for **Plymouth** (below) shows that near sea level the annual rainfall is about 1,250–2,000 mm/ 50–80 in, well distributed throughout the year, with a wetter season from July to November.

Montserrat lies in the track of violent tropical hurricanes which are most likely to develop between August and October. The severest of these storms may only strike Montserrat every few years but the appreciable rainfall they, and less violent disturbances, bring to a wider area accounts for the heavier rainfall during these months.

PLYMOUTH														MONTSERRAT
Sunshine	Temperatures							Discomfort from heat and humidity	Precipitation and humidity				Wet days	
	Average daily				Highest recorded		Lowest recorded		Relative humidity		Average monthly precipitation			
	minimum		maximum						9:00	15:00				
average hours per day	°C	°F	°C	°F	°C	°F	°C	°F		%		mm	in	more than 1 mm/0.04 in
Jan	7	21	70	28	82	32	89	17	62	Medium	69	65	122	4.8	12	Jan
Feb	7	21	70	33	83	33	91	17	62	High	66	61	86	3.4	9	Feb
March	7	21	70	29	85	34	93	17	62	Medium	65	59	112	4.4	9	March
April	8	22	72	30	86	34	94	17	63	Medium	62	59	89	3.5	8	April
May	8	23	74	31	88	36	96	19	67	High	63	60	97	3.8	10	May
June	7	24	75	31	88	37	98	19	66	High	65	63	112	4.4	13	June
July	8	24	75	31	87	37	98	21	70	High	66	64	155	6.1	14	July
Aug	8	24	75	31	88	37	98	21	69	High	68	66	183	7.2	16	Aug
Sept	7	23	74	32	89	36	97	19	67	High	68	66	168	6.6	13	Sept
Oct	8	23	74	31	87	34	94	19	67	High	69	66	196	7.7	14	Oct
Nov	7	23	73	29	85	37	98	15	59	Medium	70	68	180	7.1	16	Nov
Dec	7	22	72	28	83	33	92	18	64	Medium	70	67	140	5.5	13	Dec

Based on readings for 14 years at 16°43' N, 62°13' W, altitude 40 m/130 ft

Morocco

Morocco, a country a little smaller than France, occupies the northwestern corner of Africa. With coasts on both the Atlantic and the Mediterranean, it commands the southern shores of the narrow Straits of Gibraltar. It includes parts of the same three relief areas shown for Algeria on p. 30.

There is a narrow coastal belt with a Mediterranean climate; an interior region of high mountains and plateaux; and a southern fringe on the margin of the Sahara desert. Morocco has a long eastern border with Algeria and a short southern border with Western Sahara (formerly Spanish Sahara).

The northern coast of Morocco and the interior mountains, the Rif, have a Mediterranean climate similar to that described for Algeria. Northwestern Morocco, especially the Rif Mountains, is exposed to Atlantic depressions in winter and rainfall is moderately heavy.

The Atlantic coast as far south as Agadir receives over 200 mm/8 in of rain in winter but farther south the climate becomes progressively drier and the Sahara desert extends all the way to the Atlantic

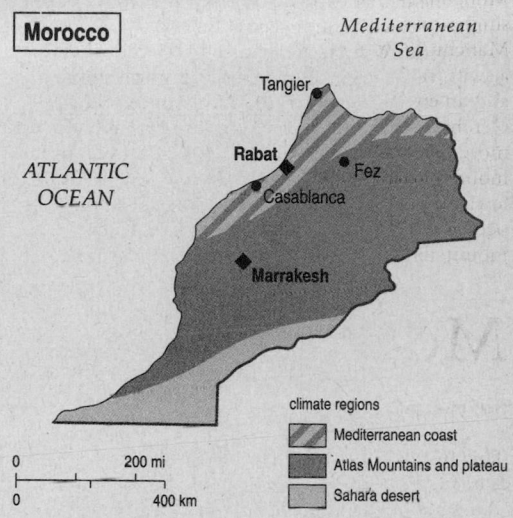

| Morocco | Mediterranean Sea |

climate regions
- Mediterranean coast
- Atlas Mountains and plateau
- Sahara desert

0 — 200 mi
0 — 400 km

coast. Rainfall increases to over 400 mm/16 in north of Casablanca. Sea and air temperatures on the Atlantic coast are kept lower than along the Mediterranean coast by the cool waters of the

RABAT

ATLANTIC MOROCCO

Sunshine	Temperatures									Discomfort from heat and humidity	Precipitation and humidity				Wet days
	Average daily				Highest recorded		Lowest recorded				Relative humidity 5:30 11:30		Average monthly precipitation		
	minimum		maximum												
average hours per day	°C	°F	°C	°F	°C	°F	°C	°F		%		mm	in	more than 0.1 mm/0.004 in
Jan	5	8	46	17	63	27	81	1	33		89	72	66	2.6	9.0	Jan
Feb	7	8	47	18	65	31	87	1	34		90	67	64	2.5	8.0	Feb
March	7	9	49	20	68	35	95	1	34		88	65	66	2.6	10.0	March
April	9	11	52	22	71	38	100	4	40		89	60	43	1.7	7.0	April
May	9	13	55	23	74	41	106	6	43	Moderate	89	61	28	1.1	6.0	May
June	10	16	60	26	78	41	105	7	45	Medium	87	60	8	0.3	2.0	June
July	11	17	63	28	82	48	118	12	53	Medium	88	59	0	0.0	0.3	July
Aug	10	18	64	28	83	45	113	10	50	Medium	91	61	0	0.0	0.3	Aug
Sept	9	17	62	27	81	44	111	8	47	Medium	92	62	10	0.4	2.0	Sept
Oct	8	14	58	25	77	39	102	7	44	Moderate	89	65	48	1.9	6.0	Oct
Nov	6	12	53	21	70	37	99	3	38		89	67	84	3.3	9.0	Nov
Dec	5	9	48	18	65	28	83	0	32		87	68	86	3.4	10.0	Dec

Based on readings for 35 years at 34°00′ N, 6°50′ W, altitude 65 m/213 ft

MARRAKESH											FOOTHILLS OF THE ATLAS MOUNTAINS		
Sunshine		Temperatures							Discomfort from heat and humidity	Precipitation and humidity			Wet days
		Average daily				Highest recorded		Lowest recorded		Relative humidity 5:30 11:30		Average monthly precipitation	
		minimum		maximum									
average hours per day		°C	°F	°C	°F	°C	°F	°C	°F	%		mm	in	more than 0.1 mm/0.004 in
Jan	7	4	40	18	65	28	83	−2	28		90	63	25	1.0	7	Jan
Feb	7	6	43	20	68	31	87	−3	27		88	58	28	1.1	5	Feb
March	8	9	48	23	74	38	100	1	33		87	53	33	1.3	6	March
April	9	11	52	26	79	39	102	2	36	Moderate	83	47	31	1.2	6	April
May	9	14	57	29	84	44	112	7	44	Medium	77	42	15	0.6	2	May
June	11	17	62	33	92	46	114	9	48	High	74	41	8	0.3	1	June
July	11	19	67	38	101	49	120	12	54	Extreme	69	36	3	0.1	1	July
Aug	11	20	68	38	100	47	117	14	57	Extreme	69	37	3	0.1	1	Aug
Sept	10	17	63	33	92	45	113	11	51	High	74	40	10	0.4	3	Sept
Oct	8	14	57	28	83	38	101	4	40	Medium	77	45	23	0.9	4	Oct
Nov	7	9	49	23	73	35	95	1	33		80	49	31	1.2	3	Nov
Dec	7	6	42	19	66	27	81	−2	29		84	57	31	1.2	7	Dec

Based on readings for 34 years at 31°36′ N, 8°01′ W, altitude 460 m/1509 ft

Canaries current. Along this coast summer temperatures are significantly cooler than inland and the cold offshore water causes some cloud and fog in summer. Winters on the Atlantic coast are very mild and snow is unknown.

The table for **Rabat** (p. 245) illustrates conditions on the Atlantic coast.

Inland in the high Atlas Mountains the weather and climate are much influenced by height. The Atlas Mountains here are at their grandest with the highest point rising to 4,163 m/13,655 ft. Winter snowfall can be heavy and the highest areas are snow-covered well into the summer. Inland at lower levels the summers are very hot, while in winter and spring winds blowing off the mountains can cause some very chilly days. At medium altitudes the climate of Morocco is healthy and very pleasant around the

year. Summers are hot but the humidity is quite low, while the winters are generally mild and sunny despite some spells of changeable weather (see the table for **Marrakesh** above).

The climate of the Saharan region of Morocco is similar to that described for Algeria on p. 31 except that in the south, where the desert reaches the coast, summer temperatures are moderated by the cool ocean waters and persistent daytime sea breezes. Here winter temperatures are also milder than inland.

Daily hours of sunshine on the Atlantic coast average nine to ten as compared with up to twelve inland in the desert. Cloud in the Atlas Mountains also reduces summer sunshine to some extent. In winter sunshine hours range from five to six a day in the north to as many as eight south of Agadir.

Mozambique

See map page 21

Mozambique is three times the size of the United Kingdom. It is situated on the east coast of southern Africa between 11° and 27° S with a coastline of over 1,900 km/1,200 mi. It is bordered on the west by Malawi, Zimbabwe, and South Africa. Although it extends outside the tropics, in the extreme south the whole country has a typically tropical climate.

The extensive coastal lowlands are warm to hot for most of the year, while the interior plateau and the hills along the border with Malawi and Zimbabwe are mild to warm even in the cooler dry season from April to September.

The warm Mozambique current flows southwards along the coast and is an important influence on the climate of the country. The whole country experiences a single rainy season at the time of high sun, when the intertropical belt of cloud and rain is farthest south.

The wettest regions are the highlands on the Malawi and Zimbabwe borders and the southeast coast between Beira and Maputo which are more exposed to the southeast trade winds throughout the year. Here annual rainfall is between 1,000 mm/40 in and 1,500 mm/60 in.

The driest areas are the lowlands inland, particularly the Zambezi valley, with between 500–750 mm/20–30 in of rainfall a year. In some places there is as little as 375 mm/15 in. In the south most of the rain falls between December and March but farther north this period lengthens by a few weeks.

The coast of northern Mozambique is occasionally affected by tropical cyclones in the Indian Ocean. These move south between Madagascar and the mainland but the majority pass east of Madagascar and hardly affect Mozambique. These cyclones bring heavy rain and strong winds which can cause extensive damage.

One reason for the comparatively low rainfall over much of the coastal lowlands is the shelter provided by the large mountainous island of Madagascar, which is fully exposed to the moist southeast trades. The eastern side of Madagascar is particularly wet as

MAPUTO										SOUTH COASTAL MOZAMBIQUE			
Sunshine		Temperatures						Discomfort from heat and humidity	Precipitation and humidity				Wet days
		Average daily		Highest recorded		Lowest recorded			Relative humidity		Average monthly precipitation		
		minimum	maximum						9:00	15:00			
average hours per day		°C °F	°C °F	°C °F		°C °F			%		mm	in	more than 1 mm/0.04 in
Jan	8	22 71	30 86	43 110		16 61		High	72	66	130	5.1	9	Jan
Feb	8	22 71	31 87	39 103		17 62		High	73	65	125	4.9	8	Feb
March	8	21 69	29 85	40 104		16 60		Medium	75	67	125	4.9	9	March
April	8	19 66	28 83	39 102		11 52		Medium	72	63	53	2.1	5	April
May	8	16 60	27 80	38 101		8 46		Medium	71	61	28	1.1	3	May
June	8	13 56	25 77	34 94		8 46		Moderate	70	57	20	0.8	2	June
July	8	13 55	24 76	36 96		7 45		Moderate	71	59	13	0.5	2	July
Aug	8	14 57	26 78	38 100		8 47		Medium	68	60	13	0.5	2	Aug
Sept	8	16 61	27 80	46 114		9 49		Medium	65	63	28	1.1	3	Sept
Oct	7	18 64	28 82	45 113		12 53		Medium	65	66	48	1.9	5	Oct
Nov	7	19 67	28 83	44 112		11 52		Medium	67	67	81	3.2	7	Nov
Dec	7	21 69	29 85	44 112		15 59		Medium	69	66	97	3.8	9	Dec

Based on readings for 42 years at 25°58′ S, 32°36′ E, altitude 59 m/194 ft

SOFALA

CENTRAL COASTAL MOZAMBIQUE

	Sunshine	Temperatures								Discomfort from heat and humidity	Precipitation and humidity				Wet days	
	average hours per day	Average daily				Highest recorded		Lowest recorded			Relative humidity 9:30 15:30		Average monthly precipitation		more than 1 mm/0.04 in	
		minimum		maximum												
		°C	°F	°C	°F	°C	°F	°C	°F		%		mm	in		
Jan	8	24	75	32	89	42	108	17	63	High	73	66	277	10.9	12	Jan
Feb	8	24	75	32	89	38	100	16	61	High	75	65	213	8.4	11	Feb
March	8	23	74	31	87	38	100	18	64	High	77	65	257	10.1	13	March
April	9	22	71	30	86	37	99	16	61	High	77	64	107	4.2	8	April
May	9	18	65	28	82	36	97	13	55	Medium	78	63	56	2.2	6	May
June	8	16	61	26	79	33	92	9	48	Medium	80	63	33	1.3	5	June
July	8	16	61	25	77	35	95	9	49	Moderate	81	65	31	1.2	4	July
Aug	9	17	62	26	78	36	96	10	50	Medium	78	66	28	1.1	3	Aug
Sept	9	18	65	28	82	39	103	13	55	Medium	73	66	20	0.8	3	Sept
Oct	9	22	71	31	87	42	107	13	56	High	68	66	132	5.2	3	Oct
Nov	8	22	72	31	87	43	109	16	61	High	68	67	135	5.3	7	Nov
Dec	8	23	73	31	88	41	106	17	63	High	70	66	234	9.2	10	Dec

Based on readings for 39 years at 19°50′ S, 34°51′ E, altitude 9 m/28 ft

TETE

INLAND MOZAMBIQUE

	Sunshine	Temperatures								Discomfort from heat and humidity	Precipitation and humidity				Wet days	
	average hours per day	Average daily				Highest recorded		Lowest recorded			Relative humidity 9:00 21:00		Average monthly precipitation		more than 1 mm/0.04 in	
		minimum		maximum												
		°C	°F	°C	°F	°C	°F	°C	°F		%		mm	in		
Jan	7	21	69	35	95	43	110	7	45	Extreme	70	58	152	6.0	8.0	Jan
Feb	7	22	71	34	94	43	109	8	46	High	73	59	163	6.4	9.0	Feb
March	8	21	69	33	91	43	109	9	48	High	72	62	117	4.6	6.0	March
April	8	20	68	34	93	43	110	11	52	High	71	54	13	0.5	1.0	April
May	9	17	63	33	91	40	104	10	50	High	72	64	3	0.1	0.9	May
June	8	15	59	30	86	39	102	7	45	High	71	66	3	0.1	0.4	June
July	8	14	57	29	84	36	97	8	46	Medium	69	65	3	0.1	0.4	July
Aug	9	16	60	31	88	40	104	9	49	High	68	61	3	0.1	0.2	Aug
Sept	9	18	64	35	95	44	111	10	50	High	63	50	0	0.0	0.4	Sept
Oct	9	21	69	38	101	45	113	10	50	Extreme	60	45	8	0.3	0.7	Oct
Nov	8	22	71	37	99	46	115	10	50	Extreme	64	50	28	1.1	2.0	Nov
Dec	7	21	70	37	98	44	111	11	52	Extreme	68	53	99	3.9	6.0	Dec

Based on readings for 12 years at 16°11′ S, 33°35′ E, altitude 139 m/456 ft

ZUMBO   NORTHWESTERN MOZAMBIQUE

	Sunshine	Temperatures								Discomfort from heat and humidity	Precipitation and humidity				Wet days	
		Average daily				Highest recorded		Lowest recorded				Relative humidity 9:00 15:00		Average monthly precipitation			
		minimum		maximum													
	average hours per day	°C	°F	°C	°F	°C	°F	°C	°F		%		mm	in	more than 1 mm/0.04 in	
Jan	6	22	71	32	90	42	107	17	63	High	79	60	208	8.2	13.0	Jan
Feb	6	22	71	32	90	40	104	17	62	High	78	58	170	6.7	9.0	Feb
March	7	21	70	33	91	40	104	12	54	High	76	51	104	4.1	6.0	March
April	8	19	67	33	91	41	106	11	52	High	69	45	3	0.1	0.9	April
May	9	15	59	32	89	38	101	7	44	Medium	65	42	0	0.0	0.3	May
June	9	13	55	28	83	36	96	6	42	Medium	65	42	0	0.0	0.0	June
July	9	13	55	28	83	35	95	3	38	Moderate	64	37	0	0.0	0.0	July
Aug	10	14	58	31	87	39	102	8	47	Medium	60	32	3	0.1	0.3	Aug
Sept	9	19	66	34	94	43	110	11	51	Medium	53	28	0	0.0	0.0	Sept
Oct	9	23	73	38	100	44	111	17	62	High	48	27	5	0.2	0.6	Oct
Nov	8	23	73	37	98	49	120	17	63	High	57	38	84	3.3	5.0	Nov
Dec	7	22	72	34	94	43	110	12	54	High	71	50	165	6.5	11.0	Dec

Based on readings for 15 years at 15°37′ S, 30°27′ E, altitude 343 m/1125 ft

compared with Mozambique. Temperatures on the coast and in some lowland regions can be rather sultry and oppressive and this is made worse by the high humidity during the rainy season.

Although the days may be hot inland at higher levels, there is a welcome drop in temperature at night and humidity is lower. Over most of Mozambique the weather is fairly sunny for much of the year with an average of between seven and nine hours of sunshine per day.

The tables for **Maputo** (p. 247) and **Sofala** (opposite and above) are representative of conditions on the coast in the drier south and in the wetter centre respectively.

The table for **Tete** (opposite) shows the higher temperatures and lower humidity found inland; also the low rainfall typical of some inland areas.

The table for **Zumbo** shows conditions in the extreme northwest of the country.

Myanmar

See map page 23

Myanmar, formerly Burma, is rather larger than France. It has a long mountain-backed coastline on the Bay of Bengal and a long eastern border with Thailand. In the north it borders India and China; this is a very mountainous region which includes part of the eastern Himalayas and the edge of the mountain plateau of Yunnan in southern China.

Much of Myanmar is mountainous with the main mountain and hill ranges running from north to south. The highest regions in the north rise to more than 5,500 m/18,000 ft but the average height of the mountains elsewhere is 1,200–2,400 m/4,000–8,000 ft. The centre of the country from north of Mandalay to the coast at Yangon is a lowland area in which flow the great rivers Irrawaddy and Salween. They rise in the high mountain region of the north where rainfall is heavy. Most of the eastern border with Thailand runs through a high plateau region when rainfall is also heavy.

Myanmar has a tropical monsoon type of climate with a marked difference between a cooler, dry season from November to April and a hotter, wet season from May until September or October. This seasonal contrast is a result of the great reversal of winds which occurs over south Asia. As in India, the dry season is dominated by the northeast monsoon blowing off the Indian Ocean. Differences of altitude within Myanmar and the degree of exposure to the rainy southwest monsoon, are responsible for the main differences of climate within the country.

The coastal mountains and the higher mountains of the north and east have abundant or heavy rainfall which ranges from 2,500 mm/100 in to 5,000 mm/200 in a year. The interior lowlands, sheltered from the direct effect of the southwest monsoon, receive as little as 1,000 mm/40 in or even less (see the table for **Mandalay** below). Over most of the country at least three-quarters of the annual rainfall occurs during the season of the southwest monsoon.

In the lowlands, and particularly on the coast, temperatures are hot throughout the year. The highest temperatures occur during the period March to May before the onset of the heaviest rains. Temperatures are lower in the hills but for most of

MANDALAY												INTERIOR LOWLAND MYANMAR		
Sunshine		Temperatures							Discomfort from heat and humidity	Precipitation and humidity				Wet days
		Average daily				Highest recorded		Lowest recorded		Relative humidity 8:00 18:00		Average monthly precipitation		
		minimum		maximum										
average hours per day		°C	°F	°C	°F	°C	°F	°C	°F	%		mm	in	more than 2.5 mm/0.1 in
Jan	9	13	55	28	82	33	91	7	45	Medium	79	52	3	0.1	0.1	Jan
Feb	9	15	59	31	88	37	99	8	47	Medium	66	41	3	0.1	0.3	Feb
March	9	19	66	36	97	42	108	12	54	High	53	31	5	0.2	0.5	March
April	9	25	77	38	101	43	110	18	64	High	55	33	31	1.2	2.0	April
May	8	26	79	37	98	44	111	21	69	Extreme	68	52	147	5.8	8.0	May
June	6	26	78	34	93	42	107	20	68	Extreme	78	64	160	6.3	7.0	June
July	5	26	78	34	93	41	106	22	72	Extreme	78	66	69	2.7	6.0	July
Aug	4	25	77	33	92	38	101	22	71	Extreme	83	72	104	4.1	8.0	Aug
Sept	6	24	76	33	91	39	103	21	69	Extreme	84	74	137	5.4	9.0	Sept
Oct	7	23	73	32	89	39	102	17	62	Extreme	83	78	109	4.3	7.0	Oct
Nov	8	19	66	29	85	37	98	13	56	High	83	74	51	2.0	3.0	Nov
Dec	9	14	57	27	80	32	90	7	44	Medium	82	66	10	0.4	0.8	Dec

Based on readings for 20 years at 21°59′ N, 96°06′ E, altitude 77 m/252 ft

LASHIO
COASTAL MYANMAR

	Sunshine	Temperatures							Discomfort from heat and humidity	Precipitation and humidity				Wet days	
	average hours per day	Average daily				Highest recorded		Lowest recorded			Relative humidity 9:00 18:00		Average monthly precipitation		more than 2.5 mm/0.1 in	
		minimum		maximum												
		°C	°F	°C	°F	°C	°F	°C	°F		%		mm	in		
Jan		8	46	23	74	26	79	2	35	Moderate	92	63	8	0.3	1	Jan
Feb		9	49	26	78	30	86	4	39	Moderate	82	51	8	0.3	1	Feb
March		13	56	30	86	34	93	8	47	Medium	70	37	15	0.6	1	March
April		17	62	32	89	37	99	12	54	Medium	69	44	56	2.2	5	April
May		19	67	31	87	37	98	14	57	High	80	62	175	6.9	12	May
June		21	70	29	84	35	95	17	62	High	86	79	249	9.8	15	June
July		21	70	28	83	33	92	18	64	High	88	81	305	12.0	27	July
Aug		21	70	28	83	31	88	17	62	High	90	84	323	12.7	19	Aug
Sept		20	68	29	84	32	89	14	58	High	91	82	198	7.8	14	Sept
Oct		18	64	28	82	31	88	11	51	High	93	82	145	5.7	10	Oct
Nov		13	56	25	77	29	85	8	47	Medium	93	83	69	2.7	5	Nov
Dec		9	49	23	73	26	79	3	38	Moderate	94	78	23	0.9	1	Dec

Based on readings for 10 years at 22°58′ N, 97°51′ E, altitude 854 m/2802 ft

SITTWE
COASTAL MYANMAR

	Sunshine	Temperatures							Discomfort from heat and humidity	Precipitation and humidity				Wet days	
	average hours per day	Average daily				Highest recorded		Lowest recorded			Relative humidity 8:30 17:30		Average monthly precipitation		more than 2.5 mm/0.1 in	
		minimum		maximum												
		°C	°F	°C	°F	°C	°F	°C	°F		%		mm	in		
Jan		15	59	27	81	34	94	8	47	Medium	80	65	3	0.1	0.1	Jan
Feb		16	61	29	84	35	95	9	49	Medium	75	65	5	0.2	0.4	Feb
March		20	68	31	88	38	100	12	54	High	77	70	10	0.4	0.7	March
April		24	75	32	90	37	99	17	62	Extreme	75	73	51	2.0	2.0	April
May		26	78	32	90	37	99	19	66	Extreme	79	77	391	15.4	11.0	May
June		25	77	30	86	37	98	20	68	High	90	87	1151	45.3	24.0	June
July		25	77	29	84	34	93	22	71	High	92	89	1400	55.1	28.0	July
Aug		25	77	29	84	33	91	22	71	High	90	88	1133	44.6	27.0	Aug
Sept		25	77	30	86	34	94	21	70	High	88	86	577	22.7	19.0	Sept
Oct		24	76	31	87	34	93	18	65	Extreme	86	82	287	11.3	9.0	Oct
Nov		22	71	29	85	33	91	16	60	High	84	79	130	5.1	4.0	Nov
Dec		17	63	27	81	32	89	11	51	Medium	84	73	18	0.7	0.7	Dec

Based on readings for 60 years at 20°08′ N, 92°55′ E, altitude 9 m/29 ft

YANGON												INTERIOR LOWLAND MYANMAR		
Sunshine	Temperatures							Discomfort from heat and humidity	Precipitation and humidity				Wet days	
	Average daily				Highest recorded		Lowest recorded		Relative humidity 9:00 18:00		Average monthly precipitation			
	minimum		maximum											
average hours per day	°C	°F	°C	°F	°C	°F	°C	°F		%		mm	in	more than 2.5 mm/0.1 in
Jan	10	18	65	32	89	38	100	13	55	High	71	52	3	0.1	0.3	Jan
Feb	10	19	67	33	92	38	101	13	56	High	72	52	5	0.2	0.3	Feb
March	10	22	71	36	96	39	103	16	61	Extreme	74	54	8	0.3	0.6	March
April	10	24	76	36	97	41	106	20	68	Extreme	71	64	51	2.0	2.0	April
May	7	25	77	33	92	41	105	21	69		80	76	307	12.1	14.0	May
June	4	24	76	30	86	37	98	22	71	High	87	85	480	18.9	23.0	June
July	3	24	76	29	85	34	93	21	70	High	89	88	582	22.9	26.0	July
Aug	3	24	76	29	85	34	93	20	68	High	89	88	528	20.8	25.0	Aug
Sept	5	24	76	30	86	34	94	22	72	High	87	86	394	15.5	20.0	Sept
Oct	6	24	76	31	88	35	95	22	71	High	83	77	180	7.1	10.0	Oct
Nov	6	23	73	31	88	35	95	16	61	High	79	72	69	2.7	3.0	Nov
Dec	8	19	67	31	88	36	96	13	55	High	75	61	10	0.4	0.6	Dec

Based on readings for 60 years at 16°46′ N, 96°11′ E, altitude 6 m/18 ft

the year the weather at places below 1,200 m/4,000 ft can be described as hot and tropical. The table for **Lashio** (p. 251) is representative of places inland at medium heights. On the coast the high temperatures are rendered more unpleasant because of high humidity. Even inland the heat is oppressive during the rainy season for the same reason (see the table for **Mandalay** on p. 250).

The dry season is distinctly cooler and more pleasant in the interior and particularly in the north of the country where increasing altitude lowers the temperature. The period from November to April is distinctly dry over the whole country. At this time,

when the country is dominated by the dry northeast monsoon, sunshine amounts are high, averaging from seven to ten hours a day. During the rainy season the weather is much more cloudy and from June to September daily sunshine amounts average only three to four hours a day.

Climatic conditions on the wettest parts of the coast are illustrated by the table for **Sittwe** (p. 251). The table for **Yangon** (above) shows that here, on the delta of the Irrawaddy where – formerly Rangoon – the coast runs from west to east and is low-lying, rainfall is less but temperature and humidity remain high throughout the year.

Namibia

See map page 21

Namibia is a large country almost two-thirds the size of South Africa. It is bordered by Angola on the north, Botswana on the east, and South Africa on the south. It is very sparsely populated and most of it is desert or semi-desert.

The entire coast, part of the Namib desert shared with the west coast of South Africa, receives very

little rain and is a complete desert. The table for **Walvis Bay** (opposite and above) is representative of this area.

Temperatures are kept low most of the time by the cold Benguela current. On a few days each month, particularly in winter, midday temperatures rise quite high when the berg wind blows from the interior. This is a föhn-type wind bringing very dry air which is heated as it descends to the coast. Apart

WALVIS BAY
COASTAL NAMIBIA

	Sunshine	Temperatures								Discomfort from heat and humidity	Precipitation and humidity				Wet days
		Average daily				Highest recorded		Lowest recorded			Relative humidity 7:30 14:00		Average monthly precipitation		
		minimum		maximum											
	average hours per day	°C	°F	°C	°F	°C	°F	°C	°F		%		mm	in	more than 0.25 mm/0.01 in
Jan	7	15	59	23	73	38	100	7	45	Moderate	91	73	0	0.0	1.0	Jan
Feb	7	16	60	23	74	36	97	7	45	Moderate	92	73	5	0.2	1.0	Feb
March	7	15	59	23	74	36	97	7	45	Moderate	95	74	8	0.3	2.0	March
April	8	13	55	24	75	39	103	6	43	Moderate	89	66	3	0.1	1.0	April
May	8	11	52	23	74	40	104	2	35	Moderate	88	68	3	0.1	1.0	May
June	8	9	48	23	74	36	97	2	35	Moderate	78	64	0	0.0	0.8	June
July	8	8	47	21	70	37	98	-4	25		83	65	0	0.0	1.0	July
Aug	7	8	46	20	68	37	99	1	34		89	73	3	0.1	3.0	Aug
Sept	6	9	48	19	66	38	100	0	32		90	69	0	0.0	2.0	Sept
Oct	7	11	51	19	67	36	97	0	32		91	72	0	0.0	1.0	Oct
Nov	7	12	54	22	71	35	95	6	43		90	71	0	0.0	1.0	Nov
Dec	7	14	57	22	72	33	91	7	45		90	72	0	0.0	1.0	Dec

Based on readings for 20 years at 22°56′ S, 14°30′ E, altitude 7 m/24 ft

WINDHOEK
INLAND NAMIBIA

	Sunshine	Temperatures								Discomfort from heat and humidity	Precipitation and humidity				Wet days
		Average daily				Highest recorded		Lowest recorded			Relative humidity 8:00 14:00		Average monthly precipitation		
		minimum		maximum											
	average hours per day	°C	°F	°C	°F	°C	°F	°C	°F		%		mm	in	more than 1 mm/0.04 in
Jan	9	17	63	29	85	36	97	9	49	Moderate	50	27	76	3.0	8.0	Jan
Feb	9	16	61	28	83	34	94	7	44	Moderate	62	35	74	2.9	8.0	Feb
March	8	15	59	27	80	34	94	4	39	Moderate	59	33	79	3.1	8.0	March
April	9	13	55	25	77	31	87	2	36		55	30	41	1.6	4.0	April
May	10	9	48	22	72	32	89	-2	29		51	24	8	0.3	0.9	May
June	10	7	44	20	68	26	79	-3	27		50	24	0	0.0	0.3	June
July	10	6	43	20	68	25	77	-3	27		42	18	0	0.0	0.1	July
Aug	11	8	47	23	73	29	85	-4	25		34	14	0	0.0	0.1	Aug
Sept	10	12	53	25	77	33	91	-1	31		28	11	3	0.1	0.3	Sept
Oct	10	15	59	29	84	34	93	2	35	Moderate	27	13	10	0.4	2.0	Oct
Nov	10	15	59	29	84	36	96	1	33	Moderate	34	18	23	0.9	3.0	Nov
Dec	10	17	62	30	86	36	97	3	38	Moderate	41	23	48	1.9	6.0	Dec

Based on readings for 30 years at 22°34′ S, 17°06′ E, altitude 1728 m/5669 ft

from the rare shower of rain and the frequent coastal fog, the berg is almost the only weather feature of this arid coastal region.

The interior as well is marked by low rainfall and much of it is semi-desert or desert. It receives some scanty but unreliable summer rain which increases eastwards and northwards. Like most interior deserts, Namibia's has a very sunny climate but, on the coast, cloud and fog reduce the sunshine.

The table for **Windhoek** (p. 253) is representative of the higher parts of the interior where much land is above 900 m/3,000 ft.

Nauru

See map page 17

This island republic lies next to the equator in the southwest Pacific. Geographically one of the Gilbert islands, it has an area of just 21 sq km/8 sq mi.

Very similar conditions prevail throughout the year in this typical tropical oceanic climate with high temperatures and humidity. There is abundant rainfall with occasional droughts. Being near the equator, Nauru has rainfall that is more evenly spread throughout the year than in neighbouring countries to the north and south and the country never experiences tropical cyclones.

The island has moderately large amounts of sunshine, averaging between six and eight hours a day in spite of a large number of days on which some rain falls. Much of the rainfall is in the form of short, heavy showers.

The table for **Yaren** (opposite), the capital of Nauru, shows weather typical of the island.

Nepal

See map page 23

This small, mountainous country lies on the southern side of the Himalayan mountains between Tibet to the north and India to the south. It includes within, or along its northern border, some of the highest mountains in the world; Everest rises to 8,848 m/29,028 ft. The country is only between 160 km/100 mi and 240 km/150 mi wide from north to south and in this distance the altitude decreases from the high Himalayan peaks to the lowlands of the Terai in the plain region of northern India. There is thus in Nepal a range of climatic conditions from tropical forest or jungle to the permanent snowfields and glaciers of the Himalayas.

The weather and climate are controlled by the same general features as those described on p. 174 for India: the seasonal alternation of the monsoon winds. The main rainy season in Nepal is from late June to September. This is a period of warm to hot temperatures, much cloud, and frequent heavy rain. At this time sunshine averages only two to three hours a day. During the rest of the year the weather is much more settled and pleasant. The days are mild or even warm, except on the higher mountains, and sunshine averages from six to nine hours a day.

The table for **Kathmandu** (opposite) illustrates conditions in the valleys and in the Himalayan foothill region where the majority of the population live. Rainfall in Nepal decreases from east to west so that the tables for **Darjeeling** and **Simla** (both on p. 176) in India are representative of the east and west of the country respectively. They also indicate better than the table for Kathmandu the likely temperature conditions in the more highly populated regions of Nepal.

Apart from some danger of flooding during the heaviest rains, the climate of Nepal is rarely hazardous and for much of the year is very pleasant.

YAREN

NAURU

	Sunshine	Temperatures								Discomfort from heat and humidity	Precipitation and humidity				Wet days	
		Average daily				Highest recorded		Lowest recorded			Relative humidity 9:00 14:00		Average monthly precipitation			
		minimum		maximum												
	average hours per day	°C	°F	°C	°F	°C	°F	°C	°F		%		mm	in	more than 2.5 mm/0.1 in	
Jan	6	23	74	31	88	34	94	20	68	High	75	74	315	12.4	15	Jan
Feb	5	24	75	31	88	34	93	19	66	High	75	73	206	8.1	11	Feb
March	5	24	75	32	89	34	94	21	69	Extreme	74	73	180	7.1	9	March
April	6	24	75	32	90	34	94	21	69	High	72	71	94	3.7	6	April
May	7	24	75	32	90	35	95	20	68	High	71	70	53	2.1	5	May
June	6	23	74	32	90	34	94	19	66	High	71	70	99	3.9	8	June
July	6	23	74	32	89	34	94	21	69	High	72	71	155	6.1	11	July
Aug	5	23	74	32	89	34	94	19	66	High	70	69	193	7.6	10	Aug
Sept	7	24	75	32	90	35	95	19	66	High	69	68	122	4.8	6	Sept
Oct	6	23	74	32	90	34	94	17	63	High	68	68	99	3.9	5	Oct
Nov	6	23	74	32	90	35	95	19	67	High	70	69	152	6.0	7	Nov
Dec	6	23	74	32	89	34	94	19	67	High	73	71	239	9.4	13	Dec

Based on readings for 15 years at 0°32' S, 167°03' E, altitude 27 m/87 ft

KATHMANDU

HIMALAYAN FOOTHILLS

	Sunshine	Temperatures								Discomfort from heat and humidity	Precipitation and humidity				Wet days	
		Average daily				Highest recorded		Lowest recorded			Relative humidity 8:00 17:00		Average monthly precipitation			
		minimum		maximum												
	average hours per day	°C	°F	°C	°F	°C	°F	°C	°F		%		mm	in	more than 2.5 mm/0.1 in	
Jan	6	2	35	18	65	25	77	-2	28		89	70	15	0.6	1.0	Jan
Feb	6	4	39	19	67	25	77	-1	31		90	68	41	1.6	5.0	Feb
March	8	7	45	25	77	33	92	2	35	Moderate	73	53	23	0.9	2.0	March
April	6	12	53	28	83	35	95	4	40	Medium	68	54	58	2.3	6.0	April
May	5	16	61	30	86	36	96	10	50	High	72	61	122	4.8	10.0	May
June	2	19	67	29	85	36	97	14	58	High	79	72	246	9.7	15.0	June
July	2	20	68	29	84	33	91	18	64	High	86	82	373	14.7	21.0	July
Aug	3	20	68	28	83	33	92	17	63	High	87	84	345	13.6	20.0	Aug
Sept	5	19	66	28	83	33	92	13	56	High	86	83	155	6.1	12.0	Sept
Oct	10	13	56	27	80	33	92	6	43	Medium	88	81	38	1.5	4.0	Oct
Nov	10	7	45	23	74	28	83	-1	31	Moderate	90	78	8	0.3	1.0	Nov
Dec	9	3	37	19	67	24	76	-2	29		89	73	3	0.1	0.2	Dec

Based on readings for 9 years at 27°42' N, 85°12' E, altitude 1338 m/4388 ft

Netherlands

See map page 18

The Netherlands, often known as Holland, is a small country with a long coastline on the North Sea. The greater part of the country is low-lying and does not rise more than 30 m/100 ft above sea level. Substantial portions of the provinces of north and south Holland, the offshore islands in the mouth of the Scheldt, and the West Frisian Islands are near, or below, sea level. These areas have been reclaimed from the sea over the centuries. A small area in the southern province of Limburg rises above 300 m/1,000 ft. Proximity to the sea, low elevation, and the presence of numerous sluggish rivers and canals impose a uniformity on the climate of the country so there are very small differences from place to place.

The coastal regions have the mildest climate throughout the year (see the table for **Vlissingen** opposite) and the lowest rainfall. In summer the slightly higher midday temperatures are more likely to produce thunderstorms accompanied by heavy showers. Climatic conditions inland are best shown by the table for **De Bilt** (opposite and below) near Utrecht, which is representative of the densely populated area between Rotterdam and Amsterdam.

As in most countries in northwestern Europe, the weather in the Netherlands can be very changeable from day to day at all times of the year and the character of each season may vary from one year to another. During winter spells of cold weather, lasting from one week to two months or more, rivers and canals may freeze. In mild winters this may not occur at all. In summer fine, hot weather may last for some weeks on occasions but the weather may also be cool and unsettled. Rainfall is well distributed over the year, but tends to fall on fewer days in summer and to be heavier. Average daily sunshine amounts range from about two hours in January to between seven and eight hours in June.

Gales are quite frequent on the coast, particularly in autumn and winter. The flat countryside makes the Netherlands a rather windy place at all times of the year. In the past this aspect of the weather was fully utilized by the Dutch, who built numerous windmills to pump water from the low-lying land reclaimed from the sea and the rivers.

On rare occasions in the past severe northerly gales have whipped up storm waves and a tidal surge in the North Sea sufficiently high to batter and breach the coastal dykes. This last flood occurred in January 1953 with disastrous consequences, inundating land below sea level and causing great loss of life.

Except during prolonged cold spells in winter, the weather in the Netherlands is rarely unpleasant or uncomfortable. When it does freeze, many people indulge in the traditional Dutch winter sport of skating on the numerous canals.

VLISSINGEN — COASTAL NETHERLANDS

	Sunshine average hours per day	Temperatures Average daily minimum °C	°F	maximum °C	°F	Highest recorded °C	°F	Lowest recorded °C	°F	Discomfort from heat and humidity	Relative humidity 7:00 %	13:00 %	Average monthly precipitation mm	in	Wet days more than 0.1mm/0.004in	
Jan	2	1	34	5	41	13	55	-15	6		89	82	62	2.4	20	Jan
Feb	2	1	33	5	41	17	62	-20	-3		87	80	45	1.8	17	Feb
March	4	3	37	9	47	20	69	-6	21		87	72	40	1.6	16	March
April	6	5	42	12	53	26	79	-2	28	Moderate	81	67	41	1.6	15	April
May	7	9	48	16	61	30	85	1	34		78	65	42	1.7	13	May
June	7	12	54	19	66	33	91	4	40		78	66	50	2.0	12	June
July	7	14	57	21	69	34	93	6	43		81	68	71	2.8	15	July
Aug	6	14	58	21	70	33	92	7	45		82	68	65	2.6	15	Aug
Sept	5	13	55	19	66	33	91	5	40		84	69	73	2.9	16	Sept
Oct	3	9	48	14	57	26	79	-3	27		87	74	70	2.8	19	Oct
Nov	2	5	41	9	49	17	63	-5	23		89	82	72	2.8	20	Nov
Dec	1	2	36	6	43	15	58	-14	8		89	85	58	2.3	20	Dec

Based on readings for 30 years at 51°28′ N, 3°35′ E, altitude 1 m/3 ft

DE BILT — INLAND NETHERLANDS

	Sunshine average hours per day	Temperatures Average daily minimum °C	°F	maximum °C	°F	Highest recorded °C	°F	Lowest recorded °C	°F	Discomfort from heat and humidity	Relative humidity 7:30 %	13:30 %	Average monthly precipitation mm	in	Wet days more than 0.1mm/0.004in	
Jan	2	-1	31	4	40	13	55	-25	-13		90	82	68	2.7	22	Jan
Feb	2	-1	31	5	42	17	63	-22	-7		90	76	53	2.1	19	Feb
March	4	1	34	10	49	21	71	-12	11		86	65	44	1.7	16	March
April	5	4	40	13	56	26	79	-4	24		79	61	49	1.9	16	April
May	7	8	46	18	64	32	90	-3	27		75	59	52	2.1	14	May
June	7	11	51	21	70	37	98	1	33		75	59	58	2.3	14	June
July	6	13	55	22	72	34	93	4	40		79	64	77	3.0	17	July
Aug	6	13	55	22	71	35	94	4	39		82	65	87	3.4	18	Aug
Sept	5	10	50	19	67	34	94	0	32		86	67	72	2.8	19	Sept
Oct	3	7	44	14	57	26	78	-8	18		90	72	72	2.8	20	Oct
Nov	2	3	38	9	48	18	64	-8	18		92	81	70	2.8	21	Nov
Dec	1	1	33	5	42	14	58	-15	4		91	85	64	2.5	21	Dec

Based on readings for 30 years at 52°06′ N, 5°11′ E, altitude 3 m/10 ft

WILLEMSTAD												CURAÇAO ISLAND		
Sunshine		Temperatures							Discomfort from heat and humidity	Precipitation and humidity				Wet days	
		Average daily				Highest recorded		Lowest recorded			Relative humidity 8:30 14:30		Average monthly precipitation		
average hours per day		minimum		maximum										more than 1 mm/0.04 in	
		°C	°F	°C	°F	°C	°F	°C	°F		%		mm	in	
Jan	8	24	75	28	83	31	87	20	68	Medium	77	69	53	2.1	14	Jan
Feb	9	23	74	29	84	33	91	19	66	Medium	78	68	25	1.0	8	Feb
March	9	23	74	29	84	32	90	17	63	Medium	76	66	20	0.8	7	March
April	8	24	76	30	86	33	91	20	68	High	76	67	28	1.1	4	April
May	7	25	77	30	86	36	96	21	70	High	76	68	20	0.8	4	May
June	8	26	78	31	87	34	94	22	71	High	76	68	25	1.0	7	June
July	9	25	77	31	87	34	94	22	72	High	77	68	38	1.5	9	July
Aug	9	26	78	31	88	35	95	22	71	High	77	67	31	1.2	8	Aug
Sept	9	26	78	32	89	36	96	22	71	High	77	67	28	1.1	6	Sept
Oct	8	26	78	31	88	34	94	21	70	High	77	70	107	4.2	9	Oct
Nov	8	24	76	30	86	33	92	20	68	High	79	72	112	4.4	15	Nov
Dec	7	24	75	29	84	33	91	21	69	High	78	71	99	3.9	16	Dec

Based on readings for 24 years at 12°06′ N, 68°56′ W, altitude 23 m/75 ft

Netherlands Antilles

See map page 15

The Netherlands Antilles consist of two distinct groups which are, politically, an integral part of the Netherlands. Close to the coast of Venezuela in 12° to 13° N, the three islands of Curaçao, Aruba, and Bonaire have a total land area of about 940 sq km/360 sq mi. Another group of three very small islands with an area of 68 sq km/26 sq mi lies east of Puerto Rico in 18° N. The larger southern islands have a dry climate for this latitude and the climatic conditions throughout the year are represented by the table for **Willemstad** (above) on the island of Curaçao. The islands share this relative aridity with the narrow coastal strip of northern Venezuela described on p. 417.

Temperature and humidity in both groups of islands are typical of the Caribbean area. But the northern group of tiny islands has similar weather throughout the year to that described for the Caribbean Islands in general on pp. 92–3.

NOUMEA														SOUTHWESTERN NEW CALEDONIA		
Sunshine	Temperatures								Discomfort from heat and humidity	Precipitation and humidity					Wet days	
	Average daily				Highest recorded		Lowest recorded			Relative humidity 9:00 15:00		Average monthly precipitation				
	minimum		maximum													
average hours per day	°C	°F	°C	°F	°C	°F	°C	°F		%		mm	in		more than 0.25 mm/0.01 in	
Jan	8	22	72	30	86	36	97	18	64	High	72	70	94	3.7	10	Jan
Feb	8	23	73	29	85	37	99	18	64	High	75	72	130	5.1	12	Feb
March	7	22	72	29	85	35	95	17	63	High	76	73	145	5.7	16	March
April	7	21	70	28	83	36	96	16	61	Medium	77	74	132	5.2	13	April
May	6	19	66	26	79	33	91	13	56	Medium	75	71	112	4.4	15	May
June	6	18	64	25	77	32	89	13	55	Medium	76	70	94	3.7	13	June
July	6	17	62	24	76	31	87	11	52	Moderate	76	69	91	3.6	13	July
Aug	7	16	61	24	76	29	85	12	54	Moderate	72	68	66	2.6	12	Aug
Sept	7	17	63	26	78	32	90	13	55	Medium	70	67	64	2.5	8	Sept
Oct	9	18	65	27	80	34	93	13	56	Medium	68	66	51	2.0	7	Oct
Nov	8	20	68	28	83	34	94	16	60	Medium	69	67	61	2.4	7	Nov
Dec	8	21	70	30	86	37	98	17	63	High	70	68	66	2.6	6	Dec

Based on readings for 22 years at 22°16′ S, 166°27′ E, altitude 9 m/30 ft

New Caledonia

See map page 17

This overseas territory of France centres on the large and mountainous island which gives its name to the whole, but also includes several smaller islands in the Chesterfield and Loyalty groups.

The territory shares with others in the western Pacific near the equator the features of a tropical oceanic climate. Very similar conditions prevail throughout the year with high temperatures and humidity. The daily range of temperature is quite small – about 4°–5° C/10° F. There is abundant rainfall. Being south of the equator, New Caledonia has its season of maximum rainfall between November and April. On some islands there is no great difference between the amount of rain from month to month. Tropical cyclones are less frequent than in the Pacific north of the equator.

Except in the wettest places, where cloud is more frequent, the country has moderately large amounts of sunshine, averaging from six to eight hours a day. Much of the rainfall comes in short, heavy showers, often after a sunny morning, but longer periods of heavy rain lasting a day or so occur in the wetter months.

In this area of the Pacific the principal difference in the weather and climate is the amount of rainfall per month. Temperature and humidity are very similar from one island to another but the amount of rainfall varies with altitude and with exposure of the coast to the dominant southeast trade winds. The number of wet days varies from island to island much less than the amount of rain does.

The climate may generally be described as pleasant and healthy, although the combination of high temperature and humidity can be a little oppressive when not tempered by sea breezes or a brisk wind.

The climatic table for **Nouméa** (above), on the western coast of New Caledonia, shows the rather less wet weather that is typical of places in the southwestern Pacific that are protected from the prevailing southeast trade winds.

New Zealand

See map page 17

New Zealand consists of two main islands – North and South – together with some small offshore islands. It is situated between 34° and 47° S in the South Pacific and has an area a little larger than the United Kingdom.

Situated 1,900 km/1,200 mi from the nearest large land mass, in the belt of disturbed westerly winds, it has a very equable maritime climate more like that of western Britain than that of Portugal, with which it can be compared in latitude.

Weather in New Zealand is very changeable throughout the year and all months are moderately wet. Fine sunny spells of weather can occur at any time of year, however, and the country has more sunshine than might be expected in such a variable climate. Daily hours of sunshine average from between four to five in winter to six or seven in summer in most parts of New Zealand. The north of the country and the east coasts are rather more sunny than the extreme south and the wetter west coast of South Island.

Both North and South Islands are hilly and mountainous. The western coast of South Island is backed by the high New Zealand Alps with Mount Cook, the highest peak the range, rising to more than 3,700 m/12,000 ft. There are several volcanic peaks in North Island, some rising above 2,400 m/8,000 ft.

These higher mountains carry snow throughout the year. In the New Zealand Alps there are extensive snowfields and glaciers as precipitation on the western side of South Island is heavy; as much as 2,000–2,500 mm/ 80–100 in and over 5,000 mm/200 in falls in the mountains each year.

Snow can occur almost anywhere at sea level in New Zealand but is very rare in the extreme north of North Island. Here the climate is almost subtropical with very mild winters and warm, humid, summers. The table for **Auckland** (below) is representative of this, the warmest part of the country.

The tables for **Wellington** (opposite) and **Napier** (opposite and below) show that temperatures are only a little lower elsewhere in North Island, where

AUCKLAND													NORTH ISLAND	
Sunshine		Temperatures							Discomfort from heat and humidity	Precipitation and humidity				Wet days
		Average daily				Highest recorded		Lowest recorded		Relative humidity		Average monthly precipitation		
		minimum		maximum						9:00	15:00			
average hours per day		°C	°F	°C	°F	°C	°F	°C	°F		%	mm	in	more than 0.25 mm/0.01 in
Jan	7	16	60	23	73	32	90	7	45	Moderate	71	62	79	3.1	10	Jan
Feb	7	16	60	23	73	32	90	8	47	Moderate	72	61	94	3.7	10	Feb
March	6	15	59	22	71	30	86	6	42		74	65	81	3.2	11	March
April	5	13	56	19	67	27	81	4	39		78	69	97	3.8	14	April
May	4	11	51	17	62	23	73	2	36		80	70	127	5.0	19	May
June	4	9	48	14	58	21	70	2	35		83	73	137	5.4	19	June
July	4	8	46	13	56	19	67	1	33		84	74	145	5.7	21	July
Aug	5	8	46	14	58	19	67	1	34		80	70	117	4.6	19	Aug
Sept	5	9	49	16	60	22	71	1	34		76	68	102	4.0	17	Sept
Oct	6	11	52	17	63	24	75	2	36		74	66	102	4.0	16	Oct
Nov	7	12	54	19	66	27	81	5	41		71	64	89	3.5	15	Nov
Dec	7	14	57	21	70	32	89	6	43		70	64	79	3.1	12	Dec

Based on readings for 36 years at 36°47′ S, 174°39′ E, altitude 26 m/85 ft

WELLINGTON
NORTH ISLAND

	Sunshine	Temperatures								Discomfort from heat and humidity	Precipitation and humidity				Wet days	
	average hours per day	Average daily				Highest recorded		Lowest recorded			Relative humidity 9:00 15:00		Average monthly precipitation		more than 0.25mm/0.01 in	
		minimum		maximum												
		°C	°F	°C	°F	°C	°F	°C	°F		%		mm	in		
Jan	8	13	56	21	69	29	85	4	39		73	67	81	3.2	10	Jan
Feb	7	13	56	21	69	31	88	5	41		75	71	81	3.2	9	Feb
March	6	12	54	19	67	27	81	4	39		76	69	81	3.2	11	March
April	5	11	51	17	63	23	74	2	36		79	76	97	3.8	13	April
May	4	8	47	14	58	22	71	0	32		80	77	117	4.6	16	May
June	4	7	44	13	55	21	69	-1	30		81	78	117	4.6	17	June
July	3	6	42	12	53	19	66	-2	29		81	76	137	5.4	18	July
Aug	4	6	43	12	54	19	66	-2	29		80	74	117	4.6	17	Aug
Sept	5	8	46	14	57	21	69	-1	31		76	75	97	3.8	15	Sept
Oct	6	9	48	16	60	24	75	1	34		75	74	102	4.0	14	Oct
Nov	7	10	50	17	63	27	81	2	36		76	69	89	3.5	13	Nov
Dec	7	12	54	19	67	28	83	3	38		74	69	89	3.5	12	Dec

Based on readings for 65 years at 41°16′ S, 174°46′ E, altitude 127 m/415 ft

NAPIER
NORTH ISLAND

	Sunshine	Temperatures								Discomfort from heat and humidity	Precipitation and humidity				Wet days	
	average hours per day	Average daily				Highest recorded		Lowest recorded			Relative humidity 9:30 15:30		Average monthly precipitation		more than 0.25mm/0.01 in	
		minimum		maximum												
		°C	°F	°C	°F	°C	°F	°C	°F		%		mm	in		
Jan	8	14	57	24	75	34	94	5	41	Moderate	63	60	74	2.9	8	Jan
Feb	7	14	57	23	74	34	94	3	38	Moderate	71	60	76	3.0	8	Feb
March	7	13	55	22	71	32	89	4	39		77	69	74	2.9	8	March
April	5	10	50	19	67	29	84	-1	31		80	68	76	3.0	8	April
May	5	8	47	17	62	25	77	-1	31		81	68	89	3.5	10	May
June	5	5	41	14	57	27	81	-2	29		80	68	86	3.4	11	June
July	5	5	41	13	56	22	71	-3	27		83	70	102	4.0	12	July
Aug	5	6	42	14	58	22	71	-3	27		77	69	84	3.3	12	Aug
Sept	6	7	45	17	62	27	80	-1	31		73	68	56	2.2	10	Sept
Oct	7	9	49	19	66	27	81	-1	31		68	63	56	2.2	9	Oct
Nov	7	11	51	21	69	32	89	2	35		67	61	61	2.4	9	Nov
Dec	8	13	55	23	73	34	93	3	38	Moderate	65	61	58	2.3	8	Dec

Based on readings for 34 years at 39°29′ S, 176°55′ E, altitude 2 m/5 ft

CHRISTCHURCH
SOUTH ISLAND

Sunshine	Temperatures								Discomfort from heat and humidity	Precipitation and humidity				Wet days
	Average daily				Highest recorded		Lowest recorded			Relative humidity 9:00 14:30		Average monthly precipitation		
	minimum		maximum											
average hours per day	°C	°F	°C	°F	°C	°F	°C	°F		%		mm	in	more than 0.25 mm/0.01 in
Jan	7	12	53	21	70	35	96	1	34		65	59	56	2.2	10	Jan
Feb	7	12	53	21	69	34	94	2	35		71	60	43	1.7	8	Feb
March	5	10	50	19	66	32	90	-1	30		75	69	48	1.9	9	March
April	5	7	45	17	62	28	82	-3	26		82	71	48	1.9	10	April
May	4	4	40	13	56	26	78	-6	21		85	69	66	2.6	12	May
June	4	2	36	11	51	21	69	-6	22		87	72	66	2.6	13	June
July	4	2	35	10	50	21	70	-5	23		87	76	69	2.7	13	July
Aug	5	2	36	11	52	21	70	-5	23		81	66	48	1.9	11	Aug
Sept	5	4	40	14	57	27	81	-5	23		72	69	46	1.8	10	Sept
Oct	6	7	44	17	62	31	88	-3	26		63	60	43	1.7	10	Oct
Nov	7	8	47	19	66	32	90	-1	31		64	64	48	1.9	10	Nov
Dec	7	11	51	21	69	33	92	1	33		67	60	56	2.2	10	Dec

Based on readings for 52 years at 43°32′ S, 172°37′ E, altitude 10 m/32 ft

DUNEDIN
SOUTH ISLAND

Sunshine	Temperatures								Discomfort from heat and humidity	Precipitation and humidity				Wet days
	Average daily				Highest recorded		Lowest recorded			Relative humidity 9:00 15:00		Average monthly precipitation		
	minimum		maximum											
average hours per day	°C	°F	°C	°F	°C	°F	°C	°F		%		mm	in	more than 0.25 mm/0.01 in
Jan	6	10	50	19	66	34	94	2	36		69	68	86	3.4	14	Jan
Feb	6	10	50	19	66	32	90	3	37		71	68	71	2.8	11	Feb
March	5	9	48	17	63	29	85	1	34		74	70	76	3.0	13	March
April	5	7	45	15	59	29	85	-1	31		77	71	71	2.8	13	April
May	4	5	41	12	53	22	72	-2	29		76	76	81	3.2	14	May
June	3	4	39	9	49	20	68	-4	24		77	76	81	3.2	13	June
July	4	3	37	9	48	19	66	-5	23		77	74	79	3.1	13	July
Aug	4	3	38	11	51	21	70	-4	25		73	73	76	3.0	13	Aug
Sept	5	5	41	13	55	25	77	-2	29		71	70	69	2.7	14	Sept
Oct	5	6	42	15	59	28	83	-1	30		67	69	76	3.0	14	Oct
Nov	6	7	45	17	62	29	85	0	32		68	69	81	3.2	14	Nov
Dec	6	9	48	18	65	31	88	2	35		73	71	89	3.5	15	Dec

Based on readings for 77 years at 45°52′ S, 170°32′ E, altitude 73 m/240 ft

HOKITIKA   SOUTH ISLAND

	Sunshine	Temperatures								Discomfort from heat and humidity	Precipitation and humidity			Wet days
	average hours per day	Average daily				Highest recorded		Lowest recorded			Relative humidity 9:00	Average monthly precipitation		more than 0.25 mm/0.01 in
		minimum		maximum										
		°C	°F	°C	°F	°C	°F	°C	°F		%	mm	in	
Jan	7	12	53	19	66	26	79	2	35		80	262	10.3	14	Jan
Feb	6	12	53	19	67	29	84	3	37		80	191	7.5	12	Feb
March	5	11	51	18	65	29	84	2	35		83	239	9.4	14	March
April	5	8	47	16	61	23	74	-1	31		87	236	9.3	15	April
May	4	6	42	14	57	22	72	-2	28		87	244	9.6	15	May
June	4	3	38	12	53	18	64	-3	26		88	231	9.1	15	June
July	4	3	37	12	53	18	65	-4	25		86	218	8.6	16	July
Aug	5	3	38	12	54	19	67	-3	26		84	239	9.4	16	Aug
Sept	5	6	42	13	56	20	68	-3	27		80	226	8.9	17	Sept
Oct	5	8	46	15	59	23	74	-1	30		78	292	11.5	19	Oct
Nov	6	9	48	16	61	23	74	0	32		78	267	10.5	18	Nov
Dec	7	11	51	18	64	26	79	1	33		80	262	10.3	16	Dec

Based on readings for 42 years at 42°43′ S, 170°58′ E, altitude 4 m/12 ft

frost is very rare on the coast but can be quite frequent inland.

The tables for **Christchurch** (opposite and above), **Dunedin** (opposite), and **Hokitika** (above) all in South Island show that temperatures there are a little lower throughout the year. Extremes of heat and cold, however, are very rare in New Zealand, thanks to the dominant influence of the ocean.

Hokitika on the west coast is much wetter in all months than Christchurch or Dunedin. The table for Christchurch is representative of the Canterbury Plains, the driest part of the country, but inland winter temperatures are rather lower and frost more

frequent. The lowlands to the east of the New Zealand Alps are often affected by a warm, very dry wind which suddenly raises the temperature for a few hours or a day or so. This is a föhn-type wind and occurs when strong westerly winds crossing the mountains are warmed as the air descends on the lee side. The wind melts snow in winter but can desiccate crops in summer.

New Zealand as a whole has a very healthy and pleasant climate with few weather hazards. The combination of weather, altitude, and scenery provide excellent opportunities for a range of sport and outdoor activities.

MANAGUA										PACIFIC-LOWLAND NICARAGUA	
Sunshine		Temperatures						Discomfort from heat and humidity	Precipitation and humidity		Wet days
average hours per day		Average daily		Highest recorded		Lowest recorded			Relative humidity	Average monthly precipitation	more than 1 mm/0.04 in
		minimum	maximum								
		°C	°F	°C	°F	°C	°F	°C	°F	%	mm	in	
Jan	7	20	68	31	88						5	0.2	3	Jan
Feb	8	21	70	32	90						1	0.0	1	Feb
March	8	22	72	34	93						5	0.2	1	March
April	7	23	73	34	93						5	0.2	1	April
May	6	23	73	34	93						76	3.0	6	May
June	4	23	73	31	88						296	11.7	21	June
July	5	22	72	31	88						134	5.3	20	July
Aug	6	22	72	31	88						130	5.1	17	Aug
Sept	6	22	72	31	88						182	7.2	20	Sept
Oct	6	22	72	31	88						243	9.6	19	Oct
Nov	7	21	70	31	88						59	2.3	10	Nov
Dec	6	20	68	31	88						5	0.2	2	Dec

Based on readings for 10 years at 12°08′ N, 86°11′ W, altitude 56 m/184 ft

Nicaragua

See map page 14

Nicaragua is the largest of the seven countries of Central America whose weather and climate are described in more detail for Panama on pp. 278–80. Nicaragua is about as large as England or the state of Michigan and is situated between 11° and 15° N. It is not quite as mountainous as some countries of this region but there are mountains rising to between 1,500–2,100 m/5,000–7,000 ft. Most of the country is thus included in the two zones of the *tierra caliente*, the hot tropical lowland, and the *tierra templada*, the cooler hill region with a larger daily range of temperature.

The table for **Managua** (above), the capital, is representative of conditions at low levels on the Pacific side of the country.

There are very few reliable climatic statistics for the whole country; but, as a general guide, it can be assumed that the table for **San José** (p. 115) in Costa Rica is representative of the cooler *tierra templada* in Nicaragua. The Caribbean coast would be similar to that shown by the table for **Belize City** (p. 62) in Belize as regards temperature. The east coast of Nicaragua, however, is one of the wettest parts of Central America with an annual rainfall of between 2,500–3,750 mm/100–150 in.

NIAMEY											SOUTHERN NIGER		
Sunshine		Temperatures								Discomfort from heat and humidity	Precipitation and humidity				Wet days
		Average daily				Highest recorded		Lowest recorded			Relative humidity		Average monthly precipitation		
		minimum		maximum							6:00 12:00				
average hours per day		°C	°F	°C	°F	°C	°F	°C	°F		%		mm	in	more than 1 mm/0.04 in
Jan	9	14	58	34	93	39	102	8	47	Medium	32	12	0	0.0	0.0	Jan
Feb	9	18	65	37	98	43	109	10	50	Medium	28	12	0	0.0	0.1	Feb
March	9	22	71	41	105	44	112	11	51	High	26	11	5	0.2	0.2	March
April	8	25	77	42	108	46	114	17	62	High	37	18	8	0.3	0.6	April
May	9	27	80	41	106	46	114	19	67	Extreme	61	35	33	1.3	4.0	May
June	9	25	77	38	101	46	114	19	67	Extreme	74	44	81	3.2	6.0	June
July	8	23	74	34	94	40	104	18	64	High	83	56	132	5.2	9.0	July
Aug	7	23	73	32	89	38	100	17	63	High	91	68	188	7.4	12.0	Aug
Sept	8	23	73	34	93	41	105	19	67	Extreme	89	60	94	3.7	7.0	Sept
Oct	9	23	74	38	101	43	109	16	61	Extreme	78	40	13	0.5	1.0	Oct
Nov	10	18	65	38	101	43	109	12	53	High	52	17	0	0.0	0.0	Nov
Dec	9	15	59	34	94	40	104	9	48	Medium	39	14	0	0.0	0.0	Dec

Based on readings for 10 years at 13°31' N, 2°06' E, altitude 216 m/709 ft

Niger

See map page 20

Niger is a relatively large country, about the size of Egypt, but with a small and sparse population. Situated in the middle of North Africa, it has land borders with seven countries and includes a large part of the Sahara. The southern part of the country is in the Sahel belt of interior West Africa and has a sparse to moderate, but rather unreliable, rainfall.

The general features of the weather and climate of this part of Africa are described for Mali on p. 230. The table for **Niamey** (above) is representative of the southern part of Niger and here the climate is very similar to that of northern Nigeria. There is a marked rainy season at the period of high sun.

Average rainfall is moderate but unreliable. Between this southern region and the northern border, rainfall progressively decreases both in amount and reliability. The northern districts are virtually rainless.

Weather here is well represented by the tables for **Faya** (p. 95) in Chad and **In Salah** (p. 32) in Algeria. In the centre of the country, where rainfall is sparse and unreliable, conditions are represented by the table for **Timbuktu** (p. 230) in Mali.

KANO										NORTHERN NIGERIA	
Sunshine		Temperatures					Discomfort from heat and humidity	Precipitation and humidity			Wet days
		Average daily		Highest recorded	Lowest recorded			Relative humidity	Average monthly precipitation		
		minimum	maximum					6:30 15:30			
average hours per day		°C °F	°C °F	°C °F	°C °F			%	mm in		more than 0.25 mm/0.01 in
Jan	9	13 55	30 86	41 106	6 43		Moderate	40 13	0 0.0		0 Jan
Feb	9	15 59	33 91	43 110	9 48		Medium	36 13	0 0.0		0 Feb
March	9	19 67	37 98	44 112	10 50		Medium	33 11	3 0.1		0 March
April	8	24 75	38 101	46 114	14 57		Medium	47 14	10 0.4		1 April
May	9	24 75	37 99	44 111	17 62		High	72 33	69 2.7		8 May
June	9	23 73	34 94	41 105	17 62		High	81 43	117 4.6		8 June
July	8	22 71	31 88	37 98	17 62		High	90 59	206 8.1		14 July
Aug	6	21 70	29 85	36 97	16 61		Medium	94 68	310 12.2		19 Aug
Sept	8	21 70	31 88	38 100	17 62		High	93 57	142 5.6		12 Sept
Oct	9	19 67	34 94	41 106	13 56		Medium	82 32	13 0.5		1 Oct
Nov	10	16 61	33 92	42 108	11 51		Medium	52 16	0 0.0		0 Nov
Dec	9	13 56	31 87	43 110	7 45		Moderate	45 14	0 0.0		0 Dec

Based on readings for 23 years at 12°02′ N, 8°32′ E, altitude 467 m/1533 ft

Nigeria

See map page 20

Nigeria is about one-and-a-half times as large as the state of Texas and extends northwards to 14° N. It is bordered by Benin on the west, Niger on the north, and Cameroon on the east. To the south it has a coast on the Gulf of Guinea. An extensive low coastal plain rises gradually inland to hill and plateau country with an average height of 460–920 m/1,500–3,000 ft. Only in the southeast does Nigeria have any significantly higher mountains.

The key to an understanding of the weather and climate in Nigeria and neighbouring countries farther west along the coast is the annual migration of the intertropical belt of cloud and associated heavy rain, high humidity, and relatively low temperature. Drier and sunnier weather, with higher temperatures, prevails on the northern side of this belt of cloud and rain. The belt of cloud and rain lies on the southern side of the point where the southwesterly to westerly winds of the Guinea monsoon give way to the northeast trade winds, or harmattan, which are dry and bring higher temperatures. The discontinuity between these

winds, often called the intertropical convergence, lies over or near the coast in December and January and moves north to about 20° N by July and August. It then returns southwards rather more rapidly between September and December. Thus much of Nigeria and the region to the west experiences two rainy periods as the intertropical convergence moves north or south; but in the north the two rainy seasons merge to give a single wet season between July and September.

This can be seen by looking at the table for **Kano** (above) in northern Nigeria. There is a single rainy season just after the time of high sun. (A similar pattern can be seen on p. 161 in the table for **Tamale** in northern Ghana.)

On the other hand, places on or near the coast have two rainy seasons with maximum rainfall in May or June and again in October. Although in the south near the coast no month is completely dry, there are two relatively drier periods between December and February and between July and September. In the north there is a single long dry season between October and April. At this time there is very little

LAGOS — COASTAL NIGERIA

	Sunshine average hours per day	Temperatures Average daily minimum °C	°F	maximum °C	°F	Highest recorded °C	°F	Lowest recorded °C	°F	Discomfort from heat and humidity	Relative humidity 8:00 %	14:00 %	Average monthly precipitation mm	in	Wet days more than 0.25mm/0.01in	
Jan	6	23	74	31	88	35	95	17	63	High	84	65	28	1.1	2	Jan
Feb	7	25	77	32	89	36	96	19	66	High	83	69	46	1.8	3	Feb
March	6	26	78	32	89	37	99	16	60	High	82	72	102	4.0	7	March
April	6	25	77	32	89	37	99	21	69	High	81	72	150	5.9	10	April
May	6	24	76	31	87	40	104	21	69	High	83	76	269	10.6	16	May
June	4	23	74	29	85	34	93	21	69	High	87	80	460	18.1	20	June
July	3	23	74	28	83	34	93	20	68	High	87	80	279	11.0	16	July
Aug	3	23	73	28	82	36	96	19	67	Medium	85	76	64	2.5	10	Aug
Sept	3	23	74	28	83	34	94	20	68	Medium	86	77	140	5.5	14	Sept
Oct	5	23	74	29	85	36	96	21	69	High	86	76	206	8.1	16	Oct
Nov	7	24	75	31	88	37	99	21	70	High	85	72	69	2.7	7	Nov
Dec	7	24	75	31	88	37	99	19	66	High	86	68	25	1.0	2	Dec

Based on readings for 32 years at 6°27′ N, 3°24′ E, altitude 3 m/10 ft

IBADAN — INLAND SOUTHERN NIGERIA

	Sunshine average hours per day	Temperatures Average daily minimum °C	°F	maximum °C	°F	Highest recorded °C	°F	Lowest recorded °C	°F	Discomfort from heat and humidity	Relative humidity 6:30 %	12:30 %	Average monthly precipitation mm	in	Wet days more than 1 mm/0.04 in	
Jan	6	21	70	33	91	37	99	10	50	High	94	51	8	0.3	1	Jan
Feb	7	22	71	34	93	39	102	12	54	High	92	49	23	0.9	2	Feb
March	6	23	73	34	93	38	101	18	64	High	95	54	76	3.0	5	March
April	6	23	73	33	91	38	100	18	65	High	95	60	125	4.9	9	April
May	6	22	72	32	89	35	95	18	64	High	96	67	145	5.7	11	May
June	5	22	71	29	85	33	91	18	64	High	97	74	163	6.4	12	June
July	3	21	70	28	82	31	89	16	61	Medium	97	78	132	5.2	12	July
Aug	2	21	69	27	81	31	89	16	60	Medium	97	78	74	2.9	10	Aug
Sept	3	22	71	29	84	36	96	17	63	High	97	75	170	6.7	15	Sept
Oct	5	22	72	30	86	33	92	18	65	High	98	70	152	6.0	12	Oct
Nov	7	22	71	32	89	34	94	14	58	High	97	63	43	1.7	4	Nov
Dec	7	21	69	33	91	35	95	14	57	High	96	56	10	0.4	1	Dec

Based on readings for 14 years at 7°26′ N, 3°54′ E, altitude 200 m/656 ft

rain in the north and temperatures are warm to hot with a very low relative humidity. During this season, the harmattan, which is often dust-laden, blows from the northeast day after day.

During the period December to February, the harmattan penetrates south so that the whole region, except a strip along the coast, is affected by it. For most of the year the coast has southwesterly winds; but on a few days these are overcome by the harmattan which brings its higher temperatures, lower humidity, and dusty air right to the coast. This brings some relief from the heat and humidity which prevail here for most of the year.

On the coast the period from December to February is least likely to experience rainy days and this dry period is more clearly recognizable than the 'little dry season' between July and September. Inland, and particularly towards the north, the time of arrival of the rains and the amount of rain may vary from year to year.

The wettest parts of Nigeria are the coastal region of the Niger delta and the mountainous border with Cameroon in the southeast. Here the annual rainfall exceeds 2,500 mm/100 in, as compared with 1,250–1,500 mm/50–60 in in much of the west and centre of Nigeria. In the far north annual rainfall is below 1,000 mm/40 in almost everywhere and in places it is as low as 600 mm/24 in. Here the rainy season is rather short and the dry period is prolonged.

The table for **Lagos** (p. 267) is representative of the southern coast of Nigeria, that for **Ibadan** (p. 267) of the inland districts of the centre and west, and that for **Kano** (p. 266) of the dry northern region.

Temperatures rise very high in the north from March to May before the arrival of the rains, but the rainy season may be equally unpleasant because of the higher humidity brought by the moist southwesterly winds. On the coast high humidity and constant high temperatures with very little relief make the weather uncomfortable throughout the year.

Hours of sunshine average from six hours a day during the rainy season to as many as ten in the dry season in the north of the country. Near the coast they average about three hours a day in the wettest months to six or seven hours during the driest period of the year.

Niue

See map page 17

This South Pacific island – self-governing in association with New Zealand – lies east of Tonga and west of the more southerly Cook Islands.

The weather and climate are typical of a tropical oceanic environment. Very similar conditions prevail throughout the year with high temperatures and humidity. The daily range of temperature is quite small – about 4°–5° C/10° F. There is abundant rainfall. Being south of the equator, Niue has its season of maximum rainfall between November and March or April. Rainfall is moderate to heavy and occurs in all months. Tropical storms of the cyclone or typhoon type occur occasionally. Periods of continuous rain lasting a day or more are not unusual but much rain comes in heavy afternoon or evening downpours after an otherwise fine, sunny day.

The climate is generally healthy and pleasant; the moderately high temperature and humidity are tempered by brisk daytime winds, either as afternoon sea breezes or as predominant southeast trade winds.

The tables for **Papeete** (p. 149) on Tahiti and **Apia** (p. 309) in Samoa illustrate conditions on Niue.

SAIPAN

MARIANA ISLAND

Sunshine	Temperatures								Discomfort from heat and humidity	Precipitation and humidity				Wet days	
	Average daily				Highest recorded		Lowest recorded			Relative humidity 6:00 14:00		Average monthly precipitation			
	minimum		maximum												
average hours per day	°C	°F	°C	°F	°C	°F	°C	°F		%		mm	in	more than 0.25mm/0.01in	
Jan 6	22	72	27	81	29	85	19	67	Medium	85	73	69	2.7	12	Jan
Feb 7	22	72	27	81	29	85	21	69	Medium	84	70	91	3.6	11	Feb
March 8	23	73	28	82	30	86	20	68	Medium	87	71	97	3.8	13	March
April 9	23	74	28	83	31	87	21	69	Medium	87	69	71	2.8	14	April
May 9	23	74	29	84	31	87	21	69	High	89	72	94	3.7	13	May
June 9	24	75	29	84	31	87	21	70	High	88	71	130	5.1	17	June
July 6	23	74	28	83	31	88	21	69	Medium	91	78	254	10.0	23	July
Aug 7	24	75	29	84	31	87	21	69	High	91	77	333	13.1	23	Aug
Sept 6	23	74	28	83	32	89	21	70	Medium	91	79	338	13.3	22	Sept
Oct 6	24	75	28	83	31	87	21	70	Medium	91	79	290	11.4	22	Oct
Nov 7	24	75	28	83	29	85	22	71	Medium	89	78	188	7.4	19	Nov
Dec 7	23	74	28	82	29	85	21	70	Medium	86	75	137	5.4	19	Dec

Based on readings for 8 years at 15°14′ N, 145°46′ E, altitude 206 m/676 ft

Northern Marianas

See map page 17

This self-governing commonwealth of the United States, occupies the northern islands in the Marianas group, which experience much the same weather as three other island groups in the western Pacific north of the equator – the Caroline, Gilbert, and Marshall Islands. Rainfall is significantly less, though, in the northernmost islands of the country.

Conditions of temperature and humidity vary little throughout the year. The country has a typical tropical oceanic climate with moderately high temperatures and humidity. The daily range of temperature is quite small – about 4°–5° C/10° F.

There is abundant to moderately heavy rainfall with a wetter season from June to November. The actual amount of rainfall on each island depends both on the altitude of the land and on exposure to the dominant winds: the northeast trade winds in the low sun period and the southeast monsoon in the high sun period. The country is liable to tropical cyclones (the typhoons of the South China Sea) with their heavy rainfall and very strong winds, which can

do considerable damage. The main season for such storms is from July to November. The worst of them may only affect one particular island every two or three years but the much larger area of heavy rain associated with a cyclone contributes to the heavier rainfall of these months.

The Northern Marianas have moderately large amounts of sunshine, averaging between six and eight hours a day, in spite of a large number of days on which some rain falls. Much of the rainfall is in the form of short, heavy showers but whole days with continuous rain are more frequent in the wetter months.

Although the combination of temperature and humidity is often muggy and oppressive, particularly at night, the daytime temperatures are usually moderate and feel more comfortable because of the brisk winds, both the daytime sea breezes and the predominant and regular trade winds.

The table for **Saipan** (above) is representative of conditions in the Marianas.

WONSAN

NORTH KOREA

	Sunshine	Temperatures								Discomfort from heat and humidity	Precipitation and humidity				Wet days	
	average hours per day	Average daily				Highest recorded		Lowest recorded			Relative humidity 5:30 13:30		Average monthly precipitation		more than 1 mm/0.04 in	
		minimum		maximum												
		°C	°F	°C	°F	°C	°F	°C	°F		%		mm	in		
Jan	7	−8	17	1	34	12	54	−22	−7		57	42	31	1.2	5	Jan
Feb	7	−7	20	2	36	14	58	−19	−3		67	47	36	1.4	4	Feb
March	7	−2	29	7	45	24	76	−16	4		65	46	48	1.9	5	March
April	8	4	40	15	59	31	88	−4	24		72	49	71	2.8	6	April
May	8	10	50	21	69	37	99	1	34		72	50	89	3.5	7	May
June	7	15	59	24	75	38	101	7	45	Moderate	84	62	124	4.9	9	June
July	6	19	67	27	80	39	103	12	53	Medium	89	72	274	10.8	14	July
Aug	6	20	68	27	81	38	100	11	52	Medium	92	73	318	12.5	13	Aug
Sept	7	14	58	23	74	34	94	4	39	Moderate	88	65	178	7.0	9	Sept
Oct	7	8	47	18	65	31	87	−2	29		77	53	76	3.0	6	Oct
Nov	6	1	34	11	51	24	76	−13	8		67	50	66	2.6	5	Nov
Dec	6	−5	23	3	38	18	64	−20	−4		65	49	31	1.2	3	Dec

Based on readings for 29 years at 39°11′ N, 127°26′ E, altitude 37 m/120 ft

PYONGYANG

NORTH KOREA

	Sunshine	Temperatures								Discomfort from heat and humidity	Precipitation and humidity			Wet days	
	average hours per day	Average daily				Highest recorded		Lowest recorded			Relative humidity all hours	Average monthly precipitation		more than 1 mm/0.04 in	
		minimum		maximum											
		°C	°F	°C	°F	°C	°F	°C	°F		%	mm	in		
Jan	6	−13	8	−3	27						74	15	0.6	3	Jan
Feb	7	−10	14	1	33						70	11	0.4	3	Feb
March	7	−4	26	7	44						66	25	1.0	4	March
April	8	3	38	16	60						63	46	1.8	5	April
May	8	9	49	22	71						66	67	2.6	7	May
June	7	15	59	26	80					Medium	71	76	3.0	7	June
July	6	20	68	29	83					High	80	237	9.3	12	July
Aug	7	20	68	29	84					High	80	228	9.0	10	Aug
Sept	7	14	56	24	76					Moderate	75	112	4.4	7	Sept
Oct	8	6	42	18	64						73	45	1.8	6	Oct
Nov	6	−2	29	9	47						73	41	1.6	7	Nov
Dec	6	−10	15	0	32						74	21	0.8	4	Dec

Based on readings for 42 years at 39°01′ N, 125°49′ E, altitude 27 m/89 ft

North Korea

See map page 24

North Korea occupies the northern half of the Korean peninsula. It has a relatively long land border along the Yalu river with the Chinese province of Manchuria. The north is a mountainous region with many areas rising to 1,800–2,450 m/6,000–8,000 ft.

The general features of the weather and climate of North Korea are described in more detail on pp. 327–8 for South Korea. This account indicates in what ways the condition in North Korea differ from those in the south.

The climate of North Korea is rather more continental and extreme than that of the south. This is because it has a long land border and is more open to cold winds which blow from Manchuria and Siberia in winter. Conditions in winter can be very cold; rivers freeze up for between three and four months and ice forms along the coast, blocking harbours and impeding navigation. Snow falls on as many as thirty-seven days at Pyongyang, and on many more days in the far north. In the north there may be as many as 200 days with frost a year. The summer months are generally warm but, in the far north, summers are not warm enough for rice to be grown.

The tables for **Wonsan** (opposite) on the east coast and **Pyongyang** (opposite and below) in a lowland area near the west coast, show that there is no very great difference between temperatures and rainfall throughout the year from one side of the country to the other.

The most unpleasant feature of the weather and climate of North Korea is undoubtedly the extreme cold and frequent wind chill in winter. Warm clothing is necessary at this time.

Norway

See map pages 18–19

Norway extends for about 1,100 mi from south to north between 58° and 71° N and has an area of 324,000 sq km/125,000 sq mi.

The northern part of the country, within the Arctic Circle, has continuous daylight at midsummer and Arctic twilight all day in winter. Norway has a long and very indented coastline on the North Sea and Atlantic Ocean with many steep-sided inlets or fiords. There are innumerable small islands offshore.

Much of the interior is high mountain and plateau rising over 1,500 m/5,000 ft. Except in the south around Oslo, the country is narrow from east to west. There is a long land border with Sweden and, in the far north in Lapland, with Finland and Russia. The largest area of lowland is around Oslo and this is the driest and warmest part of the country in summer.

The interior highlands have an Arctic climate in winter with snow, strong winds, and severe frosts but during fine spells in summer the daytime temperatures can rise quite high with long hours of sunshine. The weather and climate are similar to that of northern Sweden (see p. 344).

By contrast, the coastal areas have comparatively mild conditions in winter, because the warm Atlantic water of the Gulf Stream reaches to the extreme north of Norway. This keeps the sea from freezing and keeps the country's harbours open throughout the year. On occasions in winter strong cold winds blow down into the fiords from the snow-covered highlands.

The climate and weather of Norway are very much influenced by Atlantic weather disturbances so that the weather is changeable throughout the year. Gales, rain, and cloud are the dominant features of this coast and rainfall is frequent and heavy (see the table for **Bergen** overleaf).

Towards the north, rainfall decreases but falls frequently, and snow is common at sea level in winter (see the table for **Narvik** overleaf).

In the more extensive areas of lowland in the south the winters are colder with more frequent frost than on the Atlantic coast but summers are warmer and drier (see the table for **Oslo** on p. 273).

The **Spitzbergen** (Svalbard) archipelago (see table p. 273) is Norwegian territory. Situated in the Arctic Ocean between 77° and 80° N, it has a severe Arctic

BERGEN   COASTAL NORWAY

Sunshine	Temperatures								Discomfort from heat and humidity	Precipitation and humidity				Wet days	
	Average daily				Highest recorded		Lowest recorded			Relative humidity 6:30 12:30		Average monthly precipitation			
	minimum		maximum												
average hours per day	°C	°F	°C	°F	°C	°F	°C	°F		%		mm	in	more than 0.1 mm/0.004 in	
Jan	1	−1	31	3	38	13	56	−14	8		80	77	143	5.6	20	Jan
Feb	2	−1	30	3	38	11	52	−11	12		80	74	142	5.6	17	Feb
March	3	0	33	6	43	20	68	−10	14		79	67	109	4.3	16	March
April	5	3	37	9	49	22	72	−6	22		80	68	139	5.5	19	April
May	6	7	44	14	58	27	81	−2	28		78	64	83	3.3	15	May
June	6	10	49	16	61	32	89	1	33		83	71	126	5.0	17	June
July	6	12	54	19	66	31	87	5	41		86	73	142	5.6	20	July
Aug	6	12	54	19	65	30	85	4	40		87	73	168	6.6	20	Aug
Sept	3	10	49	15	59	26	79	1	34		87	74	228	9.0	21	Sept
Oct	2	6	43	11	52	20	67	−3	26		85	76	235	9.3	23	Oct
Nov	1	3	38	8	46	15	60	−6	22		81	77	211	8.3	21	Nov
Dec	0	1	34	5	41	16	62	−8	17		81	79	204	8.0	22	Dec

Based on readings for 24 years at 60°24′ N, 5°19′ E, altitude 43 m/141 ft

NARVIK   NORTHERN NORWAY

Sunshine	Temperatures								Discomfort from heat and humidity	Precipitation and humidity				Wet days	
	Average daily				Highest recorded		Lowest recorded			Relative humidity 7:30 13:00		Average monthly precipitation			
	minimum		maximum												
average hours per day	°C	°F	°C	°F	°C	°F	°C	°F		%		mm	in	more than 0.1 mm/0.004 in	
Jan		−7	19	−2	29	9	48	−20	−4		75	74	55	2.2	15	Jan
Feb		−7	19	−2	29	9	48	−19	−2		75	72	47	1.9	15	Feb
March		−5	22	1	34	11	51	−18	0		76	68	61	2.4	17	March
April		−2	29	5	41	16	62	−13	10		70	62	45	1.8	15	April
May		3	37	9	49	24	75	−7	20		75	65	44	1.7	17	May
June		7	45	14	56	29	83	−1	31		78	69	65	2.6	17	June
July		11	51	18	65	30	86	4	39		81	71	58	2.3	16	July
Aug		10	49	16	62	27	81	2	36		87	75	84	3.3	19	Aug
Sept		6	43	12	53	23	73	−3	26		85	71	97	3.8	20	Sept
Oct		2	35	6	43	16	60	−9	16		78	73	86	3.4	20	Oct
Nov		−2	28	3	37	13	55	−13	8		75	74	59	2.3	15	Nov
Dec		−5	24	−1	31	11	52	−19	−2		72	73	57	2.2	16	Dec

Based on readings for 25 years at 68°25′ N, 17°23′ E, altitude 40 m/131 ft

OSLO

SOUTHERN NORWAY

Sunshine	Temperatures								Discomfort from heat and humidity	Precipitation and humidity				Wet days
	Average daily				Highest recorded		Lowest recorded			Relative humidity 6:30 12:30		Average monthly precipitation		
	minimum		maximum											
average hours per day	°C	°F	°C	°F	°C	°F	°C	°F		%		mm	in	more than 0.1 mm/0.004 in
Jan	1	-7	19	-2	28	11	51	-26	-15		86	82	49	1.9	15	Jan
Feb	3	-7	19	-1	30	14	57	-24	-12		84	74	35	1.4	12	Feb
March	5	-4	25	4	39	16	60	-20	-4		80	64	26	1.0	9	March
April	6	1	34	10	50	22	71	-15	5		75	57	43	1.7	11	April
May	8	6	43	16	61	28	83	-3	27		68	52	44	1.7	10	May
June	8	10	50	20	68	34	93	2	35		69	55	70	2.8	13	June
July	7	13	55	22	72	33	91	4	39		74	59	82	3.2	15	July
Aug	6	12	53	21	70	31	88	4	39		79	61	95	3.7	14	Aug
Sept	5	8	46	16	60	26	78	-4	26		85	66	81	3.2	14	Sept
Oct	3	3	38	9	48	20	68	-8	18		88	72	74	2.9	14	Oct
Nov	1	-1	31	3	38	13	55	-16	4		88	83	68	2.7	16	Nov
Dec	1	-4	25	0	32	11	51	-21	-5		87	85	63	2.5	17	Dec

Based on readings for 24 years at 59°56′ N, 10°44′ E, altitude 94 m/308 ft

SPITZBERGEN (SVALBARD)

ARCTIC NORWAY

Sunshine	Temperatures								Discomfort from heat and humidity	Precipitation and humidity				Wet days
	Average daily				Highest recorded		Lowest recorded			Relative humidity 7:00 13:00		Average monthly precipitation		
	minimum		maximum											
average hours per day	°C	°F	°C	°F	°C	°F	°C	°F		%		mm	in	more than 0.1 mm/0.004 in
Jan	0	-13	9	-7	19	5	41	-31	-24		83	82	26	1.0	13	Jan
Feb	0	-14	7	-7	19	4	40	-31	-24		82	82	25	1.0	12	Feb
March	2	-15	6	-9	16	4	39	-33	-27		83	83	24	0.9	12	March
April	8	-12	11	-5	22	6	42	-30	-22		82	80	15	0.6	10	April
May	8	-5	24	-1	31	13	56	-19	-2		82	80	20	0.8	10	May
June	6	1	33	4	39	13	55	-6	21		85	84	19	0.8	9	June
July	5	4	39	7	45	16	60	-1	30		89	87	25	1.0	11	July
Aug	4	3	38	6	43	13	55	-2	28		88	85	40	1.6	14	Aug
Sept	2	0	32	3	37	12	54	-9	16		84	82	36	1.4	14	Sept
Oct	1	-5	23	-1	31	8	47	-16	3		81	81	39	1.5	13	Oct
Nov	0	-8	17	-3	27	6	43	-27	-16		82	82	37	1.5	14	Nov
Dec	0	-10	13	-6	22	6	42	-27	-17		82	82	31	1.2	14	Dec

Based on readings for 10 years at 78°04′ N, 13°38′ E, altitude 7 m/23 ft

type of climate. Winters are very cold and in the short summer snow scarcely melts at sea level. In the mountainous interior there are glaciers and permanent snowfields.

The north coasts of the islands are permanently enclosed in pack ice. The islands have long been inhabited, formerly by whalers but now as a meteorological station. Coal mines are jointly worked by Norway and Russia. Winter conditions in Spitzbergen are severe and Arctic clothing is essential for survival outdoors. Similar conditions apply during the winter in northern and central Norway at higher levels.

Oman

See map page 22

This small Arab state occupies the northeastern corner of the Arabian peninsula. It has coastlines on the Gulf of Oman to the north and the Arabian Sea to the south. Inland it is bordered by the United Arab Emirates, Saudi Arabia, and Yemen.

The northern part of Oman consists of the Jebel Akhdar, a mountain range rising to just over 3,000 m/10,000 ft. The annual rainfall on the higher parts of the Jebel Akhdar probably exceeds 400 mm/20 in. In the rest of Oman the annual rainfall is below 125 mm/5 in except in the hills of Dhofar in the extreme south. Along the south coast the cloudy rainy season is between June and September but in the Jebel Akhdar and in the lowlands of the north rain may

fall at any time of the year. Very occasionally a tropical cyclone in the Arabian Sea brings a spell of very wet, windy weather to the coast of Oman and this may cause damage through wind and flood.

Temperatures and humidity are high throughout the year on the coast and the period May to September is the hottest and most unpleasant season. Temperatures rise even higher inland towards the Rub' al Khali, but here humidity is lower so that the high temperatures are more tolerable and the nights are cooler. Unless precautions are taken there is a danger of heat exhaustion or even heatstroke during the hottest weather. Sunshine amounts are high throughout the year. See the table for **Muscat** (below) and details for Saudi Arabia (p. 312).

MUSCAT — NORTHERN OMAN

	Sunshine	Temperatures								Discomfort from heat and humidity	Precipitation and humidity				Wet days
		Average daily				Highest recorded		Lowest recorded				Relative humidity		Average monthly precipitation		
		minimum		maximum								8:00	16:00			
	average hours per day	°C	°F	°C	°F	°C	°F	°C	°F			%		mm	in	more than 0.25 mm/0.01 in
Jan	9	19	66	25	77	31	87	11	51	Medium		72	71	28	1.1	2
Feb	10	19	67	25	77	32	90	12	53	Medium		73	73	18	0.7	1
March	9	22	72	28	83	42	107	17	62	Medium		71	70	10	0.4	1
April	11	26	78	32	90	41	105	19	66	High		64	68	10	0.4	1
May	12	30	86	37	98	44	112	24	75	Extreme		58	60	0	0.0	0
June	12	31	88	38	100	47	116	26	78	Dangerous		72	72	3	0.1	0
July	9	31	87	36	97	45	113	25	77	Extreme		77	77	0	0.0	0
Aug	10	29	84	33	92	42	108	24	75	Extreme		82	80	0	0.0	0
Sept	11	28	83	34	93	42	107	23	73	Extreme		75	77	0	0.0	0
Oct	10	27	80	34	93	41	105	21	69	Extreme		69	74	3	0.1	0
Nov	10	23	73	30	86	36	96	17	62	High		69	72	10	0.4	1
Dec	9	20	68	20	79	33	92	16	60			70	71	18	0.7	2

Based on readings for 24 years at 23°37′ N, 58°35′ E, altitude 5 m/15 ft

Pakistan

See map page 22

Pakistan is a large country, about one and a half times the size of France. It is situated in the northwestern part of the great Indian subcontinent. Its western border with Iran and Afghanistan is mountainous and its short northern border with China and its northeastern border with India in the Pamir and Karakoram ranges include some of the higher Himalayan peaks. On the south and east it has a long border with the Punjab and Sind provinces of India; this is a region of low-lying plains, part of the great Indus valley.

Most of the country has a climate dominated by the influence of the great seasonal wind reversal called the Asiatic monsoon. (For a fuller description of this see p. 174 for India.) The year may be divided into three principal seasons. Mid-October until late February is the cool season, when the weather is generally pleasant, sunny, and quite warm by day but with chilly nights and occasional frost. The northern and western parts of the country receive some rain at this time, brought by depressions moving in from the west.

Conditions in the higher mountains at this time are distinctly cold. During this period midday temperatures in the south and centre of the country rise to very high levels. The heat is distinctly unpleasant in spite of the low humidity. Some occasional rain, usually of a showery, thundery type, may occur at this time. Such brief storms are often preceded or accompanied by dust storms. The rainy season over most of the country is from late June until early October. This is the season of the southwest monsoon and although temperatures are a little lower, the higher humidity can cause discomfort.

Not all parts of Pakistan are equally wet during the rainy season. The desert region of the south and southeast receives little rain at this time and is sunny and hot; see the table for **Jacobabad** (below), which has the reputation of being one of the hottest places in the world from April until September. **Karachi** (see table overleaf), on the coast of the Arabian Sea, also gets little rain and, although cooler than inland, has a very unpleasant climate at this time because of the higher humidity. The mountainous regions of

JACOBABAD											SOUTHERN INLAND PAKISTAN			
Sunshine	Temperatures							Discomfort from heat and humidity	Precipitation and humidity				Wet days	
	Average daily				Highest recorded		Lowest recorded		Relative humidity		Average monthly precipitation			
average hours per day	minimum		maximum						8:00	16:00			more than 2.5 mm/0.1 in	
	°C	°F	°C	°F	°C	°F	°C	°F	%		mm	in		
Jan	8	7	44	23	73	28	83	0	32		65	34	5	0.2	0.7	Jan
Feb	8	9	49	25	77	37	98	-1	30		54	35	8	0.3	0.9	Feb
March	8	16	61	33	91	43	110	7	44	Medium	45	31	5	0.2	0.7	March
April	9	22	71	39	102	47	116	11	52	Extreme	41	30	5	0.2	0.5	April
May	10	26	78	44	111	51	123	17	62	Extreme	43	27	3	0.1	0.4	May
June	9	29	85	46	114	53	127	22	72	Extreme	57	31	8	0.3	0.3	June
July	8	30	86	43	109	52	126	24	76	Extreme	65	42	23	0.9	1.0	July
Aug	9	28	83	40	104	47	117	20	68	Extreme	71	49	23	0.9	1.0	Aug
Sept	10	24	76	39	103	45	113	16	60	Extreme	68	40	5	0.2	0.3	Sept
Oct	10	19	66	37	99	42	108	11	51	High	56	31	0	0.0	0.1	Oct
Nov	10	12	53	31	87	37	99	4	39	Medium	56	29	0	0.0	0.1	Nov
Dec	8	7	45	24	75	28	83	1	33		63	31	5	0.2	0.5	Dec

Based on readings for 10 years at 28°17′ N, 68°29′ E, altitude 57 m/186 ft

KARACHI

SOUTHERN COASTAL PAKISTAN

Sunshine	Temperatures								Discomfort from heat and humidity	Precipitation and humidity				Wet days
	Average daily				Highest recorded		Lowest recorded			Relative humidity		Average monthly precipitation		
	minimum		maximum							8:00 16:00				
average hours per day	°C	°F	°C	°F	°C	°F	°C	°F		%		mm	in	more than 2.5 mm/0.1 in
Jan	9	13	55	25	77	32	89	4	40	Moderate	63	45	13	0.5	1.0	Jan
Feb	9	14	58	26	79	34	93	6	43	Moderate	72	49	10	0.4	1.0	Feb
March	9	19	67	29	85	41	106	8	47	Medium	79	57	8	0.3	1.0	March
April	10	23	73	32	90	44	111	14	57	High	87	62	3	0.1	0.2	April
May	10	26	79	34	93	48	118	18	65	Extreme	88	68	3	0.1	0.1	May
June	8	28	82	34	93	46	114	20	68	Extreme	86	69	18	0.7	1.0	June
July	4	27	81	33	91	43	110	23	73	Extreme	88	73	81	3.2	2.0	July
Aug	5	26	79	31	88	37	99	23	73	High	90	74	41	1.6	2.0	Aug
Sept	7	25	77	31	88	41	106	21	69	High	89	71	13	0.5	1.0	Sept
Oct	9	22	72	33	91	42	108	14	57	High	83	57	0	0.0	0.1	Oct
Nov	9	18	64	31	87	38	100	9	48	Medium	68	49	3	0.1	0.3	Nov
Dec	9	14	57	27	80	33	91	4	39	Moderate	64	45	5	0.2	1.0	Dec

Based on readings for 43 years at 24°48′ N, 66°59′ E, altitude 4 m/13 ft

PESHAWAR

NORTHWESTERN PAKISTAN

Sunshine	Temperatures								Discomfort from heat and humidity	Precipitation and humidity				Wet days
	Average daily				Highest recorded		Lowest recorded			Relative humidity		Average monthly precipitation		
	minimum		maximum							8:00 15:30				
average hours per day	°C	°F	°C	°F	°C	°F	°C	°F		%		mm	in	more than 2.5 mm/0.1 in
Jan	6	4	40	17	63	24	76	-3	26		73	45	36	1.4	3	Jan
Feb	7	6	43	19	66	30	86	-1	31		75	43	38	1.5	3	Feb
March	6	11	52	24	75	34	93	2	36		68	43	61	2.4	5	March
April	8	16	60	29	85	42	108	5	41	Medium	59	39	46	1.8	4	April
May	9	21	70	37	98	48	118	11	52	High	41	28	20	0.8	2	May
June	10	25	77	41	106	49	120	18	65	Extreme	43	25	8	0.3	1	June
July	9	26	79	39	103	50	122	21	69	Extreme	61	38	33	1.3	2	July
Aug	9	26	78	37	99	48	118	20	68	Extreme	70	45	51	2.0	3	Aug
Sept	8	22	71	36	96	43	110	14	58	High	65	39	20	0.8	2	Sept
Oct	9	14	58	31	88	38	101	11	52	Medium	60	32	5	0.2	1	Oct
Nov	8	8	46	25	77	33	91	1	33	Moderate	63	40	8	0.3	1	Nov
Dec	7	4	39	19	67	28	83	-2	28		73	42	18	0.7	2	Dec

Based on readings for 30 years at 34°01′ N, 71°34′ E, altitude 354 m/1161 ft

ISLAMABAD

	Sunshine	Temperatures									Discomfort from heat and humidity	Precipitation and humidity			Wet days	
	average hours per day	Average daily				Highest recorded		Lowest recorded				Relative humidity 12:00	Average monthly precipitation		more than 2.5 mm/0.01 in	
		minimum		maximum												
		°C	°F	°C	°F	°C	°F	°C	°F			%	mm	in		
Jan	7	2	36	16	61	24	75	-4	25			44	64	2.5	7	Jan
Feb	8	6	43	19	66	31	88	-2	28			46	64	2.5	6	Feb
March	8	10	50	24	75	36	97	1	34			37	81	3.2	7	March
April	10	15	59	31	88	44	111	7	45		Medium	26	42	1.7	6	April
May	10	21	70	37	99	46	115	12	54		Medium	19	23	0.9	4	May
June	9	25	77	40	104	48	118	14	57		High	23	55	2.2	7	June
July	8	25	77	36	97	46	115	17	63		High	45	233	9.2	13	July
Aug	9	24	75	34	93	42	108	14	57		High	54	258	10.2	10	Aug
Sept	10	21	70	34	93	39	102	12	54		High	44	85	3.3	5	Sept
Oct	9	15	59	32	90	38	100	7	45		Medium	29	21	0.8	2	Oct
Nov	8	9	48	28	82	32	90	-1	30		Moderate	26	12	0.5	1	Nov
Dec	7	3	37	20	68	27	81	-3	27			39	23	0.9	3	Dec

Based on readings for 30 years at 33°35' N, 73°03' E, altitude 511 m/1644 ft

the north and west of the country receive much less rain during the period of the southwest monsoon and may be wetter during the cooler winter season; see the table for **Peshawar** (opposite), which has a sequence of weather throughout the year more like that found in Iran to the west.

It is in the eastern and central plains of the country that the full effect of the monsoon rains is felt. Here the climate throughout the year is more akin to that found in the northern plains of India (see the table for **Islamabad** above).

Sunshine amounts are high around the year in most of Pakistan, ranging from six to seven hours a day in the cool season to ten to twelve during the hot season. There is an increase in cloudiness over most of the country during the wet season, even though rainfall amounts may be small in some areas. For example, in July and August daily sunshine hours

average only four or five at Karachi, even though the rainfall is much less than in the north of the country.

Snowfall is heavy on the higher mountains in the north but reliable measurements of its actual depth are not available. The melting snow from these mountains, together with the heavy summer rainfall from the monsoon, feeds the five great rivers of the Punjab plains which unite to form the Indus. Were it not for the irrigation flow from these rivers, much of the Punjab and Sind lowlands would be a more extensive desert than they are.

In the hottest parts of Pakistan there is a danger of heat exhaustion or even heatstroke during the hot season and visitors should allow themselves a few days to become acclimatized before engaging in strenuous exercise. The heat is often so great that, without air conditioning, indoor temperatures at night are very uncomfortable.

Palau

See map page 17

This republic, comprising some 340 small islands, lies east of the Philippines and north of Indonesia in the eastern part the Caroline Islands. Palau experiences very similar conditions of temperature and humidity throughout the year and these are shared with the islands of the other main groups in the western Pacific north of the equator – the Gilbert, Marianas, and Marshall Islands. All of these island groups have a typical tropical oceanic climate with moderately high temperatures and humidity, which vary little from month to month.

The daily range of temperature is quite small – about 4°–5° C/10° F. All have abundant or moderately heavy rainfall with a wetter season from June to November. Islands near the equator have rainfall more evenly spread throughout the year. The actual amount of rainfall on each island depends on both the altitude of the land and on exposure to the dominant winds: the northeast trade winds in the low sun period and the southeast monsoon in the high sun period.

Islands more than 5° N of the equator are liable to experience tropical cyclones (the typhoons of the South China Sea) with their heavy rainfall and very strong winds which can do considerable damage.

The main season for such storms is from July to November. The worst of such storms may only affect one particular island every two or three years but the much larger area of heavy rain associated with a cyclone contributes to the heavier rainfall of these months.

Palau has moderately large amounts of sunshine, averaging between six and eight hours a day, in spite of a large number of days on which some rain falls. Much of the rainfall is in the form of short, heavy showers but days with continuous rain are more frequent in the wetter months.

Although the combination of temperature and humidity is often rather muggy and oppressive, particularly at night, daytime temperatures are usually moderate and feel more comfortable because of the brisk winds, both the daytime sea breezes and the predominant and regular trade winds.

The tables for **Saipan** (p. 269) in the Northern Marianas and **Ujelang** (p. 233) in the Marshall Islands illustrate conditions over a large area of the western Pacific. That for **Yaren** (p. 255) on Nauru is more typical of islands on or near the equator; here rainfall is more evenly distributed throughout the year and tropical cyclones are never experienced.

Panama

See map page 14

Including a description of the weather and climate of Belize, Guatemala, Honduras, El Salvador, Nicaragua, and Costa Rica.

There are seven small countries in the narrow isthmus of Central America between the southern border of Mexico and the northern border of Colombia. From north to south these countries are: Belize, Guatemala, Honduras, El Salvador, Nicaragua, Costa Rica, and Panama.

Together these countries have an area of 470,000 sq km/180,000 sq mi, a little larger than the state of California and about twice the size of the United Kingdom. The area lies between 18° and 7° N and between 85° and 95° W. The whole area is within the tropics and, because of the narrowness of the isthmus, is strongly influenced by the ocean with the

result that almost everywhere the climate is tropical with abundant rainfall.

At its narrowest point the isthmus is only about 80 km/50 mi across but in Nicaragua and Honduras it widens to about 560 km/350 mi. A chain of mountains, ranging in height from 1,200 m/4,000 ft to 4,000 m/13,000 ft, runs approximately through the centre of the isthmus.

Climate and weather in all these countries are broadly similar and are described here. Only brief notes amplifying this description, with a note of any local peculiarities, are given for individual entries.

Situated well within the tropics, but north of the equator, all these countries have a typically tropical climate with high temperatures around the year at low altitudes. Temperatures are significantly modified by altitude and a simple and useful threefold division into climatic zones can be made using the local terms: *tierra caliente*, *tierra templada*, and *tierra fria*.

In the *tierra caliente* (from sea level up to about 900 m/3,000 ft) temperatures are hot throughout the year. The *tierra templada* (from 900 m/3,000 ft to 1,800 m/6,000 ft) has cooler temperatures but many tropical or subtropical crops such as coffee are grown. Here there are many local differences in the amount of rainfall, depending on altitude and the aspect of the mountains in relation to the prevailing winds. The *tierra fria* (from 1800 m/6,000 ft to 3,000 m/10,000 ft) is limited in extent but here conditions are quite cool and typical of temperate latitudes. Frost and snow may occasionally occur but the mountains of this region are not high enough to carry permanent snow.

Over most of this region the season of maximum rainfall is between May and September, the period of high sun in the northern hemisphere. Places on the eastern coast, or the Caribbean shore, tend to be rather wetter and to have a longer rainy season than those on the Pacific coast to the west. In some places on the Caribbean shore there is a tendency for a double rainy season. All months have significant rainfall; this is well illustrated by the table for **Belize City** (p. 62). Even in the narrow isthmus of Panama,

annual rainfall at Cristobal on the Caribbean coast is double that at **Balboa Heights** (see table below) on the Pacific. Some of the wettest places in this region are where mountains face the persistent northeast to easterly trade winds which blow onshore for most of the year.

Another significant feature of the weather and climate of Central America is the liability of most of the area to suffer hurricanes between June and November. These severe tropical storms develop well to the east of the Caribbean in the central Atlantic at about 5° to 10° N. The most usual track of these storms is across the West Indian islands, after which they curve north or northeastwards. The coastal regions of Central America are affected less frequently and less severely than the islands farther east, but those hurricanes which reach the mainland can produce very heavy rainfall and their strong winds can cause extensive damage.

Costa Rica and Panama are rarely affected by the storms but the remaining countries can experience hurricanes which, even when weakening and losing the more violent winds, can add appreciably to the rainfall in the months August to October. The Pacific coastlands of Central America are also occasionally affected by less violent tropical storms which develop in the eastern Pacific Ocean.

BALBOA HEIGHTS

PACIFIC COASTAL PANAMA

	Sunshine	Temperatures								Discomfort from heat and humidity	Precipitation and humidity				Wet days	
		Average daily				Highest recorded		Lowest recorded			Relative humidity 7:30 19:30		Average monthly precipitation			
		minimum		maximum												
	average hours per day	°C	°F	°C	°F	°C	°F	°C	°F		%		mm	in	more than 1 mm/0.04 in	
Jan	10	22	71	31	88	34	93	17	63	Extreme	88	84	25	1.0	4	Jan
Feb	9	22	71	32	89	35	95	18	64	Extreme	85	81	10	0.4	2	Feb
March	8	22	72	32	90	36	96	18	65	Extreme	81	78	18	0.7	1	March
April	7	23	74	31	87	36	97	18	64	Extreme	81	81	74	2.9	6	April
May	5	23	74	30	86	36	96	21	69	High	87	88	203	8.0	15	May
June	4	23	74	31	87	35	95	21	70	Extreme	90	90	213	8.4	16	June
July	5	23	74	31	87	35	95	19	67	Extreme	90	91	180	7.1	15	July
Aug	5	23	74	30	86	34	94	20	68	Extreme	90	91	201	7.9	15	Aug
Sept	5	23	74	29	85	34	94	20	68	High	91	91	208	8.2	16	Sept
Oct	5	23	73	29	85	35	95	20	68	High	90	92	257	10.1	18	Oct
Nov	5	23	73	29	85	34	94	19	67	High	91	92	259	10.2	18	Nov
Dec	7	23	73	31	87	34	94	19	66	Extreme	90	89	122	4.8	12	Dec

Based on readings for 34 years at 8°57′ N, 79°33′ W, altitude 33 m/118 ft

In the lowlands of the *tierra caliente* temperatures remain high in all months with a very small daily range of temperature. Near the coast humidity is also high and the principal relief from this perpetually warm, humid climate is the daily sea breeze. Extremely high temperatures are never recorded on the coast and midday temperatures may even be higher inland than in the *tierra templada*. Inland and at higher levels there is a much larger daily range of temperature and the nights are pleasantly cool. This can be seen by comparing the average and extreme temperatures for **Guatemala City** (p. 167) or **San Salvador** (p. 134) with those for **Belize City** (p. 62) in the tables for the respective countries.

Sunshine amounts are quite high throughout the year in most of Central America. Average daily sunshine hours range from six to eight in the wetter months to as many as ten hours during the dry months, even though this is the time of low sun. Costa Rica and Panama have a rather more cloudy climate with more frequent rain, so that here the sunshine hours range from four to five in the wettest months to eight or nine in the driest season. Many areas in Central America had a bad reputation in the past for fever and tropical diseases. The climatic conditions of the lowlands encouraged malaria and yellow fever, but these have largely been eradicated and were only indirect effects of the climate. The climate itself, although sultry and oppressive for much of the year in the wetter lowlands, is not particularly unhealthy. Indeed, in the drier areas and in the hills it is pleasant and sunny for much of the year.

Panama itself occupies the narrowest part of the Central American isthmus. About the same size as the state of Maine, it lies between 7° and 9° N and owes its existence as an independent state to the cutting of the Panama Canal by the United States; previously it was part of Colombia. Although there are areas of lowland on both the Caribbean and Pacific coasts, much of the interior is hilly with some mountains rising above 3,300 m/11,000 ft. Within this small area, therefore, are examples of the three climatic zones described above.

The table for **Balboa Heights** (p. 279) is representative of the Pacific coast. The lowlands on the northern or Caribbean coast are almost twice as wet but temperatures are almost the same.

Papua New Guinea

See map page 17

The island of New Guinea is three times the size of the United Kingdom and lies to the north of the Australian continent between the equator and 12° S. The western half of the island is the Indonesian province of Irian Jaya and the eastern half is the main part of Papua New Guinea. The island has a single range of high mountains running from east to west with the highest peak rising to 5,000 m/ 16,400 ft. There is an extensive swampy lowland in the south.

The weather and climate of New Guinea are tropical, similar to that described in greater detail on p. 181 for Indonesia. Because of the great range of altitude and the different exposures of the north and south coasts to the seasonally alternating north and south monsoons, there are great variations in the amount of rainfall and the time of heaviest fall from place to place. Temperatures at low altitudes are high throughout the year, with little variation from month to month.

The table for **Port Moresby** (opposite and above), on the south coast, indicates the temperatures and humidity around the year at low levels. Port Moresby, however, with an annual rainfall of 1,125 mm/45 in, is one of the driest places on the island. Most places have 2,000–3,000 mm/80–120 in of rain a year and in the mountains this may rise as high as 5,000 mm/200 in. The highest mountain in western New Guinea carries permanent snow even though it is almost on the equator.

Much of the rain comes in heavy downpours, accompanied by thunder, during afternoon and evening storms; but longer periods of rain occur during the wettest months. The weather in the lowlands is sultry and humid but at higher levels the lower temperature makes for much more pleasant conditions. Much of the island is very inaccessible and some parts are still little known or explored.

Papua New Guinea includes the islands of New Britain, New Ireland, and the small islands of the Bismarck Archipelago between 2° and 6° S. The weather and climate of these islands are similar to that of the main island of New Guinea. However, the island of Bougainville, also part of Papua New Guinea (see the table for **Kieta** opposite) belongs geographically to the Solomon Islands group. It shares with them the tropical oceanic climate described on p. 320.

PORT MORESBY

COASTAL NEW GUINEA

	Sunshine	Temperatures									Discomfort from heat and humidity	Precipitation and humidity				Wet days	
	average hours per day	Average daily				Highest recorded		Lowest recorded				Relative humidity 9:00 15:00		Average monthly precipitation		more than 2.5 mm/0.1 in	
		minimum		maximum													
		°C	°F	°C	°F	°C	°F	°C	°F			%		mm	in		
Jan	6	24	76	32	89	37	98	21	69		High	72	69	178	7.0	8	Jan
Feb	5	24	76	31	87	36	96	21	69		High	73	72	193	7.6	7	Feb
March	6	24	76	31	88	36	96	21	70		High	74	73	170	6.7	9	March
April	7	24	75	31	87	36	96	18	65		High	75	74	107	4.2	5	April
May	7	24	75	30	86	34	94	21	70		High	77	77	64	2.5	2	May
June	7	23	74	29	84	33	91	18	64		High	78	77	33	1.3	3	June
July	7	23	73	28	83	32	90	19	66		Medium	78	78	28	1.1	2	July
Aug	7	23	73	28	82	32	90	19	66		Medium	77	77	18	0.7	2	Aug
Sept	7	23	74	29	84	34	94	19	66		High	78	77	25	1.0	2	Sept
Oct	7	24	75	30	86	34	94	20	68		High	75	76	36	1.4	2	Oct
Nov	8	24	76	31	88	36	96	21	69		High	73	73	48	1.9	3	Nov
Dec	7	24	76	32	90	36	97	21	70		High	72	69	112	4.4	6	Dec

Based on readings for 19 years at 9°29′ S, 147°09′ E, altitude 38 m/126 ft

KIETA

BOUGAINVILLE

	Sunshine	Temperatures									Discomfort from heat and humidity	Precipitation and humidity				Wet days	
	average hours per day	Average daily				Highest recorded		Lowest recorded				Relative humidity 8:00 14:00		Average monthly precipitation		more than 2.5 mm/0.1 in	
		minimum		maximum													
		°C	°F	°C	°F	°C	°F	°C	°F			%		mm	in		
Jan	6	24	76	31	88	35	95	18	64		High	78	79	267	10.5	15	Jan
Feb	5	24	75	31	88	35	95	19	66		High	77	76	272	10.7	14	Feb
March	5	24	76	31	88	36	96	21	70		High	78	78	285	11.2	12	March
April	6	24	76	31	87	34	94	22	71		Extreme	80	80	297	11.7	14	April
May	7	24	75	31	87	34	94	18	65		High	80	79	236	9.3	14	May
June	6	24	75	30	86	33	92	21	69		High	82	81	229	9.0	13	June
July	6	23	74	29	85	34	93	21	70		High	80	80	277	10.9	13	July
Aug	4	23	74	29	85	33	92	21	70		High	80	80	239	9.4	14	Aug
Sept	7	23	74	31	87	33	92	21	69		High	79	79	203	8.0	13	Sept
Oct	6	24	75	31	88	34	94	21	69		High	75	77	249	9.8	14	Oct
Nov	6	24	75	31	88	36	96	20	68		High	76	79	244	9.6	12	Nov
Dec	6	24	75	32	89	34	94	19	66		Extreme	75	76	239	9.4	14	Dec

Based on readings for 9 years at 6°10′ S, 155°36′ E, altitude 73 m/240 ft

Paraguay

See map page 16

Paraguay is entirely landlocked and is situated between 18° and 28° S. As large as the state of California, it is bordered on the north by Bolivia and Brazil and on the south by Argentina. Most of it lies below 450 m/1,500 ft. The northwestern part of the country lies entirely within the tropics and has a typical tropical climate with hot summers and warm winters. Most of its rain falls in the hottest months between October and March. The southeastern half of the country has temperatures a little lower in all months but the summers are sufficiently hot and wet to be typically tropical.

The northwest of Paraguay is part of the Chaco region, which extends into the adjoining regions of Bolivia and Argentina. Here annual rainfall ranges between 750 mm/30 in and 1,250 mm/50 in, increasing northwards. Occasionally in winter the region is affected by outbreaks of colder polar air from Antarctica; this cold air lowers the temperature for a day or so but frost is very rare. This is a rather desolate and sparsely populated region. It is very flat and level; the elevation of the land rises gradually towards the Bolivian border. Differences of climate and weather are small within the Chaco.

The southeastern half of the country contains some land which is a little higher, and the more southerly latitude means that the winter here is somewhat cooler. However, cold days with frost are very rare. Summer temperatures are hot to warm so that conditions are then quite tropical. Rainfall is between 1,250 mm/50 in and 1,750 mm/70 in a year and it increases eastwards. Rain can be expected on about one day in five in winter and on about one day in three in summer. The table for **Asunción** (below) illustrates conditions in the centre of the country.

To the northwest, in the Chaco, conditions are a little hotter in all months and there is less rainfall. In the southeast of the country it is rather wetter with slightly lower temperatures in all months. The southeast is the most developed and densely populated part of Paraguay.

The weather can often be distinctly sultry and oppressive during the wet summer months and this is particularly the case in the Chaco region.

ASUNCION												CENTRAL PARAGUAY	
Sunshine	Temperatures							Discomfort from heat and humidity	Precipitation and humidity				Wet days
	Average daily		Highest recorded		Lowest recorded				Relative humidity	Average monthly precipitation			
	minimum	maximum							7:00 14:00				
average hours per day	°C °F	°C °F	°C °F		°C °F				%	mm	in		more than 0.1 mm/0.004 in
Jan	9	22 71	35 95	43 109	12 54			Extreme	81 56	140	5.5	8	Jan
Feb	9	22 71	34 94	43 109	11 52			High	82 55	130	5.1	6	Feb
March	8	21 69	33 92	41 106	9 49			High	84 55	109	4.3	6	March
April	8	18 65	29 84	40 104	6 42			Medium	86 59	132	5.2	7	April
May	7	14 58	25 77	37 99	1 34			Moderate	89 62	117	4.6	6	May
June	6	12 53	22 72	37 98	-2 29				88 61	69	2.7	6	June
July	6	12 53	23 74	39 103	-2 29				84 56	56	2.2	5	July
Aug	7	14 57	26 78	38 101	-1 30			Moderate	79 53	38	1.5	4	Aug
Sept	7	16 60	28 83	41 105	3 37			Medium	76 48	79	3.1	7	Sept
Oct	8	17 62	30 86	41 106	3 38			Medium	73 50	140	5.5	8	Oct
Nov	9	18 65	32 90	42 108	7 45			High	74 53	150	5.9	8	Nov
Dec	10	21 70	34 94	43 110	8 47			High	73 50	158	6.2	7	Dec

Based on readings for 15 years at 25°17' S, 57°30' W, altitude 139 m/456 ft

Peru

See map page 16

Peru is twice the size of France or the state of Texas, extending between the equator and 18° S. It has a long coastline on the Pacific Ocean and is bordered by Ecuador on the north, Brazil and Bolivia on the east, and Chile on the south. The central portion of Peru includes the great mountain and plateau region of the Andes with numerous peaks rising to over 6,000 m/20,000 ft and with extensive plateaux districts between 3,000 m/10,000 ft and 4,300 m/14,000 ft. There is a very narrow coastal plain on the Pacific shore, while to the east of the Andes the land drops steeply to the forested lowlands of the Amazon basin.

The Pacific coastal district has a most unusual type of dry desert climate. This is caused by the cold waters of the Humboldt current, which flows northwards. This area is a continuation of the coastal desert of northern Chile. The cold ocean water maintains low temperatures for a tropical latitude almost up to the equator and there are very small differences from month to month. The dryness is so marked that in some places several years have passed without appreciable rain. In the northern coastal districts, however, there is a remarkable change of weather for a few weeks every ten or fifteen years. Temperature rises, clouds build up, and torrential rain may fall for many days.

It is as if the equatorial belt of cloud and rain, which normally lies to the north on the coasts of Ecuador and Colombia, had moved south. Such unusual and unexpected heavy rain may cause widespread damage. At the same time the temperature of the sea rises offshore and the cold current retreats southwards. The phenomenon is called El Niño, and is most likely to occur in December and January.

This otherwise arid coastal strip has frequent low cloud and fog from which a light drizzle, called locally garúa, may fall. This is another unusual feature for such a dry climate.

Representative of the climate of the coastal district is the climatic table for **Lima** (below), although the city is a short distance inland. Midday temperatures are here a little higher than on the coast. Lima has an average of only one to two hours of sunshine a

LIMA												COASTAL PERU	
Sunshine	Temperatures							Discomfort from heat and humidity	Precipitation and humidity				Wet days
	Average daily				Highest recorded		Lowest recorded		Relative humidity		Average monthly precipitation		
	minimum		maximum						7:00 13:00				
average hours per day	°C	°F	°C	°F	°C	°F	°C	°F		%		mm	in	more than 1 mm/0.04 in
Jan	6	19	66	28	82	32	89	15	59	Medium	93	69	3	0.1	0.5	Jan
Feb	7	19	67	28	83	33	92	15	59	Medium	92	66	0	0.0	0.1	Feb
March	7	19	66	28	83	33	91	16	61	Medium	92	64	0	0.0	0.1	March
April	7	17	63	27	80	34	93	13	56	Medium	93	66	0	0.0	0.2	April
May	4	16	60	23	74	29	84	11	52	Moderate	95	76	5	0.2	0.8	May
June	1	14	58	20	68	27	81	9	49		95	80	5	0.2	1.0	June
July	1	14	57	19	67	27	81	9	49		94	77	8	0.3	1.0	July
Aug	1	13	56	19	66	27	81	10	50		95	78	8	0.3	2.0	Aug
Sept	1	14	57	20	68	26	78	11	51		94	76	8	0.3	1.0	Sept
Oct	3	14	58	22	71	26	79	12	53		94	72	3	0.1	0.2	Oct
Nov	4	16	60	23	74	29	85	11	51	Moderate	93	71	3	0.1	0.2	Nov
Dec	5	17	62	26	78	31	87	13	56	Medium	93	70	0	0.0	0.1	Dec

Based on readings for 15 years at 12°05′ S, 77°03′ W, altitude 120 m/394 ft

CAJAMARCA

NORTHERN INLAND PERU

Sunshine	Temperatures								Discomfort from heat and humidity	Precipitation and humidity				Wet days
	Average daily				Highest recorded		Lowest recorded			Relative humidity 7:00 13:00		Average monthly precipitation		
	minimum		maximum											
average hours per day	°C	°F	°C	°F	°C	°F	°C	°F		%		mm	in	more than 1 mm/0.04 in
Jan	9	48	22	71	25	77	4	38		85	38	91	3.6	13	Jan
Feb	9	48	21	70	25	77	0	32		88	45	107	4.2	17	Feb
March	9	48	21	70	26	79	3	37		92	46	117	4.6	17	March
April	8	47	21	70	25	77	0	32		90	42	86	3.4	14	April
May	7	44	22	71	25	77	-1	30		86	41	43	1.7	9	May
June	6	42	21	70	25	77	-1	30		81	37	13	0.5	4	June
July	5	41	21	70	25	77	-2	28		86	33	5	0.2	2	July
Aug	6	42	22	71	26	78	-1	30		81	29	8	0.3	2	Aug
Sept	7	45	22	71	25	77	0	32		85	38	58	2.3	9	Sept
Oct	8	47	22	71	26	79	1	33		81	34	58	2.3	9	Oct
Nov	8	46	22	72	26	79	-1	31		79	33	48	1.9	8	Nov
Dec	8	47	22	71	26	79	-4	25		86	37	81	3.2	11	Dec

Based on readings for 9 years at 7°09′ S, 78°30′ W, altitude 2640 m/8662 ft

CUZCO

SOUTHERN INLAND PERU

Sunshine	Temperatures								Discomfort from heat and humidity	Precipitation and humidity				Wet days
	Average daily				Highest recorded		Lowest recorded			Relative humidity 7:00 13:00		Average monthly precipitation		
	minimum		maximum											
average hours per day	°C	°F	°C	°F	°C	°F	°C	°F		%		mm	in	more than 1 mm/0.04 in
Jan	5	7	45	20	68	28	82	3	37		79	40	163	6.4	18	Jan
Feb	4	7	45	21	69	27	81	2	36		85	37	150	5.9	13	Feb
March	5	7	44	21	70	26	79	2	35		84	31	109	4.3	11	March
April	7	4	40	22	71	26	79	-4	25		87	33	51	2.0	8	April
May	8	2	35	21	70	26	78	-4	24		89	29	15	0.6	3	May
June	8	1	33	21	69	25	77	-5	23		91	23	5	0.2	2	June
July	8	-1	31	21	70	25	77	-9	16		95	23	5	0.2	2	July
Aug	8	1	34	21	70	25	77	-5	23		90	24	10	0.4	2	Aug
Sept	7	4	40	22	71	27	81	-1	30		80	26	25	1.0	7	Sept
Oct	6	6	43	22	72	29	84	-1	30		73	27	66	2.6	8	Oct
Nov	7	6	43	23	73	28	82	1	33		71	26	76	3.0	12	Nov
Dec	5	7	44	22	71	27	81	1	34		75	33	137	5.4	16	Dec

Based on readings for 13 years at 13°33′ S, 71°55′ W, altitude 3225 m/10,581 ft

day in the low sun period, but this rises to between five to seven hours a day during the warmer months of December to April.

The Andean mountain and plateaux region of Peru has similar weather and climate to that described on p. 64 for the Andean region of Bolivia. Here the main differences are a consequence of the altitude. The tables for **Cajamarca** (opposite) in the north of the country and **Cuzco** (opposite and below) in the south illustrate the marked reduction of temperature in all months and the single rainy season at the time of high sun between November and March. The greater cloudiness during the rainy season prevents

the temperature from rising higher at this time. As another consequence of the high altitude, there is a large daily range of temperature which falls quite low at night. During the dry season, frosts may be a nightly occurrence at these heights. Above 3,000 m/10,000 ft visitors may suffer from mountain sickness as described on p. 65 for Bolivia.

The climate and weather of the eastern lowlands in the Peruvian portion of the Amazon basin are similar to those described for Brazil and Bolivia; they are illustrated by the tables for **Conceptión** (p. 66) in Bolivia and **Sena Madureira** (p. 70) in Brazil.

Philippines

See map page 23

The Philippines consists of an archipelago of over 7,000 islands in the western Pacific situated between 4° and 21° N. The largest islands are, from north to south: Luzon, Samar, Leyte, Panay, Palawan, and Mindanao. They support most of the population and the main cities. All of the larger islands are mountainous and have very indented coastlines, so that the country has a rugged and confused relief.

There are numerous mountain ranges and isolated peaks rising to 1,800–3,000 m/6,000–10,000 ft. The area of the country is 300,000 sq km/116,000 sq mi, rather larger than the United Kingdom.

The country's southern islands have an almost equatorial climate with significant rain around the year (see the table for **Zamboanga** below, on Mindanao). The central and northern islands have a tropical monsoon type of climate, similar to that of

ZAMBOANGA															MINDANAO ISLAND	
Sunshine	Temperatures								Discomfort from heat and humidity	Precipitation and humidity					Wet days	
	Average daily				Highest recorded		Lowest recorded			Relative humidity 6:00 14:00		Average monthly precipitation				
	minimum		maximum													
average hours per day	°C	°F	°C	°F	°C	°F	°C	°F		%		mm	in		more than 1 mm/0.04 in	
Jan	23	73	31	88	35	95	19	66	High	92	70	53	2.1		5	Jan
Feb	23	73	31	88	34	94	19	66	High	92	71	56	2.2		5	Feb
March	23	74	32	89	35	95	20	68	High	92	70	38	1.5		5	March
April	23	74	31	88	36	96	21	69	High	93	74	51	2.0		6	April
May	24	75	31	88	35	95	22	72	High	93	76	89	3.5		9	May
June	24	75	31	88	35	95	22	71	High	94	77	107	4.2		12	June
July	23	74	31	87	35	95	21	70	High	94	77	125	4.9		12	July
Aug	24	75	31	88	35	95	21	70	High	93	75	102	4.0		10	Aug
Sept	23	74	31	88	35	95	21	70	High	94	76	119	4.7		11	Sept
Oct	23	74	31	88	35	95	21	70	High	93	76	142	5.6		11	Oct
Nov	23	74	31	88	35	95	20	68	High	94	75	107	4.2		11	Nov
Dec	23	73	32	89	34	94	19	67	Extreme	93	73	86	3.4		9	Dec

Based on readings for 15 years at 6°54′ N, 122°05′ E, altitude 7 m/23 ft

MANILA
LUZON ISLAND

	Sunshine	Temperatures							Discomfort from heat and humidity	Precipitation and humidity				Wet days	
		Average daily				Highest recorded		Lowest recorded			Relative humidity 6:00 13:00		Average monthly precipitation			
		minimum		maximum												
	average hours per day	°C	°F	°C	°F	°C	°F	°C	°F		%		mm	in	more than 0.25 mm/0.01 in	
Jan	6	21	69	30	86	35	95	14	58	High	89	63	23	0.9	6	Jan
Feb	7	21	69	31	88	36	96	16	60	High	88	59	13	0.5	3	Feb
March	7	22	71	33	91	37	98	16	61	High	85	55	18	0.7	4	March
April	9	23	73	34	93	38	100	17	63	High	85	55	33	1.3	4	April
May	7	24	75	34	93	38	101	20	68	Extreme	88	61	130	5.1	12	May
June	5	24	75	33	91	38	100	22	71	Extreme	91	68	254	10.0	17	June
July	4	24	75	31	88	36	97	21	69	High	91	74	432	17.0	24	July
Aug	4	24	75	31	87	35	95	21	69	High	92	73	422	16.6	23	Aug
Sept	4	24	75	31	88	35	95	21	69	High	93	73	356	14.0	22	Sept
Oct	5	23	74	31	88	35	95	19	67	High	92	71	193	7.6	19	Oct
Nov	5	22	72	31	87	34	93	17	62	High	91	69	145	5.7	14	Nov
Dec	5	21	70	30	86	34	94	16	60	High	90	67	66	2.6	11	Dec

Based on readings for 60 years at 14°35′ N, 120°59′ E, altitude 14 m/47 ft

ILOILO
PANAY ISLANDS

	Sunshine	Temperatures							Discomfort from heat and humidity	Precipitation and humidity				Wet days	
		Average daily				Highest recorded		Lowest recorded			Relative humidity 6:00 14:00		Average monthly precipitation			
		minimum		maximum												
	average hours per day	°C	°F	°C	°F	°C	°F	°C	°F		%		mm	in	more than 1 mm/0.04 in	
Jan		23	73	29	85	33	92	20	68	Medium	91	68	64	2.5	9	Jan
Feb		23	74	31	87	36	96	20	68	High	90	63	46	1.8	5	Feb
March		23	74	31	88	35	95	20	68	High	89	59	33	1.3	4	March
April		24	76	33	92	37	98	22	71	High	89	59	43	1.7	5	April
May		25	77	33	91	37	98	22	72	Extreme	90	67	158	6.2	13	May
June		24	76	32	89	36	96	22	71	High	92	71	264	10.4	16	June
July		24	76	31	87	35	95	22	72	High	90	75	447	17.6	20	July
Aug		24	76	31	87	34	94	22	72	High	91	74	386	15.2	18	Aug
Sept		24	76	31	88	36	97	22	72	High	91	75	315	12.4	17	Sept
Oct		24	75	31	88	34	94	21	69	High	92	73	269	10.6	16	Oct
Nov		24	75	31	87	35	95	21	69	High	93	72	211	8.3	13	Nov
Dec		23	74	30	86	34	93	19	67	High	93	70	119	4.7	11	Dec

Based on readings for 15 years at 10°42′ N, 122°34′ E, altitude 14 m/46 ft

SURIGAO														EASTERN MINDANAO	
Sunshine	Temperatures								Discomfort from heat and humidity	Precipitation and humidity				Wet days	
	Average daily				Highest recorded		Lowest recorded			Relative humidity 6:30 14:30		Average monthly precipitation			
	minimum		maximum												
average hours per day	°C	°F	°C	°F	°C	°F	°C	°F		%		mm	in	more than 1 mm/0.04 in	
Jan	23	74	28	83	31	88	19	67	High	93	80	544	21.4	24	Jan
Feb	23	73	29	84	32	90	20	68	High	93	77	376	14.8	18	Feb
March	23	74	29	85	32	90	20	68	High	93	76	506	19.9	21	March
April	23	74	31	87	33	92	21	69	High	95	76	254	10.0	19	April
May	24	76	31	88	35	95	21	70	High	94	72	158	6.2	13	May
June	24	76	31	88	36	97	21	70	High	94	70	125	4.9	10	June
July	24	76	31	88	34	94	22	71	High	89	68	178	7.0	13	July
Aug	24	76	31	88	36	96	22	72	High	89	66	130	5.1	11	Aug
Sept	24	76	31	88	37	99	22	72	High	90	68	168	6.6	13	Sept
Oct	24	75	31	87	34	94	21	70	High	91	73	272	10.7	17	Oct
Nov	24	75	29	85	33	92	21	70	High	94	78	427	16.8	20	Nov
Dec	23	74	28	83	33	91	19	66	High	94	80	620	24.4	24	Dec

Based on readings for 15 years at 9°48' N, 125°29' E, altitude 6 m/20 ft

Indo-China, with a single season of heavy rain. In most areas the wettest time is from July to October when the wind system of the western Pacific is affected by the monsoon influence of the Asian continent. Winds are then southwesterly to southeasterly. See the tables for **Manila** (opposite and above) in Luzon and **Iloilo** (opposite) on the island of Panay.

Rainfall is particularly heavy in the period August to October when much of it comes from tropical cyclones, called typhoons, in the South China Sea. The severest of these typhoons produce very high wind speeds and torrential rain. Most of them develop east of the Philippines and move westwards into the South China Sea, where they deepen and intensify. A number of typhoons affect some part of the Philippines each year and the most severe cause widespread damage and loss of life through flooding and landslides as well as wind damage.

Annual rainfall is over 1,000 mm/40 in almost everywhere and where warm, damp Pacific air is forced to rise over coastal mountains, annual rainfall often exceeds 4,000–5,000 mm /160–200 in. Coasts facing northeast are exposed to the Pacific trade winds between November and March and these areas have their heaviest rainfall at this time. See the table for **Surigao** (above) on the eastern side of Mindanao Island.

Temperatures remain fairly high throughout the year except in the mountains but excessive heat is rare. The worst feature of the climate, apart from the occasional typhoon, is the high humidity and cloud during the rainy season; on many days the weather is muggy and oppressive.

In the dry season the weather is more pleasant with much sunshine, up to seven or eight hours a day on average, with refreshing sea breezes on the coast.

There are a number of mountain resorts, such as the summer capital, Baguio on Luzon Island. Although temperatures may be much lower here, rain and cloud increase.

Poland

See map page 19

Poland lies in eastern Europe between Germany and Russia. It has a long border with the Czech Republic and the Slovak Republic in the south and a coastline on the Baltic Sea in the north. Most of the country consists of a low-lying rolling plain below 300 m/1,000 ft but in the south part of the Sudeten Mountains fall within western Poland and part of the higher Carpathian Mountains, which rise over 1,800 m/6,000 ft, belong to eastern Poland.

Most of Poland has a very similar climate and the same sequence of weather throughout the year. Winter cold increases towards the east and in the southern mountains, while the coastlands of the Baltic Sea have slightly milder winters and cooler summers (see the table for **Gdynia** below).

Precipitation is well distributed around the year with a summer maximum of rain, often heavy and accompanied by thunder. Much of the winter precipitation is snow. Snow covers the ground for an average of forty days each winter in the north and west and for as much as sixty to seventy days in the

south and east. Snow lies for up to 100 days a year in the Carpathians and winter sports are possible here. Over most of Poland total annual precipitation is quite low, between 500 mm/20 in and 625 mm/25 in.

Summer temperatures do not differ very much over the country. It rarely gets excessively hot but fine, sunny spells of weather and occasional droughts occur. Winters are distinctly cold and the length of really cold spells varies considerably from year to year. The worst winter weather occurs when strong easterly winds blow and on these occasions the winter cold is similar to that found in Russia. The cold may be prolonged when an anticyclone becomes settled over eastern Europe in winter. However, it is more bearable as there is little wind chill in the calm air and the weather may be alternately foggy or sunny.

The tables for **Poznań** (opposite) and **Warsaw** (opposite and below) illustrate conditions over much of Poland. Those for **Kraków** and **Przemyśl** (both on p. 290) are representative of the colder south and east of the country.

GDYNIA												BALTIC COAST	
Sunshine	Temperatures							Discomfort from heat and humidity	Precipitation and humidity				Wet days
	Average daily				Highest recorded		Lowest recorded		Relative humidity		Average monthly precipitation		
	minimum		maximum						7:00	13:00			
average hours per day	°C	°F	°C	°F	°C	°F	°C	°F	%		mm	in	more than 0.1 mm/0.004 in
Jan	1	−3	27	1	35	11	52	−20	−3	86	82	33	1.3	15	Jan
Feb	3	−4	25	1	35	14	56	−24	−11	86	80	31	1.2	15	Feb
March	4	−1	30	4	40	18	65	−13	9	86	76	27	1.1	12	March
April	5	2	36	9	48	24	75	−7	20	83	71	36	1.4	13	April
May	7	7	45	15	59	31	88	−2	28	78	69	42	1.7	11	May
June	9	11	52	19	66	33	91	2	36	77	67	71	2.8	11	June
July	8	14	58	21	70	36	96	8	46	81	70	84	3.3	13	July
Aug	7	14	57	21	70	34	93	7	45	83	69	75	3.0	12	Aug
Sept	6	11	51	18	64	29	85	2	35	85	69	59	2.3	14	Sept
Oct	3	7	44	13	55	24	74	−4	26	86	72	61	2.4	15	Oct
Nov	2	2	36	7	44	16	60	−10	13	87	80	29	1.1	11	Nov
Dec	1	−1	31	3	38	12	54	−16	4	88	84	46	1.8	16	Dec

Based on readings for 14 years at 54°31′ N, 18°33′ E, altitude 5 m/16 ft

POZNAN

WESTERN POLAND

Sunshine average hours per day	Temperatures								Discomfort from heat and humidity	Precipitation and humidity				Wet days more than 0.1 mm/0.004 in
	Average daily				Highest recorded		Lowest recorded			Relative humidity 7:00 13:00		Average monthly precipitation		
	minimum		maximum											
	°C	°F	°C	°F	°C	°F	°C	°F		%		mm	in	
Jan	−5	24	1	33	11	52	−23	−9		89	83	24	0.9	15	Jan
Feb	−5	22	1	34	14	57	−28	−18		89	79	29	1.1	14	Feb
March	−1	30	7	44	21	70	−15	5		88	70	26	1.0	11	March
April	3	37	12	54	29	83	−6	21		85	60	41	1.6	14	April
May	8	47	20	67	32	89	−2	28		78	52	47	1.9	11	May
June	11	52	23	72	35	96	1	33		77	54	54	2.1	11	June
July	14	57	24	76	38	101	4	39	Moderate	83	59	82	3.2	16	July
Aug	13	55	23	73	35	94	5	41	Moderate	87	60	66	2.6	13	Aug
Sept	9	48	19	67	32	90	−2	29		91	61	45	1.8	11	Sept
Oct	5	41	13	56	25	77	−6	21		93	72	38	1.5	14	Oct
Nov	1	33	6	43	17	63	−11	12		93	83	23	0.9	12	Nov
Dec	−2	28	3	37	13	55	−23	−9		91	87	39	1.5	17	Dec

Based on readings for 14 years at 52°26′ N, 16°53′ E, altitude 83 m/272 ft

WARSAW

CENTRAL POLAND

Sunshine average hours per day	Temperatures								Discomfort from heat and humidity	Precipitation and humidity				Wet days more than 0.1 mm/0.004 in
	Average daily				Highest recorded		Lowest recorded			Relative humidity 7:00 13:30		Average monthly precipitation		
	minimum		maximum											
	°C	°F	°C	°F	°C	°F	°C	°F		%		mm	in	
Jan	−6	22	0	32	11	51	−29	−20		90	84	27	1.1	15	Jan
Feb	−6	21	0	32	13	56	−27	−16		89	80	32	1.3	14	Feb
March	−2	28	6	42	18	65	−14	6		90	70	27	1.1	11	March
April	3	37	12	53	27	80	−6	22		85	61	37	1.5	13	April
May	9	48	20	67	34	92	−3	27		80	56	46	1.8	11	May
June	12	54	23	73	34	93	3	38		82	59	69	2.7	13	June
July	15	58	24	75	35	95	7	45	Moderate	86	63	96	3.8	16	July
Aug	14	56	23	73	33	92	7	44	Moderate	90	63	65	2.6	13	Aug
Sept	10	49	19	66	31	88	1	34		92	64	43	1.7	12	Sept
Oct	5	41	13	55	26	78	−9	17		93	73	38	1.5	12	Oct
Nov	1	33	6	42	17	63	−12	10		93	83	31	1.2	12	Nov
Dec	−3	28	2	35	13	55	−26	−14		92	87	44	1.7	16	Dec

Based on readings for 14 years at 52°13′ N, 21°03′ E, altitude 110 m/361 ft

KRAKOW — SOUTHERN POLAND

Sunshine	Temperatures								Discomfort from heat and humidity	Precipitation and humidity				Wet days
	Average daily				Highest recorded		Lowest recorded			Relative humidity 7:30 13:30		Average monthly precipitation		
	minimum		maximum											more than 0.1 mm/0.004 in
average hours per day	°C	°F	°C	°F	°C	°F	°C	°F		%		mm	in	
Jan 2	−5	22	0	32	11	52	−23	−10		88	81	28	1.1	16 Jan
Feb 2	−5	22	1	34	16	60	−27	−16		87	78	28	1.1	15 Feb
March 4	−1	30	7	45	21	70	−15	5		88	71	35	1.4	12 March
April 5	3	38	13	55	29	83	−6	21		85	60	46	1.8	15 April
May 7	9	48	20	67	33	91	−2	29		80	56	46	1.8	12 May
June 7	12	54	22	72	34	93	3	37		81	60	94	3.7	15 June
July 7	15	58	24	76	35	95	9	47	Moderate	83	61	111	4.4	16 July
Aug 6	14	56	23	73	34	94	6	43	Moderate	87	63	91	3.6	15 Aug
Sept 5	10	49	19	66	30	86	−1	31		91	66	62	2.4	12 Sept
Oct 3	5	42	14	56	27	80	−4	24		92	71	49	1.9	14 Oct
Nov 2	1	33	6	44	21	70	−12	11		93	82	37	1.5	15 Nov
Dec 1	−2	28	3	37	17	62	−18	−1		90	85	36	1.4	16 Dec

Based on readings for 14 years at 50°04′ N, 19°58′ E, altitude 209 m/686 ft

PRZEMYSL — SOUTHEASTERN POLAND

Sunshine	Temperatures								Discomfort from heat and humidity	Precipitation and humidity				Wet days
	Average daily				Highest recorded		Lowest recorded			Relative humidity 7:30 13:30		Average monthly precipitation		
	minimum		maximum											more than 0.1 mm/0.004 in
average hours per day	°C	°F	°C	°F	°C	°F	°C	°F		%		mm	in	
Jan 2	−7	20	0	32	14	57	−26	−15		83	74	27	1.1	14 Jan
Feb 2	−6	21	1	34	15	59	−27	−16		82	71	24	0.9	14 Feb
March 3	−2	29	6	43	24	75	−25	−13		83	64	25	1.0	10 March
April 5	3	37	13	55	31	87	−11	12		83	59	43	1.7	13 April
May 7	8	46	19	67	31	88	−2	28		79	55	57	2.2	12 May
June 7	12	53	23	73	34	92	2	35	Moderate	82	60	88	3.5	13 June
July 7	14	57	24	75	37	98	6	43	Moderate	84	63	105	4.1	15 July
Aug 6	13	55	23	73	33	91	3	38	Moderate	88	63	93	3.7	14 Aug
Sept 5	9	48	19	67	31	88	0	31		90	63	58	2.3	12 Sept
Oct 3	5	40	14	57	30	86	−7	20		89	67	50	2.0	12 Oct
Nov 2	1	33	6	43	20	67	−16	3		90	78	43	1.7	13 Nov
Dec 1	−2	28	3	38	16	61	−17	2		86	78	43	1.7	16 Dec

Based on readings for 11 years at 49°47′ N, 22°48′ E, altitude 201 m/659 ft

As in much of western and central Europe, the weather can be changeable at all times of the year but winters are most likely to have prolonged spells of one type of weather. Daily sunshine hours average from one to two hours in midwinter to as much as six to seven hours in summer.

Portugal

Portugal is a small country in the Iberian Peninsula of southwestern Europe. About the same size as Scotland, it has a coastline on the Atlantic Ocean and a land frontier with Spain. In addition, two attractive groups of Atlantic islands are integral parts of Portugal.

THE AZORES

Including (with names of towns and cities in parentheses): CORVO, FAIAL, FLORES, GRACIOSA, PICO, SANTA MARIA, SAO JORGE, SAO MIGUEL (Ponta Delgada), and TERCEIRA (Angra do Heroismo).

See map page 20

The Azores, discovered and settled by the Portuguese in the 15th century, consist of a group of ten main islands situated about 1,300 km/800 mi west of Portugal. The land area is rather less than that of the state of Rhode Island. All the islands are hilly or mountainous with peaks rising to between 600–2,300 m/2,000–7,500 ft.

The Azores have a very mild climate throughout the year with no great extremes of temperature. Summer days are warm but never really hot and in winter cold weather with frost and snow is unknown at sea level. Winter weather can be stormy and changeable when deep Atlantic depressions track across or near the islands.

Summer is generally a more settled season but occasional storms and wet weather can occur. Sunshine amounts are only moderate for the latitude and range from an average of three to four hours a day in winter to seven to eight in summer. Rainfall is well distributed around the year but is heavier and more frequent in winter.

The table for **Angra do Heroismo** (below) shows typical conditions at or near sea level in the Azores.

ANGRA DO HEROISMO														AZORES
Sunshine	Temperatures								Discomfort from heat and humidity	Precipitation and humidity				Wet days
	Average daily				Highest recorded		Lowest recorded			Relative humidity		Average monthly precipitation		
	minimum		maximum							10:00	16:00			
average hours per day	°C	°F	°C	°F	°C	°F	°C	°F		%		mm	in	more than 0.1 mm/0.004 in
Jan	3	12	53	16	61	19	66	4	39		79	80	143	5.6	21	Jan
Feb	3	12	53	16	60	19	66	4	39		79	80	131	5.2	19	Feb
March	4	12	53	16	60	20	67	4	40		78	79	150	5.9	21	March
April	5	12	54	17	62	21	70	6	43		76	77	77	3.0	14	April
May	5	14	56	18	65	24	75	8	47		76	76	70	2.8	14	May
June	6	16	61	21	70	25	77	11	52		77	77	49	1.9	11	June
July	6	18	64	23	74	28	82	12	54	Moderate	74	74	43	1.7	9	July
Aug	7	19	66	24	76	28	83	15	59	Moderate	73	73	44	1.7	11	Aug
Sept	6	18	64	23	74	28	82	14	57	Moderate	74	75	98	3.9	13	Sept
Oct	4	16	61	21	69	25	76	10	50		75	77	126	5.0	18	Oct
Nov	3	14	58	18	65	23	73	8	46		75	78	143	5.6	19	Nov
Dec	2	13	55	17	62	21	69	5	41		78	80	112	4.4	18	Dec

Based on readings for 20 years at 38°39′ N, 27°14′ W, altitude 90 m/296 ft

FUNCHAL																MADEIRA
Sunshine	Temperatures								Discomfort from heat and humidity	Precipitation and humidity					Wet days	
	Average daily				Highest recorded		Lowest recorded			Relative humidity 9:00 15:00		Average monthly precipitation				
	minimum		maximum													
average hours per day	°C	°F	°C	°F	°C	°F	°C	°F		%		mm	in		more than 1 mm/0.04 in	
Jan	5	13	56	19	66	26	79	6	42		66	66	64	2.5	6.0	Jan
Feb	6	13	56	18	65	28	82	4	40		65	65	74	2.9	6.0	Feb
March	6	13	56	19	66	28	82	7	44		66	67	79	3.1	7.0	March
April	7	14	58	19	67	29	84	7	44		64	65	33	1.3	4.0	April
May	7	16	60	21	69	31	88	9	48		65	65	18	0.7	2.0	May
June	7	17	63	22	72	36	96	9	48		68	68	5	0.2	0.9	June
July	8	19	66	24	75	37	98	13	55	Moderate	67	67	0	0.0	0.2	July
Aug	8	19	67	24	76	39	103	11	52	Moderate	67	67	0	0.0	0.4	Aug
Sept	8	19	67	24	76	35	95	13	55	Moderate	65	67	25	1.0	3.0	Sept
Oct	7	18	65	23	74	33	92	8	47	Moderate	64	66	76	3.0	7.0	Oct
Nov	5	16	61	22	71	31	87	7	45		64	65	89	3.5	6.0	Nov
Dec	5	14	58	19	67	27	80	5	41		67	67	84	3.3	7.0	Dec

Based on readings for 30 years at 32°38′ N, 16°55′ W, altitude 25 m/82 ft

MADEIRA

Including (with towns and cities in parentheses): MADEIRA (Funchal) and PORTO SANTO.

See map page 20

The Madeira group of islands, occupied and settled by the Portuguese in the 15th century, consists of the two inhabited islands and several small uninhabited islands. The total land area is small: 790 sq km/305 sq mi.

The main island of Madeira is volcanic and mountainous, with its highest peaks rising to over 1,800 m/6,000 ft. Its mild winters and generally warm, sunny summers have made it a popular holiday resort. The islands are situated about 725 km/450 mi west of the coast of Morocco.

The climate of Madeira is similar to that found around the Mediterranean or in coastal California but the ocean waters moderate the temperature so that the island never suffer extremes of heat or cold.

The winter months are quite wet, particularly at higher levels, and stormy and cloudy conditions may last for a few days at a time. There are also spells of fine, settled weather in winter with mild to cool temperatures. There is little cloudy weather from May until September but occasional light rain may fall and fog can occur. In general, the island has a sunny climate with an average of five to six hours' sunshine a day in winter and as much as seven to eight in summer. Days can be cloudy and cool as late as April at sea level and for much longer in the mountains.

The table for **Funchal** (above) is representative of conditions at sea level on Madeira.

MAINLAND PORTUGAL

Including from north to south (with towns and cities in parentheses): the DOURO region (Pôrto, Bragança), the BEIRA region, the RIBATEJO region (Lisbon, Fátima), the ALENTEJO region, and the ALGARVE region (Faro).

See map page 18

Together with Ireland, mainland Portugal occupies the most westerly position in Europe and its weather and climate are much influenced by the Atlantic. Its southerly latitude gives it a Mediterranean type of climate, similar to that of the state of California, but one where the summer heat is tempered by the Atlantic influence.

BRAGANCA — NORTHERN PORTUGAL

Sunshine average hours per day	Temperatures								Discomfort from heat and humidity	Precipitation and humidity				Wet days more than 0.1 mm/0.004 in
	Average daily				Highest recorded		Lowest recorded			Relative humidity 5:30 11:30		Average monthly precipitation		
	minimum		maximum											
	°C	°F	°C	°F	°C	°F	°C	°F		%		mm	in	
Jan 4	0	32	8	46	18	64	–12	10		90	80	149	5.9	15 Jan
Feb 6	1	33	11	51	21	71	–11	12		88	73	104	4.1	12 Feb
March 6	3	38	13	55	25	77	–7	19		86	68	133	5.2	15 March
April 8	5	40	16	60	29	83	–4	24		83	59	73	2.9	10 April
May 9	7	45	19	65	31	88	–2	28		83	59	69	2.7	11 May
June 11	11	51	24	75	36	98	1	33	Moderate	80	53	42	1.7	7 June
July 12	13	55	28	82	40	103	3	37	Medium	76	47	15	0.6	3 July
Aug 11	13	55	28	83	38	101	1	33	Medium	77	47	16	0.6	4 Aug
Sept 8	10	50	24	74	36	96	–1	30	Moderate	82	55	39	1.5	7 Sept
Oct 6	7	44	18	64	29	83	–4	25		87	66	79	3.1	10 Oct
Nov 5	3	38	12	53	22	72	–6	20		90	74	110	4.3	14 Nov
Dec 4	1	33	8	46	17	62	–10	14		90	81	144	5.7	17 Dec

Based on readings for 30 years at 41°49′ N, 6°46′ W, altitude 720 m/2362 ft

PORTO — NORTH COASTAL PORTUGAL

Sunshine average hours per day	Temperatures								Discomfort from heat and humidity	Precipitation and humidity				Wet days more than .01 mm/.0004 in
	Average daily				Highest recorded		Lowest recorded			Relative humidity 8:30 14:30		Average monthly precipitation		
	minimum		maximum											
	°C	°F	°C	°F	°C	°F	°C	°F		%		mm	in	
Jan 5	5	40	13	56	22	71	–4	25		87	69	159	6.3	18 Jan
Feb 6	5	41	14	58	29	84	–4	25		84	65	112	4.4	15 Feb
March 6	8	46	16	61	29	83	–2	29		81	65	147	5.8	17 March
April 8	9	48	18	65	32	89	1	33		76	61	86	3.4	13 April
May 9	11	51	20	67	33	92	4	38		74	65	87	3.4	13 May
June 10	13	56	23	73	37	98	7	44	Moderate	74	64	41	1.6	7 June
July 11	15	58	25	76	40	104	9	48	Moderate	73	60	20	0.8	5 July
Aug 10	15	58	25	77	39	103	9	48	Moderate	76	60	26	1.0	6 Aug
Sept 8	14	56	24	75	37	99	6	42	Moderate	80	63	51	2.0	10 Sept
Oct 6	11	51	21	69	34	94	2	35		82	64	105	4.1	15 Oct
Nov 5	8	46	17	62	26	78	–1	30		85	68	148	5.8	18 Nov
Dec 4	5	42	14	57	22	71	–4	25		86	70	168	6.6	18 Dec

Based on readings for 30 years at 41°08′ N, 8°36′ W, altitude 95 m/312 ft

LISBON
CENTRAL COASTAL PORTUGAL

Sunshine	Temperatures								Discomfort from heat and humidity	Precipitation and humidity				Wet days	
	Average daily				Highest recorded		Lowest recorded			Relative humidity 8:30 14:30		Average monthly precipitation			
	minimum		maximum												
average hours per day	°C	°F	°C	°F	°C	°F	°C	°F		%		mm	in	more than 0.1 mm/0.004 in	
Jan 5	8	46	14	57	21	69	-1	31		85	71	111	4.3	15	Jan
Feb 7	8	47	15	59	25	78	-1	29		80	64	76	3.0	12	Feb
March 7	10	50	17	63	27	81	3	37		78	64	109	4.2	14	March
April 9	12	53	20	67	31	88	4	40		69	56	54	2.1	10	April
May 10	13	55	21	71	34	94	6	44		68	57	44	1.7	10	May
June 11	15	60	25	77	38	100	10	50	Moderate	65	54	16	0.6	5	June
July 12	17	63	27	81	40	104	12	54	Moderate	62	48	3	0.1	2	July
Aug 12	17	63	28	82	40	105	13	56	Medium	64	49	4	0.2	2	Aug
Sept 9	17	62	26	79	36	96	10	51	Moderate	70	54	33	1.3	6	Sept
Oct 7	14	58	22	72	35	96	7	44		75	59	62	2.4	9	Oct
Nov 6	11	52	17	63	27	80	4	39		81	68	93	3.7	13	Nov
Dec 5	9	47	15	58	21	70	0	32		84	72	103	4.1	15	Dec

Based on readings for 30 years at 38°43' N, 9°09' W, altitude 77 m/253 ft

FARO
SOUTHERN PORTUGAL

Sunshine	Temperatures								Discomfort from heat and humidity	Precipitation and humidity				Wet days	
	Average daily				Highest recorded		Lowest recorded			Relative humidity 8:30 14:30		Average monthly precipitation			
	minimum		maximum												
average hours per day	°C	°F	°C	°F	°C	°F	°C	°F		%		mm	in	more than 0.1 mm/0.004 in	
Jan 6	9	48	15	60	24	75	-1	31		79	72	70	2.8	9	Jan
Feb 7	10	49	16	61	23	73	-1	31		76	70	52	2.1	7	Feb
March 7	11	52	18	64	26	79	2	36		76	72	72	2.8	10	March
April 9	13	55	20	67	32	89	5	41		69	67	31	1.2	6	April
May 10	14	58	22	71	33	91	7	45		68	67	21	0.8	4	May
June 12	18	64	25	77	35	95	10	50	Moderate	66	65	5	0.2	1	June
July 12	20	67	28	83	41	106	12	54	Medium	63	62	1	0.0	0	July
Aug 12	20	68	28	83	37	99	8	46	Medium	63	63	1	0.0	0	Aug
Sept 9	19	65	26	78	34	94	10	50	Medium	67	66	17	0.7	2	Sept
Oct 8	16	60	22	72	32	89	8	46		70	68	51	2.0	6	Oct
Nov 6	13	55	19	66	28	83	5	41		75	70	65	2.6	8	Nov
Dec 6	10	50	16	61	22	71	1	34		77	70	67	2.6	9	Dec

Based on readings for 30 years at 37°01' N, 7°55' W, altitude 36 m/118 ft

On the coast the winters are particularly mild. The north and the central interior of Portugal include mountains and plateaux rising in places over 1,800 m/6,000 ft; here the summers are much cooler and winters may be quite cold (see the table for **Bragança** (p. 293), situated at medium height in the extreme north).

Winter is the wet season everywhere in Portugal, but autumn rain can sometimes be heavy in the north as the fine weather of summer breaks. The length and severity of the summer drought increases from north to south. This can be seen by comparing the monthly rainfall and number of wet days at **Porto** (p. 293), **Lisbon** (opposite), and **Faro** (opposite and below) in the climatic tables. Summer sunshine and temperature and winter mildness also increase southwards. The south-facing coast of the Algarve

region is the sunniest, driest, and warmest part of the country but the summer heat rarely reaches the unpleasant levels sometimes found in southeastern Spain. Another favourable aspect of this region for tourists is the higher sea temperatures as compared with those on the west-facing coasts farther north, where seas are most likely to be rough.

Snow is very rare at sea level in Portugal, but it becomes more frequent inland and on the higher areas of the north. Winter rainfall is rather heavy north of Lisbon and the weather in the far north is often wet and stormy. Most parts of Portugal are sunny. Daily hours of sunshine average from four to five in winter and ten to eleven in summer in the north. These figures rise to six in winter and twelve in summer in the far south.

Puerto Rico

See map page 15

Puerto Rico is the most easterly of the large islands in the central Caribbean and is situated midway between Hispaniola and the Leeward Islands. It has an area of about 8,800 sq km/3,400 sq mi.

It is a mountainous island with the highest land rising to over 1,200 m/4,000 ft, so the centre and north coast of the island, exposed to the northeast trade winds, are wetter throughout the year than the sheltered south coast. The table for **San Juan** (below), on the north coast, shows that here, as on

SAN JUAN												NORTH COAST PUERTO RICO					
Sunshine		Temperatures								Discomfort from heat and humidity	Precipitation and humidity					Wet days	
		Average daily				Highest recorded		Lowest recorded			Relative humidity		Average monthly precipitation				
		minimum		maximum							9:00	12:00					
average hours per day		°C	°F	°C	°F	°C	°F	°C	°F		%		mm	in		more than 0.25 mm/0.01 in	
Jan	7	21	70	27	80	31	88	17	63	Medium	81	75	109	4.3	20		Jan
Feb	8	21	70	27	80	33	91	17	62	Medium	79	74	69	2.7	15		Feb
March	9	21	70	27	81	33	91	17	63	Medium	76	74	74	2.9	15		March
April	9	22	72	28	82	34	93	18	65	Medium	75	75	104	4.1	14		April
May	8	23	74	29	84	34	94	19	66	High	76	75	150	5.9	16		May
June	8	24	75	29	85	34	93	19	66	High	76	77	137	5.4	17		June
July	8	24	75	29	85	33	92	21	70	High	77	78	145	5.7	19		July
Aug	9	24	76	29	85	34	93	20	68	High	77	77	160	6.3	20		Aug
Sept	7	24	75	30	86	34	94	21	69	High	78	77	158	6.2	18		Sept
Oct	8	24	75	29	85	34	94	20	68	High	79	76	142	5.6	18		Oct
Nov	7	23	73	29	84	34	93	19	66	High	80	76	160	6.3	19		Nov
Dec	7	22	72	27	81	32	90	17	62	Medium	81	77	137	5.4	21		Dec

Based on readings for 48 years at 18°29′ N, 60°07′ W, altitude 25 m/82 ft

the north coast of the Dominican Republic, the annual rainfall is well spread over the year and there is no dry season. This is rather unusual for the Caribbean and is a local effect of the moist trade winds being forced to rise over the mountains close to the coast.

Qatar

See map page 22

This small Arab country consists of a low-lying peninsula on the north coast of Saudi Arabia. It is surrounded by the waters of the Persian Gulf on three sides. It has a climate similar to that of Bahrain (p. 56) and the United Arab Emirates (p. 370). It is very hot and rainless from May until September, with occasional showery rain during the rest of the year. Winter temperatures are mild to warm and the weather is then generally sunny and pleasant.

Summers are often unpleasantly hot with some danger of heat exhaustion or heatstroke. Conditions on the coast are made even more unpleasant by the high humidity which more than cancels the slightly lower temperatures. The climatic tables for **Bahrain** (p. 56) and **Sharjah** (p. 370), United Arab Emirates, are representative of conditions throughout the year in Qatar. For more detail about the weather and climate of Arabia see the description for Saudi Arabia on p. 312.

Réunion

See map page 21

This small island is situated in latitude 21° S in the Indian Ocean. It lies 190 km/120 mi west-southwest of Mauritius and has a very similar sequence of weather around the year (see the table for **Port Louis** in Mauritius on p. 236). The island consists of a high volcanic mountain rising to 3,000 m/ 10,000 ft and rainfall is very heavy on the southern and southeastern slopes exposed to the trade winds. Like Mauritius, it is occasionally affected by tropical cyclones between December and April. Formerly a French colony, Réunion is now an overseas département of France.

Romania

See map page 19

Romania is an almost landlocked country in southeastern Europe. It has a short coastline on the Black Sea, south of the mouth of the river Danube. Its southern border is with Bulgaria; it is bordered on the west by Yugoslavia and Hungary, north by Ukraine, and east by Moldova. The east and south of the country are low-lying and rather flat; the centre and west include the Carpathian Mountains and their foothills with ridges and peaks rising from 1,800 m/6,000 ft.

Romania has a climate of the continental type, rather like that of the steppes of Ukraine, with cold, snowy winters and warm summers. Precipitation is normally rather low except in the higher parts of the Carpathians. Spring and summer are the wettest seasons when thunderstorms are most frequent.

Winter precipitation is mostly snow. Snow lies from thirty to fifty days a year at low levels and up to 100 days in the mountains. The mildest area in winter is along the coast of the Black Sea.

The table for **Constanta** (opposite and above) is representative of weather conditions along the Black Sea coast of Romania.

Inland, the Danube and other rivers usually freeze in winter. The change from winter conditions to those of summer is often abrupt and spring is a short but changeable season in Romania. Late summer and autumn are often rather dry.

The weather can be changeable at all times of the year and there are considerable variations from one year to another. In dry summers the plains in the north and east can suffer from drought as hot, dry winds blow from the east.

On the other hand, in winter the most severe weather occurs when cold winds from the same region sweep the country. Winter is the time of

CONSTANTA

BLACK SEA COAST

Sunshine average hours per day	Temperatures									Discomfort from heat and humidity	Precipitation and humidity			Wet days more than 0.1 mm/0.004 in
	Average daily				Highest recorded		Lowest recorded				Relative humidity all hours	Average monthly precipitation		
	minimum		maximum											
	°C	°F	°C	°F	°C	°F	°C	°F			%	mm	in	
Jan	-4	25	3	37	17	62	-23	-10			89	29	1.1	10	Jan
Feb	-3	28	4	40	20	67	-18	0			87	23	0.9	8	Feb
March	1	33	8	46	31	87	-13	9			83	21	0.8	7	March
April	6	42	13	56	30	85	-5	23			82	28	1.1	7	April
May	11	52	19	66	34	94	2	35			81	35	1.4	8	May
June	16	60	24	75	36	97	6	42	Moderate		78	41	1.6	8	June
July	18	64	27	81	35	94	8	47	Medium		73	35	1.4	5	July
Aug	17	63	27	80	35	94	8	46	Medium		75	31	1.2	4	Aug
Sept	14	57	23	73	32	90	-1	31	Moderate		79	24	0.9	4	Sept
Oct	9	49	17	63	29	85	-4	25			84	38	1.5	6	Oct
Nov	4	40	11	51	24	76	-11	13			89	40	1.6	10	Nov
Dec	-1	31	6	43	21	69	-16	3			90	34	1.3	9	Dec

Based on readings for 27 years at 44°11′ N, 28°40′ E, altitude 32 m/105 ft

BUCHAREST

EAST OF THE CARPATHIANS

Sunshine average hours per day	Temperatures									Discomfort from heat and humidity	Precipitation and humidity			Wet days more than 0.1 mm/0.004 in
	Average daily				Highest recorded		Lowest recorded				Relative humidity all hours	Average monthly precipitation		
	minimum		maximum											
	°C	°F	°C	°F	°C	°F	°C	°F			%	mm	in	
Jan	-7	19	1	34	16	60	-32	-26			87	46	1.8	11	Jan
Feb	-5	23	4	38	20	68	-26	-15			84	26	1.0	9	Feb
March	-1	30	10	50	29	84	-19	-2			73	28	1.1	9	March
April	5	41	18	64	32	89	-4	25			63	59	2.3	11	April
May	10	51	23	74	37	98	0	31	Moderate		63	77	3.0	13	May
June	14	57	27	81	37	99	5	40	Medium		62	121	4.8	12	June
July	16	60	30	86	39	102	8	46	Medium		58	53	2.1	10	July
Aug	15	59	30	85	41	106	7	44	Medium		59	45	1.8	7	Aug
Sept	11	52	25	78	39	101	0	33	Moderate		63	45	1.8	5	Sept
Oct	6	43	18	65	35	95	-6	21			73	29	1.1	7	Oct
Nov	2	35	10	49	24	74	-14	6			85	36	1.4	12	Nov
Dec	-3	26	4	39	18	65	-23	-9			89	27	1.1	10	Dec

Based on readings for 29 years at 44°30′ N, 26°05′ E, altitude 92 m/302 ft

ARAD										WEST OF THE CARPATHIANS		
Sunshine		Temperatures						Discomfort from heat and humidity	Precipitation and humidity		Wet days	
		Average daily				Highest recorded	Lowest recorded		Relative humidity	Average monthly precipitation		
		minimum		maximum					all hours			
average hours per day		°C	°F	°C	°F	°C	°F	°C	°F			%	mm	in	more than 0.1 mm/0.004 in
Jan	2	−5	22	2	35	16	61	−27	−17		84	36	1.4	11	Jan
Feb	3	−4	26	5	40	17	63	−30	−22		80	34	1.3	11	Feb
March	4	1	33	11	52	26	78	−14	6		68	35	1.4	11	March
April	5	5	42	17	63	33	91	−5	22		62	46	1.8	10	April
May	8	10	50	22	72	34	94	−2	29		63	64	2.5	12	May
June	9	13	56	26	78	38	100	2	36	Medium	63	68	2.7	11	June
July	9	15	58	28	83	40	103	7	44	Medium	59	54	2.1	9	July
Aug	9	14	58	28	82	40	105	5	41	Medium	60	43	1.7	8	Aug
Sept	7	11	52	24	76	40	103	−2	29	Moderate	62	41	1.6	7	Sept
Oct	5	6	43	17	63	32	90	−8	18		72	44	1.7	9	Oct
Nov	2	3	37	10	50	23	73	−11	13		81	52	2.1	12	Nov
Dec	2	−2	29	5	41	18	65	−23	−9		84	41	1.6	12	Dec

Based on readings for 28 years at 46°10' N, 21°19' E, altitude 116 m/381 ft

heaviest rainfall. Summers in Romania are generally warm and sunny with an average of nine to ten hours of sunshine a day. Winter sunshine is rather low, averaging only two to three hours a day.

Away from the Black Sea coast there are no great differences in climate from one part of the country to another, apart from the cooler and wetter summers in the Carpathians. During cold spells in winter frost may be as severe in the plains as in the mountains.

The climatic table for **Bucharest** (p. 297) shows weather conditions east of the Carpathians. The table for **Arad** (above) represents the conditions west of the Carpathians.

Russian Federation

Russia is a vast country comprising a large part of eastern Europe and the whole of northern Asia. The traditional geographical division between Europe and Asia is the Ural Mountains, which split the country from north to south in about longitude 60° E. The whole of northern Russia is within the Arctic Circle.

In this large country the climate ranges from cold Arctic conditions to hot desert and subtropical lands where tea and rice are grown. The dominant feature of Russian weather and climate is the extreme cold of winter, which prevails in all but a small part of the south of the country.

This harsh Russian winter has helped to defeat invaders such as Napoleon and Hitler and it affects most aspects of Russian life even today. Adaptation to the Russian winter is a necessary but difficult process. Anyone intending to visit the country between late October and April should study the temperatures in the accompanying tables and take appropriate clothing! Only Antarctica, Greenland, Alaska, and Northern Canada experience comparable cold, frost, and snow as are found in winter over most of Russia.

Surprisingly, over much of the country temperatures in summer are quite warm, even during the short summers in northern and eastern Siberia. There is a rapid rise of temperature in spring, the season of the thaw (*rasputitsa*), and an equally rapid fall of temperature in the autumn.

In effect, over much of the country there are only two seasons, winter and summer. This is a characteristic feature of what climatologists call a continental climate and some of the best examples of this can be found in Russia.

There are two principal reasons for the cold of the Russian winter: first is the great size of the land mass of Europe and Asia, which means that the country is isolated from the moderating influence of warm ocean waters; and second the high latitude of much of the country, whose northern coastline on the Arctic Ocean remains frozen for most of the year.

The severity of the Russian winter is significant for transport. Except in the extreme south of the country the rivers are frozen for prolonged periods in winter and inland water transport comes to a halt. Road transport is also difficult and therefore the railways and air services are particularly important. The period when rivers are completely frozen varies from 70 days a year in the west of the country to as much as 250 days in northern Siberia.

The severity and length of winter increases eastwards. The only harbours normally ice free throughout the year are those on the Black Sea coast and around Murmansk and Archangel, where the influence of the Gulf Stream from the Atlantic raises sea temperatures. A shipping route from the Atlantic to the Pacific along the Arctic coast is open briefly in summer with the aid of powerful ice-breakers.

So intense is the cold in winter that northern and eastern Siberia experience a phenomenon called permafrost. Here the subsoil remains frozen all the year although the topsoil may thaw out during the summer. This raises special problems for building construction and the laying of pipelines.

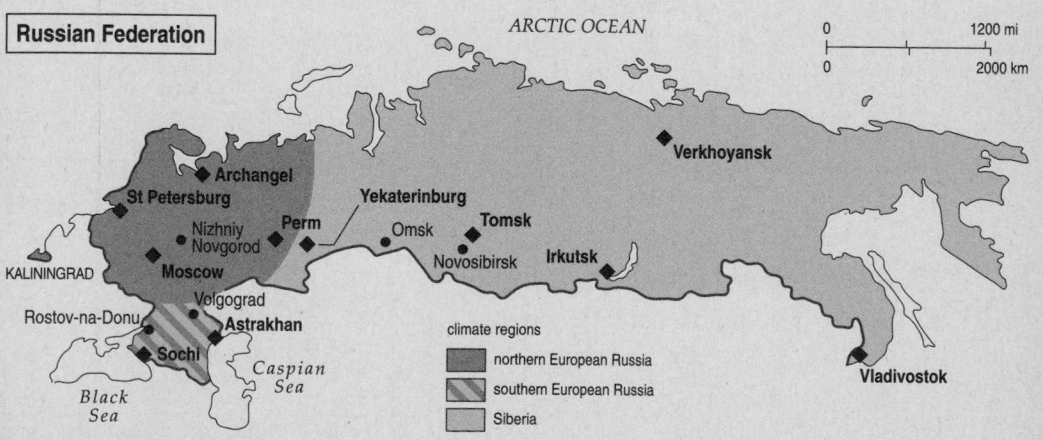

Almost everywhere in the country precipitation is rather low. In some of the major grain-producing areas of southern Russia, drought can drastically reduce crop yields in some years. Spring and early summer months are the wettest over much of the country with rainfall of the showery, thundery type. Winter snowfall, although frequent, is rarely very heavy and strong winds, the *buran* or blizzard, often sweep the ground bare of snow.

NORTHERN AND CENTRAL EUROPEAN RUSSIA

Including Archangel, Moscow, Nizhniy Novogorod, Perm, and St Petersburg.

This huge region extends – west to east – from the western border of Russia as far as the Ural Mountains and – north to south – from the Arctic coast as far as northeastern Ukraine.

The land is mostly below 300 m/1,000 ft and is level or gently rolling country. This part of Russia has the most variable weather both in summer and winter as it is more open to weather disturbances from the Atlantic and northwest Europe. The mildest areas in winter are near the Baltic coast but even here the sea often freezes.

The increasing severity of winters eastwards and northwards is illustrated by comparing the tables for **Moscow** (below), **Perm** (opposite) near the Urals, and **Archangel** (opposite and below) close to the Arctic Circle. Summers at **St Petersburg** (p. 302), at the head of the Gulf of Finland, are a little cooler than those inland and further east. Summers become warmer eastwards and southwards. The whole area has a summer maximum of precipitation. Hours of sunshine are low in winter over the whole region and average only an hour or two a day but in summer this rises to between eight and ten hours. In summer the increasing day length in the north is important for both warmth and sunshine.

SOUTHERN EUROPEAN RUSSIA

Including Astrakhan, Rostov-na-Donu, Sochi, and Volgograd.

Although the winters are still cold here and spells of extremely cold weather occur when easterly winds blow from Siberia, the winter is shorter and the spring thaw comes earlier. The tables for **Kiev** (p. 369) in the Ukraine and **Chisinau** (p. 242) in Moldova show weather that is very similar to that in most of southern Russia. Towards the southeast, in the steppe region north of the Caucasus and west of the Caspian Sea, the climate becomes distinctly

MOSCOW												NORTHERN EUROPEAN RUSSIA				
Sunshine	Temperatures							Discomfort from heat and humidity	Precipitation and humidity				Wet days	
	Average daily				Highest recorded		Lowest recorded			Relative humidity		Average monthly precipitation			
	minimum		maximum							8:30	14:30				
average hours per day	°C	°F	°C	°F	°C	°F	°C	°F		%		mm	in	more than 0.1 mm/0.004 in	
Jan	1	–16	3	–9	15	2	36	–32	–25		82	77	39	1.5	18	Jan
Feb	3	–14	8	–6	22	3	37	–32	–25		82	66	38	1.5	15	Feb
March	4	–8	18	0	32	16	61	–28	–18		82	64	36	1.4	15	March
April	5	1	34	10	50	25	76	–26	–14		73	54	37	1.5	13	April
May	8	8	46	19	66	30	86	–2	28		58	43	53	2.1	13	May
June	9	11	51	21	70	30	87	1	34		62	47	58	2.3	12	June
July	9	13	55	23	73	32	89	5	41		68	54	88	3.5	15	July
Aug	8	12	53	22	72	31	88	3	37		74	55	71	2.8	14	Aug
Sept	6	7	45	16	61	28	83	–2	28		78	59	58	2.3	13	Sept
Oct	3	3	37	9	48	24	74	–15	5		81	67	45	1.8	15	Oct
Nov	1	–3	26	2	35	12	53	–22	–7		87	79	47	1.9	15	Nov
Dec	0	–10	15	–5	24	5	41	–27	–17		85	83	54	2.1	23	Dec

Based on readings for 8 years at 55°45′ N, 37°34′ E, altitude 156 m/512 ft

PERM

NORTHERN EUROPEAN RUSSIA

	Sunshine	Temperatures								Discomfort from heat and humidity	Precipitation and humidity				Wet days
	average hours per day	Average daily				Highest recorded		Lowest recorded			Relative humidity 10:00 16:00		Average monthly precipitation		more than 0.1 mm/0.004 in
		minimum		maximum											
		°C	°F	°C	°F	°C	°F	°C	°F		%		mm	in	
Jan	1	–20	–5	–13	9	1	34	–44	–47		79	76	40	1.6	21	Jan
Feb	3	–18	0	–9	15	5	40	–41	–41		79	69	28	1.1	15	Feb
March	4	–11	12	–2	28	10	50	–34	–30		77	61	29	1.1	16	March
April	7	–1	30	9	47	25	77	–22	–7		61	50	26	1.0	10	April
May	8	5	42	17	62	29	85	–10	13		58	49	62	2.4	14	May
June	7	9	48	20	68	35	94	–3	27		60	53	73	2.9	16	June
July	8	13	55	24	75	35	94	3	38	Moderate	71	61	89	3.5	14	July
Aug	8	10	50	20	68	30	86	0	32		69	57	67	2.6	13	Aug
Sept	4	6	42	14	57	27	80	–4	25		73	61	52	2.1	15	Sept
Oct	2	–1	30	4	40	17	63	–20	–3		79	72	60	2.4	21	Oct
Nov	1	–8	18	–2	28	10	49	–29	–21		83	80	51	2.0	20	Nov
Dec	1	–16	3	–9	16	4	40	–41	–41		79	77	43	1.7	19	Dec

Based on readings for 8 years at 58°01′ N, 56°18′ E, altitude 161 m/528 ft

ARCHANGEL

NORTHERN EUROPEAN RUSSIA

	Sunshine	Temperatures								Discomfort from heat and humidity	Precipitation and humidity				Wet days
	average hours per day	Average daily				Highest recorded		Lowest recorded			Relative humidity 8:30 14:30		Average monthly precipitation		more than 0.1 mm/0.004 in
		minimum		maximum											
		°C	°F	°C	°F	°C	°F	°C	°F		%		mm	in	
Jan	0	–20	–5	–12	10	3	38	–40	–39		82	81	31	1.2	21	Jan
Feb	2	–18	0	–10	13	2	36	–41	–42		81	75	19	0.8	17	Feb
March	4	–13	9	–4	25	9	48	–35	–30		83	70	25	1.0	18	March
April	6	–4	24	5	41	16	61	–22	–7		74	60	29	1.1	12	April
May	7	2	35	12	53	26	79	–10	15		65	55	42	1.7	11	May
June	10	6	44	17	63	28	83	–3	26		63	53	52	2.1	14	June
July	9	10	50	20	68	31	88	0	33		71	58	62	2.4	15	July
Aug	7	10	49	19	65	31	88	–4	25		80	65	56	2.2	16	Aug
Sept	3	5	41	12	53	26	79	–8	18		87	73	63	2.5	18	Sept
Oct	1	–1	31	4	40	14	57	–20	–4		88	83	63	2.5	22	Oct
Nov	0	–7	20	–2	29	9	48	–37	–34		90	88	47	1.9	22	Nov
Dec	0	–15	6	–8	18	4	40	–40	–41		83	83	41	1.6	24	Dec

Based on readings for 8 years at 64°35′ N, 40°30′ E, altitude 13 m/43 ft

ST PETERSBURG — NORTHERN EUROPEAN RUSSIA

	Sunshine average hours per day	Temperatures Average daily minimum		Average daily maximum		Highest recorded		Lowest recorded		Discomfort from heat and humidity	Precipitation and humidity Relative humidity 8:00	14:00	Average monthly precipitation mm	in	Wet days more than 0.1 mm/0.004 in	
		°C	°F	°C	°F	°C	°F	°C	°F		%		mm	in		
Jan	0	-13	8	-7	19	3	38	-32	-25		86	84	35	1.4	21	Jan
Feb	2	-12	11	-5	22	3	38	-33	-27		81	73	30	1.2	17	Feb
March	4	-8	18	0	32	12	54	-26	-16		85	70	31	1.2	14	March
April	5	0	33	8	46	20	68	-13	8		79	65	36	1.4	12	April
May	8	6	42	15	59	27	81	-4	24		69	57	45	1.8	13	May
June	10	11	51	20	68	29	85	2	35		68	53	50	2.0	12	June
July	9	13	55	21	70	33	91	5	41		75	61	72	2.8	13	July
Aug	8	13	55	20	69	31	88	1	34		79	61	78	3.1	14	Aug
Sept	5	9	47	15	60	29	84	-2	29		86	68	64	2.5	17	Sept
Oct	2	4	39	9	48	18	65	-8	17		88	78	76	3.0	18	Oct
Nov	1	-2	28	2	35	12	54	-18	-1		89	85	46	1.8	18	Nov
Dec	0	-8	18	-3	26	5	41	-23	-10		88	86	40	1.6	22	Dec

Based on readings for 8 years at 59°58′ N, 30°18′ E, altitude 4 m/13 ft

ASTRAKHAN — SOUTHERN EUROPEAN RUSSIA

	Sunshine average hours per day	Temperatures Average daily minimum		Average daily maximum		Highest recorded		Lowest recorded		Discomfort from heat and humidity	Precipitation and humidity Relative humidity 9:00	15:00	Average monthly precipitation mm	in	Wet days more than 0.1 mm/0.004 in	
		°C	°F	°C	°F	°C	°F	°C	°F		%		mm	in		
Jan	2	-9	15	-2	28	13	55	-29	-21		87	75	16	0.6	11	Jan
Feb	3	-9	15	-1	31	14	58	-29	-20		84	68	11	0.4	8	Feb
March	5	-3	27	6	43	18	65	-22	-7		79	56	14	0.5	9	March
April	8	4	40	17	62	29	84	-6	22		52	35	14	0.5	5	April
May	10	12	53	25	78	34	93	0	33		45	31	16	0.6	5	May
June	10	16	61	29	83	38	100	6	43	Medium	51	37	19	0.8	6	June
July	11	18	65	31	88	39	102	11	52	Medium	48	35	10	0.4	4	July
Aug	9	17	62	30	86	39	102	6	43	Medium	51	37	25	1.0	5	Aug
Sept	8	11	53	24	75	33	92	1	33		60	40	22	0.9	5	Sept
Oct	6	5	40	16	60	26	79	-9	16		72	50	16	0.6	6	Oct
Nov	3	0	32	8	46	20	67	-12	11		85	69	16	0.6	9	Nov
Dec	2	-5	23	1	34	11	51	-24	-11		88	78	17	0.7	11	Dec

Based on readings for 8 years at 46°16′ N, 48°02′ E, altitude 18 m/59 ft

drier. This steppe is rather windswept and hot, dry winds in summer (the *sukhovey*) raise temperatures and bring very low humidity which harms crops. The opposite of this hot wind is the *buran*, a bitterly cold wind often associated with blizzards in winter.

The table for **Astrakhan** (p. 301), where the Volga river enters the Caspian Sea, shows the near-desert climate of southeastern Russia.

One small area in southern Russia is particularly favoured with mild winters: the eastern shore of the Black Sea. This area is sometimes called the Russian Riviera and is a popular summer holiday resort. Although the summer climate here is sunny, with ten or more hours of sunshine a day, rain falls all the year round and can be particularly heavy.

The table for **Sochi** (below) on the eastern shore of the Black Sea shows the weather conditions that are typical of the 'Russian Riviera'.

SIBERIA

Including Yekaterinburg, Irkutsk, Novosibirsk, Omsk, Tomsk, Verkhoyansk, Vladivostok

This region extends from the Urals to the Pacific Ocean in the east and from the Arctic Ocean to the borders of Kazakhstan, Mongolia, and China. Western Siberia is mostly low-lying and flat.

Towards the east and northeast, however, the country becomes more mountainous with deeper valleys. It is still a remote and sparsely populated region north of the band of southern settlement along the Trans-Siberian railway. There are few significant differences of weather and climate within this vast territory.

Winter precipitation is quite light and all of it falls as snow. Winters are everywhere very cold and prolonged but the short summers can be quite warm and pleasant by day once the winter snow has melted. Summers become shorter northwards, but even as far north as **Verkhoyansk** (see overleaf) the brief summer has some very warm days. Summer is everywhere the wettest season.

The Siberian town of Verkhoyansk is reputed to be one of the coldest spots on earth and of having the largest difference between summer and winter temperatures.

The tables for **Yekaterinburg** (overleaf), **Tomsk** (p. 305), and **Irkutsk** (p. 305), all in approximately the same latitude in southern Siberia, show the similarity of temperatures from west to east.

SOCHI — SOUTHERN EUROPEAN RUSSIA

	Sunshine	Temperatures								Discomfort from heat and humidity	Precipitation and humidity				Wet days	
		Average daily				Highest recorded		Lowest recorded			Relative humidity		Average monthly precipitation			
		minimum		maximum							8:30	14:30				
	average hours per day	°C	°F	°C	°F	°C	°F	°C	°F		%		mm	in		more than 0.1 mm/0.004 in
Jan	2	3	38	10	51	20	68	-13	8		71	68	201	7.9	17	Jan
Feb	4	4	39	10	51	21	69	-12	10		69	65	126	5.0	14	Feb
March	4	5	42	13	55	25	76	-3	26		73	68	130	5.1	15	March
April	6	9	48	16	61	29	84	-2	28		74	69	116	4.6	14	April
May	7	13	55	21	69	31	88	6	42		75	68	93	3.7	12	May
June	8	16	61	24	75	33	92	8	47	Moderate	73	68	101	4.0	10	June
July	9	19	66	26	80	35	96	13	55	Medium	74	69	60	2.4	7	July
Aug	9	19	66	27	80	35	96	13	56	Medium	72	68	101	4.0	9	Aug
Sept	7	16	62	25	76	32	90	9	48	Moderate	69	63	106	4.2	9	Sept
Oct	7	12	53	20	68	29	84	-3	26		71	64	91	3.6	9	Oct
Nov	5	10	49	17	62	26	79	-1	31		69	63	143	5.6	12	Nov
Dec	3	6	43	13	56	23	73	-7	19		71	66	183	7.2	15	Dec

Based on readings for 8 years at 43°35′ N, 39°43′ E, altitude not known

VERKHOYANSK — SIBERIA

Sunshine	Temperatures								Discomfort from heat and humidity	Precipitation and humidity				Wet days	
	Average daily				Highest recorded		Lowest recorded			Relative humidity		Average monthly precipitation			
	minimum		maximum							7:00	13:00				
average hours per day	°C	°F	°C	°F	°C	°F	°C	°F		%		mm	in	more than 0.1 mm/0.004 in	
Jan	0	-53	-63	-48	-54	-17	2	-67	-89		70	70	5	0.2	8	Jan
Feb	3	-49	-56	-41	-41	-10	14	-68	-90		71	69	5	0.2	7	Feb
March	7	-39	-39	-25	-13	3	38	-60	-77		74	60	3	0.1	4	March
April	10	-23	-10	-7	19	11	52	-54	-66		74	50	5	0.2	4	April
May	10	-5	23	6	42	26	79	-28	-19		63	47	8	0.3	5	May
June	10	9	48	16	60	34	94	-7	19		62	45	23	0.9	7	June
July	8	8	47	19	66	37	98	-2	29		72	49	28	1.1	8	July
Aug	7	4	40	14	58	33	92	-8	18		79	54	25	1.0	8	Aug
Sept	4	-3	27	6	43	25	77	-17	2		87	61	13	0.5	7	Sept
Oct	2	-19	-3	-11	12	13	55	-44	-48		84	70	8	0.3	7	Oct
Nov	1	-40	-40	-35	-31	1	34	-57	-70		79	78	8	0.3	8	Nov
Dec	1	-49	-56	-47	-52	-11	13	-64	-84		75	75	5	0.2	8	Dec

Based on readings for 24 years at 67°34′ N, 133°51′ E, altitude 100 m/328 ft

YEKATERINBURG — SIBERIA

Sunshine	Temperatures								Discomfort from heat and humidity	Precipitation and humidity				Wet days	
	Average daily				Highest recorded		Lowest recorded			Relative humidity		Average monthly precipitation			
	minimum		maximum							7:00	13:00				
average hours per day	°C	°F	°C	°F	°C	°F	°C	°F		%		mm	in	more than 0.1 mm/0.004 in	
Jan		-21	-5	-14	-5	4	40	-43	-45		84	79	13	0.5	12	Jan
Feb		-17	1	-10	14	3	38	-42	-44		85	72	10	0.4	8	Feb
March		-12	10	-4	25	14	58	-37	-35		86	63	13	0.5	8	March
April		-3	26	6	42	23	73	-21	-5		77	49	18	0.7	7	April
May		4	39	14	57	31	88	-8	17		70	47	48	1.9	13	May
June		9	49	18	65	32	90	-2	28		74	51	69	2.7	14	June
July		12	54	21	70	34	94	3	37		79	55	66	2.6	14	July
Aug		10	50	18	65	32	89	-1	30		85	59	69	2.7	15	Aug
Sept		5	41	12	54	30	86	-8	18		87	61	41	1.6	14	Sept
Oct		-2	28	3	37	21	69	-21	-6		86	69	31	1.2	13	Oct
Nov		-12	11	-7	20	10	50	-39	-39		86	78	28	1.1	14	Nov
Dec		-18	0	-12	10	4	39	-43	-45		86	82	20	0.8	14	Dec

Based on readings for 29 years at 56°49′ N, 60°38′ E, altitude 273 m/894 ft

TOMSK — SIBERIA

Sunshine	Temperatures								Discomfort from heat and humidity	Precipitation and humidity				Wet days	
	Average daily				Highest recorded		Lowest recorded			Relative humidity 7:00 13:00		Average monthly precipitation			
	minimum		maximum												
average hours per day	°C	°F	°C	°F	°C	°F	°C	°F		%		mm	in	more than 0.1 mm/0.004 in	
Jan	2	−24	−12	−18	0	2	36	−50	−58		82	78	28	1.1	20	Jan
Feb	3	−22	−7	−13	8	4	40	−47	−52		83	70	18	0.7	14	Feb
March	5	−17	2	−6	22	9	49	−42	−44		83	61	20	0.8	13	March
April	7	−7	20	3	38	24	76	−27	−17		79	55	23	0.9	11	April
May	9	3	37	12	54	29	84	−17	1		70	50	41	1.6	14	May
June	10	9	48	19	67	35	95	−2	28		76	55	69	2.7	15	June
July	10	12	54	23	73	36	96	2	35		83	58	66	2.6	13	July
Aug	8	10	50	20	68	32	89	−2	29		88	62	66	2.6	15	Aug
Sept	6	4	40	14	57	28	83	−6	21		89	61	41	1.6	13	Sept
Oct	3	−3	27	3	37	22	72	−29	−20		87	70	51	2.0	18	Oct
Nov	2	−14	6	−9	15	8	47	−47	−53		85	77	46	1.8	20	Nov
Dec	1	−22	−7	−16	4	3	37	−49	−57		84	81	38	1.5	22	Dec

Based on readings for 20 years at 56°30′ N, 84°58′ E, altitude 122 m/399 ft

IRKUTSK — SIBERIA

Sunshine	Temperatures								Discomfort from heat and humidity	Precipitation and humidity				Wet days	
	Average daily				Highest recorded		Lowest recorded			Relative humidity 7:00 13:00		Average monthly precipitation			
	minimum		maximum												
average hours per day	°C	°F	°C	°F	°C	°F	°C	°F		%		mm	in	more than 1 mm/0.04 in	
Jan	3	−26	−15	−16	3	2	36	−50	−58		84	75	13	0.5	3	Jan
Feb	5	−25	−13	−12	10	5	41	−44	−47		85	63	10	0.4	3	Feb
March	7	−17	2	−4	25	14	58	−37	−34		85	53	8	0.3	2	March
April	7	−7	20	6	42	29	85	−31	−24		75	43	15	0.6	4	April
May	8	1	33	13	56	31	88	14	6		67	40	33	1.3	8	May
June	8	7	44	20	68	35	95	4	24		73	47	56	2.2	7	June
July	8	10	50	21	70	37	98	1	33		83	56	79	3.1	9	July
Aug	7	9	48	20	68	33	92	−3	27		87	59	71	2.8	11	Aug
Sept	6	2	35	14	57	29	84	−10	14		89	54	43	1.7	8	Sept
Oct	5	−6	21	5	41	23	73	−31	−23		88	56	18	0.7	6	Oct
Nov	3	−17	2	−7	20	13	56	−39	−39		89	71	15	0.6	4	Nov
Dec	2	−24	−12	−16	4	3	37	−46	−51		88	85	15	0.6	4	Dec

Based on readings for 10 years at 52°16′ N, 104°19′ E, altitude 467 m/1532 ft

VLADIVOSTOK									SIBERIA	

Sunshine	Temperatures					Discomfort from heat and humidity	Precipitation and humidity		Wet days	
	Average daily		Highest recorded	Lowest recorded			Relative humidity	Average monthly precipitation		
average hours per day	minimum	maximum					7:00 13:00		more than 1 mm/0.04 in	
	°C °F	°C °F	°C °F	°C °F			%	mm in		
Jan	6	-18 0	-11 13	3 37	-30 -22		71 58	8 0.3	2	Jan
Feb	7	-14 6	-6 22	8 46	-29 -20		72 55	10 0.4	2	Feb
March	7	-7 19	1 33	13 56	-22 -7		75 56	18 0.7	4	March
April	6	1 34	8 46	19 66	-8 17		80 59	31 1.2	5	April
May	6	6 43	13 55	23 74	-1 31		83 65	53 2.1	8	May
June	5	11 52	17 63	31 88	4 39		90 76	74 2.9	10	June
July	4	16 60	22 71	33 92	8 47		91 79	84 3.3	10	July
Aug	5	18 64	24 75	32 90	10 50	Moderate	90 74	119 4.7	9	Aug
Sept	7	13 55	20 68	29 84	4 39		85 64	109 4.3	7	Sept
Oct	7	5 41	13 55	23 73	-8 17		76 53	48 1.9	5	Oct
Nov	6	-4 24	2 36	17 63	-18 0		71 55	31 1.2	4	Nov
Dec	6	-13 8	-7 20	11 51	-26 -15		71 56	15 0.6	3	Dec

Based on readings for 14 years at 43°07´ N, 131°55´ E, altitude 29 m/94 ft

The table for **Vladivostok** (above) illustrates the rather different climate and weather experienced in a narrow strip along the coast of the Pacific. Winters are still cold and harbours freeze. This is because the dominant winter wind is from the west or northwest and brings very cold Siberian air to the coast. In summer on this coast there is a reversal of wind direction as the east Asian summer monsoon brings warm, moist winds off the Pacific Ocean so that coastal regions are comparatively wet at this time.

Rwanda

See map page 21

This small country in Central Africa – situated at about 2° S – is similar in size to its neighbour Burundi (or Israel).

Like Burundi, it is hilly and mountainous; it also has a very similar climate. Its climate and weather throughout the year are illustrated by the table for **Rubona** (opposite and above) and also by that for **Kabale** (p. 368) in Uganda.

St Helena

See map page 21

St Helena is in the South Atlantic, 1,930 km/1,200 mi from the coast of Africa in latitude 15° S. Its 122 sq km/47 sq mi are rather mountainous, with a single peak rising to 820 m/2,700 ft. This remote island has a tropical climate with no great extremes of temperature. **Jamestown** (see table opposite) on the north coast has a very low annual rainfall but this coast is sheltered from the southeast trade winds which bring a heavier fall to the south coast and the higher ground; up to 750–1,000 mm/30–40 in. On the north coast the weather is warm, sunny, and dry for much of the year. The climate is rarely unpleasant or hazardous, although Napoleon, when exiled there from 1815 until his death in 1821, found much to complain about in its climate and dampness.

RUBONA — RWANDA

Sunshine	Temperatures									Discomfort from heat and humidity	Precipitation and humidity				Wet days
	Average daily				Highest recorded		Lowest recorded				Relative humidity	Average monthly precipitation			
	minimum		maximum								all hours				
average hours per day	°C	°F	°C	°F	°C	°F	°C	°F			%	mm	in		more than 0.1 mm/0.004 in
Jan	14	57	25	77	31	87	10	50	Medium		79	111	4.4		15 Jan
Feb	13	55	25	77	30	86	11	52	Medium		78	156	6.1		15 Feb
March	14	57	25	77	30	86	12	54	Medium		78	140	5.5		18 March
April	14	57	25	77	28	82	10	50	Medium		83	183	7.2		22 April
May	14	57	24	75	28	82	12	54	Moderate		72	164	6.5		18 May
June	13	55	24	75	28	82	11	52	Moderate		70	23	0.9		4 June
July	12	54	26	79	29	84	9	49	Moderate		59	7	0.3		2 July
Aug	13	55	27	81	30	86	12	54	Medium		60	27	1.1		5 Aug
Sept	14	57	27	81	31	87	12	54	Medium		60	63	2.5		11 Sept
Oct	14	57	26	79	30	86	12	54	Medium		71	102	4.0		16 Oct
Nov	14	57	25	77	29	84	11	52	Medium		76	110	4.3		20 Nov
Dec	14	57	25	77	29	84	12	54	Medium		80	93	3.7		17 Dec

Based on readings for 10 years at 2°29′ S, 29°46′ E, altitude 1706 m/5592 ft

JAMESTOWN — NORTHERN COASTAL ST HELENA

Sunshine	Temperatures									Discomfort from heat and humidity	Precipitation and humidity				Wet days
	Average daily				Highest recorded		Lowest recorded				Relative humidity		Average monthly precipitation		
	minimum		maximum								9:30	15:30			
average hours per day	°C	°F	°C	°F	°C	°F	°C	°F			%		mm	in	more than 1 mm/0.04 in
Jan	5	21	69	27	80	32	89	17	63	Medium	63	62	8	0.3	4.0 Jan
Feb	5	21	70	27	81	32	90	19	66	Medium	65	64	10	0.4	4.0 Feb
March	4	22	71	28	82	33	92	19	66	Medium	64	61	20	0.8	5.0 March
April	4	21	70	27	81	34	93	17	63	Medium	65	62	10	0.4	3.0 April
May	5	19	67	24	76	28	83	16	61	Moderate	72	70	18	0.7	4.0 May
June	4	18	65	23	74	27	81	16	61	Moderate	72	69	18	0.7	6.0 June
July	4	17	63	22	72	26	79	14	58		74	71	8	0.3	8.0 July
Aug	3	17	63	22	72	26	78	15	59		76	74	10	0.4	3.0 Aug
Sept	2	17	63	22	72	26	78	14	58		75	69	5	0.2	2.0 Sept
Oct	2	18	64	23	73	26	78	16	60	Moderate	72	70	3	0.1	0.7 Oct
Nov	2	18	65	23	74	27	80	17	62	Moderate	72	69	0	0.0	0.0 Nov
Dec	2	19	66	24	76	28	82	16	60	Moderate	65	64	3	0.1	1.0 Dec

Based on readings for 7 years at 15°55′ S, 5°43′ W, altitude 12 m/40 ft

St Kitts-Nevis

See map page 15

More properly called St Christopher and St Nevis, this hilly island pair lies in the Leeward Islands, the northern part of the Lesser Antilles. Temperature and humidity in the Leeward Islands are very similar to those described on pp. 92–3 in the general entry for the Caribbean Islands, as are the amount and distribution of sunshine. The tables for points on two other eastern Caribbean islands, **Roseau** (p. 127) on Dominica and **Plymouth** (p. 244) on Montserrat, show that, near sea level, annual rainfall is about 1,250–2,000 mm/50–80 in, well distributed throughout the year with a wetter season from July to November. The table for **Camp Jacob** (p. 167) on the island of Guadeloupe, also in the Leeward Islands, shows that rainfall increases at higher elevations and on the windward slopes exposed to the constant and moist northeast trade winds. St Kitts-Nevis lies in the track of violent tropical hurricanes which are most likely to develop between August and October. Although the severest of these storms may only strike every few years, these are always the months of heaviest rainfall.

St Lucia

See map page 15

This Caribbean island state, along with Barbados, Martinique, Grenada, and St Vincent, is one of the largest of the Windward Islands, the southern islands of the Lesser Antilles. The Windward Islands lie between 15° N and the coast of South America. Although still small, these larger islands in the Windward chain are hilly or mountainous and this tends to increase the rainfall above that of the small, flat islands in the chain. The table for **Castries** (below), the capital of St Lucia, shows that St Lucia with its higher mountains is wetter than Barbados (see p. 59) around the year. The tables for Barbados and St Lucia reflect conditions on the west coasts of the islands, which are somewhat sheltered from the

CASTRIES									WEST COAST ST LUCIA			
Sunshine	Temperatures						Discomfort from heat and humidity	Precipitation and humidity				Wet days
	Average daily				Highest recorded	Lowest recorded		Relative humidity		Average monthly precipitation		
	minimum		maximum					7:00	12:00			
average hours per day	°C	°F	°C	°F	°C	°F	°C	°F		%		mm	in	more than 1 mm/0.04 in
Jan	21	69	28	82	31	87	14	57	Medium	90	70	135	5.3	18	Jan
Feb	21	69	28	83	32	89	15	59	Medium	90	68	91	3.6	13	Feb
March	21	69	29	84	32	90	15	59	Medium	88	65	97	3.8	13	March
April	22	71	31	87	35	95	17	63	High	87	64	86	3.4	10	April
May	23	73	31	88	36	97	19	67	High	87	65	150	5.9	16	May
June	23	74	31	88	36	97	19	67	High	86	69	218	8.6	21	June
July	23	74	31	87	35	95	21	69	High	89	71	236	9.3	23	July
Aug	23	74	31	88	34	94	20	68	High	90	69	269	10.6	22	Aug
Sept	23	73	31	88	34	94	20	68	High	91	70	252	9.9	21	Sept
Oct	22	72	31	87	33	91	19	66	High	93	69	236	9.3	19	Oct
Nov	22	71	29	85	32	90	18	65	High	92	75	231	9.1	20	Nov
Dec	21	70	28	83	32	89	16	61	Medium	92	71	198	7.8	19	Dec

Based on readings for 17 years at 14°01′ N, 61°00′ W, altitude 3 m/10 ft

prevailing winds. All months receive appreciable rain but the heaviest rain is more likely to occur from July to November. This is the hurricane season and, although the most violent of these tropical storms may only strike a particular island every few years, less severe ones cause appreciable rainfall over quite a wide area. Temperature, humidity, and sunshine throughout the year are typical of the Caribbean area. (See the general entry for the Caribbean Islands on pp. 92–3.)

St Vincent and the Grenadines

See map page 15

The well forested island of St Vincent together with the Grenadine Islands group make up a Caribbean country located in the Windward Islands, the southern islands of the Lesser Antilles. The mountainous terrain of St Vincent tends to increase the rainfall above that of smaller, flatter islands in the Windward group. (Low-lying Barbados – p. 59 – is less wet around the year than Martinique – p. 243

– and St Lucia – p. 308 – both of which have higher mountains.) All months receive appreciable rain but the heaviest is more likely to occur from July to November. This is the hurricane season and, although the most violent of these tropical storms may only strike St Vincent and the Grenadines every few years, less severe ones cause rainfall over quite a wide area. Temperature, humidity, and sunshine throughout the year are typical of those described in the general entry for the Caribbean (pp. 92–3).

Samoa

See map page 17

The table for **Apia** (below), the capital of Samoa, shows weather that is typical of this constitutional monarchy in the southwest Pacific. The country comprises two volcanic islands, rising to more than 1,800 m/5,850 ft, and seven smaller islands. They share with neighbouring countries the features of a

APIA													UPOLU ISLAND, SAMOA		
Sunshine		Temperatures							Discomfort from heat and humidity	Precipitation and humidity				Wet days	
		Average daily				Highest recorded		Lowest recorded			Relative humidity 8:30 14:30		Average monthly precipitation		
		minimum		maximum											
average hours per day		°C	°F	°C	°F	°C	°F	°C	°F		%		mm	in	more than 1 mm/0.04 in
Jan	6	24	75	30	86	33	91	21	69	High	82	79	455	17.9	22	Jan
Feb	6	24	76	29	85	33	92	21	70	High	81	78	386	15.2	19	Feb
March	6	23	74	30	86	33	91	21	70	High	81	78	358	14.1	19	March
April	6	24	75	30	86	33	91	21	69	High	79	76	254	10.0	14	April
May	7	23	74	29	85	32	90	19	67	High	78	76	160	6.3	12	May
June	7	23	74	29	85	32	90	19	67	High	77	73	130	5.1	7	June
July	7	23	74	29	85	33	91	17	63	High	77	75	81	3.2	9	July
Aug	7	24	75	29	84	32	90	18	65	High	76	73	89	3.5	9	Aug
Sept	8	23	74	29	84	32	90	18	65	High	75	75	132	5.2	11	Sept
Oct	6	24	75	29	85	34	93	19	66	High	77	76	170	6.7	14	Oct
Nov	6	23	74	30	86	33	92	21	69	High	78	75	267	10.5	16	Nov
Dec	6	23	74	29	85	33	91	21	70	High	79	77	371	14.6	19	Dec

Based on readings for 19 years at 13°48′ S, 171°46′ W, altitude 2 m/7 ft

typical tropical oceanic climate. Very similar conditions prevail throughout the year with high temperatures and humidity.

The daily range of temperature is quite small – about 4°–5° C/10° F. There is abundant rainfall. Being south of the equator, Samoa has its season of maximum rainfall between November and April. On some islands there is no great difference between the amount of rain from month to month. Tropical cyclones are less frequent than in the Pacific north of the equator.

Except in the wettest places, where cloud is more frequent, the country has moderately large amounts of sunshine. They average from six to eight hours a day. Much of the rainfall comes in short, heavy showers, often after a sunny morning, but longer periods of heavy rain lasting a day or so occur in the wetter months.

In this area of the Pacific the principal difference in the weather and climate is the amount of rainfall per month. Temperature and humidity are very similar from one island to another but the amount of rainfall varies with altitude and with exposure of the coast to the dominant southeast trade winds. The number of wet days varies from island to island much less than the amount of rain.

The climate may generally be described as pleasant and healthy, although the combination of high temperature and humidity can be a little oppressive when not tempered by sea breezes or a brisk wind.

San Marino

See map page 18

This small, independent republic lies in the Appennines at an altitude of 750 m/2,500 ft inland from the Adriatic town of Rimini. It has a modified Mediterranean type of climate as described on p. 200 for peninsular Italy. The area of San Marino is about 98 sq km/38 sq mi.

SAO TOME									SAO TOME ISLAND		
Sunshine		Temperatures					Discomfort from heat and humidity	Precipitation and humidity			Wet days
		Average daily		Highest recorded		Lowest recorded		Relative humidity 9:30 15:30		Average monthly precipitation	
		minimum	maximum								
average hours per day		°C °F	°C °F	°C °F		°C °F		%		mm in	more than 1 mm/0.04 in
Jan	5	23 73	30 86	32 90		20 68	High	83	78	81 3.2	6.0	Jan
Feb	5	23 73	30 86	33 91		20 68	High	82	78	107 4.2	8.0	Feb
March	5	23 73	31 87	33 91		20 68	High	80	76	150 5.9	9.0	March
April	5	23 73	30 86	33 91		20 68	High	81	77	127 5.0	10.0	April
May	5	23 73	29 85	32 90		18 65	High	80	79	135 5.3	8.0	May
June	5	22 71	28 83	31 88		16 61	Medium	77	74	28 1.1	2.0	June
July	5	21 69	28 82	31 87		15 59	Medium	74	70	0 0.0	0.0	July
Aug	5	21 69	28 82	31 87		13 56	Medium	73	70	0 0.0	0.3	Aug
Sept	4	21 70	29 84	32 89		17 62	High	76	74	23 0.9	3.0	Sept
Oot	4	22 71	29 84	32 89		19 66	High	79	79	109 4.3	9.0	Oct
Nov	5	22 71	29 84	32 89		18 65	High	81	79	117 4.6	9.0	Nov
Dec	5	22 72	29 84	32 89		19 67	High	81	79	89 3.5	7.0	Dec

Based on readings for 10 years at 0°20′ N, 6°43′ E, altitude 5 m/16 ft

São Tomé e Príncipe

See map page 21

These two islands lie almost on the equator in the Gulf of Guinea about 274 km/170 mi from the African coast. Their land area is only 960 sq km/370 sq mi. The islands have an equatorial type of climate with high temperatures and humidity throughout the year. Rainfall is moderately heavy and the climate is rather cloudy, muggy, and oppressive.

The driest months are from June to September and rainfall outside these months is often heavy. The number of sunshine hours is rather low, averaging from four to six hours a day.

The table for **São Tomé** (above) on São Tomé Island shows weather conditions that are representative of the country as a whole.

Saudi Arabia

See map page 22

Saudi Arabia comprises the greater part of the Arabian peninsula. It is a large country, most of which is desert. It is bordered on the north by Jordan and Iraq. In the east of Saudi Arabia there is a short coastline on the Persian Gulf but there are land borders with the small Gulf states of Kuwait, Qatar, the United Arab Emirates, and Oman. There is a long land border with Oman and with Yemen on the south. In the southwest of the peninsula it also borders Yemen, to the north of which it has a long coastline on the Red Sea. The general features of the weather and climate of Arabia are described here and only briefer descriptions of the other states of the peninsula are given under the separate country headings.

Most of Arabia is desert with a low and unreliable rainfall. Where the rainfall is greater, this is a result of higher mountainous areas where the lower temperatures produce some relief from the fierce, dry summer heat. Most of the peninsula consists of a rolling plateau of low to medium elevation. It slopes northeastwards from a higher mountainous rim on the west to a low plain on the shores of the Gulf.

In the southwest the mountains of the Asir province of Saudi Arabia and of Yemen rise to between 2,400 m/8,000 ft and 3,600 m/12,000 ft. In the northeast of the peninsula the Jebel Akhdar mountains of Oman rise to just over 3,000 m/10,000 ft. Along the south coast of the peninsula there is a narrow coastal plain on the Arabian Sea. This is separated from the sandy desert of the Rub' al Khali by ranges of hills in Hadhramaut and Dhofar. At the foot of the western mountains there is a narrow coastal plain fronting the Red Sea, behind which there is a steep rise inland so that the climate of the plain is hotter and more humid than that found inland.

Only in the higher areas, the mountains of Yemen and Oman, does the annual rainfall exceed 400 mm/20 in. Elsewhere it is low and unreliable; below 200 mm/8 in and often less than 100 mm/4 in. North of Jiddah, Riyadh, and Muscat rainfall is almost confined to the period from November to April or May and is brought by weak disturbances coming from the Mediterranean or North Africa. In the southern part of Arabia and particularly in the mountains of Yemen and Oman some rain may fall in any month; along the south coast and in Yemen mountains it falls mainly in the period May to October, when it is associated with the southwest monsoon which dominates the Arabian Sea and India at this time.

Over much of Arabia, with the exception of the mountains, temperatures from May to September rise very high and this is one of the few areas of the world where temperatures above 48° C/120° F are not unusual. Inland the daytime humidity falls quite low and there is usually a sharp drop of temperature at night. Although midday temperatures do not rise so high on the coast, conditions here may be even more uncomfortable because of the high humidity; the nights are particularly unpleasant. This can be seen by comparing the tables for **Riyadh** (opposite) and **Jiddah** (opposite and below) with those for **Sharjah** (p. 370) in the United Arab Emirates and **Kuwait City** (p. 211). These last two stations are on the Gulf coast while Jiddah is on the Red Sea coast.

In the interior, and in the higher mountains in the northwest of Saudi Arabia, winter temperatures occasionally fall low enough for frost and snow to occur. Winter nights in the desert are distinctly chilly. Any strong wind is likely to raise dust and sand which can add to the unpleasant conditions, whether it is a cold winter blast or a burning dry wind in summer. Sunshine amounts are very large over most of Arabia, ranging from six to eight hours a day in winter to as much as twelve to thirteen in summer. In the mountains of Yemen and in the hills facing the Arabian Sea in Oman and Muscat, the period from June to September is much cloudier than elsewhere in Arabia, since the dominant southwest monsoon is very warm and moist; low clouds, drizzle, and light rain are frequent.

Any visitor to the states of the Arabian peninsula should be prepared for very hot conditions between May and October. Both in the very hot, dry interior and on the muggy coasts of the Gulf and Red Sea there are occasions when heat exhaustion and heatstroke can be a threat, particularly to new arrivals and those who do not take sensible precautions.

RIYADH

INLAND SAUDI ARABIA

Sunshine	Temperatures									Discomfort from heat and humidity	Precipitation and humidity					Wet days
	Average daily				Highest recorded		Lowest recorded				Relative humidity		Average monthly precipitation			
	minimum		maximum								5:00	16:00				
average hours per day	°C	°F	°C	°F	°C	°F	°C	°F			%		mm	in		more than 1 mm/0.04 in
Jan 7	8	46	21	70	30	86	-7	19			70	44	3	0.1		1 Jan
Feb 8	9	48	23	73	33	91	-2	29			63	37	20	0.8		1 Feb
March 7	13	56	28	82	38	101	1	33		Moderate	65	36	23	0.9		3 March
April 8	18	64	32	89	40	104	2	36		Medium	64	34	25	1.0		4 April
May 9	22	72	38	100	43	110	15	59		High	51	31	10	0.4		1 May
June 11	25	77	42	107	45	113	19	67		Extreme	47	31	0	0.0		0 June
July 11	26	78	42	107	45	113	19	67		High	33	19	0	0.0		0 July
Aug 10	24	75	42	107	44	112	17	62		High	35	19	0	0.0		0 Aug
Sept 9	22	72	39	102	44	111	17	63		High	42	24	0	0.0		0 Sept
Oct 10	16	61	34	94	38	101	10	50		Medium	47	25	0	0.0		0 Oct
Nov 9	13	55	29	84	34	94	2	35		Medium	60	33	0	0.0		0 Nov
Dec 7	9	49	21	70	31	87	0	32			75	52	0	0.0		0 Dec

Based on readings for 3 years at 24°39′ N, 46°42′ E, al.0titude 590 m/1938 ft

JIDDAH

RED SEA COAST

Sunshine	Temperatures									Discomfort from heat and humidity	Precipitation and humidity					Wet days
	Average daily				Highest recorded		Lowest recorded				Relative humidity		Average monthly precipitation			
	minimum		maximum								8:00	14:00				
average hours per day	°C	°F	°C	°F	°C	°F	°C	°F			%		mm	in		more than 1 mm/0.04 in
Jan	19	66	29	84	33	92	9	49		Medium	58	54	5	0.2		0.8 Jan
Feb	18	65	29	84	35	95	11	52		Medium	52	52	0	0.0		0.3 Feb
March	19	67	29	85	38	101	13	55		Medium	52	52	0	0.0		0.3 March
April	21	70	33	91	40	104	12	54		High	52	56	0	0.0		0.5 April
May	23	74	35	95	42	108	13	55		Extreme	51	55	0	0.0		0.0 May
June	24	75	36	97	47	117	19	67		Extreme	56	55	0	0.0		0.0 June
July	26	79	37	99	42	108	21	70		Extreme	55	50	0	0.0		0.0 July
Aug	27	80	37	99	42	108	23	73		Extreme	59	51	0	0.0		0.0 Aug
Sept	25	77	36	96	42	108	21	70		Extreme	65	61	0	0.0		0.0 Sept
Oct	23	73	35	95	41	105	20	68		Extreme	60	61	0	0.0		0.0 Oct
Nov	22	71	33	91	41	105	17	63		High	55	59	25	1.0		2.0 Nov
Dec	19	67	30	86	34	93	10	50		Medium	55	54	31	1.2		1.0 Dec

Based on readings for 5 years at 21°28′ N, 39°10′ E, altitude 6 m/20 ft

Senegal

See map page 20

Including a description of the climate and weather of the Gambia and Guinea-Bissau.

Senegal is on the west coast of Africa between 12° and 16° N. Its northern border with Mauritania is along the Senegal river. It has an eastern border with Mali and a southern border with Guinea and Guinea-Bissau. Senegal has a tropical climate with a single short rainy season between June and September at the time of high sun.

Temperatures are high throughout the year but there is a relatively cooler period from December to April during which rain is very rare. The following description of the climate and weather of Senegal is also applicable to the Gambia and Guinea-Bissau. All three countries are low-lying with very little land higher than 200 m/650 ft above sea level.

The chief factors controlling the climate of these countries are latitude and distance from the sea. Rainfall increases from north to south in Senegal. The north of the country is affected by the

intertropical belt of cloud and rain between June and September; during these months rain only falls on twenty to thirty days and the average annual rainfall is about 300–350 mm/12–14 in. In the south annual rainfall increases to between 1,000–1,500 mm/40–60 in and falls on between sixty and ninety days. Here the rainy season extends into October.

The table for **Dakar** (below) shows that, in the centre of the country, rainfall amounts are between these two extremes. Northern Senegal, on the edge of the Sahara, experiences conditions similar to the Saharan districts of Mali to the east and Mauritania to the north.

There is a marked seasonal contrast between the wet season, when winds are from the southwest and west, blowing from the South Atlantic, and the dry season, when they blow from the northeast out of the Sahara. The southwesterlies are warm and humid while the northeasterly harmattan wind is hot and dry and frequently dust-laden.

This contrast can be seen in the values for the relative humidity at Dakar and also those for

DAKAR										CENTRAL COASTAL SENEGAL			
Sunshine	Temperatures						Discomfort from heat and humidity	Precipitation and humidity				Wet days	
	Average daily		Highest recorded		Lowest recorded			Relative humidity		Average monthly precipitation			
	minimum		maximum					6:00	13:00				
average hours per day	°C	°F	°C	°F	°C	°F	°C	°F		%	mm	in	more than 1 mm/0.04 in
Jan	8	18	64	26	79	39	102	13	56	Moderate	1	45	0	0.0	0.0	Jan
Feb	9	17	63	27	80	38	100	14	58	Moderate	80	45	0	0.0	0.1	Feb
March	10	18	64	27	80	43	109	15	59	Medium	87	51	0	0.0	0.1	March
April	10	18	65	27	81	38	101	16	61	Medium	86	55	0	0.0	0.0	April
May	10	20	68	29	84	38	100	16	61	Medium	86	59	0	0.0	0.0	May
June	9	23	73	31	88	38	100	18	65	High	85	62	18	0.7	2.0	June
July	7	24	76	31	88	37	99	21	69	High	84	66	89	3.5	7.0	July
Aug	6	24	76	31	87	37	99	21	69	High	87	74	254	10.0	13.0	Aug
Sept	7	24	76	32	89	38	100	21	69	High	88	72	132	5.2	11.0	Sept
Oct	8	24	76	32	89	38	101	21	70	High	86	65	38	1.5	3.0	Oct
Nov	9	23	73	30	86	37	99	18	64	Medium	80	50	3	0.1	1.0	Nov
Dec	8	19	67	27	81	35	95	12	53	Moderate	70	46	8	0.3	0.1	Dec

Based on readings for 16 years at 14°42' N, 17°29' W, altitude 40 m/131 ft

Banjul (p. 151) in the Gambia; both these stations are on the coast and the humidity is increased by the frequent sea breezes. Inland the humidity is much lower during the time of the harmattan.

Temperatures are also considerably higher inland than on the coast during the dry season but they fall lower at night. The climate of Senegal is most oppressive during the wet season, particularly on the coast, where there is a combination of high humidity and high night-time temperatures.

Hours of sunshine average nine to ten a day throughout the year; sunshine hours are lower on the coast where there is more cloud and in the higher parts during the dry season.

Seychelles

See map page 21

The Seychelles consist of over ninety small islands with a total land area similar to that of the Virgin Islands in the Caribbean. They are situated between 4° and 5° S in the Indian Ocean. Most of the islands are low-lying but the largest island, Mahé, has hills rising to 900 m/3,000 ft.

The islands are about 1,300 km/800 mi from the coast of eastern Africa. They have a tropical climate and have recently become particulary well known as a tourist resort.

The table for **Port Victoria** (below) shows typical temperatures and humidity throughout the year.

The amount of rainfall round the year varies with altitude and is higher on the southern sides of the islands, which are exposed to the dominant southeast trade winds. Rainfall is everywhere moderate to heavy and the wettest months are November to March.

The Seychelles are rarely if ever affected by tropical cyclones. The combination of moderately high temperature and high humidity is tempered by regular daytime sea breezes.

The nights may feel muggy and oppressive, particularly to the visitor who is not yet acclimatized, but the climate is neither hazardous nor unpleasant.

PORT VICTORIA — MAHE ISLAND

	Sunshine average hours per day	Average daily minimum °C	°F	maximum °C	°F	Highest recorded °C	°F	Lowest recorded °C	°F	Discomfort from heat and humidity	Relative humidity 9:30 %	15:30 %	Average monthly precipitation mm	in	Wet days more than 2.5 mm/0.1 in	
Jan	6	24	76	28	83	31	88	21	69	Medium	79	78	386	15.2	15	Jan
Feb	6	25	77	29	84	32	89	22	71	High	77	76	267	10.5	10	Feb
March	7	25	77	29	85	32	90	21	69	High	75	74	234	9.2	11	March
April	8	25	77	30	86	33	92	22	71	High	74	74	183	7.2	10	April
May	8	25	77	29	85	33	91	21	69	High	75	74	170	6.7	9	May
June	7	25	77	28	83	32	89	19	67	Medium	77	75	102	4.0	9	June
July	7	24	75	27	81	30	86	19	67	Medium	77	76	84	3.3	8	July
Aug	7	24	75	27	81	31	87	20	68	Medium	76	75	69	2.7	7	Aug
Sept	7	24	76	28	82	31	88	20	68	Medium	76	75	130	5.1	8	Sept
Oct	7	24	75	28	83	32	89	20	68	Medium	76	75	155	6.1	9	Oct
Nov	7	24	75	29	84	32	89	20	68	High	75	74	231	9.1	12	Nov
Dec	6	24	75	28	83	33	91	21	69	Medium	78	78	340	13.4	15	Dec

Based on readings for 60 years at 4°37′ S, 55°27′ E, altitude 5 m/15 ft

Sierra Leone

See map page 20

Including a description of the climate and weather of Guinea and Liberia.

The three countries of Sierra Leone, Guinea, and Liberia lie on the west coast of Africa between 4° and 12° N. Each of them has a coastline facing southwest towards the Atlantic Ocean and includes an extensive coastal plain rising inland to a plateau area where heights exceed 1,000 m/3,300 ft. This similarity of situation and relief gives these countries a broadly similar climate.

In this part of Africa the intertropical belt of cloud and rain migrates northwards and southwards with the apparent movement of the overhead sun but lagging behind by some four to six weeks. From October to March, during the period of low sun, the weather is generally dry with many fine, hot, sunny days. The season of high sun, from April to September, is the rainy season.

The rainfall increases to a peak in July and August and then decreases until rain has almost ceased by November. In the north of Guinea the rainy season is a little shorter than in Liberia to the south.

Along the coast of these three countries, however, there is not much difference in the total annual rainfall, which is heavy everywhere and between 3,500 mm/160 in and 4,000 mm/180 in. This can be seen by comparing the table for **Freetown** (opposite and above) in Sierra Leone, with those for **Conakry** (p. 169) in Guinea and **Monrovia** (p. 217) in

Liberia. Annual rainfall only falls below 2,000 mm/80 in inland in the extreme east of Guinea, near Senegal's border with Mali.

Temperatures are consistently high around the year on the coast and, during the dry season, rise even higher inland. During the rainy season the coastal region is most uncomfortable because of the high relative humidity which rarely drops below 80 percent during the daytime.

The climate of this part of Africa has for long had an unenviable reputation; Sierra Leone was known as 'the white man's grave'. The high death rate among Europeans living there was due more to tropical diseases than to the direct effects of the climate. There is no doubt, however, that the combination of constant high temperature and humidity makes this an uncomfortable climate. The higher temperatures inland are to some extend mitigated by the lower humidity. The harmattan, a persistent northeast wind, which blows during the dry season, is often dust-laden.

Sunshine amounts are low on the coast, particularly during the wet season when they average two to three hours a day. These figures rise inland, particularly in eastern Guinea. During the dry season they rise to eight to nine hours a day inland but in some places on the coast they may be as low as five to six.

The table for **Freetown** (opposite and above) illustrates conditions around the year in the coastal districts of Sierra Leone.

Singapore

See map page 23

This tiny state consists of Singapore island with a total area of 581 sq km/224 sq mi at the southern tip of the Malay Peninsula. Until 1965 it formed part of the Federation of Malaysia but since then it has been an independent state of the British Commonwealth.

It has a climate similar in all respects to that described on pp. 225–8 for Malaysia.

It is hot, wet, and distinctly humid throughout the year. The most unpleasant months are March and September when winds are light. See the table opposite for characteristic conditions.

FREETOWN — COASTAL SIERRA LEONE

	Sunshine average hours per day	Temperatures Average daily min °C	°F	Average daily max °C	°F	Highest recorded °C	°F	Lowest recorded °C	°F	Discomfort from heat and humidity	Relative humidity 8:00 %	14:00 %	Average monthly precipitation mm	in	Wet days more than 0.25 mm/0.01 in	
Jan	8	24	75	29	85	33	91	20	68	Medium	82	67	13	0.5	0.8	Jan
Feb	8	24	76	30	86	34	93	21	70	High	80	67	3	0.1	0.7	Feb
March	8	25	77	30	86	35	95	21	70	High	81	69	13	0.5	2.0	March
April	7	25	77	31	87	35	95	21	70	High	81	71	56	2.2	6.0	April
May	6	25	77	30	86	34	94	21	69	High	83	74	160	6.3	15.0	May
June	5	24	75	30	86	33	92	20	68	High	86	76	302	11.9	23.0	June
July	3	23	74	28	83	32	90	21	69	High	89	81	894	35.2	27.0	July
Aug	2	23	73	28	82	31	88	20	68	High	91	82	902	35.5	28.0	Aug
Sept	4	23	74	28	83	32	90	21	69	High	90	81	610	24.0	25.0	Sept
Oct	6	23	74	29	85	33	91	19	67	High	87	77	310	12.2	23.0	Oct
Nov	7	24	75	29	85	34	94	20	68	High	85	75	132	5.2	12.0	Nov
Dec	7	24	76	29	85	32	89	19	67	High	82	71	41	1.6	4.0	Dec

Based on readings for 14 years at 8°30' N, 13°14' W, altitude 11 m/37 ft

SINGAPORE — SINGAPORE

	Sunshine average hours per day	Temperatures Average daily min °C	°F	Average daily max °C	°F	Highest recorded °C	°F	Lowest recorded °C	°F	Discomfort from heat and humidity	Relative humidity 9:00 %	15:00 %	Average monthly precipitation mm	in	Wet days more than 0.25 mm/0.01 in	
Jan	5	23	73	30	86	34	93	20	68	High	82	78	252	9.9	17	Jan
Feb	7	23	73	31	88	34	94	19	66	High	77	71	173	6.8	11	Feb
March	6	24	75	31	88	34	94	19	67	High	76	70	193	7.6	14	March
April	6	24	75	31	88	35	95	21	70	High	77	74	188	7.4	15	April
May	6	24	75	32	89	36	97	21	70	Extreme	79	73	173	6.8	15	May
June	6	24	75	31	88	35	95	21	70	High	79	73	173	6.8	13	June
July	6	24	75	31	88	34	93	21	70	High	79	72	170	6.7	13	July
Aug	6	24	75	31	87	34	93	21	69	High	78	72	196	7.7	14	Aug
Sept	5	24	75	31	87	34	93	21	69	High	79	72	178	7.0	14	Sept
Oct	5	23	74	31	87	34	93	21	69	High	78	72	208	8.2	16	Oct
Nov	5	23	74	31	87	33	92	21	69	High	79	75	254	10.0	18	Nov
Dec	4	23	74	31	87	34	93	21	69	High	82	78	257	10.1	19	Dec

Based on readings for 39 years at 1°18' N, 103°50' E, altitude 10 m/33 ft

KOSICE

NORTHEASTERN SLOVAK REPUBLIC

average hours per day	Sunshine	Average daily minimum °C	Average daily minimum °F	Average daily maximum °C	Average daily maximum °F	Highest recorded °C	Highest recorded °F	Lowest recorded °C	Lowest recorded °F	Discomfort from heat and humidity	Relative humidity 7:30 %	Relative humidity 14:30 %	Average monthly precipitation mm	Average monthly precipitation in	Wet days more than 0.1 mm/0.004 in	
Jan	2	-7	19	0	33	10	51	-27	-16		87	78	30	1.2	13	Jan
Feb	3	-6	22	2	35	13	55	-24	-12		86	72	30	1.2	13	Feb
March	4	-2	29	8	47	21	70	-17	1		83	59	26	1.0	10	March
April	6	3	38	15	60	29	84	-7	20		77	51	38	1.5	11	April
May	8	8	47	21	69	31	87	-3	27		74	51	57	2.2	13	May
June	8	12	53	24	74	34	92	2	36	Moderate	75	55	84	3.3	14	June
July	8	13	56	26	78	35	95	4	40	Moderate	77	53	84	3.3	13	July
Aug	8	13	55	25	78	39	103	3	37	Moderate	80	53	80	3.2	13	Aug
Sept	6	9	47	21	71	33	91	-1	30		86	53	47	1.9	9	Sept
Oct	4	3	38	14	58	27	81	-11	12		89	61	41	1.6	10	Oct
Nov	2	0	33	7	45	17	63	-14	7		90	76	49	1.9	13	Nov
Dec	1	-3	27	3	37	15	58	-18	-1		90	82	39	1.5	15	Dec

Based on readings for 15 years at 48°42′ N, 21°16′ E, altitude 232 m/761 ft

BRATISLAVA

SOUTHWESTERN SLOVAK REPUBLIC

average hours per day	Sunshine	Average daily minimum °C	Average daily minimum °F	Average daily maximum °C	Average daily maximum °F	Highest recorded °C	Highest recorded °F	Lowest recorded °C	Lowest recorded °F	Discomfort from heat and humidity	Relative humidity 7:00 %	Relative humidity 14:00 %	Average monthly precipitation mm	Average monthly precipitation in	Wet days more than 0.1 mm/0.004 in	
Jan	2	-3	27	2	36	15	59	-18	0		84	77	43	1.7	12	Jan
Feb	3	-2	28	3	37	16	61	-23	-9		81	70	47	1.9	12	Feb
March	5	1	32	9	48	24	75	-11	12		79	58	42	1.7	10	March
April	7	6	43	16	61	28	82	-4	25		73	49	42	1.7	11	April
May	9	11	52	21	70	33	91	-3	27		72	49	61	2.4	11	May
June	9	14	57	24	75	37	99	5	41	Moderate	72	50	64	2.5	11	June
July	9	16	61	26	79	38	100	9	48	Moderate	73	49	73	2.9	11	July
Aug	9	15	59	26	79	37	99	8	46	Moderate	75	51	69	2.7	10	Aug
Sept	7	12	54	22	72	33	91	1	2		78	52	40	1.6	8	Sept
Oct	5	7	45	15	59	27	81	-5	23		84	62	54	2.1	11	Oct
Nov	2	3	37	8	46	20	68	-7	19		86	76	55	2.2	13	Nov
Dec	1	0	32	4	32	15	59	-21	6		87	80	59	2.3	14	Dec

Based on readings for 43 years at 48°10′ N, 17°08′ E, altitude 153 m/502 ft

Slovak Republic

See map page 19

The Slovak Republic is rather more hilly than the neighbouring Czech Republic and includes part of the western Carpathian Mountains, whose higher peaks reach over 1,500 m/5,000 ft. The chief differences of weather and climate within the country occur as a result of height; the Carpathians are wetter and more snowy than the southern region. Otherwise there is little difference of weather from one area to another and everywhere it can be changeable at all times of the year. The longest spells of settled weather occur during calm but cold days in winter; snow may lie from 40 to 100 days,

depending on altitude and the nature of a particular winter. The most unpleasant weather occurs in winter when easterly winds from Russia may bring very low temperatures for several days. Spring and summer are wettest. Summers are moderately warm but fine weather is often broken by thunderstorms; extreme heat is rare. Spells of disturbed summer weather are often brought by disturbances originating over the northern Mediterranean. The number of wet days is rather less than in western Europe and the hours of sunshine rather more. Summer sunshine averages as much as eight hours per day. The tables for **Kosice** (opposite) and **Bratislava** (opposite and below) are representative.

Slovenia

See map page 19

The best known and most visited part of Slovenia is the northern segment of the Dalmatian coast. This region has a Mediterranean type of climate with mild winters and warm, sunny summers. The coast

is backed by high mountains, and winter rainfall is heavy. The table for **Dubrovnik** (p. 117) in Croatia is characteristic of weather on the Dalmatian coast. The one unpleasant feature of the winter weather is a cold gusty wind, the *bora*, which brings cold air from central and eastern Europe down to the coast

LJUBLJANA														SLOVENIA
Sunshine	Temperatures							Discomfort from heat and humidity	Precipitation and humidity				Wet days	
	Average daily				Highest recorded		Lowest recorded		Relative humidity		Average monthly precipitation			
	minimum		maximum						7:00	14:00				
average hours per day	°C	°F	°C	°F	°C	°F	°C	°F		%		mm	in	more than 0.1 mm/0.004 in	
Jan	2	−4	25	2	36	14	57	−27	−16		91	81	88	3.5	13	Jan
Feb	3	−4	25	5	41	19	66	−28	−18		90	70	89	3.5	11	Feb
March	4	0	32	10	50	23	73	−16	4		88	60	76	3.0	11	March
April	5	4	40	15	60	30	85	−5	22		87	56	98	3.9	13	April
May	6	9	48	20	68	31	88	−3	27		88	56	121	4.8	16	May
June	7	12	54	24	75	38	100	4	39	Moderate	87	56	133	5.2	16	June
July	8	14	57	27	80	39	102	7	45	Medium	89	54	113	4.5	12	July
Aug	7	14	57	26	78	35	95	4	40	Moderate	93	55	127	5.0	12	Aug
Sept	5	11	51	22	71	31	88	1	35		95	62	142	5.6	10	Sept
Oct	3	6	43	15	59	27	80	−2	28		95	70	151	5.9	14	Oct
Nov	1	2	36	8	47	20	68	−11	13		93	80	131	5.2	15	Nov
Dec	1	−1	30	4	39	16	60	−15	6		93	86	114	4.5	15	Dec

Based on readings for 17 years at 46°04′ N, 14°31′ E, altitude 299 m/981 ft

for a few days at a time; it blows particularly violently in Slovenia. Summers on this coast are not entirely rainless and the fine, sunny weather is often interrupted by thunderstorms. Sunshine averages some four hours a day in winter and from ten to twelve hours a day in summer. Inland climatic conditions rapidly become more typical of eastern Europe with cold winters and warm summers and here summer is the wettest season. Slovenia includes part of the eastern Alps with weather and climate very similar to southern Austria. The table for **Ljubljana** (p. 319) illustrates weather conditions at moderate elevations inland in Slovenia.

Solomon Islands

See map page 17

The seven large volcanic islands that make up the main territory of this southwest Pacific nation are geographically a continuation of the southeastern islands of Papua New Guinea. With neighbouring countries, these islands share the features of a tropical oceanic climate. Very similar conditions prevail throughout the year with high temperatures and humidity. The daily range of temperature is quite small – about 4°–5° C/10° F. There is abundant rainfall. Being south of the equator, the Solomon Islands' season of maximum rainfall is between November and April. On some islands there is no great difference in rainfall from month to month. Tropical cyclones are less frequent than in the western Pacific north of the equator.

Except in the wettest places, where cloud is more frequent, the country has moderately large amounts of sunshine, averaging from six to eight hours a day. Much of the rainfall comes in short, heavy showers often after a sunny morning but longer periods of heavy rain, lasting for a day or so, do occur in the wetter months.

In this area of the Pacific the principal difference in the weather and climate is the amount of rainfall per month. Temperature and humidity are very similar from one island to another but the amount of rainfall varies with altitude and with exposure of the coast to the dominant southeast trade winds. The number of wet days varies from island to island much less than the amount of rain.

The climate may generally be described as pleasant and healthy, although the combination of high temperature and humidity can be a little oppressive when not tempered by sea breezes or a brisk wind.

The table for **Kieta** (p. 281) on the island of Bougainville – geographically one of the Solomon Islands – shows weather that is similar to that in the country that takes its name from the islands.

Somalia

See map pages 20–1

Somalia occupies the northeastern corner of Africa, often called the Horn of Africa. It is bordered on the west by Ethiopia and on the south by Kenya. It extends from 2° S to 12° N and has a long coastline on the Indian Ocean and Gulf of Aden.

For a country so near the equator, it has a surprisingly dry climate. Much of the country is desert or desert scrub. Almost no part has an annual rainfall exceeding 625 mm/25 in and much of it receives less than 250 mm/10 in. In the north some rain occurs during the season of low sun when temperatures are a little lower but this area is very dry for the rest of the year (see the table for **Berbera** opposite and above). Elsewhere the rainy season is the period of high sun from April to September as in most of Ethiopia. The rains are very variable from year to year and drought is a constant problem for the nomadic pastoralist.

Temperatures along the east coast from Cape Guardafui southwards are prevented from rising too high by a cold offshore current which makes the sea surface temperature in this part of the Indian Ocean surprisingly low for tropical waters. This cold water may be one of the reasons for the very low rainfall in much of the country. The table for **Mogadishu** (opposite) shows that temperatures vary little from month to month and relative humidity remains high.

By contrast, along the north coast very high temperatures are experienced between April and September as the offshore waters here are very warm. This part of Somalia and the adjoining areas around the Gulf of Aden have a most uncomfortable climate at this time, being very hot and also humid

BERBERA

	Sunshine	Temperatures								Discomfort from heat and humidity	Precipitation and humidity					Wet days	
	average hours per day	Average daily				Highest recorded		Lowest recorded			Relative humidity 6:00 15:00		Average monthly precipitation			more than 1 mm/0.04 in	
		minimum		maximum													
		°C	°F	°C	°F	°C	°F	°C	°F		%		mm	in			
Jan		20	68	29	84	34	94	14	58	Medium	87	69	8	0.3		0.6	Jan
Feb		22	71	29	84	33	92	16	60	High	87	70	3	0.1		0.6	Feb
March		23	73	30	86	35	95	17	62	High	86	71	5	0.2		0.5	March
April		25	77	32	89	42	108	19	66	Extreme	89	73	13	0.5		0.7	April
May		27	80	36	96	44	112	21	69	Extreme	80	66	8	0.3		0.8	May
June		30	86	42	107	47	117	22	72	Extreme	51	46	0	0.0		0.1	June
July		31	88	42	107	47	116	21	69	Extreme	45	43	0	0.0		0.3	July
Aug		31	87	41	106	47	116	20	68	Extreme	44	46	3	0.1		0.5	Aug
Sept		29	84	39	103	46	114	18	64	Extreme	52	50	0	0.0		0.4	Sept
Oct		24	76	33	92	42	107	17	62	High	78	65	3	0.1		0.2	Oct
Nov		22	71	31	88	37	98	16	61	High	81	66	5	0.2		0.3	Nov
Dec		20	68	29	85	36	96	15	59	Medium	84	68	5	0.2		0.4	Dec

Based on readings for 30 years at 10°26′ N, 45°02′ E, altitude 14 m/45 ft

MOGADISHU

	Sunshine	Temperatures								Discomfort from heat and humidity	Precipitation and humidity					Wet days	
	average hours per day	Average daily				Highest recorded		Lowest recorded			Relative humidity 8:00 14:00		Average monthly precipitation			more than 0.1 mm/0.004 in	
		minimum		maximum													
		°C	°F	°C	°F	°C	°F	°C	°F		%		mm	in			
Jan	8	23	73	30	86	34	94	20	68	High	80	78	0	0.0		0.3	Jan
Feb	9	23	74	30	86	32	89	18	65	High	78	75	0	0.0		0.3	Feb
March	9	24	76	31	88	33	91	20	68	High	78	75	0	0.0		1.0	March
April	8	26	78	32	90	36	97	20	68	Extreme	78	75	58	2.3		5.0	April
May	8	25	77	32	89	34	94	18	65	Extreme	82	77	58	2.3		7.0	May
June	7	23	74	29	85	32	90	20	68	High	83	79	97	3.8		14.0	June
July	7	23	73	28	83	32	89	15	59	High	84	80	64	2.5		20.0	July
Aug	8	23	73	28	83	30	86	16	60	High	85	80	48	1.9		11.0	Aug
Sept	9	23	74	29	84	32	89	18	64	High	84	80	25	1.0		7.0	Sept
Oct	9	24	76	30	86	32	90	18	65	High	82	78	23	0.9		5.0	Oct
Nov	8	24	75	31	87	32	90	21	69	High	81	78	41	1.6		5.0	Nov
Dec	8	24	75	30	86	34	93	20	68	High	81	78	13	0.5		2.0	Dec

Based on readings for 10 years at 2°02′ N, 45°21′ E, altitude 12 m/39 ft

on the coast. Inland it is even hotter but with lower humidity. Some places here have the highest mean annual temperatures in the world and there is a serious risk of heat exhaustion or even heatstroke during the hottest period.

Sunshine amounts are high in most of the country, averaging eight to ten hours a day around the year. They are lowest on the east coast during the rainy season when there is more cloud and some coastal fog as warm air passes over the cold sea surface.

South Africa

South Africa extends from 22° S to 35° S at Cape Agulhas, the most southerly point of the African continent. Much of the interior consists of extensive high plains, known in South Africa as 'veld', with an altitude between 900 m/3,000 ft and 1,800 m/6,000 ft. The interior is divided from the narrow coastal plain by a steep escarpment (The Great Escarpment) forming lofty mountains in the east and south.

The eastern shores of southern Africa are warmed by the Agulhas current, which flows southwards from tropical latitudes; while the western shores are cooled by the Benguela current, flowing northwards from the cold southern ocean surrounding Antarctica. These influences of relief and ocean currents produce a distinctive pattern of climatic regions which cut across the political boundaries separating South Africa from its neighbours.

Both the southerly latitude and the altitude of the interior regions produce a temperate climate such that only the low-lying districts in the north, along the border with Zimbabwe and Mozambique, have a

climate that is tropical. The southern part of South Africa is sufficiently far south to be influenced in winter by weather disturbances associated with the belt of westerly winds in the southern ocean. For this reason a small portion of the southwestern Cape, below the Great Escarpment, has a Mediterranean type of climate with mild, changeable winters, during which most of the annual rainfall occurs, and a warm to hot, sunny summer.

Eastwards of Cape Town this merges into a region where some rain occurs in all months but where temperature conditions are similar. In the coastlands of Kwazulu-Natal and the lowlands below the Great Escarpment up to the border with Mozambique, the climate becomes almost tropical; winters are warmer and summer is the wetter season, although rain falls throughout the year. This coast is exposed both to warm water offshore and the southeast trade winds for most of the year.

By contrast the west coast northwards from about 32° S is a desert region with a remarkably small annual temperature range. This is because the cold

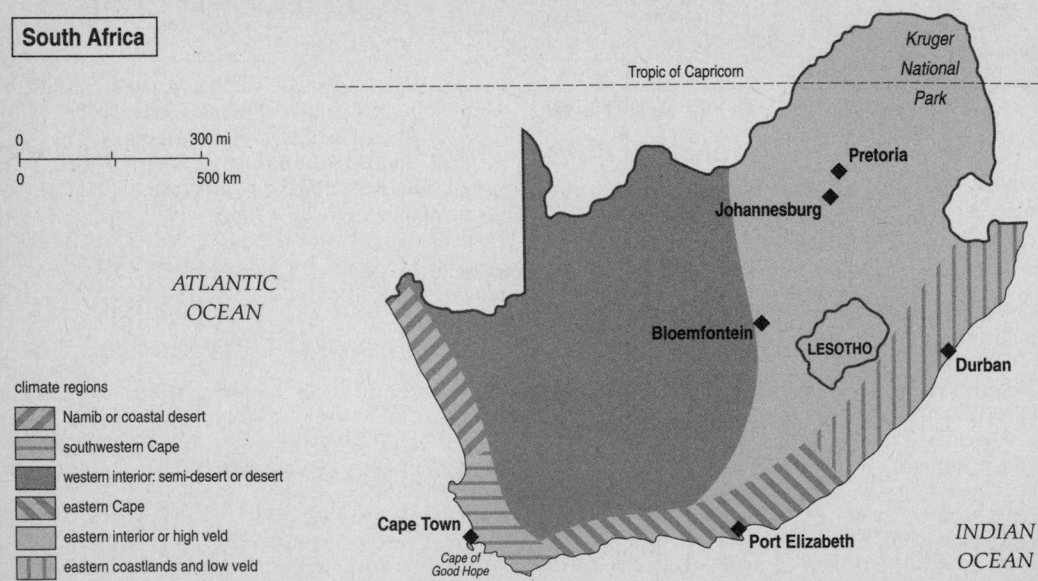

South Africa

| | 0   300 mi |
| 0   500 km |

ATLANTIC
OCEAN

climate regions
- Namib or coastal desert
- southwestern Cape
- western interior: semi-desert or desert
- eastern Cape
- eastern interior or high veld
- eastern coastlands and low veld

Tropic of Capricorn

Kruger
National
Park

Pretoria

Johannesburg

Bloemfontein

LESOTHO

Durban

Cape Town

Cape of
Good Hope

Port Elizabeth

INDIAN
OCEAN

PRETORIA												EASTERN INTERIOR	
Sunshine		Temperatures						Discomfort from heat and humidity	Precipitation and humidity				Wet days
average hours per day		Average daily		Highest recorded		Lowest recorded			Relative humidity 8:00 14:00		Average monthly precipitation		more than 1 mm/0.04 in
		minimum	maximum										
		°C	°F	°C	°F	°C	°F	°C	°F		%	mm	in
Jan	9	16	60	27	81	35	95	9	49	Moderate	71 47	127	5.0	12.0	Jan
Feb	9	16	60	27	81	33	91	9	49	Moderate	73 49	109	4.3	9.0	Feb
March	8	14	57	26	78	33	91	6	43	Moderate	75 48	114	4.5	8.0	March
April	9	10	50	24	75	28	83	1	33		74 42	43	1.7	5.0	April
May	9	6	42	21	70	26	79	-3	26		74 36	23	0.9	3.0	May
June	9	3	37	19	66	25	77	-4	24		74 32	15	0.6	1.0	June
July	9	3	37	19	66	24	75	-4	24		72 31	8	0.3	1.0	July
Aug	10	6	42	22	71	28	83	-2	28		65 29	5	0.2	0.8	Aug
Sept	10	9	49	25	77	32	89	-1	30		57 29	20	0.8	2.0	Sept
Oct	9	13	55	27	80	33	92	3	37	Moderate	60 34	56	2.2	7.0	Oct
Nov	9	14	57	27	80	36	96	5	41	Moderate	65 40	132	5.2	11.0	Nov
Dec	9	15	59	28	82	35	95	6	43	Medium	68 45	132	5.2	10.0	Dec

Based on readings for 13 years at 25°45′ S, 28°14′ E, altitude 1369 m/4491 ft

Benguela current chills the air and produces atmospheric conditions unfavourable to rainfall; fog and low cloud are frequent along this coast.

In the interior of South Africa there is a broad contrast between east and west. Total rainfall is greatest in the east and gradually decreases westwards so that much of the interior is semi-desert with a low and unreliable rainfall. The wettest regions are in high areas in the east, where both altitude and exposure to the moist air coming off the Indian Ocean produce the heaviest and most reliable rainfall. Over the whole of this interior rainfall comes mainly in the summer, much of it in thundery downpours. Because of altitude and the 'continental' influence there is a large daily and seasonal range of temperature so that frost is a frequent occurrence in winter and snow is by no means unknown above 1,500 m/5,000 ft. Winters are mainly dry and sunny and summers warm to hot.

The greater part of South Africa has a very sunny climate with much fine, settled weather. The southern coastal regions have their most disturbed and changeable weather in winter and the eastern coastlands and the interior their most disturbed and rainy weather in summer. In few parts of South Africa are the weather and climate unhealthy or likely to cause great discomfort or stress. Daily

sunshine hours are high over most of the country, averaging eight to ten hours a day around the year. The cloudiest regions are the western and eastern coasts, particularly in the summer months.

THE EASTERN INTERIOR OR HIGH VELD

Most of this area is above 1,200 m/4,000 ft. This is the most developed part of South Africa. As the tables for **Pretoria** (above), **Johannesburg** (overleaf) and **Bloemfontein** (p. 325) show, the winters are dry and mild but with frequent cold nights. Summers are warm with more frequent rain but temperatures are rarely excessively high. The low humidity and ample sunshine make for a pleasant and healthy climate for most of the year.

THE WESTERN INTERIOR

The chief feature of this large region is its low rainfall; much of it is semi-desert or even desert. Apart from the low rainfall the general features of weather and climate are similar to those of the eastern interior. The tables for **Francistown** (p. 67) in northern Botswana and **Windhoek** (p. 253) in the higher districts of Namibia are representative of much of the region.

THE NAMIB OR COASTAL DESERT

Weather and climate in this desert, which continues north along the entire coast of neighbouring Namibia, are unusual and quite distinctive. The region receives very little rain and is a complete desert but temperatures are kept low most of the time by the cold Benguela current.

On a few days each month, particularly in winter, midday temperatures rise quite high when the berg wind blows from the interior. This is a föhn-type wind bringing very dry air, which is heated as it descends to the coast. Apart from the rare shower of rain and the frequent coastal fog, the berg is almost the only weather feature of this arid region. See the table for **Walvis Bay** (p. 253) in Namibia.

THE SOUTHWESTERN CAPE

Including the coastal lowlands and southern slopes of the mountains around Cape Town.

The coastal lowlands and southern slopes of the mountains around Cape Town have mild and generally wet winters with much changeable weather and dry, settled summers similar to the climate of much of the Mediterranean or California. Summers

are not completely dry and occasional rainstorms occur. The table for **Cape Town** (opposite and below) is representative of this region, but inland some sheltered areas are warmer and drier. This was the area first settled by Europeans in the 17th century; French Huguenot settlers introduced the grape vine, which grows well in this climate.

THE EASTERN CAPE

The weather and climate of this region are intermediate between those of the southwestern Cape and the eastern coastlands regions. The main difference is that rainfall is well distributed around the year and disturbed weather can occur in both winter and summer (see the table for **Port Elizabeth** on p. 326).

THE EASTERN COASTLANDS AND LOW VELD

This is the part of southern Africa where the climate comes nearest to being tropical. The summers are warm and humid on the coast, particularly towards the north in Zululand, where conditions are similar to those found in southern Mozambique (see the table for **Maputo** on p. 247). Summer is the wettest season but some rain falls in all months. The table

JOHANNESBURG														EASTERN INTERIOR	
Sunshine	Temperatures								Discomfort from heat and humidity	Precipitation and humidity				Wet days	
	Average daily				Highest recorded		Lowest recorded			Relative humidity		Average monthly precipitation			
	minimum		maximum							8:00	14:00				
average hours per day	°C	°F	°C	°F	°C	°F	°C	°F		%		mm	in	more than 1 mm/0.04 in	
Jan	8	14	58	26	78	33	91	6	42	Moderate	75	50	114	4.5	12.0	Jan
Feb	8	14	58	25	77	33	91	7	45	Moderate	78	53	109	4.3	9.0	Feb
March	8	13	55	24	75	31	88	5	41	Moderate	79	50	89	3.5	9.0	March
April	8	10	50	22	72	29	85	-1	30		74	44	38	1.5	4.0	April
May	9	6	43	19	66	26	78	-6	22		70	36	25	1.0	3.0	May
June	9	4	39	17	62	24	76	-7	19		70	33	8	0.3	1.0	June
July	9	4	39	17	63	23	74	-7	19		69	32	8	0.3	0.9	July
Aug	10	6	43	20	68	26	79	-7	20		64	29	8	0.3	0.9	Aug
Sept	10	9	48	23	73	30	86	-3	27		59	30	23	0.9	2.0	Sept
Oct	9	12	53	25	77	32	90	0	32		64	37	56	2.2	7.0	Oct
Nov	8	13	55	25	77	34	93	2	35	Moderate	67	45	107	4.2	10.0	Nov
Dec	8	14	57	26	78	33	92	6	42	Moderate	70	47	125	4.9	11.0	Dec

Based on readings for 18 years at 26°14′ S, 28°09′ E, altitude 1665 m/5463 ft

BLOEMFONTEIN

EASTERN INTERIOR

	Sunshine	Temperatures									Discomfort from heat and humidity	Precipitation and humidity						Wet days	
		Average daily				Highest recorded		Lowest recorded				Relative humidity 7:30 13:30		Average monthly precipitation					
	average hours per day	minimum		maximum														more than 1 mm/0.04 in	
		°C	°F	°C	°F	°C	°F	°C	°F			%		mm	in				
Jan	10	16	60	30	86	38	100	6	42	Medium		62	33	91	3.6			8	Jan
Feb	10	15	59	28	83	35	95	4	39	Medium		71	42	79	3.1			9	Feb
March	9	13	55	26	79	34	93	3	37	Moderate		73	42	76	3.0			8	March
April	9	8	47	23	73	31	88	-2	28			72	38	56	2.2			6	April
May	8	4	39	19	66	27	81	-6	22			75	36	25	1.0			4	May
June	9	1	33	17	62	26	78	-9	16			74	33	8	0.3			1	June
July	9	1	33	16	61	23	73	-8	17			71	32	10	0.4			2	July
Aug	10	3	38	19	67	27	80	-9	16			60	29	20	0.8			2	Aug
Sept	10	6	43	23	73	32	90	-6	21			51	25	20	0.8			2	Sept
Oct	10	10	50	26	78	35	95	-2	28			55	28	51	2.0			5	Oct
Nov	10	12	54	27	81	34	94	2	35	Moderate		53	27	66	2.6			5	Nov
Dec	10	14	58	29	85	36	97	3	37	Moderate		56	29	61	2.4			7	Dec

Based on readings for 14 years at 29°07′ S, 26°11′ E, altitude 1419 m/4665 ft

CAPE TOWN

CAPE MEDITERRANEAN SOUTH AFRICA

	Sunshine	Temperatures									Discomfort from heat and humidity	Precipitation and humidity						Wet days	
		Average daily				Highest recorded		Lowest recorded				Relative humidity 7:00 13:00		Average monthly precipitation					
	average hours per day	minimum		maximum														more than 1 mm/0.04 in	
		°C	°F	°C	°F	°C	°F	°C	°F			%		mm	in				
Jan	11	16	60	26	78	37	99	7	44	Moderate		72	54	15	0.6			3	Jan
Feb	10	16	60	26	79	38	100	5	41	Moderate		77	54	8	0.3			2	Feb
March	9	14	58	25	77	39	103	6	42	Moderate		85	57	18	0.7			3	March
April	8	12	53	22	72	39	102	3	38			90	60	48	1.9			6	April
May	6	9	49	19	67	35	95	-1	31			91	65	79	3.1			9	May
June	6	8	46	18	65	29	85	-2	29			91	64	84	3.3			9	June
July	6	7	45	17	63	29	84	-2	28			91	67	89	3.5			10	July
Aug	7	8	46	18	64	32	89	-1	31			90	65	66	2.6			9	Aug
Sept	8	9	49	18	65	34	93	1	33			87	62	43	1.7			7	Sept
Oct	9	11	52	21	70	32	90	1	34			79	58	31	1.2			5	Oct
Nov	10	13	55	23	73	34	93	4	40			74	56	18	0.7			3	Nov
Dec	11	14	58	24	76	38	100	5	41	Moderate		71	54	10	0.4			3	Dec

Based on readings for 19 years at 33°54′ S, 18°32′ E, altitude 17 m/56 ft

PORT ELIZABETH

EASTERN CAPE LOWLANDS

	Sunshine average hours per day	Temperatures										Discomfort from heat and humidity	Precipitation and humidity				Wet days more than 1 mm/0.04 in	
		Average daily				Highest recorded		Lowest recorded					Relative humidity 7:30 13:30		Average monthly precipitation			
		minimum		maximum														
		°C	°F	°C	°F	°C	°F	°C	°F				%		mm	in		
Jan	9	16	61	26	78	34	94	7	45			Medium	77	64	31	1.2	11	Jan
Feb	8	17	62	26	78	40	104	8	46			Medium	82	67	33	1.3	10	Feb
March	8	16	60	24	76	40	104	7	45			Moderate	86	67	48	1.9	10	March
April	7	13	55	23	73	38	101	6	42			Moderate	83	64	46	1.8	7	April
May	7	10	50	22	71	35	95	-1	31				83	58	61	2.4	4	May
June	7	7	45	20	68	30	86	1	33				83	56	46	1.8	3	June
July	7	7	45	19	67	32	90	0	32				82	57	48	1.9	4	July
Aug	8	8	47	20	68	37	98	0	32				83	59	51	2.0	5	Aug
Sept	8	10	50	20	68	39	103	2	35				81	65	58	2.3	7	Sept
Oct	8	12	54	21	70	36	97	4	39				78	68	56	2.2	11	Oct
Nov	9	14	57	22	72	40	104	6	42				76	66	56	2.2	12	Nov
Dec	9	15	59	24	75	36	96	7	44			Moderate	74	65	43	1.7	13	Dec

Based on readings for 14 years at 33°59′ S, 25°36′ E, altitude 58 m/190 ft

DURBAN

EASTERN COASTAL SOUTH AFRICA

	Sunshine average hours per day	Temperatures										Discomfort from heat and humidity	Precipitation and humidity				Wet days more than 1 mm/0.04 in	
		Average daily				Highest recorded		Lowest recorded					Relative humidity 8:00 14:00		Average monthly precipitation			
		minimum		maximum														
		°C	°F	°C	°F	°C	°F	°C	°F				%		mm	in		
Jan	6	21	69	27	81	33	92	14	57			Medium	77	72	109	4.3	10	Jan
Feb	7	21	69	27	81	32	89	15	59			Medium	79	73	122	4.8	9	Feb
March	7	20	68	27	80	32	90	14	58			Medium	80	74	130	5.1	9	March
April	7	18	64	26	78	37	99	11	51			Medium	78	71	76	3.0	7	April
May	7	14	57	24	75	35	95	7	44			Moderate	72	66	51	2.0	4	May
June	8	12	53	23	73	32	90	5	41			Moderate	69	61	33	1.3	3	June
July	7	11	52	22	72	33	92	4	39				71	61	28	1.1	3	July
Aug	7	13	55	22	72	32	89	5	41				75	68	38	1.5	4	Aug
Sept	6	15	59	23	73	42	107	8	46			Moderate	74	71	71	2.8	4	Sept
Oct	6	17	62	24	75	31	87	10	50			Moderate	75	73	109	4.3	10	Oct
Nov	5	18	65	25	77	39	102	11	51			Medium	76	74	122	4.8	11	Nov
Dec	6	19	67	26	79	32	90	13	56			Medium	75	73	119	4.7	10	Dec

Based on readings for 15 years at 29°50′ S, 31°02′ E, altitude 5 m/16 ft

for **Durban** (opposite and below) is representative of the coastal lowlands. The heat and humidity are here moderated by daily sea breezes but conditions are often sultry in summer. Winters are mild to warm. Inland, and at medium altitudes below the Great Escarpment, temperatures are lower, particularly in winter, but rainfall is greater (see the table for **Mbabane** in Swaziland, p. 341).

South Korea

See map page 24

South Korea occupies the southern half of the Korean peninsula, between the Yellow Sea and the Sea of Japan. In area the country is a little smaller than England. It has a border with North Korea approximately along the 38° parallel of latitude. Much of the country is hilly or even mountainous; in the east there are many hills rising above 915 m/ 3,000 ft. The largest areas of lowland are in the west.

The general features of the weather and climate of the Korean peninsula are described here. Where conditions are different in North Korea they are mentioned on p. 271.

Situated on the eastern side of the great land mass of Eurasia, Korea has a rather extreme continental climate considering that it is surrounded by water on three sides. The winters are very cold. Nowhere else in the world, in a similar latitude, are winters so cold with such frequent frost and snow. Summers are warm and, at times, hot. Most of the rainfall occurs between June and September. Some precipitation occurs in all months but, from November until early April, this is often snow. Snow falls on an average of twenty-eight days a year at **Seoul** (below) and on about ten days in the far south.

The transition from the cold, dry winter to the warm, wet summer occurs rather quickly between April and early May, and there is a similar abrupt return to winter conditions in late October and early November. Over most of the country summer temperatures are high enough for rice to be grown extensively.

Korea is one of the most northerly countries to be affected by the great seasonal wind reversal called the Asiatic monsoon. In winter the winds are

SEOUL															SOUTH KOREA
Sunshine	Temperatures							Discomfort from heat and humidity	Precipitation and humidity					Wet days	
	Average daily				Highest recorded		Lowest recorded			Relative humidity		Average monthly precipitation			
	minimum		maximum							5:30	13:30				
average hours per day	°C	°F	°C	°F	°C	°F	°C	°F		%		mm	in	more than 1 mm/0.04 in	
Jan	6	-9	15	0	32	12	54	-22	-8		78	51	31	1.2	8	Jan
Feb	7	-7	20	3	37	16	61	-19	-3		77	47	20	0.8	6	Feb
March	7	-2	29	8	47	22	72	-15	5		77	46	38	1.5	7	March
April	8	5	41	17	62	28	83	-4	25		83	46	76	3.0	8	April
May	8	11	51	22	72	32	90	2	36		87	51	81	3.2	10	May
June	7	16	61	27	80	37	98	9	49	Medium	87	54	130	5.1	10	June
July	6	21	70	29	84	37	98	13	55	Medium	91	67	376	14.8	16	July
Aug	7	22	71	31	87	37	99	14	58	High	90	62	267	10.5	13	Aug
Sept	7	15	59	26	78	33	91	3	38	Moderate	89	55	119	4.7	9	Sept
Oct	8	7	45	19	67	30	86	-4	25		88	48	41	1.6	7	Oct
Nov	6	0	32	11	51	23	74	-12	11		83	52	46	1.8	9	Nov
Dec	6	-7	20	3	37	14	58	-24	-12		79	52	25	1.0	9	Dec

Based on readings for 22 years at 37°34′ N, 126°58′ E, altitude 87 m/285 ft

PUSAN										SOUTH KOREA		
Sunshine	Temperatures						Discomfort from heat and humidity	Precipitation and humidity				Wet days
average hours per day	Average daily				Highest recorded	Lowest recorded		Relative humidity 5:30 13:30		Average monthly precipitation		more than 1 mm/0.04 in
	minimum		maximum									
	°C	°F	°C	°F	°C	°F	°C	°F	%		mm	in	
Jan	7	−2	29	6	43	18	65	−14	7		57	41	43	1.7	5	Jan
Feb	7	−1	31	7	45	18	64	−12	11		61	45	36	1.4	3	Feb
March	7	3	37	12	53	21	69	−7	19		65	50	69	2.7	7	March
April	7	8	47	17	62	26	78	−2	29		73	59	140	5.5	8	April
May	8	13	55	21	69	29	84	6	42		75	59	132	5.2	7	May
June	7	17	62	24	75	33	92	9	49	Moderate	82	71	201	7.9	10	June
July	6	22	71	27	81	34	94	14	57	Medium	90	76	295	11.6	10	July
Aug	7	23	73	29	85	36	96	16	60	High	87	71	130	5.1	8	Aug
Sept	6	18	65	26	78	32	90	9	49	Medium	82	64	173	6.8	8	Sept
Oct	7	12	54	21	70	27	80	2	36		73	54	74	2.9	5	Oct
Nov	7	6	43	15	59	24	75	−3	26		69	52	41	1.6	4	Nov
Dec	6	1	33	9	48	19	67	−12	10		65	49	31	1.2	3	Dec

Based on readings for 29 years at 35°06′ N, 129°01′ E, altitude 13 m/41 ft

predominantly from the west and north, bringing very cold but dry air from north China and Siberia. In summer the winds are mainly from the east and south, bringing warm, moist air from the Pacific Ocean. The weather can be somewhat variable from day to day at all seasons, since the country is affected by frontal systems and depressions moving from the west. These bring rain or snow and occasional thaws in winter. In summer these disturbances are associated with the spells of heaviest rainfall. About once a year a typhoon moves up from the South China Sea and brings very heavy rain and strong winds at any time between June and September.

A surprising feature of the Korean winter is the large amount of sunshine, averaging as much as six to seven hours a day. Even when temperatures remain below freezing all day the sun may shine from a clear blue sky while the cold is intensified by the strong wind. Hours of sunshine are rather less during the wetter period in summer. The strong wind chill factor intensifies the cold so that warm winter clothing is essential. Otherwise the climate is not particularly uncomfortable and is generally healthy. Humidity is higher in the summer and some days may feel distinctly muggy and uncomfortable.

Temperatures decrease from south to north, particularly in winter, so that South Korea is rather warmer than the north around the year. The tables for **Seoul** (p. 327) near the border with North Korea, and for **Pusan** (above) in the south of the country, show the warmer conditions farther south.

Spain

Spain is a almost as large as France. On the west it shares a long border with Portugal, and the two countries form a large peninsula, with the Atlantic Ocean on its western and northern side and the Mediterranean Sea to its south and east. The large size of the peninsula and the different influences of the Atlantic and Mediterranean result in a variety of climates within Spain. It is a mistake to think of the whole country as having a Mediterranean climate such as is found in the tourist areas along the east and south coasts and in the Balearic Islands.

In the north the Pyrenees and Cantabrian Mountains rise to between 1,800 m/6,000 ft and 3,000 m/ 10,000 ft. Much of interior Spain is a plateau with an average height of 450 m–900 m /1,500 ft–3,000 ft, crossed by a number of mountain ranges (sierras). In Andalusia the valley of the Guadalquivir river forms a wide lowland, to the south of which lies the high Sierra Nevada, dominating narrow Mediterranean coastlands. These large differences of altitude and the contrast between coast and interior give Spain a range of climatic and weather conditions.

Although most of the country is hot and sunny in summer there are great differences of temperature in winter; coastal areas are mild but the interior is frequently cold and snowy. Skiing can be enjoyed on the nearest mountain ranges to most of the large towns of the country.

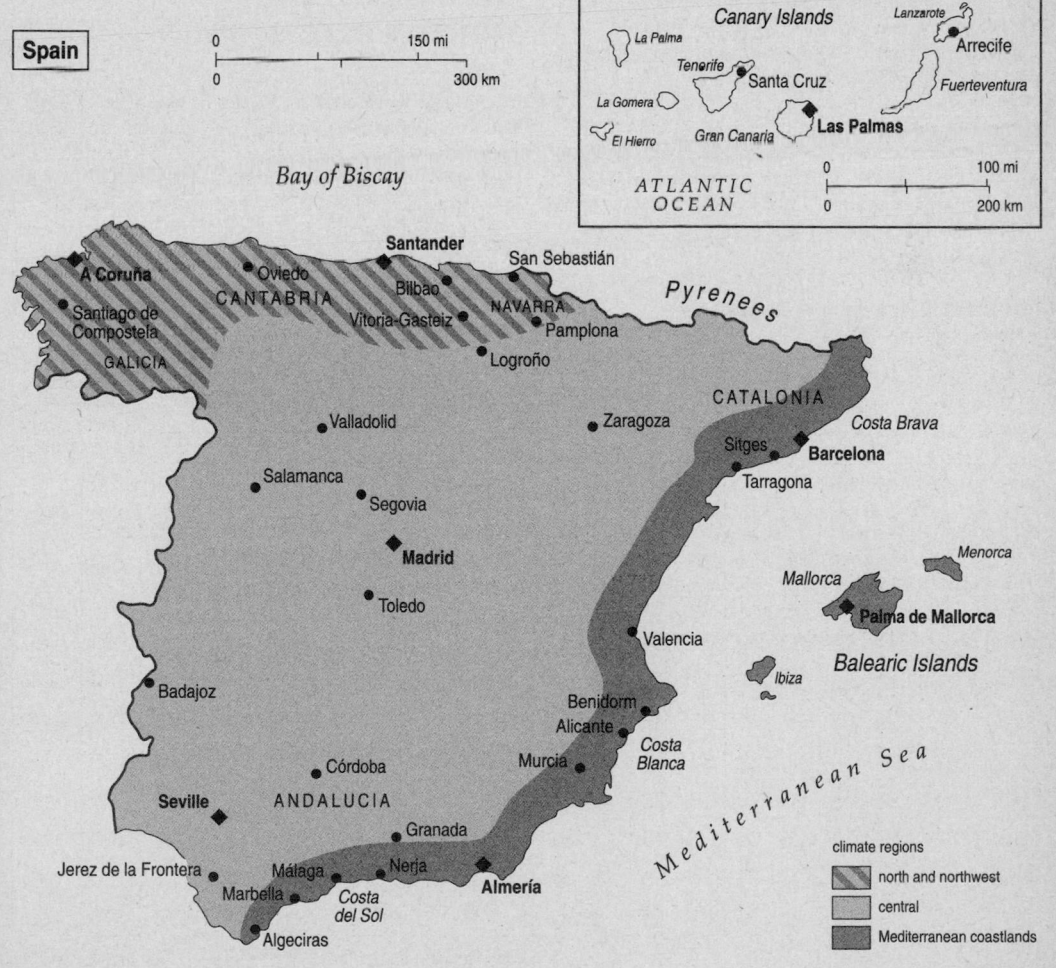

Spain can be divided into three climatic regions: the Canary Islands, the north and northwest, central Spain, and the Mediterranean coastlines of the east and south including the Balearic Islands.

CANARY ISLANDS

Including (with towns and cities in parentheses): EL HIERRO, GRAN CANARIA (Las Palmas), FUERTEVENTURA, LA GOMERA, LANZAROTE (Arrecife), LA PALMA, and TENERIFE (Santa Cruz).

The Canaries form an archipelago of seven main islands in about latitude 28° N, some 100 km/60 mi off the coast of North Africa. They are rugged volcanic islands with the highest peak, on the island of Tenerife, rising to 3,700 m/12,200 ft. This high mountain is snowcapped around the year, in marked contrast to the mild temperatures experienced at or near sea level in winter. The waters of the Atlantic Ocean are here rather cool because of the cold Canaries current; thus, summer temperatures rarely rise very high, while winters are mild.

The warmest days in summer occur when hot, dry air is drawn out from the Sahara desert and reaches as far as the islands. This air may sometimes be laden with fine dust particles blown from the desert.

However, it reaches the islands with a raised relative humidity and lower temperatures after its passage across the cool ocean water. The weather may be disturbed for a few days at a time in winter under the influence of an Atlantic depression but such stormy and wet periods are not frequent. Some fog and cloud may occur in the summer months, which are usually dry and sunny with no very hot days. The northern shores of the islands, being more exposed to the predominant northeast trade winds, are rather wetter than the sheltered southern coasts. Daily sunshine hours range from an average of six in winter to as many as eleven in the summer months.

Administratively the islands are an integral part of Spain, having been occupied by Spain in the 15th century. The table for **Las Palmas** (below) is representative of conditions at or near sea level.

NORTHERN AND NORTHWESTERN SPAIN

Including (with towns and cities in parentheses): GALICIA (A Coruña, Santiago de Compostela); most of ASTURIAS (Oviedo), CANTABRIA (Santander), and PAIS VASCO (Bilbao, Vitoria-Gasteiz); and northwestern NAVARRA (Pamplona, San Sebastián).

LAS PALMAS									CANARY ISLANDS					
Sunshine	Temperatures							Discomfort from heat and humidity	Precipitation and humidity				Wet days	
	Average daily				Highest recorded		Lowest recorded			Relative humidity		Average monthly precipitation		
	minimum		maximum							8:00	15:00			
average hours per day	°C	°F	°C	°F	°C	°F	°C	°F		%		mm	in	more than 0.1 mm/0.004 in
Jan	6	14	58	21	70	30	86	8	46		72	71	36	1.4	8.0	Jan
Feb	6	14	58	22	71	29	84	8	47		74	72	23	0.9	5.0	Feb
March	7	15	59	22	71	30	86	8	47		73	72	23	0.9	5.0	March
April	8	16	61	22	71	33	91	10	50		73	72	13	0.5	3.0	April
May	8	17	62	23	73	31	88	12	54	Moderate	72	72	5	0.2	1.0	May
June	9	18	65	24	75	32	89	14	58	Moderate	73	74	0	0.0	0.9	June
July	9	19	67	25	77	35	95	16	60	Medium	77	76	0	0.0	0.8	July
Aug	9	21	70	26	79	37	99	17	62	Medium	75	76	0	0.0	0.8	Aug
Sept	8	21	69	26	79	36	96	15	59	Medium	75	75	56	0.2	1.0	Sept
Oct	7	19	67	26	79	35	95	13	56	Medium	75	74	28	1.1	5.0	Oct
Nov	6	18	64	24	76	31	88	11	52	Moderate	74	74	53	2.1	7.0	Nov
Dec	6	16	60	22	72	29	85	8	47		73	73	41	1.6	8.0	Dec

Based on readings for 45 years at 28°11′ N, 15°28′ W, altitude 6 m/20 ft

This is the part of the country most influenced by depressions travelling in from the Atlantic, particularly in autumn and winter. It is the rainiest and cloudiest part of Spain.

Although summers are cooler, cloudier, and wetter than elsewhere in the country, there is still a considerable amount of warm, sunny weather. Rainfall decreases from west to east in the Pyrenees but is quite high on the seaward slopes of the Cantabrians and in the extreme northwest (Galicia). Daily hours of sunshine average from three in winter to seven or eight in summer.

See the tables for **A Coruña** (below) in Galicia and **Santander** (overleaf).

CENTRAL SPAIN

Including (with towns and cities in parentheses): ARAGON (Zaragoza), CASTILLA-LEON (Salamanca, Segovia, Valladolid), CASTILLA-LA MANCHA (Toledo), EXTREMADURA (Badajoz), LA RIOJA (Logroño), and MADRID (Madrid); inland ANDALUCIA (Córdoba, Granada, Jerez de la Frontera, Seville) and Andalucia's Atlantic coast; southern inland parts of ASTURIAS, CANTABRIA, NAVARRA, and PAIS VASCO; and western inland parts of CATALONIA, MURCIA, and VALENCIA.

Rainfall is generally rather low over most of the interior although winter snowfall may be quite heavy and lie for a long time on the mountains. In late summer much of the country has a burnt and barren appearance after the long summer drought.

The old French saying, 'Africa begins at the Pyrenees', has some truth in it if it is taken to refer to the heat and dry appearance of much of the countryside in summer. Summers are generally hot, particularly in the Guadalquivir valley in the south, where some of the highest temperatures in Europe are recorded.

Spring and early summer tend to be the wettest seasons in many parts of central Spain but the rainfall is light and not very effective as it often falls in short, heavy showers. Winters have frequent cold spells with biting winds blowing off the snow-covered sierras. Dust and hot winds are the most unpleasant features of the summer weather but low humidity makes the heat more bearable than in some of the coastal regions.

The length of the dry summer season increases from north to south. Sunshine amounts are quite high throughout the year, ranging from an average of five hours a day in winter to as much as twelve hours in midsummer.

A CORUNA — NORTHWESTERN SPAIN

	Sunshine average hours per day	Temperatures								Discomfort from heat and humidity	Precipitation and humidity				Wet days more than 0.1 mm/0.004 in	
		Average daily minimum		Average daily maximum		Highest recorded		Lowest recorded			Relative humidity 6:30	Relative humidity 12:30	Average monthly precipitation			
		°C	°F	°C	°F	°C	°F	°C	°F		%	%	mm	in		
Jan		7	45	13	55	20	69	-2	28		81	74	118	4.7	19	Jan
Feb		7	44	13	55	27	81	-3	27		82	71	80	3.2	15	Feb
March		8	47	15	59	27	80	1	34		82	70	92	3.6	16	March
April		9	48	16	61	30	85	2	36		81	69	67	2.6	12	April
May		11	51	18	64	29	83	3	38		83	71	54	2.1	12	May
June		13	55	20	68	31	87	7	45		83	73	45	1.8	9	June
July		15	58	22	71	34	92	10	50		84	71	28	1.1	8	July
Aug		15	59	23	73	34	92	9	49	Moderate	86	70	46	1.8	9	Aug
Sept		14	57	22	71	31	87	7	44		87	72	61	2.4	11	Sept
Oct		12	53	19	66	31	88	5	40		85	72	87	3.4	14	Oct
Nov		9	49	15	60	25	77	1	34		84	74	124	4.9	17	Nov
Dec		8	46	13	56	20	68	-1	30		84	77	135	5.3	19	Dec

Based on readings for 27 years at 43°22′ N, 8°25′ W, altitude 58 m/190 ft

SANTANDER — NORTHERN SPAIN

	Sunshine	Temperatures								Discomfort from heat and humidity	Precipitation and humidity				Wet days
		Average daily				Highest recorded		Lowest recorded			Relative humidity 6:30 12:30		Average monthly precipitation			
		minimum		maximum												
	average hours per day	°C	°F	°C	°F	°C	°F	°C	°F		%		mm	in	more than 0.1 mm/0.004 in	
Jan	3	7	44	12	53	21	70	-2	28		78	72	119	4.7	16	Jan
Feb	4	7	44	12	54	26	79	-4	25		80	71	88	3.5	14	Feb
March	5	8	47	14	58	30	86	-4	24		79	69	78	3.1	13	March
April	6	10	49	15	60	33	92	2	36		82	72	83	3.3	13	April
May	6	11	53	17	62	31	88	4	38		85	75	89	3.5	14	May
June	6	14	58	20	68	34	93	8	46		86	76	63	2.5	13	June
July	7	16	61	22	71	35	94	11	52		85	75	54	2.1	11	July
Aug	6	16	62	22	72	40	104	12	53		87	75	84	3.3	14	Aug
Sept	5	15	59	21	70	34	93	3	37		86	74	114	4.5	14	Sept
Oct	4	12	54	18	65	30	85	5	41		84	72	133	5.2	14	Oct
Nov	3	10	49	15	59	24	74	2	35		80	72	125	4.9	15	Nov
Dec	2	8	46	13	55	21	71	0	32		79	72	159	6.3	18	Dec

Based on readings for 27 years at 43°28′ N, 3°49′ W, altitude 66 m/217 ft

MADRID — CENTRAL SPAIN

	Sunshine	Temperatures								Discomfort from heat and humidity	Precipitation and humidity				Wet days
		Average daily				Highest recorded		Lowest recorded			Relative humidity 7:00 13:00		Average monthly precipitation			
		minimum		maximum												
	average hours per day	°C	°F	°C	°F	°C	°F	°C	°F		%		mm	in	more than 0.1 mm/0.004 in	
Jan	5	2	35	9	47	18	64	-10	14		86	71	39	1.5	8	Jan
Feb	6	2	36	11	52	22	72	-9	16		83	62	34	1.3	7	Feb
March	6	5	41	15	59	26	78	-4	26		80	56	43	1.7	10	March
April	8	7	45	18	65	29	85	-1	31		74	49	48	1.9	9	April
May	9	10	50	21	70	33	92	1	33		72	49	47	1.9	10	May
June	11	15	58	27	80	37	98	6	44	Moderate	66	41	27	1.0	5	June
July	12	17	63	31	87	39	102	8	47	Medium	58	33	11	0.4	2	July
Aug	11	17	63	30	85	38	100	7	45	Medium	62	35	15	0.6	3	Aug
Sept	9	14	57	25	77	36	96	4	40	Moderate	72	46	32	1.3	6	Sept
Oct	6	10	49	19	65	28	83	0	31		81	58	53	2.1	8	Oct
Nov	5	5	42	13	55	22	72	-3	27		84	65	47	1.9	9	Nov
Dec	5	2	36	9	48	16	61	-8	18		86	70	48	1.9	10	Dec

Based on readings for 27 years at 40°25′ N, 3°41′ W, altitude 660 m/2165 ft

SEVILLE										SOUTH-CENTRAL SPAIN		
Sunshine		Temperatures						Discomfort from heat and humidity	Precipitation and humidity			Wet days
		Average daily		Highest recorded		Lowest recorded			Relative humidity 6:30 12:30		Average monthly precipitation	
average hours per day		minimum	maximum									more than 0.1 mm/0.004 in
		°C	°F	°C	°F	°C	°F	°C	°F		%	mm	in

	Sunshine	min °C	min °F	max °C	max °F	High °C	High °F	Low °C	Low °F	Discomfort	RH 6:30	RH 12:30	mm	in	Wet days	
Jan	6	6	42	15	59	24	76	-3	27		87	75	66	2.6	8	Jan
Feb	6	7	44	17	63	27	80	-3	26		85	69	61	2.4	6	Feb
March	6	9	48	20	69	32	90	1	34		84	67	90	3.5	9	March
April	8	11	52	24	74	36	97	2	36	Moderate	80	61	57	2.2	7	April
May	9	13	56	27	80	42	108	3	37	Medium	77	57	41	1.6	6	May
June	11	17	63	32	90	44	110	5	41	High	73	48	8	0.3	1	June
July	12	20	67	36	98	46	114	11	52	High	67	43	1	0.0	0	July
Aug	11	20	68	36	97	49	120	12	54	High	70	45	5	0.2	0	Aug
Sept	9	18	64	32	90	41	105	9	49	High	73	53	19	0.8	2	Sept
Oct	7	14	57	26	78	39	102	4	39	Medium	82	65	70	2.8	6	Oct
Nov	6	10	50	20	68	32	89	0	32		86	72	67	2.6	7	Nov
Dec	5	7	44	16	60	24	75	-3	27		88	73	79	3.1	8	Dec

Based on readings for 27 years at 37°24′ N, 6°00′ W, altitude 9 m/30 ft

The table for **Madrid** (opposite) is representative of the conditions in the higher parts of interior Spain, while that for **Seville** (above) in the Guadalquivir valley, is typical of the lower and hotter parts of Andalucia.

MEDITERRANEAN SPAIN

Including (with towns and cities in parentheses): southeastern ANDALUCIA: Costa del Sol (Almería, Málaga, Nerja); coastal CATALONIA: Costa Brava (Barcelona, Sitges, Tarragona); most of MURCIA (Murcia); coastal VALENCIA: Costa Bianca (Valencia); and the BALEARIC ISLANDS.

This area includes the internationally famous tourist resorts – the Costa Brava in the north and the Costa del Sol in the south. Sunshine amounts are high: from six hours a day in winter to twelve in midsummer. Winters are mild and much warmer than inland. While summers are hot and at times humid, the afternoon heat is usually tempered by sea breezes. In the south conditions can occasionally become rather unpleasant when a hot, dry wind (the *leveche*) blows from North Africa. In much of the region rain is very rare during the months June to August but north of Valencia the coast is liable to occasional heavy downpours of thundery rain in summer. Around Barcelona and farther north autumn tends to be wetter than winter; here the total rainfall is greater than in the south, some parts of which are dry even in winter. In the drier regions there are considerable differences in the amount of rainfall from year to year. See the tables for **Barcelona** (overleaf), which is representative of the northern coastal regions, and **Almería** (overleaf), which is typical of the drier regions in the south. See also the table and description for Gibraltar (p. 162).

The Balearic Islands, which include Mallorca, Menorca, and Ibiza, are situated 170–250 km/100–150 mi to the east of Spain and are a popular winter and summer resort for visitors from northern Europe. They have a climate similar to that of southeastern Spain. See the table for **Palma de Mallorca** (p. 335).

BARCELONA

Sunshine		Temperatures								Discomfort from heat and humidity	Precipitation and humidity				Wet days	
		Average daily				Highest recorded		Lowest recorded			Relative humidity 7:00 13:00		Average monthly precipitation			
		minimum		maximum												
average hours per day		°C	°F	°C	°F	°C	°F	°C	°F		%		mm	in	more than 0.1 mm/0.004 in	
Jan	5	6	43	13	55	23	73	-2	28		74	61	31	1.2	5	Jan
Feb	6	7	45	14	57	21	71	-7	20		71	58	39	1.5	5	Feb
March	6	9	48	16	60	24	76	1	33		75	60	48	1.9	8	March
April	7	11	52	18	65	28	82	4	39		73	59	43	1.7	9	April
May	8	14	57	21	71	32	90	5	41		72	59	54	2.1	8	May
June	9	18	65	25	78	35	94	11	52	Moderate	68	59	37	1.5	6	June
July	10	21	69	28	82	35	96	14	58	Medium	70	59	27	1.1	4	July
Aug	9	21	69	28	82	36	97	13	56	Medium	75	63	49	1.9	6	Aug
Sept	7	19	66	25	77	32	89	10	51	Moderate	79	66	76	3.0	7	Sept
Oct	5	15	58	21	69	28	82	5	41		77	64	86	3.4	9	Oct
Nov	4	11	51	16	62	25	76	3	37		75	64	52	2.1	6	Nov
Dec	4	8	46	13	56	21	70	-3	28		72	62	45	1.8	6	Dec

Based on readings for 27 years at 41°24′ N, 2°09′ E, altitude 93 m/305 ft

ALMERIA

Sunshine		Temperatures								Discomfort from heat and humidity	Precipitation and humidity				Wet days	
		Average daily				Highest recorded		Lowest recorded			Relative humidity 7:00 13:00		Average monthly precipitation			
		minimum		maximum												
average hours per day		°C	°F	°C	°F	°C	°F	°C	°F		%		mm	in	more than 0.1 mm/0.004 in	
Jan	6	8	46	16	60	23	73	2	35		78	70	31	1.2	6	Jan
Feb	7	9	47	16	61	26	78	0	32		78	70	21	0.8	4	Feb
March	7	11	51	18	64	27	80	3	37		78	68	21	0.8	5	March
April	9	13	55	20	68	30	85	5	42		78	67	28	1.1	5	April
May	10	15	59	22	72	35	95	8	47		77	67	18	0.7	3	May
June	11	18	65	26	78	36	97	13	55	Medium	77	67	4	0.2	1	June
July	12	21	70	29	83	38	100	15	58	Medium	77	67	0	0.0	0	July
Aug	11	22	71	29	84	37	99	16	60	Medium	79	68	6	0.2	1	Aug
Sept	9	20	68	27	81	36	97	10	50	Medium	79	68	16	0.6	3	Sept
Oct	7	16	60	23	73	32	89	8	46	Moderate	79	68	25	1.0	5	Oct
Nov	6	12	54	19	67	27	80	5	40		79	70	27	1.1	4	Nov
Dec	5	9	49	17	62	25	78	3	37		77	70	36	1.4	5	Dec

Based on readings for 27 years at 36°50′ N, 2°28′ W, altitude 6 m/20 ft

PALMA DE MALLORCA											MEDITERRANEAN SPAIN	
Sunshine	Temperatures						Discomfort from heat and humidity	Precipitation and humidity				Wet days
average hours per day	Average daily		Highest recorded		Lowest recorded			Relative humidity 7:00 13:00		Average monthly precipitation		more than 0.1mm/.004 in
	minimum	maximum										
	°C	°F	°C	°F	°C	°F	°C	°F		%	mm	in	
Jan	5	6	43	14	57	22	71	-3	27		83	72	39	1.5	8	Jan
Feb	6	6	44	15	59	23	73	-4	25		82	70	34	1.3	6	Feb
March	6	8	46	17	62	24	74	-1	30		81	69	51	2.0	8	March
April	7	10	51	19	66	26	79	1	33		77	66	32	1.3	6	April
May	10	13	55	22	71	31	88	5	40		77	67	29	1.1	5	May
June	10	17	62	26	79	37	98	8	47	Medium	70	65	17	0.7	3	June
July	11	20	67	29	84	39	101	12	54	Medium	70	65	3	0.1	1	July
Aug	10	20	68	29	84	37	99	11	52	Medium	75	65	25	1.0	3	Aug
Sept	8	18	65	27	80	35	94	4	40	Medium	79	69	55	2.2	5	Sept
Oct	6	14	57	23	73	31	88	1	34	Moderate	83	71	77	3.0	9	Oct
Nov	5	10	50	18	65	26	78	1	33		83	72	47	1.9	8	Nov
Dec	4	8	46	15	59	24	74	-1	31		82	72	40	1.6	9	Dec

Based on readings for 27 years at 39°33′ N, 2°39′ E, altitude 10 m/33 ft

Sri Lanka

See map page 23

Sri Lanka is a large island in the Indian Ocean immediately south of India. It consists of extensive lowland regions around the coast and a large mountainous interior where the highest peaks rise to more than 2,400 m/8,000 ft. Situated between 6° and 10° N, Sri Lanka has a typical tropical climate which is somewhat modified by the seasonal wind reversal of the Asiatic monsoon (see p. 174 in the entry for India).

At lower levels temperatures remain high throughout the year and the high humidity and warm nights may feel uncomfortable to the visitor who has not yet become acclimatized. On the coast, however, the heat is modified by afternoon sea breezes so that it is rarely dangerous.

In the interior highlands temperatures are significantly reduced by altitude with the result that the climate is delightful for most of the year; rarely too hot by day and rarely so chilly as to be uncomfortable at night; frost is a very rare occurrence here.

Most of the country has an abundant or moderate rainfall which is well distributed throughout the year. The southwestern coast and southwestern mountain slopes are the wettest regions and here rainfall is greatest during the periods April to June and October to November.

The northeastern side of the island, particularly the lowlands, is much drier, with little rain between February and September. The main rainy season here is between October and January when the northeast monsoon blows onshore. This area is often called the 'dry zone' but the term is a relative one.

The southwest monsoon brings rather more rain to the southwestern side of the island between May and September but its arrival does not mark the same abrupt transition between a hot, dry season and a warm, wet season such as occurs in much of the Indian subcontinent.

Daily sunshine amounts vary from six to eight hours over much of the country, being least during the rainiest seasons, when cloudy disturbed weather may last for spells of two or three days. In many parts of

COLOMBO — SOUTHWESTERN LOWLANDS

	Sunshine average hours per day	Temperatures										Discomfort from heat and humidity	Precipitation and humidity				Wet days more than 1 mm/0.04 in	
		Average daily				Highest recorded		Lowest recorded					Relative humidity 9:30 15:30		Average monthly precipitation			
		minimum		maximum														
		°C	°F	°C	°F	°C	°F	°C	°F				%		mm	in		
Jan	8	22	72	30	86	34	94	15	59			High	73	67	89	3.5	7	Jan
Feb	9	22	72	31	87	36	96	16	61			High	71	66	69	2.7	6	Feb
March	8	23	74	31	88	36	96	18	64			High	71	66	147	5.8	8	March
April	7	24	76	31	88	33	92	21	70			High	74	70	231	9.1	14	April
May	6	26	78	31	87	33	91	21	69			High	78	76	371	14.6	19	May
June	5	25	77	29	85	32	89	22	72			High	80	78	224	8.8	18	June
July	6	25	77	29	85	31	88	22	71			High	79	77	135	5.3	12	July
Aug	6	25	77	29	85	31	88	22	71			High	78	76	109	4.3	11	Aug
Sept	6	25	77	29	85	32	89	22	71			High	76	75	160	6.3	13	Sept
Oct	7	24	75	29	85	32	89	21	69			High	77	76	348	13.7	19	Oct
Nov	6	23	73	29	85	32	90	19	66			High	77	75	315	12.4	16	Nov
Dec	8	22	72	29	85	33	91	17	63			Medium	74	69	147	5.8	10	Dec

based on readings for 25 years at 6°54′ N, 79°52′ E, altitude 7 m/24 ft

TRINCOMALEE — NORTHEASTERN LOWLANDS

	Sunshine average hours per day	Temperatures										Discomfort from heat and humidity	Precipitation and humidity				Wet days more than 1 mm/0.04 in	
		Average daily				Highest recorded		Lowest recorded					Relative humidity 9:30 15:30		Average monthly precipitation			
		minimum		maximum														
		°C	°F	°C	°F	°C	°F	°C	°F				%		mm	in		
Jan	7	24	75	27	80	33	92	18	65			Medium	79	78	173	6.8	10	Jan
Feb	9	24	76	28	82	36	96	19	66			Medium	72	70	66	2.6	4	Feb
March	9	24	76	29	85	38	101	19	67			High	72	70	48	1.9	4	March
April	9	26	78	32	89	39	102	19	67			High	69	68	58	2.3	5	April
May	8	26	79	33	92	40	104	19	67			High	67	61	69	2.7	5	May
June	7	26	79	33	92	39	103	22	71			High	65	54	28	1.1	2	June
July	7	26	78	33	92	38	101	21	70			High	65	53	51	2.0	3	July
Aug	7	25	77	33	92	39	102	21	69			High	65	56	107	4.2	6	Aug
Sept	8	25	77	33	92	39	102	21	70			High	65	61	107	4.2	6	Sept
Oct	6	24	76	31	88	39	102	21	69			High	72	69	221	8.7	13	Oct
Nov	6	24	75	29	84	36	97	19	67			High	80	78	358	14.1	17	Nov
Dec	6	24	75	27	81	33	91	19	66			Medium	80	79	363	14.3	16	Dec

Based on readings for 25 years at 8°35′ N, 81°15′ E, altitude 7 m/24 ft

NUWARA ELIYA										INTERIOR HIGHLANDS	
Sunshine	Temperatures							Discomfort from heat and humidity	Precipitation and humidity			Wet days
	Average daily				Highest recorded		Lowest recorded		Relative humidity	Average monthly precipitation		
	minimum		maximum							8:00 17:00		
average hours per day	°C	°F	°C	°F	°C	°F	°C	°F		%	mm	in	more than 2.5 mm/0.1 in
Jan	8	47	19	67	24	76	-3	27		89	69	170	6.7	13	Jan
Feb	7	44	21	70	24	75	-2	29		87	68	43	1.7	6	Feb
March	8	46	22	71	24	75	0	32		84	66	109	4.3	11	March
April	9	49	22	71	24	76	3	38		89	79	119	4.7	15	April
May	12	53	21	70	26	78	1	33		88	79	175	6.9	18	May
June	13	55	19	66	24	75	7	45		89	86	277	10.9	25	June
July	13	55	18	65	24	76	7	45		89	83	300	11.8	25	July
Aug	12	54	19	67	23	74	7	44		89	83	196	7.7	22	Aug
Sept	12	53	19	67	24	75	5	41		88	84	226	8.9	20	Sept
Oct	11	52	20	68	24	75	5	41		89	85	269	10.6	22	Oct
Nov	11	51	20	68	23	74	1	33		89	83	241	9.5	22	Nov
Dec	9	48	20	68	23	74	-1	30		91	80	203	8.0	17	Dec

Based on readings for 9 years at 6°58′ N, 80°46′ E, altitude 1880 m/6168 ft

the country much rainfall comes in afternoon showers accompanied by thunder. The tables for **Colombo** (opposite and above) and **Trincomalee** (opposite) are representative of the lowlands of the southwest and northeast respectively. That for **Nuwara Eliya** (above) shows the cooler conditions experienced in the higher parts of the interior.

Sudan

See map page 20

The Sudan is the largest country in Africa with an area of nearly 2.5 million sq km/1 million sq mi. It lies entirely within the tropics between 22° and 4° N. The northern part of the country is desert and has a climate similar to that of the Egyptian, Libyan, and Algerian Sahara. From Khartoum southwards to the southern border there is a progressive increase in the annual rainfall from 150 mm/6 in to over 1,000 mm/40 in. Rainfall in the north is rare and very sporadic in time and place. The southern margin of the Sahara effectively is where annual rainfall is about 400 mm/16 in, since evaporation is high during the very hot summer.

The rainy season in the Sudan is almost everywhere the period between April and October, although in the extreme south some rain may occur in any month. The length of the rainy season decreases from six to eight months in the south to as little as two months on the southern margins of the desert. The northern part of the Sudan experiences almost constant northeasterly winds throughout the year. In this dry air-mass humidity is low during the day and this makes the very high daytime temperatures more tolerable. During the cooler winter months temperatures may occasionally fall quite low and early-morning frost is not unknown in the desert. There is a progressive increase of temperature to the maximum levels reached in July and August when, even at night, the thermometer rarely falls below 24° C/75° F.

During the rainy season in the south and centre of the Sudan, southerly and southwesterly winds replace the northeasterlies. They bring slightly lower temperatures, higher humidity, and more cloud. In the far south monthly temperatures vary little around the year and are highest just before the

KHARTOUM

Sunshine	Temperatures								Discomfort from heat and humidity	Precipitation and humidity					Wet days
	Average daily				Highest recorded		Lowest recorded			Relative humidity		Average monthly precipitation			
	minimum		maximum							8:00	14:00				
average hours per day	°C	°F	°C	°F	°C	°F	°C	°F		%		mm	in		more than 1 mm/0.04 in
Jan	11	15	59	32	90	40 104		5 41		Medium	37	20	0.0	0.0	0	Jan
Feb	11	16	61	34	93	44 111		7 44		Medium	28	15	0.0	0.0	0	Feb
March	10	19	66	38 100		45 113		9 49		Medium	21	11	0.0	0.0	0	March
April	11	22	72	41 105		47 117		12 53		High	18	10	0.0	0.0	0	April
May	10	25	77	42 107		47 117		16 61		High	24	13	2.5	0.1	1	May
June	10	26	79	41 106		48 118		19 67		High	38	18	7.0	0.3	1	June
July	9	25	77	38 101		47 117		18 65		High	57	33	53.0	2.1	5	July
Aug	9	24	76	37 98		43 109		18 64		High	67	41	71.0	2.8	6	Aug
Sept	10	25	77	39 102		45 113		16 61		Extreme	55	30	18.0	0.7	2	Sept
Oct	10	24	75	40 104		45 113		17 62		High	38	21	5.0	0.2	1	Oct
Nov	11	20	68	36 97		42 107		13 55		Medium	34	19	0.0	0.0	0	Nov
Dec	11	17	62	33 92		40 104		7 45		Medium	38	21	0.0	0.0	0	Dec

Based on readings for 46 years at 15°37´ N, 32°33´ E, altitude 390 m/1279 ft

PORT SUDAN

Sunshine	Temperatures								Discomfort from heat and humidity	Precipitation and humidity					Wet days
	Average daily				Highest recorded		Lowest recorded			Relative humidity		Average monthly precipitation			
	minimum		maximum							8:30	14:30				
average hours per day	°C	°F	°C	°F	°C	°F	°C	°F		%		mm	in		more than 1 mm/0.04 in
Jan	7	20	68	27	81	32	89	10	50	Medium	66	65	5	0.2	0.9	Jan
Feb	8	19	66	27	81	32	90	11	52	Medium	65	66	3	0.1	0.3	Feb
March	9	19	67	29	84	35	95	12	53	Medium	64	63	0	0.0	0.1	March
April	10	22	71	32	89	38 101		14	58	High	56	59	0	0.0	0.2	April
May	11	24	75	35	95	44 111		15	59	High	45	51	0	0.0	0.2	May
June	10	26	78	39 102		47 117		20	68	Extreme	37	45	0	0.0	0.1	June
July	9	28	83	41 106		47 117		20	68	Extreme	39	44	8	0.3	0.8	July
Aug	10	29	84	41 105		47 117		19	67	Extreme	41	47	3	0.1	0.6	Aug
Sept	10	26	79	38 100		45 113		14	57	Extreme	47	51	0	0.0	0.0	Sept
Oct	10	24	76	34	93	42 107		16	61	Extreme	66	64	10	0.4	1.0	Oct
Nov	8	23	74	31	88	36	96	11	52	High	68	64	43	1.7	4.0	Nov
Dec	7	22	71	28	83	34	93	12	53	Medium	69	66	23	0.9	2.0	Dec

Based on readings for 30 years at 19°37´ N, 37°13´ E, altitude 5.5 m/18 ft

JUBA															SOUTHERN SUDAN	
Sunshine		Temperatures								Discomfort from heat and humidity	Precipitation and humidity					Wet days	
average hours per day		Average daily				Highest recorded		Lowest recorded			Relative humidity 8:00 14:00		Average monthly precipitation			more than 1 mm/0.04 in	
		minimum		maximum													
		°C	°F	°C	°F	°C	°F	°C	°F		%		mm	in			
Jan	9	20	68	37	99	42	108	16	60	High	54	26	5	0.2		1	Jan
Feb	8	22	71	38	100	43	109	16	60	High	56	28	15	0.6		2	Feb
March	7	22	72	37	99	42	108	16	61	High	65	34	33	1.3		6	March
April	7	22	72	36	96	42	108	18	64	High	75	44	122	4.8		9	April
May	8	22	71	33	92	44	111	17	63	High	82	54	150	5.9		10	May
June	7	21	69	33	91	38	101	16	61	High	83	56	135	5.3		9	June
July	6	20	68	31	88	37	98	17	62	High	87	60	122	4.8		10	July
Aug	7	20	68	31	88	36	97	16	61	High	88	59	132	5.2		9	Aug
Sept	8	20	68	33	91	38	100	16	61	High	83	53	107	4.2		8	Sept
Oct	8	20	68	34	94	39	103	14	57	High	80	48	94	3.7		8	Oct
Nov	8	20	68	36	96	41	105	13	56	High	75	40	36	1.4		4	Nov
Dec	9	20	68	37	98	41	105	15	59	High	64	33	18	0.7		1	Dec

Based on readings for 26 years at 4°51′ N, 31°37′ E, altitude 460 m/1509 ft

arrival of the rains. This moist southerly air has its origins in the South Atlantic or Congo basin and is the source of the Sudan's summer rain. During the rainy season there are spells of dry and sunny weather and even in the wettest areas rain only falls on about one day in three. The higher humidity during the rainy season does not make the lower temperatures any more comfortable. From April to September some heat stress can be experienced in all parts of the country.

An unpleasant and occasionally dangerous feature of the weather is the *haboob,* a local Arabic name for a violent but brief squall of wind which can raise a thick pall of dust or sand. *Haboobs* are most likely to occur in the afternoon and evening before, or at the beginning of, the rainy season. They often precede a thunderstorm which brings rain and lays the dust and sand.

The tables for **Khartoum** (opposite and above) and **Port Sudan** (opposite) are representative of the northern desert regions of the Sudan. On the coast of the Red Sea and in the hills behind there is some sporadic rainfall during the months October to December. The table for **Juba** (above) shows conditions throughout the year in the extreme south.

In the north annual sunshine amounts are almost the maximum possible, ranging from eleven to thirteen hours a day. Sunshine is least in the far south where, during the rainy season, it averages six to seven hours a day. During the dry season in the south sunshine averages nine to ten hours a day.

PARAMARIBO													COASTAL SURINAM
Sunshine	Temperatures								Discomfort from heat and humidity	Precipitation and humidity			Wet days
	Average daily				Highest recorded		Lowest recorded			Relative humidity 8:30 14:30		Average monthly precipitation	
average hours per day	minimum		maximum										more than 1 mm/0.04 in
	°C	°F	°C	°F	°C	°F	°C	°F		%		mm	in	
Jan	6	22	72	29	85	35	95	17	62	High	92	77	213	8.4	18	Jan
Feb	6	22	71	29	85	33	92	17	63	High	90	74	165	6.5	13	Feb
March	6	22	72	29	85	34	94	17	62	High	89	75	201	7.9	14	March
April	6	23	73	30	86	34	93	17	62	High	89	75	229	9.0	16	April
May	5	23	73	30	86	34	94	18	64	High	90	79	310	12.2	23	May
June	6	23	73	30	86	34	94	19	66	High	91	80	302	11.9	23	June
July	8	23	73	31	87	34	94	17	62	High	90	76	231	9.1	20	July
Aug	9	23	73	32	89	34	94	18	65	High	88	70	158	6.2	14	Aug
Sept	9	23	73	33	91	35	95	18	65	High	87	66	79	3.1	9	Sept
Oct	9	23	73	33	91	37	98	19	67	Extreme	87	67	76	3.0	9	Oct
Nov	8	23	73	32	89	37	99	19	66	High	88	71	125	4.9	12	Nov
Dec	6	22	72	30	86	34	94	17	63	High	91	77	224	8.8	18	Dec

Based on readings for 35 years at 5°49′ N, 55°09′ W, altitude 4 m/12 ft

Surinam

See map page 16

Surinam, formerly Dutch Guiana, is situated between 2° and 6° N on the Atlantic coast of South America between Guyana to the west and French Guiana to the east. In area it is smaller than Guyana and is about as large as England and Wales together. The general nature of the climate and weather of this whole area is described on p. 168 for Guyana.

The table for **Paramaribo** (above) is representative of the lowland coastal area of the country. It shows conditions almost identical with those for **Georgetown** (p. 169) in Guyana. The southern half of the country is part of the plateau region which extends eastwards from Venezuela through Guyana. Here the climatic conditions are well represented by the table for **Santa Elena** (p. 418) in Venezuela.

MBABANE													HIGHLAND SWAZILAND	
Sunshine		Temperatures							Discomfort from heat and humidity	Precipitation and humidity				Wet days
		Average daily				Highest recorded		Lowest recorded		Relative humidity 8:00		Average monthly precipitation		
		minimum		maximum										
average hours per day		°C	°F	°C	°F	°C	°F	°C	°F		%	mm	in	more than 1 mm/0.04 in
Jan	8	15	59	25	77	33	92	9	49	Medium	78	254	10.0	15	Jan
Feb	8	15	59	25	77	35	95	8	47	Medium	79	213	8.4	14	Feb
March	8	14	57	24	75	33	92	7	45	Medium	81	193	7.6	13	March
April	7	12	53	23	74	33	92	3	38	Moderate	76	71	2.8	8	April
May	8	8	47	21	70	29	85	-1	31		71	33	1.3	4	May
June	8	6	42	19	66	29	85	-4	25		64	20	0.8	3	June
July	8	6	42	19	67	27	81	-2	28		64	23	0.9	3	July
Aug	8	7	45	21	70	32	89	-5	23		67	28	1.1	4	Aug
Sept	9	9	49	23	73	37	99	-2	28		59	61	2.4	7	Sept
Oct	9	12	54	24	75	36	96	3	38	Moderate	68	127	5.0	12	Oct
Nov	8	13	56	24	76	36	96	4	40	Moderate	73	170	6.7	14	Nov
Dec	7	14	58	25	77	36	97	8	46	Medium	76	208	8.2	16	Dec

Based on readings for 20 years at 26°19′ S, 31°08′ E, altitude 1163 m/3816 ft

Swaziland

See map page 21

This small landlocked country lies in 27° S between South Africa and Mozambique. It is rather smaller than Wales or Israel. The western part includes high veld like that of the neighbouring region of South Africa. The winters are dry and mild but with frequent cold nights. Summers are warm with more frequent rain but temperatures are rarely excessively high. The low humidity and large number of sunshine hours make for a pleasant and healthy climate for most of the year.

The table for **Mbabane** (above) illustrates weather throughout the year in the higher, western parts of the country.

The country slopes eastwards until, along the Mozambique border, it is low-lying and almost tropical in climate. The summers are warm and humid with conditions similar to those found in southern Mozambique (see the table for **Maputo** on p. 247) and Kwazulu-Natal (see the table for **Durban** on p. 326) in South Africa.

Sweden

Two important influences on the climate of Sweden are its northern latitude, between 55° and 69° N, and the shelter from milder and wetter Atlantic winds provided by the high mountains and plateaux along the country's western border with Norway.

Most of Sweden has a typical continental climate with a moderate to large temperature range between summer and winter. The one exception to this is the southwest of the country from Göteborg to Malmö, where winter temperatures are modified by an open ocean that rarely freezes.

The enclosed waters of the Baltic Sea often freeze, in whole or in part, in winter. Therefore, the east coast of Sweden is much colder, particularly towards the north where the waters of the Gulf of Bothnia freeze each winter.

The high latitude means that much of the country has very long hours of daylight in summer and very long nights in winter. North of the Arctic Circle at 66° N, this amounts to 24 hours of sun and 24 hours of Arctic twilight in midsummer and midwinter respectively.

Precipitation is relatively low except on the higher mountains and is rather greater in summer than winter. North of Stockholm much of the winter precipitation falls as snow.

Winters become progressively longer and colder towards the north of the country. The average number of days with a mean temperature below freezing point increases from 71 at Malmö to 120 at Stockholm and 184 at Haparanda near the Arctic Circle.

Temperatures are surprisingly similar in midsummer over much of Sweden. The long summer days help to raise temperatures in the north of the country, so that on fine days temperatures may be as high here as in the south.

Because of the generally changeable nature of Swedish summer weather, however, the visitor should not expect fine weather every day. A wet, cool spell in summer in northern Sweden can be rather miserable.

The country can be divided broadly into three climatic regions: central and southern Sweden, the northeast or the low-lying shores of the Gulf of Bothnia, and the northwest or far north.

CENTRAL AND SOUTHERN SWEDEN

Including Göteborg, Malmö, and Stockholm.

The tables for **Göteborg** (opposite) and **Stockholm** (opposite and below) are representative of conditions in central and southern Sweden.

This is the part of the country approximately south of a line from the Oslo fiord to Uppsala on the east coast. Much of this area is low-lying with numerous lakes. It is the most densely populated and agriculturally productive part of the country. Although the winters are quite cold and shorter than those in the north, the summers are relatively warm.

Precipitation is nowhere heavy; most rain falls during summer and early autumn and much of the winter precipitation falls as snow. In some winters the snow cover may be prolonged and the harbours on the east coast have to be kept clear with icebreakers. Snow falls on an average of sixty days at Stockholm but it does not lie so long on the west coast. Summer

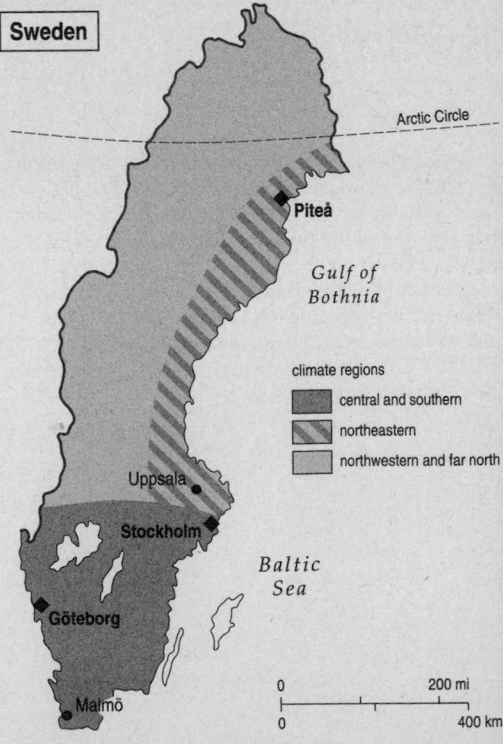

Sweden

Arctic Circle

Piteå

Gulf of Bothnia

climate regions

central and southern

northeastern

northwestern and far north

Uppsala

Stockholm

Baltic Sea

Göteborg

Malmö

0   200 mi

0   400 km

GOTEBORG

SOUTHWESTERN SWEDEN

Sunshine	Temperatures								Discomfort from heat and humidity	Precipitation and humidity				Wet days	
	Average daily				Highest recorded		Lowest recorded			Relative humidity 7:00 13:00		Average monthly precipitation			
	minimum		maximum												
average hours per day	°C	°F	°C	°F	°C	°F	°C	°F		%		mm	in	more than 0.1 mm/0.004 in	
Jan	2	-3	26	1	34	8	46	-26	-15		85	81	51	2.0	15	Jan
Feb	3	-4	25	1	34	9	48	-20	-4		85	76	34	1.3	12	Feb
March	5	-2	29	4	39	17	63	-19	-3		83	67	29	1.1	10	March
April	7	3	37	9	49	22	68	-11	12		77	59	39	1.5	12	April
May	9	7	45	16	60	28	83	-2	29		70	54	34	1.3	10	May
June	10	12	53	19	66	32	90	3	37		73	58	54	2.1	12	June
July	9	14	57	21	70	32	90	8	46		77	62	86	3.4	14	July
Aug	8	13	56	20	68	30	86	5	41		81	63	84	3.3	14	Aug
Sept	6	10	50	16	61	25	77	0	32		84	67	75	3.0	16	Sept
Oct	3	6	43	11	51	20	68	-6	21		84	72	65	2.6	15	Oct
Nov	2	3	37	6	43	13	55	-8	18		85	80	62	2.4	16	Nov
Dec	1	0	32	4	38	11	52	-16	4		86	83	57	2.2	17	Dec

Based on readings for 30 years at 57°42′ N, 11°58′ E, altitude 41 m/135 ft

STOCKHOLM

SOUTHEASTERN SWEDEN

Sunshine	Temperatures								Discomfort from heat and humidity	Precipitation and humidity				Wet days	
	Average daily				Highest recorded		Lowest recorded			Relative humidity 7:00 13:00		Average monthly precipitation			
	minimum		maximum												
average hours per day	°C	°F	°C	°F	°C	°F	°C	°F		%		mm	in	more than .01 mm/.004 in	
Jan	1	-5	23	-1	30	10	49	-28	-19		85	83	43	1.7	16	Jan
Feb	3	-5	22	-1	30	12	53	-25	-13		83	77	30	1.2	14	Feb
March	5	-4	26	3	37	15	59	-22	-8		82	68	25	1.0	10	March
April	7	1	34	8	47	20	68	-12	11		76	60	31	1.2	11	April
May	9	6	43	14	58	28	82	-3	26		66	53	34	1.3	11	May
June	11	11	51	19	67	32	90	1	34		68	55	45	1.8	13	June
July	10	14	57	22	71	35	94	8	46		74	59	61	2.4	13	July
Aug	8	13	56	20	68	31	88	5	41		81	64	76	3.0	14	Aug
Sept	6	9	49	15	60	26	78	0	32		87	69	60	2.4	14	Sept
Oct	3	5	41	9	49	17	63	-7	20		88	76	48	1.9	15	Oct
Nov	1	1	34	5	40	12	54	-11	12		89	85	53	2.1	16	Nov
Dec	1	-2	29	2	35	12	54	-16	3		88	86	48	1.9	17	Dec

Based on readings for 30 years at 59°21′ N, 18°04′ E, altitude 44 m/144 ft

PITEA											NORTHEASTERN SWEDEN			
Sunshine		Temperatures							Discomfort from heat and humidity	Precipitation and humidity				Wet days
		Average daily				Highest recorded	Lowest recorded			Relative humidity 7:30 13:30		Average monthly precipitation		
		minimum		maximum										
average hours per day		°C	°F	°C	°F	°C	°F	°C	°F		%		mm in		more than 0.1 mm/0.004 in
Jan	1	-13	8	-6	21	8	46	-38	-36		82	82	37	1.5	13	Jan
Feb	2	-14	6	-6	22	9	47	-37	-34		82	79	25	1.0	13	Feb
March	5	-11	12	-1	31	12	53	-31	-24		80	71	23	0.9	9	March
April	7	-4	25	5	40	18	64	-23	-9		77	66	28	1.1	10	April
May	9	2	35	11	53	25	77	-8	18		65	56	30	1.2	8	May
June	10	8	46	17	62	32	90	-1	30		66	57	47	1.9	11	June
July	10	12	53	21	69	35	95	3	38		70	61	50	2.0	12	July
Aug	7	10	50	19	65	28	83	-1	30		78	65	68	2.7	12	Aug
Sept	5	5	42	13	55	24	75	-7	20		83	69	69	2.7	12	Sept
Oct	3	0	31	6	42	20	68	-20	-3		86	77	48	1.9	12	Oct
Nov	1	-6	22	0	32	11	52	-27	-17		87	86	48	1.9	14	Nov
Dec	0	-10	14	3	26	8	46	-31	-24		84	83	44	1.7	15	Dec

Based on readings for 30 years at 65°19′ N, 21°28′ E, ltitude 6 m/20 ft

temperatures are similar to those experienced in southern England but there are more hours of sunshine than in England.

NORTHEASTERN SWEDEN

Including Piteå and Uppsala.

Here winters are severe and become longer and colder northwards. The short summers are surprisingly warm for the high latitude, near or north of the Arctic Circle. Precipitation is quite low near the coast but snow may lie on the ground for up to 120 days and this figure increases inland as altitude rises. Summers are sunnier and less cloudy than in the mountains along the Norwegian border. (See the table for **Piteå** above).

THE NORTHWEST AND NORTH

This is mostly a plateau of moderate to high elevation. Temperatures are largely controlled by altitude and at the higher levels snow cover persists throughout the year. In sheltered valleys precipitation may be much less than on the surrounding hills. Here, during fine weather, winter temperatures sink very low while summer temperatures may rise surprisingly high. The greater part of the area, however, has a severe winter climate with short, changeable summers.

Switzerland

This small, mountainous, landlocked country has a wide variety of climatic conditions because of its great range of altitude. The higher peaks of the Alps rise to over 3,600 m/12,000 ft and are snow-covered throughout the year.

At lower levels in the Alpine valleys and on the central Swiss plateau, summers can be quite warm but this is also the wettest period of the year in Switzerland. Much of the summer rainfall is heavy and is often accompanied by severe thunderstorms. Like other parts of west-central Europe, Switzerland is open to climatic influences from the Atlantic and from eastern Europe and the weather at all times of the year is changeable.

The most settled weather occurs when the country is influenced by an anticyclone. In summer this brings

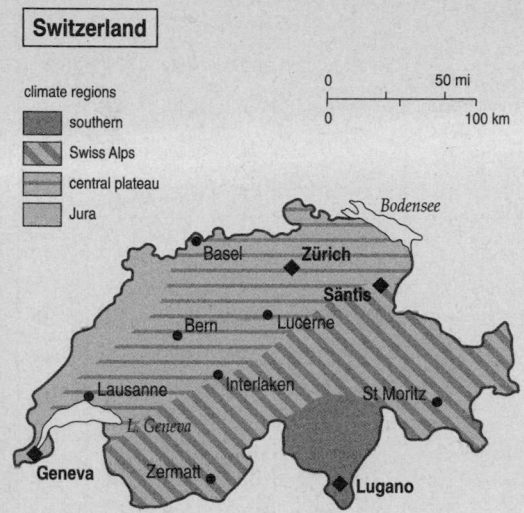

Switzerland

climate regions
- southern
- Swiss Alps
- central plateau
- Jura

0 — 50 mi
0 — 100 km

Bodensee

Basel · Zürich
Säntis
Bern · Lucerne
Lausanne · Interlaken · St Moritz
L. Geneva
Geneva · Zermatt · Lugano

SOUTHERN SWITZERLAND

Including (with towns and cities in parentheses): TICINO (Lugano) and southwestern GRISONS.

This small area around lakes Maggiore and Lugano is the warmest part of the country in summer and at low levels the winters are relatively mild. It lies south of the main Alpine ranges and is, from time to time, influenced by warmer Mediterranean air. Summers are rather similar to those of the adjoining north Italian plain but are distinctly wet with the rain occurring in heavy downpours. In settled weather it can be quite hot and sunny here. At low levels prolonged frost is rare in winter (see the table for **Lugano** below).

THE ALPS

Including (with towns and cities in parentheses): southeastern VAUD, southern BERN and central and southern ST GALLEN (Säntis); GLARUS, SCHWYZ, UNTER WALDEN, and URI; and VALAIS (Zermatt) and most of GRISONS (St Moritz).

The Alpine ranges cover half the country and extend from Geneva to the Austrian border. There are great differences between the climate of the valleys and the higher mountains. In winter the valleys are

warm, sunny weather, but in winter it may bring either cold, sunny weather or easterly winds with cloudy skies. Midwinter, rather than midsummer, is more likely to be a time of settled weather.

The country can be divided into four climatic regions: the extreme south, the Alps, the central or Swiss plateau, and the Jura mountains.

LUGANO												SOUTHERN SWITZERLAND	
Sunshine	Temperatures							Discomfort from heat and humidity	Precipitation and humidity				Wet days
	Average daily				Highest recorded	Lowest recorded			Relative humidity		Average monthly precipitation		
	minimum		maximum						7:00	13:00			
average hours per day	°C	°F	°C	°F	°C	°F	°C	°F		%		mm	in	more than 0.25 mm/0.01 in
Jan	4	-2	29	6	43	25	76	-11	13		76	56	63	2.5	7	Jan
Feb	5	-1	31	9	48	25	76	-11	13		74	52	67	2.6	7	Feb
March	6	3	37	13	56	27	81	-7	20		76	50	99	3.9	9	March
April	6	7	44	17	63	31	89	-2	28		74	50	148	5.8	11	April
May	6	10	50	21	69	33	91	1	33		77	53	215	8.5	15	May
June	8	14	57	25	77	36	97	4	40	Moderate	74	50	198	7.8	13	June
July	9	16	60	27	81	38	100	8	46	Moderate	74	48	185	7.3	11	July
Aug	8	15	60	27	80	36	98	9	47	Medium	78	51	196	7.7	12	Aug
Sept	6	13	55	23	74	32	90	2	36		82	54	159	6.3	10	Sept
Oct	5	8	47	16	62	28	83	-2	28		85	57	173	6.8	10	Oct
Nov	4	3	38	11	51	23	73	-4	25		82	59	147	5.8	10	Nov
Dec	3	0	31	7	44	21	71	-9	15		79	59	95	3.7	9	Dec

Based on readings for 30 years at 46°00′ N, 8°58′ E, altitude 276 m/906 ft

SANTIS

SWISS ALPS

	Sunshine average hours per day	Temperatures										Discomfort from heat and humidity	Precipitation and humidity				Wet days more than 0.25 mm/0.01 in	
		Average daily				Highest recorded		Lowest recorded					Relative humidity 7:00 13:00		Average monthly precipitation			
		minimum		maximum														
		°C	°F	°C	°F	°C	°F	°C	°F				%		mm	in		
Jan	3	−11	13	−7	20	3	38	−26	−15				76	74	202	8.0	16	Jan
Feb	4	−11	13	−7	20	6	42	−30	−23				76	74	180	7.1	15	Feb
March	5	−9	16	−4	24	7	45	−24	−11				75	73	164	6.5	14	March
April	5	−6	20	−2	29	12	53	−19	−3				79	78	166	6.5	16	April
May	5	−2	28	3	37	18	64	−15	4				76	77	197	7.8	16	May
June	5	1	34	6	43	17	63	−8	17				77	80	249	9.8	19	June
July	6	3	37	8	47	21	69	−5	23				79	79	302	11.9	18	July
Aug	5	3	38	8	47	19	65	−5	22				78	78	278	10.9	18	Aug
Sept	5	1	34	6	43	16	61	−13	9				77	75	209	8.2	15	Sept
Oct	5	−3	27	2	35	13	55	−17	2				74	72	183	7.2	13	Oct
Nov	4	−7	20	−3	27	8	47	−19	−2				75	72	190	7.5	13	Nov
Dec	4	−10	15	−6	22	6	43	−24	−11				75	71	169	6.7	15	Dec

Based on readings for 30 years at 47°15′ N, 9°21′ E, altitude 2500 m/8202 ft

ZURICH

CENTRAL SWITZERLAND

	Sunshine average hours per day	Temperatures										Discomfort from heat and humidity	Precipitation and humidity				Wet days more than 0.25 mm/0.01 in	
		Average daily				Highest recorded		Lowest recorded					Relative humidity 7:00 13:00		Average monthly precipitation			
		minimum		maximum														
		°C	°F	°C	°F	°C	°F	°C	°F				%		mm	in		
Jan	2	−3	26	2	36	17	62	−17	2				88	74	74	2.9	14	Jan
Feb	3	−2	28	5	41	19	66	−23	−10				88	65	69	2.7	13	Feb
March	5	1	34	10	51	22	71	−11	12				86	55	64	2.5	12	March
April	6	4	40	15	59	30	87	−6	22				81	51	76	3.0	13	April
May	7	8	47	19	67	33	92	−2	29				80	52	101	4.0	14	May
June	7	12	53	23	73	36	97	4	38				80	52	129	5.1	15	June
July	8	14	56	25	76	38	100	7	44		Moderate		81	52	136	5.4	14	July
Aug	7	13	56	24	75	36	97	5	41		Moderate		85	53	124	4.9	14	Aug
Sept	6	11	51	20	69	32	89	0	32				90	57	102	4.0	12	Sept
Oct	3	6	43	14	57	27	80	−4	25				92	64	77	3.0	12	Oct
Nov	2	2	35	7	45	20	67	−9	17				90	73	73	2.9	12	Nov
Dec	1	−2	29	3	37	15	60	−13	9				89	76	64	2.5	13	Dec

Based on readings for 30 years at 47°23′ N, 8°33′ E, altitude 493 m/1618 ft

GENEVA														JURA MOUNTAINS
Sunshine	Temperatures							Discomfort from heat and humidity	Precipitation and humidity				Wet days	
	Average daily				Highest recorded		Lowest recorded			Relative humidity 7:00 13:00		Average monthly precipitation		
average hours per day	minimum		maximum											more than 0.25 mm/0.01 in
	°C	°F	°C	°F	°C	°F	°C	°F		%		mm	in	
Jan	2	−2	29	4	38	16	60	−13	10		87	78	63	2.5	11	Jan
Feb	3	−1	30	6	42	20	67	−18	−1		86	71	56	2.2	9	Feb
March	5	2	36	10	51	22	72	−10	13		84	62	55	2.2	9	March
April	7	5	42	15	59	27	81	−3	26		79	56	51	2.0	9	April
May	8	9	49	19	66	32	89	−2	29		79	58	68	2.7	11	May
June	9	13	55	23	73	36	96	4	40		78	58	89	3.5	11	June
July	10	15	58	25	77	36	98	6	43	Moderate	77	56	64	2.5	9	July
Aug	9	14	58	24	76	36	97	5	41	Moderate	82	59	94	3.7	11	Aug
Sept	7	12	53	21	69	32	90	2	36		87	65	99	3.9	10	Sept
Oct	4	7	44	14	58	25	77	−3	27		89	71	72	2.8	10	Oct
Nov	2	3	37	8	47	19	65	−7	19		88	76	83	3.3	11	Nov
Dec	1	0	31	4	40	15	59	−13	8		88	79	59	2.3	10	Dec

Based on readings for 30 years at 46°12′ N, 6°09′ E, altitude 405 m/1329 ft

frequently cloudy and foggy with persistent frost. By contrast, during settled weather, the mountains are relatively sunny and daytime temperatures may feel quite warm.

In winter the climate of the mountain resorts is thus more pleasant than that in the valleys or on the Swiss plateau. In summer, conditions may be quite the reverse: the mountains shrouded in cloud by day and the valleys basking in warm, clear weather.

In fine weather a number of local winds occur in the Alps. In the large valleys there is a tendency for daytime breezes to blow up the valley and for a reverse down-valley wind to occur at night. Near glaciers this night-time wind can be very cold.

A more widespread wind known as the föhn can affect large areas of the Alps under certain meteorological conditions. It is a warm wind, bringing air of very low relative humidity. Although it can blow in valleys on the southern side of the Alps, it is more severe on the northern side and blows particularly where valleys run from south to north. It is most noticeable in late winter and spring and can melt snow very quickly. At higher levels it can trigger dangerous avalanches and at lower levels the very dry air and strong wind increase the fire risk to wooden buildings. With the onset of a föhn wind

temperature may rise as much as 15°–20° C/ 27°–36° F within an hour. Such conditions may last for two or three days (see the table for **Säntis** opposite and above).

THE CENTRAL PLATEAU

Including (with towns and cities in parentheses): AARGAU, BASEL (Basel), FRIBOURG, LUCERNE (Lucerne), SCHAFFHAUSEN, SOLOTHURN, THURGAU, ZUG, ZURICH (Zürich); and central BERN (Bern, Interlaken), central VAUD (Lausanne), and northern ST GALLEN.

The table for **Zürich** (opposite) is representative of conditions in the central plateau of Switzerland.

This is the lowest part of the country, extending from Lake Geneva to Lake Konstanz. All the large towns of Switzerland and the majority of the population are situated here. Winters are generally cold with much persistent low cloud and fog. Conditions are very similar to those in the deeper valleys in the Alps. During severe winters, freezing conditions may last for several weeks with frequent snow.

Snow is common during milder and changeable winters. The summer are generally warm but rather wet. Summers can vary considerably from year to year in terms of the amount of cloud and the number of wet days. During wet spells in summer the rain can be heavy and prolonged.

THE JURA MOUNTAINS

Including (with towns and cities in parentheses): northern BERN and western VAUD; AND NEUCHATEL and GENEVA (Geneva).

This small, narrow part of Switzerland extends from Basel to Geneva along the French border. The Jura

rise to less than half the altitude of the Alps, but the valleys are narrow and the ridges steep.

This area is rather wetter than the Swiss plateau and in winter the mountains carry snow for long periods. In some enclosed valleys winter temperatures can sometimes sink very low as cold air drains into the valley bottom. Summers are similar to those on the Swiss plateau but rather more cloudy and wet.

The table for **Geneva** (p. 347) is representative of weather conditions in the Swiss part of the Jura.

Syria

See map page 22

The climate and weather of Syria are very similar to those in the three other countries of the eastern Mediterranean – frequently known as the Levant States: Lebanon, Israel, and Jordan. The general features of the climate of all four countries and the factors governing the climate are described here; briefer descriptions of the other three countries are given under the country headings. These countries all have a climate and sequence of weather

throughout the year that is transitional between the Mediterranean and the Arabian desert.

The summers, lasting from April or early May until September or early October, are sunny, hot, and dry with very little change of weather from day to day. During the rest of the year there is greater variability from day to day as Mediterranean depressions bring cloudy, rainy weather and also occasional cold spells in the midwinter period, during which frost and snow may occur even at low levels. These cold spells

DEIR EZ ZOR												EASTERN SYRIA
Sunshine	Temperatures							Discomfort from heat and humidity	Precipitation and humidity			Wet days
	Average daily				Highest recorded	Lowest recorded			Relative humidity	Average monthly precipitation		
	minimum		maximum						all hours			
average hours per day	°C	°F	°C	°F	°C	°F	°C	°F	%	mm	in	more than 1 mm/0.04 in
Jan	2	35	12	53	22	72	-9	16		80	41	1.6	6.0	Jan
Feb	3	38	14	58	22	72	-8	18		73	20	0.8	5.0	Feb
March	6	42	21	70	33	91	-4	24		65	8	0.3	3.0	March
April	11	52	27	80	39	103	3	37	Medium	61	20	0.8	4.0	April
May	16	61	33	92	41	105	8	46	High	45	3	0.1	0.7	May
June	21	70	37	99	44	111	7	45	High	36	0	0.0	0.1	June
July	26	78	41	105	46	114	19	67	Extreme	29	0	0.0	0.0	July
Aug	24	76	40	104	45	113	20	68	Extreme	38	0	0.0	0.0	Aug
Sept	20	68	36	97	44	111	9	48	High	39	0	0.0	0.0	Sept
Oct	13	56	30	86	36	97	6	43	Medium	48	5	0.2	2.0	Oct
Nov	8	46	22	72	32	90	-4	25		51	38	1.5	5.0	Nov
Dec	3	37	14	58	20	68	-8	17		60	23	0.9	4.0	Dec

Based on readings for 5 years at 35°21′ N, 40°09′ E, altitude 213 m/699 ft

ALEPPO										NORTHWESTERN SYRIA		
Sunshine	Temperatures							Discomfort from heat and humidity	Precipitation and humidity			Wet days
	Average daily			Highest recorded		Lowest recorded			Relative humidity	Average monthly precipitation		
average hours per day	minimum		maximum									more than 1 mm/0.04 in
	°C	°F	°C	°F	°C	°F	°C	°F	%	mm	in	
Jan	4	1	34	10	50	17	63	-13	9		89	3.5	11.0	Jan
Feb	6	3	37	13	56	21	69	-10	14		64	2.5	10.0	Feb
March	7	4	39	18	64	31	87	-7	19		38	1.5	7.0	March
April	8	9	48	24	75	34	93	-2	28		28	1.1	4.0	April
May	11	13	56	29	85	41	105	0	32		8	0.3	2.0	May
June	13	17	63	34	94	47	117	9	48		3	0.1	0.4	June
July	13	21	69	36	97	46	115	16	60		0	0.0	0.0	July
Aug	12	21	69	36	97	43	110	15	59		0	0.0	0.2	Aug
Sept	11	16	61	33	92	41	106	7	44		0	0.0	0.1	Sept
Oct	9	12	54	27	81	37	99	5	41		25	1.0	4.0	Oct
Nov	7	7	45	19	67	30	86	-3	27		56	2.2	8.0	Nov
Dec	4	3	38	12	54	18	65	-8	18		84	3.3	10.0	Dec

Based on readings for 8 years at 36°14′ N, 37°08′ E, altitude 390 m/1280 ft

are rare and less severe along the Mediterranean coast. Inland, and in the mountains, the cold spells may be severe with frequent snow.

The probability of disturbed weather with cloud and rain is greatest in the months December to February, which is the main rainy season. Even during the midwinter period, however, the weather is often sunny and dry for long periods. There is some variation from year to year in the start and end of the hot, dry, settled weather of summer so that some heavy downpours of rain may occur at the beginning and end of summer.

These brief wet spells are the 'former' and 'latter' rains referred to in the Bible (Deut. 11:14). Apart from the gradual increase of temperature from March to May and the similar decrease from September to November there is no marked spring and autumn as occurs in countries farther north. The main seasonal contrast is the beginning and end of the settled weather of summer.

One of the most notable, and certainly the most unpleasant or even dangerous, features of the weather of these countries is brief spells of hot winds blowing from the east and southeast. These winds 'import' very hot and dusty air from Arabia and, on occasion, temperatures may rise as high as 43–

49° C/110°–120° F. Such weather is named *khamsin* in Arabic or *sirocco* in Italian. They are most frequent at the beginning and end of the summer season and are rare in midsummer. In extreme cases there is a danger of heat stress or even heatstroke unless elementary precautions are taken (see p. 7).

Syria is the largest of the Levant countries and, because of its size and east to west extent, shows the greatest contrast between the milder, wetter Mediterranean conditions on the coast and the desert conditions of the interior.

About 60 percent of Syria lying east of Aleppo and Damascus has a desert or semi-desert climate with an annual rainfall below 200m m/8 in. This is the hottest region in summer and it is often quite cold in winter with occasional snow and frequent frost (see the table for **Deir ez Zor** opposite). Rainfall, although infrequent, may be quite heavy and very local causing some spectacular desert floods.

To the north and west of this desert region there is a band of steppe country where some unirrigated cultivation can be carried out. This belt, often called the Fertile Crescent, includes the large cities of **Aleppo** (see the table above) and **Damascus** (see table overleaf). Annual average rainfall is between

DAMASCUS											SOUTHWESTERN SYRIA	
Sunshine	Temperatures						Discomfort from heat and humidity	Precipitation and humidity				Wet days
	Average daily				Highest recorded	Lowest recorded		Relative humidity 8:30 14:30		Average monthly precipitation		
	minimum		maximum									
average hours per day	°C	°F	°C	°F	°C	°F	°C	°F		%	mm	in	more than 1 mm/0.04 in
Jan	5	2	36	12	53	21	69	-6	21		81	57	43	1.7	7.0	Jan
Feb	6	4	39	14	57	30	86	-5	23		78	53	43	1.7	6.0	Feb
March	7	6	42	18	65	28	83	-2	28		62	42	8	0.3	2.0	March
April	9	9	49	24	75	35	95	-1	33		50	32	13	0.5	3.0	April
May	10	13	55	29	84	38	101	7	44	Moderate	44	26	3	0.1	1.0	May
June	12	16	61	33	91	39	102	9	48	Medium	45	22	0	0.0	0.1	June
July	13	18	64	36	96	42	108	13	55	Medium	43	19	0	0.0	0.0	July
Aug	12	18	64	37	99	45	113	13	55	High	47	21	0	0.0	0.0	Aug
Sept	10	16	60	33	91	39	102	10	50	Medium	48	24	18	0.7	2.0	Sept
Oct	8	12	54	27	81	34	93	6	42	Moderate	54	31	10	0.4	2.0	Oct
Nov	7	8	47	19	67	30	86	-2	28		73	46	41	1.6	5.0	Nov
Dec	5	4	40	13	56	21	69	-5	23		81	59	41	1.6	5.0	Dec

Based on readings for 9 years at 33°30' N, 36°20' E, altitude 720 m/2362 ft

200 mm/8 in and 500 mm/20 in. Temperatures throughout the year are very similar to those found in the Syrian desert.

Between this inland steppe region and the Mediterranean there are a series of mountain ranges and hills where rainfall is much greater and there is also a good deal of snow. Except for Mount Hermon in the southwest, which has a climate similar to that of the Lebanon Mountains (see p. 214), these western hills and mountains are not quite as wet or snowy as in Lebanon. There are a number of small

mountain resorts which are popular as a relief from the summer heat of the interior and the larger cities.

Along the Mediterranean coast there is a narrow plain where conditions are very similar to those found along the coast of Lebanon (see the table for **Beirut** on p. 215). Summers are warm and humid and winters are very mild with spells of cloud and heavy rain, alternating with fine, sunny weather. Syria has a very sunny climate with an average of six to seven hours of sunshine a day in winter and as much as twelve to thirteen in summer.

Taiwan

See map page 23

Taiwan is an independent state not recognized as such by the government of mainland China. It consists of an island rather larger than Wales or the state of Vermont, situated between 22° and 25° N and lying about 160 km/100 mi off the coast of China. It is mountainous and rugged with the highest peak rising to over 4,000 m/13,000 ft. The whole island shares the tropical monsoon climate experienced on the southern Chinese mainland. Rainfall is almost everywhere over 2,000 mm/80 in a

year at low levels and much more in the mountains. More rain falls in the period May to September than in the rest of the year. Some of the heaviest falls of rain from July to September are brought by the typhoons of the South China Sea. As they move northwards towards Japan they bring strong winds and heavy rain to the whole island. In winter disturbed weather with cloud and rain affects the north and east coasts rather more than the south. This can be seen by comparing the table for **Taipei**, (opposite and above) in the north, with that for **Hengch'un** (opposite) in the extreme south of the

TAIPEI

NORTHERN TAIWAN

Sunshine	Temperatures									Discomfort from heat and humidity	Precipitation and humidity				Wet days
	Average daily				Highest recorded		Lowest recorded				Relative humidity 6:00 14:00		Average monthly precipitation		
	minimum		maximum												
average hours per day	°C	°F	°C	°F	°C	°F	°C	°F			%		mm	in	more than 1 mm/0.04 in
Jan	3	12	54	19	66	30	86	3	37		91	71	86	3.4	9	Jan
Feb	3	12	53	18	65	31	88	0	32		92	75	135	5.3	13	Feb
March	3	14	57	21	70	33	91	2	35		90	69	178	7.0	12	March
April	4	17	63	25	77	35	95	8	46	Medium	92	71	170	6.7	14	April
May	5	21	69	28	83	37	98	10	50	Medium	92	68	231	9.1	12	May
June	6	23	73	32	89	37	99	16	60	High	93	68	290	11.4	13	June
July	7	24	76	33	92	38	101	19	67	High	91	62	231	9.1	10	July
Aug	7	24	75	33	91	38	100	19	66	High	91	64	305	12.0	12	Aug
Sept	6	23	73	31	88	36	97	13	56	High	92	66	244	9.6	10	Sept
Oct	5	19	67	27	81	35	95	11	51	Medium	90	65	122	4.8	9	Oct
Nov	3	17	62	24	75	33	92	1	34	Moderate	90	65	66	2.6	7	Nov
Dec	3	14	57	21	69	31	88	2	35		90	69	71	2.8	8	Dec

Based on readings for 37 years at 25°02′ N, 121°31′ E, altitude 9 m/30 ft

HENGCH'UN

SOUTHERN TAIWAN

Sunshine	Temperatures									Discomfort from heat and humidity	Precipitation and humidity				Wet days
	Average daily				Highest recorded		Lowest recorded				Relative humidity 6:00 14:00		Average monthly precipitation		
	minimum		maximum												
average hours per day	°C	°F	°C	°F	°C	°F	°C	°F			%		mm	in	more than 1 mm/0.04 in
Jan	6	18	64	24	75	31	87	10	50	Moderate	78	62	23	0.9	4	Jan
Feb	6	17	63	24	76	31	88	10	50	Moderate	80	60	28	1.1	4	Feb
March	7	19	67	27	80	33	92	12	53	Medium	79	60	23	0.9	3	March
April	7	22	71	29	84	34	93	15	59	Medium	84	61	51	2.0	3	April
May	7	23	74	31	87	35	95	17	63	High	87	67	188	7.4	10	May
June	8	24	76	31	87	35	95	18	65	High	91	74	366	14.4	14	June
July	7	25	77	31	88	34	94	22	71	High	93	75	439	17.3	18	July
Aug	6	24	76	31	87	33	92	19	67	High	93	76	544	21.4	17	Aug
Sept	7	24	75	31	87	34	93	19	66	High	89	71	282	11.1	13	Sept
Oct	7	23	73	29	84	34	93	16	61	Medium	76	64	158	6.2	5	Oct
Nov	6	21	70	27	80	32	89	13	55	Medium	75	61	36	1.4	5	Nov
Dec	5	19	66	24	76	31	88	9	49	Moderate	76	61	18	0.7	3	Dec

Based on readings for 30 years at 22°00′ N, 120°45′ E, altitude 24 m/77 ft

country. Taipei not only has more rain in winter but on many more days.

The summer heat is made more oppressive by high humidity so that at low levels some days can be distinctly unpleasant. The winter and spring weather of Taiwan, however, can be very pleasant. The north of the island has a cooler winter than the south. The climate is quite sunny for much of the year with sunshine hours averaging six hours a day in winter to seven or eight in summer. These amounts are much reduced in the cloudy wetter hills.

Tajikistan

See map page 22

Tajikistan is part of a mountainous region on the borders of Afghanistan and China. It includes peaks rising to over 6,000 m/20,000 ft. These mountains carry snow the year round. However, because of the distance from the sea and the shelter of the Pamir and Himalayan ranges to the south and southeast, it is a rather dry region considering its height. Winters are cold but spring comes earlier than farther north.

The tables for **Almaty** (p. 206) in Kazakhstan and **Tashkent** (p. 415) in Uzbekistan illustrate conditions in the valleys of this region.

Tanzania

See map page 21

Tanzania is the largest country in East Africa. It is situated south of the equator between 1° and 12° S. It has a long coastline on the Indian Ocean. It is bordered by Kenya and Uganda on the north, by Mozambique, Malawi, and Zambia on the south, and by the Congo Democratic Republic on the west. There is a fairly narrow coastal plain in the east but most of the interior consists of a plateau 900–1,500 m/3,000–5,000 ft above sea level.

There are a number of mountain ranges which rise to between 2,100–3,000 m/7,000–10,000 ft. In the north of the country the isolated peak of Mount Kilimanjaro, the highest mountain in Africa, rises to nearly 6,000 m/20,000 ft. It has a permanent snow-cap and small glaciers.

The whole country, except the higher mountains, has a tropical climate, but above 900 m/3,000 ft it is modified by a significant reduction of temperature, particularly at night. Compare the higher temperatures recorded on the coast at **Dar es Salaam** (see table opposite and above) with those for **Dodoma** (opposite) in the central plateau. Minimum temperatures and daytime humidity are much lower at Dodoma and cause the climate to be less enervating.

The coastal regions, including the large offshore islands of Pemba and Zanzibar, have heavier and more reliable rainfall than most of the inland areas. Average annual rainfall is almost everywhere above 1,000 mm/40 in on the coast and up to 1,500 mm/60 in in the wetter places. This compares with an annual fall of between 500–1,000 mm /20–40 in over most of the interior.

Only the higher mountain areas receive more rain than the coastal region. The annual rainfall inland is notoriously unreliable and much of it is very sporadic in both time and place. Rainfall increases a little, and also becomes more reliable, towards the west and around the shores of the three great lakes which are partly included within the boundaries of Tanzania: lakes Victoria, Tanganyika, and Malawi. (See the table for **Kigoma** overleaf.)

Over most of the country there is a single rainy season with the heaviest falls between November and April; the period May to October is dry and sunny. The coastal region is an exception in that it gets some rain in all months with the main rain falling between March and May. The southern coastal district is occasionally affected by heavy rain and strong winds associated with tropical cyclones in the south Indian Ocean. Although weather on the coast is often rather oppressive because of the higher temperatures, particularly at night, and the high humidity, conditions here are not persistently uncomfortable thanks to regular daily sea breezes.

Inland, the lower humidity and cooler night temperatures mean that heat stress is rare although daytime temperatures are quite high and sunshine abundant. Much of Tanzania has a very sunny climate with many places averaging from seven to ten hours of sunshine a day with fewer hours during the rainy season. As in most other tropical countries

DAR ES SALAAM

COASTAL TANZANIA

	Sunshine average hours per day	Temperatures								Discomfort from heat and humidity	Precipitation and humidity				Wet days more than 0.25 mm/0.01 in	
		Average daily				Highest recorded		Lowest recorded			Relative humidity 8:00 14:00		Average monthly precipitation			
		minimum		maximum												
		°C	°F	°C	°F	°C	°F	°C	°F		%		mm	in		
Jan	8	25	77	31	87	35	95	21	69	High	81	74	66	2.6	8	Jan
Feb	7	25	77	31	88	35	95	20	68	High	81	74	66	2.6	6	Feb
March	7	24	75	31	88	36	96	21	69	High	85	76	130	5.1	12	March
April	5	23	73	30	86	35	95	19	66	High	88	77	290	11.4	19	April
May	7	22	71	29	85	33	91	18	64	High	87	72	188	7.4	15	May
June	7	20	68	29	84	32	90	16	60	Medium	84	64	33	1.3	6	June
July	7	19	66	28	83	32	90	16	60	Medium	85	62	31	1.2	6	July
Aug	9	19	66	28	83	32	89	15	59	Medium	84	64	25	1.0	7	Aug
Sept	9	19	67	28	83	33	91	16	61	Medium	81	67	31	1.2	7	Sept
Oct	9	21	69	29	85	33	92	17	62	High	78	70	41	1.6	7	Oct
Nov	8	22	72	30	86	34	94	19	66	High	79	73	74	2.9	9	Nov
Dec	8	24	75	31	87	35	95	21	69	High	80	75	91	3.6	11	Dec

Based on readings for 44 years at 6°50' S, 39°18' E, altitude 14 m/47 ft

DODOMA

CENTRAL TANZANIA

	Sunshine average hours per day	Temperatures								Discomfort from heat and humidity	Precipitation and humidity				Wet days more than 0.25 mm/0.01 in	
		Average daily				Highest recorded		Lowest recorded			Relative humidity 8:00 14:00		Average monthly precipitation			
		minimum		maximum												
		°C	°F	°C	°F	°C	°F	°C	°F		%		mm	in		
Jan	8	18	65	29	85	35	95	16	61	Medium	80	52	152	6.0	12.0	Jan
Feb	7	18	65	29	84	36	96	13	55	Medium	83	53	109	4.3	9.0	Feb
March	7	18	64	28	83	34	94	15	59	Medium	84	56	137	5.4	11.0	March
April	6	18	64	28	83	33	91	15	59	Medium	82	54	48	1.9	7.0	April
May	7	16	61	28	82	33	91	11	51	Medium	76	49	5	0.2	2.0	May
June	7	14	57	27	81	32	89	9	48	Moderate	75	45	0	0.0	0.2	June
July	7	13	55	26	79	31	88	8	46	Moderate	74	43	0	0.0	0.0	July
Aug	8	14	57	27	80	34	93	9	49	Moderate	74	42	0	0.0	0.0	Aug
Sept	9	15	59	29	84	33	92	11	52	Medium	71	38	0	0.0	0.0	Sept
Oct	9	17	62	31	87	36	97	13	55	Medium	70	36	5	0.2	1.0	Oct
Nov	8	18	64	31	88	36	97	14	58	Medium	71	39	23	0.9	4.0	Nov
Dec	8	18	65	31	87	36	97	14	58	Medium	77	48	91	3.6	9.0	Dec

Based on readings for 14 years at 6°10' S, 35°46' E, altitude 1120 m/3675 ft

KIGOMA														WESTERN TANZANIA
Sunshine	Temperatures							Discomfort from heat and humidity	Precipitation and humidity					Wet days
	Average daily				Highest recorded		Lowest recorded		Relative humidity 7:30 13:30		Average monthly precipitation			
	minimum		maximum											
average hours per day	°C	°F	°C	°F	°C	°F	°C	°F		%		mm	in	more than 0.25 mm/0.01 in
Jan	6	19	67	27	80	32	89	16	61	Medium	85	73	122	4.8	14	Jan
Feb	6	20	68	27	81	33	92	16	61	Medium	84	74	127	5.0	12	Feb
March	7	20	68	27	81	32	89	16	60	Medium	85	74	150	5.9	17	March
April	6	19	67	27	81	32	89	17	63	Medium	84	74	130	5.1	17	April
May	7	19	67	28	83	32	89	16	61	Medium	79	66	43	1.7	8	May
June	8	18	65	28	82	31	88	14	58	Medium	76	59	5	0.2	1	June
July	8	17	63	28	83	32	89	12	53	Medium	69	55	3	0.1	1	July
Aug	8	18	65	29	84	33	91	14	58	Medium	64	56	5	0.2	1	Aug
Sept	9	19	67	29	85	33	92	15	59	Medium	62	61	18	0.7	3	Sept
Oct	8	21	69	29	84	36	96	16	60	Medium	67	64	48	1.9	8	Oct
Nov	7	20	68	27	80	32	90	16	60	Medium	81	74	142	5.6	17	Nov
Dec	7	19	67	26	79	32	89	16	60	Medium	85	75	135	5.3	19	Dec

Based on readings for 12 years at 4°53′ S, 29°38′ E, altitude 1189 m/2903 ft

the year is usually divided into the rainy and dry seasons, since the terms winter and summer have little meaning in respect of temperature.

The table for **Kigoma** (above) on Lake Tanganyika shows the increased volume and reliability of rainfall towards the west of Tanzania.

Thailand

See map page 23

Thailand, in southeast Asia, is about the same size as France. It is bordered by Myanmar on the north and west and by Laos and Cambodia on the east. It has a coastline on the Gulf of Thailand, which is part of the Pacific Ocean. The south of the country consists of the narrow Kra Isthmus dividing the Pacific from the Indian Ocean and joining the Malayan peninsula to the mainland of southeast Asia. Situated between 6° and 20° N, the country has an equatorial climate in the extreme south while the centre and north have a tropical monsoon climate similar to that of Myanmar. The north is hilly and even mountainous with land rising over 1,000 m/3,300 ft but most of the centre and east of Thailand is low-lying with only gentle hills and slopes.

Most of Thailand has abundant, but not excessive, rainfall and this is largely confined to the months May to October. During this season the weather is dominated by the southwest monsoon blowing from the Indian Ocean and bringing warm, humid air, and much cloud. The months November to April are much drier with rain only falling on a few days a month. This is the period of the northeast monsoon when the wind is blowing overland from China or Indo-China and the air is consequently much drier. In the Kra Isthmus these winds bring more rain since they are more likely to have their origin in the Pacific Ocean or to have blown across the Gulf of Thailand. More rain falls in the south at this time but the extreme north is virtually dry for two or three months.

In the centre and south of the country there is no great variation in temperature from month to month, but in the north the period of the northeast monsoon is definitely cooler. This may be seen by comparing the table for **Chiang Mai** (opposite) in the northern hills with that for **Bangkok** (opposite and above) in the south-centre of the country. In

BANGKOK

SOUTH-CENTRAL THAILAND

Sunshine	Temperatures								Discomfort from heat and humidity	Precipitation and humidity				Wet days	
	Average daily				Highest recorded		Lowest recorded			Relative humidity 6:30 12:30		Average monthly precipitation			
	minimum		maximum												
average hours per day	°C	°F	°C	°F	°C	°F	°C	°F		%		mm	in	more than 1 mm/0.04 in	
Jan	9	20	68	32	89	38	100	13	55	High	91	53	8	0.3	1	Jan
Feb	8	22	72	33	91	41	106	13	56	High	92	55	20	0.8	1	Feb
March	9	24	75	34	93	40	104	17	62	High	92	56	36	1.4	3	March
April	8	25	77	35	95	41	106	19	67	Extreme	90	58	58	2.3	3	April
May	8	25	77	34	93	41	106	22	71	Extreme	91	64	198	7.8	9	May
June	6	24	76	33	91	38	100	21	70	Extreme	90	67	160	6.3	10	June
July	5	24	76	32	90	38	101	22	71	High	91	66	160	6.3	13	July
Aug	5	24	76	32	90	37	99	22	72	High	92	66	175	6.9	13	Aug
Sept	5	24	76	32	89	37	98	21	69	High	94	70	305	12.0	15	Sept
Oct	6	24	75	31	88	38	100	18	64	High	93	70	206	8.1	14	Oct
Nov	8	22	72	31	87	37	99	13	56	High	92	65	66	2.6	5	Nov
Dec	9	20	68	31	87	38	100	11	52	High	91	56	5	0.2	1	Dec

Based on readings for 37 years at 13°45′ N, 100°28′ E, altitude 2 m/7 ft

CHIANG MAI

NORTHERN THAILAND

Sunshine	Temperatures								Discomfort from heat and humidity	Precipitation and humidity				Wet days	
	Average daily				Highest recorded		Lowest recorded			Relative humidity 6:30 12:30		Average monthly precipitation			
	minimum		maximum												
average hours per day	°C	°F	°C	°F	°C	°F	°C	°F		%		mm	in	more than 1 mm/0.04 in	
Jan	9	13	56	29	84	36	97	6	43	Medium	96	52	0	0.0	0.5	Jan
Feb	9	14	58	32	89	36	97	9	49	Medium	93	44	10	0.4	1.0	Feb
March	9	17	63	34	94	39	102	13	55	High	88	40	8	0.3	2.0	March
April	9	22	71	36	97	41	105	15	59	High	88	49	36	1.4	5.0	April
May	8	23	73	34	94	41	106	19	67	Extreme	90	60	122	4.8	12.0	May
June	6	23	74	32	190	38	100	21	69	High	92	67	112	4.4	15.0	June
July	5	23	74	31	88	37	99	19	66	High	94	69	213	8.4	21.0	July
Aug	4	23	74	31	88	37	99	21	70	High	95	73	193	7.6	20.0	Aug
Sept	6	23	73	31	88	36	96	18	65	High	96	72	249	9.8	17.0	Sept
Oct	7	21	70	31	87	36	96	16	60	High	96	69	94	3.7	8.0	Oct
Nov	8	19	66	30	86	37	99	12	54	High	96	63	31	1.2	4.0	Nov
Dec	9	15	59	28	83	36	97	6	43	Medium	96	57	13	0.5	2.0	Dec

Based on readings for 13 years at 18°47′ N, 98°59′ E, altitude 314 m/1030 ft

most of Thailand the hottest months are April and May, before the cloudier, rainy weather brought by the southwest monsoon. Sunshine amounts are everywhere lowest during the months June to September, when they average four to five hours a day. During the rest of the year they average nine to ten hours.

The weather of the wet season is oppressive over most of Thailand because of the combination of high temperature and humidity. During the sunnier months of the dry season conditions are fresher and there is usually more wind. Although severe heat stress is rare in Thailand, visitors will find the weather of the wet season rather uncomfortable.

Togo

See map page 20

This small country is situated in West Africa between Ghana to the west and Benin to the east. It has a very short coastline on the Gulf of Guinea and extends between 6° and 11° N. It shares the same climatic belts and sequence of weather around the year as that described on p. 266 for Nigeria and adjacent countries.

As in Nigeria and other neighbouring countries, the coastal region has two rainy seasons, one peaking in May or June, the other in October, but in the north there is a single rainy season starting in May or June. However, rainfall is lower on the coast than it is a short distance inland, as in Ghana. In the north

there is a single long dry season between October and April. At this time temperatures are warm to hot with a very low relative humidity and the dust-laden harmattan wind blows from the northeast. From December to February the harmattan affects the whole country except a strip along the coast. The coast has southwesterly winds, the dry harmattan reaching right to the coast on only a few days.

On the coast the period from December to February is least likely to experience rainy days. The tables for **Accra** (p. 161) in Ghana and **Cotonou** (p. 63) in Benin are equally well representative of conditions on the coast of Togo. The north of the country is drier with a single rainy season and here the table for **Tamale** (p. 161) in Ghana is representative.

Tokelau

See map page 17

This New Zealand dependency in the southwestern Pacific lies north of Samoa. It shares with the other areas of the western Pacific near the equator the features of a tropical oceanic climate. Very similar conditions prevail throughout the year with high temperatures and humidity. The daily range of temperature is quite small – about 4°–5° C/10° F. There is abundant rainfall. Being south of the equator, Tokelau has its season of maximum rainfall between November and April. On some islands there is no great difference between the amount of rain from month to month. Tropical cyclones are less frequent than in the Pacific north of the equator.

Except in the wettest places, where cloud is more frequent, Tokelau has moderately large amounts of sunshine, averaging from six to eight hours a day. Much of the rainfall comes in short, heavy showers, often after a sunny morning, but longer periods of heavy rain lasting a day or so occur in the wetter months.

The climate may generally be described as pleasant and healthy, although the combination of high temperature and humidity can be a little oppressive when not tempered by sea breezes or a brisk wind.

The table for **Apia** (p. 309) in Samoa shows weather that is similar to that of Tokelau.

Tonga

See map page 17

This constitutional monarchy occupies 169 islands in the southwest Pacific between Fiji and Niue. They include a low-lying eastern chain of coral limestone

and a mountainous western chain with several active volcanoes. These islands share a tropical oceanic climate with other countries of the western Pacific near the equator. Very similar conditions prevail throughout the year with high temperatures and humidity. The daily range of temperature is quite small – about 4°–5° C/10° F. There is abundant rainfall. Being south of the equator, Tonga has its season of maximum rainfall between November and April. On some islands there is no great difference between the amount of rain from month to month. Tropical cyclones are less frequent than in the Pacific north of the equator.

Except in the wettest places, where cloud is more frequent, the country has moderately large amounts of sunshine, averaging from six to eight hours a day. Much of the rainfall comes in short, heavy showers, often after a sunny morning, but longer periods of heavy rain lasting a whole day or so can occur in the wetter months.

In this area of the Pacific the principal difference in the weather and climate is the amount of rainfall per month. Temperature and humidity are very similar from one island to another but the amount of rainfall varies with altitude and with exposure of the coast to the dominant southeast trade winds. The number of wet days varies from island to island much less than the amount of rain.

The climate may generally be described as pleasant and healthy, although the combination of high temperature and humidity can be a little oppressive when not tempered by sea breezes or a brisk wind.

The table for **Apia** (p. 309) in Samoa shows weather that is typical of Tonga.

Trinidad and Tobago

See map page 15

Trinidad, and the neighbouring small island of Tobago, are the most southerly islands of the Lesser Antilles. At two points Trinidad is only a few miles from the coast of Venezuela and its climate is very similar to that of the northeast coast of that country. The table for **St Clair** (below) shows that rainfall is well distributed throughout the year with a definite wetter season from June to November. Temperatures are a little higher in Trinidad than in Caribbean islands that lie farther north.

Trinidad is too far south to be affected by violent tropical storms in the form of hurricanes, which pass to the north of the island.

ST CLAIR																		TRINIDAD
Sunshine	Temperatures									Discomfort from heat and humidity	Precipitation and humidity					Wet days		
	Average daily				Highest recorded		Lowest recorded				Relative humidity		Average monthly precipitation					
	minimum		maximum								7:00	15:00						
average hours per day	°C	°F	°C	°F	°C	°F	°C	°F			%		mm	in		more than 0.25 mm/0.01 in		
Jan	21	69	31	87	35	95	14	57		High	89	68	69	2.7		14	Jan
Feb	20	68	31	88	36	96	14	57		High	87	65	41	1.6		10	Feb
March	20	68	32	89	37	98	12	54		High	85	63	46	1.8		9	March
April	21	69	32	90	37	98	13	55		High	83	61	53	2.1		9	April
May	22	71	32	90	37	99	15	59		High	84	63	94	3.7		12	May
June	22	71	32	89	37	99	16	60		High	87	69	193	7.6		19	June
July	22	71	31	88	37	98	11	52		High	88	71	218	8.6		22	July
Aug	22	71	31	88	37	99	16	61		High	87	73	246	9.7		23	Aug
Sept	22	71	32	89	38	101	14	58		Extreme	87	73	193	7.6		19	Sept
Oct	22	71	32	89	36	96	16	61		Extreme	87	74	170	6.7		18	Oct
Nov	22	71	32	89	36	96	16	60		Extreme	89	76	183	7.2		18	Nov
Dec	21	69	31	88	36	97	16	60		High	89	71	125	4.9		17	Dec

Based on readings for 49 years at 10°40′ N, 61°31′ W, altitude 20 m/67 ft

Tunisia

Tunisia is a small country on the southern shores
of the Mediterranean; most of its coastline faces
eastwards on the Gulf of Gabes. It has a western
boundary with Algeria and a southern border with
Libya. Although only about the same size as
England, it is geographically diverse. Tunisia
includes parts of the three major regions described
for Algeria (pp. 30–2); in the north a narrow coastal
strip backed by mountains; a central and western
district of mountain and plateau or 'tell' country; and
a low-lying region in the south which is either steppe
or desert, the fringe of the Sahara.

In recent years Tunisia has developed a large tourist
trade, taking advantage of a Mediterranean climate
with mild to warm, sunny winters and hot summers
which are almost completely dry. Most of the major
tourist centres and hotels are situated on the coast
and near the main towns: Tunis, Bizerta, Sfax,
and Sousse.

The coastal regions, particularly in the north, as
well as the northern mountains have a typically
Mediterranean climate with moderate winter rainfall.
Occasional rain may occur in the early summer and

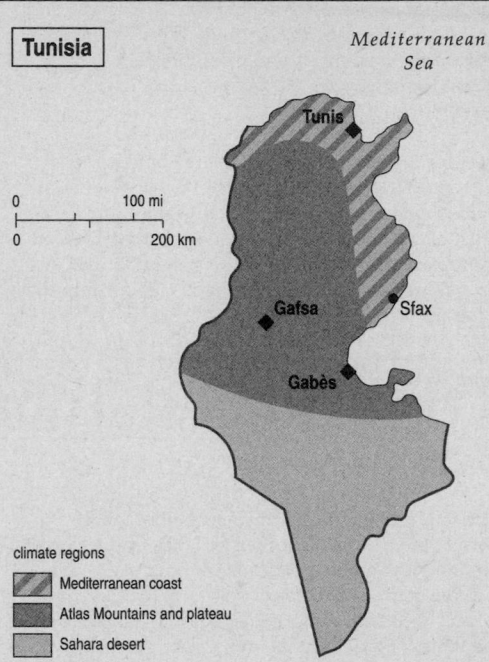

climate regions

▨ Mediterranean coast

▆ Atlas Mountains and plateau

▨ Sahara desert

TUNIS

COASTAL TUNISIA

Sunshine	Temperatures									Discomfort from heat and humidity	Precipitation and humidity					Wet days	
	Average daily				Highest recorded		Lowest recorded				Relative humidity		Average monthly precipitation			more than 0.1 mm/0.004 in	
	minimum		maximum								5:30	13:30					
average hours per day	°C	°F	°C	°F	°C	°F	°C	°F		%		mm	in		
Jan	5	6	43	14	58	25	77	-1	30		83	64	64	2.5	13	Jan
Feb	6	7	44	16	61	29	84	0	32		83	61	51	2.0	12	Feb
March	7	8	47	18	65	33	91	1	34		85	57	41	1.6	11	March
April	8	11	51	21	70	40	104	3	37		84	53	36	1.4	9	April
May	10	13	56	24	76	40	104	6	43	Moderate	79	51	18	0.7	6	May
June	11	17	63	29	84	43	109	9	48	Medium	74	45	8	0.3	5	June
July	12	20	68	32	90	48	118	10	50	Medium	75	40	3	0.1	2	July
Aug	11	21	69	33	91	47	117	11	52	High	72	47	8	0.3	3	Aug
Sept	9	19	66	31	87	44	111	11	52	Medium	80	51	33	1.3	7	Sept
Oct	7	15	59	25	77	40	104	7	45	Moderate	86	55	51	2.0	9	Oct
Nov	6	11	51	20	68	32	90	1	34		85	59	48	1.9	11	Nov
Dec	5	7	44	16	60	27	81	-1	30		85	63	61	2.4	14	Dec

Based on readings for 50 years at 36°47′ N, 10°12′ E, altitude 66 m/217 ft

GABES

COASTAL TUNISIA

Sunshine average hours per day		Temperatures								Discomfort from heat and humidity	Precipitation and humidity				Wet days more than 0.1 mm/0.004 in	
		Average daily				Highest recorded		Lowest recorded			Relative humidity 5:30 11:30		Average monthly precipitation			
		minimum		maximum												
		°C	°F	°C	°F	°C	°F	°C	°F		%		mm	in		
Jan	7	6	43	16	61	27	81	-3	27		76	54	23	0.9	4	Jan
Feb	8	7	44	18	64	31	88	-2	28		74	52	18	0.7	3	Feb
March	9	9	49	21	69	37	99	2	36		73	52	20	0.8	4	March
April	9	12	54	23	74	42	108	4	39	Moderate	79	62	10	0.4	3	April
May	10	16	61	26	79	43	109	4	39	Medium	78	64	8	0.3	2	May
June	11	19	66	28	83	46	115	6	43	Medium	76	64	0	0	2	June
July	12	22	71	32	89	50	122	9	48	High	77	60	0	0	0	July
Aug	11	22	72	33	91	47	117	14	57	High	76	60	3	0.1	1	Aug
Sept	10	21	69	31	87	49	120	12	54	High	79	62	13	0.5	3	Sept
Oct	8	17	62	27	81	44	111	6	43	Medium	82	61	31	1.2	4	Oct
Nov	8	11	52	22	72	36	97	1	34		77	51	31	1.2	4	Nov
Dec	7	7	45	17	63	27	81	0	32		75	55	15	0.6	4	Dec

Based on readings for 50 years at 33°53′ N, 10°07′ E, altitude 2 m/7 ft

GAFSA

CENTRAL TUNISIA

Sunshine average hours per day		Temperatures								Discomfort from heat and humidity	Precipitation and humidity				Wet days more than 0.1 mm/0.004 in	
		Average daily				Highest recorded		Lowest recorded			Relative humidity 5:30 11:30		Average monthly precipitation			
		minimum		maximum												
		°C	°F	°C	°F	°C	°F	°C	°F		%		mm	in		
Jan	7	4	39	14	58	25	77	-6	21		79	52	18	0.7	3	Jan
Feb	8	4	40	17	62	32	90	-4	25		71	42	13	0.5	3	Feb
March	8	7	45	21	69	35	95	-3	27		70	42	23	0.9	3	March
April	9	11	51	25	77	37	99	2	36	Moderate	74	41	15	0.6	3	April
May	10	15	59	29	85	43	109	6	43	Medium	67	36	10	0.4	3	May
June	10	19	66	34	94	49	121	9	48	Medium	62	33	8	0.3	1	June
July	12	21	70	38	101	53	127	10	50	High	59	30	3	0.1	1	July
Aug	11	21	70	38	100	48	118	12	54	High	62	31	5	0.2	1	Aug
Sept	9	18	65	33	92	45	113	10	50	High	73	40	13	0.5	3	Sept
Oct	8	14	58	27	81	39	102	3	37	Moderate	75	45	13	0.5	3	Oct
Nov	7	9	48	21	69	33	91	-3	27		75	46	18	0.7	3	Nov
Dec	7	4	40	15	59	29	84	-4	25		82	55	13	0.5	3	Dec

Based on readings for 50 years at 34°25′ N, 8°49′ E, altitude 314 m/1030 ft

autumn and this can take the form of heavy but rare downpours. Summers are fine and hot. In the wettest parts of the hills annual rainfall ranges between 600 mm/24 in and 900 mm/32 in. Snow may occur on about ten days a year in the higher parts but is very rare on the coast. The table for **Tunis** (p. 258) is representative of these regions.

Rainfall in central Tunisia and the southern hills on the Algerian border is lower. Inland winter temperatures may drop quite low with occasional frosts. Summer temperatures are higher than near the coast. The table for **Gafsa** (p. 359) illustrates inland conditions.

The climate becomes progressively drier towards the south of Tunisia and summer temperatures can rise very high inland, since this area has a virtual Sahara climate. Rainfall can occasionally be heavy in spring and autumn although days with rain are rare.

Daily sunshine amounts are everywhere large, ranging from between seven and eight hours in winter to as much as twelve hours in summer. The occasional very hot, dry, and dusty wind bringing air from the Sahara can affect any part of the country, particularly in spring, when a depression moving into the Gulf of Gabès (see the table for **Gabès** on p. 269) from the west induces southerly winds on its eastern flank.

This wind and associated weather is similar to the khamsin of Egypt but goes under the local name of *chili*. When this occurs, temperatures may rise as high as 50° C/122° F, bringing a risk of heat exhaustion or even heatstroke; but such extreme conditions are rare and for most of the year the climate of Tunisia is healthy and pleasant. Temperatures on the coast are moderated by daily sea breezes, while the higher temperatures inland are rendered less enervating by low humidity.

Turkey

See map page 22

Turkey extends for 1,600 km/1,000 mi from west to east. Turkish Thrace, west of the Bosphorus, is

geographically in Europe; it borders Greece and Bulgaria on the west and has a similar climate (see the table for **Istanbul** opposite). The rest of the country, Anatolia or Asia Minor, is strictly in Asia.

ANKARA										CENTRAL TURKEY	
Sunshine	Temperatures					Discomfort from heat and humidity	Precipitation and humidity				Wet days
	Average daily		Highest recorded	Lowest recorded			Relative humidity		Average monthly precipitation		
	minimum	maximum					7:00	14:00			
average hours per day	°C °F	°C °F	°C °F	°C °F			%		mm	in	more than 1 mm/0.04 in
Jan	3	−4 24	4 39	15 59	−25 −13		85	70	33	1.3	8	Jan
Feb	4	−3 26	6 42	18 64	−24 −12		84	67	31	1.2	8	Feb
March	6	−1 31	11 51	27 80	−16 3		81	52	33	1.3	7	March
April	7	4 40	17 63	32 89	−7 20		72	40	33	1.3	7	April
May	9	9 49	23 73	34 94	−1 31		68	38	48	1.9	7	May
June	11	12 53	26 79	37 98	2 35	Moderate	64	34	25	1.0	5	June
July	12	15 59	30 86	38 100	7 44	Medium	57	28	13	0.5	2	July
Aug	12	15 59	31 87	38 100	4 40	Medium	54	25	10	0.4	1	Aug
Sept	10	11 52	26 78	36 96	−2 29	Moderate	62	31	18	0.7	3	Sept
Oct	7	7 44	21 69	32 89	−3 27		72	37	23	0.9	5	Oct
Nov	5	3 37	14 57	26 78	−18 0		82	52	31	1.2	6	Nov
Dec	3	−2 29	6 43	17 63	−25 −13		86	71	48	1.9	9	Dec

Based on readings for 26 years at 39°57′ N, 32°53′ E, altitude 862 m/2825 ft

KARS — EASTERN TURKEY

	Sunshine	Temperatures									Discomfort from heat and humidity	Precipitation and humidity			Wet days	
		Average daily				Highest recorded		Lowest recorded				Relative humidity all hours	Average monthly precipitation			
		minimum		maximum												
	average hours per day	°C	°F	°C	°F	°C	°F	°C	°F			%	mm	in	more than 1 mm/0.04 in	
Jan	3	-18	-1	-6	21	5	41	-36	-32			65	28	1.1	7	Jan
Feb	4	-16	3	-4	25	7	44	-37	-35			68	28	1.1	7	Feb
March	5	11	12	1	34	19	66	-34	-29			71	28	1.1	8	March
April	6	-2	28	10	50	24	75	-23	-9			70	43	1.7	9	April
May	7	3	38	17	63	27	80	-7	19			69	86	3.4	15	May
June	9	6	43	21	70	29	85	-1	30			67	74	2.9	12	June
July	10	9	49	25	77	34	94	1	33	Moderate		63	53	2.1	8	July
Aug	10	9	49	26	79	34	94	1	33	Medium		60	53	2.1	7	Aug
Sept	9	4	40	22	71	32	90	-4	24			61	31	1.2	5	Sept
Oct	6	0	32	15	59	25	77	-17	1			69	41	1.6	7	Oct
Nov	5	-5	23	7	44	21	70	-24	-12			72	31	1.2	6	Nov
Dec	3	-13	9	-2	29	11	52	-35	-31			71	25	1.0	7	Dec

Based on readings for 18 years at 40°36′ N, 43°05′ E, altitude 1751 m/5741 ft

ISTANBUL — TURKISH THRACE

	Sunshine	Temperatures									Discomfort from heat and humidity	Precipitation and humidity				Wet days	
		Average daily				Highest recorded		Lowest recorded				Relative humidity 7:00 14:00		Average monthly precipitation			
		minimum		maximum													
	average hours per day	°C	°F	°C	°F	°C	°F	°C	°F			%		mm	in	more than 0.1 mm/0.004 in	
Jan	3	3	37	8	46	19	66	-8	18			82	75	109	4.0	18	Jan
Feb	4	2	36	9	47	22	71	-8	18			82	72	92	3.6	14	Feb
March	4	3	38	11	51	28	82	-6	21			81	67	72	2.8	14	March
April	6	7	45	16	60	30	85	-1	31			81	62	46	1.8	9	April
May	9	12	53	21	69	35	94	3	38			82	61	38	1.5	8	May
June	11	16	60	25	77	37	99	8	47	Moderate		79	58	34	1.3	6	June
July	12	18	65	28	82	38	100	9	49	Medium		79	56	34	1.3	4	July
Aug	11	19	66	28	82	41	105	11	53	Medium		79	55	30	1.2	4	Aug
Sept	8	16	61	24	76	38	100	6	43	Moderate		81	59	58	2.3	7	Sept
Oct	6	13	55	20	68	33	91	1	35			83	64	81	3.2	11	Oct
Nov	4	9	48	15	59	27	80	-4	25			82	71	103	4.0	14	Nov
Dec	3	5	41	11	51	23	73	-9	16			82	74	119	4.7	18	Dec

Based on readings for 25 years at 41°06′ N, 29°03′ E, altitude 114 m/374 ft

Anatolia consists of a high plateau which becomes more mountainous towards the east, where Turkey borders Georgia, Armenia, and Iran. Anatolia is enclosed by the Pontic ranges in the north and the Taurus and Anti-Taurus in the south. These mountains and isolated volcanic peaks, such as Mount Ararat in eastern Turkey, rise to over 3,000 m/10,000 ft and may carry snow throughout the year.

There are thus considerable differences of climate within Turkey. The narrow coastlands and mountain slopes facing the Black Sea on the north, the Aegean on the west, and the Mediterranean on the south have wetter and milder winters than the interior. The interior plateau has low rainfall and cold or very cold winters. Towards the east the winter cold is similar to that found in parts of Russia.

Except at higher levels, summers in the interior are warm or even hot with occasional thunderstorms. Winter precipitation here falls mostly as snow and towards the east this may lie on the ground for between three and four months. (Compare winter temperatures in the tables for **Ankara** and **Kars** on p. 360–1).

The coastal regions have much milder winters and here snow is rare. Turkish Thrace, around Istanbul and the Black Sea coast, is a little colder in winter than the west and south coasts (see the climatic table for the Black Sea town of **Samsun** below). The Black Sea coast has some rain all the year round and east of Samsun this becomes heavy in the summer and autumn.

Summers are here warm and humid and the weather is often changeable and cloudy. South of Istanbul the Aegean and Mediterranean coasts have a typical Mediterranean climate with increasingly dry, hot summers (see the table for **Izmir** opposite). Here midwinter is the rainy season when most of the disturbed weather occurs.

The hottest and driest area of Turkey in summer is the low-lying plain at the foot of the Taurus Mountains along the border with Syria. Here conditions become typical of the Middle East. The region is a semi-arid steppe with only winter rain.

Except for the eastern part of the Black Sea coastlands, most of Turkey has a very sunny climate even in winter. Average daily sunshine amounts range from three to four hours in midwinter to as much as twelve to thirteen hours in summer.

Although summer temperatures are rather high, the heat is tempered by the low humidity inland and the

SAMSUN										BLACK SEA COAST		
Sunshine	Temperatures							Discomfort from heat and humidity	Precipitation and humidity		Wet days	
	Average daily			Highest recorded		Lowest recorded			Relative humidity	Average monthly precipitation		
average hours per day	minimum		maximum						all hours			more than 1 mm/0.04 in
	°C	°F	°C	°F	°C	°F	°C	°F	%	mm	in	
Jan	3	3	38	10	50	22	72	–7	20		69	74	2.9	10	Jan
Feb	3	3	38	11	51	25	77	–7	20		72	66	2.6	10	Feb
March	4	4	40	12	54	32	90	–7	20		75	69	2.7	11	March
April	5	7	45	15	59	34	94	–2	28		77	58	2.3	9	April
May	7	12	53	19	67	37	99	2	36		79	46	1.8	8	May
June	9	16	60	23	74	35	95	8	46	Moderate	75	38	1.5	6	June
July	10	18	65	26	79	39	103	11	51	Medium	73	38	1.5	4	July
Aug	9	18	65	27	80	39	102	9	49	Medium	72	33	1.3	4	Aug
Sept	7	16	61	24	75	34	94	7	44	Moderate	74	61	2.4	6	Sept
Oct	5	13	56	21	69	35	95	3	38		75	81	3.2	7	Oct
Nov	4	9	49	17	62	32	90	–3	27		72	89	3.5	8	Nov
Dec	3	6	43	13	55	24	76	–5	23		68	86	3.4	9	Dec

Based on readings for 24 years at 41°17′ N, 36°19′ E, altitude 40 m/131 ft

IZMIR													MEDITERRANEAN COAST
Sunshine	Temperatures								Discomfort from heat and humidity	Precipitation and humidity			Wet days
average hours per day	Average daily				Highest recorded		Lowest recorded			Relative humidity 7:00 14:00		Average monthly precipitation	more than 1 mm/0.04 in
	minimum		maximum										
	°C	°F	°C	°F	°C	°F	°C	°F		%		mm in	
Jan	4	4	39	13	55	23	73	-11	12		75	62	112 4.4	10	Jan
Feb	6	4	40	14	57	23	73	-11	12		75	51	84 3.3	8	Feb
March	6	6	43	17	63	29	84	-7	19		72	52	76 3.0	7	March
April	8	9	49	21	70	33	91	-1	30		69	48	43 1.7	5	April
May	10	13	56	26	79	41	106	3	37	Moderate	65	45	33 1.3	4	May
June	12	17	63	31	87	41	105	10	50	Medium	56	40	15 0.6	2	June
July	13	21	69	33	92	42	108	11	52	Medium	53	31	5 0.2	0	July
Aug	12	21	69	33	92	42	107	12	53	Medium	57	37	5 0.2	1	Aug
Sept	10	17	62	29	85	39	103	6	42	Medium	64	42	20 0.8	2	Sept
Oct	8	13	55	24	76	37	98	-1	31		71	49	53 2.1	4	Oct
Nov	6	9	49	19	67	32	89	-7	19		77	58	84 3.3	6	Nov
Dec	4	6	42	14	58	26	79	-7	20		77	64	122 4.8	10	Dec

Based on readings for 39 years at 38°27′ N, 27°15′ E, altitude 28 m/92 ft

sea breezes along the coast. Occasionally the nights may be sticky and humid on the Aegean and Mediterranean coasts. The worst feature of the climate is the severe cold experienced in the interior in winter and occasionally in early spring.

ASHGABAT														SOUTH-CENTRAL TURKMENISTAN	
Sunshine		Temperatures								Discomfort from heat and humidity	Precipitation and humidity				Wet days
		Average daily				Highest recorded		Lowest recorded			Relative humidity 6:30 13:30		Average monthly precipitation		
		minimum		maximum											
average hours per day		°C	°F	°C	°F	°C	°F	°C	°F		%		mm	in	more than 0.1 mm/0.004 in
Jan	4	−4	25	3	38	23	74	−23	−9		87	69	25	1.0	10	Jan
Feb	4	−1	31	8	47	28	82	−26	−14		84	60	20	0.8	7	Feb
March	5	4	39	13	55	33	92	−14	7		80	54	48	1.9	10	March
April	7	9	49	21	70	36	97	−4	25		71	45	36	1.4	8	April
May	9	16	60	23	73	43	110	6	42		61	36	31	1.2	7	May
June	11	19	67	33	92	43	110	8	46	Medium	53	29	8	0.3	2	June
July	12	22	71	36	97	45	113	9	49	High	54	28	3	0.1	1	July
Aug	11	19	67	35	95	43	110	9	48	Medium	57	27	3	0.1	1	Aug
Sept	10	14	58	30	86	42	107	3	37	Medium	61	30	3	0.1	1	Sept
Oct	8	8	46	22	72	39	102	2	25		71	39	13	0.3	4	Oct
Nov	5	3	38	14	57	32	90	−15	5		84	57	20	0.8	7	Nov
Dec	4	0	32	8	47	26	79	−17	1		86	65	18	0.7	6	Dec

Based on readings for 20 years at 37°57′ N, 58°20′ E, altitude 226 m/741 ft

Turkmenistan

See map page 22

Most of this central Asian republic is steppe and desert. The summers are warm to hot but the heat is made more bearable by the low humidity. The winters are cold but generally dry and sunny over most of the region.

The table for **Ashgabat** (above) in Turkmenistan indicates the weather conditions inland.

The table for **Krasnovodsk** (opposite and above) on the Caspian shores shows an unusually mild winter compared with the rest of the country. This is a result of the moderating influence of the sea.

Turks and Caicos

See map page 15

This British dependency, a geographical extension of the Bahamas chain, comprises two groups of low-lying islands with a warm and pleasant climate. Because the land is low, annual rainfall is rather less than some other islands in the Caribbean (see pp. 92–3). Unlike the Bahamas (p. 55), they do not experience cold waves in winter or spring.

The table for the island of **Grand Turk** (opposite) is representative of weather in the Turks and Caicos.

KRASNOVODSK

COASTAL TURKMENISTAN

	Sunshine	Temperatures								Discomfort from heat and humidity	Precipitation and humidity				Wet days	
	average hours per day	Average daily				Highest recorded		Lowest recorded			Relative humidity 7:00 13:00		Average monthly precipitation			more than 0.1 mm/0.004 in	
		minimum		maximum													
		°C	°F	°C	°F	°C	°F	°C	°F		%		mm	in		
Jan		0	32	3	38	16	61	-17	1		77	69	13	0.5	5	Jan
Feb		2	35	6	42	19	66	-13	8		75	66	13	0.5	4	Feb
March		4	40	11	51	26	79	-10	14		73	62	18	0.7	6	March
April		9	49	16	61	28	83	-2	29		70	56	23	0.9	5	April
May		16	61	24	75	36	96	8	46		60	48	10	0.4	3	May
June		21	70	29	84	40	104	10	50	Medium	58	45	10	0.4	1	June
July		24	76	32	90	42	108	12	53	Medium	55	42	5	0.2	1	July
Aug		24	75	32	89	39	103	14	57	Medium	52	41	5	0.2	1	Aug
Sept		19	66	27	80	37	98	7	45	Moderate	56	45	5	0.2	1	Sept
Oct		13	55	19	67	29	85	1	33		61	51	10	0.4	2	Oct
Nov		7	44	12	54	24	75	-13	8		69	60	13	0.5	4	Nov
Dec		3	38	8	46	18	65	-13	8		76	68	13	0.5	6	Dec

Based on readings for 25 years at 40°00′ N, 52°59′ E, altitude 21 m/68 ft

GRAND TURK

THE TURKS

	Sunshine	Temperatures								Discomfort from heat and humidity	Precipitation and humidity			Wet days	
	average hours per day	Average daily				Highest recorded		Lowest recorded			Relative humidity	Average monthly precipitation		more than 0.25 mm/0.01 in	
		minimum		maximum											
		°C	°F	°C	°F	°C	°F	°C	°F		%	mm	in		
Jan	7	21	70	27	81	30	86	16	60			56	2.2	13	Jan
Feb	8	21	70	27	81	31	88	16	61			36	1.4	8	Feb
March	9	22	71	28	82	32	90	17	63			28	1.1	8	March
April	9	23	73	29	84	33	91	19	67			38	1.5	6	April
May	9	24	75	30	86	34	93	19	66			66	2.6	8	May
June	8	25	77	31	87	36	96	20	68			41	1.6	9	June
July	9	25	77	31	88	33	91	21	70			43	1.7	10	July
Aug	9	26	78	32	89	34	94	22	71			51	2.0	12	Aug
Sept	7	25	77	31	88	35	95	19	66			81	3.2	11	Sept
Oct	7	24	76	31	87	34	93	21	70			102	4.0	13	Oct
Nov	7	23	73	29	84	33	91	18	65			114	4.5	14	Nov
Dec	7	22	71	28	82	32	89	19	66			69	2.7	13	Dec

Based on readings for 10 years at 21°29′ N, 71°07′ W, altitude 3 m/11 ft

Tuvalu

See map page 17

Tuvalu occupies nine islands as well as numerous islets and reefs in the southwest Pacific, east of the Solomon Islands. The country shares with its neighbours the features of a typical tropical oceanic climate. Very similar conditions prevail throughout the year with high temperatures and humidity. The daily range of temperature is quite small – about 4°–5° C/10° F. There is abundant rainfall. Being south of the equator, Tuvalu has its season of maximum rainfall between November and April. On some islands there is no great difference between the amount of rain from month to month. Tropical cyclones are less frequent than in the western Pacific north of the equator.

Except in the wettest places, where cloud is more frequent, the country has moderately large amounts of sunshine, averaging from six to eight hours a day.

Much of the rainfall comes in short, heavy showers, often after a sunny morning, but periods of heavy rain lasting a day or so occur in the wetter months.

In this area of the Pacific the principal difference in the weather and climate is the amount of rainfall per month. Temperature and humidity are very similar from one island to another, but the amount of rainfall varies with altitude and with exposure of the coast to the dominant southeast trade winds. The number of wet days varies from island to island much less than the amount of rain. The climate may generally be described as pleasant and healthy, although the combination of high temperature and humidity can be a little oppressive when not tempered by sea breezes or a brisk wind.

The tables for **Kieta** (p. 281) on the island of Bougainville and **Apia** (p. 319) in Samoa show weather that is similar to Tuvalu's.

Uganda

See map page 21

Uganda is a landlocked East African country about the same size as the United Kingdom; it is situated between 4° N and 1° S. It includes within its borders about half of Lake Victoria, the largest lake in Africa, about half of Lake Albert, and the whole of the smaller Lake Kioga. These lakes form part of the source region of the White Nile, fed by the equatorial rains of Uganda and adjacent countries. The country is bordered on the north by the Sudan, east by Kenya, south by Tanzania and Rwanda, and west by the Congo Democratic Republic.

Uganda shares with Kenya and the Congo the same features of equatorial climate; this is modified by the elevation of the country, most of which is a plateau 1,000–1,400 m/3,500–4,500 ft above sea level. In the west and southwest there are high mountains, including the Ruwenzori Range, which rise well over 3,000 m/10,000 ft.

The sequence of weather and climate around the year is similar to that described for Kenya on pp. 207–10. Much of Uganda, however, is wetter than Kenya. This is because of the influence of Lake Victoria, an important local source of atmospheric moisture and thunderstorms; in addition, the west of the country is often influenced by moist

southwesterly winds bringing rains from the Congo Democratic Republic. The wettest areas are along the shores of Lake Victoria and in the western mountain districts; these receive over 1,500 mm/60 in of rain per year. Parts of central and northeastern Uganda receive less than 1,000 mm/40 in of rain per year; this is often much less since rainfall is unreliable from year to year.

Most of Uganda has the typical double rainy season found in the Kenya Highlands, but towards the north these two rainy seasons tend to merge into a single long wet period with a single dry period. Over most of Uganda the weather is pleasant and not uncomfortable for much of the year. There is much sunny weather with daily hours of sunshine averaging from six to eight and only much less than this in the wetter mountain districts. Temperatures are never excessively high and humidity does not reach the consistently high levels found in equatorial lowlands. Wet spells lasting a day or two are not unusual but much of the rain comes in heavy thundery showers. There is no real cool season but the daily range of temperature is enough to make the nights cool rather than chilly.

The table for **Entebbe** (opposite and above) shows the influence of Lake Victoria on rainfall and humidity. Compared **Kampala** (opposite), which is

ENTEBBE

LAKESHORE UGANDA

Sunshine	Temperatures								Discomfort from heat and humidity	Precipitation and humidity				Wet days
	Average daily				Highest recorded		Lowest recorded			Relative humidity 7:30 13:30		Average monthly precipitation		
	minimum		maximum											
average hours per day	°C	°F	°C	°F	°C	°F	°C	°F		%		mm	in	more than 0.25 mm/0.01 in
Jan 8	18	64	27	80	32	89	14	57	Medium	85	63	66	2.6	9 Jan
Feb 7	18	64	27	80	32	90	14	57	Medium	85	65	91	3.6	11 Feb
March 7	18	65	26	79	33	91	14	57	Medium	86	69	160	6.3	16 March
April 6	18	65	26	78	28	83	15	59	Medium	86	72	257	10.1	22 April
May 6	18	65	25	77	28	82	15	59	Medium	87	74	244	9.6	23 May
June 6	17	63	25	77	29	84	14	58	Medium	86	72	122	4.8	14 June
July 6	17	62	24	76	28	82	12	54	Moderate	86	70	76	3.0	10 July
Aug 6	17	62	25	77	29	84	13	56	Medium	87	70	74	2.9	12 Aug
Sept 6	17	62	26	78	31	87	14	57	Medium	85	68	74	2.9	11 Sept
Oct 7	17	63	26	79	29	85	14	57	Medium	82	66	94	3.7	13 Oct
Nov 7	18	64	26	79	32	89	14	58	Medium	84	67	132	5.2	17 Nov
Dec 7	17	63	26	79	29	85	14	57	Medium	85	66	117	4.6	12 Dec

Based on readings for 15 years at 0°04′ N, 32°29′ E, altitude 1182 m/3878 ft

KAMPALA

LAKESHORE UGANDA

Sunshine	Temperatures								Discomfort from heat and humidity	Precipitation and humidity				Wet days
	Average daily				Highest recorded		Lowest recorded			Relative humidity 7:30 13:30		Average monthly precipitation		
	minimum		maximum											
average hours per day	°C	°F	°C	°F	°C	°F	°C	°F		%		mm	in	more than 0.25 mm/0.01 in
Jan 5	18	65	28	83	33	92	12	54	Medium	78	54	46	1.8	9 Jan
Feb 6	18	65	28	82	36	97	14	57	Medium	81	56	61	2.4	9 Feb
March 5	18	64	27	81	33	92	13	56	Medium	84	62	130	5.1	14 March
April 4	18	64	26	79	33	91	14	57	Medium	88	69	175	6.9	19 April
May 4	17	63	25	78	29	84	15	59	Medium	89	72	147	5.8	19 May
June 6	17	63	25	77	29	85	12	53	Moderate	88	69	74	2.9	11 June
July 6	17	62	25	77	29	85	12	53	Moderate	89	66	46	1.8	10 July
Aug 5	16	61	25	78	29	85	12	53	Moderate	89	66	86	3.4	14 Aug
Sept 5	17	62	27	80	31	88	13	56	Medium	86	65	91	3.6	12 Sept
Oct 5	17	63	27	81	32	90	13	56	Medium	83	64	97	3.8	14 Oct
Nov 5	17	63	27	80	32	89	14	58	Medium	83	63	122	4.8	16 Nov
Dec 4	17	63	27	80	32	90	12	53	Medium	81	62	99	3.9	12 Dec

Based on readings for 15 years at 0°02′ N, 32°36′ E, altitude 1312 m/4304 ft

KABALE										SOUTHWESTERN UGANDA		
Sunshine		Temperatures							Discomfort from heat and humidity	Precipitation and humidity			Wet days
		Average daily				Highest recorded		Lowest recorded		Relative humidity 7:30 13:30		Average monthly precipitation	
		minimum		maximum									
average hours per day		°C	°F	°C	°F	°C	°F	°C	°F	%		mm	in	more than 0.25 mm/0.01 in
Jan	5	9	49	24	75	29	85	4	40	Moderate	94	55	58	2.3	11	Jan
Feb	6	11	51	24	75	29	85	6	43	Moderate	94	57	97	3.8	13	Feb
March	5	11	51	23	74	28	83	7	44	Moderate	95	61	130	5.1	16	March
April	4	11	52	23	73	27	81	7	44	Moderate	96	66	125	4.9	20	April
May	4	11	52	22	72	26	79	6	43		96	68	91	3.6	16	May
June	6	9	49	22	72	27	81	4	40		94	62	28	1.1	5	June
July	6	8	47	23	74	28	82	3	38		90	53	20	0.8	3	July
Aug	5	9	49	23	74	29	85	3	37		91	49	58	2.3	8	Aug
Sept	5	10	50	24	75	28	83	6	42	Moderate	92	55	97	3.8	15	Sept
Oct	5	11	51	23	74	27	81	6	43	Moderate	93	60	99	3.9	18	Oct
Nov	5	11	51	23	73	28	82	6	43	Moderate	94	64	109	4.3	19	Nov
Dec	4	10	50	23	73	26	79	5	41	Moderate	95	61	86	3.4	15	Dec

Based on readings for 14 years at 1°17′ S, 29°59′ E, altitude 1871 m/6138 ft

a few miles from the lakeshore. These tables are representative of much of Uganda except the drier north and centre. The table for **Kabale** (above), which is situated in the hillier southwest and is sheltered from heavy rains on the mountains, shows the greater reduction of temperature during all months as a result of higher altitude.

Ukraine

See map page 19

Although the winters are cold in Ukraine and spells of extremely cold weather occur when easterly winds blow from Siberia, the winter is shorter than in the neighbouring areas of northern and central European Russia and the spring thaw comes earlier.

The table for **Kiev** (opposite and above) shows weather typical of north-central Ukraine. Towards the south, the climate becomes warmer. The south coast of the Crimean peninsula has mild winters, and it is a popular summer holiday resort. Although the summer climate here is sunny, with ten or more hours of sunshine a day, rain falls all the year round.

The table for **Simferopol** (opposite) shows weather conditions that are typical of the south coast of the Crimean peninsula.

KIEV

NORTHERN UKRAINE

Sunshine	Temperatures							Discomfort from heat and humidity	Precipitation and humidity				Wet days
	Average daily				Highest recorded		Lowest recorded			Relative humidity 8:00 14:00		Average monthly precipitation	
	minimum		maximum										
average hours per day	°C	°F	°C	°F	°C	°F	°C	°F		%		mm	in	more than 0.1 mm/0.004 in
Jan	1	-10	14	-4	24	8	46	-25	-13		87	81	58	2.3	18	Jan
Feb	2	-8	17	-2	28	9	49	-22	-8		87	75	59	2.3	18	Feb
March	4	-4	25	3	37	22	72	-25	-13		86	69	51	2.0	16	March
April	6	5	41	14	56	27	81	-6	21		77	56	45	1.8	11	April
May	9	11	51	21	69	30	86	-1	31		69	50	49	1.9	13	May
June	9	14	56	24	75	34	93	4	39	Moderate	71	51	55	2.2	11	June
July	10	15	59	25	77	34	94	9	48	Moderate	73	53	91	3.6	13	July
Aug	8	14	58	24	76	35	94	3	38	Moderate	78	55	91	3.6	12	Aug
Sept	7	10	50	20	68	30	85	2	35		80	54	30	1.2	8	Sept
Oct	5	6	42	13	56	26	79	-5	23		87	65	33	1.3	10	Oct
Nov	2	0	32	6	42	18	65	-17	1		92	82	56	2.2	15	Nov
Dec	1	-6	22	-1	30	11	51	-24	-12		89	84	59	2.3	19	Dec

Based on readings for 8 years at 50°24′ N, 30°27′ E, altitude 179 m/587 ft

SIMFEROPOL

CRIMEAN PENINSULA

Sunshine	Temperatures							Discomfort from heat and humidity	Precipitation and humidity				Wet days
	Average daily				Highest recorded		Lowest recorded			Relative humidity 8:30 14:30		Average monthly precipitation	
	minimum		maximum										
average hours per day	°C	°F	°C	°F	°C	°F	°C	°F		%		mm	in	more than 0.1 mm/0.004 in
Jan	2	-5	24	3	37	17	63	-20	-3		87	89	46	1.8	15	Jan
Feb	4	-3	26	5	40	21	69	-21	-5		84	73	37	1.5	15	Feb
March	5	-1	31	9	47	28	82	-14	8		79	61	40	1.6	12	March
April	7	5	41	16	60	31	88	-9	15		67	49	28	1.1	9	April
May	10	10	50	22	71	32	89	1	34		62	47	38	1.5	9	May
June	11	14	57	25	78	34	94	7	44	Moderate	64	47	35	1.4	9	June
July	11	16	60	28	82	35	94	10	50	Medium	63	45	64	2.5	8	July
Aug	10	15	60	28	82	37	98	4	39	Medium	64	42	39	1.5	6	Aug
Sept	9	12	53	23	74	36	97	3	38		70	46	36	1.4	7	Sept
Oct	8	7	44	17	63	30	85	-5	23		79	52	24	0.9	6	Oct
Nov	4	4	40	12	54	26	80	-10	14		86	71	43	1.7	13	Nov
Dec	2	0	32	7	44	21	70	-18	1		87	81	52	2.1	16	Dec

Based on readings for 8 years at 45°01′ N, 33°59′ E, altitude 205 m/673 ft

SHARJAH												COASTAL UNITED ARAB EMIRATES		
Sunshine	Temperatures								Discomfort from heat and humidity	Precipitation and humidity					Wet days
average hours per day	Average daily				Highest recorded		Lowest recorded			Relative humidity 7:30 15:30		Average monthly precipitation			more than 2.5 mm/0.1 in
	minimum		maximum												
	°C	°F	°C	°F	°C	°F	°C	°F		%		mm	in		
Jan	12	54	23	74	29	85	3	37	Moderate	81	61	23	0.9	2.0		Jan
Feb	14	57	24	75	33	91	8	46	Moderate	81	63	23	0.9	2.0		Feb
March	16	60	27	80	40	104	8	46	Medium	74	61	10	0.4	1.0		March
April	18	65	30	86	39	103	12	53	High	66	63	5	0.2	0.3		April
May	22	72	34	93	43	109	16	61	Extreme	61	63	0	0.0	0.0		May
June	25	77	36	97	44	112	19	67	Extreme	64	65	0	0.0	0.0		June
July	28	82	38	100	47	117	23	73	Extreme	64	64	0	0.0	0.0		July
Aug	28	82	39	103	48	118	23	73	Extreme	66	64	0	0.0	0.0		Aug
Sept	25	77	37	99	45	113	21	69	Extreme	73	64	0	0.0	0.0		Sept
Oct	22	71	33	92	40	104	18	64	High	77	62	0	0.0	0.0		Oct
Nov	18	64	31	87	36	97	12	54	High	78	59	10	0.4	0.2		Nov
Dec	14	58	26	78	31	88	8	47	Medium	82	62	36	1.4	2.0		Dec

Based on readings for 11 years at 25°20′ N, 55°24′ E, altitude 5.5 m/18 ft

United Arab Emirates

See map page 22

This territory consists of a union of seven small Arab sheikhdoms formerly under British protection and, at that time, called the Trucial Oman. They lie on the southern shore of the Arabian (Persian) Gulf between Qatar on the west and Oman on the east. They have a land boundary with Saudi Arabia on the northern fringes of the Rub' al Khali. Most of the country is flat and consists of a sandy or rocky desert. Annual rainfall is very low and mostly occurs between November and March. Temperatures are very high between May and September and warm to mild for the rest of the year. Winters are warmer than in Kuwait or the interior of Saudi Arabia.

Summer conditions are most unpleasant on the coast where humidity is high. Both inland and on the coast there is some danger of heat exhaustion and heatstroke during the hottest weather. The table for **Sharjah** (above) is representative of conditions on the coast. For more details about the weather and climate of Arabia see the description for Saudi Arabia on p. 312.

United Kingdom

The United Kingdom consists of England, Scotland, Wales, and Northern Ireland. Situated off the northwest coast of Europe, these islands extend between 50° and 60° N. The climate of Britain is notoriously variable and changeable from day to day. Weather is generally cool to mild with frequent cloud and rain but occasional settled spells of weather occur at all seasons.

Visitors are often surprised by the long summer days, which are a consequence of the northerly latitude; in the north of Scotland in midsummer the day is eighteen hours long and twilight lasts all night. Conversely, winter days are short.

The frequent changes of weather affect all parts of the country in very much the same way; there are no

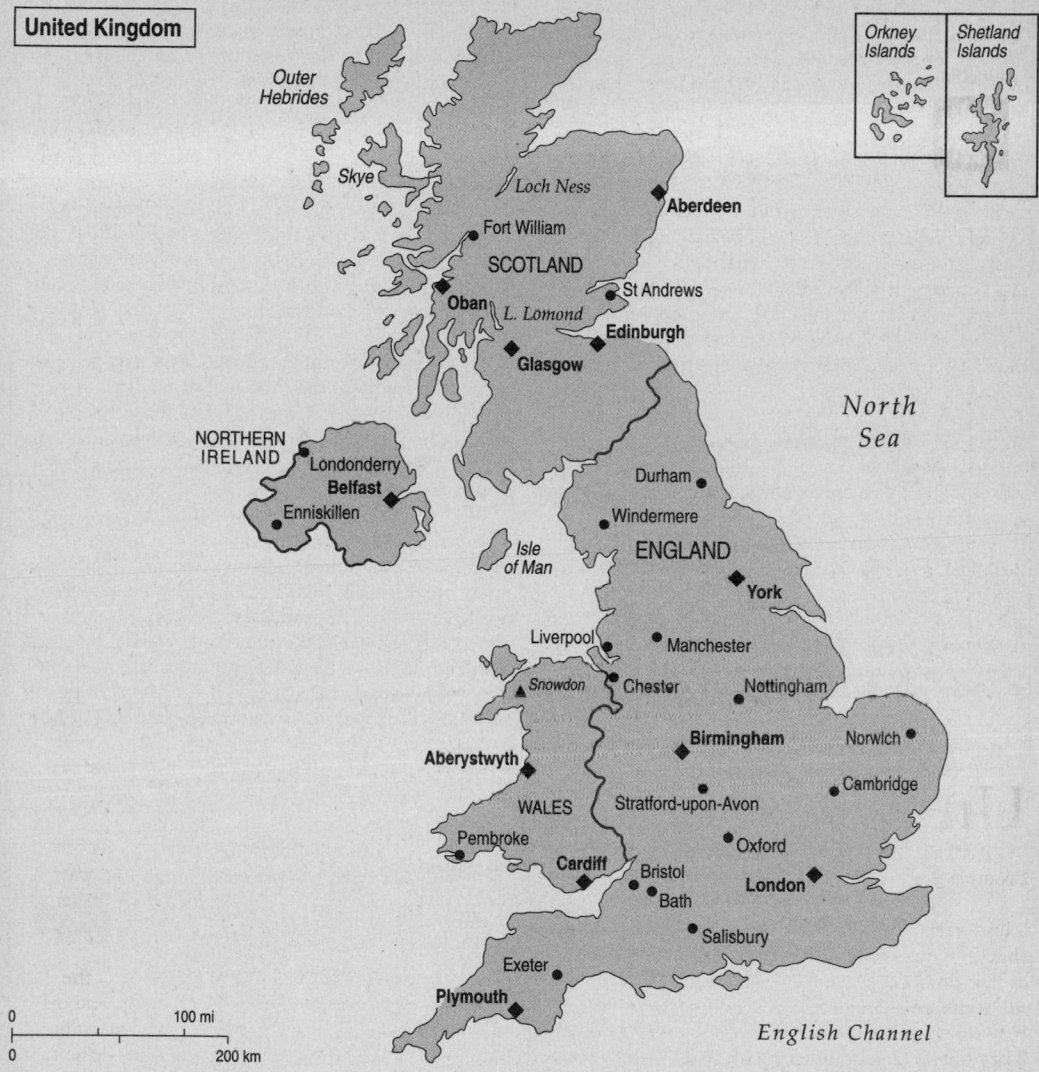

United Kingdom

Outer
Hebrides

Orkney
Islands

Shetland
Islands

Skye

Loch Ness

Aberdeen

Fort William

SCOTLAND

Oban

St Andrews

L. Lomond

Edinburgh

Glasgow

North
Sea

NORTHERN
IRELAND

Londonderry

Belfast

Enniskillen

Durham

Windermere

Isle
of Man

ENGLAND

York

Liverpool

Manchester

Snowdon

Chester

Nottingham

Birmingham

Norwich

Aberystwyth

Cambridge

WALES

Stratford-upon-Avon

Pembroke

Oxford

Cardiff

Bristol

London

Bath

Salisbury

Exeter

Plymouth

English Channel

0   100 mi

0   200 km

great differences from one part of the country to another.

While the south is usually a little warmer than the north and the west wetter than the east, the continual changes of British weather mean that, on occasions, these differences may be reversed. Extremes of weather are rare in Britain but they do occur. For example, in December 1981 and January 1982, parts of southern and central England experienced for a few days lower temperatures than central Europe and Moscow! During the long spells of hot, sunny weather in the summers of 1975 and 1976, parts of Britain were drier and warmer than many places in the western Mediterranean.

The greatest extremes of weather and climate in Britain occur in the mountains of Scotland, Wales, and northern England. Here at altitudes exceeding 600 m/2,000 ft conditions are wet and cloudy for much of the year with annual rainfall exceeding 1,500 mm/60 in and in places reaching as much as 5,000 mm/200 in. These are among the wettest places in Europe. Winter conditions may be severe with very strong winds, driving rain, or blizzards.

In spite of occasional heavy snowfalls on the Scottish mountains, conditions are not really good for skiing and there has been only a limited development of winter sports resorts. Because of severe conditions which can arise very suddenly on mountains, walkers and climbers who go unprepared face the risk of exposure or even frostbite. Conditions may be vastly different from those suggested by the weather at lower levels.

Virtually all permanent settlement in Britain lies below 300 m/1,000 ft and at these levels weather conditions are usually much more congenial. As a general rule the western side of Britain is cloudier, wetter, and milder in winter, with cooler summers than the eastern side of the country. See tables for **Oban** (below) on the west coast of Scotland, for **Belfast** (opposite) in Northern Ireland, and for **Cardiff** (opposite and below) and **Aberystwyth** (p. 374), both in Wales.

The eastern side of Britain is drier the year round, with a tendency for summer rain to be heavier than that of winter. The east is a little colder in winter and warmer in summer. See the tables for **London** (p. 374) in southeastern England, **York** (p. 375) in northeastern England, and **Edinburgh** (p. 375) in eastern Scotland.

Much of central England (see the table for **Birmingham** on p. 376) has very similar weather to that of the east and south of the country.

The table for **Plymouth** (p. 376) shows that

southwestern England shares the greater summer warmth of southern England but experiences rather milder and wetter winters than the east of the country.

The average number of hours of sunshine is greatest in the south and southeast of England and least in the north and west. Western Scotland, Wales, and Northern Ireland have rather less sunshine than most of England. In Britain daily sunshine hours range from between one and two in midwinter to between five and seven in midsummer.

Winter sunshine is much reduced in Britain because of frequent fogs and low cloud. This is a consequence of winds from the Atlantic and seas surrounding Britain, which bring high humidity. For the same reason, British mountains are particularly cloudy and wet.

The chief differences of weather and climate in Britain can be summed up by saying that Scotland is rarely much colder than England despite its more northerly latitude. Summers in Scotland, however, are usually shorter and rather cooler. Wales, western Scotland, and Northern Ireland are wetter the year round than most of England. Northwestern England and the Lake District are, however, particularly wet and cloudy.

OBAN											WESTERN SCOTLAND		
Sunshine		Temperatures							Discomfort from heat and humidity	Precipitation and humidity			Wet days
		Average daily				Highest recorded		Lowest recorded		Relative humidity	Average monthly precipitation		
average hours per day		minimum		maximum									more than 0.25 mm/0.01 in
		°C	°F	°C	°F	°C	°F	°C	°F	%	mm	in	
Jan	1	2	35	6	43	13	56	−8	17		146	5.8	20	Jan
Feb	2	1	35	7	44	13	55	−7	20		109	4.3	17	Feb
March	3	3	37	9	48	19	67	−6	22		83	3.3	15	March
April	5	4	40	11	52	21	69	−2	29		90	3.5	17	April
May	7	7	44	14	58	26	78	−4	25		72	2.8	16	May
June	6	9	49	16	61	29	84	3	37		87	3.4	16	June
July	4	11	51	17	63	29	85	5	41		120	4.7	20	July
Aug	4	11	51	17	63	27	81	3	38		116	4.6	19	Aug
Sept	4	9	49	15	60	24	75	1	33		141	5.6	19	Sept
Oct	2	7	44	12	54	22	72	−5	23		169	6.7	21	Oct
Nov	1	4	40	9	49	16	60	−5	23		146	5.8	20	Nov
Dec	1	3	37	7	45	14	58	−6	21		172	6.8	22	Dec

Based on readings for 30 years at 56°25′ N, 5°30′ W, altitude 69 m/226 ft

BELFAST

NORTHERN IRELAND

	Sunshine	Temperatures									Discomfort from heat and humidity	Precipitation and humidity				Wet days
		Average daily				Highest recorded		Lowest recorded				Relative humidity 8:30 14:30		Average monthly precipitation		
		minimum		maximum												
	average hours per day	°C	°F	°C	°F	°C	°F	°C	°F			%		mm	in	more than 0.25 mm/0.01 in
Jan	1	2	35	6	43	13	56	-13	9			92	87	80	3.2	20	Jan
Feb	2	2	35	7	44	14	57	-12	11			91	80	52	2.1	17	Feb
March	3	3	37	9	49	19	67	-12	10			88	74	50	2.0	16	March
April	5	4	39	12	53	21	69	-4	24			83	69	48	1.9	16	April
May	6	6	43	15	59	26	79	-3	26			79	66	52	2.1	15	May
June	6	9	49	18	64	28	83	-1	31			80	71	68	2.7	16	June
July	4	11	52	18	65	29	85	4	39			84	73	94	3.7	19	July
Aug	4	11	51	18	65	28	82	1	34			87	75	77	3.0	17	Aug
Sept	4	9	49	16	61	26	78	-2	28			89	78	80	3.2	18	Sept
Oct	3	7	44	13	55	21	70	-4	24			91	80	83	3.3	19	Oct
Nov	2	4	39	9	48	16	61	-6	21			92	85	72	2.8	19	Nov
Dec	1	3	37	7	44	14	58	-11	13			92	89	90	3.5	21	Dec

Based on readings for 30 years at 54°39′ N, 6°13′ W, altitude 67 m/217 ft

CARDIFF

WALES

	Sunshine	Temperatures									Discomfort from heat and humidity	Precipitation and humidity			Wet days
		Average daily				Highest recorded		Lowest recorded				Relative humidity 9:00	Average monthly precipitation		
		minimum		maximum											
	average hours per day	°C	°F	°C	°F	°C	°F	°C	°F			%	mm	in	more than 0.25 mm/0.01 in
Jan	2	2	35	7	45	15	59	-17	2			89	108	4.3	18	Jan
Feb	3	2	35	7	45	16	61	-9	15			87	72	2.8	14	Feb
March	4	3	38	10	50	20	68	-8	18			82	63	2.5	13	March
April	5	5	41	13	56	24	75	-3	27			74	65	2.6	13	April
May	6	8	46	16	61	29	84	-1	31			74	76	3.0	13	May
June	7	11	51	19	68	31	87	4	39			73	63	2.5	13	June
July	6	12	54	20	69	31	88	7	44			76	89	3.5	14	July
Aug	6	13	55	21	69	33	91	6	43			78	97	3.8	15	Aug
Sept	5	11	51	18	64	28	83	2	35			81	99	3.9	16	Sept
Oct	3	8	46	14	58	25	77	-3	26			85	109	4.3	16	Oct
Nov	2	5	41	10	51	18	65	-3	26			88	116	4.7	17	Nov
Dec	2	3	37	8	46	15	59	-7	19			89	108	4.3	18	Dec

Based on readings for 30 years at 51°30′ N, 3°10′ W, altitude 62 m/203 ft

ABERYSTWYTH — WALES

Sunshine average hours per day	Temperatures										Discomfort from heat and humidity	Precipitation and humidity				Wet days more than 0.25 mm/0.01 in	
	Average daily				Highest recorded		Lowest recorded					Relative humidity	Average monthly precipitation				
	minimum		maximum														
	°C	°F	°C	°F	°C	°F	°C	°F				%	mm	in			
Jan 2	2	36	7	44	14	57	-11	12					97	3.8	21	Jan
Feb 3	2	35	7	44	15	59	-9	16					72	2.8	17	Feb
March 4	3	38	9	49	20	68	-7	20					60	2.4	16	March
April 5	5	41	11	52	23	73	-3	27					56	2.2	16	April
May 6	7	45	15	58	26	78	-1	30					65	2.6	16	May
June 7	10	50	17	62	31	87	4	39					76	3.0	16	June
July 5	12	54	18	64	31	88	6	43					99	3.9	19	July
Aug 5	12	54	18	65	29	85	5	41					93	3.7	18	Aug
Sept 4	11	51	16	62	26	78	2	36					108	4.3	19	Sept
Oct 3	8	46	13	56	25	77	-2	28					118	4.7	20	Oct
Nov 2	5	41	10	50	17	63	-3	27					111	4.4	20	Nov
Dec 2	4	38	8	47	15	59	-6	22					96	3.8	22	Dec

Based on readings for 30 years at 52°25' N, 4°03' W, altitude 138 m/453 ft

LONDON — SOUTHEASTERN ENGLAND

Sunshine average hours per day	Temperatures										Discomfort from heat and humidity	Precipitation and humidity					Wet days more than 0.25 mm/0.01 in	
	Average daily				Highest recorded		Lowest recorded					Relative humidity 9:00 15:00		Average monthly precipitation				
	minimum		maximum															
	°C	°F	°C	°F	°C	°F	°C	°F				%	%	mm	in			
Jan 1	2	36	6	43	14	58	-10	15				86	77	54	2.1	15	Jan
Feb 2	2	36	7	44	16	61	-9	15				85	72	40	1.6	13	Feb
March 4	3	38	10	50	21	71	-8	18				81	64	37	1.5	11	March
April 5	6	42	13	56	26	78	-2	28				71	56	37	1.5	12	April
May 6	8	47	17	62	30	86	-1	30				70	57	46	1.8	12	May
June 7	12	53	20	69	33	91	5	41				70	58	45	1.8	11	June
July 6	14	56	22	71	34	93	7	45				71	59	57	2.2	12	July
Aug 6	13	56	21	71	33	92	6	43				76	62	59	2.3	11	Aug
Sept 5	11	52	19	65	30	86	3	37				80	65	49	1.9	13	Sept
Oct 3	8	46	14	58	26	78	-4	26				85	70	57	2.2	13	Oct
Nov 2	5	42	10	50	19	66	-5	23				85	78	64	2.5	15	Nov
Dec 1	4	38	7	45	15	59	-7	19				87	81	48	1.9	15	Dec

Based on readings for 30 years at 51°28' N, 0°19' W, altitude 5 m/16 ft

YORK

NORTHEASTERN ENGLAND

	Sunshine average hours per day	Temperatures								Discomfort from heat and humidity	Precipitation and humidity			Wet days more than 0.25 mm/0.01 in	
		Average daily				Highest recorded		Lowest recorded			Relative humidity 9:00	Average monthly precipitation			
		minimum		maximum											
		°C	°F	°C	°F	°C	°F	°C	°F		%	mm	in		
Jan	1	1	33	6	43	15	59	−14	7		89	59	2.3	17	Jan
Feb	2	1	34	7	44	17	62	−10	14		87	46	1.8	15	Feb
March	3	2	36	10	49	21	70	−13	9		81	37	1.5	13	March
April	5	4	40	13	55	24	75	−3	27		73	41	1.6	13	April
May	6	7	44	16	61	29	85	−1	30		71	50	2.0	13	May
June	6	10	50	19	67	32	90	2	36		71	50	2.0	14	June
July	6	12	54	21	70	31	88	5	41		74	62	2.4	15	July
Aug	5	12	53	21	69	33	92	4	39		77	68	2.7	14	Aug
Sept	4	10	50	18	64	29	84	−1	31		80	55	2.2	14	Sept
Oct	3	7	44	14	57	26	78	−4	24		85	56	2.2	15	Oct
Nov	2	4	39	10	49	19	66	−7	20		88	65	2.6	17	Nov
Dec	1	2	36	7	45	16	60	−8	18		88	50	2.0	17	Dec

Based on readings for 30 years at 53°57′ N, 1°05′ W, altitude 17 m/56 ft

EDINBURGH

EASTERN SCOTLAND

	Sunshine average hours per day	Temperatures								Discomfort from heat and humidity	Precipitation and humidity			Wet days more than 0.25 mm/0.01 in	
		Average daily				Highest recorded		Lowest recorded			Relative humidity 9:00	Average monthly precipitation			
		minimum		maximum											
		°C	°F	°C	°F	°C	°F	°C	°F		%	mm	in		
Jan	2	1	34	6	42	14	57	−8	17		84	57	2.2	17	Jan
Feb	3	1	34	6	43	14	58	−9	15		83	39	1.5	15	Feb
March	4	2	36	8	46	20	68	−6	21		81	39	1.5	15	March
April	5	4	39	11	51	22	72	−4	25		75	39	1.5	14	April
May	6	6	43	14	56	24	76	−1	31		76	54	2.1	14	May
June	6	9	49	17	62	28	83	3	37		75	47	1.9	15	June
July	5	11	52	18	65	28	83	6	42		78	83	3.3	17	July
Aug	4	11	52	18	64	28	82	4	40		80	77	3.0	16	Aug
Sept	4	9	49	16	60	25	77	1	33		80	57	2.2	16	Sept
Oct	3	7	44	12	54	20	68	−2	28		82	65	2.6	17	Oct
Nov	2	4	39	9	48	19	67	−4	24		83	62	2.4	17	Nov
Dec	1	2	36	7	44	14	58	−7	20		84	57	2.2	18	Dec

Based on readings for 30 years at 55°55′ N, 3°11′ W, altitude 134 m/440 ft

BIRMINGHAM — MIDLANDS OF ENGLAND

	Sunshine average hours per day	Temperatures — Average daily				Highest recorded		Lowest recorded		Discomfort from heat and humidity	Relative humidity 9:00	15:00	Average monthly precipitation mm	in	Wet days more than 0.25 mm/0.01 in	
		minimum °C	°F	maximum °C	°F	°C	°F	°C	°F		%					
Jan	1	2	35	5	42	13	56	-12	11		89	82	74	3.0	17	Jan
Feb	2	2	35	6	43	16	60	-9	16		89	76	54	2.1	15	Feb
March	3	3	37	9	48	21	69	-7	19		85	68	50	2.0	13	March
April	5	5	40	12	54	24	75	-2	29		75	58	53	2.1	13	April
May	5	7	45	16	60	29	85	-1	30		74	58	64	2.5	14	May
June	6	10	51	19	66	31	87	3	37		74	59	50	2.0	13	June
July	5	12	54	20	68	32	90	6	43		75	62	69	2.7	15	July
Aug	5	12	54	20	68	33	91	6	43		80	64	69	2.7	14	Aug
Sept	4	10	51	17	63	27	81	3	37		84	67	61	2.4	14	Sept
Oct	3	7	45	13	55	25	77	-2	28		88	73	69	2.7	15	Oct
Nov	2	5	40	9	48	19	67	-4	24		90	80	84	3.3	17	Nov
Dec	1	3	37	6	44	14	58	-6	21		90	84	67	2.6	18	Dec

Based on readings for 30 years at 52°29′ N, 1°56′ W, altitude 163 m/535 ft

PLYMOUTH — SOUTHWESTERN ENGLAND

	Sunshine average hours per day	Temperatures — Average daily				Highest recorded		Lowest recorded		Discomfort from heat and humidity	Relative humidity 8:30	14:30	Average monthly precipitation mm	in	Wet days more than 0.25 mm/0.01 in	
		minimum °C	°F	maximum °C	°F	°C	°F	°C	°F		%					
Jan	2	4	39	8	47	14	57	-9	16		89	81	99	3.9	19	Jan
Feb	3	4	38	8	47	15	59	-8	17		88	78	74	2.9	15	Feb
March	4	5	40	10	50	19	67	-5	23		86	74	69	2.7	14	March
April	6	6	43	12	54	22	72	-2	29		78	69	53	2.1	12	April
May	7	8	47	15	59	26	79	-1	31		77	71	63	2.5	12	May
June	7	11	52	18	64	28	82	2	35		80	73	53	2.1	12	June
July	6	13	55	19	66	29	84	7	45		81	74	70	2.8	14	July
Aug	6	13	55	19	67	31	88	4	39		83	75	77	3.0	14	Aug
Sept	5	12	53	18	64	27	81	3	37		86	75	78	3.1	15	Sept
Oct	4	9	49	15	58	23	74	-2	29		88	77	91	3.6	16	Oct
Nov	2	7	44	11	52	17	63	-4	25		88	79	113	4.5	17	Nov
Dec	2	5	41	9	49	14	58	-5	23		89	82	110	4.3	18	Dec

Based on readings for 30 years at 50°21′ N, 4°07′ W, altitude 27 m/89 ft

Snow may occur anywhere in Britain in winter or even spring but, except on the hills, it rarely lies for more than a few days. In some winters there may be very little snow, but every fifteen or twenty years it may lie for some weeks during a prolonged cold spell.

Visitors to Britain will rarely experience severe or unpleasant weather for long unless they venture on

the hills. They should be prepared for rapid changes of weather at all seasons, however, and recognize that there is good reason for weather being a major talking point in Britain.

Visitors to Northern Ireland should consult the description of weather for the Republic of Ireland (p. 190) which applies to the whole of the island.

United States of America

See map p. 378

The United States is the fourth largest country in the world with an area of over 7.8 million sq km/ 3 million sq mi. It is bordered on the north by Canada and on the south by Mexico.

The area described here is situated between 25° and 49° N and lies entirely outside the tropics. It includes areas with a very great range of weather and climatic conditions around the year. On occasions parts of the USA experience extremes of heat and cold characteristic of hot tropical deserts or cold Arctic continental regions. Another feature of the weather and climate of the United States is the variation of weather over quite short periods at all seasons of the year.

The reason for this variation of weather is the country's position in the belt of disturbed westerly winds so that, for much of the year, most regions of the USA are affected by cyclonic storms or depressions with their associated warm and cold fronts. Most of the southwest to east or northeast winds bring cloud, precipitation, and disturbed, changeable weather. The central and northeastern parts of the USA are particularly liable to sudden changes of temperature during such periods of disturbed weather.

The central part of the USA – the Great Plains – which extend from the Rockies in the west to the Appalachian Mountains in the east, is mainly flat and mostly below 600 m/2,000 ft in height. This area is wide open to the influence of two very contrasting types of air-masses. Cold polar and Arctic air can sweep southwards from the Canadian Arctic regions and warm, humid tropical air can move north from the Caribbean and the Gulf of Mexico. Each imports its own properties of temperature and humidity. When one air-mass replaces another, particularly during winter and spring, the temperature may change by as much as 22°C/40°F and 28°C/50°F within a few hours. Such sudden changes may also occur in the northeast of

the country as far south as Virginia; farther south on the Atlantic and Gulf coasts the temperature changes are less dramatic but still produce a significant weather change.

On the Pacific coast and west of the main chain of the Rocky Mountains the influence of the Pacific Ocean makes for a more equable climate with a much smaller range of temperatures from winter to summer or from day to day. The maritime influences are to a large extent excluded from the centre of the country by the great mass of mountains and plateaux country which comprises the Rockies – the Western Cordillera.

The large size of the North American continent also makes for seasonal extremes of temperature: winter cold and summer heat. Only the Pacific shores and, to a lesser extent, the coast of the Gulf of Mexico and the Atlantic south of Virginia, benefit from the sea's moderating effect of keeping temperatures more equable around the year.

Compared with countries of western Europe in the same latitude, the United States has greater extremes of temperature and daily or weekly changes are more noticeable. Much of the Midwest has a more extreme or continental climate than central or eastern Europe. Only Canada or Russia east of the Urals are more extreme in terms of their annual range of temperature.

Some parts of the USA are liable to experience two particularly violent and destructive weather phenomena: hurricanes and tornadoes. Hurricanes affect the southeastern states bordering the Gulf of Mexico and the Atlantic once or twice in most years. These tropical storms, which bring very strong winds and torrential rainfall, move northeastwards from the Caribbean region before dying out in mid-Atlantic. They are described in more detail for the Caribbean Islands on p. 93.

A tornado is a very much more local and destructive storm of wind, often described as a 'whirlwind' or, in the USA, as a 'twister'. Tornadoes can cause almost complete destruction of buildings on a narrow path not more than a few hundred yards wide. They mainly occur in spring and summer on days when there are violent thunderstorms associated with rapid changes of temperature along, or near, a cold front.

Much of the western third of the United States consists of a series of high mountain chains and interior plateaux and basins which are collectively termed the Rockies or the Western Cordillera. Weather and climate are here very variable from place to place depending on altitude and the degree of exposure or shelter. There are many lofty mountain ranges with peaks above 4,250 m/14,000 ft, extensive high plateaux between 1,200 m/4,000 ft and 2,000 m/7,000 ft, and some small areas, such as Death Valley and the Salton Sink in southern California, which are below sea level.

This makes for a great variety of climatic conditions with some very wet and snowy mountain regions and some semi-arid or even desert lowlands with great extremes of temperature. By contrast, in the central plains of the USA and, to a lesser extent, on the

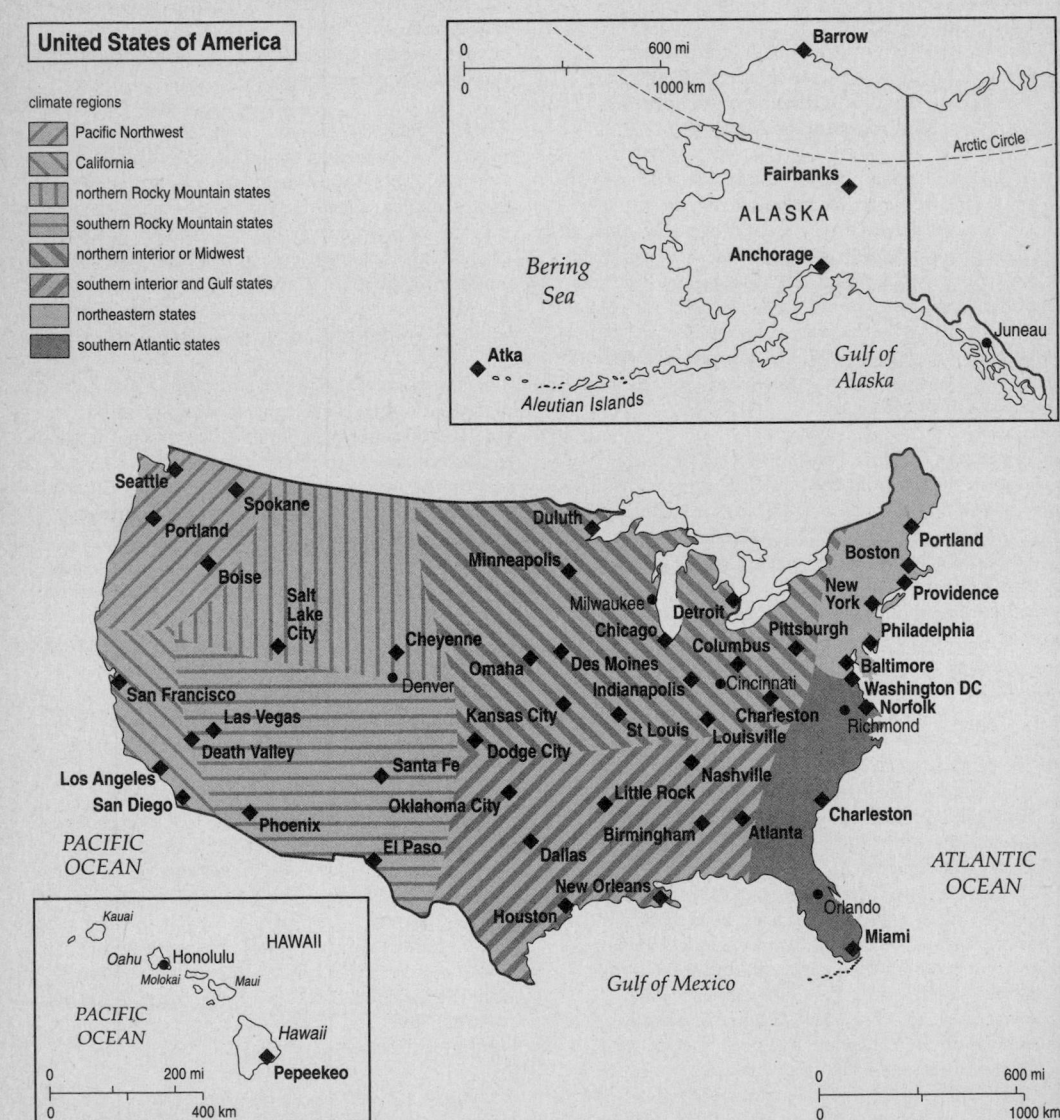

United States of America

climate regions

- Pacific Northwest
- California
- northern Rocky Mountain states
- southern Rocky Mountain states
- northern interior or Midwest
- southern interior and Gulf states
- northeastern states
- southern Atlantic states

Atlantic coast, changes of weather and climate are much more gradual and almost imperceptible over great distances.

For a more detailed account of the weather and climate of this large country it is convenient to divide the USA into the following climatic regions, broadly coinciding with particular groups of states: the northeastern states, the southern Atlantic states, the Midwest or northern interior, the southern interior and the Gulf states, the states of the Rocky Mountains regions, the states of the Pacific northwest, California, and Alaska. Climatic tables for the more important and representative places are included with the description of each region.

THE NORTHEASTERN STATES

Including (with towns and cities in parentheses): CONNECTICUT, DELAWARE, the DISTRICT OF COLUMBIA (Washington, DC), MAINE (Portland), MASSACHUSETTS (Boston), NEW HAMPSHIRE, NEW JERSEY, RHODE ISLAND (Providence) and VERMONT; the eastern parts of of NEW YORK (New York) and PENNSYLVANIA (Philadelphia); and northern MARYLAND (Baltimore).

This region can experience changeable weather around the year with moderate amounts of precipitation in all months. Towards the north the winters are wet and usually snowy but south of New York summer tends to be slightly wetter. Summer heat waves can produce temperatures over 38° C/ 100° F for a few days and such hot spells are usually made the more uncomfortable because the humidity on or near the coast is high. In the great cities of this densely populated area heat waves are even more uncomfortable for the temperatures in the city streets are often a few degrees higher than those recorded at meteorological stations, usually in large parks or rural districts.

Very cold spells can affect the whole region from time to time in winter or even in spring, with very severe snowfalls likely in the north. The region includes the northern Appalachian Mountains, whose heights rise to between 1,200–1,800 m/4,000–6,000 ft. At these higher levels winters can be prolonged and severe and there are many opportunities for winter sports.

In summer the mountains provide resorts where relief can be obtained from the heat and humidity of the extensive coastal plains which contain the largest cities. This region has a more extreme or continental climate than the British Isles; summers are warmer and winters colder. It is also more extreme in other respects; day-to-day changes in temperature can be much greater and individual falls of rain and snow are often heavier than in most parts of Britain.

Although this is one of the less sunny parts of the country, the northeastern states receive more sunshine round the year than most of northwestern Europe. Daily sunshine hours on the coast, and at lower levels inland, average from four to five in winter and as much as nine or ten in summer.

Locally, sunshine may be reduced on the coast by fog both in summer and winter; inland, or in the larger cities, winter fog may reduce the sunshine. Some valleys in the Appalachians are particularly foggy because of a combination of industrial pollution and valley mists in winter.

Characteristic weather for this region is represented by the the tables for **Baltimore, Maryland** (overleaf), **Boston, Massachusetts** (overleaf), **New York** (p. 381), **Philadelphia, Pennsylvania** (p. 381), **Portland, Maine** (p. 382), **Providence, Rhode Island** (p. 382), and **Washington, District of Columbia** (p. 383).

BALTIMORE, MARYLAND

NORTHEASTERN USA

	Sunshine	Temperatures								Discomfort from heat and humidity	Precipitation and humidity				Wet days	
		Average daily				Highest recorded		Lowest recorded			Relative humidity		Average monthly precipitation			
		minimum		maximum							8:00	12:00				
	average hours per day	°C	°F	°C	°F	°C	°F	°C	°F		%		mm	in	more than 0.25 mm/0.01 in	
Jan	5	-2	28	6	42	26	79	-21	-6		72	58	86	3.4	11	Jan
Feb	6	-2	28	6	43	28	83	-22	-7		70	56	81	3.2	10	Feb
March	6	2	35	11	51	32	90	-15	5		69	53	94	3.7	12	March
April	7	7	45	17	63	34	94	-9	15		65	50	89	3.5	11	April
May	8	13	56	23	74	37	98	1	34		67	51	91	3.6	11	May
June	10	18	65	28	82	41	105	8	46	Medium	70	53	97	3.8	11	June
July	10	21	69	30	86	42	107	12	54	Medium	71	52	112	4.4	11	July
Aug	9	19	67	29	84	41	105	11	51	Medium	74	55	114	4.5	11	Aug
Sept	8	16	61	26	78	38	101	4	39	Moderate	75	56	89	3.5	8	Sept
Oct	7	10	50	19	67	36	97	-1	30		74	53	76	3.0	8	Oct
Nov	5	4	40	12	54	28	82	-11	12		72	55	71	2.8	9	Nov
Dec	5	-1	31	7	44	23	74	-19	-3		71	58	79	3.1	10	Dec

Based on readings for 48 years at 39°17′ N, 76°37′ W, altitude 4 m/14 ft

BOSTON, MASSACHUSETTS

NORTHEASTERN USA

	Sunshine	Temperatures								Discomfort from heat and humidity	Precipitation and humidity				Wet days	
		Average daily				Highest recorded		Lowest recorded			Relative humidity		Average monthly precipitation			
		minimum		maximum							8:00	12:00				
	average hours per day	°C	°F	°C	°F	°C	°F	°C	°F		%		mm	in	more than 0.25 mm/0.01 in	
Jan	5	-7	20	2	36	21	70	-25	-13		72	63	91	3.6	12	Jan
Feb	6	-6	21	3	37	20	68	-28	-18		71	61	84	3.3	10	Feb
March	7	-2	28	6	43	30	86	-22	-8		70	58	97	3.8	12	March
April	7	3	38	12	54	32	89	-12	11		69	57	89	3.5	11	April
May	9	9	49	19	66	36	97	-1	31		70	61	79	3.1	11	May
June	10	14	58	24	75	38	100	5	41	Moderate	72	59	81	3.2	10	June
July	11	17	63	27	80	40	104	10	50	Medium	71	66	84	3.3	10	July
Aug	9	17	62	26	78	38	101	8	46	Medium	76	61	91	3.6	10	Aug
Sept	8	13	55	22	71	39	102	1	34		77	62	81	3.2	9	Sept
Oct	7	8	46	17	62	32	90	-4	25		75	58	84	3.3	9	Oct
Nov	5	2	35	9	49	26	78	-19	-2		73	65	91	3.6	10	Nov
Dec	5	-4	25	4	40	21	69	-27	-17		74	62	86	3.4	11	Dec

Based on readings for 59 years at 42°22′ N, 71°04′ W, altitude 38 m/124 ft

NEW YORK CITY — NORTHEASTERN USA

Month	Sunshine average hours per day	Average daily minimum °C	°F	Average daily maximum °C	°F	Highest recorded °C	°F	Lowest recorded °C	°F	Discomfort from heat and humidity	Relative humidity 7:30 %	12:00 %	Average monthly precipitation mm	in	Wet days more than 0.25 mm/0.01 in	Month
Jan	5	-4	24	3	37	20	68	-21	-6		72	60	94	3.7	12	Jan
Feb	6	-4	24	3	38	23	73	-26	-14		70	58	97	3.8	10	Feb
March	7	-1	30	7	45	29	84	-16	3		70	55	91	3.6	12	March
April	7	6	42	14	57	33	91	-11	12		68	53	81	3.2	11	April
May	8	12	53	20	68	35	95	1	34		70	54	81	3.2	11	May
June	10	16	60	25	77	36	97	7	44	Moderate	74	58	84	3.3	10	June
July	10	19	66	28	82	39	102	12	54	Medium	77	58	107	4.2	12	July
Aug	9	19	66	27	80	39	102	11	51	Medium	79	60	109	4.3	10	Aug
Sept	8	16	60	26	79	38	100	4	39	Medium	79	61	86	3.4	9	Sept
Oct	7	9	49	21	69	32	90	-3	27		76	57	89	3.5	9	Oct
Nov	6	3	37	11	51	24	75	-14	7		75	60	76	3.0	9	Nov
Dec	5	-2	29	5	41	21	69	-25	-13		73	61	91	3.6	10	Dec

Based on readings for 46 years at 40°43' N, 74°00' W, altitude 96 m/314 ft

PHILADELPHIA, PENNSYLVANIA — NORTHEASTERN USA

Month	Sunshine average hours per day	Average daily minimum °C	°F	Average daily maximum °C	°F	Highest recorded °C	°F	Lowest recorded °C	°F	Discomfort from heat and humidity	Relative humidity 8:00 %	13:30 %	Average monthly precipitation mm	in	Wet days more than 0.25 mm/0.01 in	Month
Jan	5	-3	26	4	40	23	73	-21	-5		75	65	84	3.3	12	Jan
Feb	6	-3	27	5	41	26	79	-24	-11		74	62	84	3.3	11	Feb
March	7	1	33	9	49	30	86	-15	5		73	60	86	3.4	12	March
April	8	6	43	16	61	34	93	-10	14		69	56	79	3.1	11	April
May	8	12	54	22	72	36	96	2	35		70	55	84	3.3	11	May
June	10	17	62	27	80	39	102	8	46	Medium	72	56	81	3.2	10	June
July	10	20	68	29	85	40	104	11	52	Medium	73	56	104	4.1	11	July
Aug	8	19	67	28	83	41	106	11	51	Medium	76	58	117	4.6	11	Aug
Sept	8	16	60	24	76	39	102	4	40	Moderate	77	59	79	3.1	8	Sept
Oct	7	10	50	19	66	34	94	-2	29		75	56	71	2.8	8	Oct
Nov	5	4	39	12	53	26	78	-13	8		74	62	69	2.7	9	Nov
Dec	5	-1	30	6	43	21	70	-21	-5		74	63	86	3.4	10	Dec

Based on readings for 58 years at 39°57' N, 75°09' W, altitude 8 m/26 ft

PORTLAND, MAINE

	Sunshine	Temperatures								Discomfort from heat and humidity	Precipitation and humidity				Wet days	
		Average daily				Highest recorded		Lowest recorded			Relative humidity		Average monthly precipitation			
		minimum		maximum							8:00	12:00				
	average hours per day	°C	°F	°C	°F	°C	°F	°C	°F		%		mm	in	more than 0.25 mm/0.01 in	
Jan	5	-9	15	-1	31	18	65	-28	-18		75	62	102	4.0	12	Jan
Feb	6	-9	16	0	32	14	58	-28	-18		74	61	99	3.9	11	Feb
March	6	-3	26	4	40	26	79	-22	-7		71	60	102	4.0	13	March
April	7	2	35	10	50	32	89	-13	9		68	57	89	3.5	11	April
May	8	8	46	16	61	36	96	-3	27		70	58	84	3.3	12	May
June	10	12	54	22	71	36	96	3	38		73	60	84	3.3	12	June
July	10	16	60	24	76	39	103	9	48	Moderate	75	63	84	3.3	12	July
Aug	9	15	59	23	74	37	98	7	44	Moderate	78	62	81	3.2	11	Aug
Sept	8	11	52	20	68	36	96	0	32		79	63	81	3.2	10	Sept
Oct	7	6	42	14	57	29	85	-6	22		77	60	81	3.2	10	Oct
Nov	5	0	32	7	45	23	74	-21	-6		76	63	89	3.5	11	Nov
Dec	5	-6	21	1	34	18	65	-29	-21		75	64	99	3.9	12	Dec

Based on readings for 67 years at 43°39' N, 70°15' W, altitude 31 m/103 ft

PROVIDENCE, RHODE ISLAND

	Sunshine	Temperatures								Discomfort from heat and humidity	Precipitation and humidity				Wet days	
		Average daily				Highest recorded		Lowest recorded			Relative humidity		Average monthly precipitation			
		minimum		maximum							7:30	13:30				
	average hours per day	°C	°F	°C	°F	°C	°F	°C	°F		%		mm	in	more than 0.25 mm/0.01 in	
Jan	5	-6	22	3	37	20	68	-23	-9		72	60	89	3.5	12	Jan
Feb	6	-6	21	3	37	21	69	-27	-17		72	59	74	2.9	10	Feb
March	7	-2	29	8	46	32	90	-16	4		69	55	89	3.5	12	March
April	7	3	38	13	56	33	91	-12	11		66	51	84	3.3	11	April
May	8	9	48	20	68	35	95	0	32		67	52	71	2.8	11	May
June	10	14	57	24	76	37	98	4	39	Moderate	71	57	79	3.1	11	June
July	10	17	63	28	82	38	100	10	50	Medium	74	58	81	3.2	10	July
Aug	8	17	62	27	80	38	100	7	44	Medium	76	57	84	3.3	9	Aug
Sept	8	13	55	23	73	35	95	1	33		78	59	84	3.3	9	Sept
Oct	7	7	45	17	63	31	88	-4	25		76	55	71	2.8	9	Oct
Nov	5	2	35	11	51	24	75	-13	9		76	60	81	3.2	10	Nov
Dec	5	-4	25	4	40	20	68	-24	-12		72	60	89	3.5	10	Dec

Based on readings for 43 years at 41°50' N, 71°25' W, altitude 49 m/159 ft

WASHINGTON, DISTRICT OF COLUMBIA

NORTHEASTERN USA

	Sunshine average hours per day	Temperatures								Discomfort from heat and humidity	Precipitation and humidity				Wet days more than 0.25 mm/0.01 in	
		Average daily				Highest recorded		Lowest recorded			Relative humidity 7:30 13:30		Average monthly precipitation			
		minimum		maximum												
		°C	°F	°C	°F	°C	°F	°C	°F		%		mm	in		
Jan	5	−3	27	6	42	25	77	−26	−14		73	56	86	3.4	11	Jan
Feb	6	−2	28	7	44	29	84	−26	−15		71	53	76	3.0	10	Feb
March	7	2	35	12	53	34	93	−16	4		72	48	91	3.6	12	March
April	8	7	44	18	64	35	95	−9	15		68	45	84	3.3	11	April
May	9	12	54	24	75	36	97	1	33		72	48	94	3.7	12	May
June	9	17	63	28	83	39	102	6	43	Medium	75	52	99	3.9	11	June
July	9	20	68	31	87	41	106	11	52	Medium	79	53	112	4.4	11	July
Aug	8	19	66	29	84	41	106	9	49	Medium	80	53	109	4.3	11	Aug
Sept	8	15	59	26	78	40	104	2	36	Moderate	81	53	94	3.7	8	Sept
Oct	7	9	48	19	67	36	96	−3	26		81	50	74	2.9	8	Oct
Nov	5	3	38	13	55	28	83	−12	11		77	51	66	2.6	9	Nov
Dec	4	−2	29	7	45	23	74	−25	−13		74	55	79	3.1	10	Dec

Based on readings for 78 years at 38°54′ N, 77°03′ W, altitude 22 m/72 ft

THE SOUTHERN ATLANTIC STATES

Including (with towns and cities in parentheses): southern MARYLAND and most of FLORIDA (Miami, Orlando), GEORGIA, NORTH CAROLINA, SOUTH CAROLINA (Charleston), and VIRGINIA (Richmond, Norfolk).

Characteristic weather for this region is represented by the the tables for **Charleston, South Carolina** (below), **Miami, Florida** (opposite), and **Norfolk, Virginia** (opposite and below).

There is a gradual increase in the warmth of winter southwards along the Atlantic coast, so that Florida has an almost tropical climate with only very rare and short cold spells when frost and snow occur. The northern part of Virginia and much of West Virginia in the Appalachian Mountains have winter conditions more typical of the northeastern region. On the other hand there is much less difference between the north and south of this region in terms of summer temperatures. The contrast is rather in the length of the summer season and the warmth of spring and autumn.

Florida has a very oceanic climate, being much influenced by the surrounding warm Atlantic waters, so that summer temperatures do not reach the heights sometimes recorded as far north as New York. On the other hand, Florida and the coastal lowlands of Georgia and the Carolinas have mild winters and frost and snow are much less frequent than in Washington, DC, or North Virginia. In northern Florida and southern Georgia snow only falls every ten or fifteen years but in southern Virginia it falls in at least two years out of three.

The proportion of the annual rainfall coming in the summer months increases southwards and a significant amount of this is associated with thunderstorms. Florida has more thunderstorms than any other state in the USA – over a hundred a year in parts of the state. This region is also affected by hurricanes, or less severe tropical storms, at least once or twice a year and they account for some of the heavier falls of rain in the months July to October.

This is the sunniest part of the eastern United States, with sunshine hours averaging from about six in winter to as much as nine or ten in summer. Florida is particularly sunny in winter which, combined with its much warmer temperature at this time, makes it a popular winter resort. The summer months in Florida are slightly less sunny than in areas farther north because of the regular afternoon build-up of cloud leading to thunderstorms.

CHARLESTON, SOUTH CAROLINA

SOUTHERN ATLANTIC USA

	Sunshine	Temperatures									Discomfort from heat and humidity	Precipitation and humidity				Wet days	
		Average daily				Highest recorded		Lowest recorded				Relative humidity		Average monthly precipitation			
		minimum		maximum								7:30	12:00				
	average hours per day	°C	°F	°C	°F	°C	°F	°C	°F			%		mm	in	more than 0.25 mm/0.01 in	
Jan	6	6	43	14	58	28	82	-12	10			81	64	74	2.9	10	Jan
Feb	7	7	44	15	59	28	82	-14	7			80	63	84	3.3	9	Feb
March	8	10	50	19	66	34	94	-4	24			79	62	86	3.4	9	March
April	10	14	57	23	73	34	93	0	32	Moderate		75	61	71	2.8	8	April
May	10	19	66	27	80	37	99	7	45	Medium		75	63	81	3.2	8	May
June	11	23	73	30	86	40	104	9	49	High		77	65	119	4.7	11	June
July	10	24	75	31	88	40	104	16	61	High		79	67	185	7.3	13	July
Aug	9	24	75	31	87	39	102	17	62	High		82	68	168	6.6	13	Aug
Sept	8	22	71	28	83	38	100	9	49	Medium		83	68	130	5.1	10	Sept
Oct	7	16	61	24	75	35	95	3	37	Moderate		80	62	81	3.2	6	Oct
Nov	7	11	51	19	66	28	83	-5	23			79	61	58	2.3	7	Nov
Dec	6	7	44	15	59	27	81	-11	12			81	65	71	2.8	9	Dec

Based on readings for 75 years at 32°47′ N, 79°55′ W, altitude 3 m/9 ft

MIAMI, FLORIDA
SOUTHERN ATLANTIC USA

	Sunshine	Temperatures							Discomfort from heat and humidity	Precipitation and humidity				Wet days	
		Average daily				Highest recorded		Lowest recorded			Relative humidity 7:30 12:00		Average monthly precipitation			
		minimum		maximum												
	average hours per day	°C	°F	°C	°F	°C	°F	°C	°F		%		mm	in	more than 0.25mm/0.01in	
Jan	8	16	61	23	74	29	85	-2	29		81	66	71	2.8	9	Jan
Feb	8	16	61	24	75	31	88	-3	27	Moderate	82	63	53	2.1	6	Feb
March	9	18	64	26	78	33	92	1	34	Medium	77	62	64	2.5	7	March
April	9	19	67	27	80	34	93	7	45	Medium	73	64	81	3.2	7	April
May	9	22	71	29	84	34	94	10	50	Medium	75	67	173	6.8	12	May
June	9	23	74	30	86	34	94	16	61	High	75	69	178	7.0	13	June
July	9	24	76	31	88	36	96	19	66	High	75	68	155	6.1	15	July
Aug	8	24	76	31	88	36	96	16	60	High	76	68	160	6.3	15	Aug
Sept	7	24	75	31	87	35	95	17	62	High	79	70	203	8.0	18	Sept
Oct	6	22	72	28	83	34	93	11	52	Medium	80	69	234	9.2	16	Oct
Nov	7	19	66	26	78	31	88	2	36	Medium	77	64	71	2.8	10	Nov
Dec	7	17	62	24	76	33	91	-1	30	Moderate	82	65	51	2.0	7	Dec

Based on readings for 51 years at 25°48′ N, 80°12′ W, altitude 8 m/25 ft

NORFOLK, VIRGINIA
SOUTHERN ATLANTIC USA

	Sunshine	Temperatures							Discomfort from heat and humidity	Precipitation and humidity				Wet days	
		Average daily				Highest recorded		Lowest recorded			Relative humidity 7:30 13:30		Average monthly precipitation			
		minimum		maximum												
	average hours per day	°C	°F	°C	°F	°C	°F	°C	°F		%		mm	in	more than 0.25mm/0.01in	
Jan	6	1	34	9	49	27	80	-15	5		79	62	81	3.2	11	Jan
Feb	6	1	34	10	50	28	82	-17	2		77	56	86	3.4	11	Feb
March	7	4	40	14	58	33	92	-10	14		77	56	97	3.8	11	March
April	8	9	48	19	66	35	95	-5	23		74	53	84	3.3	10	April
May	9	14	58	24	76	37	98	1	33	Moderate	76	54	94	3.7	11	May
June	11	19	66	28	83	39	102	9	49	Medium	79	58	107	4.2	11	June
July	10	22	71	31	87	40	104	14	57	High	81	61	147	5.8	13	July
Aug	9	21	70	29	85	41	105	13	56	Medium	82	62	132	5.2	11	Aug
Sept	8	18	65	27	80	38	100	4	40	Medium	82	63	97	3.8	8	Sept
Oct	7	13	55	21	70	34	94	-1	31		81	59	76	3.0	8	Oct
Nov	6	7	45	16	60	28	82	-8	17		80	58	64	2.5	8	Nov
Dec	6	2	36	11	51	24	76	-15	5		79	60	56	3.2	10	Dec

Based on readings for 74 years at 36°51′ N, 76°17′ W, altitude 3 m/11 ft

THE NORTHERN INTERIOR

Including (with towns and cities in parentheses) all those states between the western Appalachians and the foothills of the Rocky Mountains approximately to the north of 37° N: ILLINOIS (Chicago), INDIANA (Indianapolis), IOWA (Des Moines), KANSAS (Kansas City, Dodge City), KENTUCKY (Louisville), MICHIGAN (Detroit), MINNESOTA (Duluth, Minneapolis), MISSOURI (St Louis), NEBRASKA (Omaha), NORTH DAKOTA, OHIO (Cincinnati, Columbus), SOUTH DAKOTA, WEST VIRGINIA (Charleston), and WISCONSIN (Milwaukee); and the west of NEW YORK, PENNSYLVANIA (Pittsburgh), and VIRGINIA.

Characteristic weather for this region is represented by the the tables for **Charleston, West Virginia** (opposite), **Chicago, Illinois** (opposite and below), **Columbus, Ohio** (p. 388), **Des Moines, Iowa** (p. 388), **Detroit, Michigan** (p. 389), **Dodge City, Kansas** (p. 389), **Duluth, Minnesota** (p. 390), **Indianapolis, Indiana** (p. 390), **Kansas City, Missouri** (p. 391), **Louisville, Kentucky** (p. 391), **Minneapolis, Minnesota** (p. 392), **Omaha, Nebraska** (p. 392), **Pittsburgh, Pennsylvania** (p. 393), **St Louis, Missouri** (p. 393).

There are extensive plains in the valleys of the Ohio, Missouri, and northern Mississippi. Much of this region goes by the name of the Midwest. Most of it is below 600 m/2,000 ft and much of it is below 300 m/1,000 ft. It has the most continental climate of any part of the United States. Winters are cold and summers warm with quite frequent heat waves and drought. There is a gradual increase in summer warmth southwards but a more noticeable increase in the severity and length of winter northwards. Winter precipitation is light, particularly in the west of this region, and much of it falls as snow. In the north, along the Canadian border and around the Great Lakes, winter conditions can occasionally be very severe with blizzards, as very cold air sweeps south from the Canadian Arctic.

There is a gradual decrease in the amount of annual precipitation westwards and the western plains suffer most frequently from drought. The eastern states of Michigan, Indiana, Illinois, and Kentucky have a heavier annual precipitation with much wetter winters than those farther west. An unpleasant feature of the weather in the north of this region is the frequent occurrence of freezing rain in winter as rain falls from a warm air-mass onto ground previously frozen hard. This is a serious danger to road traffic and may occur on as many as five to ten days a year.

Almost the whole of the region has at least one winter month with an average temperature below freezing but, since the weather is frequently changeable, unseasonably mild conditions may occur for a few days even in midwinter. Clear skies and abundant sunshine are a feature of the weather for much of the time, even in winter. Sunshine hours a day average from four to five in winter and as much as ten or eleven in summer.

A feature of the western part of this region at the foot of the Rockies is the occasional warm dry wind, the chinook, which raises temperature and quickly melts snow in winter and spring. This is a föhn-type wind, warmed as the air descends to the east of the mountains.

CHARLESTON, WEST VIRGINIA

NORTHERN INTERIOR USA

	Sunshine	Temperatures							Discomfort from heat and humidity	Precipitation and humidity			Wet days
	average hours per day	Average daily				Highest recorded		Lowest recorded			Relative humidity	Average monthly precipitation		more than 0.25 mm/0.01 in
		minimum		maximum										
		°C	°F	°C	°F	°C	°F	°C	°F		%	mm	in	
Jan		−3	26	10	50	26	79	−23	−9			97	3.8	13	Jan
Feb		−3	27	11	51	27	80	−24	−11			89	3.5	11	Feb
March		2	35	16	61	33	92	−12	10			109	4.3	12	March
April		6	42	21	70	36	96	−8	18			94	3.7	12	April
May		11	52	26	79	37	98	−1	31			102	4.0	11	May
June		16	61	29	85	39	103	5	41			112	4.4	11	June
July		18	64	32	89	41	106	9	48			107	4.2	10	July
Aug		18	63	31	87	42	108	9	48			114	4.5	10	Aug
Sept		14	58	29	84	38	101	1	33			76	3.0	7	Sept
Oct		7	45	22	72	36	96	−7	20			74	2.9	8	Oct
Nov		2	35	16	61	29	85	−14	6			79	3.1	9	Nov
Dec		−2	28	11	51	25	77	−27	−17			86	3.4	11	Dec

Based on readings for 24 years at 38°21′ N, 81°38′ W, altitude 188 m/615 ft

CHICAGO, ILLINOIS

NORTHERN INTERIOR USA

	Sunshine	Temperatures								Discomfort from heat and humidity	Precipitation and humidity				Wet days
	average hours per day	Average daily				Highest recorded		Lowest recorded			Relative humidity 7:00 12:00		Average monthly precipitation		more than 0.25 mm/0.01 in
		minimum		maximum											
		°C	°F	°C	°F	°C	°F	°C	°F		%		mm	in	
Jan	4	−8	18	0	32	18	65	−29	−20		80	70	51	2.0	11	Jan
Feb	5	−7	20	1	34	20	68	−29	−21		79	69	51	2.0	10	Feb
March	7	−2	29	6	43	17	62	−24	−12		77	64	66	2.6	12	March
April	7	4	40	13	55	33	91	−8	17		74	61	71	2.8	11	April
May	9	10	50	18	65	37	98	−3	27		73	59	86	3.4	12	May
June	10	16	60	24	75	39	102	2	35	Moderate	76	61	89	3.5	11	June
July	10	19	66	27	81	41	105	9	49	Medium	75	58	84	3.3	9	July
Aug	9	18	65	26	79	39	102	8	47	Medium	79	61	81	3.2	9	Aug
Sept	8	14	58	23	73	38	100	−2	29		80	59	79	3.1	9	Sept
Oct	7	8	47	16	61	31	88	−10	14		78	59	66	2.6	9	Oct
Nov	5	1	34	8	47	26	78	−19	−2		79	65	61	2.4	10	Nov
Dec	4	−5	23	2	36	20	68	−31	−23		80	72	51	2.0	11	Dec

Based on readings for 75 years at 41°53′ N, 87°38′ W, altitude 251 m/823 ft

COLUMBUS, OHIO

NORTHERN INTERIOR USA

Sunshine average hours per day	Temperatures Average daily minimum °C	°F	maximum °C	°F	Highest recorded °C	°F	Lowest recorded °C	°F	Discomfort from heat and humidity	Relative humidity 7:30 12:00 %	Average monthly precipitation mm	in	Wet days more than 0.25 mm/0.01 in	
Jan	3	-6	22	3	37	22	72	-29	-20		83 72	79	3.1	14	Jan
Feb	4	-5	23	4	39	22	72	-29	-20		82 72	69	2.7	12	Feb
March	6	0	32	9	49	29	84	-18	0		79 64	86	3.4	14	March
April	7	6	42	16	61	32	90	-9	15		74 61	74	2.9	12	April
May	8	11	52	22	72	36	96	-1	31		75 59	89	3.5	12	May
June	10	16	61	27	81	39	102	4	39	Medium	77 58	86	3.4	12	June
July	10	18	65	29	85	41	106	9	49	Medium	77 53	91	3.6	11	July
Aug	10	17	63	28	83	39	103	6	42	Medium	79 57	81	3.2	10	Aug
Sept	9	14	57	25	77	37	99	0	32	Moderate	80 58	64	2.5	9	Sept
Oct	7	8	46	18	65	32	90	-7	20		81 60	64	2.5	9	Oct
Nov	5	2	35	10	50	26	78	-21	-5		82 68	71	2.8	11	Nov
Dec	3	-3	26	4	39	19	67	-24	-12		83 74	69	2.7	13	Dec

Based on readings for 68 years at 39°58′ N, 83°00′ W, altitude 221 m/724 ft

DES MOINES, IOWA

NORTHERN INTERIOR USA

Sunshine average hours per day	Temperatures Average daily minimum °C	°F	maximum °C	°F	Highest recorded °C	°F	Lowest recorded °C	°F	Discomfort from heat and humidity	Relative humidity 7:00 12:00 %	Average monthly precipitation mm	in	Wet days more than 0.25 mm/0.01 in	
Jan	5	-11	12	-1	30	18	65	-34	-30		83 68	28	1.1	8	Jan
Feb	6	-9	15	1	33	26	78	-32	-26		82 66	28	1.1	8	Feb
March	6	-3	27	8	46	31	88	-23	-10		79 56	46	1.8	9	March
April	8	4	40	16	61	33	92	-12	11		76 53	74	2.9	10	April
May	9	11	51	22	71	37	98	-3	26		76 49	112	4.4	12	May
June	10	16	61	27	80	39	102	3	37	Medium	79 55	122	4.8	11	June
July	11	18	65	30	86	43	109	9	48	Medium	78 51	86	3.4	9	July
Aug	10	17	63	29	84	43	110	4	40	Medium	82 54	91	3.6	9	Aug
Sept	9	13	55	24	76	37	99	-3	26	Moderate	83 55	91	3.6	9	Sept
Oct	8	6	43	18	64	33	91	-14	7		80 52	64	2.5	8	Oct
Nov	6	-1	30	9	48	26	79	-23	-10		80 63	38	1.5	7	Nov
Dec	4	-8	18	1	34	21	69	-29	-21		82 69	31	1.2	8	Dec

Based on readings for 52 years at 41°35′ N, 93°37′ W, altitude 244 m/800 ft

DETROIT, MICHIGAN
NORTHERN INTERIOR USA

	Sunshine	Temperatures							Discomfort from heat and humidity	Precipitation and humidity				Wet days	
		Average daily				Highest recorded		Lowest recorded			Relative humidity 7:30 12:00		Average monthly precipitation			
		minimum		maximum												
	average hours per day	°C	°F	°C	°F	°C	°F	°C	°F		%		mm	in	more than 0.25 mm/0.01 in	
Jan	3	−7	19	−1	31	19	66	−27	−16		86	76	53	2.1	13	Jan
Feb	4	−8	18	0	32	18	65	−29	−20		84	74	53	2.1	12	Feb
March	5	−3	27	6	42	27	81	−22	−7		80	67	64	2.5	13	March
April	7	3	37	13	55	31	88	−13	8		75	62	64	2.5	11	April
May	8	9	48	19	67	35	95	−2	28		73	59	84	3.3	13	May
June	10	14	58	25	77	40	104	3	38	Moderate	74	58	91	3.6	11	June
July	9	17	63	28	82	41	105	9	48	Medium	73	53	84	3.3	9	July
Aug	9	17	62	27	80	40	104	6	43	Medium	77	53	69	2.7	9	Aug
Sept	8	13	55	23	73	38	100	−1	30		80	59	71	2.8	10	Sept
Oct	6	7	44	16	60	32	89	−6	22		81	62	61	2.4	10	Oct
Nov	3	1	33	8	46	24	75	−18	0		82	71	61	2.4	12	Nov
Dec	3	−4	24	2	35	18	65	−31	−24		84	78	58	2.3	14	Dec

Based on readings for 73 years at 42°24′ N, 83°00′ W, altitude 189 m/619 ft

DODGE CITY, KANSAS
NORTHERN INTERIOR USA

	Sunshine	Temperatures							Discomfort from heat and humidity	Precipitation and humidity				Wet days	
		Average daily				Highest recorded		Lowest recorded			Relative humidity 6:30 12:00		Average monthly precipitation			
		minimum		maximum												
	average hours per day	°C	°F	°C	°F	°C	°F	°C	°F		%		mm	in	more than 0.25 mm/0.01 in	
Jan	7	−8	17	5	41	26	79	−29	−20		80	54	10	0.4	4	Jan
Feb	7	−6	21	8	46	29	84	−32	−26		80	50	18	0.7	5	Feb
March	8	−2	29	13	56	37	98	−23	−10		76	46	23	0.9	6	March
April	9	5	41	19	67	35	95	−11	13		77	48	48	1.9	7	April
May	9	11	51	24	75	38	101	−7	19	Moderate	80	51	74	2.9	11	May
June	12	16	61	29	85	42	107	2	36	Medium	80	48	81	3.2	9	June
July	11	19	66	32	90	42	108	8	46	Medium	78	43	79	3.1	8	July
Aug	11	18	64	32	89	41	105	6	43	Medium	80	43	66	2.6	7	Aug
Sept	10	13	56	28	82	39	102	−1	30	Medium	81	45	48	1.9	5	Sept
Oct	8	6	43	21	69	34	94	−12	10		79	47	36	1.4	5	Oct
Nov	7	−1	30	13	56	29	85	−25	−13		79	49	20	0.8	4	Nov
Dec	6	−6	21	7	44	26	79	−26	−15		80	56	15	0.6	4	Dec

Based on readings for 56 years at 37°46′ N, 99°58′ W, altitude 791 m/2594 ft

DULUTH, MINNESOTA

NORTHERN INTERIOR USA

Sunshine	Temperatures							Discomfort from heat and humidity	Precipitation and humidity				Wet days	
	Average daily				Highest recorded		Lowest recorded		Relative humidity 7:00 12:00		Average monthly precipitation			
	minimum		maximum											
average hours per day	°C	°F	°C	°F	°C	°F	°C	°F		%		mm	in	more than 0.25 mm/0.01 in	
Jan	5	–18	–1	–9	16	13	55	–41	–41		88	80	25	1.0	10	Jan
Feb	6	–16	3	–7	20	14	58	–38	–36		87	78	25	1.0	9	Feb
March	7	–9	16	0	32	27	81	–32	–26		83	69	38	1.5	10	March
April	7	–2	29	7	45	29	85	–17	1		87	62	51	2.0	9	April
May	8	3	38	13	56	35	95	–9	16		75	60	81	3.2	12	May
June	10	9	48	19	67	36	97	–1	31		80	66	104	4.1	13	June
July	10	12	54	23	73	41	106	6	42	Moderate	81	65	97	3.8	12	July
Aug	9	12	54	22	71	36	97	3	38		83	65	81	3.2	11	Aug
Sept	7	8	47	17	63	34	94	–4	25		84	69	89	3.5	11	Sept
Oct	6	3	37	11	51	29	85	–13	8		83	68	61	2.4	10	Oct
Nov	4	–5	23	3	37	23	73	–34	–29		85	74	38	1.5	9	Nov
Dec	4	–13	8	–5	23	13	56	–37	–35		88	82	28	1.1	11	Dec

Based on readings for 72 years at 46°47′ N, 92°06′ W, altitude 344 m/1128 ft

INDIANAPOLIS, INDIANA

NORTHERN INTERIOR USA

Sunshine	Temperatures							Discomfort from heat and humidity	Precipitation and humidity				Wet days	
	Average daily				Highest recorded		Lowest recorded		Relative humidity 7:30 12:00		Average monthly precipitation			
	minimum		maximum											
average hours per day	°C	°F	°C	°F	°C	°F	°C	°F		%		mm	in	more than 0.25 mm/0.01 in	
Jan	4	–6	22	2	36	21	70	–32	–25		83	69	76	3.0	13	Jan
Feb	5	–5	23	4	39	23	73	–28	–18		81	67	69	2.7	11	Feb
March	7	0	32	9	49	29	84	–21	–5		78	60	102	4.0	13	March
April	7	6	43	16	61	32	90	–7	19		73	55	91	3.6	12	April
May	9	12	54	22	72	36	96	–1	31		72	51	99	3.9	13	May
June	10	17	63	28	82	38	101	4	39	Medium	74	53	102	4.0	11	June
July	10	19	67	30	86	41	106	9	48	Medium	72	49	99	3.9	10	July
Aug	10	18	65	29	84	39	103	7	44	Medium	77	53	84	3.3	9	Aug
Sept	9	14	58	25	77	38	100	–1	30	Moderate	79	54	81	3.2	9	Sept
Oct	7	8	47	18	65	32	89	–6	22		79	55	71	2.8	9	Oct
Nov	5	2	35	10	50	26	78	–21	–5		79	64	84	3.3	11	Nov
Dec	4	–3	26	4	39	15	59	–26	–15		82	71	76	3.0	12	Dec

Based on readings for 76 years at 39°46′ N, 86°10′ W, altitude 216 m/718 ft

KANSAS CITY, MISSOURI

NORTHERN INTERIOR USA

	Sunshine average hours per day	Average daily minimum °C	Average daily minimum °F	Average daily maximum °C	Average daily maximum °F	Highest recorded °C	Highest recorded °F	Lowest recorded °C	Lowest recorded °F	Discomfort from heat and humidity	Relative humidity 6:30 %	Relative humidity 12:00 %	Average monthly precipitation mm	Average monthly precipitation in	Wet days more than 0.25mm/0.01in	
Jan	4	-6	22	3	38	21	70	-29	-20		78	64	33	1.3	7	Jan
Feb	6	-4	24	5	41	27	81	-30	-22		78	59	43	1.7	8	Feb
March	6	1	34	12	53	33	91	-19	-3		75	53	66	2.6	9	March
April	8	8	46	18	65	35	95	-9	16		74	51	81	3.2	11	April
May	9	13	56	23	74	39	103	-3	27		75	54	125	4.9	12	May
June	11	18	65	28	83	42	108	7	44	Medium	78	56	122	4.8	11	June
July	11	21	70	32	89	43	110	12	53	High	76	51	104	4.1	9	July
Aug	10	20	68	31	87	45	113	8	46	Medium	78	52	104	4.1	9	Aug
Sept	9	16	60	27	80	42	107	1	34	Medium	79	54	117	4.6	10	Sept
Oct	8	9	49	20	68	37	98	-8	17		76	53	71	2.8	7	Oct
Nov	6	2	36	12	53	28	83	-16	4		74	57	48	1.9	6	Nov
Dec	5	-3	26	5	41	23	74	-25	-13		78	64	33	1.3	7	Dec

Based on readings for 58 years at 39°07' N, 94°35' W, altitude 226 m/741 ft

LOUISVILLE, KENTUCKY

NORTHERN INTERIOR USA

	Sunshine average hours per day	Average daily minimum °C	Average daily minimum °F	Average daily maximum °C	Average daily maximum °F	Highest recorded °C	Highest recorded °F	Lowest recorded °C	Lowest recorded °F	Discomfort from heat and humidity	Relative humidity 7:30 %	Relative humidity 12:00 %	Average monthly precipitation mm	Average monthly precipitation in	Wet days more than 0.25mm/0.01in	
Jan	3	-3	27	6	43	25	77	-29	-20		78	67	104	4.1	12	Jan
Feb	5	-2	29	7	45	26	78	-26	-14		77	64	89	3.5	10	Feb
March	6	3	37	13	55	31	88	-16	3		75	56	109	4.3	12	March
April	7	8	47	19	66	33	91	-6	21		71	52	102	4.0	12	April
May	9	13	56	24	76	37	98	1	33	Moderate	72	53	97	3.8	11	May
June	10	18	65	29	84	39	102	6	43	Medium	74	54	102	4.0	11	June
July	10	21	69	31	88	42	107	9	49	Medium	74	51	94	3.7	10	July
Aug	9	19	67	30	86	41	105	7	45	Medium	78	53	81	3.2	9	Aug
Sept	9	16	61	27	80	39	102	2	36	Medium	79	55	69	2.7	8	Sept
Oct	7	9	49	21	69	33	91	-5	23		79	54	71	2.8	8	Oct
Nov	5	3	38	13	55	28	82	-17	1		76	61	91	3.6	10	Nov
Dec	4	-2	29	7	45	23	74	-22	-7		78	67	94	3.7	11	Dec

Based on readings for 75 years at 38°15' N, 85°45' W, altitude 160 m/525 ft

MINNEAPOLIS, MINNESOTA

NORTHERN INTERIOR USA

Sunshine	Temperatures									Discomfort from heat and humidity	Precipitation and humidity			Wet days	
	Average daily				Highest recorded		Lowest recorded				Relative humidity 12:00	Average monthly precipitation			
	minimum		maximum												
average hours per day	°C	°F	°C	°F	°C	°F	°C	°F			%	mm	in	more than 0.25 mm/0.01 in	
Jan	4	−14	6	−6	22	14	58	−37	−34		71	25	1.0	8	Jan
Feb	6	−13	8	−4	25	18	64	−36	−32		72	25	1.0	7	Feb
March	6	−6	22	3	38	28	83	−33	−27		59	41	1.6	8	March
April	7	2	36	13	56	33	91	−14	6		51	58	2.3	10	April
May	8	9	48	20	68	41	106	−6	22		49	86	3.4	12	May
June	9	14	58	25	77	40	104	1	34	Moderate	56	112	4.4	12	June
July	10	17	63	28	83	42	108	7	44	Medium	52	86	3.4	9	July
Aug	9	16	61	27	80	39	103	6	42	Medium	51	86	3.4	9	Aug
Sept	8	11	52	22	72	40	104	−3	26		56	86	3.4	9	Sept
Oct	7	5	41	15	59	32	90	−12	10		56	53	2.1	9	Oct
Nov	4	−3	26	4	40	25	77	−25	−13		65	36	1.4	7	Nov
Dec	4	−11	12	−3	27	17	63	−33	−27		73	31	1.2	8	Dec

Based on readings for 57 years at 44°53′ N, 93°13′ W, altitude 253 m/830 ft

OMAHA, NEBRASKA

NORTHERN INTERIOR USA

Sunshine	Temperatures									Discomfort from heat and humidity	Precipitation and humidity				Wet days	
	Average daily				Highest recorded		Lowest recorded				Relative humidity 6:30 12:00		Average monthly precipitation			
	minimum		maximum													
average hours per day	°C	°F	°C	°F	°C	°F	°C	°F			%		mm	in	more than 0.25 mm/0.01 in	
Jan	5	−11	13	−1	30	19	67	−36	−32		81	66	18	0.7	7	Jan
Feb	6	−8	17	2	35	26	78	−32	−26		80	63	23	0.9	6	Feb
March	6	−2	28	8	47	33	91	−22	−8		76	54	33	1.3	7	March
April	8	6	42	16	61	34	94	−14	6		74	54	69	2.7	10	April
May	9	12	53	22	72	37	99	−4	25		74	53	94	3.7	12	May
June	10	17	62	27	81	41	105	6	42	Medium	77	56	117	4.6	11	June
July	11	19	67	30	86	43	109	10	50	Medium	75	52	102	4.0	9	July
Aug	9	18	65	29	84	44	111	7	44	Medium	78	54	86	3.4	9	Aug
Sept	9	14	57	24	76	39	102	−1	30	Moderate	80	54	84	3.3	9	Sept
Oct	8	7	45	18	64	33	92	−13	8		76	52	58	2.3	7	Oct
Nov	6	−1	30	9	48	27	80	−26	−14		77	62	31	1.2	5	Nov
Dec	5	−7	19	2	35	22	71	−29	−20		81	68	23	0.9	7	Dec

Based on readings for 58 years at 41°18′ N, 95°54′ W, altitude 298 m/978 ft

PITTSBURGH, PENNSYLVANIA — NORTHERN INTERIOR USA

	Sunshine average hours per day	Temperatures									Discomfort from heat and humidity	Precipitation and humidity				Wet days more than 0.25mm/0.01in	
		Average daily				Highest recorded		Lowest recorded				Relative humidity 7:30 12:00		Average monthly precipitation			
		minimum		maximum													
		°C	°F	°C	°F	°C	°F	°C	°F			%		mm	in		
Jan	3	-4	24	3	38	24	75	-27	-16			80	69	76	3.0	16	Jan
Feb	4	-5	23	4	39	25	77	-29	-20			79	68	66	2.6	14	Feb
March	6	-1	31	9	49	29	84	-18	-1			76	61	76	3.0	15	March
April	7	5	41	16	61	32	90	-12	11			72	57	76	3.0	13	April
May	8	11	52	22	72	35	95	-3	27			72	55	79	3.1	13	May
June	10	16	60	27	80	37	98	4	38		Medium	74	56	94	3.7	12	June
July	9	18	64	29	84	39	103	8	46		Medium	75	54	107	4.2	12	July
Aug	8	17	63	28	82	39	103	7	45		Medium	78	57	81	3.2	10	Aug
Sept	8	14	57	24	76	39	102	1	34		Moderate	80	57	64	2.5	9	Sept
Oct	7	8	46	18	64	33	91	-7	20			80	60	66	2.6	10	Oct
Nov	5	2	36	11	51	26	79	-17	1			77	67	58	2.3	12	Nov
Dec	4	-3	27	5	41	23	73	-23	-9			78	71	71	2.8	14	Dec

Based on readings for 73 years at 40°26′ N, 80°00′ W, altitude 238 m/749 ft

ST LOUIS, MISSOURI — NORTHERN INTERIOR USA

	Sunshine average hours per day	Temperatures									Discomfort from heat and humidity	Precipitation and humidity				Wet days more than 0.25mm/0.01in	
		Average daily				Highest recorded		Lowest recorded				Relative humidity 7:00 12:00		Average monthly precipitation			
		minimum		maximum													
		°C	°F	°C	°F	°C	°F	°C	°F			%		mm	in		
Jan	4	-4	24	4	40	23	74	-30	-22			79	64	58	2.3	9	Jan
Feb	6	-3	26	6	43	29	84	-28	-18			78	62	64	2.5	9	Feb
March	7	2	36	12	54	33	92	-16	3			76	56	89	3.5	11	March
April	8	8	47	18	65	34	93	-18	0			72	55	97	3.8	11	April
May	9	14	57	24	75	36	96	0	32		Moderate	74	56	114	4.5	11	May
June	10	19	66	29	84	40	104	7	44		Medium	75	55	114	4.5	11	June
July	10	22	71	31	88	43	110	13	55		Medium	74	50	89	3.5	9	July
Aug	9	21	69	31	87	42	108	11	52		Medium	77	53	86	3.4	8	Aug
Sept	9	17	62	27	80	39	103	2	36		Medium	79	56	81	3.2	8	Sept
Oct	8	10	50	20	68	34	93	-6	21			77	54	74	2.9	8	Oct
Nov	6	3	38	12	54	28	83	-16	3			75	61	71	2.8	8	Nov
Dec	4	-2	28	6	43	24	75	-26	-15			78	65	64	2.5	9	Dec

Based on readings for 75 years at 38°28′ N, 90°12′ W, altitude 173 m/568 ft

THE SOUTHERN INTERIOR AND GULF STATES

Including (with towns and cities in parentheses): ALABAMA (Birmingham), ARKANSAS (Little Rock), LOUISIANA (New Orleans), MISSISSIPPI (Jackson), OKLAHOMA (Oklahoma City), TENNESSEE (Nashville), and most of TEXAS (Dallas, Houston); and the west of GEORGIA (Atlanta), FLORIDA, NORTH CAROLINA, and SOUTH CAROLINA.

This large region includes the states roughly south of 37° N between the Rockies and the Appalachians and those with a coastline on the Gulf of Mexico. The general sequence of weather and climate around the year is rather similar to that in the Midwest; but, being in a more southerly latitude and more open to the flow of warm tropical air from the Atlantic and the Gulf of Mexico, the winters are both warmer and shorter than those farther north.

It is rare for a winter month here to have an average temperature below freezing point but occasional very cold spells may last for a few days when Arctic air penetrates this region from the north. Occasional snow and frost can occur as far south as the shores of the Gulf of Mexico and in western Texas such cold spells are more frequent and more severe.

Summers are a little warmer than farther north but the increasing length of the summer period and the warmth of spring and autumn are more noticeable.

The eastern part of this region is much wetter than the west. Annual precipitation is almost everywhere between 1,000 mm/40 in and 1,250 mm/50 in in the east but it falls as low as 350 mm/15 in and 500m/20 in in the west. Summer is the wettest season and thunderstorms are very frequent in the east of this region. Parts of the states of Tennessee and Alabama include the southern Appalachian Mountains; here winter precipitation is heavier and the weather and climate are more like those of the eastern Atlantic states.

Most of the region has a sunny climate, particularly the western parts of Texas and Oklahoma. Sunshine averages five to six hours a day in winter to ten or eleven in summer. The summer heat is rarely unpleasant, except along the coast of the Gulf of Mexico, where the combination of heat and humidity can be trying. Compare the afternoon relative humidity at **New Orleans, Louisiana** (see table on p. 398) with that at **Dallas, Texas** (table on p. 396) or **Oklahoma City** (table on p. 398).

Weather characteristic of this region is also shown by the climatic tables for **Atlanta, Georgia** (opposite and above), **Birmingham, Alabama** (opposite), **Houston, Texas** (p. 396), **Little Rock, Arkansas** (p. 397), **Nashville, Tennessee** (p. 397).

This region is the most affected by weather hazards: hurricanes and tornadoes, mentioned in the general account of the United States (p. 377).

ATLANTA, GEORGIA

SOUTHERN INTERIOR USA

Sunshine	Temperatures								Discomfort from heat and humidity	Precipitation and humidity				Wet days
	Average daily				Highest recorded		Lowest recorded			Relative humidity 7:30 12:00		Average monthly precipitation		
	minimum		maximum											
average hours per day	°C	°F	°C	°F	°C	°F	°C	°F		%		mm	in	more than 0.25 mm/0.01 in
Jan	5	2	35	11	51	24	76	-19	-2		80	67	125	4.9	12	Jan
Feb	5	3	37	12	54	26	78	-22	-8		78	66	122	4.8	11	Feb
March	6	6	43	17	62	31	87	-13	8		76	57	140	5.5	11	March
April	8	11	51	22	71	34	93	-4	25		73	54	94	3.7	10	April
May	9	16	60	26	79	36	97	3	38	Moderate	74	55	91	3.6	10	May
June	10	19	67	30	86	39	102	4	39	Medium	77	55	94	3.7	11	June
July	9	21	70	31	87	39	103	14	58	High	82	57	119	4.7	13	July
Aug	9	21	69	30	86	38	101	13	55	Medium	84	59	109	4.3	12	Aug
Sept	8	18	64	28	82	39	102	6	43	Medium	81	57	81	3.2	8	Sept
Oct	7	12	54	22	72	34	94	-2	28		78	56	66	2.6	7	Oct
Nov	6	6	43	16	61	28	82	-10	14		77	60	79	3.1	8	Nov
Dec	5	3	37	11	52	24	75	-17	1		79	66	114	4.5	11	Dec

Based on readings for 68 years at 33°45′ N, 84°23′ W, altitude 321 m/1054 ft

BIRMINGHAM, ALABAMA

SOUTHERN INTERIOR USA

Sunshine	Temperatures								Discomfort from heat and humidity	Precipitation and humidity				Wet days
	Average daily				Highest recorded		Lowest recorded			Relative humidity 7:00 12:00		Average monthly precipitation		
	minimum		maximum											
average hours per day	°C	°F	°C	°F	°C	°F	°C	°F		%		mm	in	more than 0.25 mm/0.01 in
Jan	4	3	37	13	55	25	77	-17	1		79	59	137	5.4	11	Jan
Feb	6	3	38	14	57	28	82	-23	-10		76	57	122	4.8	10	Feb
March	7	8	46	19	66	32	90	-11	12		75	51	150	5.9	11	March
April	9	12	53	23	73	32	90	-2	28		74	50	127	5.0	9	April
May	9	16	61	27	81	37	99	3	38	Medium	77	54	109	4.3	10	May
June	10	20	68	31	88	38	101	8	47	Medium	78	54	112	4.4	10	June
July	9	21	70	32	90	42	107	14	57	High	83	55	132	5.2	12	July
Aug	9	21	70	32	90	39	103	13	55	High	85	55	107	4.2	11	Aug
Sept	8	19	66	30	86	41	106	5	41	Medium	82	51	79	3.1	7	Sept
Oct	7	13	55	24	76	34	94	-3	27		79	49	61	2.4	6	Oct
Nov	6	7	44	18	64	29	84	-10	14		77	54	89	3.5	8	Nov
Dec	5	3	38	13	55	25	77	-15	5		79	61	122	4.8	10	Dec

Based on readings for 35 years at 33°34′ N, 86°45′ W, altitude 186 m/610 ft

DALLAS, TEXAS

SOUTHERN INTERIOR USA

	Sunshine average hours per day	Temperatures											Discomfort from heat and humidity	Precipitation and humidity				Wet days more than 0.25 mm/0.01 in	
		Average daily				Highest recorded		Lowest recorded						Relative humidity 6:30 12:00		Average monthly precipitation			
		minimum		maximum															
		°C	°F	°C	°F	°C	°F	°C	°F					%		mm	in		
Jan	5	2	36	13	55	31	88	−19	−3					79	60	64	2.5	9	Jan
Feb	6	4	40	16	60	34	93	−17	2					78	56	61	2.4	7	Feb
March	7	8	46	19	67	36	96	−12	11					74	50	84	3.3	7	March
April	8	13	55	24	75	36	96	−1	30			Moderate		77	51	107	4.2	9	April
May	9	17	63	28	82	39	103	7	44			Medium		82	55	114	4.5	9	May
June	11	22	71	32	90	41	105	12	53			High		81	53	97	3.8	7	June
July	11	24	75	34	94	41	105	13	56			High		76	48	71	2.8	5	July
Aug	10	23	74	34	94	43	110	14	57			High		77	46	76	3.0	6	Aug
Sept	9	20	68	31	88	41	106	2	36			Medium		80	49	69	2.7	6	Sept
Oct	8	14	57	26	78	38	100	−3	26			Moderate		81	51	71	2.8	7	Oct
Nov	7	8	47	19	66	31	87	−7	19					78	52	69	2.7	6	Nov
Dec	6	3	38	14	57	27	81	−12	10					78	55	64	2.5	7	Dec

Based on readings for 34 years at 32°46′ N, 96°47′ W, altitude 156 m/512 ft

HOUSTON, TEXAS

GULF COAST USA

	Sunshine average hours per day	Temperatures											Discomfort from heat and humidity	Precipitation and humidity				Wet days more than 0.25 mm/0.01 in	
		Average daily				Highest recorded		Lowest recorded						Relative humidity 6:30 12:00		Average monthly precipitation			
		minimum		maximum															
		°C	°F	°C	°F	°C	°F	°C	°F					%		mm	in		
Jan	5	7	44	17	62	29	84	−15	5					85	66	89	3.5	9	Jan
Feb	6	8	46	18	65	31	87	−14	6					85	61	76	3.0	8	Feb
March	7	12	54	22	72	34	94	−5	23					84	59	84	3.3	8	March
April	7	16	60	26	78	33	92	1	34			Moderate		86	59	91	3.6	7	April
May	9	19	66	29	84	37	98	7	45			Medium		87	60	119	4.7	7	May
June	11	22	72	32	90	39	103	13	55			High		87	60	117	4.6	8	June
July	10	23	74	33	92	40	104	13	55			High		88	57	99	3.9	10	July
Aug	10	23	74	34	93	42	108	12	54			High		88	54	99	3.9	10	Aug
Sept	9	21	70	31	88	38	101	8	47			High		88	58	104	4.1	8	Sept
Oct	8	16	61	27	81	37	99	1	33			Medium		86	54	94	3.7	5	Oct
Nov	6	11	52	22	71	32	89	−5	23					84	58	89	3.5	8	Nov
Dec	5	7	45	17	63	28	83	−9	15					84	64	109	4.3	10	Dec

Based on readings for 34 years at 29°46′ N, 95°22′ W, altitude 13 m/41 ft

LITTLE ROCK, ARKANSAS

SOUTHERN INTERIOR USA

Sunshine	Temperatures								Discomfort from heat and humidity	Precipitation and humidity				Wet days	
	Average daily				Highest recorded		Lowest recorded			Relative humidity 7:00 12:00		Average monthly precipitation			
	minimum		maximum												
average hours per day	°C	°F	°C	°F	°C	°F	°C	°F		%		mm	in	more than 0.25 mm/0.01 in	
Jan	4	1	34	10	50	27	81	-22	-8		79	65	122	4.8	10	Jan
Feb	5	2	36	12	54	31	87	-24	-12		78	61	97	3.8	9	Feb
March	6	7	44	17	63	32	90	-12	11		76	55	114	4.5	10	March
April	8	12	53	22	72	34	94	-2	28		77	54	130	5.1	10	April
May	9	16	61	26	79	36	97	4	39	Moderate	80	57	125	4.9	10	May
June	10	21	69	31	87	41	105	11	51	High	81	57	97	3.8	10	June
July	10	22	72	32	90	42	108	14	58	High	82	53	86	3.4	9	July
Aug	10	22	71	32	90	43	110	11	52	High	84	53	94	3.7	9	Aug
Sept	9	18	65	29	84	40	104	3	37	Medium	84	54	79	3.1	7	Sept
Oct	8	12	54	23	74	34	93	-3	27		82	55	71	2.8	7	Oct
Nov	6	6	43	16	61	29	84	-12	10		80	59	104	4.1	8	Nov
Dec	5	2	36	11	52	26	78	-15	5		80	63	104	4.1	9	Dec

Based on readings for 67 years at 34°45' N, 92°16' W, altitude 109 m/357 ft

NASHVILLE, TENNESSEE

SOUTHERN INTERIOR USA

Sunshine	Temperatures								Discomfort from heat and humidity	Precipitation and humidity				Wet days	
	Average daily				Highest recorded		Lowest recorded			Relative humidity 7:00 12:00		Average monthly precipitation			
	minimum		maximum												
average hours per day	°C	°F	°C	°F	°C	°F	°C	°F		%		mm	in	more than 0.25 mm/0.01 in	
Jan	4	-1	31	8	47	26	78	-23	-10		81	65	117	4.6	12	Jan
Feb	5	1	33	10	50	26	79	-25	-13		80	62	104	4.1	11	Feb
March	6	4	40	15	59	32	89	-16	3		77	55	130	5.1	12	March
April	8	9	49	21	69	32	90	-4	25		74	50	109	4.3	11	April
May	8	14	58	26	78	36	96	2	36	Moderate	77	54	97	3.8	11	May
June	10	19	67	30	86	38	101	6	42	Medium	78	54	104	4.1	11	June
July	10	21	70	32	89	41	106	12	54	High	79	51	102	4.0	11	July
Aug	10	20	68	31	88	41	105	11	51	Medium	83	54	91	3.6	9	Aug
Sept	8	17	62	28	82	40	104	3	38	Medium	84	53	84	3.4	8	Sept
Oct	7	10	50	22	72	33	92	-3	26		83	53	66	2.6	7	Oct
Nov	6	4	40	14	58	29	85	-13	8		80	60	89	3.5	9	Nov
Dec	4	1	33	9	49	24	75	-19	-2		81	64	102	4.0	11	Dec

Based on readings for 75 years at 36°10' N, 87°47' W, altitude 166 m/546 ft

NEW ORLEANS, LOUISIANA

GULF COAST USA

	Sunshine average hours per day	Temperatures Average daily				Highest recorded		Lowest recorded		Discomfort from heat and humidity	Precipitation and humidity Relative humidity 7:00 12:00		Average monthly precipitation		Wet days more than 0.25 mm/0.01 in	
		minimum		maximum												
		°C	°F	°C	°F	°C	°F	°C	°F		%		mm	in		
Jan	5	8	47	17	62	28	83	-9	15		85	69	117	4.6	10	Jan
Feb	6	10	50	18	65	29	84	-14	7		85	66	107	4.2	12	Feb
March	7	13	55	22	71	32	90	-2	28		85	64	119	4.7	9	March
April	8	16	61	25	77	32	90	3	38	Moderate	83	62	122	4.8	7	April
May	9	20	68	28	83	36	96	11	52	Medium	82	61	114	4.5	8	May
June	9	23	74	31	88	39	102	14	58	High	81	62	140	5.5	13	June
July	8	24	76	32	90	39	102	19	66	High	83	63	168	6.6	15	July
Aug	8	24	76	32	90	38	100	17	63	High	84	63	147	5.8	14	Aug
Sept	8	23	73	30	86	37	99	12	54	High	84	62	122	4.8	10	Sept
Oct	8	18	64	26	79	34	94	4	40	High	82	60	89	3.5	7	Oct
Nov	6	13	55	21	70	32	89	-2	29		83	63	97	3.8	7	Nov
Dec	5	9	48	18	64	29	84	-7	19		84	68	117	4.6	10	Dec

Based on readings for 73 years at 29°57' N, 90°04' W, altitude 2 m/8 ft

OKLAHOMA CITY, OKLAHOMA

SOUTHERN INTERIOR USA

	Sunshine average hours per day	Temperatures Average daily				Highest recorded		Lowest recorded		Discomfort from heat and humidity	Precipitation and humidity Relative humidity 6:30 12:00		Average monthly precipitation		Wet days more than 0.25 mm/0.01 in	
		minimum		maximum												
		°C	°F	°C	°F	°C	°F	°C	°F		%		mm	in		
Jan	5	-2	28	8	47	28	83	-24	-11		81	62	33	1.3	6	Jan
Feb	7	-1	30	11	51	32	90	-27	-17		79	54	25	1.0	5	Feb
March	7	4	39	17	62	36	97	-17	1		76	48	56	2.2	7	March
April	8	9	49	22	71	36	96	-7	20		77	51	84	3.3	8	April
May	9	14	58	26	78	37	99	1	33	Moderate	82	57	130	5.1	10	May
June	11	19	67	31	87	42	107	8	46	High	82	55	89	3.5	8	June
July	11	22	71	33	92	43	109	13	55	High	80	48	74	2.9	7	July
Aug	11	21	70	33	92	45	113	9	49	High	80	46	69	2.7	7	Aug
Sept	10	17	63	29	85	41	105	2	35	Medium	82	51	76	3.0	7	Sept
Oct	8	11	52	23	73	36	97	-9	16		79	55	76	3.0	6	Oct
Nov	7	4	39	16	60	30	86	-13	9		79	58	51	2.0	5	Nov
Dec	6	-1	30	9	49	26	79	-19	-2		80	59	41	1.6	6	Dec

Based on readings for 56 years at 35°29' N, 97°32' W, altitude 382 m/1254 ft

THE STATES OF THE ROCKY MOUNTAINS REGION

Including the mountainous country comprising all or large parts of: ARIZONA (Phoenix), COLORADO (Denver), IDAHO, MONTANA, NEVADA (Las Vegas), NEW MEXICO (Santa Fe), UTAH (Salt Lake City), and WYOMING (Cheyenne); and western TEXAS (El Paso).

It is possible to make a broad distinction between the three northern states of Idaho, Montana, Wyoming, and the rest of the mountainous country of the great Western Cordillera. In general these northern states are cooler in both winter and summer, have a much longer cold season, and are generally wetter than those farther south. Within this whole region, however, there are so many local variations of temperature and precipitation, because of the range of altitude, that one can find cold spots in the southern parts of the region and some dry areas in the north.

The tables for this region give a good indication of the range of altitude and its effect on temperature in each month. For example, there is no great difference between precipitation and temperatures for **Cheyenne, Wyoming** (see table overleaf) and **Santa Fe, New Mexico** (see table p. 402), both of which are above 1,800 m/6,000 ft. On the other hand, temperatures are very much higher in all months at **Phoenix, Arizona** (see table p. 401)at 330 m/1,083 ft than at Santa Fe.

Much of this region has a low precipitation, particularly in the south where large areas of Arizona, New Mexico, Utah, and Colorado are desert or semi-desert with annual precipitation below 300 mm/12 in or even 200 mm/8 in. This is a consequence of the rain shadow of the western mountains in California, which extract much of the moisture from air which comes in from the Pacific. It is also a result of the frequent and persistent anticyclonic weather which prevails in this region.

The table for **El Paso, Texas** (overleaf) has been included with those for this region, for this part of western Texas is mountainous.

The highest-recorded and lowest-recorded temperatures in the tables show that some extremely high and also extremely low temperatures have been recorded at different places in this mountain region: very low temperatures in the north and very high temperatures in the south.

The southern part has the sunniest climate in the United States; both Phoenix and **Las Vegas, Nevada** (see table p. 401)have about eight hours sunshine a day in winter and between twelve and thirteen hours in the summer months.

The high summer temperatures in this area are made more bearable by the low humidity and the climate of this whole region is generally healthy. Under extreme conditions, however, both heat stress and cold stress can be experienced.

See also the climatic table for **Salt Lake City, Utah** on p. 402.

CHEYENNE, WYOMING

ROCKY MOUNTAIN USA

	Sunshine	Temperatures								Discomfort from heat and humidity	Precipitation and humidity				Wet days	
		Average daily				Highest recorded		Lowest recorded			Relative humidity 6:00 12:00		Average monthly precipitation				
		minimum		maximum													
	average hours per day	°C	°F	°C	°F	°C	°F	°C	°F		%		mm	in	more than 0.25 mm/0.01 in	
Jan	6	–9	15	2	36	18	64	–39	–38		61	49	10	0.4	6	Jan
Feb	7	–9	16	3	38	19	66	–37	–34		65	49	15	0.6	6	Feb
March	8	–6	22	7	44	25	77	–29	–21		67	49	25	1.0	8	March
April	8	–2	29	12	53	28	82	–21	–6		71	49	48	1.9	10	April
May	8	3	38	17	62	31	88	–13	8		73	46	61	2.4	12	May
June	10	8	47	23	74	36	97	–2	28		70	42	41	1.6	9	June
July	10	12	53	27	80	38	100	1	33	Moderate	69	40	53	2.1	11	July
Aug	9	11	52	26	79	36	96	–4	25	Moderate	70	39	41	1.6	10	Aug
Sept	9	6	43	22	71	33	91	–9	16		66	40	31	1.2	6	Sept
Oct	8	0	32	14	58	29	85	–21	–5		64	46	25	1.0	6	Oct
Nov	6	–5	23	8	46	24	75	–29	–21		60	48	13	0.5	5	Nov
Dec	5	–8	18	4	39	21	69	–33	–28		61	51	13	0.5	5	Dec

Based on readings for 74 years at 41°09′ N, 104°49′ W, altitude 1871 m/6139 ft

EL PASO, TEXAS

ROCKY MOUNTAIN USA

	Sunshine	Temperatures								Discomfort from heat and humidity	Precipitation and humidity				Wet days	
		Average daily				Highest recorded		Lowest recorded			Relative humidity 6:00 12:00		Average monthly precipitation				
		minimum		maximum													
	average hours per day	°C	°F	°C	°F	°C	°F	°C	°F		%		mm	in	more than 0.25 mm/0.01 in	
Jan	8	0	32	14	57	25	77	–21	–6		60	37	10	0.4	3	Jan
Feb	9	3	37	17	62	30	86	–15	5		54	32	13	0.5	3	Feb
March	10	6	42	21	69	34	93	–10	14		46	26	8	0.3	3	March
April	11	10	50	25	77	35	95	–3	26		40	21	5	0.2	2	April
May	12	14	58	30	86	39	102	2	36	Moderate	38	20	8	0.3	2	May
June	13	19	67	34	94	41	106	8	46	Medium	43	22	15	0.6	3	June
July	11	21	70	34	93	41	105	13	56	Medium	60	33	46	1.8	9	July
Aug	11	20	68	33	91	39	103	11	52	Medium	65	36	41	1.6	9	Aug
Sept	11	17	63	30	86	38	100	5	41	Medium	63	35	33	1.3	6	Sept
Oct	10	11	52	25	77	34	94	–3	26		60	36	18	0.7	4	Oct
Nov	9	4	40	19	66	29	85	–12	11		60	36	13	0.5	3	Nov
Dec	8	1	33	14	57	25	77	–21	–5		62	42	13	0.5	4	Dec

Based on readings for 60 years at 31°48′ N, 106°24′ W, altitude 1194 m/3920 ft

LAS VEGAS, NEVADA

ROCKY MOUNTAIN USA

	Sunshine	Temperatures								Discomfort from heat and humidity	Precipitation and humidity				Wet days	
	average hours per day	Average daily minimum		Average daily maximum		Highest recorded		Lowest recorded			Relative humidity 5:00 17:00		Average monthly precipitation		more than 0.25 mm/0.01 in	
		°C	°F	°C	°F	°C	°F	°C	°F		%		mm	in		
Jan	8	-2	29	16	60	27	80	-13	8		59	33	18	0.7	2	Jan
Feb	9	1	34	19	67	32	89	-12	10		56	25	13	0.5	2	Feb
March	10	4	39	22	72	36	96	-9	16		47	21	8	0.3	2	March
April	11	7	45	27	81	39	102	-3	26		41	16	8	0.3	1	April
May	12	11	52	32	89	46	114	-2	28	Moderate	31	12	5	0.2	1	May
June	14	16	61	37	99	45	113	2	35	Medium	26	10	5	0.2	1	June
July	12	20	68	39	103	46	115	4	40	High	30	14	13	0.5	2	July
Aug	12	19	66	39	102	46	114	8	47	High	32	15	13	0.5	2	Aug
Sept	12	14	57	35	95	42	108	3	38	Medium	30	13	8	0.3	1	Sept
Oct	10	8	47	29	84	38	101	-2	29	Moderate	39	18	8	0.3	1	Oct
Nov	9	2	36	22	71	32	89	-10	14		49	25	5	0.2	1	Nov
Dec	10	-1	30	16	61	33	91	-11	12		61	35	10	0.4	2	Dec

Based on readings for 20 years at 36°10' N, 115°09' W, altitude 612 m/2006 ft

PHOENIX, ARIZONA

ROCKY MOUNTAIN USA

	Sunshine	Temperatures								Discomfort from heat and humidity	Precipitation and humidity				Wet days	
	average hours per day	Average daily minimum		Average daily maximum		Highest recorded		Lowest recorded			Relative humidity 5:30 17:30		Average monthly precipitation		more than 0.25 mm/0.01 in	
		°C	°F	°C	°F	°C	°F	°C	°F		%		mm	in		
Jan	8	4	39	18	65	29	84	-9	16		69	39	20	0.8	4	Jan
Feb	10	6	43	21	69	33	92	-4	24		67	34	20	0.8	4	Feb
March	11	8	47	24	75	35	95	-1	30		61	28	18	0.7	4	March
April	12	12	53	28	82	39	103	2	35	Moderate	51	21	10	0.4	2	April
May	13	16	60	33	91	46	114	4	39	Medium	42	16	3	0.1	1	May
June	14	21	69	38	101	48	118	9	49	Medium	37	14	3	0.1	1	June
July	13	25	77	40	104	48	118	17	63	High	53	24	25	1.0	5	July
Aug	12	24	76	38	101	46	115	14	58	High	60	27	25	1.0	6	Aug
Sept	12	21	69	36	97	45	113	9	49	High	56	27	18	0.7	3	Sept
Oct	10	13	56	30	86	41	105	2	36	Medium	56	30	10	0.4	2	Oct
Nov	9	7	45	24	75	36	96	-3	27		64	38	15	0.6	3	Nov
Dec	9	4	40	19	66	29	84	-6	22		67	40	23	0.9	4	Dec

Based on readings for 52 years at 33°28' N, 112°04' W, altitude 330 m/1083 ft

SALT LAKE CITY, UTAH   ROCKY MOUNTAIN USA

	Sunshine	Temperatures							Discomfort from heat and humidity	Precipitation and humidity				Wet days	
		Average daily				Highest recorded		Lowest recorded			Relative humidity		Average monthly precipitation			
		minimum		maximum							5:30 12:00					
	average hours per day	°C	°F	°C	°F	°C	°F	°C	°F		%		mm	in	more than 0.25 mm/0.01 in	
Jan	4	–8	17	2	35	17	62	–29	–20		75	64	33	1.3	10	Jan
Feb	6	–4	24	5	41	20	68	–25	–13		73	59	38	1.5	9	Feb
March	7	–1	31	11	51	26	78	–18	0		65	49	51	2.0	10	March
April	9	3	38	17	62	29	85	–8	18		60	44	51	2.0	9	April
May	11	7	45	23	73	34	93	–4	25		57	36	51	2.0	8	May
June	12	11	52	28	82	39	103	0	32	Moderate	49	28	20	0.8	5	June
July	12	16	61	33	92	41	105	6	43	Medium	46	29	15	0.6	4	July
Aug	11	16	60	32	90	39	102	6	42	Medium	47	30	20	0.8	6	Aug
Sept	10	9	49	26	79	36	97	–2	29	Moderate	50	34	25	1.0	5	Sept
Oct	8	4	40	19	66	31	88	–6	22		59	42	38	1.5	7	Oct
Nov	6	–2	28	9	49	23	74	–19	–2		65	53	36	1.4	7	Nov
Dec	4	–6	22	4	40	20	68	–23	–10		74	62	36	1.4	10	Dec

Based on readings for 19 years at 40°46′ N, 111°54′ W, altitude 689 m/4260 ft

SANTA FE, NEW MEXICO   ROCKY MOUNTAIN USA

	Sunshine	Temperatures							Discomfort from heat and humidity	Precipitation and humidity				Wet days	
		Average daily				Highest recorded		Lowest recorded			Relative humidity		Average monthly precipitation			
		minimum		maximum							6:00 12:00					
	average hours per day	°C	°F	°C	°F	°C	°F	°C	°F		%		mm	in	more than 0.25 mm/0.01 in	
Jan	7	–7	19	4	40	24	76	–25	–13		64	51	18	0.7	6	Jan
Feb	8	–5	23	6	43	24	75	–24	–11		66	49	20	0.8	6	Feb
March	8	–2	29	11	51	28	82	–19	–2		60	45	20	0.8	7	March
April	10	2	35	15	59	29	84	–12	11		54	37	25	1.0	6	April
May	11	6	43	20	68	32	89	–7	20		49	31	33	1.3	7	May
June	12	11	52	26	78	33	92	1	33	Moderate	47	31	28	1.1	6	June
July	10	14	57	27	80	36	96	6	43	Moderate	61	38	61	2.4	13	July
Aug	10	13	56	26	79	36	97	4	40	Moderate	65	39	58	2.3	12	Aug
Sept	9	9	49	23	73	32	90	–6	21		62	39	36	1.4	8	Sept
Oct	9	3	38	17	62	29	85	–11	13		59	38	31	1.2	5	Oct
Nov	8	–2	28	10	50	25	77	–24	–11		59	42	18	0.7	4	Nov
Dec	7	–7	20	4	40	18	65	–25	–13		65	54	18	0.7	6	Dec

Based on readings for 54 years at 35°41′ N, 105°57′ W, altitude 2134 m/7000 ft

THE STATES OF THE PACIFIC NORTHWEST

Including (with towns and cities in parentheses): WASHINGTON (Seattle, Spokane), OREGON (Portland), and western IDAHO (Boise).

This climatic region has weather and climate very similar to that of northwestern Europe and Britain in particular. Some parts of the state of Idaho in the Rocky Mountain region have similarities with it. This region includes a number of high mountains, part of the Western Cordillera, which rise to over 4,250 m/14,000 ft and are snow-covered throughout the year. Thus the higher parts of these two states have some similarity with the weather and climate of the northern part of the Rocky Mountains.

The coastal districts have the smallest annual range of temperatures anywhere in the United States; winters are mild and summers only moderately warm. It is a cloudy region and the least sunny part of the USA with a large number of rainy days. Some of the mountain areas are very wet with as much as 2,500–3,000 mm/100–120 in of precipitation a year.

By contrast, in the sheltered valleys and in some of the extensive high plateaux districts, annual precipitation is as low as 300m/12 in. This is also the one region of the country where winter is the wettest season, although some rain and changeable weather can occur in all months. There is no real summer drought such as occurs farther south in California.

The tables for **Seattle, Washington** (overleaf) and **Portland, Oregon** (overleaf) are representative of the coastal districts, while those for **Spokane, Washington** (p. 405) and **Boise, Idaho** (below) are typical of areas farther inland at moderate height. Sea fog in summer can affect some of the coastal regions and reduce sunshine and lower temperature.

The region owes its wetness and mildness to the influence of the Pacific Ocean and the frequent passage of cyclonic depressions which originate on the North Pacific polar front. The air-masses involved in these depressions do not have the extreme conditions of temperature which give so much of the interior of the United States a continental type of climate with frequent alternations of warm and very cold weather as well as a great contrast between summer heat and winter cold.

The average number of sunshine hours per day ranges from two to three hours in winter and nine to ten in summer on the coast. Inland and at higher levels the winters are sunnier with as much as five to six hours a day.

BOISE, IDAHO

PACIFIC NORTHWEST USA

Sunshine average hours per day	Temperatures Average daily minimum °C	°F	maximum °C	°F	Highest recorded °C	°F	Lowest recorded °C	°F	Discomfort from heat and humidity	Relative humidity 5:30 %	17:30	Average monthly precipitation mm	in	Wet days more than 0.25mm/0.01 in
Jan	3	−6	22	3	38	17	62	−33 −28		82	70	48	1.9	11	Jan
Feb	5	−3	27	6	43	21	69	−25 −13		79	59	36	1.4	9	Feb
March	7	1	33	12	53	28	83	−21 −5		74	46	41	1.6	9	March
April	9	3	38	17	62	33	92	−12 11		70	37	31	1.2	7	April
May	11	7	45	22	71	38 100	−4 25		70	34	36	1.4	7	May
June	12	11	51	27	80	43 109	−1 30	Moderate	67	30	20	0.8	5	June
July	14	14	58	32	90	45 113	4 40	Medium	54	21	5	0.2	2	July
Aug	12	13	56	31	88	44 112	0 32	Medium	52	22	5	0.2	2	Aug
Sept	11	8	47	24	76	39 103	−5 23		61	31	13	0.5	3	Sept
Oct	8	4	39	18	64	35	95	−10 14		70	42	28	1.1	5	Oct
Nov	5	−1	31	10	50	29	85	−23 −10		74	57	36	1.4	8	Nov
Dec	4	−4	24	4	40	21	70	−28 −18		84	74	43	1.7	10	Dec

Based on readings for 62 years at 43°34' N, 115°13' W, altitude 867 m/2844 ft

PORTLAND, OREGON

PACIFIC NORTHWEST USA

	Sunshine	Temperatures								Discomfort from heat and humidity	Precipitation and humidity				Wet days	
		Average daily				Highest recorded		Lowest recorded			Relative humidity		Average monthly precipitation			
		minimum		maximum							4:30	16:30				
	average hours per day	°C	°F	°C	°F	°C	°F	°C	°F		%		mm	in	more than 0.25 mm/0.01 in	
Jan	2	1	34	7	44	18	65	-19	-2		86	78	155	6.1	19	Jan
Feb	3	2	36	9	48	20	68	-14	7		85	71	132	5.2	17	Feb
March	4	4	39	12	54	28	83	-7	20		85	61	117	4.6	17	March
April	6	6	43	16	61	34	93	-2	28		84	54	71	2.8	14	April
May	7	8	47	19	66	37	99	0	32		84	51	53	2.1	13	May
June	7	12	53	22	72	39	102	4	39		83	51	41	1.6	10	June
July	10	13	56	25	77	42	107	6	43	Moderate	82	45	13	0.5	3	July
Aug	8	13	56	25	77	39	102	6	43	Moderate	84	46	15	0.6	4	Aug
Sept	7	11	52	22	71	39	102	2	35		86	53	46	1.8	8	Sept
Oct	4	8	47	17	62	31	88	-2	29		89	66	84	3.3	12	Oct
Nov	3	5	41	12	53	23	73	-12	11		88	77	158	6.2	17	Nov
Dec	2	3	37	8	46	18	65	-16	3		86	80	178	7.0	19	Dec

Based on readings for 72 years at 45°32' N, 122°40' W, altitude 47 m/154 ft

SEATTLE, WASHINGTON

PACIFIC NORTHWEST USA

	Sunshine	Temperatures								Discomfort from heat and humidity	Precipitation and humidity				Wet days	
		Average daily				Highest recorded		Lowest recorded			Relative humidity		Average monthly precipitation			
		minimum		maximum							4:30	16:30				
	average hours per day	°C	°F	°C	°F	°C	°F	°C	°F		%		mm	in	more than 0.25 mm/0.01 in	
Jan	2	2	36	7	45	19	67	-16	3		86	79	122	4.8	18	Jan
Feb	4	3	37	9	48	21	70	-16	4		85	73	94	3.7	16	Feb
March	5	4	39	11	52	27	81	-7	20		85	65	79	3.1	16	March
April	7	6	43	14	58	31	87	-1	30		85	58	58	2.3	13	April
May	8	8	47	18	64	33	92	2	36		85	56	46	1.8	12	May
June	8	11	52	21	69	37	98	4	40		84	54	36	1.4	9	June
July	10	12	54	22	72	38	100	8	46		85	51	15	0.6	4	July
Aug	8	13	55	23	73	36	96	8	46		87	54	18	0.7	5	Aug
Sept	7	11	52	19	67	33	92	2	36		89	61	43	1.7	8	Sept
Oct	4	8	47	15	59	28	82	-2	29		90	73	74	2.9	13	Oct
Nov	3	5	41	11	51	20	68	-9	15		88	80	122	4.8	17	Nov
Dec	2	3	38	8	47	18	65	-11	12		87	81	142	5.6	19	Dec

Based on readings for 57 years at 47°36' N, 122°20' W, altitude 38 m/125 ft

SPOKANE, WASHINGTON

PACIFIC NORTHWEST USA

	Sunshine	Temperatures									Discomfort from heat and humidity	Precipitation and humidity					Wet days	
		Average daily				Highest recorded		Lowest recorded				Relative humidity 5:00 17:00		Average monthly precipitation				
		minimum		maximum													
	average hours per day	°C	°F	°C	°F	°C	°F	°C	°F			%		mm	in	more than 0.25 mm/0.01 in	
Jan	2	–6	22	1	33	17	62	–34	–30		86	78	53	2.1	14	Jan
Feb	4	–4	24	4	39	16	60	–31	–23		85	68	43	1.7	12	Feb
March	6	–1	31	9	49	23	74	–23	–10		79	51	31	1.2	11	March
April	9	3	38	15	60	32	90	–10	14		75	39	28	1.1	9	April
May	10	7	45	20	68	36	97	–2	29		74	37	33	1.3	9	May
June	10	11	51	24	75	38	100	1	34		70	33	33	1.3	8	June
July	13	13	56	29	84	42	108	5	41	Moderate	63	24	15	0.6	4	July
Aug	11	12	54	28	83	40	104	3	37	Moderate	63	25	15	0.6	4	Aug
Sept	9	8	47	22	72	37	98	–6	22		73	35	23	0.9	7	Sept
Oct	5	3	38	16	60	31	87	–13	9		81	49	28	1.1	8	Oct
Nov	3	–1	31	7	44	21	70	–25	–13		86	73	53	2.1	13	Nov
Dec	2	–3	26	2	36	16	60	–28	–18		86	81	53	2.1	14	Dec

Based on readings for 66 years at 43°37′ N, 117°31′ W, altitude 719 m/2357 ft

CALIFORNIA

California enjoys a very distinctive climate of the Mediterranean type and this climatic region is almost coincident with the state boundary. The northern coast of California has a climate similar to the coastal districts of the northwest but there is a gradual increase in summer temperature southwards and a decrease of rainfall until the summers become completely dry in central and southern California.

In the southeast of the state precipitation decreases until conditions become similar to those of the desert regions of neighbouring Arizona and northern Mexico. Most of California enjoys mild and moderately wet winters and warm to hot and very dry summers. There are some large mountain regions within the state: the coast ranges and the Sierra Nevada, which rise to over 3,700 m/12,000 ft. These mountains have a heavy precipitation and, at higher levels, much of this is snow so there are many opportunities for winter sports within a state which is often associated with sun, sea, and warmth.

The tables for **San Francisco** (p. 408), **Los Angeles** (opposite) and **San Diego** (p. 408) are representative of the coastal region. San Francisco is unusual in having cool to mild summers. This is a very local feature caused by the frequent sea fog which sweeps into the bay through the Golden Gate gap in the coast range. Elsewhere this sea fog rarely affects the land but the cool waters of the California current help to maintain much lower summer temperatures on the coast than inland.

In the Great Valley of California and in the desert areas in the southeast, summer temperatures are much higher. Frost and snow are very rare occurrences on the coast but occur more frequently inland in winter. The table for **Death Valley** (opposite) shows the extremely high temperatures here in summer. This place has not only experienced the highest temperatures in the United States but some of the highest recorded anywhere in the world.

The winter precipitation of California is caused but the same sequence of cyclonic depressions as bring rain to the sates of the northwest. In summer such disturbances are pushed farther north by the almost permanent presence of the North Pacific subtropical anticyclone. It brings calm, settled, sunny weather.

This anticyclone is also responsible, however, for the most unpleasant and dangerous weather phenomenon which particularly affects the great urban area of Los Angeles: urban smog. This is a combination of fog and pollution from automobiles and industry. The pollution is trapped beneath a layer of warm air which overlies the coast; the light winds are unable to disperse it beyond the encircling hills and mountains.

Apart from this particular hazard, most of California has a very agreeable and healthy climate throughout the year: sunny and dry with only short periods of relatively cold weather in winter. The visitor should obviously avoid going to such 'hot spots' as Death Valley without taking sensible precautions or ignoring the fact that very heavy snowstorms can occur in the mountains of California.

California is one of the sunniest states in the country. Sunshine hours a day average from seven to eight in winter to as many as twelve to fourteen in summer in the driest regions inland. On the coast they are rather less: from six to seven in winter and nine to ten in summer. The reduction in summer sunshine on the coast is because of sea fog.

DEATH VALLEY
CALIFORNIA

	Sunshine	Average daily minimum		Average daily maximum		Highest recorded		Lowest recorded		Discomfort from heat and humidity	Relative humidity	Average monthly precipitation		Wet days more than 0.25 mm/0.01 in	
	average hours per day	°C	°F	°C	°F	°C	°F	°C	°F		%	mm	in		
Jan		3	38	19	66	29	85	−9	15			3	0.1	1.0	Jan
Feb		7	44	22	72	33	92	−6	21			0	0.0	1.0	Feb
March		11	51	27	81	38	100	−1	30			3	0.1	2.0	March
April		16	60	32	90	43	109	2	35			3	0.1	1.0	April
May		21	69	37	99	49	120	6	42			5	0.2	0.5	May
June		26	78	43	109	51	124	9	49			3	0.1	0.1	June
July		31	87	47	116	57	134	17	62			8	0.3	0.3	July
Aug		29	84	46	114	53	127	18	65			8	0.3	0.7	Aug
Sept		23	73	41	106	49	121	5	41			5	0.2	0.3	Sept
Oct		15	59	33	91	43	110	0	32			0	0.0	1.0	Oct
Nov		8	46	24	76	34	93	−4	24			3	0.1	1.0	Nov
Dec		4	39	19	66	30	86	−7	19			0	0.0	2.0	Dec

Based on readings for 37 years at 36°28′ N, 116°51′ W, altitude − 54 m/− 178 ft

LOS ANGELES
CALIFORNIA

	Sunshine	Average daily minimum		Average daily maximum		Highest recorded		Lowest recorded		Discomfort from heat and humidity	Relative humidity 5:00	Relative humidity 12:00	Average monthly precipitation		Wet days more than 0.25 mm/0.01 in	
	average hours per day	°C	°F	°C	°F	°C	°F	°C	°F		%	%	mm	in		
Jan	7	8	46	18	65	32	90	−2	28		67	47	79	3.1	6	Jan
Feb	8	8	47	19	66	33	92	−2	28		74	53	76	3.0	6	Feb
March	9	9	48	19	67	37	99	−1	31		77	51	71	2.8	6	March
April	9	10	50	21	70	38	100	2	36		82	55	25	1.0	4	April
May	9	12	53	22	72	39	103	4	40		86	59	10	0.4	2	May
June	10	13	56	24	76	41	105	8	46	Moderate	87	58	3	0.1	1	June
July	12	16	60	27	81	43	109	9	49	Medium	88	55	0	0.0	0	July
Aug	11	16	60	28	82	41	106	9	49	Medium	87	54	0	0.0	0	Aug
Sept	10	14	58	27	81	42	108	7	44	Medium	82	52	5	0.2	1	Sept
Oct	9	12	54	24	76	39	102	4	40		75	49	15	0.6	2	Oct
Nov	8	10	50	23	73	36	96	1	34		62	38	31	1.2	3	Nov
Dec	8	8	47	19	67	33	92	−1	30		60	44	66	2.6	6	Dec

Based on readings for 70 years at 34°03′ N, 118°15′ W, altitude 95 m/312 ft

SAN DIEGO — CALIFORNIA

	Sunshine average hours per day	Temperatures Average daily minimum °C	°F	Average daily maximum °C	°F	Highest recorded °C	°F	Lowest recorded °C	°F	Discomfort from heat and humidity	Relative humidity 4:30 %	16:30 %	Average monthly precipitation mm	in	Wet days more than 0.25 mm/0.01 in	
Jan	7	8	47	17	63	29	85	-4	25		73	67	48	1.9	6	Jan
Feb	8	9	48	17	63	32	89	1	34		79	68	53	2.1	7	Feb
March	8	10	50	18	64	37	99	2	36		80	66	38	1.5	7	March
April	8	12	53	19	66	36	96	4	39		82	68	18	0.7	4	April
May	8	13	56	19	67	37	98	7	45		83	71	8	0.3	3	May
June	8	15	59	21	69	36	96	10	50		86	72	3	0.1	1	June
July	10	17	63	23	73	38	100	12	54	Moderate	87	73	3	0.1	1	July
Aug	9	18	64	23	74	34	94	12	54	Moderate	87	73	3	0.1	1	Aug
Sept	9	17	62	23	73	43	110	10	50	Moderate	86	72	3	0.1	1	Sept
Oct	8	14	57	22	71	36	96	7	44		81	71	10	0.4	3	Oct
Nov	8	11	52	21	69	34	93	2	36		71	67	23	0.9	4	Nov
Dec	8	9	48	18	65	29	84	0	32		70	67	51	2.0	6	Dec

Based on readings for 72 years at 32°44′ N, 117°10′ W, altitude 6 m/19 ft

SAN FRANCISO — CALIFORNIA

	Sunshine average hours per day	Temperatures Average daily minimum °C	°F	Average daily maximum °C	°F	Highest recorded °C	°F	Lowest recorded °C	°F	Discomfort from heat and humidity	Relative humidity 5:00 %	12:00 %	Average monthly precipitation mm	in	Wet days more than 0.25 mm/0.01 in	
Jan	5	7	45	13	55	26	78	-2	29		85	69	119	4.7	11	Jan
Feb	7	8	47	15	59	27	80	1	33		84	66	97	3.8	11	Feb
March	8	9	48	16	61	30	86	1	33		83	61	79	3.1	10	March
April	10	9	49	17	62	32	89	4	40		83	61	38	1.5	6	April
May	11	11	51	17	63	36	97	6	42		85	62	18	0.7	4	May
June	11	11	52	19	66	38	100	8	46		88	64	3	0.1	2	June
July	10	12	53	18	65	37	99	8	47		91	69	0	0	0	July
Aug	9	12	53	18	65	33	92	8	46		92	70	0	0	0	Aug
Sept	9	13	55	21	69	38	101	8	47		88	63	8	0.3	2	Sept
Oct	8	12	54	20	68	36	96	6	43		85	58	25	1.0	4	Oct
Nov	7	11	51	17	63	28	83	3	38		83	60	64	2.5	7	Nov
Dec	6	8	47	14	57	23	74	-3	27		83	68	112	4.4	10	Dec

Based on readings for 73 years at 37°47′ N, 122°25′ W, altitude 16 m/52 ft

ALASKA

Alaska is one of the states of the USA but is described separately here because of its geographical separation from the rest of the continental United States. Twice as large as Texas, it is the largest state of the Union.

It comprises the northwestern lands of the North American continent, between 60° and 72° N and two separate and distinct appendages. There is a narrow mountainous coastal strip with numerous offshore islands extending south to 55° N to give Alaska a long land border into the North Pacific between 50° and 55° N towards the coast of Siberia.

Much of Alaska is mountainous as it includes the northern ranges of the Rocky Mountains with some of the highest mountains in North America. Large and impressive glaciers descend from the mountains almost to sea level. Inland there are extensive lowlands including the valleys of the Yukon and Porcupine rivers.

The interior and north coast of Alaska have a cold Arctic or sub-Arctic climate similar to that described on p. 89 for northern Canada. The mountains have permanent snow and ice and the lowlands suffer from permafrost. The rivers remain frozen from

September until late May. The table for **Fairbanks** (below) is representative of much of interior Alaska. The short summer can be surprisingly warm for the latitude and this is helped by the long hours of daylight and, in fine weather, the prolonged sunshine.

Winters are long and very severe. Wind chill is a serious hazard when low temperatures are accompanied by strong winds (see p. 2). The low annual precipitation is largely snow but summer is the wettest season and some rain occurs then.

The table for **Barrow** (overleaf) on the shores of the Arctic Ocean shows that summer here is colder and shorter. The sea is frozen for most of the year or partially blocked by drift ice in summer.

On the Pacific coast the weather and climate are rather different. This is a region of much heavier precipitation with more changeable and disturbed weather throughout the year. Summer temperatures are cool and may be less warm than inland.

Winters are cool but mild compared with the very low temperatures inland. Weather and climate here are very much influenced by the frequent frontal depressions which develop in the North Pacific between Japan and the Aleutian Islands. Cloud and

FAIRBANKS — ALASKA

Sunshine	Temperatures								Discomfort from heat and humidity	Precipitation and humidity				Wet days	
	Average daily		Highest recorded		Lowest recorded					Relative humidity		Average monthly precipitation			
	minimum		maximum							2:00	14:00				
average hours per day	°C	°F	°C	°F	°C	°F	°C	°F		%		mm	in	more than 0.25 mm/0.01 in	
Jan	2	−29	−20	−19	−2	6	42	−54	−66		81	81	23	0.9	10	Jan
Feb	4	−23	−10	−12	11	10	50	−50	−58		80	72	13	0.5	6	Feb
March	8	−20	−4	−5	23	13	56	−49	−56		79	50	18	0.7	6	March
April	11	−8	17	6	42	21	69	−36	−32		76	41	8	0.3	4	April
May	11	2	35	15	59	30	86	−18	0		77	39	15	0.6	9	May
June	13	8	46	22	71	35	95	−2	28		83	41	33	1.3	10	June
July	9	9	48	22	72	37	99	−1	30		88	48	48	1.9	13	July
Aug	5	7	44	19	66	32	90	−7	19		90	55	53	2.1	15	Aug
Sept	5	1	33	12	54	27	80	−12	11		86	55	33	1.3	10	Sept
Oct	3	−8	18	2	35	19	67	−33	−28		84	67	20	0.8	11	Oct
Nov	2	−21	−5	−11	12	12	54	−47	−54		82	79	18	0.7	10	Nov
Dec	1	−27	−16	−17	1	14	58	−51	−59		82	83	15	0.6	7	Dec

Based on readings for 43 years at 64°51′ N, 147°43′ W, altitude 134 m/440 ft

BARROW
ALASKA

Sunshine	Temperatures								Discomfort from heat and humidity	Precipitation and humidity				Wet days	
	Average daily				Highest recorded		Lowest recorded			Relative humidity 8:00 14:00		Average monthly precipitation			
	minimum		maximum												
average hours per day	°C	°F	°C	°F	°C	°F	°C	°F		%		mm	in	more than 0.25 mm/0.01 in	
Jan	−30	−22	−23	−9	1	33	−47	−53		68	67	5	0.2	3	Jan
Feb	−32	−25	−24	−12	−1	31	−50	−56		66	66	3	0.1	3	Feb
March	−30	−22	−22	−8	−1	30	−47	−52		67	69	3	0.1	3	March
April	−22	−8	−14	7	6	42	−41	−42		76	75	3	0.1	3	April
May	−11	13	−4	24	7	45	−28	−18		88	86	3	0.1	3	May
June	−2	29	4	39	21	70	−13	8		93	92	8	0.3	4	June
July	1	33	8	46	26	78	−6	22		91	88	23	0.9	8	July
Aug	1	33	7	44	23	73	−7	20		93	89	20	0.8	10	Aug
Sept	−3	27	1	34	15	59	−16	4		92	90	13	0.5	8	Sept
Oct	−11	12	−6	22	4	40	−28	−19		87	87	13	0.5	9	Oct
Nov	−21	−5	−14	7	4	39	−40	−40		77	77	8	0.3	5	Nov
Dec	−27	−17	−20	−4	1	34	−48	−55		69	70	5	0.2	4	Dec

Based on readings for 32 years at 71°18′ N, 156°47′ W, altitude 7 m/22 ft

ANCHORAGE
ALASKA

Sunshine average hours per day	Temperatures								Discomfort from heat and humidity	Precipitation and humidity				Wet days	
	Average daily				Highest recorded		Lowest recorded			Relative humidity 6:30 12:30		Average monthly precipitation			
	minimum		maximum												
	°C	°F	°C	°F	°C	°F	°C	°F		%		mm	in	more than 0.25 mm/0.01 in	
Jan 2	−15	5	−7	19	13	56	−36	−33		75	73	20	0.8	7	Jan
Feb 3	−13	9	−3	27	13	55	−36	−32		73	62	18	0.7	6	Feb
March 6	−11	13	1	33	13	56	−28	−19		73	59	15	0.6	5	March
April 9	−3	27	7	44	17	63	−26	−15		66	51	10	0.4	4	April
May 8	2	36	12	54	22	71	−7	20		64	49	13	0.5	5	May
June 10	7	44	17	62	33	92	−2	29		68	57	18	0.7	6	June
July 8	9	49	18	65	27	81	1	34		75	63	41	1.6	10	July
Aug 6	8	47	18	64	28	82	−1	31		78	65	66	2.6	15	Aug
Sept 4	4	39	14	57	23	73	−7	19		84	66	66	2.6	14	Sept
Oct 3	−2	29	6	43	17	63	−21	−6		83	69	56	2.2	12	Oct
Nov 2	−9	15	−1	30	17	62	−28	−18		78	74	25	1.0	7	Nov
Dec 2	−14	6	−7	20	12	53	−38	−36		77	76	23	0.9	6	Dec

Based on readings for 22 years at 61°14′ N, 149°49′ W, altitude 40 m/132 ft

ATKA

Sunshine	Temperatures								Discomfort from heat and humidity	Precipitation and humidity			Wet days
	Average daily				Highest recorded		Lowest recorded			Relative humidity	Average monthly precipitation		
	minimum		maximum										
average hours per day	°C	°F	°C	°F	°C	°F	°C	°F	%	mm	in	more than 0.25 mm/0.01 in	
Jan	−1	30	3	37	10	50	−10	14			163	6.4	21	Jan
Feb	−2	29	3	37	8	47	11	12			119	4.7	17	Feb
March	−2	29	3	38	11	51	−9	15			127	5.0	19	March
April	0	32	6	42	15	59	−6	21			125	4.9	18	April
May	2	36	7	45	18	65	−4	24			122	4.8	17	May
June	4	40	11	51	22	72	−2	28			99	3.9	14	June
July	7	44	13	55	24	76	2	35			135	5.3	16	July
Aug	8	46	14	57	24	76	3	38			137	5.4	16	Aug
Sept	6	43	14	57	19	66	−2	29			180	7.1	21	Sept
Oct	3	37	8	47	14	57	−4	24			188	7.4	23	Oct
Nov	1	33	5	41	14	57	−11	13			211	8.3	23	Nov
Dec	−2	29	3	37	9	48	−11	12			155	6.1	21	Dec

Based on readings for 13 years at 52°10′ N, 174°12′ W, altitude 8 m/26 ft

fog are frequent at all seasons. The table for **Anchorage** (opposite), in a deep-sheltered bay on the west coast, shows warmer winter temperatures than inland. Anchorage, however, is much colder than both the offshore islands and the Aleutians, which benefit from the relatively warm sea temperatures of the Pacific. The coastal region and the islands have weather and climate very similar to that experienced on the coasts of Norway. The climatic table for **Atka** (above) is representative of the weather and climate of the Aleutian Islands.

HAWAII

Including (with towns and cities in parentheses): HAWAII (Pepeekeo), KAUAI, MAUI, MOLOKAI, and OAHU (Honolulu).

These islands are a state of the USA; they are situated between 18° and 22° N in the central Pacific, almost midway between North America and Japan. In area the islands are rather smaller than Wales or the state of Massachusetts; about 16,400 sq km/6,400 sq mi.

There are eight main islands; all are hilly and mountainous and consist of both extinct and active volcanoes. On the islands of Hawaii and Maui these peaks exceed 3,000 m/10,000 ft in height.

The islands have a tropical oceanic climate with temperatures much moderated both by altitude and by regular sea breezes at lower levels. As the tables show, there is no great difference in average daily temperatures around the year and, although warm or even hot, the combination of temperature and humidity is rarely unpleasant.

There are some remarkable differences in annual rainfall between the southwest coasts, which are relatively dry (see the table for **Honolulu** opposite), and the northeastern coasts exposed to the trade winds (see the table for **Pepeekeo** opposite and below), which receive much heavier rainfall in all months. In the drier parts of the islands the wettest season is the time of low sun between October and March, which is rather unusual in the tropics.

Some mountain slopes on the island of Hawaii are amongst the wettest regions in the world, with an annual rainfall exceeding 10,000 mm/400 in. The difference in the amount of cloud between the wetter and drier areas causes the average daily sunshine hours to vary between seven and ten hours throughout the year at Honolulu to a mere four to five hours at the wetter places.

The islands are occasionally affected by tropical cyclones between May and November, which otherwise is the drier time of year. Such severe storms, however, are less frequent here than in the Caribbean or the South China Sea and west Pacific.

HONOLULU

HAWAIIAN ISLANDS

Sunshine	Temperatures								Discomfort from heat and humidity	Precipitation and humidity			Wet days
	Average daily		Highest recorded		Lowest recorded					Relative humidity	Average monthly precipitation		
	minimum	maximum								8:00 12:00			
average hours per day	°C	°F	°C	°F	°C	°F	°C	°F		%	mm	in	more than 0.25 mm/0.01 in
Jan	7	21	69	24	76	29	84	12	54	Moderate	75	66	104	4.1	14	Jan
Feb	8	19	67	24	76	29	84	11	52	Moderate	75	67	66	2.6	11	Feb
March	9	19	67	25	77	29	84	12	53	Moderate	73	65	79	3.1	13	March
April	9	20	68	26	78	30	86	15	59	Medium	69	64	48	1.9	12	April
May	10	21	70	27	80	31	87	16	60	Medium	69	64	25	1.0	11	May
June	10	22	72	27	81	31	88	17	63	Medium	69	63	18	0.7	12	June
July	11	23	73	28	82	31	88	17	63	Medium	70	63	23	0.9	14	July
Aug	11	23	74	28	83	31	88	17	63	Medium	71	64	28	1.1	13	Aug
Sept	9	23	74	28	83	31	88	17	63	Medium	71	65	36	1.4	13	Sept
Oct	8	22	72	28	82	32	90	17	63	Medium	73	66	48	1.9	13	Oct
Nov	6	21	70	27	80	30	86	15	59	Medium	74	67	64	2.5	13	Nov
Dec	7	21	69	26	78	29	85	13	55	Medium	75	68	104	4.1	15	Dec

Based on readings for 40 years at 21°19' N, 157°52' E, altitude 12 m/38 ft

PEPEEKEO

HAWAIIAN ISLANDS

Sunshine	Temperatures								Discomfort from heat and humidity	Precipitation and humidity		Wet days
	Average daily		Highest recorded		Lowest recorded					Relative humidity	Average monthly precipitation	
	minimum	maximum										
average hours per day	°C	°F	°C	°F	°C	°F	°C	°F		%	mm	in	more than 0.25 mm/0.01 in
Jan	7	18	64	26	78	31	87	13	56			312	12.3	20	Jan
Feb	7	17	63	26	78	31	87	13	56			234	9.2	16	Feb
March	8	18	64	26	78	32	89	13	56			366	14.4	22	March
April	9	18	65	26	78	30	86	14	57			290	11.4	24	April
May	9	19	66	27	80	31	88	15	59			216	8.5	22	May
June	10	19	67	27	81	30	86	14	58			170	6.7	22	June
July	10	20	68	28	82	31	88	16	61			244	9.6	25	July
Aug	10	20	68	28	82	31	88	16	61			274	10.8	26	Aug
Sept	11	20	68	28	82	31	88	15	59			269	10.6	24	Sept
Oct	9	20	68	28	82	32	89	16	60			254	10.0	23	Oct
Nov	7	19	66	27	81	32	89	14	58			310	12.2	22	Nov
Dec	7	18	65	26	79	32	90	14	57			307	12.1	22	Dec

Based on readings for 34 years at 19°51' N, 155°03' W, altitude 31 m/100 ft

MONTEVIDEO
COASTAL URUGUAY

Sunshine	Temperatures								Discomfort from heat and humidity	Precipitation and humidity				Wet days	
	Average daily				Highest recorded		Lowest recorded			Relative humidity 7:00 14:00		Average monthly precipitation			
	minimum		maximum												
average hours per day	°C	°F	°C	°F	°C	°F	°C	°F		%		mm	in	more than 1 mm/0.04 in	
Jan	11	17	62	28	83	43	109	8	46	Medium	76	53	74	2.9	6	Jan
Feb	10	16	61	28	82	41	105	8	46	Medium	81	55	66	2.6	5	Feb
March	9	15	59	26	78	38	101	4	40	Moderate	85	57	99	3.9	5	March
April	8	12	53	22	71	37	98	2	36		87	61	99	3.9	6	April
May	6	9	48	18	64	31	87	-2	29		89	66	84	3.3	6	May
June	5	6	43	15	59	27	81	-4	25		89	69	81	3.2	5	June
July	5	6	43	14	58	28	83	-3	26		89	69	74	2.9	6	July
Aug	6	6	43	15	59	26	79	-4	25		88	67	79	3.1	7	Aug
Sept	7	8	46	17	63	30	86	-2	29		87	65	76	3.0	6	Sept
Oct	8	9	49	20	68	34	94	-2	29		82	62	66	2.6	6	Oct
Nov	10	12	54	23	74	37	98	3	38		77	56	74	2.9	6	Nov
Dec	10	15	59	26	79	39	102	5	41	Moderate	73	52	79	3.1	7	Dec

Based on readings for 56 years at 34°52′ S, 56°12′ W, altitude 22 m/72 ft

Uruguay

See map page 16

Uruguay is a little smaller than the United Kingdom and about the same size as the state of Washington. It lies on the east coast of South America between 30° and 35° S. It is bordered on the north by Brazil and on the west by the river Uruguay, which forms the border with Argentina. Most of the country is low-lying and rather flat with the highest hills rising to about 450 m/1,500 ft.

The climate of Uruguay is similar to that of the Pampas region of Argentina and because of the level nature of the country there is little variation of weather and climate within Uruguay, The table for **Montevideo** (above) is representative of the coastal districts and there are only slight differences between these and the areas farther inland.

Most of Uruguay has a moderate annual rainfall of about 1,000 mm/40 in; this is well distributed throughout the year but the autumn months tend to be slightly wetter. Rain falls on a comparatively small

number of days; about one day in five at all seasons. When it occurs it is often moderate to heavy.

The summers are warm but not as hot as in some other countries in similar latitudes, such as the southern Atlantic coastlands of the USA or parts of southeastern Australia. Winters are mild and frost and snow are very rare. Southerly winds can bring occasional spells of colder weather, which may be associated with squally winds or gales in the estuary of the river Plate. However, such outbreaks of colder polar air from Antarctica are much modified after they have crossed some thousands of miles of warmer water in the South Atlantic.

Inland the summer temperatures are a little higher than those found on the coast. Sunshine hours are high in Uruguay, ranging from five to six hours a day in winter to as much as nine to ten in summer. The climate of Uruguay is rarely uncomfortable or unpleasant and can be described as healthy for most of the year.

TASHKENT

EASTERN UZBEKISTAN

	Sunshine	Temperatures							Discomfort from heat and humidity	Precipitation and humidity				Wet days
		Average daily				Highest recorded		Lowest recorded			Relative humidity 7:00 13:00		Average monthly precipitation		more than 0.1 mm/0.004 in
		minimum		maximum											
	average hours per day	°C	°F	°C	°F	°C	°F	°C	°F		%		mm	in	
Jan	4	–6	21	3	37	19	66	–28	–19		82	63	53	2.1	10	Jan
Feb	4	–3	27	7	44	24	76	–26	–14		78	58	28	1.1	8	Feb
March	5	3	37	12	53	30	86	–19	–3		77	55	66	2.6	12	March
April	8	8	47	18	65	33	91	–5	23		72	52	58	2.3	10	April
May	10	13	56	26	78	39	103	1	33	Moderate	66	42	36	1.4	7	May
June	12	17	62	31	87	41	106	6	43	Medium	59	34	13	0.5	4	June
July	13	18	64	33	92	41	106	9	48	Medium	63	33	5	0.2	1	July
Aug	12	16	60	32	89	39	102	8	46	Medium	61	32	3	0.1	1	Aug
Sept	10	11	52	27	80	36	96	1	33	Moderate	66	34	3	0.1	1	Sept
Oct	8	5	41	18	65	35	95	–6	21		76	43	31	1.2	5	Oct
Nov	5	2	35	12	53	27	81	–22	–7		79	55	38	1.5	7	Nov
Dec	4	–2	29	7	44	22	72	–24	–12		79	62	41	1.6	9	Dec

Based on readings for 19 years at 41°20' N, 69°18' E, altitude 478 m/1569 ft

Uzbekistan

See map page 22

This is one of the driest countries in central Asia. It includes extensive lowland deserts as well as semi-arid steppes. The summers in the low country are warm to hot but the heat is made more bearable by the low humidity. The winters are cold but generally dry and sunny over most of the region. The table for **Kazalinsk** (p. 206) in Kazakhstan gives an indication of the weather in these regions.

The east of the country borders on high mountains that carry snow the year round. However, because of the distance from the sea and the shelter of the Pamir and Himalayan ranges to the south and southeast, it is a rather dry region considering its height. Winters are cold in the mountains but spring comes earlier than farther north. The table for **Tashkent** (above) illustrates conditions in the valleys of Uzbekistan's mountainous eastern region.

TANNA											NEW HEBRIDES	
Sunshine	Temperatures						Discomfort from heat and humidity	Precipitation and humidity			Wet days	
	Average daily				Highest recorded	Lowest recorded		Relative humidity 9:00 21:00		Average monthly precipitation		
	minimum		maximum									
average hours per day	°C	°F	°C	°F	°C	°F	°C	°F	%		mm	in	more than 2.5 mm/0.1 in
Jan	23	73	28	83	32	89	19	66	High	80	87	257	10.1	12	Jan
Feb	23	74	29	84	32	90	19	66	High	83	88	272	10.7	12	Feb
March	23	73	29	84	34	94	18	65	High	82	87	282	11.1	11	March
April	22	72	27	81	31	88	16	60	Medium	82	85	338	13.3	13	April
May	21	70	26	79	29	85	15	59	Medium	77	82	244	9.6	9	May
June	19	67	25	77	30	86	14	57	Medium	78	83	127	5.0	9	June
July	19	67	24	76	30	86	14	57	Medium	78	83	158	6.2	9	July
Aug	18	65	24	76	29	85	12	54	Medium	72	80	125	4.9	5	Aug
Sept	19	67	24	76	29	85	13	55	Medium	77	81	99	3.9	7	Sept
Oct	20	68	26	78	29	84	13	55	Medium	77	82	137	5.4	8	Oct
Nov	21	70	27	80	30	86	16	61	Medium	76	83	165	6.5	7	Nov
Dec	22	72	28	82	31	88	17	62	High	79	86	201	7.9	10	Dec

Based on readings for 8 years at 19°30′ S, 169°20′ E, altitude 38 m/125 ft

Vanuatu

See map page 17

This southwest Pacific republic comprises thirteen main islands and numerous smaller ones. The large islands are mountainous and hilly. Vanuatu shares with neighbouring countries the features of a tropical oceanic climate.

Very similar conditions prevail throughout the year with high temperatures and humidity. The daily range of temperature is quite small – about 4°–5° C/10° F. There is abundant rainfall. Being south of the equator, Vanuatu has its season of maximum rainfall between November and April. On some islands there is no great difference between the amount of rain from month to month. Tropical cyclones occasionally cause devastating damage.

Except in the wettest places, where cloud is more frequent, the country has moderately large amounts of sunshine, averaging from six to eight hours a day.

Much of the rainfall comes in short, heavy showers, often after a sunny morning, but longer periods of heavy rain lasting a whole day or so occur in the wetter months.

In this area of the Pacific the principal difference in the weather and climate is the amount of rainfall per month. Temperature and humidity are very similar from one island to another but the amount of rainfall varies with altitude and with exposure of the coast to the dominant southeast trade winds. The number of wet days varies from island to island much less than the amount of rain.

The climate may generally be described as pleasant and healthy, although the combination of high temperature and humidity can be a little oppressive when not tempered by sea breezes or a brisk wind.

The table for **Tanna** (above) in the New Hebrides shows weather that is typical of Vanuatu.

Venezuela

See map page 16

Venezuela is the most northerly country in South America, situated between 1° and 12° N. It is rather more than twice the size of France or the state of Texas. It has a long coastline on the Caribbean Sea and is bordered on the west by Colombia, on the east by Guyana, and on the south by Brazil.

In Venezuela the main chain of the Andes mountains runs from west to east, thus leaving a narrow coastal plain on the Caribbean shore. In the west there is a more extensive marshy lowland around Lake Maracaibo. To the south of the Andes there is a large lowland area in the valley of the river Orinoco, known as the Llanos; this has a typical tropical climate with a single rainy season. In the southeast of the country the land rises to a plateau, extending into Guyana, with an average height of some 600 m/2,000 ft; from this plateau numerous hills rise to more than 1,800 m/6,000 ft.

Venezuela is unusual among South American countries in that almost everywhere the main rainy season is from April to October at the time of high

sun. Towards the west of the country there is a tendency for a double rainy season, as in Colombia. The northern lowland, particularly in the west, has a surprisingly dry climate for a tropical coast. This is thought to be a consequence of the direction of the coastline in relation to the frequent northeast trade winds.

The Andes in Venezuela are lower and narrower than in Colombia, Peru, and Bolivia but there are a number of individual peaks rising above 4,600m/ 15,000 ft which carry snow throughout the year. There are many local variations of weather and climate as a result of altitude; the threefold division into *tierra caliente* (lowlands), *tierra templada* (middle elevations), and *tierra fria* (highland), described on p. 66 for Bolivia, applies to this region.

The northern slopes of the Andes tend to have less rainfall than the southern side. **Caracas** (see table below), at an altitude of 1,040 m/3,400 ft, has a climate typical of the *tierra templada* but shows traces of the relative dryness which affects the whole north coast. Over most of this area sunshine amounts are moderately high as a consequence of

CARACAS												NORTHERN VENEZUELA	
Sunshine	Temperatures								Discomfort from heat and humidity	Precipitation and humidity			Wet days
	Average daily		Highest recorded		Lowest recorded					Relative humidity	Average monthly precipitation		
	minimum		maximum										
average hours per day	°C	°F	°C	°F	°C	°F	°C	°F	%		mm	in	more than 0.25 mm/0.01 in
Jan	8	13	56	24	75	28	83	8	47			23	0.9	6	Jan
Feb	9	13	56	25	77	31	88	8	46			10	0.4	2	Feb
March	8	14	58	26	79	33	91	7	45			15	0.6	3	March
April	7	16	60	27	81	32	89	11	51			33	1.3	4	April
May	6	17	62	27	80	32	89	11	52			79	3.1	9	May
June	7	17	62	26	78	30	86	12	53			102	4.0	14	June
July	8	16	61	26	78	29	84	11	52			109	4.3	15	July
Aug	8	16	61	26	79	30	86	12	53			109	4.3	15	Aug
Sept	7	16	61	27	80	29	85	12	53			107	4.2	13	Sept
Oct	7	16	61	26	79	30	86	12	54			109	4.3	12	Oct
Nov	7	16	60	25	77	29	84	11	51			94	3.7	13	Nov
Dec	7	14	58	26	78	28	83	8	47			46	1.8	10	Dec

Based on readings for 21 years at 10°30′ N, 66°56′ W, altitude 1042 m/3418 ft

MARACAIBO

COASTAL VENEZUELA

Sunshine	Temperatures								Discomfort from heat and humidity	Precipitation and humidity				Wet days
	Average daily				Highest recorded		Lowest recorded			Relative humidity		Average monthly precipitation		
average hours per day	minimum		maximum							7:00 13:00				more than 0.25 mm/0.01 in
	°C	°F	°C	°F	°C	°F	°C	°F		%		mm	in	
Jan	9	23	73	32	90	37	98	19	66	High	80	61	3	0.1	0.5	Jan
Feb	9	23	73	32	90	36	97	20	68	High	80	61	0	0.0	0.3	Feb
March	8	23	74	33	91	37	98	19	67	High	78	61	8	0.3	1.0	March
April	6	24	76	33	92	39	102	20	68	High	78	61	20	0.8	1.0	April
May	6	25	77	33	92	38	100	20	68	High	82	63	69	2.7	6.0	May
June	7	25	77	34	93	38	100	21	69	Extreme	80	60	56	2.2	6.0	June
July	8	24	76	34	94	38	101	21	70	Extreme	81	62	46	1.8	5.0	July
Aug	8	25	77	34	94	39	102	21	69	Extreme	82	62	56	2.2	7.0	Aug
Sept	7	25	77	34	94	39	102	20	68	Extreme	84	62	71	2.8	6.0	Sept
Oct	6	24	76	33	92	37	99	20	68	High	84	62	150	5.9	9.0	Oct
Nov	7	24	76	33	91	37	98	21	70	High	83	63	84	3.3	8.0	Nov
Dec	8	24	75	33	91	36	96	20	68	High	82	62	15	0.6	2.0	Dec

Based on readings for 12 years at 10°39′ N, 71°36′ W, altitude 6 m/20 ft

SANTA ELENA

GUYANA PLATEAU, VENEZUELA

Sunshine	Temperatures								Discomfort from heat and humidity	Precipitation and humidity				Wet days
	Average daily				Highest recorded		Lowest recorded			Relative humidity		Average monthly precipitation		
average hours per day	minimum		maximum							8:00 14:00				more than 0.25 mm/0.01 in
	°C	°F	°C	°F	°C	°F	°C	°F		%		mm	in	
Jan	6	16	61	30	86	33	91	13	55	High	89	63	51	2.0	13	Jan
Feb	7	17	62	31	87	33	91	13	55	High	89	62	61	2.4	11	Feb
March	7	18	64	31	88	35	95	12	53	High	83	57	94	3.7	15	March
April	6	18	64	30	86	34	93	14	57	High	86	61	137	5.4	18	April
May	5	18	65	29	84	32	89	14	57	Medium	90	69	213	8.4	28	May
June	5	18	64	28	82	31	88	15	59	Medium	93	73	252	9.9	28	June
July	6	17	62	28	82	30	86	14	57	Medium	95	73	216	8.5	27	July
Aug	6	17	63	28	83	31	88	12	54	Medium	95	74	173	6.8	26	Aug
Sept	8	17	63	29	84	33	92	13	56	Medium	90	59	94	3.7	19	Sept
Oct	8	17	63	29	85	34	93	13	55	Medium	90	55	89	3.5	15	Oct
Nov	7	17	62	30	86	34	93	13	55	Medium	86	57	130	5.1	18	Nov
Dec	6	17	63	29	84	32	90	14	57	Medium	88	61	119	4.7	17	Dec

Based on readings for 7 years at 4°36′ N, 61°07′ W, altitude 859 m/2816 ft

the lack of cloud and rain; ranging from six hours a day in the wetter months to as much as eight hours in the drier months. Annual rainfall in the mountains is usually over 1,000 mm/40 in but is less in some sheltered valleys and on the northern slopes. On the coast the rainfall increases from the very low annual totals around Lake Maracaibo (see the table for **Maracaibo** opposite) to as much as 1,000 mm/40 in in the east. The lowlands around Lake Maracaibo are particularly hot in all months.

In the Llanos region of the Orinoco valley there is a typical hot, tropical climate with a single wet season between April and October. Over most of this region

annual rainfall is 1,000–1,500 mm/40–60 in. Temperature varies little from month to month and there is never any really cool weather. The wet months are the most uncomfortable because of the combination of heat and high humidity.

In the southeast on the Guyana plateau rainfall is rather heavier, generally above 1,500 mm/60 in per year, but with a definite dry season at the time of low sun. Temperatures are moderated by the higher altitude and humidity is rather lower than in the Llanos. The table for **Santa Elena** (opposite and below) is representative of this plateau region.

Vietnam

See map page 23

Vietnam is a country of southeast Asia, rather larger than Britain and about half the size of the state of Texas. Extending between 9° and 23° N, it lies entirely within the tropics. It has a long coastline on the Gulf of Tonkin and the South China Sea. On the landward side it borders China in the north and Laos and Cambodia in the west. Like the other countries of the region, it has a tropical monsoon

type of climate dominated by south to southeasterly winds from May until September and northerly to northeasterly winds between October and April. There is a twice-yearly period of variable winds at the time of transition from the north to south monsoon. There are considerable areas of high land rising to over 2,450 m/8,000 ft, particularly in the northwest and in the central highlands facing the South China Sea. In the north around **Hanoi** (see table below), the capital city, and in the south

HANOI													NORTHERN VIETNAM	
Sunshine		Temperatures							Discomfort from heat and humidity	Precipitation and humidity				Wet days
		Average daily				Highest recorded		Lowest recorded		Relative humidity		Average monthly precipitation		
		minimum		maximum						10:00	16:00			
average hours per day		°C	°F	°C	°F	°C	°F	°C	°F	%		mm	in	more than 1 mm/0.04 in
Jan	1	13	56	20	68	33	92	6	42		78	68	18	0.7	7	Jan
Feb	1	14	58	21	69	34	94	6	43		82	70	28	1.1	13	Feb
March	1	17	63	23	74	37	98	12	53	Moderate	83	76	38	1.5	15	March
April	2	20	69	28	82	39	103	10	50	Medium	83	75	81	3.2	14	April
May	4	23	74	32	90	43	109	16	60	High	77	69	196	7.7	15	May
June	5	26	78	33	92	40	104	21	69	Extreme	78	71	239	9.4	14	June
July	5	26	78	33	91	40	104	22	71	Extreme	79	72	323	12.7	15	July
Aug	4	26	78	32	90	38	101	21	70	Extreme	82	75	343	13.5	16	Aug
Sept	4	24	76	31	88	37	99	17	63	High	79	73	254	10.0	14	Sept
Oct	4	22	71	29	84	36	96	14	57	Medium	75	69	99	3.9	9	Oct
Nov	3	18	64	26	78	36	97	7	44	Medium	74	68	43	1.7	7	Nov
Dec	2	15	59	22	72	37	98	7	44		75	67	20	0.8	7	Dec

Based on readings for 33 years at 21°02′ N, 105°52′ E, altitude 16 m/53 ft

HO CHI MINH CITY
SOUTHERN VIETNAM

Sunshine	Temperatures								Discomfort from heat and humidity	Precipitation and humidity				Wet days
	Average daily				Highest recorded		Lowest recorded			Relative humidity		Average monthly precipitation		
	minimum		maximum							10:00 16:00				
average hours per day	°C	°F	°C	°F	°C	°F	°C	°F		%		mm	in	more than 1 mm/0.04 in
Jan	5	21	70	32	89	37	98	14	57	High	69	61	15	0.6	2	Jan
Feb	6	22	71	33	91	39	102	16	61	High	66	56	3	0.1	1	Feb
March	5	23	74	34	93	39	103	18	64	High	63	58	13	0.5	2	March
April	6	24	76	35	95	40	104	20	68	Extreme	63	60	43	1.7	4	April
May	4	24	76	33	92	39	102	21	70	Extreme	71	71	221	8.7	16	May
June	4	24	75	32	89	38	100	21	69	Extreme	77	78	330	13.0	21	June
July	4	24	75	31	88	34	94	19	67	Extreme	79	80	315	12.4	23	July
Aug	5	24	75	31	88	35	95	20	68	High	77	78	269	10.6	21	Aug
Sept	5	23	74	31	88	36	96	21	69	Extreme	78	80	335	13.2	21	Sept
Oct	4	23	74	31	88	34	94	20	68	Extreme	77	80	269	10.6	20	Oct
Nov	4	23	73	31	87	35	95	18	64	High	74	75	114	4.5	11	Nov
Dec	4	22	71	31	87	36	97	14	57	High	72	68	56	2.2	7	Dec

Based on readings for 31 years at 10°47' N, 106°42' E, altitude 9 m/30 ft

DA NANG
COASTAL VIETNAM

Sunshine	Temperatures								Discomfort from heat and humidity	Precipitation and humidity			Wet days
	Average daily				Highest recorded		Lowest recorded			Relative humidity	Average monthly precipitation		
	minimum		maximum							all hours			
average hours per day	°C	°F	°C	°F	°C	°F	°C	°F		%	mm	in	more than 1 mm/0.04 in
Jan		19	66	24	75	31	87	11	52	Medium	86	102	4.0	15	Jan
Feb		20	68	26	78	37	98	14	58	Medium	86	31	1.2	7	Feb
March		21	69	27	81	36	97	15	60	Medium	86	12	0.5	4	March
April		23	73	30	86	40	104	18	64	High	85	18	0.7	4	April
May		24	76	33	91	39	102	22	71	Extreme	81	47	1.9	8	May
June		25	77	34	94	40	104	23	73	Extreme	77	42	1.7	7	June
July		25	77	34	92	38	100	22	71	Extreme	78	99	3.9	11	July
Aug		25	76	34	93	39	102	21	71	Extreme	77	117	4.6	12	Aug
Sept		24	75	31	88	37	97	21	70	Extreme	84	447	17.6	17	Sept
Oct		23	73	28	83	34	92	17	63	High	85	530	20.1	21	Oct
Nov		22	71	27	80	31	88	15	59	Medium	86	221	8.7	21	Nov
Dec		20	68	25	77	31	87	13	56	Medium	86	209	8.2	20	Dec

Based on readings for x years at 16°05' N, 108°13' E, altitude 3 m/10 ft

around **Ho Chi Minh City** (see table opposite) there are extensive low-lying regions in the Red River delta and the Mekong delta respectively. These two lowlands contain a large proportion of the population and the productive rice-growing areas.

The general features of the climate of Vietnam also apply to the two adjoining countries, Laos and Cambodia; all three countries are often grouped together under the name Indo-China. Over most of Indo-China there is a single rainy season at the time of the south monsoon between May and September. During the rest of the year rainfall is infrequent and light. Annual rainfall is almost everywhere above 1,000 mm/40 in and rises to between 2,000 mm/80 in and 2,500 mm/100 in on the hills, particularly those facing the sea.

On the coast and in those parts of the central highlands which face northeast, the season of maximum rainfall is between September and January (see the table for **Da Nang** opposite and below). This area often receives heavy rain from typhoons, or severe tropical storms, which develop in the western Pacific at this time of year.

This is also a time of much cloud and frequent drizzle (called locally the *crachin*). In the north of Vietnam there are more cloudy days with occasional light rain during the period of the northeast monsoon. The south of the country is more likely to be dry and sunny at this time.

In the southern and central parts of Indo-China temperatures remain high around the year but in the north there is a definite cooler season as the north monsoon brings colder air from central China from time to time. Frost and occasional snow only occur on the highest mountains in the north for a few days a year. In the south of Vietnam, and in Cambodia and Laos, the lowlands are sheltered from any such outbreaks of colder northerly air and the dry season is warm to hot with much sunshine.

The weather of Vietnam, Laos, and Cambodia is rather sultry and oppressive during the rainy season and the humidity is high at this time. On the coast and in the hills the frequent cloud and high humidity combine with lack of sunshine to make this time of the year rather unpleasant in spite of the reduction of temperatures with height.

Virgin Islands

See map page 15

These 100 or so islands are the northernmost group of the Leeward islands, the northerly islands of the Lesser Antilles. The British Virgin Islands are administered from a capital at Road Town on the island of Tortola, the American Virgin Islands from a capital at Charlotte Amalie on the island of St Thomas.

Temperature and humidity around the year in the Leeward Islands are very similar to those described in the general entry for the Caribbean (pp. 92–3), as are the amount and distribution of sunshine. The tables for points on two other islands in the eastern Caribbean, **Roseau** (p. 127) on Dominica and

Plymouth (p. 244) on Montserrat, show that near sea level, the annual rainfall is about 1,250–2,000 mm/50–80 in, well distributed throughout the year, with a wetter season from July to November. The table for **Camp Jacob** (p. 167) on the island of Guadeloupe, also in the Leeward Islands, shows that rainfall increases at higher elevations and on the windward slopes exposed to the constant and moist northeast trade winds.

The Virgin Islands lie in the track of violent tropical hurricanes which are most likely to develop between August and October. Although the severest of these storms may only strike once every few years, these are always the months of heaviest rainfall.

Wallis and Futuna

See map page 17

This group of islands in the southwest Pacific – an overseas territory of France – shares with neighbouring countries the features of a typical tropical oceanic climate. Very similar conditions prevail throughout the year with high temperatures

and humidity. The daily range of temperature is quite small – about 4°–5° C/10° F. There is abundant rainfall. Being south of the equator, Wallis and Futuna have their season of maximum rainfall between November and April. On some islands there is no great difference between the amount of rain from month to month. Tropical cyclones are less frequent than in the Pacific north of the equator. Except in the wettest places, where cloud is more frequent, the country has moderately large amounts of sunshine, averaging from six to eight hours a day. Much of the rainfall comes in short, heavy showers, often after a sunny morning, but longer periods of heavy rain lasting a whole day or so occur in the wetter months.

In this area of the Pacific the principal difference in the weather and climate is the amount of rainfall per month. Temperature and humidity are very similar from one island to another but the amount of rainfall varies with altitude and with exposure of the coast to the dominant southeast trade winds. The number of wet days varies from island to island much less than the amount of rain.

The climate may generally be described as pleasant and healthy, although the combination of high temperature and humidity can be a little oppressive when not tempered by sea breezes or a brisk wind.

The table for **Apia** (p. 309) in neighbouring Samoa shows weather that is typical of Wallis and Futuna.

Western Sahara

See map page 20

This territory on the coast of northwest Africa between Morocco and Mauritania was formerly the Spanish colony of Spanish Sahara. In 1975 it was partitioned between Morocco and Mauritania after an agreement with Spain. In 1979, however, it was united with Morocco. Since then it has been disputed between Morocco and the local population. It has an area about as large as the United Kingdom but a very small population.

The whole territory is part of the Sahara and it has a similar climate to the adjacent parts of southern Morocco (pp. 245–6) and northern Mauritania (p. 235).

Yemen

See map page 22

This mountainous country lies in the southwestern portion of the Arabian peninsula. It has a narrow coastal plain on the Red Sea, a long coastline on the Arabian Sea, and land borders with Saudi Arabia and Oman.

The land rises steeply to a mountainous interior over 3,600 m/12,000 ft above sea level. It is an exceptional part of Arabia, since the mountains receive moderate to abundant rainfall between March and September so that coffee and a wide variety of crops are grown.

In the higher regions temperatures are much lower than elsewhere in Arabia. Here the climate is quite pleasant with mild winters and warm, moist, but generally sunny summers. No reliable climatic data is available for the higher part of the country and the description above is based on travellers' accounts.

The interior includes a small portion of the great sand desert of the Rub' al Khali which is mainly in Saudi Arabia (see p. 312). Between this desert and the coast there are ranges of hills within which runs a broad valley, the Wadi Hadhramaut. This area receives rather more rainfall and is settled and more densely populated.

Climatic conditions along the southern coast are represented by the table for **Khormaksar** (opposite and above), the airport of Aden.

On the southern coast rainfall is low throughout the year and most of the coastal plain is desert. Temperatures and humidity are high and the period from June to September is the most uncomfortable time when midday temperatures regularly rise to near 38° C/100° F with a high humidity. Daily sea breezes help to mitigate the heat on the coast. Inland in the hills both temperatures and humidity are a little lower. Here rainfall is a little more and mostly falls between May and September.

In the lowland along the Red Sea coast the weather is hot and humid for most of the year and similar to that on the Red Sea coast of Saudi Arabia. In this lowland the rainfall is rather low, averaging about 100 mm/4 in a year, and may occur in both winter and summer.

Conditions on the Red Sea coast are represented by the table for **Kamaran Island** (opposite).

KHORMAKSAR

GULF OF ADEN COAST

	Sunshine	Temperatures								Discomfort from heat and humidity	Precipitation and humidity				Wet days	
		Average daily				Highest recorded		Lowest recorded			Relative humidity 3:00 15:00		Average monthly precipitation			
		minimum		maximum												
	average hours per day	°C	°F	°C	°F	°C	°F	°C	°F		%		mm	in	more than 1 mm/0.04 in	
Jan	9	22	72	28	82	30	86	16	61	Medium	78	63	5	0.2	1.0	Jan
Feb	9	23	73	28	83	31	87	17	63	Medium	79	65	0	0.0	0.5	Feb
March	9	24	76	30	86	35	95	19	67	High	82	66	5	0.2	0.3	March
April	10	25	77	32	89	37	99	20	68	High	83	66	0	0.0	0.0	April
May	10	27	81	34	93	39	103	24	75	Extreme	83	66	0	0.0	0.0	May
June	9	29	84	37	98	41	106	26	79	Extreme	76	51	0	0.0	0.0	June
July	7	28	83	36	97	40	104	23	73	High	76	49	5	0.2	1.0	July
Aug	8	28	82	36	96	38	101	23	74	Extreme	78	50	3	0.1	0.7	Aug
Sept	9	28	83	36	96	38	101	25	77	Extreme	78	56	0	0.0	0.2	Sept
Oct	10	24	76	33	91	38	100	19	66	High	77	58	0	0.0	0.2	Oct
Nov	10	23	73	30	86	33	91	18	65	High	77	61	0	0.0	0.2	Nov
Dec	9	23	73	28	83	31	87	17	62	Medium	76	62	5	0.2	2.0	Dec

Based on readings for 6 years at 12°50′ N, 45°01′ E, altitude 7 m/22 ft

KAMARAN ISLAND

RED SEA COAST

	Sunshine	Temperatures								Discomfort from heat and humidity	Precipitation and humidity				Wet days	
		Average daily				Highest recorded		Lowest recorded			Relative humidity 9:00 15:00		Average monthly precipitation			
		minimum		maximum												
	average hours per day	°C	°F	°C	°F	°C	°F	°C	°F		%		mm	in	more than 1 mm/0.04 in	
Jan		23	74	28	82	31	88	19	66	Medium	79	69	5	0.2	0.6	Jan
Feb		23	74	28	83	32	89	19	67	Medium	77	65	5	0.2	0.9	Feb
March		25	77	30	86	34	94	21	70	High	75	65	3	0.1	0.6	March
April		26	79	32	89	37	98	23	73	High	74	61	3	0.1	0.3	April
May		28	82	35	95	39	102	23	74	Extreme	70	56	3	0.1	0.2	May
June		29	84	36	97	40	104	24	75	Extreme	67	55	0	0.0	0.1	June
July		29	85	37	98	41	105	22	72	Extreme	63	52	13	0.5	2.0	July
Aug		29	85	36	97	39	103	22	72	Extreme	67	55	18	0.7	1.0	Aug
Sept		29	84	36	97	40	104	23	74	Extreme	71	58	3	0.1	0.5	Sept
Oct		28	82	34	93	39	102	23	73	High	67	57	3	0.1	0.5	Oct
Nov		26	78	31	87	34	94	20	68	High	74	63	10	0.4	0.8	Nov
Dec		24	75	28	83	32	90	20	68	Medium	77	68	23	0.9	2.0	Dec

Based on readings for 26 years at 15°20′ N, 42°37′ E, altitude 6 m/20 ft

PODGORICA   MONTENEGRO

Sunshine	Temperatures								Discomfort from heat and humidity	Precipitation and humidity				Wet days	
	Average daily				Highest recorded		Lowest recorded			Relative humidity		Average monthly precipitation			
	minimum		maximum							7:30	14:30				
average hours per day	°C	°F	°C	°F	°C	°F	°C	°F		%		mm	in	more than 0.1 mm/0.004 in	
Jan	4	2	36	9	48	18	64	−9	16		77	63	163	6.4	13	Jan
Feb	4	3	37	11	52	20	68	−10	14		79	63	179	7.1	14	Feb
March	6	5	41	14	57	26	79	−5	23		71	54	146	5.7	11	March
April	7	9	48	19	66	31	88	1	34		70	50	98	3.9	10	April
May	8	14	57	24	75	33	91	5	41	Moderate	69	50	105	4.1	11	May
June	10	18	64	29	84	38	100	10	50	Medium	61	43	59	2.3	6	June
July	11	21	70	33	91	41	106	14	57	Medium	53	37	38	1.5	5	July
Aug	11	21	70	33	91	41	106	9	48	Medium	53	36	51	2.0	4	Aug
Sept	8	17	63	27	81	39	102	10	50	Moderate	64	45	110	4.3	7	Sept
Oct	6	12	54	21	70	30	86	3	37		75	55	230	9.1	11	Oct
Nov	4	8	46	15	59	23	73	−5	23		83	67	213	8.4	16	Nov
Dec	3	4	39	12	54	19	66	−7	19		82	67	225	8.9	15	Dec

Based on readings for 22 years at 42°26′ N, 19°17′ E, altitude 16 m/52 ft

BELGRADE   SERBIA

Sunshine	Temperatures								Discomfort from heat and humidity	Precipitation and humidity				Wet days	
	Average daily				Highest recorded		Lowest recorded			Relative humidity		Average monthly precipitation			
	minimum		maximum							7:30	14:30				
average hours per day	°C	°F	°C	°F	°C	°F	°C	°F		%		mm	in	more than 0.1 mm/0.004 in	
Jan	2	−3	26	3	37	20	68	−25	−12		85	75	47	1.9	14	Jan
Feb	3	−2	29	5	42	21	70	−21	−5		83	67	46	1.8	13	Feb
March	5	2	36	11	52	30	86	−14	8		77	56	46	1.8	12	March
April	6	7	45	18	64	31	87	−6	21		72	49	54	2.1	13	April
May	7	12	54	23	73	34	94	−1	29		73	51	74	2.9	14	May
June	9	15	59	26	79	37	98	6	43	Moderate	74	51	96	3.8	13	June
July	10	17	62	28	83	39	103	8	47	Medium	71	47	61	2.4	9	July
Aug	9	17	62	28	83	39	103	8	46	Medium	73	46	55	2.2	9	Aug
Sept	8	13	56	24	76	42	107	2	35		76	47	50	2.0	8	Sept
Oct	3	8	47	18	64	35	94	−7	20		82	58	55	2.2	11	Oct
Nov	3	4	39	11	51	23	74	−8	17		85	71	61	2.4	14	Nov
Dec	2	0	32	5	42	21	70	−19	−3		85	76	55	2.2	14	Dec

Based on readings for 30 years at 44°48′ N, 20°28′ E, altitude 132 m/433 ft

Yugoslavia

See map page 19

Yugoslavia, comprising Serbia and Montenegro, has a varied climate and geography. That part best known and most visited by tourists is the Dalmatian coast of Montenegro. It has a Mediterranean type of climate with mild winters and sunny, warm summers. The coast is backed by mountains. Winter rainfall here is heavy and parts of Montenegro are among the wettest places in Europe.

The table for **Podgorica** (opposite) shows weather typical of southwestern Montenegro near the coast. For conditions typical of the coast itself see the table for **Dubrovnik** (p. 117) in southern Croatia.

The one unpleasant feature of the winter weather is a cold gusty wind, the *bora*, which brings cold air from central and eastern Europe down to the coast for a few days at a time. Summers on the coast are not entirely rainless and the fine, sunny weather is often interrupted by thunderstorms. Sunshine averages some four hours a day in winter and from ten to twelve hours a day in summer.

Inland climatic conditions rapidly become more typical of eastern Europe with cold winters and warm summers and here summer is the wettest season. Much of Serbia is mountainous or hilly and snow lies for long periods in the higher regions. Serbia includes much low-lying land in the valleys of the Danube, Drave, and Save; here winters are rather cold and rainfall lower.

The table for **Belgrade** (opposite and below) shows conditions in lowland areas of Serbia. Although this table shows many days with rain during the summer months, the rain is often of a showery, thundery type so that the hours of sunshine in summer are not all that fewer than on the Adriatic coast.

Zambia

See map page 21

Including a description of the weather and climate of Zimbabwe and Malawi.

Zambia, Zimbabwe, and Malawi, three landlocked countries in south-central Africa between 8° and 22° S, all have a broad similarity of weather and climate. Any significant differences from place to place are a consequence of the range of altitude found in each country.

All three countries include extensive areas between 900 m/3,000 ft and 1,500 m/5,000 ft above sea level. Only in the valleys of the major rivers (the Zambezi, which forms the border between Zambia and Zimbabwe; the Limpopo, which is the border between Zimbabwe and South Africa; and their tributaries, such as the Shire in Malawi) are there areas of land below 600 m/2,000 ft. In these lowland areas the climate is typically tropical with no real cool season and high temperatures during the period of overhead sun between October and February. This period of high sun is also the rainy season in all these countries. The climate of these lowlands is oppressive and sultry, particularly during the rainy season, and has a bad reputation for the health of humans and animals because of the prevalence of both malaria and sleeping sickness.

By contrast, the lower temperatures on the upland plateaux which make up the greater part of these countries are much more healthy and pleasant. Above 1,200 m/4,000 ft temperatures around the year are typical of warm-temperate rather than tropical climates. During the long dry season there is abundant sunshine and the sun's rays are more powerful as a consequence of the altitude. The air temperature, however, is rarely so high as to cause stress or discomfort and it is mitigated by the generally low humidity.

The most uncomfortable season is the period from November to February, when both temperature and humidity are greatest and there is a smaller daily temperature range so that nights are not so cool. At altitudes above 1,000 m/4,000 ft and 1,500 m/5,000 ft frost is not uncommon at night during the dry season from April to August. This is a period of low sun and some days may be chilly if there is much cloud.

Rainfall is largely confined to the period October to March, with a maximum in the months December to February, when the intertropical belt of cloud and rain is farthest south. It then lies across southern Zambia and Malawi. Much of the rain is heavy and showery and accompanied by thunder but periods of almost continuous rain lasting two or three days are

NDOLA — NORTH-CENTRAL ZAMBIA

Sunshine average hours per day	Temperatures Average daily				Highest recorded		Lowest recorded		Discomfort from heat and humidity	Precipitation and humidity Relative humidity		Average monthly precipitation		Wet days more than 0.25 mm/0.01 in	
	minimum		maximum							8:30	14:00				
	°C	°F	°C	°F	°C	°F	°C	°F		%		mm	in		
Jan 4	17	62	26	79	30	86	12	54	Medium	87	63	351	13.8	22.0	Jan
Feb 4	17	62	26	79	30	86	12	54	Medium	88	61	264	10.4	19.0	Feb
March 6	16	61	26	79	30	86	11	52	Moderate	87	51	234	9.2	17.0	March
April 8	13	56	27	81	31	87	7	45	Moderate	78	43	33	1.3	4.0	April
May 9	9	49	26	79	30	86	1	34	Moderate	71	32	3	0.1	0.5	May
June 9	5	41	24	76	28	83	0	32		65	29	0	0.0	0.0	June
July 9	5	41	25	77	29	84	-2	28		62	24	0	0.0	0.0	July
Aug 10	7	45	27	80	32	89	2	35	Moderate	50	21	0	0.0	0.0	Aug
Sept 9	12	53	30	86	34	93	5	41	Moderate	43	17	0	0.0	0.1	Sept
Oct 9	15	59	32	89	36	97	9	49	Medium	45	20	18	0.7	3.0	Oct
Nov 7	17	62	29	84	34	94	13	55	Medium	66	42	140	5.5	13.0	Nov
Dec 5	17	62	27	80	32	89	12	53	Medium	81	61	252	9.9	19.0	Dec

Based on readings for 10 years at 12°59′ S, 28°37′ E, altitude 1269 m/4163 ft

KASAMA — NORTHEASTERN ZAMBIA

Sunshine average hours per day	Temperatures Average daily				Highest recorded		Lowest recorded		Discomfort from heat and humidity	Precipitation and humidity Relative humidity		Average monthly precipitation		Wet days more than 0.25 mm/0.01 in	
	minimum		maximum							8:30	14:00				
	°C	°F	°C	°F	°C	°F	°C	°F		%		mm	in		
Jan 4	16	61	26	79	30	86	14	57	Moderate	83	59	272	10.7	24.0	Jan
Feb 4	17	62	26	79	30	86	13	56	Moderate	84	59	252	9.9	19.0	Feb
March 6	17	62	26	78	29	84	14	58	Moderate	85	56	277	10.9	21.0	March
April 8	16	60	26	79	29	84	11	51	Moderate	77	51	71	2.8	7.0	April
May 9	13	56	26	78	29	85	7	44	Moderate	71	40	13	0.5	1.0	May
June 9	11	51	24	76	28	82	4	39		61	33	0	0.0	0.0	June
July 10	10	50	24	76	28	83	4	40		61	29	0	0.0	0.1	July
Aug 10	11	52	26	79	31	87	6	42		57	22	0	0.0	0.1	Aug
Sept 10	14	58	29	85	34	93	8	47	Moderate	47	20	0	0.0	0.2	Sept
Oct 9	17	62	31	87	35	95	12	53	Moderate	44	19	20	0.8	3.0	Oct
Nov 7	17	62	28	83	34	93	13	55	Moderate	63	38	163	6.4	16.0	Nov
Dec 5	17	62	27	80	31	87	14	58	Medium	79	55	241	9.5	22.0	Dec

Based on readings for 10 years at 10°12′ S, 31°11′ E, altitude 1385 m/4544 ft

LUSAKA									SOUTH-CENTRAL ZAMBIA			
Sunshine	Temperatures							Discomfort from heat and humidity	Precipitation and humidity			Wet days
☀ average hours per day	Average daily		Highest recorded		Lowest recorded				Relative humidity 8:30 14:00		Average monthly precipitation	🌧 more than 0.25 mm/0.01 in
	minimum	maximum										
	°C	°F	°C	°F	°C	°F	°C	°F		%	mm	in
Jan	5	17	63	26	78	31	88	14	58	Medium	84	71	231	9.1	21.0	Jan
Feb	5	17	63	26	79	31	87	13	56	Medium	85	70	191	7.5	17.0	Feb
March	7	17	62	26	78	30	86	13	55	Moderate	83	56	142	5.6	15.0	March
April	9	15	59	26	79	31	87	10	50	Moderate	71	47	18	0.7	3.0	April
May	9	12	54	25	77	29	85	8	47		59	37	3	0.1	0.9	May
June	9	10	50	23	73	28	83	4	39		56	32	0	0.0	0.4	June
July	9	9	49	23	73	28	83	4	40		54	28	0	0.0	0.1	July
Aug	10	12	53	25	77	31	87	6	43		46	26	0	0.0	0.0	Aug
Sept	9	15	59	29	84	35	95	8	46	Moderate	41	19	0	0.0	0.4	Sept
Oct	9	18	64	31	88	38	100	12	54	Medium	39	23	10	0.4	3.0	Oct
Nov	7	18	64	29	84	37	98	13	55	Medium	57	46	91	3.6	11.0	Nov
Dec	6	17	63	27	80	34	93	14	57	Medium	76	61	150	5.9	17.0	Dec

Based on readings for 10 years at 15°25′ S, 28°19′ E, altitude 1277 m/4191 ft

by no means unusual. Except in the higher mountainous areas of Malawi, rainfall is very rare during the period April to September.

Zambia is the largest of the three countries. It has the greatest extent both from east and west and north to south. It is bordered on the north by the Congo Democratic Republic and Tanzania, east by Malawi, south by Zimbabwe, and west by Angola. In the northern part of Zambia the rainy season is a few weeks longer than elsewhere, since it is nearest to the equator. The tables for **Ndola** (opposite and above), near the border with the Congo Democratic Republic, and for **Kasama** (opposite), in the northeast, are representative of wetter parts of the country. That for **Lusaka** (above), farther south, is typical of the drier parts. All three places, however, show very little difference in temperature, since they are at similar altitudes. The higher temperatures in the lowlands can be represented by the table for **Zumbo** (p. 249), which is in the Zambesi valley in Mozambique. The southwestern parts of Zambia and the valleys of the Zambesi and its tributary, the Luangwa, are the driest regions.

Zimbabwe

See map page 21

Zimbabwe is the most southerly of the three countries of south-central Africa which share a similar climate and which are described in more detail for Zambia (pp. 425–7). In area Zimbabwe is almost twice as large as the United Kingdom. It is bordered on the north by Zambia, east by Mozambique, south by South Africa, and west by Botswana. Most of the country consists of a plateau with an average height of over 1,200 m/4,000 ft. Along the eastern border with Mozambique there are hills rising to over 2,400 m/8,000 ft, while in the north and south of the country, in the valleys of the Zambesi and Limpopo respectively, altitude falls below 450 m/1,500 ft.

The low-lying parts of the country have a rather dry climate with an unreliable rainfall of between 400 mm/16 in and 600 mm/24 in. In the eastern highlands annual rainfall is as much as 1,500 mm/60 in and 200 mm/80 in. Over most of the country annual rainfall is between 750 mm/30 in and 1,000 mm/40 in. Most of the rain falls during the period November to March at the time of high sun.

Except in the lower regions, temperatures are warm but rarely hot around the year. Hours of sunshine average eight to nine a day during the dry season and as much as six to seven during the rainy season.

Most of Zimbabwe has a healthy and generally pleasant climate around the year. The tables for **Bulawayo** (opposite) and **Harare** (opposite and below) are typical of the upland regions between 1,200 m/4,000 ft) and 1,500 m/5,000 ft. The table for **Zumbo** (p. 249), in the Zambezi valley but actually in Mozambique, is typical of conditions in the lower parts of northern Zimbabwe.

BULAWAYO

UPLAND ZIMBABWE

Sunshine	Temperatures									Discomfort from heat and humidity	Precipitation and humidity				Wet days
average hours per day	Average daily				Highest recorded		Lowest recorded				Relative humidity 8:30 15:00		Average monthly precipitation		more than 0.25mm/0.01in
	minimum		maximum												
	°C	°F	°C	°F	°C	°F	°C	°F			%		mm	in	
Jan	16	61	27	81	36	96	9	49	7	Medium	70	51	142	5.6	14.0	Jan
Feb	16	61	27	80	34	94	8	46	8	Medium	74	52	109	4.3	11.0	Feb
March	15	59	26	79	34	93	9	48	8	Moderate	72	48	84	3.3	9.0	March
April	13	56	26	79	33	91	3	38	9	Moderate	63	39	18	0.7	4.0	April
May	9	49	23	74	31	87	1	33	9		56	33	10	0.4	2.0	May
June	7	45	21	69	28	82	-2	28	10		56	33	3	0.1	0.9	June
July	7	45	21	70	28	83	0	32	9		52	29	0	0.0	0.5	July
Aug	9	48	23	74	32	89	0	32	10		46	26	0	0.0	0.4	Aug
Sept	12	54	27	81	36	96	3	37	10	Moderate	42	24	5	0.2	1.0	Sept
Oct	15	59	29	85	36	97	7	44	9	Moderate	41	26	20	0.8	4.0	Oct
Nov	16	61	29	84	37	99	9	49	8	Medium	53	41	81	3.2	10.0	Nov
Dec	16	61	28	82	35	95	11	51	8	Medium	62	49	122	4.8	12.0	Dec

Based on readings for 15 years at 20°09′ S, 28°37′ E, altitude 1341 m/4405 ft

HARARE

UPLAND ZIMBABWE

Sunshine	Temperatures									Discomfort from heat and humidity	Precipitation and humidity				Wet days
average hours per day	Average daily				Highest recorded		Lowest recorded				Relative humidity 8:30 14:00		Average monthly precipitation		more than 0.25mm/0.01in
	minimum		maximum												
	°C	°F	°C	°F	°C	°F	°C	°F			%		mm	in	
Jan	16	60	26	78	32	90	8	47	6	Moderate	74	57	196	7.7	18.0	Jan
Feb	16	60	26	78	31	88	9	49	7	Moderate	77	53	178	7.0	15.0	Feb
March	14	58	26	78	30	86	8	46	7	Moderate	75	52	117	4.6	13.0	March
April	13	55	26	78	32	89	6	43	9	Moderate	68	44	28	1.1	5.0	April
May	9	49	23	74	28	83	2	36	9		60	37	13	0.5	2.0	May
June	7	44	21	70	26	79	0	32	9		58	36	3	0.1	1.0	June
July	7	44	21	70	28	82	0	32	9		56	33	0	0.0	0.7	July
Aug	8	47	23	74	31	88	1	34	10		50	28	3	0.1	0.6	Aug
Sept	12	53	26	79	33	92	3	37	10		43	26	5	0.2	1.0	Sept
Oct	14	58	28	83	34	93	7	44	10	Moderate	43	26	28	1.1	4.0	Oct
Nov	16	60	27	81	35	95	8	46	7	Moderate	56	43	97	3.8	11.0	Nov
Dec	16	60	26	79	33	92	9	49	7	Moderate	67	57	163	6.4	16.0	Dec

Based on readings for 15 years at 17°50′ S, 31°08′ E, altitude 1473 m/4831 ft

Glossary

Agulhas current A current of warm ocean water flowing westwards along the south coast of South Africa, It is a common local name for the Mozambique current (q.v.).

air mass An extensive mass of air with broadly similar properties, particularly surface temperature and humidity: for example, warm and dry, cold and humid, etc. Different types of weather are associated with different air masses.

anticyclone An area where the atmospheric pressure is high relative to the areas surrounding it and thus forms a distinctive pattern on a weather map. The weather is usually calm and settled at or near the centre of an anticyclone.

Bai-U The Japanese name for early summer rains that make the transition from the winter monsoon to the rainy season of the summer monsoon.

Benguela current A current of cold ocean water flowing northwards along the west coast of southern Africa. It lowers the coastal temperatures from Cape Town northwards to about latitude 10° S as compared with the east coast of southern Africa washed by the Mozambique current (q.v.).

berg wind A wind in the coastal districts of South Africa and Namibia. It blows from the interior and brings high temperatures and low humidity, particularly in the winter season.

bora A cold, dry, and gusty wind which blows from the land along the Adriatic coast of Yugoslavia and also affects the Italian shores of the Adriatic. It is particularly strong in the area of Trieste and most frequent in winter and spring.

buran A Russian word applied to a bitterly cold wind which is often associated with blizzard conditions, particularly in Siberia.

Californian current A current of cold ocean water flowing southwards along the west coasts of Mexico and California. It has the effect of reducing the temperature of the coastal regions and is responsible for the frequent sea fogs on this coast.

Canaries current A current of cold ocean water flowing southwards along the coast of northwest Africa. It has a similar effect to that of the Californian current (q.v.). It particularly affects the Canary Islands and – on the mainland of North Africa – Morocco and Mauritania.

chinook A warm dry wind of the föhn type (q.v.) which blows from the west immediately to the east of the Rocky Mountains in Canada and the United States. In winter and spring it melts snow rapidly.

continental climate A climate with a large seasonal range of temperature as found in the interior of a large land mass, particularly in temperate latitudes. The opposite of a maritime climate (q.v.).

crachin A French term for light rain or drizzle occurring on parts of the coast and northern mountain slopes in Vietnam during the cool season.

cyclone A particularly severe type of tropical storm with very low atmospheric pressure at the centre and strong winds blowing around it. Violent winds and heavy rain may affect an area of some hundreds of square miles. The name applies to such storms in the Indian Ocean. 'Typhoon' and 'hurricane' are other names applied to the same phenomena in the Pacific and Atlantic Oceans respectively.

depression A region where the surface atmospheric pressure is low. A distinctive feature on a weather map and the opposite of an anticyclone (q.v.). Usually associated with cloud and rain and sometimes with strong winds. A less severe weather disturbance than a tropical cyclone.

doldrums The old term used by sailors for the belt of light winds or calms in tropical and equatorial latitudes between the regular and constant trade winds and monsoons (q.v.). The modern meteorological term ITCZ (Intertropical Convergence Zone) (q.v.) is now used more frequently.

El Niño A Spanish term given to a warm ocean current, and to the unusually warm and rainy weather associated with it, which sometimes occurs for a few weeks off the coast of Peru (which is otherwise an extremely dry and cool region of the tropics). Several years may pass without this current appearing.

etesian wind The constant northerly to northwesterly winds which blow between June and September in the Aegean and the eastern Mediterranean. During this season the weather remains fine and sunny but the sea may be rough at times.

föhn A warm and very dry wind which blows in some valleys in the Alps. It can melt snow very rapidly and during a spell of föhn there is a greatly increased fire risk. Similar winds in other parts of the world are the chinook and the berg wind (q.v.).

garúa The light coastal drizzle falling frequently on the coast of Peru and northern Chile, which are otherwise very dry regions.

ghibli The Arabic name given in Libya to a hot, dry, and often dusty wind blowing from the south which raises coastal temperatures to very high levels for brief periods, particularly between March and early June.

Guinea monsoon The warm and humid southwesterly winds which blow to the south of the ITCZ (q.v.) in West Africa between April and September and are associated with the rainy season.

Gulf Stream A current of warm surface ocean water in the North Atlantic flowing from the Gulf of Mexico towards northwestern Europe. Also called the North Atlantic Drift, it is an important influence in keeping winters mild in the British Isles and along the coast of Norway, an influence that reaches to beyond the Arctic Circle.

haboob An Arabic word used in the Sudan for a wind squall lasting for an hour or so. The strong wind may raise a wall of dust particles as the squall advances, usually from an easterly direction.

harmattan The name given in West Africa to the northeast trade winds which blow from the Sahara desert towards the ITCZ (q.v.). During the dry season from October to March the harmattan sometimes reaches the coast of the Gulf of Guinea. The wind is associated with the hot, dry, and dusty weather of the dry season. The opposite of the Guinea monsoon (q.v.).

high sun A convenient term used in tropical countries for the season when the sun is at its maximum noon altitude. In the tropics there is no real winter in the sense of the word in temperate latitudes. In most parts of the tropics the high-sun period is the wettest period of the year.

Humboldt current A current of cold surface water moving northwards along the Pacific coast of South America almost as far north as the equator. It lowers the temperature of the coastlands of northern Chile and Peru.

hurricane The name applied in the Caribbean and United States to tropical cyclones (q.v.). West Indian islands and the coasts of Mexico and the southern United States are often struck by severe hurricanes.

ITCZ (Intertropical Convergence Zone) The doldrums (q.v.). The area of light winds in the tropics between the trade winds and monsoons blowing from opposite directions. Cloud and rain are often frequent and heavy in this zone.

khamsin The Arabic name given in Egypt, Palestine, Syria, and Lebanon to a hot, dry southerly or easterly wind blowing from the interior, which raises temperature in the coastal regions, particularly between March and early June. Often associated with dust storms or a hazy atmosphere.

Labrador current A current of cold surface water moving southwards along the east coast of Canada as far south as Newfoundland. It carries icebergs and is an important influence in keeping temperatures on the Labrador coast cool in summer.

land and sea breezes A local wind system which occurs during fine, calm weather on most coasts in the tropics and on most tropical islands; also around the Mediterranean in the summer months. A light wind or breeze blows from the sea by day and from the land by night. The sea breeze is usually welcome since it arrives at the hottest time of day and has a distinct cooling effect.

leveche The name given in the coastal regions of southern Spain to a hot, dry wind which blows from North Africa and is associated with a heat wave.

low sun The opposite season to that of high sun (q.v.) in the tropics. Usually the drier period of the year when the sun is at its minimum noonday elevation.

maritime climate A term used to denote a climate with both a small annual and daily range of temperature such as is found on most coasts, but particularly on west coasts in mid-latitudes, for example, the British Isles and the states of Washington and Oregon, also New Zealand and oceanic islands.

Mediterranean climate A distinctive seasonal rhythm of weather and climate such as is found in most countries around the Mediterranean. Characterized by warm to hot and dry summers with mild to cool winters with more disturbed weather and rain. Also found in California, Australia, South Africa, and Chile.

mistral A blustery wind which blows in the South of France, particularly in the lower Rhône valley. In winter and spring it brings cold air to this region. It may blow strongly at any time of the year and in summer it can greatly increase the risk of forest fires.

monsoon rains The name given in India and other parts of Asia to the heavy rains of the wet season. Also frequently used to describe the rains in Ethiopia and West Africa.

monsoon winds A term usually applied in Asia but also used for East and West Africa and Australia. The seasonal reversal of wind direction when the winds are predominantly off the ocean during the wet season and blow outwards from the land during the dry season: for example, in India the northeast monsoon blows off the land and the southwest monsoon blows from the ocean.

mountain and valley winds The daily reversal of wind which occurs in the valleys of mountain regions, such as the Alps in fine settled weather. During the day winds tend to blow up the valley and during the night down the valley. The wind direction may be quite different at higher levels on the mountains.

Mozambique current A current of warm surface water moving south along the coast of Mozambique and Natal which helps to maintain higher temperatures along the coast, particularly during the season of low sun (q.v.), when it may be much cooler inland.

permafrost The permanently frozen ground as occurs in north Canada, northern Russia, and Alaska. Although the top few feet of soil and rock may thaw out during the short summer, the ground remains permanently frozen below this layer.

polar front The boundary zone between cold air of Arctic or polar origin and warm air of tropical origin. The polar front is an important feature in the weather and climate of mid-latitudes, because many weather disturbances develop in this region of contrasting air masses, particularly in the North Atlantic and North Pacific.

rasputitsa The Russian name for the short period in spring when the snow melts and the ground thaws out.

shamal The Arabic name for a northwesterly wind that blows persistently between June and September in Iraq and the Persian Gulf when the weather is very hot and dry.

sharav The Hebrew name used in Israel for the hot dry khamsin (q.v.) blowing from the south and east.

sirocco (or scirocco) The name widely applied in the Mediterranean region, particularly in Greece and Italy, to a warm southerly wind. Of the same origin as other hot winds in this region: ghibli, khamsin, leveche, and sharav (q.v.). On the northern shores of the Mediterranean the sirocco is warm and humid.

smog A combination of atmospheric pollution and fog. When thick or toxic it may cause severe distress through irritation of the eyes, nose, throat, and lungs. Sometimes applied to a badly polluted atmosphere in the absence of visible fog as in large cities, such as Los Angeles, Tokyo, Athens, etc., under calm and sunny conditions.

sukhovey A warm, desiccating south or southeast wind in southern Russia. If it blows for a few days at a time it can be harmful to crops.

tierra caliente A term used in the Spanish-speaking countries of Central and South America for the lower slopes of the mountains (below about 900 m/3,000 ft) where the climate is tropical all the year round, generally hot, and with abundant rain.

tierra fria A term used in Central and South America for the higher mountain regions (from 1,800–3,000 m/6,000–10,000 ft) where temperatures are much reduced by altitude and frost and even snow may occur.

tierra templada The intermediate slopes of mountains in Central and South America between the *tierra fria* and the *tierra caliente*. Temperatures are rarely excessively hot and never really cold. A tropical upland climate such as the Kenyan highlands.

tornado The name given in the United States to a very strong and damaging whirlwind with a clearly visible dark, snake-like funnel extending from a thunder cloud to the ground. The track of a tornado at ground level is rarely very wide, but buildings, trees, and crops may be totally devastated.

trade winds The very constant winds found over most oceans within the tropics. These winds blow towards the equator as the northeast trades in the northern hemisphere and as the southeast trades in the southern hemisphere. They were of great importance to shipping in the days of sail; hence the name.

typhoon The name given in the western Pacific and particularly in the China Sea to violent tropical storms or cyclones (q.v.).

willy willies A colloquial Australian term for a violent tropical storm or cyclone (q.v.) affecting the coasts of northern Australia.

Index

Some locations included in this index appear only on maps. To find out about their weather, look up the relevant country for general information. In addition, you should look on the map for a nearby black diamond ♦ in the same climate region. When you look up the location marked by the diamond you will find a table with detailed weather information.

With guidebooks for every kind of travel—from weekend getaways to island hopping to adventures abroad—it's easy to understand why smart travelers go with **Fodor's**.